WORD ORDER IN DISCOURSE

TYPOLOGICAL STUDIES IN LANGUAGE (TSL)

A companion series to the journal "STUDIES IN LANGUAGE"

Volumes in this series will be functionally and typologically oriented, covering specific topics in language by collecting together data from a wide variety of languages and language typologies. The orientation of the volumes will be substantive rather than formal, with the aim of investigating universals of human language via as broadly defined a data base as possible, leaning toward cross-linguistic, diachronic, developmental and live-discourse data. The series is, in spirit as well as in fact, a continuation of the tradition initiated by C. Li (*Word Order and Word Order Change, Subject and Topic, Mechanisms for Syntactic Change*) and continued by T. Givón (*Discourse and Syntax*) and P. Hopper (*Tense-Aspect: Between Semantics and Pragmatics*).

Volume 30

Pamela Downing and Michael Noonan (eds)

Word Order in Discourse

WORD ORDER IN DISCOURSE

Edited by

PAMELA DOWNING

MICHAEL NOONAN

University of Wisconsin-Milwaukee

JOHN BENJAMINS PUBLISHING COMPANY
AMSTERDAM/PHILADELPHIA

The paper used in this publication meets the minimum requirements of American National Standard for Information Sciences — Permanence of Paper for Printed Library Materials, ANSI Z39.48-1984.

Library of Congress Cataloging-in-Publication Data

Word order in discourse / edited by Pamela Downing, Michael Noonan.
p. cm. -- (Typological studies in language, ISSN 0167-7373; v. 30)
1. Grammar, Comparative and general--Word order. 2. Typology (Linguistics) 3. Discourse analysis. I. Downing, Pamela. II. Noonan, Michael (Michael P.) III. Series.
P295.W66 1995
415--dc20 94-44088
ISBN 90 272 2921 X (hb.) / 90 272 2922 8 (pb.) (European; alk. paper) CIP
ISBN 1-55619-424-2 (hb.) / 1-55619-636-9 (pb.) (U.S.; alk. paper)

John Benjamins Publishing Co. • P.O.Box 75577 • 1070 AN Amsterdam • The Netherlands
John Benjamins North America • P.O.Box 27519 • Philadelphia PA 19118-0519 • USA

Preface

The present volume constitutes a selection from the more than fifty papers presented at a symposium entitled *Word Order in Discourse* held at the University of Wisconsin-Milwaukee, April 12-14, 1991. The symposium was the twentieth in a series of linguistics symposia held at UWM and was chaired by Edith Moravcsik and me.

The topic of this symposium grew out of an idea I had for a conference on verb-initial languages and the ways in which these languages exploit word order variation in discourse. Somewhere along the way, the scope of the symposium broadened to include word order variation in discourse in all languages. The topic proved to be a popular one, since the fifty or so papers presented at the symposium were selected from among the more than one hundred twenty abstracts we received after the symposium was announced.

The UWM Linguistics Symposia are community endeavors and would not be possible without the untiring assistance of dozens of people. I would like to take this opportunity to thank the following who, together with Edith and me, served on the organizing committee: Michael Darnell, Fred Eckman, Gregory Iverson, and Patricia Kilroe. The following campus units offered financial support: the Center for Twentieth Century Studies, the College of Letters and Science, the Department of English and Comparative Literature, the Department of German, the Department of Linguistics, the Department of Philosophy, the Department of Slavic Languages, the Department of Spanish and Portuguese, the Department of Speech Pathology and Audiology, the Division of Outreach and Continuing Education, the Graduate School, the Intensive English as a Second Language Program, the Language Resource Center, the Master of Arts in Foreign Language and Literature Program, the School of Allied Health Professions, and the School of Education. To all these units, I would like to express my sincere appreciation for their support, which, for many of these units, has continued over many years.

Michael Noonan

Contents

List of Abbreviations

ABL	ablative
ACC	accusative
ACT	active
ADJ	adjective
ADV	adverb
ART	article
ASP	aspect
ATT	attributive
AUX	auxiliary
CAUS	causative
CL	clitic
CLASS	classifier
COMP	complementizer
COND	conditional
CONT	continuative
COP	copula
DAT	dative
EMP	emphatic
FEM	feminine
FOC	focus
FUT	future
GEN	genitive
HON	honorific
IMP	imperative
IMPERF	imperfect
INDEF	indefinitive
INF	infinitive
INSTR	instrumental
INT	intransitive
LOC	locative
MASC	masculine
NEG	negative
NOM	nominative
OBJ	object
OBL	oblique
PART	particle
PASS	passive
PAST	past
PERF	perfect
PL	plural
POSS	possessive
PRED	predicate
PRES	present
PRET	preterite
PROG	progressive
Q	question
QUOT	quotative
RED	reduplicative
REL	relative
SG	singular
STAT	stative
SUBJ	subject
TAG	tag question
TAM	tense-aspect modality
TOP	topic
TRANS	transitive
VOC	vocative

Word order in discourse

By way of introduction*

Pamela Downing
University of Wisconsin-Milwaukee

1. Introduction

As the papers in this volume demonstrate, word order variation, both inter-linguistic and intra-linguistic, is not random, boundless, and unpredictable. Because all languages are put to similar uses in the human communities in which they are spoken, it is common to find that speakers of a language use distinct word order patterns for such universally relevant discourse tasks as signalling the introduction of a new participant into a narrative or marking disagreement with the claims of another speaker. And because users of all human languages share common cognitive capacities, the word order variations permitted in any language must conform to the constraints imposed by those capacities.

We also find that, on the basis of the word order variants which they permit, we can classify languages into a limited number of *types*, each characterized by a *cluster* of co-occurring traits. If we can identify the type to which a particular language belongs, we will be able to predict with relative confidence that it will possess a whole range of properties characteristic of languages of that type. Thus, for instance, if the language belongs to the verb-final type, we might predict that it will also exhibit suffixes rather than prefixes, postpositions rather than prepositions, post-verbal rather than pre-verbal auxiliaries, and so on, since these traits typically co-occur with clause-final verb placement in the languages that have thus far been studied.[1]

In addition to these predictions about *invariant* properties characteristic of languages of particular types, it is also possible to make predictions about

Table 1. Patterns of word order variation for different basic word order types (from Steele 1978: 601).

	VOS	VSO	SOV	SVO
Very common (over 50% of lges)	VSO SVO	VOS	OSV	
Common (at least 50% of lges)		SVO	SVO	
Not uncommon (slightly less than 50%)				V S
Uncommon (substantially less than 50%)		OVS OSV SOV SV	OVS VOS VSO V S	VOS VSO SOV OSV OVS
Nonexistent	SOV OSV			

which *alternative* word orders will be permitted, and, in some cases, about what discourse functions these alternative word orders will serve, in languages of particular types. Susan Steele, in an early paper on word order typology (Steele 1978), for instance, presented the chart shown in Table 1,[2] which demonstrates striking differences in the predilections of languages of different types to exploit word order variation.

Not only do languages of different types appear to be differentially susceptible to the use of particular alternative word orders; these particular alternative orders may also tend to be confined, in languages of a particular type, to particular discourse contexts. This tendency is illustrated by the papers in this volume which discuss the use of non-verb-initial clauses in basically verb-initial languages. R. E. Longacre, for instance, concentrates on three "strongly VSO languages",[3] Trique (Otomanguean), Luwo (Nilotic), and Biblical Hebrew, and catalogues a number of uses of non-verb-initial structures, all of them sharing the function of marking "a departure from the primary storyline into setting, background, or explanation." Doris Payne also describes a pattern common to a number of verb-initial Austronesian languages whereby pre-verbal phrases are allowed, as in the languages described by Longacre, in clauses which are descriptive, which initiate new subsections of the text, or which "lay foundations," i.e. "concepts to which subsequent information is specifically mapped."

The tendency to exploit non-verb-initial structures in this way is but one of a number of linguistic properties characteristic of verb-initial languages. The fact that syntactic language types are characterized not just by the defining trait (such as a predominance of verb-initial clauses), but also by a number of other correlated traits, suggests that the distribution of these properties is not arbitrary. In other words, we are invited to consider the question of possible motivations for the correlations observed.

From the functionalist perspective represented by most of the papers in this volume, the answer to such questions can be found, as can the key to language variation within a single language, in the constraints imposed by the social system within which language is used and by the cognitive abilities of its users. Since human language is universally put to such uses as conversational exchange or storytelling, each language will need to develop structures that facilitate the performance of these functions. And since all human beings share a particular cognitive architecture, each human language will be constrained to develop in a way that can be readily manipulated by this system. Individual languages may realize one of a limited number of alternative ways of meeting these requirements; from this perspective, we can see each type-specific cluster of traits as one possible response to the array of social and cognitive constraints within which all languages must operate.

Bruce Harold begins to identify some of these alternative responses in his paper in this volume. VSO languages, Harold argues, may choose "predictability" ("the degree to which the listener can predict the presence and role of a particular concept") as a syntactic organizing principle, placing verbs in initial position in most cases but also permitting indefinites and pragmatically marked NPs in this slot because of their unpredictability. Languages of some other types may organize instead on the basis of "availability" ("the ease with which a listener can access a concept"), thereby assigning indefinite noun phrases to slots late in the clause because they are not available. Both of these organizing principles can be seen as responses to the cognitive limitations of human language users, but as *alternative* responses. Each pattern is thus cognitively *motivated*, but because of the existence of competing, equally well-motivated options, we cannot *predict* which option a given language may choose.

Once a language has chosen a particular option, let's say predictability-oriented verb-initiality, a number of other features characteristic of the type may follow. Because the ease of processing of one part of a sentence depends on the organization of the preceding parts, the choice of the verb-initial option may predispose the language to choose other options (which come to be characteristic of the type) as well. Thus, to take a simple if somewhat controversial example[4], if the head constituent of the verb phrase, the verb, precedes its dependents, this may exert pressure on the head of the adpositional phrase, the adposition, to precede its dependents as well, guaranteeing a consistent (and therefore less cognitively stressful) processing order (head before dependents) for phrases of both types. In other words, although there are languages in which adpositions appear before their dependents and languages in which adpositions appear after their dependents, in principle allowing for a particular language to adopt either option, if that language also possesses verbs with pre-verbal dependents, the balance may be tipped toward the use of postpositions, in order to maintain structural harmony throughout the language and to facilitate processing of the sentences of the language. It is in this way that languages with particular clusters of traits, i.e. of particular structural types, develop, in accordance with internal as well as external pressures.

2. Methods of investigation

Now, we can easily see from the recent history of the discipline that there are a number of ways in which we can go about studying constraints on word order.

2.1 *The sentence elicitation approach*

One methodology, probably the dominant one, has involved the interviewing of native speakers of the language in question, presenting them with candidate sentences and eliciting from them grammaticality judgements. While this methodology has produced some successes, it has clearly been deficient in revealing much about those cases where speakers accept as "grammatical" more than one alternative word order. Thus, in English we can use either of the alternative forms shown in (1).

(1) a. *If you're happy, I'm happy.*
    b. *I'm happy if you're happy.*

If languages eschew true synonymy, as is often claimed, why should these alternative word orders be possible?

2.2 *The text distribution approach*

Here a discourse-based approach to word order can be of help. By examining the use of these alternative orders in actual texts, we may find that, although they may be "synonymous" in some strict semantic sense, they serve very different pragmatic functions. In her research on the placement of adverbial clauses in English conversation, Cecilia Ford has examined precisely the sort of sentences shown in (1), and she has found that the placement of the conditional clause is related to its interactional function within the conversation. Consider the example, from Ford 1993: 48, in (2), where the conditional clause precedes the main clause:

(2) A: ... *So what time y'leaving f'the city.*
B: *Oh:: probly abou-t te [n-*
A: [*((ringing sound))*]
B: *-ten thirdy eleven, er- [n-d-ih .hh*
→ A: [*Oh If you wanna leave about eleven,*
[*I'll walk down with [you °cuz I haftuh go tuh school.*

Here the placement of the *if*-clause in initial position allows speaker A to select an alternative (eleven o'clock, as opposed to ten thirty) from B's preceding turn and use that as the point of departure for her offer to accompany B. As Ford points out (1993: 48), "the fact that A selects an option from B's prior talk gives a sense that the two parties are reaching a decision together." In her corpus, Ford found that initial conditional clauses were often used in this way, "to present options that follow from points reached in prior discourse, to restate options that have appeared in prior discourse, or to present possibilities as at least temporarily shared" (1993: 62). By contrast, final conditionals were not used to create discourse level linkages of this sort, as the initial conditional in example (2) does. Thus, once we examine the actual use of these alternative constructions in discourse, we find that they are not synonymous, at least not pragmatically.

In this way, ongoing work on word order in discourse has been revolutionizing our understanding of the complex web of factors that determine the word order that a particular speaker of a particular language is likely to use in a particular speech context. In some cases, these studies have involved painstaking analysis of individual examples drawn from detailed transcripts; this approach has been used to considerable profit by, for instance, practitioners of the "conversation analysis" methodology pioneered by Harvey Sacks, Emanuel Schegloff, and Gail Jefferson.[5] Other studies have been based on an assessment of the distributional properties of a large corpus of examples of the construction in question; this sort of quantitative approach is represented by most of the papers in this volume. Discourse-based work using these two approaches (or a combination of the two) has already provided us with a lengthy list of documented influences on word order, and we are now able to begin to explore the ways in which the competition among these not always compatible factors is worked out in different languages and in different contexts involving the use of the same language.

Even this very fruitful approach to the study of word order variation is not without its shortcomings, however. In the real world situations in which texts are produced, several potential determinants of word order may typically co-occur, making it difficult to see exactly which is decisive in a particular instance. Referents which are agentive, for instance, may typically be human as well, making it unclear whether a word order option used in the presence of such referents is triggered by their humanness or their agentiveness. This is a simple example; in actual texts a much larger number of influencing factors may simultaneously be at work, and the text may fail to provide the "crucial example" that will show which of the co-occurring factors is decisive.

In his paper in this volume, Russell Tomlin points out another problem with a strictly text-based methodology. When particular language structures are used in particular discourse contexts, say, in the presence of human agents, or in a passage devoted to storyline development, it is sometimes difficult to determine whether the relationship between the linguistic form and the discourse factor is causal or merely correlational. As Tomlin puts it:

> As long as one relies on textual analysis as the principal methodology for investigating functional claims, one will be hindered by the problem of distinguishing correlation from causation in functional mappings, principally because the statistical methods required to reach the kinds of theoretical conclusions functional analysis requires are not yet fully developed (Tomlin, this volume)

2.3 *The experimental approach*

To avoid these problems, it is useful to supplement the text-based methodology with work in an experimental paradigm in which the individual functional factors can be manipulated independently; this is the approach taken in this volume by Tomlin in his paper and by Ron Cowan in his. Cowan describes experiments in which he created mini-discourses that systematically manipulated several discourse factors, including animacy, the (old vs. new) information status of the referents, the role continuity of the referents, the distance since the last mention, and the perceived "negativity" of the situation described. English and Mandarin-speaking subjects were then asked to judge whether various sentences involving dative movement and passivization were appropriate completions of the mini-discourses with which they were presented. Interestingly, the responses of native English and (ESL-learning) native Mandarin speakers to English passive sentences differed, suggesting that the Mandarin speakers carried over into English their native assessment of the relative importance of the factors of information status and negativity, an assessment that differed from that of the native English speakers.

Tomlin's paper focusses on the relationship between the discourse "saliency" or "thematicity" of a referent and its syntactic treatment. Citing the difficulties that other authors have had in identifying "themes" and "topics" in textual data, Tomlin chooses as the focus of his investigation "focally attended referents", a category which overlaps considerably with the traditional "topic" and "theme", but which is easier to define operationally within the experimental paradigm which he has adopted. Using as his stimuli a set of computer-animated films depicting the actions of two fish, Tomlin first attracted the subjects' "focal attention" to one of the fish by displaying a large arrow pointed at the fish. He then showed a film sequence involving the focally attended fish and another fish, and asked the subjects to produce on-line descriptions of the action sequence. The English-speaking subjects Tomlin tested virtually unanimously assigned the "focally attended" fish to the subject slot in their descriptive sentences, even when the focal fish was the patient of the action depicted and required a passive verb form in order to be expressed as the subject.

On the basis of these results, Tomlin concludes that the functional grammar of English contains a rule which dictates that the speaker is to code as the syntactic subject of the utterance the referent which is currently focally attended. This generalization is one which would be difficult to perceive sheerly through the examination of textual data, because of the difficulties attendant on determining which referent was focally attended to by the speaker at the point at which the sentence was produced, and because of the competing influence of other discourse factors, which may in fact obscure the importance of focal attention in determining the syntactic structure of the sentence. Because it is possible to perceive in a controlled, experimental environment the influence of factors whose role may be obscured in textual analysis, this sort of research paradigm can act as a valuable supplement and corrective to the results of textual analysis, Tomlin argues.

These interesting results should not, however, lead us to forget that the behavior of subjects in an experimental situation is not necessarily identical to the behavior that subjects would exhibit in a real world language use situation, other things being equal. Several considerations suggest, for instance, that we would be premature in proposing that the regular correspondence between focal attention and subject choice which Tomlin observed in his experiments represents a rule of English "in general."

First, we should note that Tomlin's subjects were asked to give *on-line* descriptions of the scenes they viewed. This is a very specific type of task and one that is involved in a decided minority of the sentences produced by the typical English user. Because the subjects were charged, in this way, with producing on-line descriptions of a string of events of whose outcome they were unaware, it is unlikely that they were able to construct the sort of *global* textual structure that is characteristic of many narratives; this feature of the experimental design may have affected lexical and syntactic structure in a number of ways. In addition, the experimental situation was devoid of many of the social factors which can trigger linguistic adaptations. Whether focal attention would be as crucially determinative of subject choice in other sorts of language-use situations, when the speaker can use subject assignment as one of an array of politeness devices, or as a means of signalling the *global* textual status of a particular referent, remains to be seen. Clearly, there is much work ahead in integrating the findings produced by these various approaches to the study of word order variation.

3. Motivations for word order variation

In the meantime, however, there is ample evidence to continue the description of factors with an attested influence on the choice among word order options. Among the functions which language must serve for its users, the conveying of propositional information has traditionally been taken as primary. It is clear that word order has a fundamental role here — in a morphologically modest language like English, word order may in some cases be the only clue to the identity of the grammatical roles of the subject and direct object of the verb.

The information carried by word order variations is not confined to the propositional, however. Word order choices may also be dictated by the need of the speaker or writer to establish a social or affective stance, to create text-level structures from sentence-level resources, and to communicate in a way which is optimally matched to the text receiver's cognitive capacities.

3.1 *Affect marking*

The affect-marking potential of word order emerges especially clearly in conversational texts. In his paper, Kyu-hyun Kim argues, for instance, that one of the primary functions of WH-clefts in conversation is to serve as an "affect key", foregrounding the speaker's affective stance in a way that would not be possible with the non-clefted alternative word order.

Working with Sinhala and Tamil, Susan Herring and John Paolillo also point out the effect of affective stance and communicative intent on the word order of WH-questions in narratives in these SOV languages. In true information-seeking questions in Tamil narratives, the WH-word is most likely to appear in pre-verbal position, while in "classical" rhetorical questions (expected to elicit a "no" response from the hearer), it is in initial position that the WH-word is most often found. Sinhala also displays word order alternations dependent on the function of the WH-question. While the WH-word is most likely to appear in initial position in true information-seeking questions, it typically appears in post-verbal position when the function of the question is to introduce the next event in the narrative chain (e.g., "What did she do next? She dug a hole in the ground.")

3.2 *Creation of textual structure*

As for the text-level functions of word order, virtually every paper in the volume underscores the role of word order variation in creating textual structure. The way in which word order will be exploited for this purpose of course differs from text type to text type; while WH-clefts may be used in English conversations to initiate repairs or to signal disagreement with the preceding speaker, as Kyu-hyun Kim describes in his paper, the use of WH-clefts for these purposes may be entirely absent in a narrative text, for example.

Most of the papers in the volume do in fact concentrate on narrative texts, and a number of them describe ways in which word order variation is used to draw textual boundaries and define textual sub-units. In English conversational story-telling contexts, for instance, left-dislocation constructions may be used to mark the disjunctive resumption of a story, the initiation of a story, or the affectively upgraded repetition of a story, as Kyu-hyun Kim demonstrates in his paper. The papers by Longacre and Payne mentioned earlier show how non-verb-initial structures can be used in verb-initial languages to separate those sections of the text which convey the backbone of the narrative from those which merely give background information, information which is off the time line. In her paper on the "nearly free word order" *di-* clauses in Classical Malay, Susanna Cumming notes that in this language, preverbal agents occur only in clauses which also include a pre-verbal patient and which serve to "re-orient the reader/hearer to participants which are given but in a potentially new relationship," thereby initiating a text structure boundary. In the ancient non-VSO languages Hittite, Latin, and Classical Greek, verb-initial sentences were used in the context of discontinuity or unexpectedness, as when the information in a particular section of text was marked as additional, or less important, as Sylvia Luraghi explaines in her paper. And in the strict SVO language Emai, described by Ronald Schaefer, the possessor movement construction is but one of an array of linguistic devices used to mark the "peak" of the narrative storyline.

Word order variations can also be used, not simply to demarcate textual substructures, but also to indicate the textual status of the referents of individual constituents of the clause. Placement of a particular noun phrase before the predicate in a basically verb-initial language, for instance, may do more than indicate a textual break — it may also carry information about the role of the referent of that particular noun phrase in the the developing text. Certain positions appear to be reserved for referents which are "low in topicality", as indicated by lack of recent mention and failure to persist in the text. Considering the basically verb-initial language Colville-Okanagan, Michael Darnell argues in his paper that nominals may appear preverbally only if they are of low topicality and/or contrastive. Similarly, in written Guaraní folk stories, nominals representing referents of low discourse topicality are good candidates for pre-verbal placement or for incorporation into the verb, as explained by Maura Velázquez-Castillo in her paper.

By contrast, certain syntactic positions seem to be reserved for referents of high discourse topicality. As noted earlier, Tomlin argues on the basis of the on-line descriptions elicited in his experimental task that English speakers will encode the focally attended referent as the subject of the clause. Payne, in her examination of a number of verb-initial languages, argues that in languages (like Yagua and Cebuano) that allow a certain flexibility of post-verbal word order, thematic NPs are likely to appear as close after the verb as possible. And in his study of the Emai possessor movement construction, Schaefer notes that this construction allows a nominal of relatively high topicality to appear in the immediately post-verbal slot, the slot where secondary topics typically appear.

Alternative word orders are also put to use for introducing new referents into the text, especially if the role of those referents in the discourse is to be a prominent one. Robert Hetzron pointed out a number of years ago (Hetzron 1971) that many languages possess a "presentative" construction which has the effect of positioning toward the end of the sentence NPs referring to referents destined to figure prominently in the upcoming text. In her paper on ancient Indo-European languages, Luraghi describes the use of verb-initial constructions which meet this description in introductory contexts. In their paper on SOV languages, Herring and Paolillo examine presentative sentences in Sinhala and Tamil narratives and also find support for Hetzron's predictions, although the degree of compliance depends on the rigidity with which the language applies the verb-final constraint.

The fact that a number of languages not only have presentative constructions, but presentative constructions which place the presented referent in similar position within the sentence in languages of different word order types, is quite striking. It suggests that these constructions may reflect the influence of the second class of factors mentioned above — those which stem from the cognitive limitations of human language users.

3.3 *Facilitating language processing*

It is by now a commonplace in linguistics that many sorts of linguistic phenomena seem to be designed to accommodate the strengths and weaknesses of our cognitive systems. To take a simple example, it has been repeatedly observed, in a wide variety of languages, that a referent is likely to be encoded by a lexical noun when it is first introduced into a text, but with pronouns or zero anaphora (depending on the language) from then on.[6] A lexical noun may once again be used, however, when the referent has been absent from the stage for a while, whether other competing referents have entered the scene or not. This reversion to the more complete, less ambiguous form of reference has been linked to the fact that human beings seem to be able to keep information in consciousness for only a short time without rehearsing it; if the referent has been absent from the stage for a while, it is likely that it is no longer in the focus of the reader/hearer's consciousness, necessitating re-mention with the semantically richer form.[7]

This linguistic pattern reflects the temporal limitations to which our consciousness is subject. Many of the word order phenomena discussed in this volume reflect as well the limited capacity of consciousness at a single point in time. While it may in principle be possible to construct grammatical sentences, like (3),

(3) *A farmer kills a duckling.*

in which the information conveyed by the subject, the verb, and the object is all "new" to the reader/hearer, it has been repeatedly noted that the sentences used in actual texts, especially oral texts, are rarely of this sort.[8] Instead, they typically include some information with which the hearer/reader is already familiar, as well as some new information, as in (4).

(4) *He killed the duckling.*

The prevalence of this pattern is so striking that some linguists have attempted to cast it in terms of a linguistic principle. Givón, for instance, has proposed that

> there exists a strategy of information processing in language such that the amount of new information per a certain unit of *message-transaction* is restricted in a fashion—say "one unit per proposition". (Givón 1975: 202)

Similar insights underlie Chafe's "one-new-idea-at-a-time constraint" (Chafe 1992) and Du Bois' "One Lexical Argument Constraint" (Du Bois 1987). The existence of these constraints is explained in the following way: because the human language processor is incapable of assimilating large amounts of new information at once, sentences are typically composed of combinations of old and new information. As each bit of new information is assimilated, it is incorporated into a developing structure of information and is then ready to serve as part of the cognitive foundation to which further bits of information will come to be attached. Each sentence, then, both evokes this pre-existing information structure and offers new information to be added to it.

Within this model, it will of course be to the language processor's advantage if s/he can readily discriminate between the old and the new information, and between the crucial, foundation-building new information and the not-so-important, prop-like new information. It is precisely these distinctions that are marked, our authors argue, by many of the word order variations discussed in this volume.

3.3.1 *The theme-first pattern*

Cowan, for instance, discusses the importance of the "Old Things First Principle" (OTFP) for English. Even though English has fairly rigid SVO word order, it does show some flexibility in the positioning of recipient noun phrases relative to patient noun phrases, and on the basis of experimental evidence, Cowan argues that the OTFP predicts the choice between sentence pairs like those shown in (5).

(5) a. *He walked across the room and gave the package to Mary.*
 b. *He walked across the room and gave Mary the package.*

In Cowan's study, subjects given a sample discourse containing information about the package, but not about Mary, tended to choose sentence (5a) as the preferred completion to the sample discourse. It is of course this alternative which presents the old information first, in accordance with Cowan's principle.

The governing principle discussed by Cowan here has much in common with what the Prague School linguists have termed "communicative dynamism". As defined by Firbas (1966: 270), the communicative dynamism of a linguistic element is "the extent to which the sentence element contributes to the development of the communication, to which, as it were, 'it pushes the communication forward.'" Within this framework, elements with the lowest degree of communicative dynamism (CD) are called "thematic", those with higher degrees "rhematic". The influence of degree of CD on word order has been much discussed with respect to languages like Czech and Russian, where it can be claimed that it is not the grammatical roles of the sentence elements, but rather their degree of CD, that serves as the fundamental word ordering principle within the sentence, with themes tending to appear early in the sentence, and rhemes appearing later. LaPolla argues that similar factors are crucial to the description of Chinese, where it is "focus structure,"[9] rather than syntactic relations, that determine word order variation.

It has been suggested that this same principle lies behind the fact that languages in which objects typically precede subjects are statistically quite rare; since continuing topics of talk tend to be made subjects (Prince 1992), and since themes tend to precede rhemes, subjects tend to precede objects (Mallinson and Blake 1981: 154). Similarly, even in languages with fairly rigid word order, like English, the preference for theme – rheme order may contribute to findings like those discussed by Cowan.

3.3.2 *The rheme-first pattern*

Not all languages with flexible word order, however, appear to follow the much discussed theme to rheme pattern. In the 70s, Creider (1977) and Tomlin and Rhodes (1979) began to call our attention to languages, like Ojibwa and Nandi, which appeared to place rhematic information early in the sentence. In this volume, papers by Mithun, Payne and others discuss additional languages which break with the theme → rheme pattern, placing "newsworthy" (rhematic) information of various sorts toward the beginning, rather than the end, of the clause. In some of these languages, e.g. Iroquois, as discussed in the paper by Mithun, the pattern seems to be the exact opposite of the theme–rheme pattern: words are linearly arranged from the most to the least newsworthy. In other cases, as in Maasai and Yagua as analyzed in the paper by Payne, clauses may begin with highly newsworthy elements, but the clause as a whole does not represent a progression from highest to lowest rhematicity. Rather, post-verbal NPs tend to assume an order in which the more thematic precede the rhematic, thwarting attempts to come up with a simple overall characterization of the pattern of information distribution within the clause.

3.3.3 *Cognitive explanations*

The utility for the text-receiver of either the theme → rheme pattern or the rheme → theme pattern is apparent, since both reserve a particular sentence position for the crucial high CD (rhematic) material. What might be less obvious is the way in which these two patterns correlate with the propensities of the human cognitive apparatus. Since two completely distinct, in fact, completely opposite, strategies are used for the purpose of distinguishing thematic and rhematic material, how is it possible to claim that either is cognitively motivated?

Here again we should keep in mind the fact that *motivation* is different from *prediction*. Although the co-presence of these two patterns demonstrates that neither is a necessary outcome of the structure of cognition, it is in fact possible to argue that each exploits independently demonstrable tendencies, albeit *different* tendencies, of our cognitive systems.

3.3.3.1 *Cognitive explanations for the theme-first pattern*

Consider the theme-rheme pattern. If it is in fact the case that our understanding of a text is dependent on the increasing elaboration of a cognitive representation of the information carried by the text, as is suggested, for instance, by Gernsbacher and Hargreaves (1988), it makes sense that one fruitful strategy would be to present the thematic material first, in order to provide an anchor, as it were, to which the subsequent rhematic material can be attached. The importance of this strategy has been demonstrated with respect to other linguistic phenomena: Fox and Thompson's recent work on relative clauses in English conversation (Fox and Thompson 1990), for instance, shows that relatives which modify subjects are much more likely to provide "grounding" for the referent of the subject than are relatives which modify direct objects. Fox and Thompson explain this discrepancy in the role of the relative clauses by pointing out that the subjects typically appear early in the clause, at a point where the speaker may not yet have been able to warrant the introduction of the referent by relating it to another (anchoring) referent already established in the discourse. By the time that the direct object NP appears later in the sentence, however, it is likely that the speaker will have been able to ground it by other means, making the use of a grounding relative clause unnecessary. The theme → rheme order, then, like subject relatives, has the advantage of providing grounding information early in the sentence; in fact, it grounds the new information in advance of its presentation.

This pattern also has the advantage of placing the most highly rhematic material in clause-final position, a position which has been demonstrated to be of high memorability. In a series of experiments conducted by Jarvella (Jarvella 1979), for instance, it was found that when subjects were asked to provide verbatim recall of segments from a recorded passage, they could recall all the words of the last clause heard without substantial difficulty, but were able to recall the first and last words in the previous clause better than words in the adjacent positions, which in turn were better remembered than words in the center positions in the clause.

Taken together, these considerations help to explain Hetzron's observation that presentative constructions do more than simply move presented referents to a marked position somewhere in the clause — that marked position tends to be late in the clause, i.e. in a position of inherent cognitive salience which follows slots that can be devoted to grounding the presented referent.

3.3.3.2 *Cognitive explanations for the rheme-first pattern*

Not all the cognitive advantages, however, accrue to the theme-rheme pattern. In psycholinguistic studies like those conducted by Jarvella and Gernsbacher and Hargreaves, subjects charged with identifying the words contained in sentences which they had read or listened to found elements placed in clause-initial position, or even in the first NP position, to be especially memorable. From this perspective, rheme → theme languages and verb-initial languages which place "pragmatically marked" elements in initial position are making good use of another slot which is of high cognitive salience. The frequency with which languages of all types exploit clause-initial position for special purposes is reflected in the Functional Grammar designation of a special "P1" slot, which is often devoted to constituents with a Topic or Focus function (Dik 1989). The exploitation of the clause-initial slot for such "special purposes" can occur even in a language which generally seems to reflect a theme to rheme pattern of organization; on the basis of conversational data, Ocampo reports in his paper here that this is the case in Spanish.

In her paper, Mithun also suggests that the rheme-initial pattern may be especially useful because it places the rhematic material in a position of natural prosodic prominence. Given evidence that, in most languages, the pitch and amplitude of intonation units tends to progressively decrease, placement of a newsworthy element at the beginning of an intonation unit will tend to increase its auditory prominence. To the extent that sentences and intonation units are co-extensive, exploitation of the "newsworthy first" principle will thus supplement the natural salience of sentence-initial position with auditory reinforcement.

4. Remaining problems

The papers in this volume and others I have referred to attest to the tremendous progress that is being made in our understanding of the functions of word order variation in language. It is essential to notice, however, that the enterprise is still plagued by a number of problems areas which urgently require attention.

4.1 *Terminology*

One of these problem areas involves the very terminology we have been using to describe our findings. Especially when everyday words like "topic" and "focus" have been drafted for technical purposes, the assumption has been that "we all know roughly what we're talking about," and the new terms have been applied to language after language without benefit of any clear guiding criteria. Frequently, clarification of the term (and sometimes the corresponding *concept* as well) has taken place only upon encountering a language which does not appear to be describable in terms that were previously thought to be universally applicable. An interesting case in point is the term "subject", which elicited a flurry of definitional activity[10] as linguists wrestled with ergative and Philippine-type languages (see Schachter 1976). In his paper in this volume, Darnell illustrates the difficulty inherent in applying the trusty concept of "clause" to the Salish languages, in which any independent word can serve as a predicate.

Some of the papers in this volume argue that certain traditional terms should be abandoned, or at least supplemented with additional terms which mark better defined, more finely discriminated categories. Tomlin, for instance, argues that the "theoretically undefinable and empirically vague pragmatic notions of theme or topic" should be discarded in favor of experimentally manipulable concepts like "focal attention". Cumming too expresses dissatisfaction with attempts to account for the various information statuses of referents in terms of a single "topicality" continuum; she suggests establishing independent dimensions of "accessibility", "referentiality", etc., and adding to the list the quality of "protagonism", i.e. the importance of the participant to the story as a whole. Herring and Paolillo argue for further refinement of the use of the term "focus", suggesting that attempts to identify a "focus position" in language of particular types has suffered from a failure to recognize that "presentational focus", "informational WH-focus", etc., may elicit distinct linguistic treatments.

Of course, not all the papers in the volume reflect these terminology-related suggestions, and there is considerable variation, as there is in the field as a whole, in the use of terms. In editing the volume, however, we have made an effort to ensure that all the authors make explicit their definitions for contested categories such as "topic", "theme", etc. This is probably the most we can hope for until a consensus based on the analysis of a large pool of typologically diverse languages has been worked out.

4.2 *Criteria for typing languages*

A number of the papers in the volume also address another difficult methodological issue — how to identify a particular language as a member of a given syntactic type. A number of issues are tied up together here. The first of these involves the identification of the sentence elements on which useful typologies can be based. A glance at the recent literature reveals a remarkable profusion of proposed typological parameters: the position of the verb (Payne 1990), the position of the subject (Keenan 1978), the relative positions of the subject, verb, and object (Greenberg 1963), whether the language exhibits grammatical or pragmatic word order (Thompson 1978), whether it is head-marking or dependent-marking (Nichols 1986), whether it is configurational or non-configurational (Hale 1983). The list goes on and on.

The striking profusion of classificatory schemes here is due in part to our discovery, over the years, that not all languages are necessarily describable in the same terms. While Greenberg's seminal work in syntactic typology relied on the analysis of sentences into the trusty elements subjects, verbs, and objects, for example, subsequent research revealed the existence of languages in which it is difficult to justify calling any particular noun phrase the subject (Schachter 1976).

But even if we confine our attention to languages which do clearly possess the elements on which the proposed typology is based, let's say subjects, objects, and verbs, it is still not always a straightforward task to assign these languages to types defined by the relative order of these three elements. This is because, as we have seen, all languages in discourse exhibit some word order variability, and it is up to the analyst to decide upon one of these orders as "basic" or "unmarked" or "dominant", if the language is to be typed.[11]

Within the typological tradition, the nod has often been given in cases of competition to the most frequently occurring surface word orders; in cases of close calls, however, a variety of criteria are invoked (Keenan 1976; Hawkins 1983; Givón 1979). Do clauses exhibiting the potentially "unmarked" word order allow the full range of tense, mood, aspect, and voice distinctions permitted within the language? Are clauses with this word order usable in contexts that are relatively free of presupposition, or does use of the construction carry some "special" pragmatic force, such as contrastive emphasis? Is this construction used in a wide range of pragmatic contexts, and within texts of all sorts, and does it appear relatively frequently within all these contexts?

In some cases, a single word order may elicit a "yes" answer to all these questions; in other cases, conflicts among criteria may arise. For instance, the word order that is used introducing referents often deviates from that which is used once they have been incorporated into the text. In such a case, the "freedom from presupposition" criterion may single out the introductory construction, while the range and frequency criteria may point to other constructions as more basic.

The dilemma I have described here can be quite real, and even functionally oriented typologists can differ from one another on the conclusions they draw in such cases. The paper by Matthew Dryer focuses on precisely this issue, re-analyzing the decisions about "unmarked word order" that have been made by other authors with respect to such languages as Tojolabal, Ojibwa, and Yagua. Dryer contends that the unmarked word order is not necessarily the most frequent. Rather, it is the default, "elsewhere" order used in situations which fail to satisfy the concisely characterizable conditions for the use of alternative (marked) word orders. While this word order may be the most frequently used, it need not be.

Dryer's approach to the discovery of the unmarked word order of a language, like those of most other scholars who have confronted the question, skirts another important issue with significant implications for the syntactic typing of languages: if textual data are to serve as the grounds for assigning a language to a particular word order type, *which* sort of text should be used?

This is a critical question, for, as Alan Kim's paper elegantly demonstrates, the word order options available may differ dramatically in accordance with the formality, genre, and modality of the text. In considering Japanese texts produced by a number of authors, for example, Kim found that the N(X)Q "Q-Float" numeral construction was common in oral and colloquial written texts, but rare in formal written texts, where the QN construction was preferred. When written and spoken word order options differ, or when the patterns used in narrative differ from those used in conversation, which sort of text (if either) should be given priority?

For years, linguists have written grammars that have served as the basis for typological descriptions without explicitly addressing this important issue. In most cases, grammars were based, without explicit discussion, on decontextualized elicited sentences or on transcriptions of oral narratives. In his paper, Longacre argues that it is indeed proper to use narratives as the foundation for language typing, since monologue is a better guide than dialogue to standard word order, and since narrative is "the most universal and most highly structured type of monologue discourse." Longacre thus proposes that "if storyline clauses in narrative discourse in a given language are VSO then that language should be classified as a VSO language."

Longacre's view is not universally held, however. Among linguists who have concerned themselves with the question, an increasing number argue that we should look instead to conversational texts as our primary source of data. As Kyu-hyun Kim puts it in his paper, "conversation is the primordial mode of language use which constitutes the basis of human social interaction and social organization." From this perspective, one might argue that the peculiarities of conversational texts should be seen as fundamental indicators of the syntactic capabilities of the language, rather than as deviations from the standard, especially if, as Kim suggests, "a grammar of a language is bound to be shaped by or adapted to the primordial interactional context where it is situated and actualized."

A full recognition of the implications of this controversy will eventually require a re-analysis of of the typological status of languages which have been classified on the basis of evidence from just one text type or from an indiscriminate mélange of text types, for, as Payne puts it, "most claims about word order have undoubtedly been based on narrative data and, without conscious awareness, the typological cubbyholes to which languages have been assigned are likely biased by formal features correlating with temporal sequentiality." In the meantime, we should take care to note what sort of data has served as the basis for a particular analysis, and we can make a plea for more papers entitled, "Word order in X oral narratives", as opposed to "Word order in X."

4.3 *Predicting the outcome of competitions among motivating factors*

The next "problem area" that I would like to draw your attention to has been slowly emerging as we have learned more and more about the plethora of factors that can have an influence on word order. Let us concentrate for the moment on a single genre of language activity — conversation. It should be clear, even from the brief discussion here, that the grammar of any language will be hard-pressed to encode all the sorts of information speakers may wish to convey in conversation and do it in a way that facilitates both cognitive processing and orderly interaction among the participants in the conversation.

Consider for instance the placement of relative clauses. If, as Fox and Thompson have suggested, the referents introduced into conversation must be grounded *at the point when they are introduced*, and if relative clauses can serve this grounding function, would it not be preferable for relative clauses in English conversation to precede, rather than follow, the noun which they modify? Although the answer to this question might be "yes", Hawkins (1983) has pointed out the fact that in prepositional languages (like English), relative clauses, which have a tendency to be long and heavy, have a greater tendency to follow the noun than do other nominal modifiers such as adjectives, genitives, numerals, and demonstratives. This peculiarity of relative clauses is often attributed to the fact that their placement before the noun would significantly delay the hearer's processing of the basic constituent structure of the sentence. If the relative clause preceded the modified noun, the hearer might in fact misinterpret a noun phrase within the relative clause as the head noun, further delaying the correct interpretation of the sentence. So in this case one might wish to claim that efficient sentence parsing demands that the relative clause be placed after the head noun, even though accurate interpretation of the text, and the referent's role in it, might be better served by placing the relative before the head noun.

This is a simple example, but it illustrates quite clearly, I think, the fact that not all the forces which act on word order are in league with each other to produce the same result. Furthermore, there is clearly no one algorithm for resolving conflicts among competing motivations. If there were, we would presumably not see all the typological variation that we do, since the competititon would shake out in the same way in each case. The fact that different languages do exhibit different word order patterns suggests that different factors from the pool we have discussed dominate the syntactic organization of different languages. On the other hand, the fact that many of these languages can be grouped into a limited number of frequently occurring types suggests that there may be some favored strategies for resolving the competition.

Many of the papers in the volume take up the topic of the competition among the various factors motivating word order. Harold's paper discusses the conflict between availability and predictability as syntactic organizing principles and characterizes the way in which the conflict is likely to be resolved, through different strategies, in languages of different types. In the competition between these two motivating factors, there is no pre-determined outcome. In the competition between referential coherence and thematic coherence as determinants of word order variation, on the other hand, Givón (1993) argues that when the two are in conflict, "the grammar parts company with the former and remains sensitive to the latter."

Clearly, much work remains to be done in this area. Exceptions to the predictions of functionally-oriented linguistic hypotheses are often explained as being due to the temporary victory of some competing motivating factor. Yet, in the absence of a model which specifies the conditions under which each competing factor is likely to prevail, such an appeal to competing motivations may seem to be little more than a *deus ex machina*. Given the complex and shifting array of contextual factors which come into play in determining the word order in a particular text, it is not surprising that it is often difficult to *predict* how a given competition will be resolved, given our current state of understanding. In fact, the taste and style of an individual speaker, very difficult to quantify, may have a significant impact on word order, making absolute predictability an unachievable goal. In spite of these difficulties, however, it is important not to give up the quest prematurely, since an understanding of the relative weight of competing factors can contribute not only to a model of grammar and text production, but also to our understanding of how and why languages change.

4.4 *Explaining language change*

The issue of language change presents a serious challenge, as well as a source of important data, for functional syntacticians. If a language is composed of cognitively tailored structures designed to perform the various functions demanded by the speech community, then why, one should ask, does the language inevitably change? In other words, why fix it if it ain't broke?

Several of the papers in the volume tackle this question and come up with different pieces of a possible answer. In some cases, a given linguistic structure may with time be re-interpreted in accordance with the speech contexts in which it is typically used, i.e. re-interpreted as the marker of a factor which regularly correlates with the factor it marked originally. What is initially seen as a plural marker may, for instance, be re-interpreted as a politeness marker because of its frequent exploitation in polite contexts (Brown and Levinson 1987: 198). In this volume, Harold views such re-interpretations as crucial determinants of the common pattern of historical drift from SOV to free word order to VSO to SVO.

And once one structure in a language has changed, it may provoke changes in other areas of the grammar. Mithun's paper offers a detailed discussion of a number of Siouan, Caddoan, and Iroquoian languages which are all remotely related genetically but which now exhibit strikingly different word orders. Tracing the development of these languages from a fixed SOV proto-language to the present, Mithun links shifts in word order to other language-internal developments, such as the rise of case marking in certain Siouan languages, referential third person pronominal prefixes in the Iroquoian languages, and an increase in noun incorporation in certain Caddoan languages.

In cases like some of those discussed by Mithun, the development of one particular language structure may promote change in another because the two represent alternative means of fulfilling the same linguistic function. The historic rigidification of word order and loss of case marking in English are often cited as an example of this sort, since both structures are capable of clarifying the grammatical roles of the NPs in the clause. In other cases the development of new structures, especially structures which are frequently used, may trigger other changes which have the effect of establishing (processing-enhancing) structural harmony throughout the language. In this regard, Dryer raises the case of O'odham (Papago), arguing that the recent change from GenN toward NGen order, and from postpositions to prepositions, can be seen as the result of the fact that VS and VO (as opposed to SV and OV) word orders have become more frequent. Although it can be argued that these verb-initial structures are not unmarked in O'odham (Payne 1987), their prevalence in frequency has been sufficient to motivate the use of right-branching structures elsewhere in the language, Dryer contends.

Language-external social factors may also leave their mark. Cowan suggests, for example, that the "adversative" constraint on the Mandarin *bei* passive is being lost under the influence of Russian and English. Velázquez-Castillo's paper similarly links the decline of a strictly topicality-based distribution of noun phrases in Guaraní to the introduction of definite articles borrowed from Spanish.

5. Conclusion

As the closing pages of this paper have pointed out, there is still much to be done in working out a consensus on the nature of the constraints governing word order variation. Even if we concentrate solely on the last-mentioned problem — constructing a coherent, psychologically and socially plausible model of syntactic change — it is clear that we face a daunting task; arriving at a *predictive* model of syntactic variation remains an even more distant goal.

I trust, however, that these pages have also demonstrated the tremendous amount of progress that has been made toward clarifying and reaching these goals in the last twenty years. We will undoubtedly continue to encounter new questions which may at times obscure the path, but it is clear that the journey is safely under way; we hope that the papers in this volume will be seen as an important contribution to the enterprise.

Notes

* I wish to thank Pat Clancy, Ceci Ford, and Mickey Noonan for their helpful comments on an earlier version of this paper.

1. For a recent elaboration on these correlations based on a database of 543 languages, see Dryer (1992).

2. Steele's stance in undertaking this study was that "all languages have a dominant word order, a surface ordering of subject, object and verb relative to one another that is at least more common than other possible orders" (p. 587), and she identified the basic order for each language in her sample "on the statement of the person who described it" (p. 591), or, if she was familiar with it, on the basis of her own analysis. She concentrated her analysis on the word order manifested in declarative main clauses and accepted as "variant" word orders only those which were neither characterized as "marked" by the investigator nor distinguished by phonological or syntactic peculiarities from the basic word order of the language.

   It is also important to note Steele's method for identifying subjects and objects. As she puts it, (p. 591): "although *subject* is a term linguists use regularly and with confidence, a precise characterization of the notion eludes us. A similar situation may pertain as regards the notion *object*. I am not going to agonize over the problem. In languages where I am dependent on someone else's description I simply accepted their decision as to what was a subject and what was an object. In languages with which I was familiar I didn't use any formal criteria to identify subject and object, but rather assumed the validity of such concepts, and, with no obvious evidence to the contrary, expected that they would correspond roughly to ENGLISH."

   As the subsequent discussion will demonstrate, not all typologists share Steele's views on these matters, and it is crucial to keep in mind the assumptions which guided her data analysis when interpreting the results presented in Table 1.

3. In justifying his characterization of these languages as "strongly VSO", Longacre notes that
   a) they conform to Greenberg's generalization that VSO languages are verb-initial and prepositional and use noun-genitive and noun-adjective orders, and
   b) storyline clauses in narrative discourse in these languages are VSO.

4. Dryer (1992) argues, for instance, that it is not a consistent pattern in head-dependent ordering which lies behind these regularities, but rather the tendency of languages to be consistently right-branching or consistently left-branching.

5. For examples of work done in this tradition, see Kyu-hyun Kim's paper in this volume, Fox (1987), Ford (1993), or Schegloff (1988).

6. Whether the option of the pronoun/zero anaphor is chosen in a particular textual context will also depend, of course, on other factors, such as the presence or absence of other referents, the textual status of the referent (as hero or prop), etc. For a detailed treatment of the effect of these factors on lexical choice in Japanese narratives, see Clancy (1980).

7. Givón (1990) suggests that the use of these different sorts of nominals may act as text-processing instructions to the reader/hearer. Thus the use of the zero anaphoric form instructs the text receiver to continue the activiation of the referents which were active in the preceding clause, while the use of a full NP instructs the text receiver to terminate the current activation.

8. See, for instance, Lambrecht (1987), for a description and explanation of the "preferred clause structure" of modern spoken French, and Du Bois (1987) for a discussion of a "type-independent Preferred Argument Structure" found in both accusative and ergative languages.

9. Following Lambrecht (to appear), LaPolla intends by this term "a grammatical system used to mark the focus of the assertion in a sentence by setting it off against the pragmatic presupposition."

10. See the papers, especially those by Keenan and by Li and Thompson, in Li (1976).

11. Of course, it is possible that some languages, especially those which exhibit "pragmatic word order" (Thompson 1978), cannot usefully be assigned to any basic word order type. See Mithun (1987) for discussion of this issue.

References

Brown, Penelope and Stephen C. Levinson. 1987. *Politeness: Some universals in language usage*. Cambridge: Cambridge University Press.

Chafe, Wallace L. 1992. "The flow of ideas in a sample of written language." *Discourse Description: Diverse linguistic analyses of a fund-raising text* ed. by William C. Mann and Sandra A. Thompson, 267-94. Amsterdam/Philadelphia: John Benjamins.

Clancy, Patricia M. 1980. "Referential choice in English and Japanese narrative discourse." *The Pear Stories: Cognitive, cultural, and linguistic aspects of narrative production* ed. by Wallace L. Chafe, 127-202. Norwood, N.J.: Ablex.

Creider, Chet. 1977. "Functional sentence perspective in a verb-initial language." *Language and Linguistic Problems in Africa* ed. by P.F. Kotey and H. Der-Houssikian, 330-43. Columbia, S.C.: Hornbeam Press.

Dik, Simon C. 1989. *The Theory of Functional Grammar. Part 1: The Structure of the Clause*. Dordrecht: Foris.

Dryer, Matthew. 1992. "The Greenbergian word order correlations." *Language* 68.81-138.

Du Bois, John. 1987. "The discourse basis of ergativity." *Language* 63.805-55.

Firbas, Jan. 1966. "On defining the theme in functional sentence analysis." *Travaux linguistiques de Prague* 1.267-80.

Ford, Cecilia E. 1993. *Grammar in Interaction: the pragmatics of adverbial clauses in American English conversation.* Cambridge: Cambridge University Press.

Fox, Barbara. 1987. *Discourse Structure and Anaphora*. Cambridge: Cambridge University Press.

Fox, Barbara and Sandra A. Thompson. 1990. "A discourse explanation of the grammar of relative clauses in English conversation." *Language* 66.297-316.

Gernsbacher, Morton Ann and David J. Hargreaves. 1988. "Accessing sentence participants: the advantage of first mention." *Journal of Memory and Language* 27.699-717.

Givón, T. 1975. "Focus and the scope of assertion: some Bantu evidence." *Studies in African Linguistics* 6.185-205.

Givón, T. 1979. *On Understanding Grammar*. New York: Academic Press.

Givón, T. 1990. *Syntax: A Functional-Typological Introduction*, Vol. 2. Amsterdam/ Philadelphia: John Benjamins.

Givón, T. 1993. "The pragmatics of word-order in Early Biblical Hebrew: referential vs. thematic coherence." Ms.

Greenberg, Joseph. 1963. "Some universals of grammar with particular reference to the order of meaningful elements." *Universals of Language* ed. by Joseph Greenberg, 58-90. Cambridge, Mass.: MIT Press.

Hale, Ken. 1983. "Warlpiri and the grammar of non-configurational languages." *Natural Language and Linguistic Theory* 1.5-47.

Hawkins, John A. 1983. *Word Order Universals.* New York: Academic Press.

Hetzron, Robert. 1971. "Presentative function and presentative movement." *Studies in African Linguistics* Suppl. 2. 79-105.

Jarvella, Robert J. 1979. "Immediate memory and discourse processing." *The Psychology of Learning and Motivation: Advances in research and theory, Vol. 13* ed. by Gordon H. Bower, 379-421. New York: Academic Press.

Keenan, Edward L. 1976. "Towards a universal definition of 'subject'." *Subject and Topic* ed. by Charles N. Li, 303-33. New York: Academic Press.

Keenan, Edward L. 1978. "The syntax of subject-final languages." *Syntactic Typology* ed. by Winfred P. Lehmann, 267-327. Austin: University of Texas Press.

Lambrecht, Knud. 1987. "On the status of SVO sentences in French discourse." *Coherence and Grounding in Discourse* ed. by Russell S. Tomlin, 217-61. Amsterdam/Philadelphia: John Benjamins.

Li, Charles N. and Sandra A. Thompson. 1976. "Subject and topic: a new typology of language." *Subject and Topic* ed. by Charles N. Li, 457-89. New York: Academic Press.

Mallinson, Graham and Barry J. Blake. 1981. *Language Typology.* Amsterdam: North Holland.

Mithun, Marianne. 1987. "Is basic word order universal?" *Coherence and Grounding in Discourse* ed. by Russell S. Tomlin, 281-328. Amsterdam/Philadelphia: John Benjamins.

Nichols, Johanna. 1986. "Head-marking and dependent-marking grammar." *Language* 62.56-119.

Payne, Doris. 1987. "Information structuring in Papago narrative discourse." *Language* 63.783-804.

Payne, Doris. 1990. *The Pragmatics of Word Order: Typological dimensions of verb initial languages.* Berlin: Mouton de Gruyter.

Prince, Ellen. 1992. "The ZPG letter: subjects, definiteness, and information-status." *Discourse Description: Diverse linguistic analyses of a fund-raising text* ed. by William C. Mann and Sandra A. Thompson, 295-326. Amsterdam/Philadelphia: John Benjamins.

Schachter, Paul. 1976. "The Subject in Philippine languages: topic, actor, actor-topic, or none of the above." *Subject and Topic* ed. by Charles N. Li, 491-518. New York: Academic Press.

Schegloff, Emanuel. 1988. "Description in the social sciences I: talk-in-interaction." *Papers in Pragmatics* 2.1-24.

Steele, Susan. 1978. "Word order variation: a typological study." *Universals of Human Language. Vol. 4 Syntax* ed. by Joseph Greenberg, 585-623. Stanford, Ca.: Stanford University Press.

Thompson, Sandra A. 1978. "Modern English from a typological point of view: some implications of the function of word order." *Linguistische Berichte* 54.19-35.

Tomlin, Russell and Richard Rhodes. 1979. "An introduction to information distribution in Ojibwa." *Papers from the Fifteenth Regional Meeting of the Chicago Linguistic Society* ed. by Paul R. Clyne et al., 307-20. Chicago: Chicago Linguistic Society.

What are discourse principles made of?*

Ron Cowan
University of Illinois

The goal of this paper is to refine the characterization of so-called pragmatic principles which have been proposed to account (in part) for word order variation in discourse, e.g. "information predictability" (Givón 1988), "first things first" (Gundel 1988), the "newsworthiness" principle (Mithun 1987) and "discourse iconicity" (Hetzron 1975). To date these have been formulated from the perspective of information structuring in communication and in the broadest possible manner. Unfortunately, the desire to achieve maximum generality through broad definitions has directed interest away from studying other discourse variables which may interact with these principles to produce word order variation in a language. Moreover, there are attested cases of syntactic structures whose occurrence is definitely determined by discoursal factors that do not fall within the bounds of currently proposed pragmatic principles. In this paper I will report three experiments undertaken to correct these two shortcomings. This research proceeds from a psycholinguistic perspective where pragmatic principles (henceforth 'discourse principles') are viewed as statements of the knowledge that speakers bring to bear in deciding whether a syntactic structure can be fit to a developing discourse.

My program for demonstrating the validity and advantages of looking at discourse pragmatics in this light is as follows. I will begin by defining two kinds of discourse principles, 'cognitive' and 'rhetorical.' Data from two experiments will be presented which show that several variables interact with an oft-cited cognitive principle to determine speakers' sensitivity to it when processing English discourse. Rhetorical principles will then be exemplified in Mandarin. They will be shown to represent knowledge that differs from that embodied in cognitive principles, knowledge so robust that it is transferred in processing a second language. Finally, the acquisition, origin and diachronic life span of rhetorical principles is discussed.

Cognitive discourse principles are applied in the production and comprehension of running discourse to facilitate ease of processing. As Givón (1988:278) points out, processing proceeds smoothly when sentences are structured in such a way that they maximize the "ease of recall" and minimize the "degree of effort" involved in relating in-coming information to the already comprehended text. One of the more widely discussed cognitive discourse principles that operates in English and many other SVO languages is shown in (1).

(1) *The Principle of "Old Things First"* [1]
Each sentence added to a discourse should be structured so that (old/given) thematic material precedes rhematic (new) material.

First discussed by Vilém Mathesius (1928), one of the founders of the Prague Linguistic Circle, this information structuring principle has been cited as the basis for triggering or blocking the application of specific syntactic rules, e.g. relative clause extraposition (Ziv 1975), dative movement (Erteschik-Shir 1979) and the passive (Ross 1975). While these claims are based on the intuitions of the linguist in each case, there has, nevertheless, been some empirical investigation of the extent to which the "Old Things First" principle (OTFP) may increase or decrease the probability of a syntactic rule being deployed at a particular point in a discourse. Using interview data from 44 native speakers of different social classes, ages and races, Weiner and Labov (1983) examined the contribution of the OTFP and parallel structure on the production of agentless passives in English. Krauthamer (1981) studied the effect of given and new information co-varied with the noun feature ±animate on the production of passives with agents. Her subjects, 96 adult native speakers of English, were asked to produce written sentences based on illustrations, some of which they were to view as cartoon sequences, and others as individual pictures.

The methodologies used in these two studies are not without their limitations and problems. Sociolinguists generally view the total number of tokens of a syntactic structure found in a corpus of natural speech as the most conservative and scientifically valid evidence. However, it is well known that the number of examples of a specific syntactic structure can vary widely from corpus to corpus (see Greenbaum 1988:83-84 for examples) and the use of corpora limits the investigator to a single style of speech (Weiner and Labov 1983:56). As many child language researchers have discovered, the use of pictures to stimulate sentence production frequently results in a large number of sentences which are semantically plausible in terms of the illustration but are regrettably not examples of the structure under investigation. The discourse completion task, first developed by Greenbaum (1970, 1973, 1977) and Greenbaum and Quirk (1970), and more recently modified by second language researchers to study cross-cultural and interlanguage pragmatics, e.g. Blum-Kulka (1982), Blum-Kulka and Olshtain (1986), House and Kaspar (1987), Olshtain and Weinbach (1987), avoids the problems associated with the methodologies used in the above studies while providing excellent control of independent variables in discourse which could force a choice of syntactic structures. The experimental task requires the subject to complete a discourse with one of several alternative sentences, only one of which matches the prediction which follows from the investigator's hypothesis. To control for an order effect each subject is presented with a different order of alternative completions. Data can also be in the form an elicited utterance that terminates a discourse. The two experiments described below, which were run on 441 native speakers of English, elicited both types of data.[2] In each experiment the subjects received the following instructions: "please read the passage below and indicate whether you think sentence (a) or (b) is the best completion for it. If you think both are equally good, indicate this by choosing (c)."[3]

The first experiment used five texts to examine whether the OTFP affects the application of dative movement under different conditions. The initial goal was to determine whether the dative movement rule would be blocked or applied depending upon whether the direct or indirect object was established as old information by the preceding discourse. Thus the first text, shown in (2), mentioned the direct object, the two weapons, in the lead-in sentence. According to the OTFP this should be sufficient to block the application of dative movement and force a statistically significant choice of the prepositional pattern in (a). And in fact this was the result, as a sample of 32 native speakers revealed ($\chi^2 = 12.52$ $p < .01$).

(2) You are both aware of the rules of the duel, but I will go over them for the benefit of your seconds. *I have two pistols here — a Colt 45 and a German Luger.*[4]

a. *I'm going to give the Colt to Fred and the Luger to Alex.* They will both walk in opposite directions for a distance of ten paces, turn, and fire.

b. *I'm going to give Fred the Colt and Alex the Luger.* They will both walk in opposite directions for a distance of ten paces, turn, and fire.

The same two alternatives were then used in the next text, where the second sentence of the lead-in discourse was changed to mention only the indirect objects: *You all know the two antagonists, Fred and Alex.* This was sufficient to produce a significant choice in favor of the sentence where the dative movement rule has has applied, i.e. (b), with a sample of 34 subjects ($\chi^2 = 6.76$ $p < .05$). The lead-in text was then changed as shown in (3) to examine the effect of mentioning both the direct and indirect objects prior to their appearance in the target sentences. Despite the fact that the direct objects are referred to only indirectly, i.e. as weapons, the subjects were apparently unable to decide what constituted old and new information. As a result, the choice between the two possible alternatives was not significant with a sample of 26 native speakers ($\chi^2 = 2.32$ n.s.).

(3) I will now explain the rule of the duel for the benefit of everyone else. *The two duelists, Fred and Alex, will receive the weapons they chose earlier.*

The same effect was found in a production test like the one shown in (4). Here the subjects were not confronted with alternative choices but, instead, were asked to make up a sentence that they felt was a viable completion in terms of the lead-in discourse and was cooperative in terms of the request set forth in the scenario. Once again, there was no significant difference in the choice of either the prepositional pattern or the dative movement pattern by the 15 subjects who participated ($\chi^2 = 1.66$ n.s.).

(4) *The Helpful Mailroom Worker Scenario*
You are working, sorting mail in a local post office. One day the police show up and ask your help in averting a potential tragedy. They have good information that terrorists have placed a bomb in one of two pieces of mail which you have just sorted and sent out a few minutes ago. *The bomb is either in a package or a letter.* They also know that the bomb is destined *for either a Mr. Brown or a Mr.*

Green. You remember which name was on which item. This is all the information that the police need to know to avoid the tragedy. You want to help them. Tell them which item was sent to which person. Do this by finishing the sentence below.

I sent ... (finish the sentence)

Finally, the text shown in (5) was used to examine how distance, defined in terms of clauses separating an NP which appears in the lead-in sentence of the discourse and is rementioned in a later (target) sentence, might affect the strength of the OTFP in biasing speakers' choice of either the prepositional or the dative movement pattern. The discourse in (5), which has 9 clauses intervening between the lead-in sentence and the target alternatives (a), (b) and (c), was tested with 30 subjects. No significant choice of sentence pattern was found. The discourse was then systematically manipulated by subtracting a single clause over a series of 9 trials to determine at what point the a significant choice of the pattern predicted by the OTFP would occur. A total of 270 subjects, 30 per each trial, were tested with variations of this discourse.

(5) Fred walked along, head into the wind, *with the package under his arm.* It was a cold, blustery day. Large, grey, scudding clouds marched across the sky. He had to bend forward and actually lean into the wind as walked down the dirt road toward his destination. When he finally arrived at the cottage, he saw that the party was in full swing. He opened the door and stepped inside. The room was full of people.

(a) He walked across the room *and gave the package to Mary.*
(b) He walked across the room *and gave Mary the package.*
(c) Either (a) or (b) is equally good.

Table 1 shows that the OTFP exercises a robust influence up to a separation of six clauses, significantly biasing the subjects' choice in favor of the prepositional phrase pattern, in which the NP, *the package*, appropriately occupies the position of old information. However, when the distance is increased to 7 clauses, the subjects' selection of a single alternative falls below significance (χ^2 at 2 df = 5.99 for $p < .05$). As the distance is increased to 9 clauses, the speakers' sense that either alternative is equally acceptable increases dramatically, as is evidenced by the rise in choice of the dative movement pattern and the category, *either pattern is equally good.*

Table 1. Effect of distance on choice of sentence pattern with indirect object

Number of clauses	Prep phrase pattern	Dative movement pattern	Both patterns	χ^2
1	24	4	2	29.6***
2	20	7	3	15.8***
3	21	5	4	18.2***
4	18	5	7	9.8***
5	17	7	6	7.4*
6	23	3	4	25.4***
7	16	7	7	5.44
8	15	7	8	4.3
9	14	8	8	2.4

*p< 0.05 ***p< 0.001

The next experiment investigated the validity of a long-standing claim (Ross 1975), that the passive rule in English is deployed in discourse as a result of native speakers' sensitivity to the OTFP. The first goal was to determine if the native speakers would rely on the passive within a sentence for the purpose of facilitating the processing of pronoun-antecedent connections. There is a fair amount of empirical evidence (Cowan, 1978, 1980, 1985; Ehrlich 1980; Grober, Beardsley and Caramazza 1978) supporting the processing strategy in (6). Native speakers of English regularly deploy it as a default strategy (Cowan 1985) when no other salient clues such as semantic features of verbs or broader contextual clues are readily available in the preceding discourse for resolving ambiguous cases of anaphora.

(6) *The Parallel Function Strategy*
If more than one NP can, on the basis of semantic and syntactic features, qualify as a potential antecedent of a following or preceding pronoun, the NP which has the same grammatical function as the pronoun will be selected.

Notice that passivization within the second of the coordinated clauses in (7a) produces (7b), where the antecedent of the pronoun is detectable by following the parallel function strategy. (7a), on the other hand, conflicts with the strategy. Coreference will, of course, be resolved in (7a), but to do so the reader must activate her/his internalized knowledge of the contrastive stress, which is required on the pronoun *him* if the sentence is to make any sense.

(7) a. In the French Open Andre Agassi beat Boris Becker, but Jim Currier beat him.
b. In the French Open Andre Agassi beat Boris Becker, but he was beaten by Jim Currier.

The choice of (7b) over (7a) is therefore not simply a matter of stylistic preference, rather it is motivated by a cognitive consideration — passivizing the second clause facilitates processing. We would expect this to be reflected in speakers' preference for (7b), and in a test of 33 subjects who were asked if they felt one of these sentences was easier to understand, a highly significant difference in favor of (7b) was found ($\chi^2 = 12.87$ $p < .01$).[5]

The passage in (8) was then used to determine whether native speakers' sensitivity to the OTFP as it is manifested beyond the sentence level within a developing discourse in the sense of Haviland and Clark (1974) would force a selection of a passive sentence at a given point in a text. Although nearly all of the sentences in (8) are active, the continual repetition of the the subject pronoun, *he*, establishes it as given information. The OTFP predicts that the final sentence in (8) should be completed by (b), since this passive would place the given information before the new information, thereby making this sentence congruent with the others that comprise the rest of the discourse. In a sample of 31 students this prediction was overwhelmingly confirmed ($\chi^2 = 14.5$ $p < .001$).

(8) Fred was having a terrible day. He woke up a half hour late because his alarm clock didn't go off. At breakfast he burned his toast, and when he opened his mail he discovered that he was going to be audited by the IRS. He arrived at work almost 45 minutes late, a fact that did not go unnoticed by his boss. And then, to top it all off, ...[6]

a. Coral, my pet cobra, bit him.
b. He was bitten by my pet cobra, Coral.

To summarize, the results of the first experiment demonstrate that either the OTFP must be rephrased to include the conditions in discourse which affect its saliency with respect to syntactic rules, e.g. the presence of a single unambiguous NP qualifying as old information and the distance separating such an NP from the point where a decision has to be made to apply a rule, or the concept "old information" must be more precisely defined. The second experiment demonstrated that two processing strategies such as parallel function and the OTFP may converge to trigger the application of a syntactic rule in English. The OTFP is thus a major factor in determining word order in English even though its application in the creation of discourse is subject to some variation.

In other languages the functional equivalent of the English passive rule will be deployed by native speakers as a result of a distinctly different kind of discourse principle, which I will call rhetorical. Rhetorical principles are not based on processing considerations, rather they depend on the situation, mood or set of circumstances that have been developed in the discourse prior to the point where the speaker or writer is planning a new sentence. The construct is easier to illustrate than to characterize with great precision. An example from Chinese may serve to clarify the foregoing description. The *bei* passive in Mandarin is formally almost identical to the English passive. As (9b) shows, it involves an exchange of the subject and object of a corresponding active, (9a), and the insertion of a particle *bei* before the new object.

(9) a. *Zhang da le wo*
(name) hit PERF I/me
'Zhang hit me.'

b. *Wo bei Zhang da le*
I PASS (name) hit PERF
'I was hit by Zhang.'

As with the English passive, the agent may be freely deleted and the rule is subject to certain lexical constraints — the logical object tends to be animate (Cheng, personal communication) and the verb is usually one of "disposal," i.e. it describes how the object is "dealt with, manipulated or handled in some way" (Li and Thompson 1981:501).[7] A sentence like (10) is thus ungrammatical because the verb does not express disposal.

(10) * *Ta bei ta de tongxue hen le*
he PASS he NOM classmates hate PERF
' He was hated by his classmates.'

A major difference between the English passive and the Mandarin *bei* passive is that the latter is not used in discourse to facilitate processing and maintain the appropriate sequence of given and new information, rather it is deployed in response to a rhetorical principle that is established by the content of preceding sentences. A rough formulation of this is shown in (11).

(11) *The Adversity Principle*
Deploy the *bei* passive construction to complete a discourse if previous sentences describe the development or occurrence of an unfortunate or adverse event which the NP promoted to subject is involved in.

The Adversity Principle (AP) stipulates that the *bei* passive in (12) is the appropriate completion for a discourse in Mandarin like the English text in (8), but not for the reason that it is appropriate in English. Rather, a *bei* passive like (12) is appropriately added to (8) because the preceding sentences in that discourse describe a series of unfortunate events which happened to the NP promoted to subject in this passive construction.

(12) *Ta bei she yao le*
he PASS snake bite PERF
'He was bitten by a snake.'

In contrast, the Mandarin discourse in (13), for which in English a passive sentence would be an appropriate continuation precisely because it maintains the given-new order specified by the OTFP, would be completed by an entirely different construction in Chinese, as (14) demonstrates.

(13) *Jien tien women zhai ke tang shan tao lun yi ben*
today we in class discuss one CLASS
shu ta miao xue le zhang zheng gei ren min dai lai
book it describe PERF war CAUS people bring
de ku nan
NOM hardship
'In class today we were talking about a book that describes the war. It relates the hardships that people endured (then).'

(14) *nei ben shu shi wo mugin xie de*
that CLASS book is my mother write NOM
'That book was written by my mother.'

The robustness of this rhetorical principle can be tested in the context of second language learning. If the rhetorical conditions embodied in AP are indeed the basis for triggering the *bei* passive in Chinese, we might expect

Chinese learners of English to transfer them when processing English, i.e. they should deploy the equivalent of the *bei* passive in the target language when the rhetorical conditions in an English discourse match those stipulated in the AP. To test this hypothesis an experiment was run with 36 native speakers of Chinese who were studying at the University of Illinois and 18 native speakers of English, also students, who served as a control group. The Chinese subjects were divided into two proficiency groups — intermediate and advanced — on the basis of their TOEFL scores.[8]

All of the subjects viewed 60 sequences of three slides in Chinese and English, 40 of which were experimental sequences and 20 of which were distractor sequences. The first two slides of each sequence developed an episode and the third slide contained the a picture of an action which completed the episode. Beneath the depiction of the action in the third slide were two sentences, an active and a passive. Experimental sequences were classified as positive or negative depending on the contextual features of the episode. Negative episodes were operationally defined as those in which the subject was damaged, killed, injured or otherwise adversely affected, or the action depicted was of a negative nature, such as boys stealing candy or a cat eating a cake. Positive episodes were defined as those in which there was no such damage or negative effect or where the action was of a positive or neutral nature such as someone helping someone else or someone buying something.

Identical sequences were constructed in English and Chinese. The Chinese sentences were translated directly from the English, with passives rendered as *bei* constructions. The only exception occurred with those English sentences using the verb 'help.' The corresponding Chinese verb *bhang zhu* does not take the *bei* construction without a resultative complement. Therefore, in a sentence like 'the boy was helped by the other boy,' the verb 'help' was replaced by a more specific verb like 'save,' *jiu hao*. The experimental sequences were balanced to insure that an equal number of animate and inanimate objects were present and that within positive and negative situations passives were used the same number of times as active sentences to maintain the given–new order which had been established in the first two pictures. Maintenance of the given–new order between the second and target sentences was operationalized as follows: sequences in which an NP that was the focus of attention in the second sentence, i.e. its subject, was moved into the position of old information by a passive in one of the target sentences were designated as 'topic up' sequences, since the selection of that passive alternative would maintain the given-new order throughout the entire discourse. An example of a topic up discourse describing a negative situation is shown in (15).

(15) *Topic up, negative situation*
Picture 1: A boy was walking along.
Picture 2: He wasn't watching where he was going.
Picture 3: a. The boy was hit by a truck.
b. A truck hit the boy.

Sequences in which an NP moved into subject position by a passive in a target sentence was not the subject of or was absent from the second sentence were designated as 'topic down' sequences, since the choice of the passive would not maintain the given–new order throughout the entire discourse. The example in (16) shows a topic down discourse which describes a negative situation.

(16) *Topic down, negative situation*
Picture 1: A little girl was playing with her ball.
Picture 2: A small dog was watching her..
Picture 3: a. The ball was taken by the dog.
b. The dog took the ball.

Final copies of the English and Chinese sentences were given to three native speakers of each language to check for naturalness of discourse and correct written representation. In order to minimize the effect of English vocabulary on the Chinese subjects, all sentences used lexical items below 2000 as listed in Carroll, Davies and Richman (1971). The position of the passive sentences in the last frame was randomized. The sixty sequences were randomized into four running orders. For the first two frames of every sequence there was a tape recording which described the action being portrayed. The recordings for the Chinese sequences were made by a female native Chinese speaker from Taiwan using a standard Mandarin dialect and accent. The recordings for the English test were made by a native-speaking male.

The Chinese subjects were assigned to one of four groups composed of from seven to ten subjects. Each group received an English test running order and a Chinese test running order. The control group subjects were also assigned to three groups. Each group was given sixty-item response sheets. The subjects were told that they were participating in a test of style and that they were to indicate their preference for one sentence or the other (the passive or the active) in the third slide by marking either (a) or (b) on the response sheet.

They were instructed to indicate their interpretation of each sequence as either negative or positive by marking a plus or a minus beside their selection. Negative and positive situations were defined for the subjects as previously described, and two examples, one positive and one negative, were then shown. The sequences were then projected while the accompanying recorded sentences for the first two pictures were played. A three second pause separated the first, second and third frame of each sequence. A seven second pause, in which the subjects marked their choice and indicated their perception of the sequence as positive or negative, separated the last frame from the next sequence. The Chinese subjects were given the Chinese test first and the English test seven days later. All subjects were paid for their participation.

The subjects' interpretations of the episodes as positive or negative were obviously of considerable importance for this experiment. To determine whether both groups were sensitive and consistent in their interpretations of the rhetorical dimension in the experimental discourses, correlations using a Phi coefficient were run between their plus and minus responses and the original sequence division of the target sentences. These turned out to be quite high: .8145 for the Chinese subjects and .8852 for the English control group. A number of analyses of variance (ANOVAS) were then run on the Chinese and English speakers' data. Due to multiple analysis of the same data sets, an acceptable level of significance was set at .025 in order to maintain an overall significance level of .05.

The first ANOVA, a 2 language x 2 proficiency x 2 rhetorical situation (negative vs. positive) x 2 object (animate vs. inanimate) x 2 given-new order (maintained vs. not maintained) x 2 sentence type analysis, was run on just the Chinese speakers' data. Significant effects were found for rhetorical situation ($F(1,34) = 69.0593$ $p < .00001$), object ($F(1,34)= 6.4919$ $p < .0155$), and given-new sequence ($F(1,34) =19.1233$ $p < .0001$). There was a strong influence on the use of the passive exerted in negative situations with animate objects. The lack of a main effect for language simply indicates that the Chinese subjects did not perform any differently on the English or the Chinese sequences with regard to their selection of passives. Similarly, the lack of a main effect for proficiency indicates that there was no significant difference in performance on both tests attributable to knowledge of English.

There was also a strong interaction effect for rhetorical situation x given new sequence ($F(1, 34) = 5.9078$ $p <.0205$). This interaction, which operates across languages and proficiency levels, is shown in Figure 1.

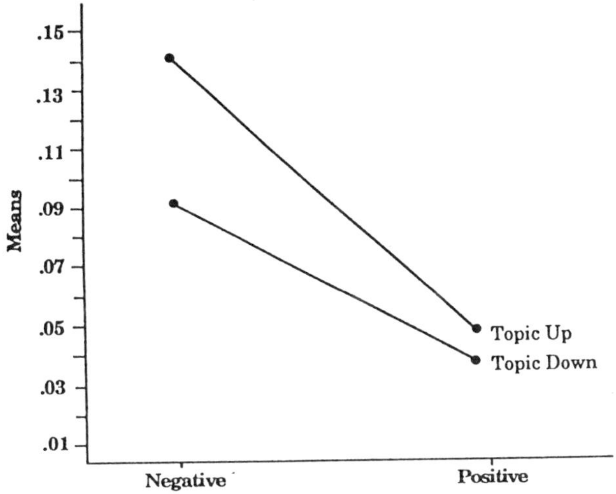

Figure 1. Situation x given–new order interaction Chinese subjects' performance

Although the presence of a sentence which maintains established given-new order exerts a stronger influence within negative situations than it does in positive situations, it is nevertheless clear that rhetorical situation is the dominant influence, with negative, adverse situations constituting the optimal condition for the Chinese subjects selection of passive sentences in both languages. Of course this does not prove that Chinese transfer their preference for the passive in negative situations in second language learning. Evidence in support of this hypothesis can only be found by comparing the Chinese speakers' performance on the English passive with that of the control group, which is what the next ANOVA did.

A 2 (language group: Chinese vs. English) x 2 rhetorical situation x 2 object x 2 given–new order ANOVA was performed on the data. Main effects were found for language group (F (1,52) = 10.6498 p < .0019), situation (F (1,52) = 28.9301 p < .00001) and given–new order (F (1,52) = 19.434 p < .00001). The Chinese subjects chose the passive significantly more than the American subjects. This result is due to the fact that in some of the positive situations they selected the passive, whereas in the negative situations they always selected the passive. The decisive evidence that the Chinese subjects

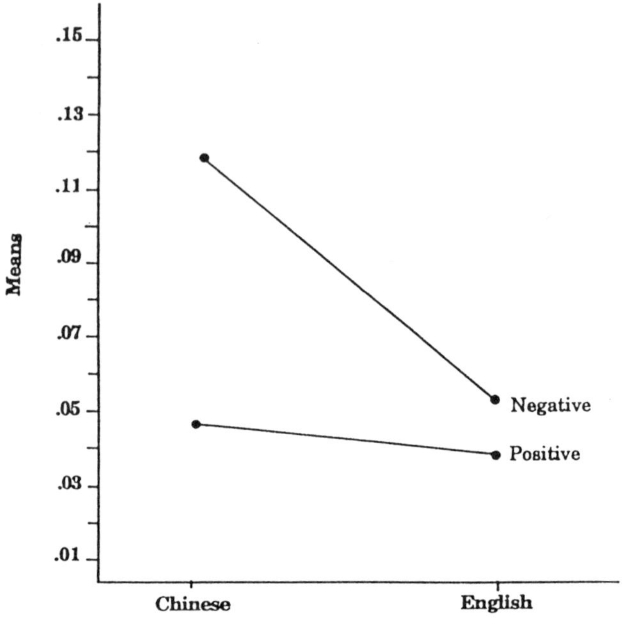

Figure 2. Language group x situation interaction performance on English passives

were partial to discourse contexts characterized by the AP in their use of the English passive is to be seen in the significant interaction effect between language group and rhetorical situation ($F(1,52) = 5.2731$ $p < .025$), shown in Figure 2.

It is clear that the Chinese subjects were much more constrained by the rhetorical situation in their choice of the passive in both languages than the American subjects. Although the American control group did choose the passive more often in negative than in positive situations, Figure 2 shows this difference to be quite small, suggesting that, on the whole, they are not sensitive to rhetorical situation. To clarify this tendency among the American control group subjects, an ANOVA was performed on their data alone. The factors included situation, object and given–new order. Predictably, the only factor showing a significant effect alone was given–new order ($F(1,17) = 11.8959$ $p < .003$), indicating that the American subjects were guided by the OTFP in their selections. The results thus indicate that the Chinese subjects' preference for using a passive in response to rhetorical values in discourse is sufficiently robust to be transferred in second language learning regardless of proficiency in the second language. They also provide one possible explanation for second language learners' failure to master the organizational structure of the target language discourse.

The construct of a rhetorical principle suggests a natural explanation of how native speakers acquire the knowledge which restricts the deployment of a particular syntactic structure like the *bei* passive. The most intuitive account would be that native speakers become aware of and internalize the conditions embodied in a rhetorical principle as a result of repeatedly encountering a particular syntactic structure in discourses where sentences that precede it describe a clearly defined, restricted rhetorical content. When the connection is made, the native speaker has acquired the knowledge embodied in the rhetorical principle, and it can be manifested in several ways: the native speaker uses the structure in just the appropriate discourses, extends it to similar sentences in second language learning, and is able to describe an entailment that the structure conveys out of context, even when the structure is extended in sentences containing a lexical class that does not normally appear with it. Thus in the case of the *bei* passive, if a neutral verb like 'see' is used with the *bei* passive in a sentence like *wo bei lao shi kan jian le* 'he was seen by the teacher,' native speakers of Mandarin will volunteer some implicature that is congruent with the conditions embodied in the AP, e.g. the sentence implies that the subject, for some reason, did not want to be seen (Li and Thompson 1981:495).

The acquisition process provides us with a more precise characterization of rhetorical principles — they are representations of implicatures which have become bound to a particular syntactic structure. Rhetorical principles describe very specific rhetorical values which a speaker must search for in preceding discourse when obeying the Maxim of Relevance with regard to a given structure. What conditions are conducive to a syntactic structure developing a special implicature which it formerly did not possess? Hypotheses about this are risky, but one which enjoys some current support is that more marked structures in a language have the best chance of undergoing this development. In her insightful article on peculiar passives Davison (1980) suggests something along these lines. She develops a markedness hierarchy for English passives based on an NP's potential for promotion to subject and then shows that one of the more marked passives has a tendency to develop special implicatures. In this regard it is interesting to note that passives in different languages, in particular agentless passives, have often been cited as structures which carry an adversive, or conversely, a favorable meaning. Kuno (1973) and Shibatani (1990) note that Japanese passives formed with the verbal affix -*(r)are* can impart the notion that the subject has suffered some adverse effect.[9] Lee (1974) describes a similar situation for Korean with three verbal suffixes (-*mac*, *-tangha*, and *-tit*) which produce passives with an adverse or favorable interpretation, and Noss (1964) cites examples with an auxiliary of the passive that results in either of these two interpretations in Thai. This suggests that the presence of morphology which distinguishes one structure from other alternatives may also be a necessary condition for this kind of development.[10] There is also some evidence from Sanskrit and Hindi (cf. Davison 1980:62) which indicates that this innovation may often have a literary source. Cross-linguistic comparisons of the discourses in which these constructions with adversive meanings occur and diachronic examinations of their development (where documents permit this) would be very useful for shedding light on how structures develop restricted implicatures.

If the acquisition of a rhetorical restriction by a specific syntactic structure is a matter of conjecture, the loss of such a restriction is not. Typically the influence of a prestige dialect works to widen the usage of the structure and break down the restricted meaning associated with it. More than one example of this kind of on-going syntactic change exists; I will cite only two recently documented examples of this process. Kachru (1975) notes that the *dvara* passive in Hindi, which formerly occurred only with impersonal agents and was restricted to formal communication, has, under the influence of the English passive, been extended to informal contexts where it has taken on personal agents. Similarly, the *bei* passive's rhetorical restriction has begun to be broadened to include more discourse contexts, initially as a result of copious translations of Russian scientific literature (Kierman 1969) in which the rhetorical restrictions in the native language were disregarded, and more recently under the influence of English, which has gained currency as the foreign language most studied in Mainland China. In an experiment similar to the one reported above, Reed and Cowan (1988) found that many Chinese scholars are still sensitive to the rhetorical restrictions embodied in the AP, but this is diminishing to the point where the *bei* passive will be employed in non-adverse discourses. This appears to be particularly prevalent with agentless passives. A verb like 'tell,' which was formerly restricted to active sentences, e.g. *renjia gaosugou wo* 'people have told me', now regularly appears in *bei* passive constructions, e.g. *wo bei gaosu* 'I have been told.' Pei and Chi (1987) have observed similar changes which they ascribe to translations of English which are widely disseminated via Reference News broadcasts in Mainland China. Whether this will result in the eventual eradication of the AP remains to be seen, but it indicates that rhetorical principles are more susceptible to diachronic extinction than their cognitive counterparts.

Previous discussions of the role that discourse pragmatics plays in determining word order variation in natural language have focused on information structuring and have invoked some version of the principle formulated as the OTFP in this paper. Indeed, virtually every paper in the symposium that led to this volume has followed this orientation. I have presented evidence that this conception of discourse pragmatics is not sufficient to account for all types of word order variation. In addition to recognizing other factors which interact with information structuring principles, I have shown the need for recognizing two kinds of knowledge that speakers use when producing and processing sentences to be integrated into on-going discourse. These two kinds of knowledge, which I have called cognitive and rhetorical discourse principles, are acquired as a consequence of speakers' exposure to discourse in their native languages. Epiphenominal to the grammar, they guide the speaker's choice of grammatical structures in the processing and production of discourse.

Cognitive and rhetorical discourse principles differ from one another in several ways. Cognitive discourse principles characterize knowledge which will affect the application of more than one rule and more than one grammatical process, i.e. deletion as well as movement. Recently Cheng (1988, 1990) has shown that a descriptively adequate account of pro drop in Chinese requires the recognition of two cognitive principles, the "Opening Principle" and the "Recency Principle," both of which are predicated on the assumption that a discourse consists of topic continuities. It follows that cognitive discourse principles are doubtlessly universal and, if not a consequence of word order (Herring 1990), at least to some extent dependent upon it, e.g. (Dryer this volume). In contrast, rhetorical discourse principles have a much narrower scope of application than cognitive discourse principles. They embody knowledge which the speaker brings to bear in deciding whether to deploy a single syntactic structure. Furthermore, the origin of rhetorical discourse principles — the conventionalization of an implicature — truly qualifies them to be called pragmatic principles. There is no evidence that the binding of a special implicature to a syntactic structure is in any way dependent on word order. Finally, rhetorical discourse principles are likely to have a limited diachronic existence, since the structures to which they pertain will, under the pressure of prestige dialects and borrowing in a multilingual environment, be extended to other discourse contexts, thereby nullifying their restricted meanings.

Notes

* I am grateful to Brad Reed for granting permission to use the data from the experiment with the Chinese subjects. Both he and I thank Yokiko Abe for her assistance in analysing the data obtained therefrom. I benefited considerably from a discussion with Hans Hock concerning passives in various languages. Pamela Downing and Mickey Noonan provided enormously detailed and insightful comments which greatly improved the clarity and quality of the earlier version of this paper. None of the above-mentioned helpful individuals should be held responsible for any of the opinions or shortcomings contained in this revision.

1. This principle tends to be renamed by each investigator who studies it. The formulation here is mine; the designation is Ross's (1975). There are clearly exceptions to the formulation in (1), e.g. if the preceding discourse describes a situation which would incline a writer or speaker to prefer a continuation using a sentence with emphatic word order.

2. Each experiment run with native speakers used a different group of subjects, all of whom were drawn from the undergraduate population at the University of Illinois. Only sophomores, juniors and seniors participated.

3. Alternative (c) was always: "either (a) or (b) is equally good." A typical example is shown in (5). Each subject saw a different order of alternatives, where sentences (a) and (b) were reversed. Alternative (c) always appeared as the last of the three possible choices.

4. None of the stimulus sentences in the experimental materials contained noun phrases highlighted in italic script as they do in the examples throughout this paper.

5. All stimuli in this second experiment which investigated the application of parallel function strategy and the OTFP in regard to English passives were presented in written form. The subjects indicated their preferences by circling one of the three alternatives available as in the previous experiment.

6. This example is a slightly altered version of the one found in Ross (1975).

7. Chao (1968:706) notes some exceptions to the general rule requiring verbs of disposal — certain verbs of perception e.g. *ting jian* 'hear,' *kan jian* 'see,' may appear in *bei* passives when used as verbs of actual perception as opposed to their citation forms, *ting* 'listen,' and *kan* 'see.'

8. The TOEFL scores of the first group ranged from 540 to 550, with a mean of 530. The range of the advanced group was from 557 to 640, the mean score being 586. The mean United States residency of the participants in the intermediate group was 6.61 months. The advanced group had a mean residency of 9.56 months. All of the Chinese subjects were enrolled at the University of Illinois.

9. However, Shibatani (1990:326-27) supplies examples demonstrating that the *-(r)are* passive does not always have an adverse meaning with respect to the subject.

10. Caution should be exercised in postulating that passives *per se* are subject to developing conventionalized implicatures since there are obvious counterexamples, e.g. French, where the alternative expression used to circumvent the restriction on agentless passives, i.e. *on* in an active sentence,has not taken on a special meaning. I suspect that a combination of several factors may be responsible for this development, one of which is morphological marking. Davison (1980) makes a good case for her thesis, but some of her conditions for the development of a "special" meaning derived by applying Gricean maxims are questionable. For example, the general condition that an agentless passives like (1) below will have a modal meaning of "possibility" equivalent to the paraphrase in (2), provided that the NP moved into subject position bears no marks from the action executed upon it, seems contradicted by (3), where the promoted NP fits the condition.

    (1) This peak has been climbed many times.
    (2) It is possible (even easy) to climb this peak.
    (3) This road has been walked down many times.

    It would appear that other factors beside the conditions cited by Davison may assist in the imparting of special implicatures, not the least of which is the preceding context which the structure is to be integrated into.

References

Blum-Kulka, S. 1982. "Learning how to say what you mean in a second language: A study of speech act performance of learners of Hebrew as a second language". *Applied Linguistics* 3.29-59.

Blum-Kukla, S. and E. Olshtain. 1986. "Too many words: Length of utterance and pragmatic failure". *Journal of Pragmatics* 8.47-61.

Carroll, J., P. Davies and B. Richman 1971. *The American Heritage Word Frequency Book.* New York: Houghton Mifflin

Chao, Y. R. 1968. *A Grammar of spoken Chinese.* Berkeley and Los Angeles, CA: University of California Press.

Cheng, C.C. 1988. "Communication-based Chinese discourse grammar". *Shije Hanyu Jiaoxue* 1.6-13. (In Chinese.)

Cheng, C.C. 1990. "Toward a theory of Chinese anaphora interpretation". Paper presented at the Second Northeast Conference on Chinese Linguistics.

Cowan, JR. 1978. "Investigating the psychological basis of anaphora". Paper presented at the 53rd annual meeting of the Linguistic Society of America.

Cowan, JR. 1980. "The significance of parallel function in the assignment of intersentential anaphora". *Papers from the Parasession on Pronouns and Anaphora* ed. by J. Kreiman and A.E. Ojeda, 110-24. Chicago: Chicago Linguistic Society.

Cowan, JR. 1985. "Mechanisms of anaphora". Paper presented at the International Symposium on Anaphora, Kleve, Germany (University of Nijmegen).

Davison, A. 1980. "Peculiar passives". *Language* 56.42-66.

Dryer, M. 1991. This volume. "Frequency and pragmatically unmarked word order".

Ehrlich, K. 1980. "Comprehension of pronouns'. *Quarterly Journal of Experimental Psychology* 32. 247-55.

Erteschik-Shir, N. 1979. "Discourse constraints on dative movement." *Discourse and Syntax* ed. by T. Givón. New York: Academic Press [*Syntax and Semantics* 12].

Givón, T. 1988. "The pragmatics of word order: predictability, importance and attention." Studies in Syntactic Typology ed. by M. Hammond, E.A. Moravcsik an J.R. Wirth, 243-84. Amsterdam/Philadelphia: John Benjamins.

Greenbaum, S. 1970. *Verb-Intensifier Collocations in English: An experimental approach.* The Hague: Mounton.

Greenbaum, S. 1973. "Informant elicitation of data on syntactic variation". *Lingua* 31. 201-72.

Greenbaum, S. 1977. "The linguist as experimenter". *Current Themes in Linguistics* ed. by F.R. Eckman, 125-44. New York: Wiley.

Greenbaum, S. 1988. *Good English and the Grammarian* .London:Longman.

Greenbaum, S. and Randolf Quirk. 1970. *Elicitation Experiments in English: Linguistic Studies in Use an Attitude.* London: Longman.

Grober, E.H., Beardsley, H. and A. Caramazza. 1978. "Parallel function strategy in pronoun assignment". *Cognition* 6. 117-33.

Gundel, J.K. 1988. "Universals of topic-comment structure." *Studies in Syntactic Typology* ed. by M. Hammond, E.A. Moravcsik and J.R. Wirth, 209-42. Amsterdam/ Philadelphia: John Benjamins.

Haviland, S.E. and H.H. Clark. 1974. "What's new? Acquiring new information as a process in comprehension". *Journal of Verbal Learning and Verbal Behavior* 13. 512-21.

Herring, S.C. 1990. "Information structure as a consequence of word order type". *Proceedings of Sixteenth Annual Meeting of the Berkeley Linguistics Society* ed. by K. Hall, J.P. Koenig, M. Meacham, S. Reinman and L.A. Sutton, 163-74. Berkeley: Berkeley Linguistics Society.

Hetzron, R. 1975. "The presentative movement, or why the ideal word order is V.S.O.P.". *Word Order and Word Order Change* ed. by C.N. Li, 347-88. Austin: University of Texas Press.

House, J. & G. Kaspar. 1987. "Interlanguage pragmatics: Requesting in a foreign language". *Perspectives on Language in Performance: Festschrift for Werner Hüllen* ed. by W. Loerscher and R. Schulze, 1250-88. Tübingen: Narr.

Kachru, B.B. 1979. "The Englishization of Hindi: Language rivalry and language change". *Linguistic Method* ed. by Irmgard Rauch and G.F. Carr, 199-212. The Hague: Mounton.

Kierman, Frank A. Jr. 1969. "Night thoughts and the passive". *Unicorn* 5. 72-78.

Krauthamer, H. 1981. "The prediction of passive occurrence". *Linguistics* 19. 307-24.

Kuno, S. 1973. *The Structure of the Japanese Language.* Cambridge, Mass.: Harvard University Press.

Lee, C.M. 1974. *Abstract Syntax and Korean with Reference to English*. Seoul: Pan Korea Book Corp.

Li, C.N. and S.A. Thompson. 1981 *Mandarin Chinese: A functional reference grammar*. Berkeley: University of California.

Mathesius, V. 1928. "On linguistic charactorology with illustrations from modern English". Reprinted 1967 in *A Prague School Reader in Linguistics*, compiled by J. Vachek, 54-67. Bloomington: Indiana University Press.

Mithun, M. 1987. "Is basic word order universal?" *Coherence and Grounding in Discourse* ed. by R.S. Tomlin, 281-99. Amsterdam/Philadelphia: John Benjamins.

Noss, R.B. 1964. *Thai Reference Grammar*. Washington D.C.: Foreign Service Institute.

Olshtain, E. and L. Winebach. 1987. "Complaints: A study of speech act behavior among native and non-native speakers of Hebrew". *The Pragmatic Perspective* ed. by J. Verschueren and M. Bertucelli-Papi, 195-208. Amsterdam/Philadelphia: John Benjamins.

Pei, Z.Z. and F.W. Chi. 1987. "The two faces of English in China: Englishization of Chinese and nativization of English". *World Englishes* 6. 111-26.

Reed, B. and JR. Cowan. 1988. "Applying an experimental approach to the investigation of syntactic change". *Synchronic and Diachronic Approaches to Linguistic Variation and Change* ed. by T.J. Walsh, 260-67. Washington D.C.: Georgetown University Press.

Ross, J.R. 1975. "Parallels in phonological and semantic organization". *The Role of Speech in Language* ed. by J.F. Kavanaugh and J.E. Cutting, 283-304. Cambridge, Mass: MIT Press.

Shibatani, M. 1990. *The Languages of Japan*. Cambridge: Cambridge University Press.

Weiner, E.J. and W. Labov. 1983. "Constraints on the agentless passive". *Journal of Linguistics* 19. 29-58.

Ziv, Y. 1975. "On the relevance of content to the form-function correlation". *Papers from the Parasession on Functionalism* ed. by R. E. Grossman, L. J. San and T. J. Vance, 568-579. Chicago: Chicago Linguistic Society.

Agent position in the *Sejarah Melayu*

Susanna Cumming
University of California, Santa Barbara

1. Introduction

Classical Malay is the name commonly given to the language of court literature in the cultural centers of the Malay peninsula and what is now western Indonesia. It is known today from manuscripts produced between the 17th and 19th centuries. Unlike most modern Malay varieties, it is a "typical" Western Austronesian language, similar in several respects to the Batak and Philippine languages. As in these languages, word order and voice (marked by verb prefix) are the most central devices for signalling the discourse statuses of clauses and their arguments. In Malay, the use of these two coding devices in transitive clauses is closely connected. One transitive clause type, marked by a prefix of *meN-*[1] on the verb, has fixed word order, i.e. Agent > Verb > Patient (AVP):[2]

(1)

Agent		**Verb**			**Patient**	
kedua	*baginda*	*memakai*	*dengan*	*selengkap*	*pakaian*	*kerajaan.*[3]
both	3	AT:wear	with	complete	clothes	kingship

'Both of them dressed entirely in royal garments'

The other, associated with the *di-* verbal prefix, has nearly free word order. A few of the possibilities are illustrated here:

(2)

	Verb	**Agent**			**Patient**		
Maka	*dilihat*	*oleh*	*Sang*	*Sapurba*	*sebuah*	*kuala*	*sungai*
CONJ	PT:see	by	Sang	Sapurba	one:CL	mouth	river
terlalu	*besar*						
very	big						

'Sang Sapurba saw a great river-mouth'

(3)

	Verb	**Patient**		**Agent**			
maka	*disambut*	*bunga*	*itu*	*oleh*	*bini*	*perdana*	*menteri.*
CONJ	PT:welcome	flower	that	by	wife	prime	minister

'The flowers were welcomed by the wife of the prime minister'

(4)

	Agent				**Patient**		
maka	*oleh*	*Demang*	*Lebar*	*Daun*	*saudaranya*	*yang*	*muda*
CONJ	by	Demang	Lebar	Daun	sibling:3	REL	young

Verb			
ditinggalkan	*di*	*negeri*	*Palembang.*
PT:leave	at	country	Palembang

'Demang Lebar Daun left his young brother in Palembang'

(5)

Patient							
anak	*ceteria*	*Cina*	*yang*	*beristerikan*	*Puteri*	*Tunjung*	*Bueh,*
child	prince	China	REL	marry:CAUS	Puteri	Tunjung	Bueh

Agent			**Verb**			
oleh	*Sang*	*Sapurba*	*dirajakan*	*baginda*	*di*	*negeri*
by	Sang	Saprba	PT:king:CAUS	3:HON	at	country

Palembang
Palembang

'Sang Sapurba made the Chinese prince who had married Princess Tunjung Bueh the king of Palembang'

A good deal of research has focussed on the factors conditioning the relative position of the verb and the patient in the Classical Malay *di-* clause (Hopper 1983; 1987; Rafferty 1987; Cumming 1991). However, very little has been written about the factors conditioning the position of the *agent* in this clause type. In this paper I propose to address this issue (along with a number of interacting morphosyntactic alternations), and furthermore to explore the implications of my findings for our understanding of the nature of the mappings between linguistic forms and discourse-semantic functions.

In the remainder of this section I will describe the database on which the present study is based, and then review the findings of various authors relating to the factors conditioning which prefix is used and the position of the patient in the *di-* clause. Section 2 will describe the grammatical possibilities for agent coding, and Section 3 will discuss the discourse factors that condition the various alternants. Section 4 will interpret these results in terms of a general understanding of the relation between discourse and grammar.

1.1 *Database*

The database for this study consists of the entire text of Chapter 2 (715 clauses) of the *Sejarah Melayu* or the 'Malay Annals', probably the most well-known Classical Malay text. It is a "history" of the ruling family of the Malacca/Johor empire, concerned with legitimizing the royal line by tracing it back to the union of Alexander the Great with a Tamil princess. Chapter 2 describes the arrival of Sang Sapurba and his two brothers (grandsons of Alexander) in Palembang; Sang Sapurba's marriage and coronation; a voyage in which he seeks a new place to found a kingdom, and in the process creates political alliances by marrying relatives and dependents to local rulers at various stopping points; and finally his settling and founding a kingdom upriver in Kuantan, after proving his legitimacy by having one of his followers kill a serpent that had been terrorizing the local population.

Like most Classical Malay *hikayat* (a term which can be translated as 'history' or 'romance', depending on your point of view), the *Sejarah Melayu* represents a compilation of material drawn from various sources at various times; however, the bulk of the version used for this study (the Situmorang-Teeuw romanization of the Abdullah edition — Situmorang and Teeuw 1958) was probably composed in the mid-17th century.[4] The *Sejarah Melayu* was chosen because previous analysis has shown that it contains greater syntactic diversity, especially in terms of constituent order, than most other *hikayat* (Cumming 1991:144 — this may be why Sir Richard Winstedt called it "the most famous, distinctive, and best of all Malay literary works" (1961:129)). In particular, unlike some other *hikayat*, it exhibits preverbal "patient-trigger' (PT) agents. Thus, some of the findings reported here may not be generalizable to other Classical Malay texts.

1.2 *Prefix choice and constituent order in Classical Malay*

Like many other Western Austronesian languages, Classical Malay can be described as "patient-prominent", in the sense that in most transitive clauses the patient rather than the agent has "pivot" properties (as defined in Foley and Van Valin 1984). The "pivot" is the argument which can be omitted in a dependent clause; in the *me-* clause, this is the agent, and in the *di-* clause, it is the patient. Hereafter I will call the argument with pivot properties the "trigger"; a *me-* clause is thus an "agent-trigger" or (AT) clause, a *di-* clause is a "patient-trigger" (PT) clause.[5] In practice, this means that the prefix of a transitive verb which shares an argument with another predicate is determined by the role of the shared argument: if it is an agent, the verb must have the *me-* form; if it is a patient, it must have the *di-* form. The following examples illustrate this restriction for several types of clause combination. (The clause which is affected by the constraint is enclosed in angled brackets; the shared argument is in boldface.)

Relative clauses

(6) *Maka tumpatlah rupa laut itu daripada kebanyakan*
CONJ solid:EVT face sea that from quantity
*perahu **orang** <yang mengiringkan baginda itu>.*
ship person REL AT:accompany 3 that
'The sea appeared solid from the number of ships of those that were accompanying him.'

(7) *Maka segala Minangkabau terlalu heran melihat baik*
CONJ all Minangkabau very amazed AT:see good
paras baginda,
looks 3
*dan melihat **makota** <yang dipakai baginda itu>*
and AT:see crown REL PT:wear 3 that
'All the Minangkabaus were amazed to see his beauty and to see the crown which he was wearing'

Serial verbs

(8) *Maka **Bat** berdiri <memuji Sang Sapurba.>*
CONJ Bat stand AT:praise Sang Sapurba
'Bat stood praising Sang Sapurba'

Complement clauses

(9) *Syahadan, berapa lamanya Sang Sapurba diam di*
CONJ some long:3 Sang Sapurbastay at
Palembang,
Palembang
*maka **baginda** berkira-kira hendak <melihat laut>.*
CONJ 3 think:REDUP want AT:see ocean
'Sang Sapurba stayed at Palembang for a while, then he thought he would like to see the ocean.'

Adverbial clauses

(10) *Maka* ***Wan Empo' dan Wan Malini pun*** *heran*
CONJ Wan Empo' and Wan Malini TOP amazed
<*melihat hal yang demikian itu*>.
AT:see thing REL thus that
'Wan Empo' and Wan Malini were amazed to see a thing like that.'

(11) *Telah pagi hari dilihat-nya* ***puteri itu*** *kedal tulah*
PFV morning day PT:see:3 princess that skin: disease
<*sebab dijamah baginda itu*>.
because PT:touch 3 that
'In the morning he saw that the girl had "kedal" (skin disease characterized by whitish spots) because she had been touched by him.'

Conjoined clauses

(12) *Setelah ular itu melihat manusia datang,*
after snake that AT:see human come
maka ***ia pun*** *menggerak dirinya;*
CONJ 3 TOP AT:move self:3;
<*maka segera ditetak Permasku Mambang penggal tiga*
CONJ at:once PT:chop Permasku Mambang piece three
lalu mati.>
then die
'After the snake saw a human coming, it moved; then Permasku Mambang immediately chopped (it) into three pieces, and (it) died.'

(13) *maka* ***Sang Sapurba pun*** *bersalin kain selengkap tubuh,*
CONJ Sang Sapurba TOP change cloth entire body
<*lalu memakai pakaian darapati darmani namanya*>
CONJ AT:wear clothes darapati darmani name:3
'Sang Sapurba changed all his clothing, and put on clothes called "Darapati Darmani"'

The fact that the role of the shared argument — which is necessarily "given" in the dependent clause — determines verb prefixation has led some linguists to assume that prefix choice is always determined by the information status of the arguments, i.e. that AT clauses are associated with given agents and PT clauses with given patients.[6] However, I have argued elsewhere (Cumming in press) that this is a mistaken conclusion: text counts reveal that speakers choose constructions with a shared patient in the secondary clause only when there are independent reasons for using a *di-* verb, related to the considerations (described below) which determine the use of this verb form in a main clause. Otherwise, speakers can simply use two independent clauses, of which the second contains a pronoun, rather than an argument-sharing construction.

In addition to this syntactic constraint, there is another context which "forces" choice of one or the other prefix: the use of the particle *pun*, often glossed as a "topic marker" (in e.g. Becker 1979; Ajamiseba 1983) since it marks given arguments in initial poisition. A *pun*-marked argument must be the trigger of its clause: if it is an agent, the clause must be agent-trigger, while if it is a patient, it must be patient-trigger. This is illustrated in the following examples.

(14) *maka* ***ular*** ***itu*** ***pun*** *mencium bau manusia*
CONJ snake that TOP AT:smell odor human
'The snake smelled the odor of a human'

(15) *Maka* ***anak*** ***raja*** ***itu*** ***pun*** *dibawanya kembali ke rumahnya.*
CONJ child king that TOP PT:take:3 back to house:3
'They took those king's sons back to their house'

If *pun* were indeed simply a marker of "topic", this pattern would provide additional support to the idea that the information status of the arguments determines both word order and prefix in Classical Malay. However, I have argued extensively elsewhere (Cumming 1991:90-107) that the best characterization of the function of *pun* has to do with non-expectedness or unpredictability, which can come from various sources: a switch in the semantic role of the *pun* argument, "potential interference" from a semantically compatible argument in the immediately preceding context, contrast situations (including parallel lists), and counter-expectation from general knowledge. The following passage contains several typical uses of *pun*:

(16) *Maka ada seorang hulubalang baginda, Permasku Mambang*
CONJ be one:CL commander 3 Permasku Mambang
namanya,
name:3
maka ialah dititahkan oleh baginda membunuh ular itu;
CONJ 3:EVT PT:order by 3 AT:kill snake that
dan pedang Corek Semandang Kini itu dikurniakan baginda;

and sword Corek Semandang Kini that PT:present 3
maka ***ia pun*** *pergilah.*
CONJ 3 TOP go:EVT
Setelah datang pada tempat ular itu,
after come to place snake that
maka ***ular itu pun*** *mencium bau manusia,*
CONJ snake that TOP AT:smell odor human
maka ***ia pun*** *keluarlah daripada lengkarannya.*
CONJ 3 TOP go:out:EVT from coil:3
'There was a commander of his [Sang Sapurba's] named Permasku Mambang; he [S.S.] ordered him [P.M.] to kill the snake, and he [S.S.] gave him [P.M.] the sword Corek Simandang Kini; then he [P.M.] went. When he came to the snake's place, the snake smelled a human, and came out of its coil.'

In the above passage, the first two instances of *pun* represent a switch in the actor. The third instance is perhaps attributable to the fact that the snake, being lower in animacy than Permasku Mambang, is less expected as an actor even though it has just been mentioned in the same role. Thus, *pun* arguments are indeed topical in the sense of being "given" information, but they are not highly continuous in the sense of being predictable. Nor are they noticeably high in overall importance in the text, a quality which I will call "protagonism". If we define the "protagonism" of a referent as the total number of references to that referent in a text, we can compute the average protagonism of a coding type by summing the protagonism scores of the referents of each NP of a that type and dividing by the number of such NPs.[7] Applying this procedure, the difference between the average number of mentions for the referents of *pun* and non-*pun* arguments is very small (50 to 47). Thus, the choice of *pun* is evidently related primarily to the local consideration of preceding context.

The relative frequency of clause types provides further evidence that "topicality" or "givenness" are not good predictors of prefix in Classical Malay. As we would expect cross-linguistically, the agent is nearly always more continuous (topical or "given"), according to any measure that can be applied (cf. the "Given A constraint" of Du Bois 1987). Figure 1 illustrates the relative "referential distance" (RD: distance in clauses to last mention) of agents, patients, and intransitive arguments or "Ss".[8] As this figure shows, As are associated with shorter RDs and Ps with longer ones; Ss are in between.

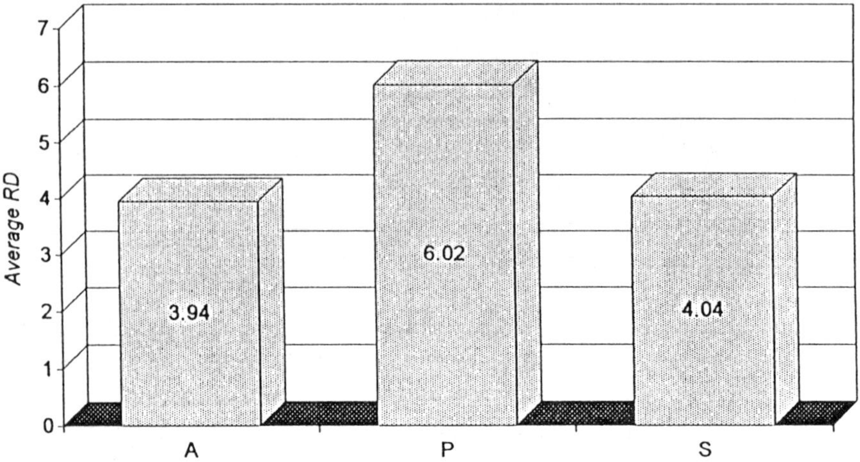

Figure 1. Average RD by role

Another measure is to look at the type of NP used to code the referents in the three roles. Pronouns, of course, represent the most accessible information (excluding "zeros"). Names represent an intermediate status between pronouns and lexical NPs (see e.g. Hopper 1989): like pronouns they are generally anaphoric (a speaker/author is not licensed to refer to a person by name until the person has been introduced), and moreover they are available primarily to human referents, which tend to be accessible; but unlike pronouns, and like lexical NPs, they typically carry enough information to pick a specific referent out of a group of competing referents. Lexical NPs can be used for first mentions of human participants and for any mention of (typically non-accessible) non-human participants; they are also typically longer than names. Figure 2 shows that As are associated with smaller referring expressions and Ps are associated with larger referring expressions, while Ss are in between.[9]

Since agents are more topical, if verb prefixation were determined by information status, we would expect that the *me-* (AT) clause type would be much more frequent in discourse. But this is not the case, as Figure 3 shows.

What, then, does condition the prefix alternation if not information status of the arguments? A number of studies suggest that properties of the predication are more central: patient-trigger voice is associated with high "eventiveness" — punctuality, telicity, sequencedness, foregrounding, and in gen-

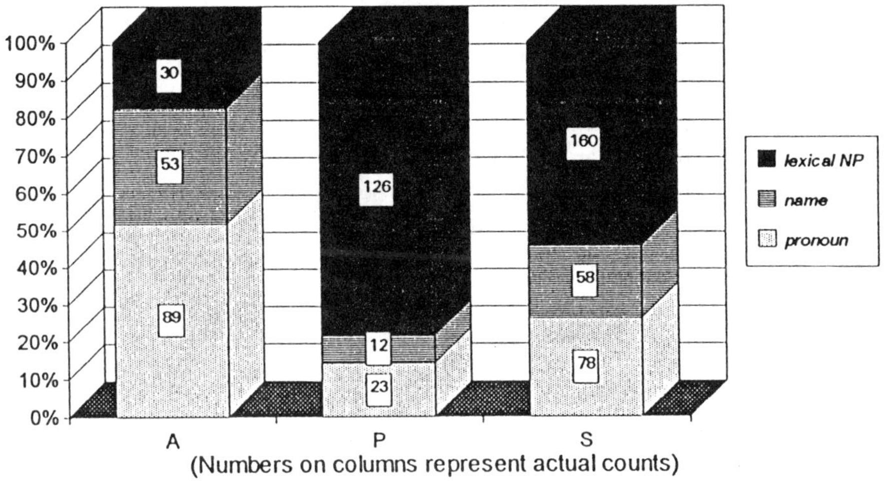

Figure 2. NP type by role

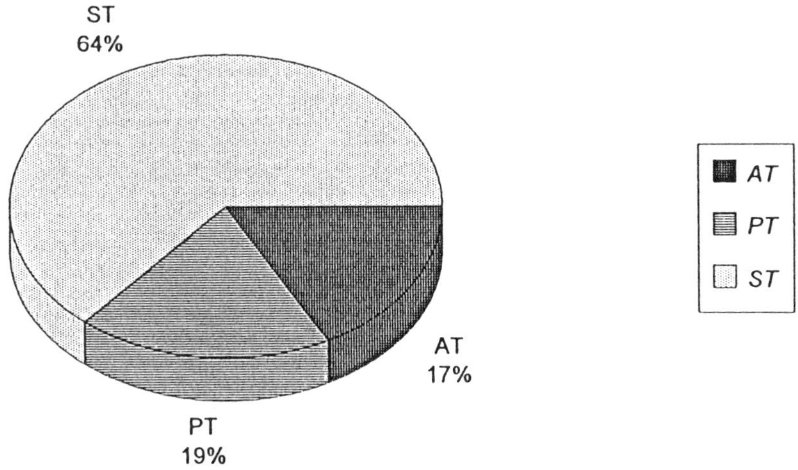

Figure 3. Trigger role

eral with those of Hopper and Thompson's (1980) "transitivity parameters" which have to do with properties of predicates, while the agent-trigger form is associated with background or non-sequenced clauses (see Hopper 1983; Rafferty 1987; and Cumming 1991 for text counts in support of this claim in various Classical and Early Modern Malay texts). As suggested above, this effect can be seen in dependent clauses involving argument sharing as well as in main ones. Thus, the transitive verb prefixes are probably best interpreted as relating primarily to properties of predicates (like e.g. aspect markers) rather than to properties of arguments (like e.g. voice systems, according to most interpretations); and indeed, glossing AT and PT clauses with the terms "active" and "passive" can be highly misleading. (Another indication of this is that glossing PT clauses with English passives usually leads to very strange-sounding sentences; in most cases I have translated PT clauses as actives.) For the same reasons I have avoided the terms "subject" and "object" to refer to the arguments of transitive clauses.

Having discussed the factors relating to prefix choice, we can return to the relative position of the verb and the trigger. In fact, these variables are not independent. In intransitive clauses, where the transitive verb prefixes aren't available to mark aspect, eventiveness is coded primarily by V>S constituent order (usually in conjunction with the particle *-lah* marking the predicate). In the transitive clause this correlation occurs as well: the more eventive *di-* clause is the only one which allows verb-initial order. The correlation of verb-initial order and event-line narration in predominantly verb-initial languages is well-attested in the literature: see for instance the papers by Longacre and Payne in this volume, as well as Myhill (1985), Givón (1987), Hopper (1987), Mithun (1987), Payne (1990).

Finally, it is important to bear in mind throughout the remainder of this paper that the clause type which we will be discussing below — the PT clause — generally occurs in sequenced, event-line narrative, and that therefore the range of information statuses of the agent in this clause type is relatively narrow: agents in narrative clauses are overwhelmingly highly continuous. What factors, then, condition the alternations in agent position that we do find?

2. Coding possibilities for the agent

In this section, I will describe the forms and positions in which agents of *di-* clauses occur in the *Sejarah Melayu*, and discuss the grammatical restrictions on those forms and positions.

2.1 *No agent*

An agent may be "omitted", as in the following example.

(17) *maka diambil baginda akan menantu,*
CONJ PT:take 3 as son-in-law
dikawinkan (ø) dengan Tuan-Puteri Cendera Dewi
PT:marry:CAUS (ø) with princess Cendera Dewi
'He [Sang Sapurba] took (him [the king of Majapahit]) as a son-in-law; (he) married (him) to Princess Cendera Dewi'

2.2 *Clitic agents*

An agent may be cliticized to the verb. The agents in the following examples are considered to be clitics because they cannot be separated from the verb; moreover, the monosyllabic enclitics cause a stress shift from the penult to the last syllable of the root.[10] The monosyllabic clitics *ku-* 'I', *kau-* 'you', *-nya* 'he/she/it/they' (which at least historically are allomorphs of the full forms *aku, engkau,* and *ia* or *dia* respectively) are normally written as part of the word they attach to; in this section I write them with a hyphen to make it easier to identify them.

Proclitics are used when the agent is a speech participant (first or second person). When a proclitic is present, the PT prefix *di-* (otherwise obligatory) is missing.

(18) *Baik* ***ku-****intai, supaya* ***aku*** *ketahui apa juga makan dia*
good 1SG:watch so:that 1SG know what also eat 3
'I'd better watch (it), so that I can find out what is eating it'

(19) ***kamu*** *tunjukkan tempat ular itu pada aku*
2 show:BEN place snake that to 1SG
'Show me where that snake is'

The evidence that proclitic-agent clauses should still be considered PT clauses, even in the absence of the *di-* prefix, is primarily syntactic: in clause combining they have the same properties as other PT clauses. In cases where the pivot argument is a patient and the agent in the secondary clause is first or second person, the agent is invariably proclitic, as in the following patient relative:

(20) *Inilah hal <yang* ***kita*** *lihat semalam itu>*
this:EVT matter REL 1INCL see yesterday that
'This is the thing that we saw last night'

Since proclitics can only have first or second person reference, they are invariably pronominal in function, but the class of "pronouns" in Malay is quite large and includes many polite forms — both honorific and deprecatory — that could equally function as third person referring expressions:

(21) *akan pinta bapak itu* ***hamba*** *kabulkanlah*
to request father that slave consent:EVT
'I (=slave) consent to your (=father's) request'

(22) *Jikalau anak patik* ***tuan-ku*** *peristeri, nescaya kedal ia*
if child slave lord:1SG CAUS:wife must disease 3
'If you (=my lord) marry my (=slave's) child, she will inevitably get *kedal'*

Third person agents which are not marked by the "optional" agent preposition *oleh* (explained below) are coded as enclitics. This includes both pronominal and lexical forms.

(23) *Maka anak raja itu pun dibawa-**nya** kembali ke*
CONJ child king that TOP PT:take:3 back to
rumahnya.
house:3
'They took the princes back to their house'

(24) *dan pedang Corek Semandang Kini itu dikurniakan* ***baginda***
and sword Corek Semandang Kini that PT:bless 3
'He blessed the sword Corek Semandang Kini'

(25) *Maka Nila Pahlawan dan Kerisna Pandita pun*
CONJ Nila Pahlawan and Kerisna Pandita TOP
dikawinkan
PT:marry:CAUS
Bat *dengan Wan Empo' dan Wan Malini*
Bat with Wan Wmpo' and Wan Malini
'Bat married Nila Pahlawan and Kerisna Pandita to Wan Empo' and Wan Malini'

2.3 *Oleh agents*

Non-clitic agents must be marked with the preposition *oleh*. Like most prepositional phrases, an *oleh* phrase can occur in any position in the clause; thus, with a third person agent, *oleh* is obligatory in every possible clause order except VAP (and it is still possible even in this clause order). Examples of the various possibilities were given above in (2)-(5).[11]

Oleh agents may be cross-referenced with a clitic. See example (5) above, and the following:

(26) *Maka padinya pun dituai-nya oleh Wan Empo' dan*
CONJ rice:3 TOP PT:cut:3 by Wan Empo' and
Wan Malini.
Wan Malini
'Wan Empo' and Wan Malini harvested their rice'

(27) *Maka* ***oleh Raja Aftabu'l-Ardz*** *diberi-**nya** seekor lembu*
CONJ by Raja Aftabu'l-Ardz PT:give:3 one:CL ox
yang amat putih
REL very white
'Raja Aftabu'l-Ardz gave (them) a very white ox'

(28) *Maka* ***oleh Sang Sapurba*** *akan ananda baginda Sang*
CONJ by Sang Sapurba to child 3 Sang
Nila Utama itu
Nila Utama that
*dianugerahi-**nya*** ***baginda*** *suatu makota kerajaan*
PT:bestow:3 3 one crown kingship
'Sang Sapurba gave his son Sang Nila Utama a king's crown'

It seems probable that example (28) actually contains *three* references to the agent, Sang Sapurba: in the *oleh* phrase, as a clitic *-nya*, and again as a cliticized honorific pronoun *baginda*.[12]

3. Functions of the contrasts

In this section I will describe the discourse factors which condition the choice among the various possibilities for agent coding.

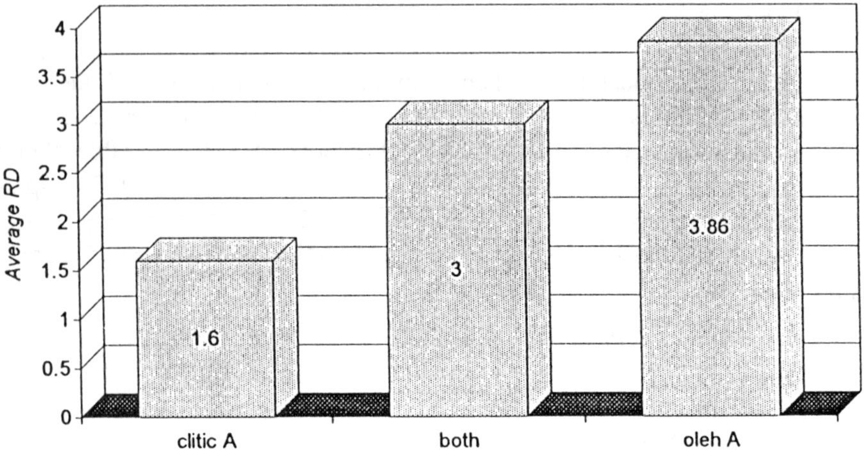

Figure 4. Average RD by type

3.1 *Oleh vs. clitic agents*

The function of *oleh* has been studied in Modern Indonesian in Cumming (1986) and Myhill (1988a). These two authors agree that the contrast is primarily related to the information status of the agent, with more continuous agents tending to cliticize. The Classical Malay data exhibits a similar pattern. As in Modern Indonesian, clitics are associated with highly continuous agents, as Figure 4 shows. (In this and subsequent figures, the category "both" refers to clauses in which the agent is "cross-referenced" — that is, coded by *both* a clitic and an *oleh*-phrase.[13])

Moreover, Classical Malay shows a tendency (not observed in Modern Indonesian) for agents to cliticize when they are specific but their identity is unimportant. These agents are usually coded with the word *orang* 'person', as in the following example:

(29) *Maka gendang nobat pun dipalu* ***oranglah.***
CONJ drum coronation TOP PT:beat person:EVT
'They (people) beat the coronation drum'

The fact that *orang* is in fact cliticized to the verb here is demonstrated by the attachment of the particle *-lah*, which normally attaches to predicates, to the

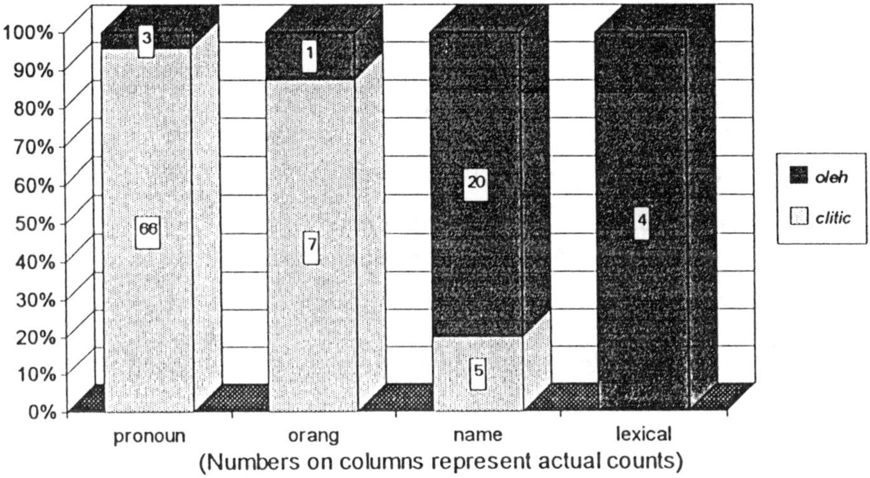

Figure 5. Agent coding and NP type

agent — or more properly, to the predicate phrase which includes the agent; this is characteristic of *orang*. Figure 5 shows the relationship between noun phrase type (including *orang*) and use of *oleh*.

As this figure shows, the "heavier" a noun phrase gets, the less likely it is to cliticize. *Orang* agents probably have the position they do because, while not accessible in the sense of having an easily retrieved referent, they are still low in information. Moreover, they have in common with pronouns the feature of being low in "categoriality" in the sense of Hopper and Thompson (1984). Myhill (1988a,b) argues persuasively that a number of syntactic phenomena, including the Modern Indonesian analogue of agent cliticization, can be explained in terms of a tendency for syntactic elements which are low in categoriality to "cluster" with a high-categoriality element (such as, in this case, the verb); this approach provides a pleasing explanation for this phenomenon.

These tendencies, especially the very strong associations between pronounhood and cliticization and between *oleh* and lexical status, provide further evidence for the claim that cliticization reflects high continuity or accessibility. However, Figure 5 is also consistent with the hypothesis that mere length, rather than a more cognitive quality like accessibility, is the primary conditioning factor. As a counterargument to that hypothesis, I can offer examples where agents which are relatively long and internally complex — but nonetheless expected and accessible — are cliticized:

(30) *hendaklah* ***tuan-ku*** *bunuhkan ular itu*
will:EVT lord:1SG kill:BEN snake that
'Let my lord (=you) kill that snake for us'

(31) *dianugerahkan* ***Allah subhanahu wa ta'ala*** *pada*
PT:bestow Allah may:he:be:praised and exalted to
segala
all
raja-raja Melayu, tiada pernah memberi aib pada
king:REDUP Malay not ever AT:give shame to
segala hamba Melayu
all slave Malay
'Allah — may he be praised and exalted — granted to all the Malay kings never o shame any Malay slave'

The agent in example (31) is lengthy, but it is probably unanalyzed: it is in Arabic rather than Malay, and it is a formulaic and entirely predictable way of referring to Allah. Moreover, although the current database contained no examples, it is in fact possible for lexical NPs to occur in enclitic position if they are sufficiently predictable and/or unimportant; consider example (32), from Chapter 3 of the *Sejarah Melayu*.

(32) *Maka kenaikan itu pun keairan, maka*
CONJ vehicle that TOP affected:by:water CONJ
dipertimba orang,
PT:CAUS:bucket person
tiada tertimba air ruang lagi.
NEG scoopable water hold more
→ *Maka disuruh* ***penghulu kenaikan*** *membuang;*
CONJ PT:order captain vehicle AT:throw:out
maka beberapa harta yang dibuangkan,
CONJ several goods REL PT:throw:out:CAUS
tiada berapa lagi yang tinggal.
NEG so:much more REL remain
'The vessel was shipping water, and people bailed it out, (until) the water in the hold couldn't be scooped out any more. Then **the**

> **captain of the vessel** ordered (them) to throw out (ballast etc.); and (they) threw out so much stuff, there was barely anything left.'

This captain has not been previously mentioned; however, his presence is predictable from the previous mention of the ship. Moreover, he is "anchored" to the ship in this mention of him: the NP *penghulu kenaikan* contains mentions of both.

Having established that accessibility is the most important factor affecting whether or not an agent is cliticized, we can go on to ask whether a purely local kind of accessibility is most relevant, or conversely whether protagonism, the importance of a participant in the story as a whole, is more important. In the case of cliticization, it is easy to demonstrate that local accessibility is the overriding factor. The first column of Figure 6 gives the total number of mentions in the database for the seven most frequently mentioned referents, and the way they are coded when they occur as As of PT clauses (two of the referents never occur in this role).

As this figure shows, Sang Sapurba is by far the most important participant, mentioned almost four times as often as anyone else. This is because he is the central character in Chapter 2: he appears in the second episode of the chapter (the first episode serves to set the scene for his arrival), and is the central character in every subsequent episode. The other participants with high protagonism values are centrally connected with Sang Sapurba (Demang Lebar Daun is his father-in-law and chief minister; Nila Utama and Kerisna Pandita are his brothers, and Wan Empo' and Wan Malini become their wives; and Permaisuri Iskandar Syah becomes his son's mother-in-law) and

Referent	Mentions	clitic	both	oleh
Sang Sapurba	236	32	2	13
Demang Lebar Daun	59	2	0	3
Nila Utama	55	0	0	0
Kerisna Pandita	54	0	0	0
Wan Malini	50	5	1	4
Wan Empo'	49	5	1	4
Perm. Iskandar Syah	28	6	0	0

Figure 6. Protagonism (top 7 participants)

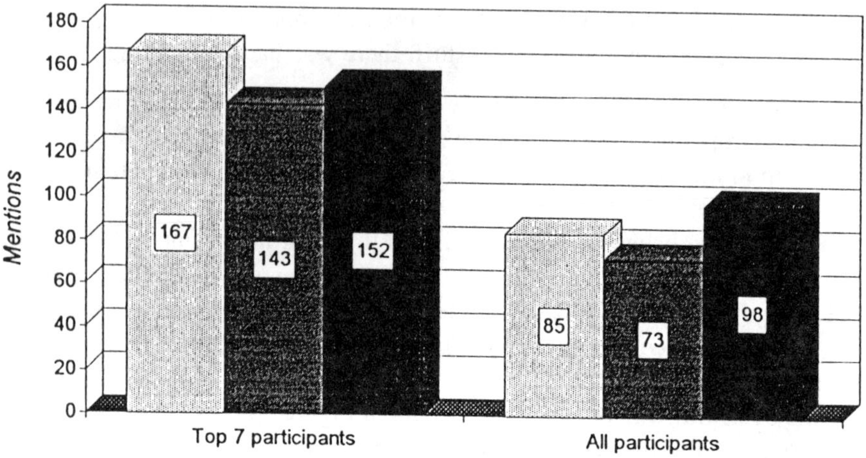

Figure 7. Average number of mentions and coding

appear in several episodes each. Other human participants appear in only one or two episodes (the next most frequently mentioned referent only occurs 17 times).

Given these protagonism values, we can look at the relationship between protagonism and the clitic/*oleh* contrast. Figure 7 gives the average protagonism scores for the three coding types for the seven participants listed in Figure 6, and for all of the participants in the text that are mentioned more than once.

Among the "top seven" referents, the average protagonism of an *oleh* agent is slightly less than that of a clitic agent; among all referents it is slightly more. In neither case is the difference large.

Another approach to determining the relationship of protagonism to agent coding is to look at the references to Sang Sapurba, the primary protagonist of the chapter. If cliticization reflected protagonist status, we might expect that a higher percentage of clitic agents would refer to Sang Sapurba than of *oleh* agents. In fact, the percentages are almost the same, as is shown in Figure 8.

These measures establish that local accessibility, rather than global measures of importance, is most useful in determining the presence of *oleh* in *di-* clauses.

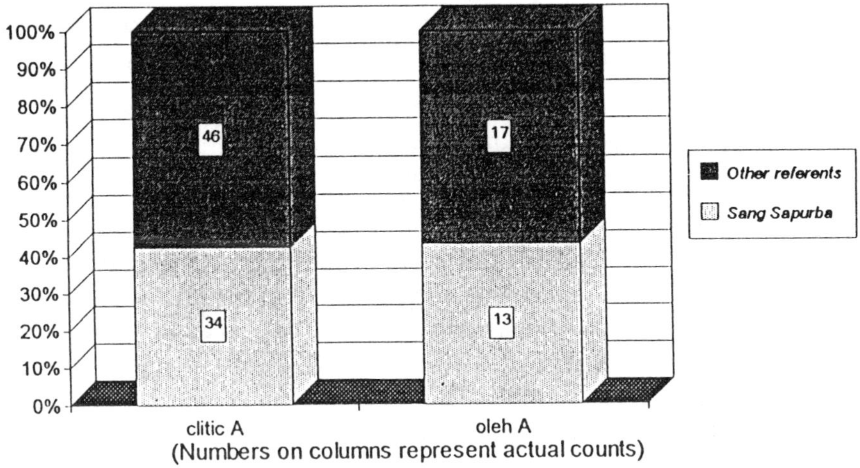

Figure 8.Proportion of Sang Sapurba references

3.2 *Clitic agents and missing agents*

Agent omission is relatively rare in Classical Malay; it accounts for about 20% of *di-* clauses in this corpus, whereas in Modern Indonesian novels approximately 50% of *di-* clauses are agentless (Cumming 1986, 1991).[14] There are three distinct kinds of environments which lead to agent omission. The most common environment (accounting for 14 of the 28 instances in my corpus) is that of example (17) (repeated here as (33)), in which the agent is specific, referential, continuous and recoverable from the context; these examples are similar to examples with clitic pronouns.

(33)	*maka*	*diambil*	*baginda*	*akan*	*menantu,*
	CONJ	PT:take	3	as	son-in-law
→	*dikawinkan*	*dengan*	*Tuan-Puteri*	*Cendera*	*Dewi*
	PT:marry:CAUS	with	princess	Cendera	Dewi

'He [Sang Sapurba] took (him [the king of Majapahit]) as a son-in-law; (he) married (him) to Princess Cendera Dewi'

An exploration of the motivation for the omission of the agent rather than the use of a clitic is beyond the scope of this paper, since "zero" agents cannot be said to have a position in the clause; but it merits further research.

The second type of environment is illustrated in (34); here the referent is not recoverable, but it is unimportant.

(34) *yang bungsunya dinamai Nila Utama*
REL youngest:3 PT:name Nila Utama
'The youngest was named Nila Utama'

These examples are similar to those with clitic *orang* for unimportant referents. They differ principally in that in all of the examples with *orang*, the clause is realis and on the event line; in the agentless examples, the predication refers to an event which is off the event line in the past, irrealis or generic. One way to capture this distinction is to describe the "zero" agents as non-referential and the *orang* agents as referential but unimportant.[15]

The third type of environment is the imperative, illustrated in example (35).

(35) *apabila adalah cap serupa ini, maka terimalah;*
if be:EVT seal like this CONJ accept:EVT
nyatalah daripada raja Melayu.
clear:EVT from king Malay
→ *Jikalau tiada jangan diterima.*
if NEG NEG:IMPER PT:accept
'If there is a seal like this, accept it; it is clearly from a Malay king. If there isn't, don't accept (it).'

In this type of example the omission of the agent is usually assumed to be associated with politeness; but an imperative — and especially a negative imperative, as in this example — is also irrealis, so nonreferentiality may also be a factor for at least some of these clauses.

To recapitulate, then, I have argued that *oleh* is associated with referents whose identity is important (as opposed to *orang* agents and some zeros) but which are not locally accessible (as opposed to clitic agents and other zeros).

3.3 *Oleh agents: position and cross-referencing*

Now that the issue of the factors conditioning the presence or absence of *oleh* has been addressed, we can proceed to consider the factors determining the position of the *oleh* agent and the occurrence of a cross-referencing clitic on the verb. One hypothesis suggests that the majority of *oleh* phrases would appear separated from the verb, since it is superficially plausible that a motivation for the use of *oleh* is to allow the agent to occur in other positions. This hypothesis is easily disconfirmed: agents usually follow the verb directly, even if marked by *oleh*. Figure 9 compares the relative position of *oleh* agents and patients in PT clauses with respect to distance from the verb. The numbers on the x-axis represent position relative to the verb and to other constituents, including clitics (thus, a constituent with position "1" is immediately after the verb, "2" is after the verb with but separated from it by one constituent, "-1" is immediately before the verb, "-2" is before the verb but separated from it by one constituent, and so forth). This figure shows that the large majority of *oleh* agents follow the verb directly with no intervening material, just as clitics do. Thus, freedom of position cannot be a major factor in the choice of *oleh*.

Clitic cross-referencing is strongly associated with preverbal As in this corpus: 5 out of the 6 examples of cross-referencing clitics relate to preverbal As, while 5 out of the 7 preverbal As are cross-referenced by clitics. There are enough exceptions to the pattern to show that the correlation is not grammaticized, but an analysis of the factors conditioning cross-referencing will have to await a larger corpus.

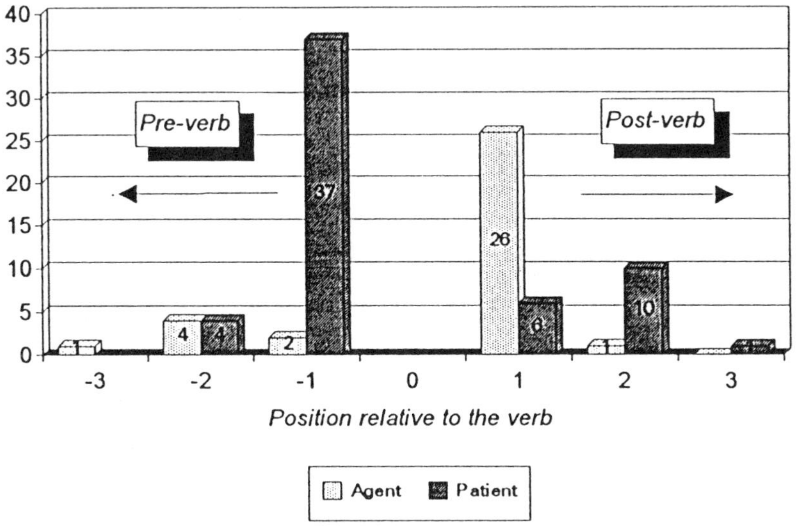

Figure 9. Role and position

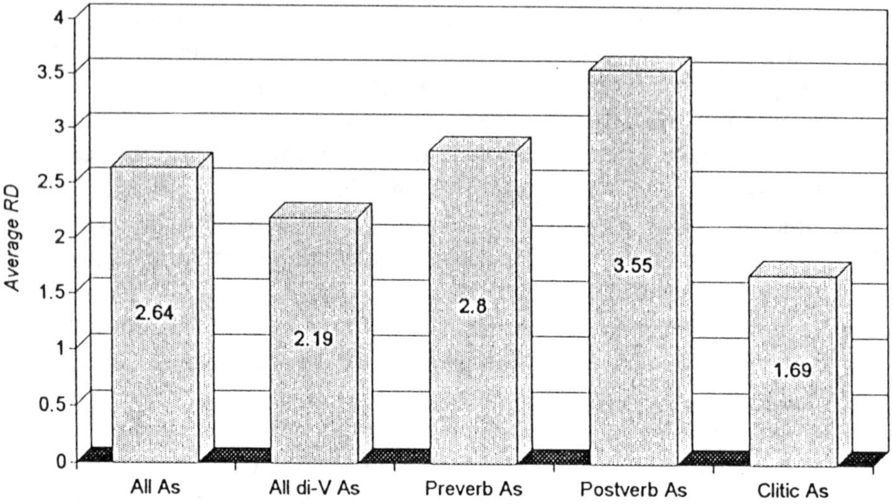

Figure 10. RD and agent position

Brand-new As never occur preverbally; preverbal As are often somewhat discontinuous, but they are identifiable and accessible. Figure 10 shows that preverbal *oleh* As are more continuous (in terms of referential distance) than postverbal *oleh* As, though both types of course have higher referential distance than clitic As (or even than agents in all clause types, including *me*-clauses).

However, we plainly still need a more adequate characterization of the distinction. In my corpus, preverbal agents invariably occur in clauses in which there is also an overt P which is also preverbal, and the clause is introduced by a text-structure marker such as *maka*. They apparently function to create a text structure boundary. A qualitative examination of instances of preverbal As reveals that they are associated with the beginnings of sequences of clauses joined together by argument sharing and other cohesive devices (such as subordinators and possessor overlap) involving syntactic dependency. I will call such sequences "clause chains".[16] Clause chains are smaller units than "episodes" (sequences of events taking place in one location and involving the same participants), though of course episode boundaries always involve beginning a new clause chain. Consider the following example, which gives the context for (28) above:

(36) *Maka Sang Nila Utama, anak Sang Sapurba, diabmil baginda akan menantu, didudukkan baginda dengan anaknya baginda yang bernama Wan Seri Beni itu; maka dinobatkan sekali akan gantinya.*
Maka ***oleh Sang Sapurba akan ananda baginda Sang Nila Utama itu*** *dianugerahinya baginda suatu makota kerajaan, tiada bahana kelihatan masnya daripada kebanyakan permata dan ratna mutu maknikam yang terkena pada makota itu; dan dianugerahi cap kempa kerajaan, seperti cap baginda juga rupanya.*
'Then she took Sang Nila Utama, Sang Sapurba's son, as her son-in-law, settling him with her daughter Wan Seri Beni; then she crowned him king in her place.
Then **Sang Sapurba** gave **his son Sang Nila Utama** a royal crown whose gold couldn't be seen clearly from the quantity of jewels of various sorts which were inlaid in it; and he gave him a royal seal, just like his own seal.'

The preverbal arguments here mark a change from the previous passage, which describes the actions of Queen Iskandar Syah, to a section describing the actions of Sang Sapurba. Sang Sapurba has been mentioned in the previous context, but only as the father of the queen's new son-in-law. It seems likely that in this type of sentence the occurrence of two arguments in preverbal position serves to *reorient* the reader/hearer to participants which are given but in a potentially new relationship. This is a function which is cross-linguistically associated with "left-dislocation" constructions (Keenan and Schiefflin 1976, Duranti and Ochs 1979, Foley and Van Valin 1985), and the prevalence of the cross-referencing clitic in this context makes the resemblance to left-dislocation even stronger.[17] Moreover, a resumptive function for initial position is characteristic of verb-initial languages. However, what is uncharacteristic of this pattern in Classical Malay is that it is strongly associated with *two* preposed arguments, rather than one. It seems as though a principle of attraction were at work, whereby if one direct argument is preverbal through being the head of a clause chain, the other direct argument follows along. The presence of case-marking morphology (i.e. *oleh* and, in some cases such as the above example, an *akan* which signals that the trigger is semantically a goal or recipient) serves to make explicit the new role relationship between them.

This observation is reinforced by looking at the relative position of the preverbal A and the preverbal P. In these instances, it is always the case that the argument that precedes is the more resumptive one — that is, the one with a *longer* referential distance (and, typically, correspondingly "heavy" NP coding). Consider the following examples:

RD of A: 6. RD of P: 51. Order: PAV

(37) *Sebermula, diceriterakan oleh setengah ceritera*
to:begin PT:tell by half story
bahwa anak ceteria Cina yang beristerikan Puteri Tunjung
that child prince China REL wife:CAUS Puteri Tunjung
Bueh,
Bueh
***oleh Sang Sapurba** dirajakan baginda di negeri*
by Sang Sapurba PT:king:CAUS 3 at country
Palembang
Palembang
'The story has it that Sang Sapurba made the Chinese prince who had married Princess Tunjung Bueh the king of Palembang'

RD of A: 25. RD of P: 3. Order: APV

(38) *Maka oleh orang Kuantan Sang Sapurba dirajakannya*
CONJ by people Kuantan Sang Sapurba PT:king:CAUS:3
'The people of Kuantan made Sang Sapurba their king'

Both of these examples occur, like the other preverbal agent examples, at the beginning of clause chains. Example (36) is episode-initial (as is clearly indicated by the presence of the linker *sebermula* with a return to the narrative frame, which only occurs at major text-structure boundaries). Example (37) occurs after a description of the killing of the serpent by Sang Sapurba's follower Permasku Mambang; the Kuantan inhabitants who requested this deed haven't been mentioned since the beginning of this scene. It is chain initial position which licenses both the preverbal agents and the patients; but apparently even in this context considerations of relative recency can determine the relative position of the agents and the patients.

3.4 *Preverbal oleh agent vs. pun agent*

While up to now we have been discussing only the statuses accorded to agents of *di-* clauses, there is one other type of construction that needs to be taken into account: the *pun*-marked agent of a *me-* clause. As illustrated above in Section 1.1, arguments marked by *pun* must be the triggers of their clauses.

Moreover, the functions that have been ascribed to *pun* (a resumptive function associated with text-structure boundaries as well as other contexts) overlap with the functions that I have described as characterizing preverbal *oleh* agents.

In general, however, the environments which elicit *pun* are more local than the kind of higher-level text-structure boundaries which elicit preverbal *oleh* arguments. The relatively local nature of the *pun* preverbal argument is demonstrated by the fact that, unlike preverbal *oleh*, *pun* often marks pronouns.

Moreover, it should be noted that unlike preverbal *oleh*, *pun* is available for arguments of both transitive and intransitive clauses; where an episode begins with an intransitive clause (for instance a verb of motion), as is frequently the case, the preverbal *oleh* phrase is not available, and a *pun* phrase may stand in instead to reorient the reader to the participants. Consider the following example:

(39) *Setelah ular itu melihat manusia datang,*
after snake that AT:see human come
maka ***ia pun*** *menggerak dirinya;*
CONJ 3 TOP AT:move self:3;
maka segera ditetak Permasku Mambang penggal tiga
CONJ at:once PT:chop Permasku Mambang piece three
lalu mati.
then die
→ *Maka* ***Permasku Mambang pun*** *kembali menghadap Sang*
CONJ Permasku Mambang TOP return AT:face Sang
Sapurba
Sapurba
persembahkan ular itu sudah mati,
present snake that PFV dead
syahadan ***pedang itu pun*** *dipersembahkan kepada Sang*
CONJ sword that TOP PT:present to Sang
Sapurba.
Sapurba
'After the snake saw a human coming, it moved; then Permasku Mambang immediately chopped (it) into three pieces, and (it) died. Then Permasku Mambang returned to pay homage to Sang Sapurba and present the dead snake; he (also) gave the sword to Sang Sapurba.'

The second *pun* phrase here occurs at an episode boundary, in exactly the kind of context which if it were transitive might elicit a preverbal *oleh* phrase.

4. Conclusions

While the picture given above of the factors relating to positional variation — and related matters — among agents in Classical Malay is not entirely complete,[18] I hope to have at least indicated the degree of complexity attached to the coding of this role. In this section I will discuss some of the implications of these findings for theories of language, specifically theories concerned with specifying the relations between forms and functions/meanings. Figure 11 schematizes some aspects of the relationships discussed above. While this figure does not do justice to all the complexities,[19] it does illustrate several generalizations that I hope have emerged from this study.

4.1 *Constituent order cannot be studied in isolation*

Even in a relatively "morphology-free" language like Malay, constituent order alternation interacts crucially with other morphosyntactic alternations. For instance, preverbal agents can be associated with several very different discourse functions, ranging from highly accessible (proclitic first- and sec-

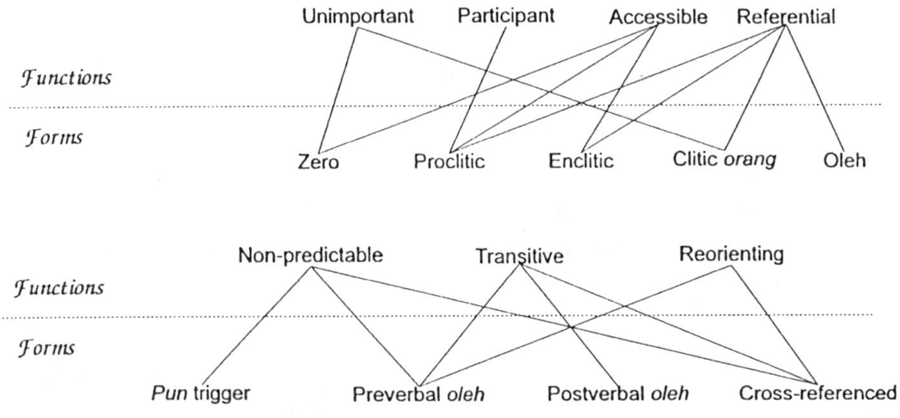

Figure 11. A few function–form mappings

ond-person pronominals), through moderately inaccessible (*pun* agent triggers) to very inaccessible (cross-referenced, sentence-initial *oleh* agents marking resumptive arguments at major text-structure boundaries). The different functions associated with early position are distinguished by various other morphosyntactic characteristics: the presence of lexical material such as *oleh* and *pun*, the presence or absence of additional material between agent and verb, most probably intonational differences, verb prefixation and cross-referencing, and the form of the agent itself.

4.2 *Form-function mappings are many-to-one and one-to-many*

A given meaning or function tends to be expressed by a cluster of forms, while a given form is usually associated with several (usually — but not always — covarying) meanings/functions. It is precisely this complexity that allows for the reanalysis of the mappings between forms and functions which characterizes syntactic change. Approaches to language which explicitly or implicitly assume a strict isomorphism between categories of form and of meaning/function — including the approaches of many linguists who characterize their work as "cognitive" or "functional" — will not be able to capture this complexity, and thus will not be able to account for change.

4.3 *Discourse-functional statuses are diverse*

To adequately account for occurring variation, a wide range of *different* functional statuses must be taken into account. While there is some contingent covariation among these statuses (for instance, "speech act participants" are generally "accessible") and some implicational structure (for instance, all "accessible" referents must by definition be "referential"), in most cases each category represents an independent dimension. This represents a departure from work which assumes that information status represents a single continuum (of e.g. "topicality"), and that a wide range of forms can be distinguished merely by their relative position on that continuum.[20]

This complexity must at least in part be derived from the fact that natural language must accomodate both the speaker's and the hearer's mental processes. Some of it reflects the variety of mental statuses a referent can have for a hearer (as argued in e.g. Givón 1989 and his paper in this volume), where activation level in the hearer's mind, expectedness for the hearer, and location in the hearer's memory all independently require appropriate coding on the part of the speaker; the categories of "accessibility", "predictability" and "reorientation" presumably relate primarily to these matters. Additional complexity is added from a partially overlapping set of categories related to the speaker's cognitive representations (as argued in e.g. Chafe 1980, 1987; Tomlin 1987, and Tomlin's paper in this volume). Plausibly, "importance" and "referentiality" relate primarily to speakers' representations.[21] Thus, a sophisticated mental interpretation of grammatical alternation can go a long way towards motivating the richness and complexity we find in natural language texts.

Appendix: Glossing conventions

Punctuation in the examples reflects that in the edition I used as a source; this does not however necessarily reflect the original manuscript, which does not contain punctuation. For the sake of brevity, I have not indicated the complete morphological analysis of every form; morphemes are only glossed separately when they relate to the topic of this paper or to understanding the example.
The following abbreviations are used in the glosses:

1SG, 2, 3 1INCL, 1EXCL 3PL	First, second, and third person pronouns, including both free and cliticized forms. The same forms are used for clausal arguments and for possessors. There is no distinct second person plural form, and most third-person forms can be used for either number. Numerous forms, expressing different kinds of honorification, correspond to each of these person/number categories; I have not usually attempted to include social information in the glosses.
REDUP	Reduplication, indicating plural, repeated action, distributiveness etc.
BEN	The benefactive suffix *-kan*
CAUS	A causative morpheme, including causative *-kan* and the prefix *per-*
CL	A numeral classifier
PT	The "Patient Trigger" prefix
EVT	*-lah*, a particle marking "eventive" predicates and imperatives
CONJ	Conjunctions which do not have a good English equivalent (especially *maka*, 'sequenced event-line action')
AT	The 'Agent Trigger" prefix *me-*
NEG	A negative morpheme
PFV	A perfective auxiliary (*sudah* or *telah*)
TOP	The "resumptive topic" particle *pun*
REL	The relative clause introducer *yang*

Notes

* This paper has benefitted most directly from interactions with T. Givón, Bob Longacre, and Doris Payne in Milwaukee; written comments from the editors and from Sandy Thompson; e-mail discussions with Tom Payne; and much invaluable feedback from Barbara Fox and the Colorado Discourse and Grammar Group.

1. The final nasal of this prefix assimilates in place to the first consonant of the root; if this consonant is a voiceless stop, it is then dropped. Since *me-* is the invariant part of this prefix, I will henceforth refer to it as the *me-* prefix.

2. Following Comrie (1981), I use the term "A" or "agent" to refer to the direct argument of a transitive clause which is "most actor-like", and "P" or "patient" to refer to the direct argument which is "most undergoer-like"; these will often not be "prototypical" semantic agents and patients. I prefer this terminology to Dixon's A/O system because — as will become evident — O or "object" has syntactic overtones which are misleading in the majority of cases for Classical Malay.

3. Glossing conventions for this and the following examples are listed in the Appendix.

4. For a discussion of the various recensions of this text, see Iskandar and Kaeh (1978), and Liaw (1975).

5. For arguments against the use of the terms "subject" or "pivot" for this syntactic role, see Cumming (1991:33); some of the reasons will become apparent in the course of this paper, as will reasons for avoiding the Philippinist term "topic". Briefly, in the most frequent clause type, triggers do not have the pragmatic properties associated with subjects and/or topics. Related objections apply to the use of the terms "active" and "passive" for the clause types I have labelled AT and PT, and to "object" for the non-trigger argument of a transitive clause. See Cumming and Wouk (1987) for arguments against the use of the term "ergative" for the PT clause type.

6. This is for instance the assumption underlying Foley and Van Valin's characterization of Indonesian as a "pragmatic pivot" language, i.e. a language in which "the pivot is crucially associated with pragmatic notions of discourse topicality" (Foley and Van Valin 1985:305).

7. In previous work I have followed Nichols (1984) and others in using the term "thematicity" in this sense; however, recently I have been persuaded that this term is too ambiguous to be useful. Therefore I hesitantly introduce the term "protagonism", in the hope that its novelty is outweighed by its transparency. (The participant structure of this corpus will be discussed in more detail in Section 3.1.) In the protagonism measures used in this paper, references to sets (including plurals as well as conjoined NPs) are counted as references to each member of the set. Only those NPs whose referents are mentioned more than once in the corpus are included in the counts; this is an attempt to include only those referents which are truly "referential", or "trackable" in the sense of Du Bois (1980).

8. The technique of measuring accessibility in terms of distance to the last mention is due to Givón (1983), but I have used a slightly different method than proposed there. The averages given in this paper represent only the values for referents with RDs of less than 20; they do not include first mentions. A value of 0 is possible if a referent has been mentioned in the same clause.

9. Actually, by the RD measure Ss look very similar to As; this is doubtless due to the fact that "brand-new" referents are excluded from these counts.

10. While stress information is not available for Classical Malay, evidence for the stress shift before *-nya* goes back to the 7th century stone inscriptions, written in an Indic script in which vowel length marking was used to transcribe stress in Malay words (Cœdès 1930).
    Myhill (1988a) argues that what I am calling cliticization should actually be regarded as a kind of incorporation. There are indeed certain typological parallels to incorporation constructions in other languages, but the usual extreme referentiality of the agent argues against this analysis.

11. One of these orders — VPA — is so rare that it did not occur in the *Sejarah Melayu* database; example (3) is from the *Hikayat Indraputra*, Mulyadi (1983).

12. It is also possible that *baginda* cross-references the recipient, Sang Sapurba's son. We know from the verb form, which contains the suffix -i, that the recipient is the trigger of the clause. However, in this text it is usually the case that when two human participants interact, they are distinguished by honorification, with the honorific being reserved for the higher-status referent, which in this case is Sang Sapurba; moreover, there are no clear examples elsewhere in the text of *trigger* cross-referencing.

13. The number of cross-referenced agents in this corpus is small (six), and therefore their statistical characteristics are not significant; I separate them out in the tables because it is not evident whether they should be included with the *oleh* or clitic agents (or neither). For some discussion of the characteristics of this class of agents see Section 3.3.

14. This difference is one of the reasons why the *di-* clause is more passive-like in Modern Indonesian than in Classical Malay.

15. Since neither type of "unimportant" agent is ever "tracked" in the ensuing discourse, it is impossible to verify this by discourse measures; and discourse-functional (rather than semantic; c.f. Du Bois 1980) approaches to referentiality cannot capture the distinction.

16. Longacre (1985) uses the term "co-ranking structures" to refer to this type of sequence, reserving the term "clause chain" for switch-reference languages with a medial/final distinction. In my view this distinction is incidental, hinging only on which end of the chain is the most fully specified. In fact there are several parallels between the use of switch-reference markers and the Malay verb prefixes to keep track of referents in medial clauses. See also Cumming (1984) on clause chains and "sentences" in Chinese.

17. It is worth noting that only *di-* verb agents (and, in a construction not discussed here, possessors) can be cross-referenced in this way. If cross-referencing is viewed as a kind of agreement, this fact poses additional problems for the analysis of trigger as subject.

18. Among the issues left unresolved here are the distinction between clitic and "zero" agents, and the distinction between cross-referenced and non-cross-referenced preverbal agents.

19. Specifically, this figure avoids the issue of which forms "really code" each function and which forms merely correlate with it. In some cases I have addressed this issue above; in others insufficiency of data has prevented a conclusive treatment; and in yet others there is probably systematic indeterminacy in the language.

20. This characterizes some of the work inspired by the collection in Givón (1983), though a close reading of Givón's own introduction to that volume indicates a more sophisticated view.

21. Some linguists would want to add social or interactional motivations as a third category which would supplement or replace speaker-oriented and hearer-oriented motivations. In my interpretation, interactional motivations can be analyzed into speaker's representations, speaker's goals and speaker models of hearer states. Since they include real-time production and reaction in their database, however, interactional explanations can often go farther than purely internal ones in bringing out the non-arbitrariness of certain patterns of form–function mappings.

References

Ajamiseba, Danielo. 1983. *A Classical Malay Text Grammar: Insights into a non-Western text tradition.* Canberra: Pacific Linguistics. [*Pacific Linguistics Series D,* No. 56; *Materials in Languages of Indonesia,* 21.]

Becker, A. L. 1979. "The figure a sentence makes: an interpretation of a Classical Malay sentence." *Discourse and Syntax* ed. by T. Givón, 243-60. New York: Academic Press. [*Syntax and Semantics* 12.]

Chafe, Wallace L. 1980. "The deployment of consciousness in the production of a narrative." *The Pear Stories: Cognitive, cultural and linguistic aspects of narrative production* ed. by Wallace L. Chafe, 9-50. Norwood, NJ: Ablex.

Chafe, Wallace L. 1987. "Cognitive constraints on information flow." *Coherence and Grounding in Discourse* ed. by Russell S. Tomlin, 21-51. [*Typological Studies in Language* 11]. Amsterdam/Philadelphia: John Benjamins.

Cœdès, G. 1930. "Les inscriptions Malaises de Çrivijaya." *Bulletin de l'Ecole Française de l'Extrème-Orient* 30. 29-80.

Comrie, Bernard. 1981. *Language Universals and Linguistic Typology.* Chicago: University of Chicago Press.

Cumming, Susanna. 1984. "The sentence in Chinese." *Studies in Language* 8. 365-395.

Cumming, Susanna. 1986. "The function of *oleh.*" *Proceedings of the First Annual Pacific Linguistics Conference,* 69-84.

Cumming, Susanna. In press. "Multifunctionality and the realization problem in modeling discourse production." Forthcoming in a secret festschrift.

Cumming, Susanna. 1991. *Functional Change: The case of Malay constituent order.* Berlin: Mouton de Gruyter.

Cumming, Susanna and Fay Wouk. 1987. "Is there 'discourse ergativity' in Austronesian languages?" *Studies in Ergativity* ed. by R.M.W. Dixon, 271-97. Amsterdam: North Holland. (Also published as *Lingua* 71.)

Du Bois, John W. 1980. "Beyond definiteness: the trace of identity in discourse." *The Pear Stories* ed. by Wallace L. Chafe, 203-75. Norwood, NJ: Ablex.

Du Bois, John W. 1987. "The discourse basis of ergativity." *Language* 63. 805-856.

Duranti, Alessandro and Elinor Ochs. 1979. "Left-dislocation in Italian conversation." *Discourse and Syntax* ed. by T. Givón, 377-415. New York: Academic Press. [*Syntax and Semantics* 12].

Foley, William A. and Robert D. Van Valin. 1984. *Functional Syntax and Universal Grammar.* Cambridge: Cambridge University Press. [*Cambridge Studies in Linguistics* 38.]

Foley, William A. and Robert D. Van Valin. 1985. "Information packaging in the clause." *Language Typology and Syntactic Description,* Vol. 1: *Clause structure* ed. by Timothy Shopen, 282-364. Cambridge; Cambridge University Press.

Givón, T. ed. 1983. *Topic Continuity in Discourse.* Amsterdam/Philadelphia: John Benjamins. [*Typological Studies in Language,* 3].

Givón, T. 1987. "The pragmatics of word-order: predictability, importance, and attention." *Studies in Syntactic Typology* ed. by Michael Hammond et al, 243-284. Amsterdam: Benjamins.

Givón, T. 1989. *Mind, Code and Context.* Norwood, NJ: Ablex.

Hopper, Paul J. 1979. "Aspect and foregrounding in discourse." *Discourse and Syntax* ed. by T. Givón, 213-24. New York: Academic Press. [*Syntax & Semantics* 12].

Hopper, Paul J. 1983. "Ergative, passive and active in Malay narrative." *Discourse Perspectives on Syntax* ed. by Flora Klein-Andreu, 67-88. New York: Academic Press.

Hopper, Paul J. 1987. "Stability and change in VN/NV alternating languages: a study in pragmatics and linguistic typology." *The Pragmatic Perspective: Selected papers from the 1985 International Pragmatics Conference* ed. by Jef Verschueren & Marcella Bertuccelli-Papi, 455-476. Amsterdam/Philadelphia: John Benjamins.

Hopper, Paul J. 1989. "The emergence of the category 'proper name' in discourse". *Redefining Linguistics* ed. by H. Davis and T. J. Taylor, 149-162. Londen/New York: Routledge.

Hopper, Paul J. and Sandra A. Thompson. 1980. "Transitivity in grammar and discourse." *Language* 56. 251-299.

Hopper, Paul J. and Sandra A. Thompson 1984. "The discourse basis for lexical categories in universal grammar." *Language* 60. 703-752.

Iskandar, Yusoff and Abdul Rahman Kaeh. 1978. *Sejarah Melayu (Edisi Shellabear): satu pembicaraan kritis dari pelbagai bidang.* Kuala Lumpur: Heinemann Educational Books Ltd.

Keenan, Elinor Ochs and Bambi Schiefflin. 1976. "Foregrounding referents: a reconsideration of left-dislocation in discourse." *Proceedings of the Second Annual Meeting of the Berkeley Linguistics Society,* 240-57. Berkeley: Berkeley Linguistics Society.

Liaw, Yock Fang. 1975. *Sjarah Kesusastraan Melayu Klassik.* Singapore: Pustaka Nasional.

Longacre, Robert E. 1985. "Sentences as combinations of clauses." *Language Typology and Syntactic Description,* Vol. 2: *Complex constructions* ed. by Timothy Shopen, 235-286. Cambridge; Cambridge University Press.

Mithun, Marianne. 1987. "Is basic word order universal?" *Coherence and Grounding in Discourse* ed. by Russell S. Tomlin, 280-328. Amsterdam/Philadelphia: John Benjamins. [*Typological Studies in Language* 11].

Mulyadi, Sri Wulan Rujiati. 1983. *Hikayat Indraputra: a Malay romance.* Dordrecht: Foris. [*Koninklijk Instituut voor Taal-, Land- en Volkenkunde, Bibliotheca Indonesica* 23].

Myhill, John. 1982. "Word order and marginal ergativity." *Proceedings of the 18th Annual Meeting of the Chicago Linguistic Society,* 377-389. Chicago: Chicago Linguistic Society.

Myhill, John. 1985. "Pragmatic and categorial correlates of VS word order." *Lingua* 66. 177-200.

Myhill, John. 1988a. "Nominal agent incorporation in Indonesian." *Journal of Linguistics* 24. 111-136.

Myhill, John. 1988b. "Categoriality and clustering." *Studies in Language* 12. 261-297.

Nichols, Johanna. 1984. "The grammatical marking of theme in literary Russian." *UCLA Slavic Studies* 11 ed. by M. Flier and R. Brecht, 170-86. Columbus: Slavica.

Payne, Doris L. 1990. *The Pragmatics of Word Order: Typological dimensions of verb-initial languages.* Berlin: Mouton de Gruyter.

Rafferty, Ellen. 1985. "Changing Discourse Strategies in Malay Texts of the 1920s." Unpublished Ms.

Rafferty, Ellen. 1987. "Word order in High and Low Malay of the late 19th Century." *Coherence and Grounding in Discourse* ed. by Russell S. Tomlin, 361-382. Amsterdam/Philadelphia: John Benjamins. [*Typological Studies in Language* 11].

Situmorang, T.D. and A. Teeuw (eds). 1958. *Sedjarah Melaju menurut terbitan Abdullah.* Penerbit Jambatan.

Tomlin, Russell S. 1987. "Linguistic reflections of cognitive events." *Coherence and grounding in discourse,* 455-80. Amsterdam/Philadelphia: John Benjamins. [*Typological Studies in Language* 11].

Winstedt, Richard O. 1961. *A History of Classical Malay Literature* (Revised edition). *Journal of the Royal Asiatic Society, Malayan Branch* 31, part 3, No. 183. [*Monographs on Malay Subjects* 5].

Preverbal nominals in Colville-Okanagan

Michael Darnell
University of Wisconsin - Milwaukee

1. Introduction

Colville, a Salish language spoken in Eastern Washington and British Columbia, has been analyzed as having clauses whose major constituent order is verb-initial. It is the function of those clauses which do not fit that typical pattern, namely preposing constructions, that is of interest in this study. The conclusions that I draw about these constructions must be qualified in two ways. First, I examine only narrative discourse, and though the claims made about preposing constructions may at some point be shown to hold for other discourse genres, such generality is not assumed here. Furthermore, the text, Peter Seymour's *The Golden Woman*, is assumed to be representative of Colville narratives, but is still the work of a single narrator. The second limitation of this paper is that it examines only nominal arguments in preverbal position. Full pronouns, always considered contrastive/emphatic, are rare in Colville narrative discourse since grammatical roles are referenced by clitics or affixes on the verb.

In the first section some preliminary remarks about the text and this study's methodology are presented. Also, the crucial problem of determining clausal boundaries in Colville is examined and a diagnostic method proposed to separate preposed nominals from what appear to be separate clauses. Given these preliminaries and a detailed examination of clauses containing these preverbal nominals, I conclude, following Mattina (1973), that preverbal nominals in Colville in many instances function as markers of contrastive information. However, not all such preverbal nominals can be analyzed as contrastive. In those instances in which preverbal nominals are non-contrastive they must code referents which are not topical in the following discourse, and thus such constructions do not function primarily as a method of marking shifts in discourse topics.

2. Preliminaries

In the following subsections I discuss the text and my methodological approach to it in greater detail, and offer a diagnostic for determining clause boundaries. In the case of the latter, I will propose a method which is used in this study to separate what I call, for the lack of a better term, 'true' preposed nominals from those nominals which seem to be clauses unto themselves.

2.1 *The Golden Woman*

In *The Golden Woman* (Mattina 1985), Mattina has transcribed and edited several days of tape-recording sessions into a single complete narrative and additional appendices containing sections of the text which were repeated during the taping sessions. As a database I used this single version of the story. The edited version of this text is approximately 2800 clauses in length. Mattina sections the text by numbering 'sentences'. Working with a detailed analysis of the first 160 clauses (an analysis which serves later as a base for comparisons of topicality measures), an average of 4 clauses appeared in each 'sentence', thus the approximation of the text's length.

2.2 *Methodology*

Variations from a basic word order generally indicate that a clause has a different discourse function than a clause with the basic order. Two possibilities that are often mentioned with regard to preposing constructions are contrast and topicalization. An analysis which characterizes a construction as contrastive can be based on the work of Chafe (1976) and Prince (1982). The notion of contrastive information may be nicely delimited by appealing to Chafe's three requirements: shared background knowledge, the existence of a set of possible candidates, and the assertion of the correct candidate. However, Chafe's (1976) characterization of shared background can be too restrictive in some cases, i.e. this characterization seems to depend solely on linguistic or extralinguistic context. In his example, 'Rónald made the hamburgers,' where contrastive stress falls on the subject, the shared background knowledge that 'someone made the hamburgers' exists due to the previous discourse or the situation. However, as Prince (1982) notes, nominals are able to be topicalized, or left dislocated (and available for contrast), if they can be evoked not only by context, but also by a salient set relationship or a semantic frame. For example, Prince (1982:6) provides these two examples from Studs Terkel's book, *Working*.

(1) I don't want my son to have it [long hair]. Now *the sideburns* I wear because I do TV commericals and stuff. (Terkel 1974:191)

(2) [But I graduated from high school] an average student. My initiative didn't carry me any further than average. *History* I found to be dry. *Math courses* I was never good at. (Terkel 1974:590)

These examples illustrate two points relevant to this discussion. First, in both cases, the existence of shared background knowledge can be construed. In (1), the extralinguistic context (i.e. the interview situation) may provide the background knowledge, but a set relationship may also exist (i.e. long hair and sideburns could be considered in a set relationship considering the American social climate in 1974). In (2), a semantic frame is evoked by the mention of high school and is alone responsible for the existence of shared background knowledge. Second, in (1) some sort of contrast exists, though it does not seem appropriate to say that the mention of sideburns constitutes an assertion of the correct candidate. In (2) it is difficult to say that the left-dislocation is contrastive. Thus, considering these examples, some care is taken to note other possible analyses of preposed constituents beyond those contrastive situations described by Chafe (1976). In this paper I depend on both of these approaches not only to show how my analysis concurs with Mattina's claims that preverbal nominals are contrastive, but also to note situations where the term does not seem to adequately describe the situation.

Classifying constructions as topicalizations has often been based on subjective judgements. In order to eliminate this subjectivity, the quantitative methodology pioneered by T. Givón (1983) is employed here[1]. By counting the number of clauses in which a referent appeared previously in the text and the number of clauses in which that referent continues to appear in the subsequent discourse, one may realize a quantitative measure of a referent's topicality. To illustrate, referents which appear in clauses as anaphoric pronouns, affixes, or zero anaphors typically will have been mentioned before in one of the previous three clauses, if not the immediately preceding clause. Referents which appear as nominals typically will not have been mentioned very recently in the preceding discourse. Thus, by comparing the number of clauses since the last mention of the referent, a quantitative difference in topicality between the occurrence of anaphoric mentions and nominals can be realized. Therefore, in a less subjective way, one can claim that referents coded by anaphors have been topical in the preceding discourse, while those coded by nominals usually have not.

In the same way, by considering the number of clauses in which a referent continues to be mentioned in the following discourse, those referents which appear in a greater number of the following clauses can be claimed to be more topical than those which do not appear as often. In this approach there is a certain amount of ambiguity in terminology; topicality has been defined according to both the previous and subsequent discourse. Since the focus of this paper is on nominals, the previous discourse is not crucial to my discussion of topicality. However, due to the fact that I discuss topicality in previous discourse, I will borrow Givón's (1991) term 'anaphoric' to refer to topicality in these situations. To determine whether or not a referent introduced by a nominal is topical, the subsequent discourse is the crucial environment. If that referent has a high persistence count, i.e. continues to be mentioned in the discourse, then it can be objectively called a topic. Again following Givón, I employ the term 'cataphoric' topicality to refer to these situations.

2.3 *Determining clausal boundaries*

In many languages clauses are analyzable by noting the presence of some finite or non-finite verb form. Salish languages are problematic in this respect. The clause in (3) illustrates the problem.

(3) *t'əxʷ axà? táwn*
indeed DEICTIC town
'It is a town.'[2]

While (3) is punctuated as a clause, and is marked for stress in a manner consistent with clauses (a matter discussed below), it has no verb or verbal element[3]. The lack of a copula in the language, not unusual in verb-initial languages, is not the central problem. Rather, the ability of any independent word, as opposed to a clitic, in Colville to be a predicate can present a problem in determining whether a clause is indeed a preposing construction. Given a construction with what may seem straightforwardly a preverbal argument (i.e. this particular constituent is an argument of the following verb), it is still necessary to consider the possibility that the preverbal constituent is actually a clause. While the construction in (4) will be analyzed as a case of 'true' preposing, it can serve now to illustrate the problem.

(4)	*axaʔ*	*mnìmɬ-əmp*	*p*	*q'wíq'ʷəɬ-t*
	DEICTIC	folks-2PL:POSS	2PL:SUBJ	smart-STAT

'You folks are smart.'

It might be argued that /axaʔ mnimɬəmp/ is itself a clause that could be translated as 'It is you folks'. The entire construction then could be translated as two independent clauses, i.e. 'It is you folks. You (pl.) are smart.'

In resolving this problem, the following two criteria were used as a first step to determine clause boundaries and delimit 'true' preposing. First, the presence of a verbal (i.e. an independent word which takes verbal, as opposed to nominal, inflections) in a construction was considered an indication of a clause. Second, in cases like (3), in which no verbal was present, clausal stress patterns seemed a useful indicator since the pattern of stress on the clause level is quite consistent. As one would expect, independent words can bear stress while particles or clitics cannot. Secondary stress may fall on deictics or other words with restricted distributions. Most importantly, though a clause may have secondary stress occurring on independent words, it will have only one primary stress, which will typically fall on the last word in the clause. In both (3) and (4), primary stress falls on the predicative word while secondary stress appears on the deictic and the nominal. The use of stress patterns provided a consistent method of determining that non-verbal constructions like (3) were independent clauses, and provided an initial indication that examples like (4) might qualify as preposing constructions.

In cases where the above criteria failed to provide clear results, additional factors needed to be considered. The next step was to consider the presence of particles, deictics, or articles between a nominal and a following verb, as some of these morphemes appear to mark clause boundaries. Each case is illustrated below. For the purposes of the present study, I conclude that only those instances where so-called 'independent clause particles' appear between the nominal and the verb qualify as preposing constructions.

Colville employs a number of clause-initial particles to indicate interclausal relations and tense and modality. These particles can be divided into two sets: independent and dependent (Mattina1973:126). The set of independent particles which includes tense and modality markers occurs with independent clauses, clause-initially for the most part, but some freedom is exhibited by the tense and modality markers. Dependent particles, on the other hand, indicate that what follows is a subordinate clause. In the case where neither set appeared between the nominal and the verb, such constructions were treated as 'true' preposing. (4), reprinted here as (5), is an example of this case.

(5)	*axaʔ*	*mnìmɫ-əmp*	*p*	*q'wíɫq'ʷəɫ-t*
	DEICTIC	folks-2PL:POSS	2PL:SUBJ	smart-STAT
	'You folks are smart.'			

These constructions position an argument of the predicate preverbally and contain a single primary stress. The use of the clitic morpheme /p/ in this construction to indicate grammatical role, person, and number would be obligatory in both a preposing construction and the verb-initial norm.

In (6) a member of the independent particle set intervenes between the nominal and verb.

(6)	*uɫ*	*n'ìn'wiʔ*	*t*	*nƛ'ləltàn*	***mi***	*ƛ'lál*
	and	until	INSTR	one's death	***FUT***	die
	'And until from his death he'll die.'					

Since the future marker co-occurs with an independent clause, there is no question that (6) is a single clause with a preposed oblique object.

While the few instances of subordinating conjunctions posed little problem for this analysis, another more common particle was more problematic. In (7) and (8) the particle /kiʔ/, with its variant [kəʔ]) appears in the crucial position. In (9) the particle does not appear.

(7)	*illìʔ*	*ḷ*	*nəqs-lùp*	*kəʔ*	*ct'ʔ ák'ʷ*
	DEICTIC	in	one-place	***REL***	comes up
	'It is in one place that she comes up.'				

(8)	*k'əl*	*nəspìlem*	***kiʔ***	*kən*	*xʷúy'*
	to	place name	***REL***	1SG.SUBJ	go
	'It was to Nespelem that I went.'				

(9) *k'əl nəspìlem kən xʷúy'*
to place name 1SG:SUBJ go
'To Nespelem I went.'

Mattina (1973:126) calls /kiʔ/ a relativizing particle. Despite the similarity in terminology, he does not, I believe, mean to imply that what follows the particle is a relative clause. The presence of prepositions and casemarking (in other examples) which indicate the nominal's grammatical role in the following clause seems quite odd if indeed the following clause is a relativization on the nominal. These clauses appear to be clefts. Following Mattina's analysis, I considered (8) and (9) different clause types: (8), a cleft, and (9), a preposing construction.

In addition, deictic words and articles must also be noted as markers of clause boundaries. Colville has a rich deictic system with forms which distinguish, for example, between source and location, with each possibility characterized as proximate and obviate as well (Mattina, 1973). These seldom appear before a nominal in the fashion of English's "that man". The most common use of such deictics is in constructions where the deictic appears initially, followed by a "simple sentence, [consisting of a] predicate and optional complement(s)" (Mattina 1973:144-5). Since this clause-initial position is so regular, I have ruled out constructions like (10) as examples of 'true' preposing.

(10) *ixìʔ sənk'ʷəstʔìwtx*
DEICTIC youngest one
illìʔ *ck'əlʔìm-st-ə-s l a-ksəntq'ʷútn'*
DEICTIC waits for-TRANS-2SG:OBJ-3SG:SUBJ in 2POSS-bed
'There is the youngest one. There she waits for you in your bed.'(lit.)

In this case, though the stress pattern is suggestive of a single clause, the deictic before the verb, 'waits', indicates that this construction is two clauses, the first stative, the second in which the referent appears as an anaphoric agent. Further evidence for analyzing these as separate clauses comes from the fact that nominal agents in transitive clauses must appear with the case marker /t/, which is absent in (10). The appearance of this morpheme can be seen in (13) below.

Finally, while the article /iʔ/ appears before nominals to signal definite reference[4] as in (11), the article at times appears between a possibly preposed nominal and a following verb as in (12).

(11) *ixì? c?àcqa?-st-Ø-s i? sqláw-s*
DEICTIC take out-TRANS-3SG:OBJ-3SG:SUBJ ART money-3POSS
'He took out his money.'

(12) *axà? n-?əɬna?sqìlxʷtn i? kíc-ənt-Ø-əm*
DEICTIC LOC-man eater ART arrive-TRANS-3SG:OBJ-1PL:SUBJ
'This is a maneater's where we are going.'

Clauses like the one in (12) seem to be relative clauses. The position of an article which specifies a nominal is always, as it is in (11), before the nominal. In every case in the translations of clauses like (12) relativization is indicated. The semantic relationship between the nominal and the verb is one of modification or limitation. Also, this is the first mention of this referent in the text, and it seems to be introduced with the most typical strategy, a stative clause. Lastly, other article-verb constructions appear in clauses as arguments of verbs. Though we normally expect a nominalizer to appear in these cases, the presence of the article appears to be sufficient. All of these facts suggest that these constructions are relatives, rather than preposing constructions.

2.4 *Possible grammatical/semantic roles in 'true' preposing*

There seems to be no restriction on the grammatical or semantic role of the referent which appears to the left of the verb. In the examples above an intransitive subject/patient is preposed in (5), in (6) an oblique. The examples below further illustrate the range; an agentive subject and a direct object appear in (13) and (14), respectively.

(13) *axa? t i? i-səxʷk'ʷùlem n'ín'wi? ch'ʷúl-ɬəm-s*
DEICTIC OBL ART 1SG:POSS-man FUT care for-DITR-3SG:SUBJ
'My hired hand will care for them (for you).'

(14) *axà? i? sk'ʷƛ̕'təm-s qɬqíɬ-nt-Ø-s*
DEICTIC ART brother-3SG:POSS wake up-TRANS-3SG:OBJ-3SG:SUBJ[5]
'He woke up his brothers.'

While we will see in the next section that the topicality of the various grammatical and semantic roles varies quite greatly, no particular role is clearly prohibited from appearing in preverbal position.

3. The function of preverbal nominals

In this section I analyze the function of preposing constructions in the narrative. The first subsection compares the topicality measures of non-nominal references (affixes, clitics and zero anaphors) and postverbal nominals with those of preverbal nominals. My conclusion is that preposing constructions cannot be considered topicalizations. Next, I examine the constructions in view of Mattina's (1973) contrastive analysis, and discuss examples which I find difficult to analyze as contrastive. From this analysis I propose a constraint on the preverbal position involving the referent's cataphoric topicality.

Before moving to these subjects, the infrequency of such preposing constructions should be noted. The narrative is approximately 2800 clauses long; only 45 clauses are claimed to be instances of 'true' preposing.

3.1 *Topicality of postverbal nominals and anaphoric mentions*

In Table 1 the means for referential distance and persistence for postverbal nominals of various grammatical types and referents represented by clitics, affixes, and zero anaphors are presented. In all of the tables which follow, referential distance — the number of clauses since the last mention of the referent — is referred to as RD. Likewise, persistence — the number of clauses in which the referent appeared out of the following ten clauses — is referred to as P. The 'n=' column notes the total number of occurrences of each type. The referents coded in the text as affixes, clitics or zero anaphors form the bulk of the sample; only 43 clauses did not contain a referent coded in this way.

Table 1. Topicality of postverbal arguments (means from a sample of 160 clauses.)

	RD	*P*	*n=*
Non-nominal subjects	1.6	4.7	117
Non-nominal objects	1	5	10
Subject nominals	10	3	28
Object nominals	13	2	25
Oblique nominals	15.6	0.5	12
Oblique agents	5.5	3.6	6

Non-nominal subjects are highly topical referents both in anaphoric topicality and cataphoric, having a very low referential distance (RD = 1.6) and high persistence (P = 4.7), i.e. on average these referents appeared in the previous clause or the one before that and continued to appear in 5 of the next 10 clauses. Non-nominal objects, likewise, are topical in this dual way (RD = 1) and (P = 5)[6]. The high topicality of these referents can be explained by the fact that in half of these instances the object affix codes a speech act participant, and in two others the arguments coded as direct objects are recipients of ditransitive verbs. Turning to the more relevant nominal types, postverbal subject nominals are not as topical in the preceding discourse (RD = 10), but do tend to persist in the following discourse (P = 3). The object nominals' anaphoric topicality is slightly less than subject nominals' in that the average RD is higher (RD = 13), and the average P is somewhat lower (P = 2), indicating lower cataphoric topicality. Oblique nominals[7] are the least topical in both senses (RD = 15.6, P = 0.5). Since the focus of this paper is on whether or not certain referents persist in the following discourse, the important differences are between the persistence averages for the three types of nominals discussed so far. Both subjects and objects (to a lesser degree) appear to introduce referents which are topical in the cataphoric sense, which persist in the following discourse. Oblique nominals do not.

The category called 'oblique agents' is an interesting one. These agents are marked with the same morpheme, /t/, as oblique objects, and typically occur with detransitivizing verbal morphology. However, they do occur with regular transitive verb morphology (e.g. (21) and (22)) in rare cases. Thus I have used the term 'oblique', but do not mean to imply that these are functionally equivalent to other oblique nominals.[8] Both the general trend of detransitivization and the low frequency of the non-detransitivized cases indicate that a separate category is required for this grammatical role. The referents which are coded by this category are somewhat topical in both senses (RD = 5.5, P = 3.6).

Taken as a whole, Table 1 suggests a pattern that has been reported in studies which employ this methodology, and others similar to it (see Givón 1983; Du Bois 1987). Major and minor participants and important props are introduced into the text as nominals in the grammatical role of subject or object. Once introduced they can appear as anaphors. Reintroduction or ambiguity causes their reappearance as nominals. Incidental props and locations appear in the oblique slot and fail to continue to be mentioned in the discourse.

Table 2. Topicality of preverbal nominals.

	RD	*P*	*n=*
subject nominals	15	2.8	22
object nominals	16	2.3	7
oblique nominals	20	0	11
oblique agents	14	0.6	5

3.2 *Topicality of preverbal nominals*

In Table 2 the average referential distance and persistence for preverbal nominals is presented. In the cases of subject, object, and oblique nominals in preverbal position some slight differences in the means can be noted between the preverbal occurrences and their postverbal counterparts. Quite a difference seems to exist, however, between preverbal and postverbal oblique agents.

Looking first at the non-agentive oblique nominals in Table 2, we see that the conclusions drawn above about both the anaphoric and cataphoric topicality of referents which surface as obliques holds for preverbal instances as well as postverbal. Most are new mentions, and in neither preverbal or postverbal position do such referents persist in the following discourse. None of the preverbal obliques appeared in the following ten clauses and only one postverbal oblique (in that particular sample) persisted for 2 clauses.

The difference between preverbal and postverbal oblique agents seems quite striking, and suggests that while postverbal oblique agents are somewhat topical, preverbal are not. However, since the number of these constructions appearing in the sample and the text is small, and arithmetic means based on small samples can be deceiving, examining the frequency distributions can provide a more reliable characterization.

In Table 3 preverbal and postverbal oblique agents are compared in this fashion. In the RD columns the distribution range is listed, beginning with the highest referential distance, (20). The numbers in the column indicate the range from the previous number to the number listed (e.g. 10 = 19 through 10, 5 = 9 through 5, etc.). In the 'n=' column the number of occurrences in each range is listed. The same is true of the persistence (P) measures. The ranges for

Table 3. Frequency distributions for oblique agents

Preverbal				Postverbal			
RD	n=	P	n=	RD	n=	P	n=
20	3	0	4	20	1	0	3
10	0	1	0	10	0	1	1
5	2	3	1	5	2	3	0
3	0	5	0	3	1	5	0
1	0	10	0	1	2	10	2

RD and P are in opposite orders, but this has been done so that in both columns the measures indicating low topicality (20 for RD and 0 for P) appear at the top of the column and those indicating high topicality at the bottom.

In the case of preverbal oblique agents the means of both RD and P do not prove deceptive. The high RD and low P means of these preverbal nominals is fairly representative of the facts. Three instances of preverbal obliques have the maximum RD count, 20; two instances are bit more topical in the previous discourse with RD measures of between 9 and 5. But again the persistence measure is the crucial factor. Four of the five preverbal oblique agents fail to appear in the any of the following 10 clauses; the fact that only one persists in the subsequent discourse at all argues against a topicalization analysis of preposing in these cases.

The means for postverbal oblique agents suggest that these referents are somewhat topical, having a low RD (5.5) and a high P (3.6). Examining the frequency distribution bears this conclusion out for the most part. Instances of topical referents do occur; for example, two cases occur in which referents appeared in the previous clause (RD =1), and two in which referents persisted for all 10 of the following clauses (P =10). Yet, three other cases show up in which the referents did not appear in any of the 10 subsequent clauses, and in one case, in only one of the following 10.

Part of the reason that referents in the postverbal oblique agent category can be more topical than other oblique nominals in the preceding and subsequent discourse is because of their animacy and grammatical role. However, these facts do not explain their appearance in an oblique case. I have not fully investigated voice distinctions in Colville, but a cursory look at them suggests that they are similar to other Salish languages. In light of that similarity, I offer a few speculations. In narrative discourse situations often arise in which two participants are involved in transitive events; each of the participants may be at one point agent, at the next patient. Considering the ambiguity which can arise if only affixes are generally used to code the referents, the language must have a method to clarify the participants' roles. This clarification seems to be accomplished by voice. Whether the best structural analysis of these cases is one that argues for passive voice or inverse constructions is not the crucial point. What is central is the function of these constructions. Two nominals can appear in these constructions with one marked clearly as agent, disambiguating the situation. Throughout the Salish language family, it is common for various detransitivizing verbal morphology and oblique case marking to appear in clauses with two nominals. Again, whether passive or inverse is the best analysis of these constructions is not as important to this paper as the need to distinguish these oblique case agents from other more typical obliques. Furthermore, these agents seem better compared to postverbal subjects than other obliques when discussing their anaphoric and cataphoric topicality.

The topicality, in both senses, of preverbal oblique agents, however, is quite low. The generalization that seems to hold for this small sample is that the preverbal position, in conjunction with voice (in some instances) and case marking requirements, is the position in which new referents can be introduced as agents without giving them much prominence. An example like (13) presents a contrastive situation (the hired hand rather than others will care for their horses). The oblique agent slot in this case is an economical construction, introducing and contrasting a new referent at the same time. As we will see below, contrast is not always involved, but it seems that once again the preverbal position can be equated with low cataphoric topicality even when the role is one that is usually a topical slot, i.e. agent/subject.

Table 4. Frequency distributions for pre- and postverbal objects

Preverbal				Postverbal			
RD	n=	P	n=	RD	n=	P	n=
20	4	0	3	20	13	0	11
10	1	1	2	10	5	1	2
5	1	3	1	5	4	3	4
3	0	5	1	3	0	5	6
1	1	10	0	1	3	10	2

In Table 4 the frequency distribution for pre- and postverbal objects is presented. For preverbal objects the tendency to have low anaphoric topicality is evident in the distribution and not unexpected since the referents are coded as nominals. Four of the seven preverbal objects in the sample have not been mentioned in the previous twenty clauses. The lack of cataphoric topicality is fairly evident; only 28.5% of the time did a preverbal object persist for 3 or more clauses. In the case of postverbal object nominals a different situation appears. Again, since these arguments are nominals, high RD counts are not surprising. More importantly, the persistence measures show that these postverbal objects are mentioned more frequently in the following discourse; 46.1% persist for 3 or more clauses. Certainly, a larger sample would prove more reliable, but the facts so far suggest at least that the preverbal position does not topicalize object nominals.

Looking finally at the subject measures in Table 5, we can see a similar pattern in their distribution. Preverbal subjects generally are relatively new to the discourse, and persist in the following discourse for 3 or more clauses only 40.9% of the time. While this is a better percentage than that of objects, it does not match the 64.2% figure for postverbal subject nominals.

My analysis then makes two claims about the data. First, in Colville, the grammatical role in which a referent is introduced can be an indication of its cataphoric topicality. A hierarchy of grammatical roles according to the importance in the subsequent discourse a referent may have can be posited as follows: Subject > Object > Oblique nominal. This is not controversial. The placement of oblique agents in this hierarchy, I believe, is inappropriate as these clauses are marked in regard to voice and frequency. While this hierarchy holds for both preverbal and postverbal nominals, the difference between the two positions lies in the fact that the preverbal nominals are consistently

Table 5. Frequency distribution of pre- and postverbal subjects.

Preverbal				Postverbal			
RD	n=	P	n=	RD	n=	P	n=
20	11	0	10	20	12	0	7
10	3	1	3	10	2	1	3
5	2	3	4	5	3	3	9
3	3	5	3	3	10	5	2
1	3	10	2	1	1	10	7

lower in persistence measures. While the sample is indeed small, this consistency suggests that preposing constructions cannot be considered as topicalizations, despite the fact that some topical referents do appear preverbally.

3.3 *Contrast and the preverbal position*

In many cases the analysis Mattina argues for, i.e. preverbal is contrastive, is in fact correct. However, not all instances of preposing can be clearly accounted for under such an analysis; some do not seem to be the focus of contrast.

In (15) I roughly formulate the conditions for preposing and possibilities associated with that clausal position.

(15)

Effect	*Cataphoric topicality*	*Preposing possible*
Contrast	Low	Yes
Contrast	High	Yes
Non-contrast	Low	Yes
Non-contrast	High	No

The crucial case in (15) is the last. No non-contrastive nominals appeared preverbally if that nominal encoded a topical referent. In the following examples I illustrate each of the possible cases and discuss the constraint present in the last.

In (16) and (17) preverbal nominals of low cataphoric topicality, but ones which provide contrastive information, are cited.

(16)

nixʷ	*t*	*k'ʷə-k'ʷ y-inaʔ*	*iʔ*	*t*	*sqlaw'*	*xʷic-əxt-xʷ*
also	OBL	a little	ART	OBL	money	give-DITR-2SG:SUBJ

'Also a little money you give to him.'

(17)

way'	*kɬ-c'ik'ʷəsxən.*	*kəl*	*sksək'ʷtikst*	*kɬ-ənsp'ustin*
well	have-light	LOC	other hand	have-sword

'Well she has a light. In the other hand she has a sword.'

In (16) the oblique case-marked object stands in contrast to the previous action in the narrative[9]. The chief had prepared his three oldest sons for a journey, supplying them with horses, clothes, and money (the narrator points out that it is quite a sum). His youngest son is dismayed at being left at home. In order to assuage the youngest's feelings, his mother tells her husband, the chief, to give him an old horse, and in contrast to the large sums given to the older sons, a little money. In (17) the sons have been taken in, both deceived and sheltered by a monster, a man-eater. As they sleep she mounts the stairs to slay them. We assume from the context in the first clause the light is held in her hand; the contrastive information follows in the preverbal position of the second clause.

Examples (18) and (19) illustrate topical arguments in contrastive contexts.

(18) *axaʔ mnìmɬ-əmp p q'wíɬq'ʷel-t*
DEICTIC folks-2PL:POSS 2PL:SUBJ smart-STAT
'You folks are smart.'

(19) *axaʔ iʔ k'wƛ'et iʔ sqilxʷ*
DEICTIC ART rest of ART people
lut kʷu t'ə ckəlq'ʷ-ist-nt-səlx
NEG 1SG:OBJ EMP touch-arm-TRANS-3PL:SUBJ
'The rest of the people can't even touch my arm' *(lit.* 'arm-touch me').

uɬ axaʔ smyɬ-tətwit kʷən-nu-nt-Ø-s
and DEICTIC amazing-boy grab-success-TRANS-3SG:OBJ-3SG:SUBJ
'And this amazing boy managed to grab it.'

(18) appears in a situation where the youngest son, after discussing his own inadequacies, explains to his older brothers how they will escape from a monster. The brothers are quite topical anaphorically and in their persistence in the following text. In (19) the youngest son is being discussed by the Golden Woman, whom he has captured. In the second clause of the passage he is contrasted with 'the rest of the people' who cannot even touch her arm. The boy is topical both anaphorically and in the following discourse.

On the other hand, the first clause in (19) offers an example of a non-contrastive, non-topical preverbal nominal. This is its first and only mention in the text (it refers to other adventurers who have tried and failed to capture the Golden Woman). The same seems to be true of (20).

(20) *way' iʔ t ƛ'ut miy-nt-Ø-s*
well ART INSTR rocks put on-TRANS-3SG:OBJ-3SG:SUBJ
sənt'əpt'paqsəs
corners
'Well he put on the corners the rocks.'

As in the first clause in (19), this is the single mention of this referent (the rocks) in the text. Considering Chafe's (1976) criteria for contrast and Prince's (1982) discussion, it is not clear that either of these two clauses code contrastive information. First, no shared background knowledge, in the textual sense, seems to be present. In the discourse previous to (19) only the hero's age and appearance are discussed. The actual capture occurs earlier in the text, but is somewhat distant at this point, leading me to believe that no semantic frame still exists to provide that background knowledge. The same lack of shared background knowledge is true of (20). The context does not clearly require the hero's action, i.e. securing the corners of a handkerchief, and the previous narration focuses on the abilities of the Golden Woman. Second, since neither evokes other possible candidates, it is difficult to say that an assertion of the *correct* candidate has occurred.

The same situation can be seen in a word order variation involving two otherwise virtually identical clauses. Early in the narrative the youngest son's magical horse explains to him what will happen when he reaches a monster's dwelling. (21) occurs in this episode. The monster's dogs are mentioned only once in the episode.

(21) *uɫ n'in'w'iʔ cəm' ixiʔ wah-ənt-s-is*
and FUT might DEICTIC bark-TRANS-2SG:OBJ-3SG:SUBJ
iʔ t k-kəwapaʔ
ART OBL RED-dog
'And then the dogs will bark at you.'

Much later in the text the adventures of the youngest son and his brothers are recounted in a storytelling session and the incident with the dogs is related in (22).

(22) *n'in'w'iʔ cəm' iʔ t k-kəwapaʔ wah-ənt-s-is*
FUT might ART OBL RED-dog bark-TRANS-2SG:OBJ-3SG:SUBJ
'And then the dogs will bark at you.'

In this situation, as in the first, the dogs are mentioned only once. In neither case are the dogs or the dogs' actions constrasted with other animals or their actions. In each the dogs are the first thing encountered by the boy when he arrives. Also, in neither case does the interpretation seem to be 'the dogs and nothing else'. This interpretation seems especially unlikely given the meaning of the verb /wah/, 'dog bark'. The possibility, but not the necessity, to place this non-topical referent before the verb exists without any clear contrastive interpretation.

The examples above illustrate the first three parts of the formulation in (15); the last remains. If topicality constrains the preverbal position as stated in (15), then no topical referents should appear in the preverbal position without being subject to a contrastive interpretation. This is the case. All the major participants and props are introduced postverbally with one exception, the hero, the youngest son. While he is mentioned as one of the chief's four sons previous to the clause in (23), this is the first specific mention of him as an individual. The situation is clearly contrastive. In the previous episode (this shift in major participants seems to mark an episode boundary) his brothers are preparing for their journey. The youngest son, on the other hand, can do none of these things.

(23) *way' axaʔ iʔ stətʔiwtaʔx putiʔ* x^{w}*up-t*
well DEICTIC ART youngest one still do nothing-STAT
'And the youngest one still is unable to do anything.'

Throughout the text, while referents of varying degrees of importance to the following discourse may be freely introduced postverbally, the constraint on the preverbal position formulated in (15) holds.

4. Conclusion

In this study I hope to have accomplished two things. First, a conservative diagnostic has been proposed to segment this particular text into clauses. This diagnostic is crucial to the examination of texts in Colville, and, I believe, raises some issues relevant to texts in other Salish languages. The central claim of this paper is that the preposing constructions in Colville never function as topicalization devices, but also that such constructions are not always signals of contrast. The preverbal position is available to referents in non-contrastive situations only if the referent is low in cataphoric topicality, relatively unimportant in the subsequent discourse.

Notes

1. For a complete discussion of the methodology, and studies employing the methodology, see Givón (1983).
2. In the examples the abbreviation DITR is used for a ditransitive suffix (for standard abbreviations, see list on p. ix). In the earlier sections, stress is discussed. Stress markings appear directly above the vowel with /´/ indicating primary stress and /`/ indicating

secondary stress. In all cases these markings should not be confused with the diacritcs indicating ejectives which follow consonants, e.g. /p'/. The free glosses are in the main taken from the interlinear translation. In a few cases a literal translation appears instead of the interlinear one offered in Mattina (1985). These exceptions are marked by *lit.*, i.e. 'literal'.

3. Some deictics on occasion may take verbal inflection; however, these cases are few . More importantly, these deictics freely co-occur with verbals in single clauses. Considering this co-occurrence, it would be, I believe, incorrect to assume that the deictic in (3) functions as a verbal.

4. For expository purposes I have called this article a signal of definite reference. Though Mattina uses this term as well, he notes that the definite/indefinite distinction may not operate in Colville. I have not investigated the distribution, but believe that it does not bear on this discussion as presented. No preverbal nominals were ignored due to the presence or absence of the article.

5. In unambigious situations the plural marker /-əlx/ is not obligatory.

6. In previous examples we have seen that 3rd person intransitive subjects and direct objects have been indexed on the verb by a zero morpheme. The category of non-nominal objects does not exclude instances where the direct object was coded solely by the zero anaphor, but in the sample the occurrence of 3rd person direct objects without a nominal was quite rare.

7. I use the term 'oblique' as a cover term for several types of grammatical roles. All nominals in this category are, however, arguments of the verbs in the clauses. Locatives with verbs of motion and three place predicators and instrumentals acting as agents are included in this category. Also, however, initial direct objects which are demoted via an antipassive construction are included. None of these demoted objects appeared preverbally. Furthermore, Colville has two ditransitive suffixes which indicate whether the direct or indirect object will appear as an oblique.

8. The differences between these two categories are discussed more fully below. However, several points should be briefly mentioned. In general, in Salish, the oblique marking of agents co-occurs with detransitive verb morphology. To my knowledge, Colville, or at least this narrator, is an exception to that general rule. Various analyses have been suggested for these constructions, in particular, passive and inverse. See Darnell (1991) for an analysis of Squamish, a relative of Colville, in terms of passive voice. Jacobs (1991) argues that an inverse analysis better characterizes these constructions in Squamish. It should be noted that comparing Colville to Squamish is not an unreasonable position as the verbal morphology is quite similar in these two langauges.

9. The oblique case-marking of the direct object in this example is not due to any voice distinction. The ditransitive nature of the clause requires that the direct object, even though the recipient/benefactee does not appear, be in the oblique case.

References

Chafe, Wallace. 1976. "Givenness, contrastiveness, definiteness, subjects, topics, and point of view." *Subject and Topic* ed. by Charles Li, 25-55. New York: Academic Press.

Darnell, Michael. 1991. "Squamish /-m/ constructions." *Proceedings of the 16th Annual Meeting of the Berkeley Linguistic Society, Special Session.* Berkeley: Berkeley Linguistic Society.

Du Bois, John. 1987. "The discourse basis of ergativity." *Language*. 63.4:804-855

Givón, T. 1983. *Topic Continuity in Discourse*. Amsterdam: John Benjamins.

Givón, T. 1991. *Syntax: A Functional-Typological Introduction*, Vol. 2. Amsterdam/ Philadelphia: John Benjamins.

Jacobs, Peter. 1991. "The Inverse in Squamish." Unpublished ms.

Mattina, Anthony. 1973. "Colville Grammatical Structure." University of Hawaii Ph.D. dissertation.

Mattina, Anthony. 1985. *The Golden Woman: The Colville narrative of Peter J. Seymour.* Tucson: The University of Arizona Press.

Mattina, Anthony. 1987. *Colville-Okanagan Dictionary*. Missoula: The University of Montana. [*University of Montana Occasional Papers in Linguistics*, 5].

Prince, Ellen F. 1982. "On the discourse functions of topicalization and left-dislocation." Paper presented at the NSF/CNRS Workshop on Discourse Comprehension, Cadarache (France).

Frequency and pragmatically unmarked word order *

Matthew S. Dryer
SUNY at Buffalo

1. Introduction

Discussions of word order in languages with flexible word order in which different word orders are grammatical often describe one of the orders as the (pragmatically) *unmarked* or neutral word order, while other grammatical orders are all described as being *marked* in some way. In most languages in which one order has been so characterized, the order described as unmarked is also the order which occurs most frequently in spoken or written texts. It is widely assumed, in fact, that this is a necessary characteristic of unmarked word order, that it is part of what it means to be unmarked that the unmarked word order be most frequent. For example, Greenberg (1966:67) claims explicitly that the unmarked order in a language is "necessarily the most frequent". There are instances, however, in which this assumption has been questioned, in which descriptions of word order in particular languages have claimed that a particular order is unmarked or neutral, even though that order is not significantly more frequent than other orders, and may in fact be less frequent than at least some other orders. I will discuss four instances from the literature in which claims of this sort have been made. The purpose of this paper is to explore the question of whether such claims make sense, whether there is a useful notion of pragmatically unmarked word order that is not necessarily the most frequent order. I will propose that a particular word order can be described as pragmatically unmarked if it is the *default* word order, if there are concise ways to characterize the situations in which other word orders are used, with the pragmatically unmarked word order being most easily characterized as the order that is used elsewhere, once the situations in which the pragmatically marked orders are used have been characterized.

I discuss a number of at least hypothetical situations where it would make sense to say that one order can reasonably be described as pragmatically unmarked, even though not more frequent than other orders. I will also show that there are possible situations where two orders might differ in relative frequency, but not differ in pragmatic markedness. But I will argue that in none of the four actual cases where a claim has been made that the pragmatically unmarked word order is not significantly more frequent than other orders is it clear that the order in question is pragmatically unmarked in the way proposed here. And while it is possible for there to be mismatches between frequency and markedness, it is often not clear when people describe a word order as pragmatically unmarked that their characterization is based on anything more than frequency. Finally, I will propose that while frequency is epiphenomenal relative to the grammars of individual languages, it plays a much larger role than pragmatic markedness in explaining why languages are the way they are.

Three of the four actual examples I discuss here involve the word order of clauses containing a lexical subject and a lexical object, but no significance should be associated with this. I assume that questions of which order is unmarked can be asked of any elements in language whose order is determined by discourse factors. In fact, a number of the cases I discuss here involve alternations other than word order alternations. I assume that these questions regarding the relationship of pragmatic markedness to frequency apply to any alternation that is governed by discourse factors. As various people have noted (cf. Du Bois 1987), clauses containing both a lexical subject and a lexical object tend to be relatively infrequent in texts, and I assume that one could also argue that such clauses are pragmatically marked, relative at least to clauses containing a single lexical argument (or no lexical argument). While I believe that typological discussion often assigns such clauses a special significance they do not deserve, it still makes sense to ask what order, if any, among such clauses is pragmatically unmarked in a language, just as it makes sense to ask of a language what the unmarked order is in noun phrases containing a demonstrative, a numeral, an adjective, and a noun, even though such noun phrases will be very infrequent in any language.

2. Case 1: Tojolabal

In order to ground the discussion, I will start off by presenting one of the four cases I will discuss in which a particular order is claimed to be pragmatically unmarked, though not most frequent. This case is a description of clause order in Tojolabal, a Mayan language of Guatemala, by Brody (1984). Brody argues that while VOS order in Tojolabal is the least marked word order, it is infrequent, particularly by comparison with SVO order, which she claims is a marked word order. But I do not find her arguments for this conclusion convincing. Her only argument that SVO order is pragmatically marked is that it involves what she calls "topicalization" of the subject. But she does not explain what discourse property is associated with what she calls "topicalization", except to say that it gives "prominence" to the subject. Since the terms "topic" and "prominence" are used by different linguists in a wide variety of ways, some of them even contradictory, this tells us very little about exactly what discourse factors are associated with SVO order in Tojolabal. For example, on one common use of the term "topic", subjects are typically topics. I assume that most linguists would not want to describe utterances in which the subject is topic in that sense as pragmatically marked.

The following quotation from Brody (1984) provides further insight into the nature of her claim that VOS is unmarked, even though less frequent than SVO:

> The VOS sentence communicates very little; in fact, it communicates nothing beyond propositional content. It reveals nothing about the speaker's prejudices or presuppositions, nothing about the direction the discourse is moving toward or coming from, and nothing about the relative importance of the participants. In every significant sense, the VOS sentence in Tojolabal is an unimportant sentence type in discourse, albeit the basic sentence by most of the criteria examined above. It is simply not a very useful kind of sentence for furthering the flow of information. It is thus not surprising that an uninformative sentence type should occur with low frequency in discourse. The SVO sentence, on the other hand, is more frequent in discourse because it is less neutral, both semantically and from a discourse perspective, and it is also more informative, giving prominence to the subject NP. (Brody 1984:726)

I have great difficulty making sense of Brody's claims. Cleft sentences in English are less neutral than basic sentences and are more informative in the sense that they give prominence to the clefted element. The logic of Brody's argument would seem to imply that cleft sentences in English should therefore be more common than non-cleft sentences. Similarly, transitive clauses in which both arguments are lexical are presumably in some sense "more informative" than clauses in which one of the arguments is pronominal. But then by Brody's logic, one might argue that transitive clauses in which both arguments are lexical ought to be the most frequent transitive clause type. But as she herself notes, such clauses are infrequent in Tojolabal, much as they are in other languages. In fact, following suggestions by Chafe (1987), we might say that such clauses are infrequent precisely because they are *too* informative, and the information expressed by such clauses is often broken down into two separate clauses. Word orders that are described as pragmatically marked often involve some sort of unexpectedness, some information that involves a change in the direction of the flow of information, either because some information is counter to expectations or because a new participant is introduced to the discourse. Word orders that are described as pragmatically unmarked, on the other hand, are often used in clauses which continue the existing flow. Brody's claim that pragmatically unmarked word order should be expected to be infrequent because it "reveals nothing ... about the direction the discourse is moving toward or coming from" ignores the fact that the default type of clause need not reveal anything of that sort, precisely because the discourse is proceeding in an expected fashion. But regardless of these problems, it is difficult to evaluate Brody's claim that SVO sentences in Tojolabal are more informative than VOS sentences in the absence of any indication as to the nature of the prominence SVO order gives to subjects.

One is tempted to respond to Brody's claim with the following counterargument. If we accept her claim that SVO order is most frequent in Tojolabal, then this fact alone tells us something about the discourse factors associated with SVO order. Namely, whatever discourse properties are associated with what she calls topics, these properties are apparently ones that subjects more often have, at least in clauses containing both a lexical subject and a lexical object. That in itself eliminates various possible interpretations of what she means by "topic", such as that associated with so-called topicalization in English, since that type of situation occurs infrequently. But it also implies that being topic is something that is normal for subjects in Tojolabal, and thus we might say that the unmarked situation in Tojolabal is for subjects to be topics. And if that is the case, we might say that SVO order is the unmarked word order, not a marked one. Conversely, although we do not know what properties are associated with subjects in VOS sentences in Tojolabal, whatever properties they are are ones that subjects more commonly lack, so we might say that VOS is a marked word order in the language.

While I think that there is some merit to this argument, and that it is at least as strong as Brody's argument for the opposite conclusion, it does beg the question being addressed in this paper, since it assumes that the most frequent order is necessarily pragmatically unmarked. The question I wish to address here is whether there exists a useful notion of pragmatically unmarked word order that is distinct from that of most frequent order. In order to do that, I turn briefly to the ways in which the terms "marked" and "unmarked" are employed in other domains, to determine whether those notions can be extended naturally into the area of discourse.

3. Markedness as a general notion

The terms "marked" and "unmarked" have been used by linguists in other domains in a wide variety of ways. It is possible to distinguish a broad and a narrow sense in which the terms are used. On its broad use (cf. Greenberg 1966; Croft 1990), markedness is an umbrella term that refers to a cluster of notions that correlate with each other or bear family resemblances to each other. On its narrow use (cf. Andersen 1988), the term is restricted to what are viewed as core instances of markedness and the other notions are simply viewed as related notions which may correlate with markedness, but which are not themselves instances of markedness. I assume that regardless of how one chooses to use the term, the broad and narrow notions must be kept distinct.

A further distinction can be made between crosslinguistic markedness and language-particular markedness. Most of the references to markedness in the typological literature involve a crosslinguistic notion of markedness that is related to naturalness. When it is claimed that [p] is typologically unmarked relative to [b], what is meant is that language-particular manifestations of the unmarked status of [p] relative to [b], such as its being the sound found when a phonemic contrast is neutralized, are to be explained in terms of the articulatory or perceptual properties of [p] compared to those of [b], the assumption being that the neutralization in the direction of [p] is a natural and explainable phenomenon. And in many cases, such as this one, the distinction between cross-linguistic markedness and language-particular markedness may not be obvious. However, when Greenberg (1966:39) notes that Oneida is exceptional in treating feminine gender as unmarked relative to masculine gender, the distinction is somewhat clearer, since the criteria that identify feminine gender as unmarked in Oneida are clearly distinct from those that identify masculine gender as the unmarked gender crosslinguistically. The crucial evidence that masculine gender is the unmarked gender crosslinguistically derives from the fact that in most languages exhibiting markedness differences between masculine and feminine, the language-specific criteria point to the masculine being unmarked. Thus language-specific markedness involves a set of traditional criteria or tests, while crosslinguistic markedness simply involves the frequency over languages in which the criteria for language-specific markedness point to the same value as the unmarked value. Hence we can say, without contradiction, that feminine gender is unmarked in Oneida despite being universally marked, since the criteria for it being universally marked only require that it be marked in a significant majority of cases. The distinction is particularly clear in the domain of unmarked word order, where the notion is usually used in a language-particular sense. While one might say that SV order is crosslinguistically unmarked, because SV order is more common, such usage is clearly irrelevant to the question whether SV or VS order in a particular language is unmarked. Similarly, one can say that SO order is crosslinguistically unmarked, but this is clearly irrelevant to whether SO or OS (if either) is pragmatically unmarked in a given language. For these reasons, I will restrict attention here to markedness in a language-particular sense.

Among the ways the term "markedness" is used in a language-particular sense in other domains, we can distinguish at least four types of markedness: formal markedness, distributional markedness, semantic markedness, and frequency (cf. Lyons 1977; Croft 1990). *Formal* markedness, sometimes referred to as morphological, morphosyntactic, or structural markedness, refers to the presence vs. absence of morphemes, or, sometimes, to the relative phonological size of morphemes. Thus *lioness* is formally marked relative to *lion*, because *lioness* contains an additional morpheme, and a passive sentence like *Mary was kissed by John* is formally marked relative to its corresponding active sentence *John kissed Mary*, since it contains two more morphemes than the active form. Word order differences in language generally do not involve differences in formal markedness, but occasionally they do. For example, in Yagua, an Amazonian language discussed by Doris Payne (1990 *inter alia*), both VS and SV order occur, as illustrated in (1).

(1) a. *sa-jṷṷ́y Anita.*
3SG-fall Anita
'Anita falls.'

b. *Anita jṷṷ́y.*
Anita fall
'Anita falls.'

VS order is formally marked in Yagua, however, since a subject clitic occurs on the verb when that order is used, as in (1a), but is absent when SV order is used, as in (1b). As discussed below, however, Payne (1990) argues that the SV order of (1b), while formally unmarked, is both less frequent and pragmatically marked. Quite apart from questions of pragmatic markedness, this case is an interesting one, since it illustrates the more unusual situation in which the formally marked member of a pair is the most frequent.

Distinct from formal markedness is the notion of *distributional* markedness: one form is said to be distributionally marked if it occurs in a proper subset of the morphosyntactic contexts in which the other occurs. This notion is relevant in the area of word order since there exist instances in which one word order has a more restricted distribution than another. In Turkish, for example, both OV and VO order are found in main clauses, while only OV order is found in relative clauses (Utschig 1985: 161); since VO has a more restricted syntactic distribution, it is distributionally marked. As with formal markedness, we may expect a distributionally marked order to be pragmatically marked as well, but this is not necessary and the fact that an order is distributionally marked in a language provides no basis for saying that it is pragmatically marked.

Text frequency is treated by some linguists, like Greenberg (1966) and Croft (1990), as a criterion for markedness, but those who use the term in a narrower sense have pointed out how frequency can deviate from markedness (cf. Andersen 1988:30, Comrie 1976:116-117). In contrast, Greenberg (1966: 67) claims that of the various criteria for markedness, only frequency is relevant to the notion of unmarked versus marked word order. He suggests, in fact, that this might provide the basis of an argument that frequency is primary as a criterion for markedness. However, if one assumes a narrower notion of markedness that excludes text frequency as a criterion, and if one accepts Greenberg's conclusion that frequency is the only notion of markedness that is applicable to the notion of unmarked word order, then one could draw a very different conclusion from Greenberg, namely that what people call marked or unmarked word order has nothing to do with markedness at all, since its only resemblance to true markedness is the family resemblance via text frequency. Or, as Andersen (1988:30) puts it, if "unmarked" means no more than "most frequent", then the former term "might as well be dispensed with".

4. Pragmatic markedness as additional meaning

There is reason to question Greenberg's assumption that frequency is the only notion of markedness that applies to marked and unmarked word order. For example, one aspect of the markedness of *lioness* relative to *lion* is that it is semantically marked in that the meaning of *lioness* involves the meaning of *lion* plus an additional component of meaning. There are alternations in discourse that seem to involve a similar kind of opposition. For example, (2b) can be construed as having the meaning of (2a), plus the additional presupposition that John saw someone.

(2) a. *John saw Mary.*
b. *It was Mary that John saw.*

Furthermore, (2a) can be used with the same presupposition, with suitable stress, as in (3), just as *lion* can be used to refer to a female lion, so the set of contexts in which (2b) is appropriate is a proper subset of the set of contexts in which (2a) is appropriate.

(3) *John saw MARY.*

In general, we can say that a construction is pragmatically marked relative to another if the range of contexts in which it is appropriate is a proper subset of the set of contexts in which the unmarked construction is used.[1]

It is not clear, however, how often discourse-governed alternations can be characterized in this way, how often a difference can be adequately characterized in terms of an added component of meaning in one alternant that is absent in the other. For example, while there have been attempts to describe the difference between active and passive sentences in English in this way, these attempts are unconvincing. Battistella (1990:108) attempts to characterize the active-passive contrast in this fashion, claiming that "passivization in effect topicalizes the promoted object, making it the information focus of the sentence". But while I think there are a variety of problems with this characterization of passive sentences, the central point is that even if it were meaningful and true, we could equally well say, stripping away the derivational terminology, that "active sentences in effect treat the 'notional subject' as topic, making it the information focus of the sentence". On such a view, active sentences would involve the addition of a component of meaning absent in the passive just as much as passive sentences involve the addition of a component of meaning absent in the active, so the argument provides no basis for identifying a sense in which passive sentences in English are pragmatically marked relative to active sentences.

5. Pragmatic markedness in terms of discourse factors

Many recent approaches to discourse-governed alternations describe the alternation, not in terms of a difference in meaning, but rather in terms of the discourse factors that govern or determine the choice of one construction over another. I assume that one component of a speaker's knowledge of a language is the discourse grammar of their language, the set of rules or principles that defines the association between particular constructions and the discourse factors that determine the use of those constructions. Thus, where languages allow flexibility of word order, I assume that the discourse grammars of those languages define exactly the circumstances in which the different orders are used. And I assume that questions about pragmatic markedness are questions about the particular rules or principles of discourse grammar, that to say that one word order is pragmatically unmarked in a language is to say something about the rules or principles of discourse grammar that govern word order in the language.

Similarly, I assume that the question of whether passive is pragmatically unmarked in English is a question about the nature of the rules or principles that govern the use of passive. Now there are theories of passive that characterize the choice between active and passive as involving some property or set of properties X such that the choice is governed by a principle like that in (4). Tomlin (this volume) assumes a theory of this form.[2]

(4) a. Passive is used when the P ("patient" / "notional object" / "undergoer") has property X;

b. Active is used when the A ("agent" / "notional subject" / "actor") has property X.

But if the choice between active and passive is governed by a principle like that in (4), then the opposition would be an equipollent one, not a privative one, to use traditional markedness terminology from Trubetzkoy (1969), and there would be no sense in which passive is pragmatically marked. In other words, if we just examine the nature of the rule in (4), we find an essentially symmetric relationship between the specification of the conditions under which passive is used and the specification of the conditions under which active is used.

But there are also theories of passive that *do* treat the opposition of active and passive as a privative opposition, with the passive pragmatically marked. Both Tomlin (1983) and Thompson (1987) discuss a principle governing the use of passive that can be loosely paraphrased as in (5).[3]

(5) Passive is used in English if and only if the P is more thematic than the A.

Exactly what "thematic" means is not crucial here; what is crucial is the logical form of the rule. Note that (5) is equivalent to the conjunction of the three propositions in (6).

(6) a. Passive is used if P is more thematic than A.
b. Active is used if A is more thematic than P.
c. Active is used if A and P are equally thematic.

Implicit in (5), and made explicit in (6c), is the claim that the active is used when the A and P are equally thematic. This is an instance of neutralization, one of the classic criteria for markedness. If an analysis like that in (5)/(6) is right, then we *do* say that the active construction is pragmatically unmarked, in that when the factor determining the choice of active versus passive is neutralized, in this case the different thematicity of the A and the P, it is the active that is used. The contrast between (4) and (5)/(6) illustrates one possible way of distinguishing oppositions that do not involve pragmatic markedness and ones that do.

The two types of cases just discussed can also be used to illustrate the relationship between pragmatic markedness and frequency. The fact that passive clauses in English, especially ones with the A expressed, are far less frequent than active clauses provides no basis in itself for concluding that passive clauses are pragmatically marked and no evidence against an analysis that takes the form of (4). For the greater frequency of active clauses might be entirely due to As having property X far more often than Ps do. The frequency of different constructions is a function of two things, the discourse factors underlying use of the construction, which are part of discourse grammar, and the frequency with which those factors tend to hold in typical human discourse, which is independent of discourse grammar. As Du Bois (1985:357) notes, "neither humanness nor agency are components of a notion of Topic ... . Rather, only at the level of discourse tokens ... do the properties of humanness, agency, and topicality or thematicity tend to appear as recurrent clusters." It is possible, therefore, for an opposition to be equipollent, i.e. without a markedness relation holding between them, while one member of the opposition is more common than the other due to the nature of typical human discourse.

Another example illustrating this general point is provided by Payne's (1987) discussion of word order in O'odham (Papago). Payne shows that there is a strong association between definiteness and the position of nominals relative to the verb: some well-defined exceptions aside, indefinite nominals tend to precede the verb while definite nominals tend to follow. Thus, oversimplifying somewhat, we could describe O'odham word order as governed by the principle in (7).[4]

(7) a. If the nominal is indefinite, then preverbal.
 b. If the nominal is definite, then postverbal.

The principle in (7) characterizes the opposition between preverbal and postverbal position in O'odham as an equipollent one, since the form of the rule provides no basis for treating one order or the other as unmarked. While Payne shows that postverbal position is more common in O'odham, this frequency difference does not in itself provide any reason to conclude that postverbal position is pragmatically unmarked. For the frequency difference can be explained entirely in terms of the fact that definite nominals tend to be more common than indefinites in typical human discourse. The difference in frequency does not reflect anything about the discourse grammar of O'odham.

These examples make clear that it is possible, at least in principle, for one word order to be more frequent than another without that order being pragmatically unmarked. Conversely, it is possible to describe at least hypothetical situations where one order is pragmatically unmarked in that it is the order that is used when the factors determining choice of order are neutralized, but where that order is not more frequent. Consider the hypothetical situation in (8).

(8) Suppose there is some property X such that
   a. order AB is used when A has property X more than B;
   b. order BA is used when B has property X more than A;
   c. order AB is used when A and B do not differ in property X.

By the criteria discussed above, order AB is pragmatically unmarked relative to order BA since it is used in neutralized contexts. Suppose further that because of *extralinguistic* factors, the relative frequencies of the three situations in (8) are as given in (9).

(9) a. A has property X more than B 20%
   b. B has property X more than A 60%
   c. A and B do not differ in property X 20%

Under such circumstances, the pragmatically marked order, namely BA, would occur more frequently than the pragmatically unmarked order AB, since BA order occurs with the single condition that arises 60% of the time. There are reasons to believe that such situations are atypical, but again the theoretical possibility of pragmatic markedness not matching up with frequency is illustrated. Because such situations are atypical, frequency may be a useful *diagnostic* for pragmatic markedness, even if ultimately it is not a defining characteristic.

Situations in which one word order is the order used when conditioning factors are neutralized is one type of situation in which a word order can be described as pragmatically unmarked. Such situations can be viewed as special instances of a more general type of situation in which one word order is the default order in the sense that the easiest way to characterize the contexts in which that order is used is to specify when other orders are used and then state that the order in question is used *elsewhere* . Such an approach is often implicit in descriptions of word order, in which linguists describe the contexts in which the marked word orders are used, with the understanding that the unmarked word order is used elsewhere. Similar comments apply to other discourse-governed alternations. For example, in her discussion of when passive is used in English, Thompson (1987) never directly addresses the question of when active is used, with the implicit understanding that active is used elsewhere. Similarly, Mithun (1990) describes a four-way contrast between four types of third person reference in Central Pomo. Her characterization of this contrast (p. 371) is summarized in (10).

(10) a. If completely new, outside of speakers' consciousness, then use full lexical NP.
b. If already within focal consciousness, then no marker ["zero pronoun"] is used.
c. If referent is entity from whose point of view information is presented, then use empathetic *t̂íi* pronoun.
d. Otherwise, use *muul* pronoun.

For the first three reference types in (10), it is possible to characterize succinctly the conditions under which that reference type occurs. But Mithun notes (p. 371) that the pronouns that she refers to as the *muul* pronouns serve a constellation of functions and that they can be most easily characterized by contrasting their use with that of the other referential forms. In other words, they are the elsewhere case, and their use is most easily characterized by describing where each of the other three types is used. This constitutes a reason to describe them as the pragmatically unmarked referential form.

While it is probably the case that the default within a range of alternatives in opposition to each other is usually the most frequent alternative, this is not a necessity. For example, while Mithun does not discuss the relative frequency of the different referential forms in Central Pomo, there is no reason to believe that the *muul* pronouns, the pragmatically unmarked option, are more frequent that the alternative forms, and her characterization of the use of zero suggests that zero may even be more common. Similarly, within the context of word order, one can imagine hypothetical situations in which the default order occurs less frequently than other orders. Consider the hypothetical situation in (11).

(11) BA if X and Y
AB otherwise

Given a rule like that in (11), we can describe AB as the pragmatically unmarked order, since it is the elsewhere case. Now suppose that as a result of extralinguistic factors, X is true 80% of the time and Y is true 80% of the time. Then the expected frequency of the different possibilities (assuming X and Y independent) will be as given in (12).

(12)

	Y	~Y
X	64%	16%
~ X	16%	4%

But then, given the frequencies in (12), it follows that BA, the pragmatically marked order, will occur 64% of the time, while AB, the unmarked order, will occur only 36% of the time. In this situation, the marked order would be more frequent than the unmarked order.

While these examples point to the conclusion that one can identify a notion of pragmatic markedness that is independent of frequency, it is not clear how often linguists use the term in this way. In languages in which one word order has been described as unmarked, there is often not clear evidence that the given order is the default order, since linguists rarely provide even observationally adequate accounts of what determines word order alternations. Rather, claims that a particular order is unmarked generally seem to be based on nothing more than an impression that that order is most frequent, the assumption being made that higher frequency necessarily entails some property of the principles underlying the word order alternations. But I have argued here that while that assumption may generally be true, it is not necessarily the case. Thus, claims that a particular order is unmarked may often mean no more than that that order is most frequent.

One possible shortcoming of the approach to pragmatic markedness I have proposed here is that it appears to be dependent on a particular analysis. This problem is especially acute if two orders are in an essentially equipollent relationship, as in (7) above, or any case of the form in (13).

(13) AB if X; BA if Y

If X and Y exhaust the set of possible situations, (13) is equivalent to both (14) and (15).

(14) AB if X; BA elsewhere.
(15) BA if Y; AB elsewhere.

But if we take the default order to be the one that is specified as occurring elsewhere, then the situation in (13) to (15) presents a problem. If we assume (14), then order BA is pragmatically unmarked; if we assume (15), then AB is pragmatically unmarked; and if we assume (13), then neither is pragmatically unmarked. But since all three analyses describe the same set of facts, this is clearly an undesirable result.

What this example illustrates is that we need to revise the notion of pragmatically unmarked word order to be a default word order, not in the sense that one *can* provide an analysis under which the order is the elsewhere case, but rather in the sense that one *cannot* easily specify when a construction is used without either listing a set of different conditions under which the order is used, or specifying the conditions in which *other* orders are used and then stating that the order in question is used elsewhere. Furthermore, we need to stipulate that a word order is pragmatically unmarked only if one *can* specify in relatively simple terms the situations in which all *other* orders are used, since one clear property that a pragmatically unmarked order must have is that it be in contrast to orders which are pragmatically marked.

The discussion so far has assumed that it makes sense to talk of the most frequent word order in a language. But in fact it is not entirely clear whether such a notion is always meaningful. Because the frequency of different linguistic constructions depends entirely on the frequency with which the different factors conditioning the choice arise, frequency will actually vary from discourse type to discourse type, from text to text, and from subtext to subtext. Where word order is sensitive to aspect, a word order that is more frequent in narrative may be less frequent than other discourse types. Where word order is sensitive to contrasting participants in a text, a text with two primary participants may exhibit rather different frequencies from one with a single primary participant. And clearly one order may be more frequent than another for similar reasons in one section of text but not in another section of the same text. Thus while the relative frequency of different orders may be well-defined for a given corpus of texts, it is less clear what it means as a feature of the language itself. In some languages, one order may be more frequent than another in most texts, and for such languages, it may make sense to say that that order is most frequent in the language. But for other languages, this may not be the case, and for such languages it presumably does not really make sense to say that one order is more frequent in the language.

6. Tojolabal again

Let me turn now to discussion of four cases from the literature where a word order has been claimed to be (pragmatically) unmarked though not significantly more frequent than some other order. The first case is the case of Tojolabal, discussed above. I argued above that the arguments by Brody (1984) for treating VOS as pragmatically unmarked are unconvincing since it is quite unclear what she means by "topic" and thus quite unclear what determines the choice of SVO versus VOS in the language. If there is some argument that the easiest way to describe where VOS is used is by describing where SVO order is used and specifying that VOS order is used elsewhere, then we would have an argument that VOS is pragmatically unmarked. But Brody gives no argument for that conclusion. Without clear claims as to what determines word order in Tojolabal, supported by evidence from texts, this case remains unconvincing.

7. Case 2: Ojibwa

The second case involves Ojibwa, an Algonquian language. Tomlin and Rhodes (1979) claim that the unmarked word order in Ojibwa is VOS. They note that this is "obscured" by a number of principles. Rhodes (personal communication) informs me that SVO order appears to be at least as common as VOS in texts, and my own text counts of Ojibwa texts in Nichols (1988) revealed the frequencies given in Table 1.[5] While the numbers here are too small to be taken too seriously, it is notable that only 5 out of 25 clauses with lexical subject and lexical object are VOS, the order claimed to be pragmatically unmarked.

The claim that VOS order is unmarked in Ojibwa is based on the fact that SVO order is claimed to occur in one of a set of marked situations, when the subject is indefinite, contrastive, or "the theme of a local section of text". VOS order is used when the subject lacks these properties. VOS order is used in situations more akin to ones where either the subject and the object are realized only by the pronominal affixes on the verb, ones where the subject or object is relatively predictable. The argument that VOS is unmarked runs as

Table 1. Ojibwa clauses with lexical subject and lexical object

SVO	12	(48%)
VOS	5	(20%)
VSO	4	(16%)
OVS	3	(12%)
SOV	1	(4%)
Total	25	

follows. It is assumed that the unmarked situation for an argument of the verb is one in which it is relatively predictable, and that the unmarked transitive clause is one in which both arguments are relatively predictable. In the majority of such clauses, one or both of the arguments is realized entirely by the verb morphology, and thus it does not contain two lexical arguments. Only in a minority of those situations in which both arguments are relatively predictable will both arguments be realized by full noun phrases, and in those cases VOS order will occur. But SVO order is as common as VOS because it is used in situations in which the subject is less predictable, and in those situations a full noun phrase is always used. Thus VOS is a subinstance of the more frequent situation in which both arguments are relatively predictable, but since it is used in only a subset of those situations, it is no more frequent than SVO.

There are a number of problems with this argument. First, it is important to realize that markedness is a *relative* notion. A category A can be marked relative to B, even though A is a subinstance of a larger construction type C which is *unmarked* relative to B. Similarly a category A can be unmarked relative to B, even though both A and B are instances of a construction type that is *marked* relative to some other category C. One can plausibly argue that transitive clauses in which both the subject and object are lexically realized are pragmatically marked, relative to clauses in which either the subject or object is pronominal, realized either by an independent pronoun or by a pronominal affix on the verb. In any language, therefore, any SVO or VOS clause with lexical subject and object will be marked relative to clauses with a pronominal subject or object. The question of whether VOS or SVO is the unmarked order in a language is thus a question of which order (if any) is unmarked relative to other clauses with lexical subject and lexical object, even though the set of such clauses are all marked relative to other clauses. The fact that the discourse conditions under which VOS order occurs more closely resemble those in which the subject and object are pronominal thus constitutes no argument that VOS order is unmarked relative to SVO.

An analogy from phonology may be useful. Although the notion of markedness in phonology may differ in some ways from the notion of markedness in the context of discourse, the general point made in the preceding paragraph still holds. Namely, we may say that voiced sounds are unmarked overall relative to voiceless sounds, since, except for obstruents, there is an overall preference for voiced sounds. Among obstruents, however, voiceless appears to be the unmarked value: in languages which lack voicing contrasts for obstruents, or for certain obstruents, the more common alternant is typically the voiceless one. The fact that voiced sounds are unmarked relative to voiceless sounds overall constitutes no argument against the claim that voiced obstruents may be marked relative to voiceless obstruents. Analogously, while transitive clauses with highly predictable subject and object might be unmarked overall, it might still be that among clauses with a lexical subject and a lexical object, the unmarked situation is one in which one of the arguments is less predictable.

To answer the question of whether postverbal position is pragmatically unmarked in Ojibwa, we must examine the form of the rule governing the distribution of the different orders. Tomlin and Rhodes' account basically is that given in (16).

(16) a. An indefinite NP follows the verb if
i. the verb is a quantifier verb, such as *baatiinak* 'be many' or *niizhig* 'be two';
ii. the NP is thematically irrelevant.
Otherwise, it precedes the verb.
b. A definite NP precedes the verb if
i. the NP is a quantifier;
ii. the NP is contrastive;
iii. the NP is the theme of the local section of text.
Otherwise, it follows the verb.

The notion of pragmatic markedness, interpreted as default choice, is relevant to the description of Ojibwa word order only in the sense that we can say that the pragmatically unmarked position for *indefinites* is preverbal while the pragmatically unmarked position for *definites* is postverbal. The reason that these are pragmatically unmarked is that the rule in (16) specifies these choices as the default or elsewhere choice. However, the form of the rule in (16) does not treat either preverbal position or postverbal position as pragmatically unmarked, since neither of these is defined as the default choice in general. In other words, the form of the rule in (16) treats the relation between preverbal position and postverbal position as equipollent. For this reason, there is no reason to say that postverbal position is pragmatically unmarked.

8. Case 3: Yagua

The third case I will discuss is Yagua, a language of eastern Peru. Payne (1990: 237) argues that VSO is the unmarked word order in Yagua. Her argument for this conclusion runs as follows. First, she argues that preverbal position for nominals is in general pragmatically marked in Yagua, regardless of their grammatical or semantic status. Second, she argues that although a variety of orders are common for clauses containing a lexical subject and a lexical object, VSO is the only order possible in which both follow the verb. Since postverbal position is in general the unmarked position for lexical noun phrases, VSO must be the unmarked order among clauses with a lexical subject and a lexical object.

VSO order is not, however, significantly more frequent than other orders. While it is true that in general, both subjects and objects more commonly follow the verb in Yagua, the data in Table 2 from Payne (1990) show that VSO order is only slightly more common than SVO in one set of texts and is found in only a minority of clauses containing a lexical subject and a lexical object.[6]

While VSO is more common than the other orders in this count, the difference is small and probably not statistically significant. Furthermore, VSO accounts for fewer than 40% of clauses containing a lexical subject and a lexical object. This would thus be a possible case of a language in which the pragmatically unmarked order is not significantly more frequent than other orders.

Table 2. Yagua clauses with lexical subject and lexical object

VSO	19	(39%)
SVO	15	(31%)
OVS	11	(22%)
O,SV	3	(6%)
S,OV	1	(2%)
Total	49	

Table 3. Types of pragmatically marked preverbal constituents in Yagua

Single focus contrast	38	(11%)	It was *Mary* that John saw.
Double focus contrast	43	(13%)	Her *husband* stayed at home to *babysit*, and *she* went to *work*.
Restatement	45	(13%)	They were eating apples; *apples they were eating*.
Added detail restatement	37	(11%)	They were eating apples; they were eating *green apples*.
(Wh-)question	81	(23%)	*Who* did Mary see?
Answer to (wh-)question	13	(4%)	John saw *Mary*.
Counter expectation	11	(3%)	He brought for us *soda pop* to drink.
Negation	4	(1%)	He doesn't want *manioc beer*.
Threats	6	(2%)	*The beetle* will plant you under the ground.
Unexplained	67	(19%)	

Payne's claim that preverbal position is pragmatically marked in Yagua is based on a detailed analysis of the types of clauses containing preverbal nominals. Her data for these types are given in Table 3.

I will discuss shortly Payne's arguments that these types are pragmatically marked. But it is worth noting first that her argument that VSO is unmarked assumes that the position of transitive subjects is governed by the same principles as those governing other nominals. However, transitive subjects precede the verb more often than intransitive subjects or objects, as shown by the frequency numbers given in Table 4, extrapolated from her data. Table 4 shows the relative frequency of the different orders of verb with respect to transitive subject (S_t), intransitive subject (S_i), and object.

Table 4 shows that while intransitive subjects and objects clearly follow the verb more often in Yagua, transitive subjects follow the verb only marginally more often.

There are three possible accounts of this difference between the figures for subjects of transitive clauses and those for intransitive subjects and objects. First, it might be random variation, without linguistic significance. However, the difference turns out to be statistically significant at the .001 level (chi-square). Second, it might be that, because of the nature of discourse, S_t's more often fall into one of the pragmatically marked categories that Payne classifies preverbal elements in Yagua as falling into. It is already known (cf. Du Bois

Table 4. Order of nominal and verb in Yagua by type

VS_t	47 (55%)	VS_i	210 (74%)	VO	186 (74%)
S_tV	39 (45%)	S_iV	75 (26%)	OV	65 (26%)

1987) that transitive subjects generally differ from intransitive subjects and objects in being lexical far less often. This might be tied to a tendency to fall into one of Payne's pragmatically marked categories more often. A third possibility is that the discourse principles governing the position of transitive subjects are somewhat different from those governing other nominals. According to Payne (1990:219), 19% of the preverbal constituents do not fall into one of her nine pragmatically marked categories and are unexplained; perhaps a higher than random proportion of these are transitive subjects. If this third possibility is true, then Payne's case that VSO is pragmatically unmarked would be severely weakened. And in the absence of an explanation for the higher frequency of S_tV order, Payne's argument that VSO order is pragmatically unmarked is unconvincing.

Payne's argument that the types of clauses in Table 3 are pragmatically marked resembles Givón's (1979) attempts to define pragmatic markedness in terms of presuppositions. She characterizes unmarked assertions as "those assertions which largely rehearse what the speaker assumes are already-established links, or which attempt to make new links of a fairly incremental nature." She claims that with marked speech acts "the major portion of the predication ... is presupposed and is not asserted" and "the speaker assumes something about what the hearer holds to be true (or at least will accept without challenging), but takes pains to modify in some specific way what the hearer takes for granted". Payne also notes (personal communication) that her notion of pragmatic markedness can be characterized in terms of a notion of counterexpectation.

Payne's characterization of pragmatic markedness can be evaluated both from the perspective of its success in describing the particular Yagua clause types in Table 3 that are associated with preverbal constituents, and in terms of the question of whether it provides a general characterization of pragmatic markedness. With respect to the Yagua clause types in Table 3, her characterization does seem to fit a number of the types, like single focus contrast, added detail restatement, answer to a wh-question, counterexpectation, and negated clauses. But it is less clear that it is successful in characterizing some of the other types, such as double focus contrast, where she herself admits (p. 202) that the situations are not necessarily taken as presupposed, and restatements, which she also admits fail to fit her characterization of pragmatic markedness. But these latter two types are in fact the two most frequent types with preverbal constituents, other than wh-questions, where the preverbal position of the interrogative expression may be grammaticized as it is in many other languages, like English. I therefore remain unconvinced that she has successfully justified her characterization of these clause types as pragmatically marked, even in her use of the term.

Payne's notion of pragmatic markedness differs from mine in that it is based on substantive pragmatic notions rather than the logical form of the underlying principles. In this respect, she is using the term "markedness" in a fashion that is different from its traditional use. Nevertheless, one might view the difference between Payne's use of the expression "pragmatic markedness" and mine as merely terminological. But the question remains whether her notion of pragmatic markedness succeeds in characterizing the range of phenomena in other languages that others might want to employ the term for. For example, if the choice between active and passive in English is governed by a principle like that in (6) above, according to which active is used in neutralized situations, then I assume we would want to say that passive is pragmatically marked relative to active. However it is quite unclear that passive would count as pragmatically marked under Payne's definition.[7] Similarly, right dislocations in English, like (17), are presumably pragmatically marked, but again Payne's characterization would not treat them as such.

(17) *They're playing better now, the Red Wings.*

The same comment applies to inverted sentences in English like (18).

(18) *Beside a pond lived a little turtle.*

The sentence in (18) is the initial sentence from a children's story.[8] But it does not seem to fit Payne's characterization of pragmatic markedness, since the speaker/writer presumably makes the fewest presuppositions at the start of a story. Yet the structure in (18) is most appropriate in precisely that kind of situation. It is therefore unclear that Payne's use of the term "pragmatic markedness" is consistent with how others use the term.

Payne's notion of pragmatic markedness seems, to some extent, to be language- specific. Even if there is some pragmatic characteristic shared by all of the preverbal types in Table 3, it does not seem to be the case that word order in other languages is defined by exactly the same notion. It does not, for example, seem to fit marked word order in Slavic languages. I assume, however, that languages can vary widely in what discourse factors are associated with pragmatically marked word order. While one language may use a marked word order in certain situations, another language may use the unmarked word order in corresponding situations, and use a marked word order in situations in which the first language uses its unmarked word order. For these reasons, on my use of the expression "pragmatic markedness", any attempt to define pragmatic markedness in universal pragmatic terms cannot succeed. I have argued that what defines pragmatically unmarked word order is the general characteristic of being the default order, and the actual discourse conditions associated with the marked orders may vary considerably from language to language.

While I find Payne's arguments that postverbal position in Yagua is pragmatically unmarked unconvincing, both because it is not clear that all of the preverbal types satisfy her notion of pragmatic markedness and because it is not clear that her notion of pragmatic markedness is consistent with how others use the term, the question remains whether postverbal position in Yagua might be pragmatically unmarked in the sense of this paper, in being the default order. The fact that Payne lists the situations in which constituents precede the verb means one could reinterpret her analysis and simply say that postverbal position is pragmatically unmarked simply because it is the default order, the order used when none of the conditions in Table 3 holds. The primary problem facing this is the fact that 19% of the preverbal constituents in the texts she examined are unexplained by her criteria. In addition, she also notes the existence of a smaller number of postverbal constituents that fall into one of the types in Table 3 generally associated with preverbal position. Thus while her account goes a long way towards describing the factors conditioning Yagua word order (it accounts for 81% of preverbal constituents and over 98% of postverbal ones), the existence of unexplained instances means that it is not possible to identify a default order, since that concept requires that we have an observationally adequate description which accounts for all instances of the different orders. What this illustrates is that it is very difficult to provide convincing evidence that a given construction is pragmatically unmarked.

9. Case 4: Macushi

Abbott (1991:25) describes OVS as the least pragmatically marked order in Macushi, a Carib language of Guyana and adjacent areas of Brazil and Venezuela. She cites text counts, however, showing 39 instances of transitive clauses with S(O)V order and 32 instances with (O)VS order, where the "(O)" signifies that transitive clauses with or without an expressed object are included. Because these counts include transitive clauses in which the object is not expressed, they really signify the relative frequency of transitive subject with respect to verb and the markedness question is thus whether VS order is the pragmatically unmarked order for transitive subject with respect to verb. Unlike the other cases discussed here, pronominal subjects as well as lexical subjects are included. Abbott claims that VS order is pragmatically unmarked despite the fact that SV order is slightly more frequent, at least in this count.

Abbott's argument that SV order is pragmatically marked is that clauses employing this order either "highlight a change of topic" (33 cases) or involve fronting the subject "for other special discourse-pragmatic effects", while VS order is used when "the subject refers to a topic previously introduced and not especially highlighted" (p. 25). Her argument thus resembles Payne's argument for Yagua in that she assumes that whether an order is pragmatically marked or not depends on the intrinsic pragmatic properties of the clause, rather than the kind of notion I have proposed here, based on default order, which is independent of the actual discourse properties associated with the different orders. Her notion of pragmatic order also clearly resembles Payne's since a pragmatically marked order is assumed to be associated with a higher degree of unexpectedness than pragmatically unmarked clauses.

Although Abbott's argument that VS is pragmatically unmarked assumes a different notion of pragmatic markedness from the one assumed in this paper, the particular characterization she gives conforms precisely to the notion of pragmatic markedness discussed in Section 5. Namely, she provides two situations in which SV order is used (change of topic or special effect) and characterizes when VS order is used at least partly in terms of the *absence* of the conditions in which SV order is used (previously introduced topic and *not* especially highlighted). Characterizing the situation in which VS order is used partly in terms of a notion "not especially highlighted" essentially involves characterizing this use in terms of the absence of the conditions for VS order and is in effect a way of saying "elsewhere".

The Macushi case comes closer than any of the first three cases to satisfying the conditions required for the most frequent order not to be the pragmatically unmarked word order, but we would have to know that Abbott's characterization describes the Macushi facts accurately before we could conclude that it is a convincing case. One initial shortcoming is the vagueness of the characterizations "not especially highlighted" and "other special discourse-pragmatic effects"; testing claims of this sort is necessarily rather difficult. Furthermore, unlike Payne's analysis of Yagua word order, which was based on a detailed empirical study, the basis for Abbott's conclusions is unclear. Examination of the sample Macushi text she provides with her description of the language reveals cases that do not seem to conform to her description. In particular, at least one sentence, her (22) on p. 156, involves a preverbal subject that continues a subject from the preceding text and does not appear to be fronted for any obvious special pragmatic reason. Conversely, at least one sentence, her (45) on p. 159, contains a postverbal subject introducing a new topic, again contrary to her principle. But if her characterization has exceptions, then, as with Payne's, we have no way to evaluate which order is the default order. As a result, this case too is unconvincing.

10. Some recent proposals by Givón

It is worth examining briefly recent proposals regarding markedness by Givón (1990). Givón discusses three notions of markedness, two of which are identical to two of the notions I have discussed here, namely formal markedness and frequency, and the third of which he calls cognitive complexity. His notion of cognitive complexity is similar to pragmatic markedness to the extent that both are cognitively-based markedness notions that are associated with, but distinct from, formal markedness and frequency. But otherwise, his notion is rather different from pragmatic markedness, at least as I use the term. As stated earlier, I assume that pragmatic markedness is a property of the rules or principles of discourse grammar, which determine the choice by speakers of a particular construction from a set of discourse-governed alternants. Since such rules or principles are relevant to explaining the choices that the speaker makes, pragmatic markedness is a speaker-based notion. But Givón's notion of cognitive complexity is purely a *hearer*-based notion. It involves the amount of effort or the number of cognitive operations that take place in the mind of the hearer in processing. Givón argues, for example, that definite nominals have greater cognitive complexity than pronouns, since processing them involves a more complex mental search for the intended referent than is the case with pronouns.

Givón's notion of cognitive complexity differs from my understanding of pragmatic markedness in a number of other ways. First, many different factors contribute to cognitive complexity, among them, formal markedness and frequency. In some cases, formally marked structures will require more processing, simply because they involve more morphemes. In other cases, apparent differences in cognitive complexity may reflect no more than differences in frequency: to some extent, structures that occur quite frequently are presumably recognized and processed more quickly than structures that occur infrequently, simply because they are more familiar as a function of frequency.

Secondly, while the choices that speakers make are often governed by their model of the hearer, particularly in the case of reference, it is not clear to what extent hearers attend to all the choices that speakers make. This is particularly relevant in the case of flexible word order. In a language which permits all six orders of subject, object, and verb, I assume that there are *some* principles or determining factors in the mind of the speaker that completely determine the choice of order for these elements for every utterance that contains these elements. But there is no reason to believe that the hearer attributes some significance to every one of these choices. It is a matter of logical necessity that there be *some* cognitive events in the mind of the speaker underlying every choice of word order, since words cannot be unordered and the order results only from something in the mind of the speaker. But it is not a matter of logical necessity that hearers attend to every fact in the order of words in utterances they process — just as they presumably do not attend to all of the phonetic details of the words they hear — and there is very little empirical evidence bearing on just what hearers do attend to, and thus no evidence that hearers do attend to all details of word order. Hence, there may be word order alternations that are governed by something in the mind of the speaker, but which are ignored by hearers, so any cognitively based theory which refers exclusively to hearers is potentially inadequate.

A third feature of Givón's notion of cognitive complexity is that it is extremely context-sensitive. Since cognitive complexity is a function of an extremely broad array of factors, the cognitive complexity of a given utterance is a function of all of these factors. While we can talk of the cognitive complexity of a given utterance in a given context, it is less clear how we can talk about the cognitive complexity of a given construction. For example, if passive sentences are cognitively less complex than active sentences in some contexts but more complex in other contexts, it is not clear how we compare the cognitive complexity of active and passive in general, or of one order compared to another, without appealing once again to frequency. Hence Givón's notion cannot provide the basis of a notion of unmarked word order distinct from frequency. Note, in contrast, that the notion of pragmatic markedness, as I am using the term, is not context-sensitive in the same way, since it is a property of discourse grammar, of the rules or principles that underly discourse-governed choices. But these rules or principles are not context-sensitive in the way cognitive complexity is. In so far as word order alternations are context-sensitive, that context sensitivity is built into the rules or principles. The rules or principles themselves do not vary with the context; rather the rules or principles define how the word order varies with the context. Hence it is possible to describe a construction as pragmatically marked or unmarked independent of the context of use. Whatever the merits of Givón's notion of cognitive complexity, it is at best a further notion of markedness, distinct from pragmatic markedness.

11. Conclusion

Let me finish with some general comments about the relative significance of frequency and pragmatic markedness. Pragmatic markedness, as I have used the term here, reflects the nature of the rules or principles underlying production, and thus is part of the grammar of particular languages. Frequency, on the other hand, is epiphenomenal relative to the cognitive structures or mechanisms underlying language production and understanding. It thus plays no role in the grammar of particular languages. On the other hand, while pragmatic markedness may play a role in the grammar of particular languages, it is not clear that it has any important role to play in explaining why languages are the way they are. Conversely, frequency, while it may be epiphenomenal relative to the grammar of particular languages, seems to play a major role in explaining why languages are the way they are. While a number of factors contribute towards differences in formal markedness, one of the primary factors appears to be what Haiman (1983) calls economic motivation, whereby the length of linguistic structures will be inversely proportional to their frequency. Similarly, Du Bois (1987:851) argues that much of the nature of language can be explained in terms of a principle that "grammars code best what speakers do most".

Such explanations assume that a notion of greater frequency is well-defined, and presumably the frequency differences in the relevant cases are sufficiently stable over texts that the greater frequency is well-defined. Furthermore, it is probably the case that the bulk of actual human discourse involves certain types of conversation and that while frequency differences may be great over different discourse types in a language, and even over different kinds of conversation, there may be certain core types of conversational discourse that occur with sufficiently high frequency relative to others that the frequency differences found in such discourse types are the ones that are crucial in driving the explanatory forces that are sensitive to frequency. It is precisely because of such considerations that a number of studies that examine the relative frequency of different constructions, with the goal of explaining why language is the way it is, base their frequency counts on conversational discourse (e.g. Thompson 1988; Fox 1987; Fox and Thompson 1990).

Within the context of word order, there are cases where word order changes seem explainable only in terms of frequency. I argue in Dryer (1989) that O'odham (Papago) has recently been undergoing a change from GenN order toward NGen order and a change from postpositions toward prepositions. This change is apparently the result of a recent change in the discourse factors governing word order variability in O'odham, with the side effect that VS and VO order have become more frequent than SV and OV. Payne (1987) argues, however, that O'odham is not grammatically VS and VO. Rather, as I discussed above, the greater frequency of VS and VO in O'odham is simply an epiphenomenal side effect of the fact that word order in O'odham is largely driven by definiteness, that VS and VO order are more frequent only because definite noun phrases happen to occur more frequently than indefinites. Thus while the greater frequency of VS and VO is epiphenomenal relative to the grammar of O'odham, it is necessary to appeal to the frequency facts in order to explain word order changes that have been occurring in the language. If all we knew was the grammar of the language, these changes would be a mystery.

Notes

* The research for this paper was supported by Social Sciences and Humanities Research Council of Canada Research Grants 410-810949, 410-830354, and 410-850540 and by National Science Foundation Research Grant BNS-9011190. I am indebted to Bill Croft, Doris Payne and Russ Tomlin for comments on earlier drafts of this paper.

1. Lambrecht (ms.) offers a definition of pragmatically unmarked word order that is similar: "Given a pair of truth-conditionally equivalent syntactic structures, one of its members may be said to be unmarked pragmatically if it can be used to express two discourse functions while the other member can express only one of them" (p. 10). The examples he discusses are all ones in which the set of contexts in which the marked construction is used is a proper subset of the set of contexts in which the unmarked construction is used. A possible problem with Lambrecht's approach, however, is that it assumes that unmarked constructions serve multiple discourse functions. Consider the analogy of instances of semantic markedness. While we might want to say that *lion* can be used for either a male of the species or a female, we presumably would not want to say that *lion* has two meanings, one for male and one for female: rather the word is simply vague or unspecified for the sex of the animal. In some cases, like the one illustrated in (2a) and (3), we may want to say that a given construction has two uses, distinguished by intonation. In other cases, however, a pragmatically unmarked construction may be appropriate in a superset of the contexts in which the marked construction is appropriate, without there being two identifiable discourse functions associated with the set of contexts in which the unmarked construction is used.

2. I assume in (4) that property X is some property that exactly one of the A and the P can possess.

3. In Thompson's analysis, the principle like (5) is only one of two principles governing use of passive.

4. The terms "definite" and "indefinite" are used here as the names for discourse-pragmatic categories rather than morphosyntactic categories. The terms "identifiable" and "non-identifiable" are alternative terms for these categories.

5. Ojibwa exhibits a contrast between two types of clauses, direct clauses and inverse clauses, and there are competing theories as to what is subject in inverse clauses. The traditional analysis assumes a notion of subject corresponding to notional subject. Rhodes (1976, 1990) provides an analysis of inverse clauses under which the notional object is the grammatical subject and the notional subject is the grammatical object. All 25 of the clauses with lexical subject and lexical object in the counts in Table 1 were direct rather than inverse clauses, so the problem of how to analyse inverse clauses does not arise.

   Proulx (1991) cites results of a count of a different set of Ojibwa texts that are similar to the ones in my count to the extent that SVO is most common: SVO – 17, VSO –7, OVS – 2, and VOS – 1. The most notable difference is that only one VOS clause occurred in the texts he examined. He apparently assumes notions of subject and object corresponding to notional subject and notional object.

6. The cases of OSV and SOV may not belong here since the initial element is separated intonationally from the rest of the clause and may better be viewed as outside the clause,

somewhat analogous to left dislocation structures in English. The number of such clauses is relatively small, however, and their inclusion does not affect the logic of the arguments presented here.

7. Givón (1979:58-59) argues that passive sentences are more presuppositional than active sentences, but his sense of presupposition seems broader than Payne's and his arguments seem unconvincing. His arguments depend crucially on the properties of agentless passives. But since the crucial question is whether *agented* passives are pragmatically marked, the properties of agentless passives are irrelevant, despite the fact that they are more frequent than agented passives.

8. *Little Turtle's Big Adventure*, by David Harrison (New York: Random House, 1969).

References

Abbott, Miriam. 1991. "Macushi." *Handbook of Amazonian Languages,* Vol. 3 ed. by Desmond Derbyshire and Geoffrey Pullum, 23-160. Berlin: Mouton de Gruyter.

Andersen, Henning. 1988. "Markedness theory: The first 150 years." *Markedness in Synchrony and Diachrony* ed. by Olga Mišeska Tomić. Berlin: Mouton de Gruyter.

Battistella, Edwin L. 1990. *Markedness: The evaluative superstructure of language.* Albany: State University of New York Press.

Brody, Jill. 1984. "Some problems with the concept of basic word order." *Linguistics* 22.711-36.

Chafe, Wallace. 1987. "Cognitive constraints on information flow." *Coherence and Grounding in Discourse* ed. by Russell Tomlin. Amsterdam/Philadelphia: John Benjamins.

Comrie, Bernard. 1976. *Aspect.* Cambridge: Cambridge University Press.

Croft, William. 1990. *Typology and Universals.* Cambridge: Cambridge University Press.

Dryer, Matthew S. 1989. "Discourse-governed word order and word order typology." *Belgian Journal of Linguistics* 4.69-90.

Du Bois, John W. 1985. "Competing motivations." *Iconicity in Syntax* ed. by John Haiman, 343-65. Amsterdam: John Benjamins.

Du Bois, John W. 1987. "The discourse basis of ergativity." *Language* 63.805-55.

Fox, Barbara. 1987. "The noun phrase accessibility hierarchy revisited." *Language* 63.856-70.

Fox, Barbara, and Sandra Thompson. 1990. "A discourse explanation of the grammar of relative clauses in English conversation." *Language* 66.297-316.

Givón, T. 1979. *On Understanding Grammar.* New York: Academic Press.

Givón, T. 1990. *Syntax: A Functional-Typological Introduction,* Vol. 2. Amsterdam/Philadelphia: John Benjamins.

Greenberg, Joseph. 1966. *Language Universals (with special reference to feature hierarchies).* The Hague: Mouton.

Haiman, John. 1983. "Iconic and economic motivation." *Language* 59.781-819.

Lambrecht, Knud. "Information structure and sentence form: the pragmatics of syntax in spoken French." Unpublished ms.

Lyons, John. 1977. *Semantics*. Cambridge: Cambridge University Press.

Mithun, Marianne. 1990. "Third person reference and the function of pronouns in Central Pomo natural speech." *International Journal of American Linguistics* 56.361-76.

Nichols, John. 1988. *An Ojibwe Text Anthology.* London, Ontario: The Centre for Research and Teaching of Canadian Native Languages, University of Western Ontario.

Payne, Doris L. 1987. "Information structuring in Papago narrative discourse." *Language* 63.783-804.

Payne, Doris L. 1990. *The Pragmatics of Word Order: Typological dimensions of verb initial languages*. Berlin: Mouton de Gruyter.

Payne, Doris L., and Thomas E. Payne. 1990. "Yagua." *Handbook of Amazonian Languages,* Vol 2 ed. by Desmond C. Derbyshire and Geoffrey K. Pullum, 249-474. Berlin: Mouton de Gruyter.

Proulx, Paul. 1991. Review of *Statement Made By Indians: A Bilingual Petitin of the Chippewas of Lake Superior, 1864*, John Nichols, ed. (1988). *Canadian Journal of Linguistics* 36.198-201.

Rhodes, Richard A. 1976. "The Morphosyntax of the Central Ojibwa Verb." University of Michigan dissertation.

Rhodes, Richard A. 1990. "Obviation, inversion and topic rank in Ojibwa." *Berkeley Linguistics Society 16, Special Session on General Topics in American Indian Linguistics*, 101-15.

Thompson, Sandra A. 1987. "The passive in English: a discourse perspective." *In Honor of Ilse Lehiste* ed. by Robert Channon and Linda Schockey. Dordrecht: Foris.

Thompson, Sandra A. 1988. "A discourse approach to the cross-linguistic category 'adjective'". *Explaining Language Universals* ed. by John A. Hawkins, 167-185. Oxford: Blackwell.

Tomlin, Russell S. 1983. "On the interaction of subject, theme, and agent in English." *Journal of Pragmatics* 7.411-432. Reprinted 1985 in *Beyond the Sentence: Discourse and Sentential Form* ed. by J. Wirth Ann Arbor: Karoma.

Tomlin, Russell S. This volume. "Focal attention, voice, and word order: an experimental, cross-linguistic study."

Tomlin, Russell S., and Richard A. Rhodes. 1979. "An introduction to information distribution in Ojibwa." *Papers from the Fifteenth Regional Meeting of the Chicago Linguistic Society*, 307-320. Reprinted in, *The Pragmatics of Word Order Flexibility* ed. by Doris Payne. Amsterdam/Philadelphia: John Benjamins.

Trubetzkoy, Nikolaj Sergeevitsch. 1969. *Principles of Phonology.* Translated by Christiane A. M. Baltaxe. Berkeley: University of California Press.

Utschig, Anne M. 1985. "Main and Subordinate Clause Word Order." Ph.D. Dissertation, Univ. of Minnesota.

Subject-verb word order and the function of early position

Bruce B. Harold
University of Michigan

1. Introduction

Previous attempts to identify the universal correlates of word order have come to a variety of conclusions that seem to be in opposition. In the traditional approach, the parameters said to favor early position were thematicity (or alternatively topicality or given-ness) and importance. Thematicity has a long history, and importance dates back at least to Jespersen (1949). More recent work by Payne (1987) and Mithun (1987) casts doubt on whether thematicity always favors early position. Givón (1988) argues that the universal parameters favoring early position are unpredictability and importance. In this paper I will try to combine the insights of these differing claims by showing how the pragmatic parameters relate to organization and how this is responsible for both the variety of patterns found in languages and the consistencies. To support and explain this analysis, I will present the language data arranged by basic word order types in the order of typical diachronic progression.[1]

2. Proposal

It is widely accepted that the beginning of a clause receives special attention. Because this is taken to be a universal fact of human cognition, we should expect that some patterns across languages will reflect this. Although I am interested in the beginning of the clause, the studies I have used to give me a wide cross-linguistic base have not included enough information to allow me to speak about first position, but only about relatively early position. Most of my information on subjects (and objects) only tells about their position relative to the verb.

Some might object that the attention in a clause goes to the peak of communication or the rheme. This is true, but it is probably a different type of attention. While I will not delve into the intricacies of attention, I can mention that rhematic attention is not tied to one position across languages. It can be marked by a variety of language-specific means including phonological stress and late position in the clause.

2.1 *Organization*

I am proposing that there is a particular function, better called a *meta-function*, of early position in the sentence and clause that is common to all languages. I will call this meta-function *organization*. I am using the term "meta-function" because organization is a combination of functions; the functions themselves are universal, but different languages use them in different combinations to define their particular version of the meta-function.

In making this proposal, I am not claiming that placing an element in early position is the only means for organization within a language. I am claiming that early position is consistently used for this purpose across languages, with different languages emphasizing different aspects. I also will argue below that the differences in emphasis are related to the basic word order types and to a possible direction of change between the types.

Sgall *et al.* (1973)[2] also comment on organizing constituents in first position, but they do not deal with the relationship of the function of early position to the word order patterns of the various language types.

I should note here that in this paper I am using the term *entity* for the referent of a noun phrase and the term *concept* as a broader term covering entities, events, properties, etc.

In the simplest case, organization requires the twin functions of *grouping* and *dividing*. These functions are "twins" because they are inevitably tied together. To group elements, one must divide them from other elements. If some clauses form a group, then the preceding and following clauses are divided (more distant) from them. These functions can work on many levels;

there can be groups of groups and the whole discourse may be grouped or bound together in some way. Each of these groupings involves divisions on the same level.

In discourse, organization involves more than hierarchical arrangement. Discourse also must relate the new structures it is creating to the existing structures in the listener's mind. The structures in the listener's mind include both those related to the listener's prior knowledge and those created by earlier parts of the same discourse. I will call this function *relating*.

This approach to organization of discourse does not imply that a discourse has a fixed organization in the speaker's mind or that the speaker is consciously trying to organize the discourse. Chafe (1979) suggests that much of the organization of discourse has to do with the flow of thought as it moves from one focus of attention to another.

2.2 *Organizers*

An *organizer* is a constituent used for the meta-function organization. In this paper, I will refer to the first major constituent as an organizer and argue that these constituents tend to have the characteristics that would assist in organization.

The ideal organizer, in this theory, would be a constituent designating a concept that groups a section of the discourse, divides or distinguishes it from adjacent sections, and relates it to something already known to the listener. A noun phrase can be used for this purpose when it designates an entity that ties together a section of the discourse or that separates a section of the discourse from another section. A constituent can separate a section of the discourse by showing a shift of attention. A noun phrase also can relate a section of the discourse to an entity known to the listener. Verbs are sometimes used as organizers to divide the details from one another.

There are other constituents that often serve this function as well; I will mention more about these at the end. Although I do not have cross-linguistic data on these, the English studies are of interest. Clauses and phrases of time and place can be used to group sections of the discourse and relate it to known concepts. Some preparatory clauses such as conditionals (Ford and Thompson 1986) and certain types of purpose clauses (Thompson 1985) perform this function on the sentence level.

2.3 *Pragmatic factors*

The usefulness of a constituent for organization can be related to various pragmatic factors that have already figured significantly in the discussion of word order. These factors apply to the referent of the constituent rather than directly to the constituent.

Each of these factors can be viewed in a fine-grained approach as a matter of degree or in a coarse-grained approach as a binary feature. The approach used at various points in this paper is determined by the issue at hand.

2.3.1 *Importance*

The first of these pragmatic factors is *importance.* Though most writers take the meaning of this term to be self-evident, I believe that we need to examine it a little more closely. There are at least two types of importance that can be distinguished.

One type of importance is integrally involved in the development of the discourse; we could call this *discourse importance.* Generally, if a section of a discourse can be said to be about a particular entity, that entity can be said to have discourse importance. The degree of discourse importance depends in part on the size of the section. Discourse importance is also affected by frequency of mention throughout the discourse. Constituents referring to entities with discourse importance tend to group a section of the discourse. Givón's tests for importance are based on discourse importance. He states, "...[O]ne can presumably assess a referent's importance in the discourse by measuring how long a referent *persists* once it has been introduced" (Givón 1988:248). He uses topic persistence to quantify this.

On the other hand some concepts are important in a discourse even though they are hardly mentioned. This indicates that there is another type and source of importance. I will designate this other type of importance *external importance.* This is importance derived not from the frequency of the concept in the discourse but from some external value or significance that the speaker wants or expects the hearer to give to the concept. External importance does not contribute to the function of grouping, but it often does relate the discourse to previous knowledge.

It may be helpful to exemplify this. The following example is from a Chinese movie. The seamstress must leave her sewing machine where she works at the side of the street and go to a local government office. A helpful person offers,

(1) *Fengrenji wo bang ni kan zhe, mei shi.*
Sewing.machine I help you watch PROG, not matter
'I'll watch the sewing machine for you. It's no problem.'

There is no reference to the sewing machine in the preceding or following discourse, but the speaker recognizes that it is a significant cause of concern to the listener at that time.

I will only use the term "external importance" for concepts that do not also have discourse importance. Most often the two sources of importance coincide because the factors contributing to external importance usually lead to frequent mention.

Because the detailed language studies that I am using do not make this distinction between external importance and discourse importance, I will not be able to use this distinction in the language data section of this paper.

2.3.2 *Availability*

Another pragmatic factor is *availability*. Availability is the ease with which the listener can access a concept. This is affected by prior knowledge, previous mention, and inferability. The more familiar a concept is, the more available it is; that is, the greater the listener's prior knowledge of the concept, the more easily the listener can access that concept. Previously mentioned concepts are most available immediately after mention and less available as more time passes. In a spreading activation network model, this would be handled by decay of activation.

This can be related to Prince's taxonomy of information statuses (Prince 1981a). Prince makes the point that entities known to both speaker and listener have a different status ("Unused") than those that are not known to the listener ("Brand-new"); this allows more distinctions than the dichotomy between "old" and "new." Entities also can become available by inference. If I talk about sailing, the concept of a boat, or even "the boat" are somewhat available even though they are not explicitly shared — the availability in this case comes from implicitly shared expectations. Prince refers to these as "Inferrable."

On the whole, Prince's taxonomy does not deal as much with degrees of availability as with causes of availability. Unused entities are not necessarily more or less available than inferable ones, but they are available based on prior knowledge rather than based on expectations coming out of the discourse. Additionally, an entity that is unused, in her sense, can be made more available by being partially inferable from context as well. The statuses she lists are neither ordered (from "given" to "new") nor mutually exclusive.

The availability of an entity makes it useful for relating information to the listener's existing knowledge structures.

2.3.3 *Predictability*

Importance and availability tend to correlate — important entities tend to recur, and previously available entities tend to be more important than new ones. This might make for a simple, strong cross-linguistic pattern if it were not for the pressures created by another pragmatic factor — *predictability*. Predictability is the degree to which the listener can predict the presence and role of a particular concept.[3] Givón (1988) lists four factors that affect an entity's predictability: distance since last mention; recent mention of other potential referents; semantic information from within the clause, and thematic information from the preceding discourse. Continuity of role also contributes to predictability, probably as part of the thematic information. A concept has maximum predictability when it has just been prominently mentioned, it is continuing in the same role, and no other concept in the immediate context would be likely to have that role.

Predictability provides a counter-pressure that keeps concepts from being used as organizers. The most predictable concepts tend not to be mentioned. It is as if there were a rule: Don't tell them what they already know. This is an example of Haiman's economic motivation (Haiman 1983). When a grammatical subject is continuing as a subject, it can often be omitted. Even in English this occurs in the restricted case of conjunction reduction. The pattern is even more obvious with clauses and phrases specifying setting. Once the speaker establishes the time and place, they are not generally repeated until there is a change worthy of mention or some need to specify that some other event did indeed happen at the same time or place.

Because of this pressure from predictability, we see that *unpredictability* can be a useful pragmatic factor for organizers. Unpredictable entities can fill the function of dividing that we discussed above. Givón (1983a, 1988) discusses the role of unpredictability and applies the measures of referential distance and potential interference to attempt to quantify it.

2.3.4 *Comparison and interaction of factors*

We must understand the nature of the difference between availability and predictability since I am using both in this analysis. Availability is the general ease of access; predictability is the level of expectation that a concept will be used at a particular point in a particular role. Any concept that is predictable must be available, though many concepts that are moderately available are not predictable — this would include inferable concepts and concepts that are well-known to the listener but have not been mentioned. Predictability is more sensitive to distance since last mention and the presence of other concepts that could fill the same role. We can see the effects of competing concepts in (2).

(2) *Barry saw Bill, but he didn't stop.*

Two concepts (designated *Barry* and *Bill*) are very available but each is less than fully predictable because of their competition; as a result, the pronoun allows two possible readings.

There are various other situations in which availability and predictability can be distinguished, including topic resumption and many cases of contrast and listing. We will discuss these below.

There is also a difference in the way in which availability and predictability are used as binary factors. An entity can be available even if it has fairly low availability, but it can only be predictable if it has fairly high predictability.

Of course, much of the time predictability and availability coincide. Much of the variety of language patterns that we will discuss arises from the competition between these two factors and the corresponding functions, dividing and relating.

Importance and unpredictability can reinforce each other because an important concept needs to receive attention at the *beginning* of its section. An element referring to an important, unpredictable concept serves both as a handle or heading to group a new section of the discourse and a distinction to separate it from the previous section. After the first clause of the new section, the concept is established and references to it have less role in organization.

Mithun's "Newsworthiness Principle" (Mithun 1987) and Givón's "urgent" (Givón 1988:275) are both a combination of importance and unpredictability. Mithun also uses the term "importance," but it seems to cover the same broad range of phenomena that "newsworthiness" covers. My approach to the pragmatic factors differs from these two approaches in that I argue that availability plays a role as well as unpredictability.

2.3.5 *Other pragmatic factors*

There are also a couple of pragmatic factors that are related to the factors we have already discussed but have additional complications.

The distinction between definite and indefinite (in terms of identifiability) does not exactly fit with either availability or predictability. Entities that are available or predictable are definite, and thus indefinites are (generally) neither predictable nor available. On the other hand, entities that are unknown to the listener but can be described with definite noun phrases are not predictable and may not be available. It seems common enough, though, for languages to treat new definite noun phrases differently from indefinites.

Givón (1988) argues that the distinction between predictable and unpredictable can be extended to include the difference between definite and indefinite. I propose that languages extend the definition of *either* predictability/ unpredictability or availability to include definiteness. (This need not affect how definiteness is determined in the language.) Whichever factor has the most effect on the word order patterns in the language is the one that should determine the placement of definite and indefinite noun phrases. Languages that use predictability to determine word order should tend to place indefinites early because they are not predictable. Languages that use availability more should place indefinites later because they are not available. In the discussion of the language data, I will assume the accuracy of this pattern — I will the use placement of definites and indefinites to argue for the influence of availability or predictability in the ordering patterns of particular languages. Definiteness will figure significantly in the language data because most studies discuss its effects.

The other special factor is set membership. In the clearest cases of contrast, the contrastive elements are members of some set. Myhill and Xing (1993) use the concept of sets to build a definition of contrast that can be objectively applied to natural texts. By virtue of common set membership, the second member of the contrast pair can be somewhat available and useful for relating the new information to the old information.

2.4 *Discourse Functions*

2.4.1 *Topic shift*

We can relate several discourse functions to the organizing functions and the pragmatic factors. I will start with simple cases and then go to some specialized cases. One basic function is topic shift. Topic shift occurs when one entity has been discussed for a few clauses and then another entity becomes the focus of attention and will continue as such for a few clauses. The noun phrase designating the new topic is useful as an organizer because it groups a section of discourse while dividing it from the previous section. This entity has at least the pragmatic factors of unpredictability and discourse importance.

2.4.2 *Contrast*

Contrast also favors organizing position for the contrasted entity. Contrast typically involves an entity that is in a set relation with another entity in the discourse and an assertion about that entity that is in tension with the assertion about the other entity. At times the alternative entity and assertion are implicit in the discourse rather than explicit.

When a pair of entities are contrasted, the first entity of the pair may or may not be unpredictable. The first entity is useful for dividing the first idea from the following idea, and for that reason can aid organization. The second entity is even more useful as an organizer; it definitely separates its section (often a single clause) from the preceding section (evidently the preferred direction for dividing) by being unpredictable. It is normally available because of its membership in a common set with the first entity as we have discussed. Often contrasted entities also have external importance — it is important to get the right entity with the right predicate (for reasons other than grouping the discourse).

Entities in implicit contrast are like the second member of a contrasting pair because the implicit member of the contrast set is treated as already known. Also any indicators of contrast (such as word order) must appear in the one explicit clause.

2.4.3 *Listing*

Another basic function is listing. Listing consists of a series of assertions, each related to a different element of a list or set. These assertions may be contrastive, very similar, or even just different. Myhill and Xing (1993) use the term "listing" only for cases in which the assertions are essentially identical; the definition I have given here overlaps contrast. Like contrast, the existence of a common set can give each element an amount of availability. When each is first mentioned it is unpredictable. Thus each element of the list can be used to divide (on a detailed level) and to relate its clause or clauses to the local structure and often to prior knowledge. This can even cause objects to appear early in the clause in English, as illustrated by *history* and *math* in (3).

(3) *[I graduated from high school as] an average student. My initiative didn't carry me any further than average. History I found to be dry. Math courses I was never good at. I enjoyed sciences...football was my bag.*[4]

Listing may also be the function motivating verb-initial languages to place the verb first in sequential narrative. The list of specific events divides the larger event, which is the whole. In this case the listener does not know the set membership beforehand. I will address the relationship between listing and verb-first order further under the discussion of VSO languages.

2.4.4 *Topic resumption*

There are a couple of more complex discourse functions that combine more factors and thus more strongly favor early position for a particular element. One such function is topic resumption. Topic resumption occurs when a previous topic is reintroduced to the focus of attention and will remain there for a few clauses. Besides serving to group and divide, as all topic changes do, topic resumption uses an entity that is available from earlier discourse to relate its section to existing knowledge.

2.4.5 *Contrastive topic shift*

Closely related to topic resumption is contrastive topic shift. Contrastive topic shift is a topic shift in which the new topic contrasts with the previous topic. This serves to group and divide as other topic shifts do. Like other cases of contrast, the topic will typically have some availability based on its relation to the previous topic as well as external importance. But this differs from the more typical cases of contrast in that the clause introducing the new topic tends not to be paired with an adjacent clause with an opposing predicate about the former topic. Often the contrastive topic will be available from recent mention as well; Payne (1987) mentions this as a characteristic of contrastive topic shift in O'odham (also called Papago).

2.5 *Organizers and Topics*

Although they may share many characteristics, organizers are not the same as topics. In the so-called "theme-rheme" languages there is a large degree of overlap; we could say that these languages tend use topics for organization.

Other languages, including the so-called "rheme-theme" languages, use only certain types of topics for organization; generally they use other constituents for this purpose.

3. Language data

3.1 *Ordering of Languages*

Givón (1977) claims that there is a common pattern of drift for many languages in the order SOV → free → VSO → SVO, though the VSO stage is probably optional. This is based on a simpler pattern suggested by Vennemann (e.g. Vennemann 1974), namely SOV → TVX → SVO. Vennemann also suggests that SVO may change to VSO. Although I do not wish to commit to a decision between these suggestions or any others, I find that the order suggested by Givón provides a meaningful arrangement of the language types for which I have data. By arranging the language types in this order, we can see both the relationship between the word order and the use of organizers and also a possible diachronic reanalysis of the meta-function of organization.

3.2 *SOV*

For the fairly strong SOV languages, I have examined studies of postposing in Turkish (Erguvanlı 1984) and Japanese (Simon 1989). Generally these languages have the subject in the organizing position when it is expressed. If the subject is omitted, the object is preferred as an organizer over the verb. My primary information on this comes from studies on postposing, so the question of interest is "When can the subject be included but not in its normal leading position?"

Postposing with an intonation break often seems to be a typical case of afterthought.[5] That is, it appears as if the speaker makes the decision to include the postposed entity after he begins the sentence. This may be due to a reevaluation by the speaker about the predictability of the entity.

Both Japanese and Turkish also have some subjects (and other entities) after the verb without an intonation break. These are often high in predictability, but both studies point out that the post-verbal information is not always predictable; it can be totally unpredictable. Erguvanlı gives these three restrictions on post-verbal material in Turkish: it cannot be stressed, it cannot be indefinite, and it cannot be a questioned constituent. In both studies it appeared that the post-verbal constituents (including subjects) were either predictable or relatively unimportant.

Erguvanlı also mentions that indefinites must be immediately pre-verbal. The verb's position at the end of the clause indicates that verbs are disfavored as organizers, though they will be in first position if there are no other constituents or if all other constituents are postposed.

We can see in this case that all three major pragmatic factors contribute to this pattern. Entities that are high in predictability or low in importance can be postposed or omitted; we have already seen why these may not be desirable for organization. Available entities are more likely to be used as organizers than the newest entities as long as the available ones are not too predictable. The entities that are lowest in availability (indefinites) are immediately preverbal and thus not usually first. Also, these languages seem to strongly resist using verbs as primary organizers, judging from their resistance to starting clauses with verbs if other constituents are present. The organizers in these languages, then, tend to be important, moderately unpredictable, and at least minimally available. This fits well with the expectations of this approach, and this is a common, stable language type.

3.3 *Post-SOV free word order*

My data for Post-SOV languages comes from Givón's study of Ute (Givón 1983b), Payne's study of O'odham (also called Papago; Payne 1987) and my own examination of the text in the *Ute Reference Grammar*. The languages discussed by Mithun (1987) seem to follow identical patterns so we should group them here as well. Both Ute and O'odham are Uto-Aztecan languages that were formerly SOV; Mithun's study shows similar patterns in unrelated languages.

Ute is closer to SOV, so we will examine that language first. Although most full noun phrases are pre-verbal, 39% of definite full noun phrase subjects are post-verbal. Indefinite subjects and all objects are much more strongly pre-verbal. This indicates a stronger effect of predictability in moving concepts away from being organizers. This effect of predictability corresponds to a stronger use of the dividing aspect of organization.

The effect of predictability can be seen in two other patterns that Givón observes. A definite full noun phrase subject is more likely to be post-verbal if it designates the entity that is the subject of the previous clause. The ones that are "same subject" are post-verbal 61% of the time; the ones that are different are post-verbal only 30% of the time. The other pattern is that subjects are more likely to be before the verb at paragraph breaks than elsewhere. Chafe has identified a correlation between typical paragraph judgments and pauses in spoken discourse (Chafe 1979). These points of pause and discontinuity reduce predictability. As a result, there is more need to establish the most basic organizer, usually the subject.

O'odham has progressed farther away from SOV, and in this language the majority of subjects and objects appear after the verb. Payne found that definiteness correlated with noun phrase position more strongly than any other factor she examined. Noun phrases, whatever their syntactic role, usually come before the verb if they are indefinite (83% SV) and after the verb if they are definite and not pragmatically marked (98% VS). Payne also noted that the indefinites that did appear after the verb tended to be unimportant. She says putting an indefinite entity post-verbally seems to tell the listener that he should not "open a file" for this entity, just as he does not need to open a file for a definite entity (which is also usually post-verbal).

The other noun phrases that tend to appear before the verb are pragmatically marked ones. These include "information in single-focus and double-focus contrast situations...information questions and answers to them...contrastive change in major topic..." (Payne 1987:787). Most topic shifts are not included, in this group; to be included, there must be an element of contrast. Most of the time, contrastive topic shifts involve topics that are mentioned within the last 12 clauses.

We can see here that predictability has been extended close to its logical limit. Almost always the least predictable element is first. Some consideration for importance limits this, apparently; this explains why some indefinites are not pre-verbal. The pattern of contrastive topic shifts illustrates one of our most ideal situations for organizers; the new topics are available from recent mention as well as unpredictable from contrast and change of topic.

Organization here is largely a matter of dividing, usually on a detailed level. We might question why typical topic shifts do not involve a pre-verbal topic; these are good for dividing and are more important than many of the other entities used for dividing in these languages. I would suggest that the use of detailed divisions undermines the usefulness of this position for larger divisions and grouping. Also the use of predictability to disqualify would-be organizers has been extended to such a degree that the typical new topic no longer qualifies.

This pattern seems much less than ideal for the theory I am proposing because it uses first position to divide on a detailed level and does not use it much for grouping or relating. It is not surprising that it is much less frequent than other word order patterns and probably less stable. One factor that may partially motivate or reinforce this pattern is that the attention given to the beginning of the clause largely overlaps the attention given to the rheme.

3.4 *VSO*

My sources for text studies on VSO are Givón's and Fox's studies of biblical Hebrew (Givón 1977; Fox 1983) and my own examination of interlinear texts from Genesis (Green 1985).

VSO languages have many of the same characteristics that we saw in the advanced free word order languages. Because the types of noun phrases that appear pre-verbally in languages like O'odham (indefinites and pragmatically marked) are not common, not much change of ordering is necessary for them to become verb-first languages.

The most strongly VS languages (stronger than biblical Hebrew) have pre-verbal subjects only in subject focus constructions (Myhill 1985); here the subject has the function of predication. In these languages, the overlap between organization and predication is close to complete. I mentioned before that not all languages going through this diachronic path have a clear VSO stage; probably many that are VSO at some point are never as rigid as this type.

Other strongly VS languages use pre-verbal position for a contrasted entity, for a topic in a topic shift or a topic resumption, or for any other entity whose action/predicate could especially easily be attributed to another entity. This is not clearly different from the pattern we found for post-SOV free word order languages. There is probably a difference in the degree of grammaticalization and fixity of order.

In biblical Hebrew, indefinites still tend to be pre-verbal. Fox found 21 pre-verbal indefinite subjects and only 10 post-verbal ones in Genesis (Fox

1983:238).

These patterns have essentially the same explanation that I offered for O'odham. VSO languages are more common than the free word order languages, but are still significantly less common than either SOV or SVO. Like the free word order languages, they are probably disfavored to some degree because of the use of the same less-than-ideal pattern of organizers.

There is another pattern in these languages that is related. In a number of these languages, the position of the verb is related to the role of the clause in the discourse. Clauses that are sequentially ordered and carry forward the "main story line" tend to be verb-initial; other clauses often have other elements before the verb (Givón 1977; Longacre this volume). This pattern is clearest in narrative — in other types of discourse sequential ordering is not as frequent or as central. This indicates that the verb in initial position is in fact used for dividing, or more specifically, for listing. Listing here is organizing by the use of subdivisions of a larger entity; it does not imply that the larger event is conceptualized as a list of actions. When the verb is an element of the main event, it is initial; Longacre describes the sequential clauses as the "backbone" of the story. When the clause is not part of the main event but only background information (including asides, descriptions, subordinate clauses), the verb is not always initial; in Hebrew, it usually cannot be initial in these cases.

Although these languages are similar to the free word order languages in their general patterns of word order on the clause level, there are apparently major changes on the phrase level. These changes involve the phrase level word orders that tend to be in harmony with the dominant order of verb and object. Dryer (1989:87) notes,

> Thus the evidence cited here is actually more consistent with an hypothesis according to which languages with discourse-governed word order tend to exhibit OV characteristics, regardless of which order of object and verb is more common. Only the diachronic evidence from Papago and a priori assumptions cast doubt on this hypothesis.

The OV characteristics he examines in his paper are Genitive-Noun order and postpositions. His findings are consistent with the belief that most of these languages are descendants of SOV languages; thus my term "post-SOV free word order languages." He argues that comparative evidence demonstrates that Papago has partially changed from more consistent OV characteristics to mixed characteristics with the OV characteristics still predominating. I am suggesting that this should be the general pattern — these languages will start with OV characteristics and change to VO characteristics only after VO order becomes predominant. So we would expect the change of correlated patterns to come in the transition between the free word order stage and the VSO stage.

3.5 *SVO*

For SVO and the drift to SVO, my major sources are Myhill (1985, 1986, 1991) and Givón (1977) supplemented by my own examination of transcripts of spoken English from Terkel (1984).

The change from VSO to SVO involves movement along what Myhill calls "the VS to SV continuum" (of VO languages). Myhill (1986, 1991) discusses how the correlates of SV order change along this continuum. As the percentage of VS order decreases, so does the correlation between sequencing and VS order. Toward the SV end of the range, indefinites begin to clearly favor VS order. Still closer to the SV end, special constructions for presentatives emerge with a grammaticalized VS syntax.

17th-century Spanish, which has more than 50% SV order, is toward the middle of this continuum (Myhill 1991). On the one hand, it has a correlation between sequenced clauses and VS word order, no correlation between presentative verbs and VS order (except as a result of other correlations), and no distinct presentative construction; in these respects it is like VSO languages. On the other hand, it has a correlation between high referential distance of the subject and VS order, and indefinites are 71% VS.

In Rumanian, which is more frequently SV, there is not only a clear correlation between indefinite subjects and VS order (even in nonpresentatives), but there is also a presentative construction that is very strongly VS (Myhill 1986). Rumanian also has no significant correlation between sequenced clauses and VS order.

Myhill suggests that in the final stages of movement toward rigid SV order, languages lose the ability to use VS order freely based on pragmatic parameters while gaining specialized syntax for the presentative function. Rumanian is in the middle of this process, but French and English have completed the change — they allow VS order only in special constructions (such as the presentative construction).

We see in these changes a distinct change of direction. Organization is no longer being increasingly affected by predictability; instead, availability is becoming a significant factor again. New elements have some inherent weaknesses as organizers: they do not help to relate to prior knowledge and they very often have little role in the discourse, so that they do not help to group sections of the discourse. Perhaps because the newest elements are not ideal for their organizing ability, the contrastive topic becomes the new center for the prototype for organizers, and there is increasing use of other entities with similar characteristics in organization. This reanalysis eventually favors availability. Because topics are most frequently grammatical subjects, this can lead to a reanalysis of pre-verbal position as subject position and of subjects as the standard organizers. I also would suggest that indefinites may shift to post-verbal position because that position, being the object position, becomes the typical position for new entities. This gives us a switch from pre-verbal focus to post-verbal focus.

The increased role of the pragmatic factor of availability correlates with an increased role of the organizational function of relating. Availability and relating favor the "old-first" ordering that seems to be such a natural analysis of many European "pragmatic word order" languages. The choice of organizers in these languages seems to match quite well with our expectations; this language type is correspondingly frequent and stable.

I would like to offer one note of caution. This preference for organizing by available entities may not always show up in counts of referential distance in the way we might expect; most pre-verbal subjects represented with a full noun phrase may still have a fairly high referential distance. If they were strongly predictable, they would usually be replaced by pronouns or zero anaphora.

The presentative constructions are part of the pattern of favoring availability. Myhill (1986) points out that some strong SVO languages require even presentatives to have some pre-verbal material; this would indicate that these verbs are not organizers. The organizing material, then, may be a locative or even the dummy existential "there" (derived from a locative) or "it." One could say that these dummy subjects relate the concept embodied in the sentence to the very general background or situation, which is "the ultimate given" as it were; Lakoff (1987) claims that existential "there" relates the new entity to a particular mental space. Some other presentatives are organized by being related to an available (or at least more stable) location.

Some languages going through this change in the definition of organization become TVX (topic-verb-rest) rather than SVO. Vennemann (1974) suggests Czech as an example of a TVX language. Although I cannot say precisely what makes the difference, I can suggest two of the important factors, which probably are closely related. These are whether the language makes increasing use of constructions that move entities that would not "normally" be the subject to the subject position (such as passivization) and whether the pre-verbal position becomes reanalyzed as a syntactic position. Both changes favor SVO instead of TVX. In the case of the change in biblical Hebrew, Givón argues that the high frequency of the use of subjects for topic-switching "automatically insures that the language will eventually gravitate toward SVO rather than TVX" (Givón 1977:216). Of course, a TVX language can proceed to change to an SVO language.

3.6 *Summary of language data*

Table 1 summarizes the language data we have discussed. The horizontal lines in the indefinite and sequenced columns show the point in the continuum where the effects of these factors change. Indefinites are said to favor VS in languages in which indefinite subjects are more likely to be post-verbal than definite ones are; this does not mean that the majority of indefinite subjects are post-verbal. These lines of division are suggestions; as more details come to light our picture will probably become more complex. The findings of Myhill (1985) suggest that the line between focus favoring SV and focus favoring VS

Table 1. Languages and some pragmatic factors affecting word order

Type	Languages	Pre-/Post-posing	Indef	Seq	Focus
SOV	Japanese	limited postposing			
	Turkish				
Post SOV	O'odham	subj often postposed	favors SV		favors SV
	Ute	subj and obj often postposed		favors VS	
VSO	Hebrew	limited preposing	--------		??
	Spanish	subj before or after		--------	
	Rumanian	limited subj postposing	favors VS	no effect	favors VS
SVO	English				

is close to the line I have drawn between indefinites favoring SV and indefinites favoring VS. We discussed above how focus clearly favors SV in Turkish and O'odham; Myhill (1985) gives similar information for VSO languages. By contrast, in Rumanian, focus favors VS, at least when marked by *şi* 'also' (Myhill 1986).

SOV languages have limited postposing. Postposing becomes more common toward the middle of the table and post-verbal position is predominant for all noun phrases in VSO or verb-1 languages. Continuing down to SVO, subjects become more commonly pre-verbal, while objects remain predominantly post-verbal. During the change from VSO to SVO, indefinites — and probably also focused subjects — cease to favor pre-verbal position and begin to favor post-verbal position (although many can still be preverbal). Farther along in the shift, sequencing ceases to favor VS order.

3.7 *The use of presentatives as evidence*

In the discussion of SVO languages above, I used presentative constructions as evidence that new entities tend to come later in the clause than old entities. However, Givón (1988) argues that existential-presentative constructions are not evidence for new information coming in later position. He offers a two-pronged argument: the existential 'be' or 'have' is grammaticalized in many languages, and there is usually other material, the "comment", after the indefinite subject.

The first problem with this argument is that, though many existential verb forms are very grammaticalized, many other presentative verbs are not (such as 'come' or 'stand'). That is, the verbs themselves are not reduced in any way although they are part of a grammaticalized construction. The ungrammaticalized verbs can be used even in strongly SVO languages like English. Several different verbs are used in Rumanian, and others can be justified as presentatives in special contexts (see Myhill 1986).

The second side of Givón's argument deals with the relevance of these constructions to the current discussion. First we should note that Givón's paper deals primarily with the distinction between "topic-comment" order and "comment-topic" order; by contrast, the current paper is dealing with subject-verb order and the function of early position. For Givón's purposes, demonstrating that existential-presentative constructions have a basic "topic-comment" order is sufficient. For our purposes, we should ask why the indefinite subjects in these constructions have a later position than most subjects.

But even when we recognize this difference of purpose, this side of Givón's argument has some difficulties. Givón only discusses the existential-presentative; in other presentatives the verbs contribute more to the total predication.

There is another possible objection to using presentatives as evidence in this discussion. Givón has claimed that the VS order in these constructions is one of several "'frozen' attestations of VS syntax" (Givón 1977:181). I believe that the data we have examined allow us to question this assertion. If these patterns are relics, the grammaticalization should have taken place during a time of predominant VS order. In fact, we find something quite different. As we discussed before, early biblical Hebrew, in the strong VSO stage, seems to prefer pre-verbal position for indefinite subjects, so the VS presentative construction in modern Israeli Hebrew (compare Givón 1988) cannot be a remnant from the time of strong VS order. Myhill (1991) argues that the presentative construction arises as a grammaticalized form only toward the SV end of the VS to SV continuum. This suggests that it is an innovation resulting from the changing use of early position rather than the relic of an older order which it superficially resembles. So it is more reasonable to take this pattern as a late grammaticalization of the patterns we first saw in 17th-Century Spanish and Rumanian. In these languages indefinites favor post-verbal position outside of presentative contexts as well as in presentative contexts.

4. Organization and other constituents

We can apply this same meta-function, organization, to other findings on the order of clause and sentence constituents.

4.1 *Time*

The patterns suggested here are based on "Language and memory" (Chafe 1973) and my own observations. Both of these were introspective studies, not text studies.

Chafe's basic suggestions are that the longer ago an event occurred, the more likely the time word is to be first, and the more important the event, the more likely the time word is to be last. I also would suggest, along the same lines, that the less the time (at least the general time) is predictable from the event, the more needed the time word is, and the more likely it is to be first. This does not include cases where the time is the main predication. Another situation that tends to use initial time words is a list of events organized by time; this would be a case of the use of organizers for the discourse function listing.

This use of time words for organizers is somewhat different in English than the use of noun phrases. There seems to be more of an emphasis on availability in noun phrases and more on unpredictability in time phrases. This may be partially a result of the fact that any absolute time phrase and most relative ones are known to the listener or at least inferable; as a result, most time phrases can be considered at least generally available. Also, time follows a natural sequence, and most narratives do not jump between blocks of time the way they do between subjects and other entities; this makes time especially useful for grouping and dividing.

Overall, in English, at least, and in Mandarin as well, based on my observations, time appears to follow much the same rules that Givón (1988) gives for subjects: Unpredictability and importance favor earlier position.[6]

4.2 *Purpose clauses*

Subordinate clauses show patterns on the sentence level that are similar to those we have been examining on the clause level.

Sandra Thompson (1985) found some related patterns in a text study of purpose clauses in English. She found that initial purpose clauses refer to purposes or goals mentioned in the previous discourse or inferable from it. Initial purpose clauses also explain more than one following clause. Final purpose clauses are rarely inferable and tend to refer only to the immediately preceding main clause. Frequently the clause cannot be changed from one position to the other in context, while in others cases the result is somewhat odd. Thompson concludes that initial purpose clauses are significant in organizing the discourse and final ones are not. This pattern may provide additional evidence for my claim that availability can favor first position, but it also could be simply a case of grouping.

In our terms, only slightly different from Thompson's, these clauses are qualified to serve as organizers because they group several clauses and relate them to previous knowledge (in the context). Their motivation is similar to that of English subjects.

4.3 *Conditional clauses*

Ford and Thompson (1986) found some similar, though not as clear, results in a text study of conditional clauses. They showed that conditional clauses generally relate the main clause to the previous discourse and can prepare for the following discourse. This relates them to the functions of grouping and relating (because the condition is implied by the context or a restatement of something in the context). So these are well qualified to serve as organizers, and, in fact, they have a strong tendency to be initial.

When conditional clauses are non-initial, it is usually because they are not as necessary for a proper understanding of the main clause or because there is something else which is better placed first. Non-initial conditional clauses also seem less useful for relating and grouping; as Ford and Thompson state it, "A non-initial *if*-clause...does not display as clear a connection with preceding and subsequent discourse as does an initial *if*-clause" (Ford and Thompson 1986: 370).

4.4 *Wh-clefts and* it-*clefts*

Prince, in her text-based study of wh-clefts and *it*-clefts in English (1978), argues that in a wh-cleft, with the wh-clause at the front of the sentence, the contents of the wh-clause are assumed to be both known to the listener and on his mind. By contrast, the wh/*that*-clause of an *it*-cleft comes later in the sentence and is generally not on the listener's mind. It may be known or inferable or it may be totally new.

These findings indicate that wh-clefting puts information that is very available in the organizing position and that *it*-clefting deals with less available information (in the non-cleft portion) and does not use the organizing position for this information. This is similar to the general pattern we have found in English of preferring availability for organization.

4.5 *Adverbs*

Adverbs are probably rarely organizers in the sense we have been discussing. On the other hand, they do have patterns that seem to be related to the same basic motivations within a different range of possibilities. These comments are based on Bolinger's work on the effects of adverb order in English (Bolinger 1952). Adverbs at the beginning of a clause modify the whole clause and not just a part of it; adverbs at the end modify a part; ones in the middle are more open to variation. Although this function is very different from that of the typical organizing noun phrase, it is related to the function of grouping, because the earlier ones have a broader scope. We would probably see the same early position favored for an adverb that modified several clauses; usually these clauses would be conjoined in a single sentence.

Bolinger also notes that most contrast between adverbs is clause-final. This may be because the contrast is not usually between two ways to characterize a whole sentence, but rather between two possible manners for a single action. If the contrast is between two different actions, then the actions or actors are usually the organizers rather than the manner. Also, contrasted adverbs are usually predicates, and predication does not normally overlap organization in an SVO language. Bolinger does give one case of initial contrast, but this involves time adverbs, which we have discussed separately.

5. Conclusions

I have attempted to show how, across various language types, the function of early position in the sentence or clause can be argued to be organization. We can explain — or at least describe — many differences in word order by the varying definitions of organization and the resulting choice of organizers. These differences arise from the variations in the relative emphasis placed on the different functions that compose organization. These functions are grouping, dividing and relating. I used these functions to explain the role of the pragmatic factors of importance, availability, and unpredictability, and the role of the discourse functions of contrast, listing, and various types of topic shifts. We also saw how different elements within the sentence may be sensitive to different pragmatic factors in determining whether or not they will be used as organizers in a particular situation.

More research is needed on a variety of details. Studies are needed to determine the patterning of time words, locatives, and other oblique noun phrases across these language types. Future research also should examine what is first and not simply when a constituent occurs before or after the verb. Also, there is a need to relate these findings to other possible paths of language change.

Notes

1. I want to express my appreciation to William Croft for his extensive guidance, comments and suggestions; his active interest in my study has made a significant contribution. I also want to extend my thanks to Pamela Downing, John Myhill, and Mickey Noonan for their comments, criticisms, insights, and information.

2. See for example Sgall *et al.* (1973:40, section 2.5).

3. This role can be either grammatical or semantic. Passives and antipassives are used to take advantage of the expectation that the entity will continue in the same grammatical role. Persistence in the same semantic role also increases predictability. Of course, the highest predictability comes when these factors coincide.

4. Studs Terkel, *Working* (New York: Avon, 1974), p. 590 as cited in Prince 1981b. The material in brackets is in Prince's citation.

5. Larry Hyman (1975) describes afterthought as involving an intonation break and the placement of an element where it is not allowed to occur. He also argues that this pattern can become standardized and contribute to word order change. In the situation he is describing, this would lead straight from SOV to SVO.

6. In Mandarin, later position for time words is after the subject; earlier position is before the subject. All time words designating a place in time normally come before the verb.

References

Bolinger, Dwight. 1952. "Linear modification." *Publications of the Modern Language Association*, 67. Reprinted 1965 in *Forms of English: Accent, morpheme, order* ed. by Isamu Abe and Tetsuya Kanekiyo, 279-307. Cambridge, Mass.: Harvard University Press.

Chafe, Wallace L. 1973. "Language and memory." *Language* 49.261-81.

Chafe, Wallace L. 1979. "The flow of thought and the flow of language." *Discourse and Syntax* ed. by T. Givón, 159-81. New York: Academic Press.

Dryer, Matthew. 1989. "Discourse-governed word order and word order typology." *Belgian Journal of Linguistics* 4.69-90.

Erguvanlı, Eser Emine. 1984. *The Function of Word Order in Turkish Grammar.* Berkeley: University of California. [*University of California Publications in Linguistics*, 106].

Ford, Cecilia E. and Sandra A. Thompson. 1986. "Conditionals in discourse: A text-based study from English." *On Conditionals* ed. by Elizabeth Closs Traugott *et al.*, 353-72. Cambridge: Cambridge University Press.

Fox, Andrew. 1983. "Topic continuity in biblical Hebrew narrative." Givón 1983a 215-54.

Givón, T. 1977. "The drift from VSO to SVO in biblical Hebrew: The pragmatics of tense-aspect." *Mechanisms of Syntactic Change* ed. by C. N. Li, 181-254. Austin: University of Texas Press.

Givón, T. (ed). 1983a. *Topic Continuity in Discourse.* Amsterdam: John Benjamins.

Givón, T. 1983b. "Topic continuity and word-order pragmatics in Ute." Givón 1983a, 141-214.

Givón, T. 1988. "Pragmatics of word order: predictability, importance and attention." *Studies in Syntactic Typology* ed. by Michael Hammond, Edith Moravcsik, and Jessica Wirth, 243-84. Amsterdam: John Benjamins.

Green, Jay P., Sr. (ed.) 1985. *The Interlinear Hebrew-Aramaic Old Testament*. Peabody, Mass.: Hendrickson.

Haiman, John. 1983. "Iconic and economic motivation." *Language* 59:4.781-819.

Hyman, Larry M. 1975. "On the change from SOV to SVO: Evidence from Niger-Congo." *Order and Word Order Change* ed. by Charles N. Li. Austin: University of Texas Press.

Jespersen, Otto. 1949. *A Modern English Grammar on Historical Principles*, Vol. VII. Allen and Unwin.

Lakoff, George. 1987. *Women, Fire, and Dangerous Things: What categories reveal about the mind*. Chicago: University of Chicago Press.

Mithun, Marianne. 1987. "Is basic word order universal?" *Coherence and Grounding in Discourse* ed. by Russell S. Tomlin, 281-328. Amsterdam/Philadelphia: John Benjamins.

Myhill, John. 1985. "Pragmatic and categorial correlates of VS word order." *Lingua* 66.177-200.

Myhill, John. 1986. "The two VS constructions in Rumanian." *Linguistics* 24.331-50.

Myhill, John. 1991. *Typological Discourse Analysis*. Oxford: Basil Blackwell.

Myhill, John, and Zhiqun Xing. 1993. "The discourse functions of patient fronting: A comparative study of biblical Hebrew and Chinese." *Linguistics* 33:1. 25-57.

Payne, Doris L. 1987. "Information structuring in Papago narrative discourse." *Language* 63:4.783-804.

Prince, Ellen. 1978. "A comparison of wh-clefts and *it*-clefts in discourse." *Language* 54:4. 883-906.

Prince, Ellen. 1981a. "Toward a taxonomy of given–new information." *Radical Pragmatics* ed. by Peter Cole, 223-55. New York: Academic Press.

Prince, Ellen. 1981b. "Topicalization, focus-movement, and Yiddish-movement: A pragmatic differentiation." *Proceedings of the Sixth Annual Meeting of Berkeley Linguistics Society* 7.249-64. Berkeley: Berkeley Linguistics Society.

Sgall, Petr, Eva Hajicova, and Eva Benesova. 1973. *Topic, Focus and Generative Semantics*. Kronberg: Scriptor.

Simon, Mutsuko Endo. 1989. "An analysis of the postposing construction in Japanese." Ph.D. Diss. University of Michigan.

Terkel, Studs. 1984. *The Good War*. New York: Pantheon Books.

Thompson, Sandra A. 1985. "Grammar and written discourse: Initial vs. final purpose clauses in English." *Text* 5:1-2. 55-84.

Vennemann, Theo. 1974. "Topics, subjects and word order: From SXV to SVX via TVX." *Historical Linguistics I: Syntax, Morphology, Internal and Comparative Reconstruction* ed. by J. M. Anderson and C. Jones, 339-76. Amsterdam: North-Holland.

Ute Reference Grammar. 1980. Ignacio, Col.: Ute Press.

Focus position in SOV languages

Susan C. Herring
University of Texas at Arlington

John C. Paolillo
University of Texas at Arlington

1. Introduction: focus and word order*

Many languages manifest a preference for placing 'focused' information — that is, information to which the speaker/writer wishes to accord particular salience — in a special position in the sentence, commonly referred to as 'focus position'. In English, especially in written English, where intonation is not available as a cue to signal saliency differences, the primary focus position is claimed to be located at or near the end of the sentence (Halliday 1967; Leech and Short 1981). There are plausible cognitive and functional motivations for placing salient information in sentence-final position: people better retain in short-term memory that which they have heard or read most recently, a tendency which takes on functional significance when the final focused element becomes the topic of the subsequent discourse, as is often the case. It should not be surprising, therefore, that sentence-final focus is not restricted to English, but has also been documented in other languages of the SVO type (e.g. French, Mandarin Chinese), and indeed in languages of different word order types as well.

The present study is concerned with the location of primary focus position in languages whose basic word order is SOV. Verb-final languages pose a unique challenge to the cross-linguistic tendency towards sentence-final focus, since in many such languages, there is a requirement that the finite verb appear in absolute final position; that is, postposed orders such as (X)VO and (X)VS are excluded, except in cases where the postposed element is an intonationally-backgrounded 'afterthought'. Given that focus of the sort we are concerned with crucially involves constituents other than the finite verb, the question naturally arises as to where focus position in SOV languages is located.

1.1 *Two conflicting views*

Readers familiar with the literature on word order and pragmatic focus may feel that this question has already been answered. In fact, however, two different answers have been proposed which taken together make conflicting claims. The most widely-held view is that in SOV languages which have a strict verb-final constraint, the position of greatest focus is immediately *preverbal.* Such languages allow rightward movement of constituents for focusing effect up to — but not beyond — the finite verb. This pattern has been described for rigid SOV languages such as Turkish (Erguvanı 1984), Kartvelian (Harris 1981), Japanese (Kuno 1978; cited in Kim 1988), and Korean (Kim 1985). Kim (1988) generalizes these observations as the 'linear order focus hypothesis', given in (1):

(1) *Linear Order Focus Hypothesis*
If L is a rigid verb-final language in its basic word order, the rhematic focus of a sentence of L is most likely to be in the position immediately preceding the finite verb. (Kim 1988:150)

Later in the same article, Kim neutralizes the distinction between rigid and non-rigid verb-final languages, provided that they are 'harmoniously head-final' languages of Greenberg's (1966) Type XXIII:

(2) If a language has a harmonious head-final property, the information flow principle will not apply beyond the verbal head of the sentence. (Kim 1988:162)

According to this view, then, the primary focus position in SOV languages is immediately preverbal, while postverbal focus is predicted never to occur.

The alternative view holds that the tendency towards *sentence-final focus* noted at the outset is a language universal, implicitly present in languages of all word order types. As such, it seeks to manifest itself in SOV languages, resulting in violations of strict verb-finality. Hetzron (1975) argues at length for the universality of sentence-final focus, citing evidence of focused elements occurring *after* the finite verb in otherwise strict SOV languages such as Amharic and Somali. Clearly, these two views make conflicting predictions regarding the preferred focus position in languages of the SOV type: is it immediately preverbal, or is it final?

1.2 *Methodological considerations*

At this point, a methodological objection might be raised. Languages employ a variety of focus types, some of which could conceivably occupy different positions within the sentence; precisely what is intended here by the use of the term 'focus'? It is noteworthy that the claims of Hetzron and Kim are based on different focus types. Hetzron's observations derive from a cross-linguistic survey of 'presentational' focus constructions[1] — that is, constructions used to 'present' referents that are new or otherwise informationally salient, and about which the speaker typically intends to comment in the subsequent discourse. The examples discussed by Hetzron include locative inversions (e.g. 'In the house (is) a man') and clefts (e.g. 'What I saw was a pink elephant'). Kim's analysis, on the other hand, concentrates on subject WH- question words and the responses they elicit. Given these differences, it is legitimate to ask whether focus position varies depending on focus type — if, for example, it could be demonstrated that WH- focus were preverbal, and presentational focus final, then the two conflicting views might be reconciled.

A second methodological concern involves the kinds of data considered. The data in both Hetzron's and Kim's studies are isolated sentences (or simple question-response sequences) drawn from secondary sources or constructed by the authors or their informants; no actual discourse or contexts of use are analyzed. Indeed, one of the justifications advanced by Kim for choosing WH- words is that they are *inherently* focused; as a consequence, "the researcher [is] relatively free from the necessity of confirming whether or not a given subject NP in the preverbal position is indeed serving as the focus of the sentence in a specific discourse context" (1988:151). However, the results of our investigation reveal that discourse variables influence the positioning of WH- words (see Sections 2.2, 3.2), and that it is not possible to identify certain types of presentational focus without taking the immediate discourse context into account (Section 3.1). The fact that neither Hetzron nor Kim analyzed actually occurring discourse, therefore, potentially skews their investigative results. Given considerations such as these, it is obvious that no definitive answer yet exists to the question of what constitutes focus position in SOV languages — further systematic, discourse-based research is required.

1.3 *Aims and methods of the present investigation*

The present investigation analyzes the relationship between focus and linear word order in two SOV languages, Sinhala (Indo-Aryan) and Tamil (Dravidian).[2] Both are harmoniously head-final type XXIII languages: each has postpositions rather than prepositions, and genitives and adjectives precede the nouns they modify. According to the predictions advanced in (1) and (2) above, focus position (at least for WH- words) in both languages should be preverbal, and final focus should never occur. Indeed, Tamil is one of the languages cited by Kim in support of the linear order focus hypothesis, and therefore any Tamil evidence which runs counter to these predictions would constitute a direct challenge to Kim's claim. In contrast, the universalist hypothesis predicts that Sinhala and Tamil should make use of final focus, at least in the presentation of informationally salient referents.

The methodology employed in this study involves the analysis of both presentational focus and WH- words in a corpus of oral and written narratives. The Sinhala corpus is made up of four oral narratives and nine short written narratives, for a total of 1154 finite clauses. The Tamil corpus consists of six oral narratives and 11 short written narratives, for a total of 1018 finite clauses.

The oral narratives were tape-recorded by the authors in Sri Lanka and in Tamil Nadu, South India, several years ago. The Sinhala oral narratives were related informally by Buddhist monks; all are folk tales involving Buddhist themes. The Tamil oral narratives were told by a variety of narrators, and include real-life accounts as well as folk tales and Hindu myths.

The written narrative texts include one children's story from each language, as well as narrative selections from pedagogical texts for adult second-language learners. Both children's stories were intended for native-speaker students at a first or second grade level. The second-language texts are the product of a single, native-speaker author in each language; the Sinhala selections are folk tales, and the Tamil selections are classical literary narratives retold in simplified, informal prose.[3] The written data represent a relatively straightforward, colloquial style, which because of its pedagogical orientation can be considered to reflect prescriptive norms of modern usage.

We analyzed the position of focus words in these data both quantitatively and qualitatively, with a view toward their functional correlates in discourse. The following section (Section 2) describes the results of our analysis for presentational and WH- focus in Sinhala. Section 3 then compares these findings with the results of a similar analysis for Tamil.

2. Sinhala

2.1 *Presentational focus in Sinhala*

Presentational focus is prototypically associated with a cluster of features, including the status of the referent as 'new' information, its resumption as 'given' or thematic information in the clauses which immediately follow, and its salience or importance relative to the ongoing discourse. Of these, newness of mention is the most consistent correlate of presentational focus, despite the fact that a very small number of 'presented' referents in our data are in fact reintroduced after having been mentioned previously.[4] We therefore analyzed new mentions with respect to their position within the sentence: do they favor immediate preverbal position, and if so, to what extent?

The results of our analysis show that new mentions in Sinhala are by no means exclusively restricted to preverbal position, but rather are distributed across initial (first and second),[5] preverbal, and final positions. However,

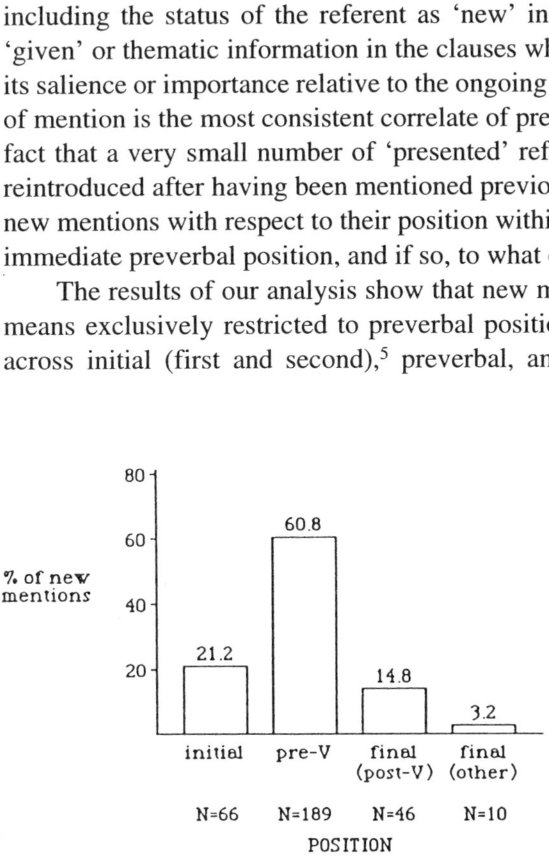

Figure 1. Distributions of new mentions in Sinhala (all grammatical roles)

about three times more new mentions (60.8%) appear in preverbal position than they do in initial (21.2%) or final positions (18.0%).[6] This is depicted graphically in Figure 1.

The high incidence of new mentions in preverbal position in Sinhala would appear to lend strong support to the linear order focus hypothesis. At the same time, one cannot rule out the possibility that new mentions occur there for other reasons, e.g. because they are grammatical objects, or are otherwise syntactically conditioned to appear directly before the finite verb. This is a hypothesis which can easily be tested. A closer examination of the data reveals that although new Os are found virtually exclusively in preverbal position, new Ss and obliques statistically favor this position as well.[7] The location of new mentions according to their grammatical role is summarized in Table 1.[8]

The fact that the overwhelming majority (94.5%) of new Os in the corpus occur in preverbal position, which is the unmarked position for direct objects in Sinhala, is not surprising, and should not be taken as evidence for preverbal focus. That is, the figure of 60.8% in Figure 1 above implies a higher degree of preverbal focus than can justifiably be claimed to exist. In order to obtain a more representative statistical measure, we calculated the percentage of non-Os (i.e. S and oblique arguments) in each of the three major positions. This calculation produces a somewhat more balanced distribution: 31.6% for initial (first and second) positions, 44.5% for preverbal position, and 19.1% and 4.8% for final positions — that is, nearly half of all non-O new mentions appear immediately preverbally, while the remainder are distributed across the other sentential positions. The adjusted distribution of new mentions in Sinhala is shown in Figure 2. These results suggest that there is a tendency — albeit not an overwhelmingly strong one — for new referents to be presented in immediate preverbal position, irrespective of their grammatical role.

Table 1. Position of Sinhala new mentions by grammatical role

	S	**O**	**Obl**	Total
initial	31.6%	0%	34.3%	N= 66
preverbal	**44.7%**	**94.5%**	**49.3%**	N=189
final	23.7%	5.5%	16.4%	N= 46
Total:	100% (N=106)	100% (N=102)	100% (N=93)	N=301

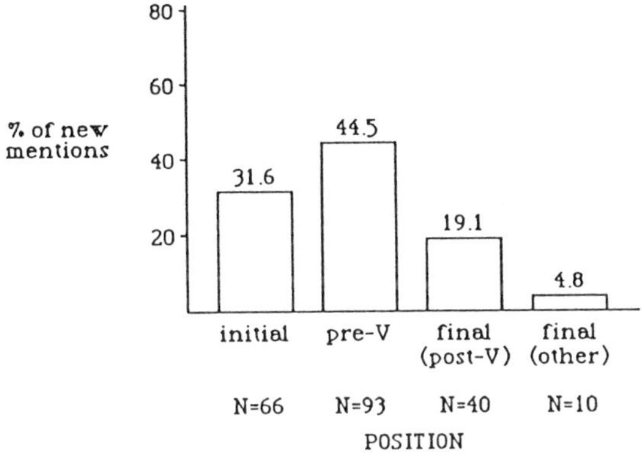

Figure 2. Distribution of non-object new mentions in Sinhala

An example of preverbal presentation from the narrative data is reproduced in (3). [9]

(3) Sinhala (written folk tale)
oya gaňg-en *e-goḍa* *eka paetta-k-a* ***loku kaelaeaewa-k***
that river-INSTR that-bank one side-INDEF-LOC **large forest-INDEF**
tibunaa.
exist-PAST
'On the far bank of that river was **a large forest**.' (lit. '**a large forest** was')

In this example, the locative adverbial 'on the far bank of that river' is in initial position, followed by the subject 'a large forest'. If the inverse order had been employed, the focus would have been on the location of the forest; as the sentence actually appears, the existence of the forest is accorded greater salience. This sentence occurs near the beginning of the narrative as part of a sequence of sentences which contain the verb *tibunaa* 'exist', and which describe the physical setting (there was a river, a forest, a village, etc.). In this sequence, all of the new referents occur in preverbal position.

In our attempts to establish preverbal focus for Sinhala, we have thus far said little about what is in fact a rather remarkable discovery in our analysis — the occurrence of presented referents in postverbal position. Although these account for only 14.8% (N=46) of new referents, the fact that they occur at all is an explicit violation of principle (2) above, which states that new information will not be introduced beyond the verbal head of the sentence. These instances are distributed relatively evenly across all of the narratives in the sample, both spoken and written. What is their function, and how does it differ from that of preverbal focus?

Postverbal new mentions are strongly associated with the presentational function. Not only are they new information, but they tend overwhelmingly to be 'important' referents which are carried over as themes in the following discourse. Example (4) below is from the same story as example (3), and also introduces a forest.[10] This time, however, the forest is not simply one of a set of background features of the general narrative orientation, but rather functions as the location in which the dramatic events of the story begin. Corresponding to its functional importance, the subject NP 'a forest' appears in the more salient postverbal position:

(4) Sinhala (written folk tale)

gaňg-en	*me-goḍa-t*	*tibunaa*	***kaelaeaewa-k.***
river-INSTR	this-bank-also	be-PAST	**forest-INDEF**

'On this bank of the river also was **a forest.'**

By the use of a marked word order, the author effectively draws the reader's attention to this particular forest, which then becomes the theme of the following sentence:

(5)

oya	*kaelaeae-we*	*hiṭiyaa*	***nariy-ek.***
that	forest-LOC	live-PAST	**jackal-INDEF**

'In that forest lived **a jackal.'**[11]

Example (5) contains yet another instance of postposed presentational focus. The jackal introduced here is a main character in the narrative, and thus is accorded positional salience. Postposing is employed in introducing the only other main character — a crocodile — as well.[12]

There appears to be a functional distinction between preverbal and postverbal presentation in Sinhala. Postverbal presentation is characteristic of the introduction of referents or features of the setting which are central to the narrative plot. Of the 13 narratives in the corpus, the Sinhala children's story illustrates this pattern most clearly. The story tells of a young boy who learns to read and write, but is sad because he has no stories to read. His writing stylus and palm-leaf notebook, seeing his condition, go off on a late-night journey, looking for a story to bring back to the boy. They meet an assortment of creatures along the way, but are unsuccessful until, at the world's end, they encounter Sarasvati, the goddess of learning, who summons for them all the pundits of the world, each of whom writes a story for the boy. The boy reads the stories and becomes a wise pundit himself. In this narrative, only four nominal referents are presented postverbally: the boy, the stylus, the palm-leaf book, and Sarasvati. These are clearly the central participants of the narrative. Secondary participants, such as the boy's mother and father, the boy's teacher, the various creatures encountered by the stylus and the palm-leaf book, and the pundits, are introduced in immediate preverbal position.

Given the existence of a postverbal focusing strategy of this type, is it reasonable to maintain that the primary focus position in Sinhala is preverbal? In terms of sheer numbers, preverbal focus predominates: more than three times the number of new referents are introduced preverbally than post-verbally. Yet of the two strategies, postverbal presentation appears to be more specialized in its focus function.

In order to quantify this observation, we calculated the percentage of overall mentions in each of the three major positions which are new. If a particular sentential position were found to contain mostly new mentions, we could then conclude that the position was specialized in the presentational function, the assumption being that the position containing the highest concentration of new mentions would be salient in this function to users of the language.

The results of this analysis reveal a profile very different from that shown by simple distribution (cf. Figure 2). Athough initial position contains a significant number of new mentions (N=66), this number is completely over-shadowed by the number of mentions which are old or accessible information (N=1245),[13] resulting in a density of new mentions of only 5.3% However, this is not surprising when we consider that initial position in subject-initial languages is conventionally reserved for thematic and/or topical information (Herring 1990). Preverbal position, on the other hand, contains relatively fewer old mentions, although the ratio of old and accessible to new is still nearly five-to-one (percentage of new mentions = 21.4%; see Figure 3 below). If initial and preverbal positions are compared, preverbal position is significantly more specialized for the presentational function than is initial position. However the issue of real importance — that is, the comparison between preverbal and final positions — remains to be considered.

Final position in Sinhala also contains elements other than new mentions. These are of two unrelated types. First, there is the so-called 'afterthought' construction, which bears a formal resemblance to the presentational construction in that both allow the postposing of nominals in all case roles, without requiring any other modifications to the morphosyntax of the sentence. The two are functional complements, however, in that information appearing after the finite verb in an 'afterthought' construction is typically contextually given, or, less commonly, new (but not crucial) information added on to an otherwise functionally complete proposition.[14] Afterthought postposings are characteristic of both written and spoken narratives, as illustrated in examples (6)-(7).

(6) Sinhala (written folk tale)

ee særee gemba ara kanda uḍa-ṭa gihin kææ gaha-nḍa
then frog that hill top-DAT go-PPLE shout-INF
paṭan gatta aliya-ṭa-t hoňdaṭa-ma watura tibaha-yi.
start-PAST elephant-DAT-also well-EMP water thirsty-PRED.
gemba-ge sadde æhi-laa aliyaa bohoma amaaruw-en
frog-GEN sound hear-PPLE elephant very difficulty-INSTR
nægga ***ara kanda-ṭa****.*
climb-PAST that hill-DAT

'Then the frog, having gone to the top of that hill, began to croak. The elephant also was very thirsty. Having heard the sound of the frog, the elephant climbed up with great difficulty, **that hill**.'

(7) Sinhala (oral folk tale)

eyaa keree mokak-da? eewaa tæn tæn wala
he do-PAST-EMP what-Q those place-place-LOC
walee dæmma, ***parissan karanna, ee kaale tibba***
bury-PAST **protect-INF that time place-PAST-ADJ**
widiya-ṭa*.*
way-DAT

'What did he do? He buried them in various places, **for safekeeping, the way they kept things at that time**.'

In (6), the postposed nominal 'that hill' is contextually given, having been mentioned two sentences earlier. In (7), the postposed elements — an infinitive phrase and a complex nominal — have not been previously mentioned, but neither do they contain information that is surprising or of particular significance to the narrative. They are added on as 'afterthoughts', i.e. for the sake of specifying additional detail to an already essentially complete utterance. In sentences with postposed presentation, in contrast, the postposed element is a vital part of the sentence's meaning; it could be moved preverbally, but the sentence would make no sense without it, given the context in which it occurs.

In distinguishing between afterthought postposing and postverbal presentation in the narrative data, we made use of three criteria. First, the postposed NP in the presentational construction is usually indefinite, while that in the afterthought construction is definite. Second, the presentational construction has an intonational peak coinciding with the postverbal constituent, whereas the corresponding intonational peak in the afterthought construction coincides with the verb itself, the postverbal material being intonationally 'backgrounded'. Finally, afterthought nominals, being non-central, are rarely if ever elaborated upon in the clauses which follow.[15] In short, although the two strategies make use of the same word order, they are sufficiently distinct in other respects that the possibility of confusion between them rarely arises.

The remaining type of postposing in Sinhala bears a functional relationship to presentational focus, yet is formally distinct. This is the so-called 'emphatic transformation' (Gair 1970), in which a special emphatic form of the finite verb is used. The 'focus' in such constructions is prototypically contrastive, as in (8) below:

(8) Sinhala (written folk tale)
mama kiya-nna ya-nne ***lankaaw-e kataawa-k nemey,***
I tell-INF go-EMP **Sri Lankan-GEN story-INDEF NEG**
indiyaaw-e kataawa-k.
Indian-GEN story-INDEF
'It is **not a Sri Lankan story** that I am going to tell, but **an Indian story**.'

At the same time, like the English *it*-cleft construction often used to translate it, the Sinhala emphatic construction has a broader functional range than the expression of simple contrast, including non-contrastive assertion and stylistic emphasis, as illustrated in example (9):

(9) Sinhala (oral folk tale)
balan iňda-laa mahawsada paṇḍitayoo dæn naagana hema
wait be-PPLE Mahawshadha Pandit now bathe-PPLE etc.

aawa.	*æwilla*	*dæn*	***baḍaginn-e-y***	*in-ne.*
come-PAST	come-PPLE	now	**hunger-LOC-FOC**	be-PRES-EMPH

'Having waited, Mahawshadha now bathed himself and came. Having come, he is now **very hungry**.' (lit. 'it is **in hunger** that he now is')

In this example, no contrast is implied; the focus construction simply emphasizes the state of being hungry.

The emphatic form of the verb, in addition to appearing in emphatic focus constructions, is also grammatically required in negated sentences and with WH- words.[16] As a consequence, the emphatic construction is extremely frequent in modern colloquial Sinhala: 10.5% of all finite clauses in the narrative corpus have the verb in the emphatic form, and the frequency is even higher in conversation, which makes greater use of contrastive assertions, negation, and questions.

The focused nominal in an emphatic construction may appear either before or after the verb. In the Sinhala narrative corpus, 28.8% of emphatics involve an initial or immediately preverbal focused element, while the remaining 71.2% are postposed, as in (8) above.[17] Thus the emphatic construction alone does not appear to require a particular word order; by virtue of its characteristic verbal morphology, the construction is always 'focused' regardless of where in the sentence the focused element occurs.

Taking into consideration postverbal mentions of all three types — presentational, afterthought, and emphatic — we arrive at a percentage of 44.7% of the total that are new. This represents a degree of specialization that is more than twice that for preverbal position. The averaged percentage is misleading, however, in that the three postposed types exhibit widely divergent degrees of specialization. The percentage of 'afterthoughts' that are new information is extremely low: 7.7%, a percentage which reflects the *negative* correlation between afterthoughts and new mentions. Postposed emphatics, on the other hand, are new one-half of the time. While this figure would seem to suggest that information status is irrelevant to the placement of focused nominals in the emphatic construction, such is not the case. At 50.0% new, postposed emphatics are nearly four times more likely to be first mentions than are preverbal emphatics, which are new only 13.3% of the time. This argues further for an association between postverbal position and the presentational function, even if newness alone cannot account for all of the instances of postposed mentions in emphatic constructions.[18]

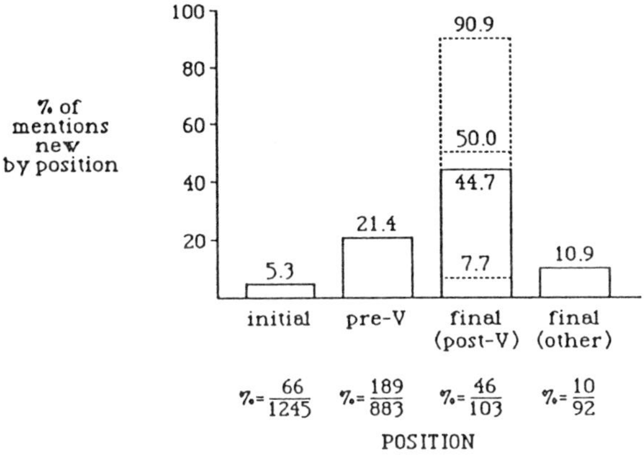

Figure 3. Specialization of positions for new mentions in Sinhala

Excluding afterthoughts and emphatics from the count, we are left with a percentage of 90.9% of simple postposings which introduce new referents — a very high percentage indeed! The relative degrees of specialization of each sentential position for new mentions are summarized in Figure 3.

Figure 3 shows that in terms of the specialization of each position for new mentions, sentence-final position, rather than immediately preverbal position, predominates. The Sinhala situation thus supports the predictions of Hetzron regarding presentational focus. In so doing, it explicitly contradicts one of the predictions made by Kim — namely, that in head-final SOV languages, focused information will not appear after the finite verb.

2.2 *WH- focus in Sinhala*

Thus far we have shown that postverbal position is more specialized for presentational focus than is preverbal position. The crosslinguistic study on which the 'linear order focus hypothesis' is based did not consider presentational focus, however, but rather WH- words. It is at least theoretically possible that WH- words in Sinhala pattern according to the principles given in (1) and (2) above — that is, that they appear preferentially in immediate preverbal position, and do not appear postverbally. In this section, the use of WH- words in the Sinhala narrative corpus is considered.

Table 2. Position of Sinhala WH-words by grammatical role

	S	**O**	**Obl**	**Adv**	Total:
initial	50.0%	17.6%	100%	36.4%	N=14
preverbal	25.0%	**47.1%**	0%	27.3%	N=12
final	25.0%	35.3%	0%	36.4%	N=11
Total:	100% (N=4)	100% (N=17)	100% (N=5)	100% (N=11)	N=37

WH- questions are relatively infrequent in narrative. Out of 1154 finite clauses, only 48 (4.2%) are WH- questions; of these, three are WH- words appearing alone as interjections, and eight contain WH- words in final position in nominal and adjectival predicate constructions, which we exclude from further consideration since they do not contain a finite verb. The remaining WH- words are of four grammatical types: subject, object, oblique (morphologically marked for an oblique case, e.g. 'with whom?', 'from where?'), and Adverb ('where', 'when', 'how'). The distribution of WH- words in Sinhala is summarized in Table 2.

It is immediately obvious upon examining Table 2 that WH- words in Sinhala do not favor preverbal position. Even object WH- words show only a slight statistical preference for preverbal position (47.1%), despite this being the canonical location for objects (compare this percentage with the percentage of presented object NPs in preverbal position (94.5%) in Figure 1). Subjects and adverbials, on the other hand, are distributed relatively evenly across the three positions,[19] while obliques cluster in initial position. Ironically, the highest overall concentration of WH- words is in initial position — the position in the sentence conventionally considered to be *least* favored for focus functions.[20] What accounts for this distribution?

The explanation, we suggest, is partially discourse-based. More than one-third (35.1%) of the WH- questions in the Sinhala narratives are rhetorical in nature. These may be of the 'classical' type, which implies a universally quantified negative response ('Where would a bird learn stories?' = 'A bird wouldn't learn stories anywhere'), or alternatively, of the 'thematicizing' type,[21] which leads into the next narrative event ('What did he do then? He buried all his possessions'). WH- words in classical rhetorical questions

(CRQs) appear exclusively in initial or preverbal positions, in contrast with genuine information-seeking questions, which may place the WH- word in final position. This contrast is illustrated in examples (10)-(11):

(10) Sinhala (written folk tale) [CRQ]
dæn pænikirilli-ṭa harima duka-yi. ara aliya-t ekka
now hummingbird-DAT very sad-PRED. that elephant-also with
harima taraha-y. eet ***moka-da*** *kara-nne?*
very angry-PRED. still **what-Q** do-PRES-EMP
'Now the hummingbird is very sad. She is very angry with that elephant. But **what** can she do?' (i.e. 'She can't do anything')

(11) Sinhala (written folk tale) [info Q]
awasarayi deeway-an wahansa, ara maagal-ee wele-nḍa
permission lord-ACC HON-VOC that mat-LOC dry-INF
daa-la tiye-nne ***monawaa-da****?*
put-PPLE be-PRES-EMP **what-Q**
'Excuse me, your highness, **what** has been set to dry on that mat?'

In the information-seeking question in (11), posed by a character in a folk tale, the WH- word follows the finite verb, which is in the emphatic form, as is grammatically required. In (10), however, the question is rhetorical — in the given context, we understand it to mean 'she can't do anything' — and the WH- word appears *before* the emphatic form of the finite verb. Classical rhetorical questions comprise only 14.3% of WH- words in initial position, however, and thus make only a minor contribution to the higher incidence of WH- words in that location.

Thematicizing rhetorical questions (TRQs), on the other hand, typically situate the WH- word in postverbal position (e.g. 'Then he did *what*?'; see

Table 3. Position of Sahala WH-words by rhetorical type

	info Q	**CRQ**	**TRQ**	Total
initial	**50.0%**	**40.0%**	0%	N=14
preverbal	29.2%	**60.0%**	25.0%	N=12
final	20.8%	0%	**75.0%**	N=11
Total:	100% (N=24)	100% (N=5)	100% (N=8)	N=37

also example (7)), where they are closest to the narrative 'answer' which follows. Rhetorical questions of this type account for more than half (54.5%) of the postverbal WH- words in the Sinhala data, a concentration which significantly influences the overall incidence of WH- words in that position. Table 3 shows the positioning of WH- questions by rhetorical type. The most obvious conclusion to be drawn from these data is that the discourse functions of WH- words can and do affect their positioning in the sentence, and hence must be taken into account. True information-seeking questions statistically favor the placement of WH- words in initial position, CRQ's favor initial or preverbal[22] (but not final) position, and TRQ's favor final (but not initial) position. In all, this evidence offers no support whatsoever for the prediction that WH- words in Sinhala will occur preferentially in preverbal position — indeed, preverbal focus is *weaker* for WH- words overall than it is for new referent presentation.

2.3 *Focus and the rigid verb-final constraint*

The Sinhala findings presented thus far argue against the generalization that the 'linear order focus hypothesis' applies to all head-final languages. Sinhala is an otherwise well-behaved head-final language, yet it has final focus for presentation and thematicizing rhetorical questions, and initial focus for other question types. In his original formulation of the hypothesis (see (1) above), however, Kim appears to suggest that the restriction against focus postposing, and the resultant specialization of preverbal position for focus, might be a characteristic of rigidly verb-final languages only. If it could be demonstrated that Sinhala were a non-rigidly verb-final language, its lack of conformity to the predicted pattern might be explained; at the very least, it would not violate the prediction in (1).

In order to arrive at a measure of verb-finality for Sinhala, we sorted all of the finite clauses in the corpus into the categories 'verb-final' ((X)V), 'verb non-final' (VX), and 'verbless'.[23] The results are summarized in Table 4.

Table 4. Verb-finality in Sinhala

	(X)V	**VX**	**verbless**
% all finite clauses	66.5%	21.4%	12.0%
% verbal clauses only	75.6%	24.4%	—

Table 4 shows that three-quarters of all verbal clauses are verb-final, which is to say that one-quarter of clauses containing a finite verb do *not* have the verb in final position.[24] Although verb-final utterances are statistically preferred overall, Sinhala cannot be considered a rigidly verb-final language. This fact may account for the possibility of focusing nominals by moving them to the end of the sentence, beyond the finite verb.

3. Tamil

Tamil, like Sinhala, is a head-final type XXIII language. Unlike Sinhala, however, Tamil is rigidly verb-final. In the 11 written Tamil narratives analyzed, each and every verbal clause has the finite verb in final position; that is, there is 100% verb-finality.[25] Oral narratives, on the other hand, allow some postposing, although the percentage of verb-final verbal clauses is still extremely high (92.9%). The combined figures regarding verb-finality in Tamil are shown in Table 5. Given its high degree of verb-finality, Tamil is thus an ideal language in which to test the linear order focus hypothesis.

Kim (1988) includes Tamil in his list of languages which "show a noticeable disposition to put their WH- words in immediately preverbal position" (154). At the same time, he admits to gathering his data from a single source, Ganesan (1975), in which "there are not enough data to test the hypothesis in terms of the position of subject WH- words in ... Tamil" (153). He does however cite Ganesan's remarks concerning general focus and word order in Tamil:

> In his comparative study of Tamil and Hindi, Ganesan (1975) remarks that the unmarked word order of Tamil sentences is typically SOV, "however the order may be OSV if the subject is to be put in focus (p.456)," as in *putakam na:n etutte:n* [sic] 'I took the book' [lit. 'book I took' - SCH]. He also notes that in bitransitive sentences the dative NP usually precedes the accusative NP but this order may be reversed "if the dative object is in focus

Table 5. Verb-finality in Tamil

	(X)V	VX	verbless
% all finite clauses	83.0%	4.0%	13.0%
% verbal clauses only	95.4%	4.6%	—

> (p. 457)." Tamil adverbs seem to behave in a similar fashion. According to Ganesan, temporal as well as spatial adverbs occur in three optional positions: sentence-initial, medial, and immediately preverbal, but those adverbs occurring in the immediately preverbal position always receive a special focus interpretation (p. 459). (Kim 1988:153-4).

In the following sections, we evaluate how well the claim that Tamil has preverbal focus fits the distribution of presentational and WH- focus in actual narrative usage.

3.1 *Presentational focus in Tamil*

In our analysis of presentational focus in Tamil, the same procedure was followed as for Sinhala. That is, new mentions were identified and classified according to position in the sentence, and a graph showing the distribution of new mentions by position was plotted. The new mentions were then further broken down by grammatical role, and new Os in preverbal position excluded. Last, the relative degree of specialization of each position for new mentions was calculated.

The Sinhala data did not display significant differences in focus strategies between the written and the oral texts, since both were of a colloquial variety. However, preferred focus strategies differ in the written and spoken Tamil texts. We therefore present the findings for each modality separately in the discussion that follows.

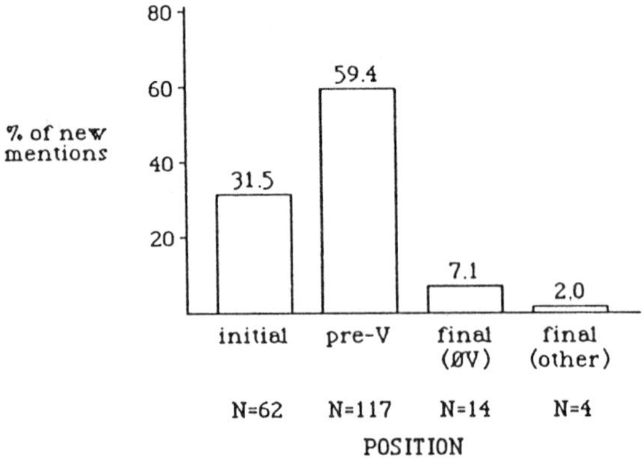

Figure 4. Distribution of new mentions in written Tamil (all grammatical roles)

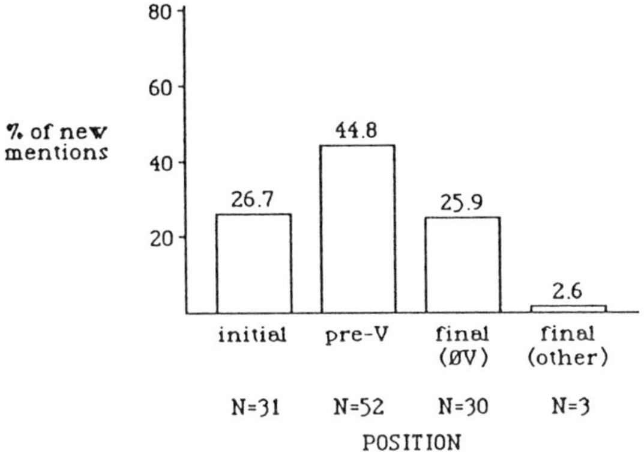

Figure 5. Distribution of new mentions in spoken Tamil (all grammatical roles)

The overall distribution of new mentions in Tamil is shown in Figures 4 and 5. As these figures show, preverbal new mentions in both written and spoken Tamil predominate numerically over new mentions in other sentential positions. The written texts have relatively more new mentions in preverbal position than the oral texts, however, and new mentions are less likely in the written texts than in the oral to appear in sentence-final position, i.e. in verbless (ØV) constructions (see below).[26] Tables 6 and 7 give the breakdown of new mentions by grammatical role.[27] New Os overwhelmingly favor preverbal position in both the written and spoken data, as was found in Sinhala. If we exclude Os, however, the two varieties display rather different patterns. New mentions in written Tamil show a preference for initial position when subjects, and preverbal position when obliques, suggesting a distributional pattern based on grammatical role (S-initial, O-preverbal), with a preference for preverbal Obliques (cf. Ganesan's observations on 'dative objects'). Spoken Tamil, in contrast, prefers to introduce new Ss in *final* position, and divides Obliques equally between initial and preverbal positions — a system in which neither grammatical conditioning nor preverbal focus plays an obvious role. The adjusted distribution of subject and oblique new mentions is represented graphically in Figure 6 (for written Tamil) and Figure 7 (for spoken Tamil).

Comparing Figure 6 with Figure 2, we see that written Tamil shows no greater degree of preverbal focus than does Sinhala. And spoken Tamil manifests no preference for preverbal focus at all — new mentions are evenly

Table 6. Position of written Tamil new mentions by grammatical role

	S	O	Obl	Total:
initial	44.8%	4.4%	34.0%	N= 62
preverbal	40.6%	**95.6%**	**66.0%**	N=115
final	14.6%	—	—	N= 14
Total:	100% (N=96)	100% (N=45)	100% (N=50)	N=191

Table 7. Position of spoken Tamil new mentions by grammatical role

	S	O	Obl	Total:
initial	26.9%	4.8%	50.0%	N=31
preverbal	28.4%	**95.2%**	50.0%	N=51
final	**44.8%**	—	—	N=30
Total:	100% (N=67)	100% (N=21)	100% (N=24)	N=112

distributed across the three major positions. These results are surprising, given that Tamil is more rigidly verb-final, and hence is predicted to have stronger preverbal focus according to the hypothesis in (1).

This is not to say that preverbal focus is non-existent in Tamil. On the contrary, the fact that many new Ss and obliques appear preverbally can be taken as evidence that the position has focus value.[28] Preverbal focus is most apparent in written Tamil; as for example in (12):

(12) Tamil (written historical narrative)
anta nātt-il ***oru aracaṉ*** *iru-nt-āṉ*
that country-LOC **one king** be-PAST-3SG:MASC
'In that country, (there) was **a king**.' (lit. '**a king** was')

As in the Sinhala example in (3), the referent is presented here as the subject of an intransitive predicate, and is situated between an initial locative adverbial and the finite verb, in this case, the verb *iru* 'to be'.

The Tamil children's story in the corpus makes systematic use of preverbal presentation. In this story, a puppy becomes separated from its master, a young boy, during the drive back from a mountain vacation resort. The puppy, although frightened, is determined to find its way back to the boy, and

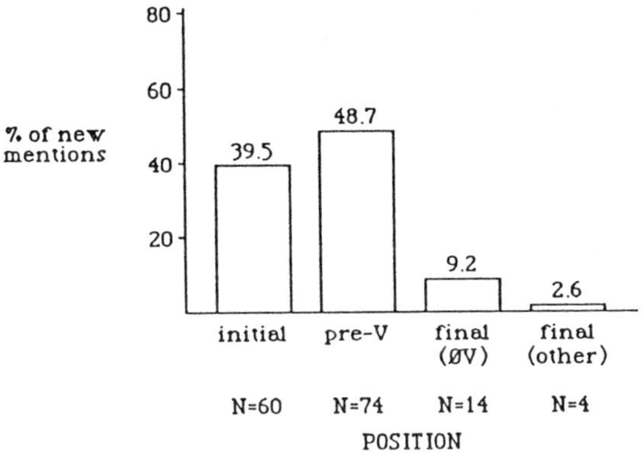

Figure 6. Distribution of non-object new mentions in written Tamil

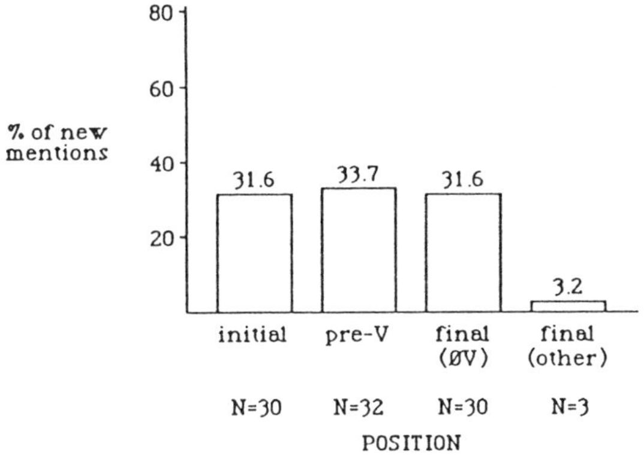

Figure 7. Distribution of non-object new mentions in spoken Tamil

sets out along the road. In the chapter analyzed, it encounters a series of larger animals — an adult dog, a mother bear and her two cubs, a lame horse — who befriend the puppy and offer it food, shelter, and advice along the way. Each of these animals is introduced preverbally, as the subject of an intransitive verb following a locative adverbial, as in example (13):

(13) Tamil (written children's story)
Pātai ōratt-il ***oru kutirai*** *mēyntu-koṇṭiru-nt-atu.*
path side-LOC **one horse** graze-CONT-PAST-3SG:N
'By the side of the path, **a horse** was grazing.'

Interestingly, however, the most central characters in this story — the puppy and the boy — are introduced not preverbally but as subjects in initial position, as in (14), the first mention of the boy.

(14) Tamil (written children's story)
avar-utaiya makaṉ katirvēl *nāy-kkuṭṭiy-iṭam aṉp-uṭaṉ*
he-GEN son Katirvel dog-child-LOC affection-with
paḻaki-va-nt-āṉ.
spend:time-come-PAST-3SG:MASC
'**His son Katirvel** used to spend time being affectionate with the puppy.'

This strategy is characteristic of main character presentation in the Tamil written narratives more generally, as reflected in the higher percentages of initial Ss in the first column in Table 6.

Preverbal focus is also employed to some extent in the oral narratives, especially in introducing non-central participants. Example (15) below is structurally and functionally analogous to written Tamil example (12) and Sinhala example (3):

(15) Tamil (oral folk tale)
Oru kāṭṭ-ile vantu, inta ***niṟaiya mirunkañ-kaḷ*** *iru-nt-atu.*
one forest-LOC TOP this **many animal-PL** be-PAST-3SG:N
'In a forest, this — there were **many animals**.' (lit. '**many animals** were')

Important referents, on the other hand, are introduced via a strategy which allows the new referent to appear in sentence-final position. Unlike in Sinhala, this is not accomplished by moving the referent to the right of the finite verb, since in Tamil postverbal position is generally reserved for intonationally backgrounded given or accessible referents.[29] Instead, the Tamil presen-tational construction omits the finite verb, resulting in an utterance type in which a nominal referent occupies absolute sentence-final position 'by default'. We refer to this phenomenon as 'verbless presentation'.[30]

As with the Sinhala postposing strategy, a verblessly presented constituent in Tamil is almost invariably new information, which is treated as given in the utterances that follow. This is illustrated in example (16), which immediately follows the utterance in (15) in the text of the narrative:

(16) Tamil (oral folk tale)
At-ile ***oru periya ciñkam****. Cinkatt-ai kaṇ-tā ellā ellā*
that-LOC **one big lion**. lion-ACC see-COND all all
animals-ukkum payam.
animals-DAT fear
'Among them, **a big lion**. Whenever (they) saw the lion, all the animals were afraid.'

The lion in this example is the villain of the story, and hence a central participant. The hero — a rabbit — is also introduced verblessly:

(17) *Appuṟam mūṉāvatu nāḷ vantu* ***oru muyal****. Cens*
then third day TOP **one rabbit**. chance
va-nt-atu.
come-PAST-3SG:N
'Then on the third day, **a rabbit**. (It's) turn came.'

In contrast, the other animals — both collectively and individually — are introduced in preverbal position, as are other secondary participants in the tale. In this respect, verbless presentation in Tamil functionally parallels presentational postposing in Sinhala, in that both specialize in the introduction of thematically important referents.

Verbless presentation is found in written Tamil as well, where it typically functions to set the physical or temporal scene:

(18) Tamil (written historical narrative)
Anta ūr-il ***oru tiruviḻā****. Tōli talaivi-ṭam, "talaivi,*
that town-LOC **one festival** friend heroine-LOC heroine
nāñkaḷ tiruviḻā pār-kka pō-kiṟ-ōm. Nīy-um vā-ȳeṉ"
we festival see-INF go-PRES-1PL you-and come-why
eṉ-ṟ-āḷ.
say-PAST-3SG:FEM
'In that town, **a festival**. Her friend said to the heroine, "Heroine, we're going to see the festival. Why don't you come along?'

Verbless presentation exhibits its own unique formal characteristics. Unlike in Sinhala, the presented NP must always be in the subject, or morphologically unmarked, case. The actual grammatical role played by the referent in the ongoing discourse is indicated by the case marking used when it is resumed in the following clause (e.g. accusative in (16) and genitive in (17); it may also be resumed inside of a quote, as in (18)). As for the 'missing' verb in such constructions, it need not be a simple verb of existence, as (17) attests; its interpretation relies heavily on the content of the immediately following utterance. Verbless presentation in Tamil is thus a grammatical strategy which can properly be understood *only* through the analysis of connected discourse.

The verbless construction, although accounting for only 13.7% of new mentions in the Tamil corpus overall, is highly specialized for new referent introduction. Out of 30 instances in the oral narratives, fully 88.2% contain new mentions or mentions reintroduced after a long hiatus. This figure subsumes two verbless construction types. The first, participant presentation as illustrated in (16) - (18), introduces referents that are new 89.3% of the time — more than five times the degree of specialization of preverbal position (17.5%). The second type is the 'dative subject' possessor construction, which occurs both with and without a finite verb. An example of the verbless variant is found in the last sentence in (16) — the expression *ellā animals-ukkum payam* literally translates as 'to all the animals, fear'. This clause introduces the notion of 'fear' into the discourse, although 'fear' is of course not a narrative participant in the same sense as is 'the lion' or 'the rabbit'. Dative subject constructions are primarily used in narrative to describe the existence (or coming into existence) of a physical or emotional state, and hence are semantically conditioned. At the same time, such constructions, *when verbless*, tend strongly to present states that are being mentioned for the first time: 83.3% of verbless dative subject constructions in the oral texts describe 'new' states of fear, anger, hunger, etc., as opposed to only 40.0% of those in which a finite verb appears. Although the dative subject construction and verbless presentation are grammatically distinct (i.e. by virtue of the presence or absence of a possessor NP in the dative case) and only partially congruent in function, it is nevertheless significant that the absence of a finite verb correlates with the presentational function in both.

The same tendencies are present in written Tamil, although to a weaker extent. Final verbless constructions, at 60.9% new, are considerably more specialized for new information than any other sentence position. Presentational-type constructions contain 64.7% new mentions, and dative-subject constructions contain new mentions exactly half the time. Interestingly, the majority (78%) of verbless constructions in the written data are not presentational but rather of the dative subject type, while the inverse is true in the oral

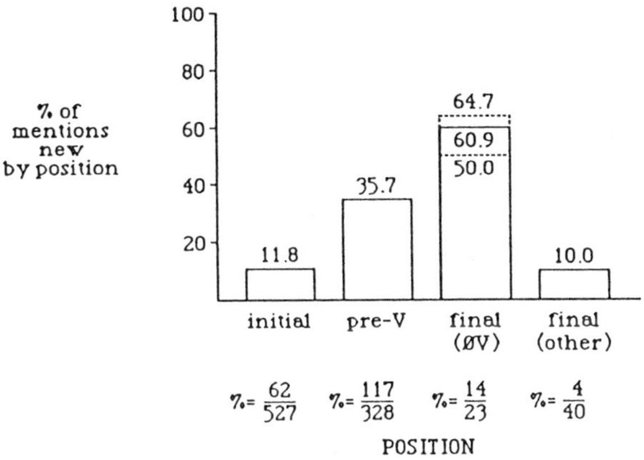

Figure 8. Specialization of positions for new mentions in written Tamil

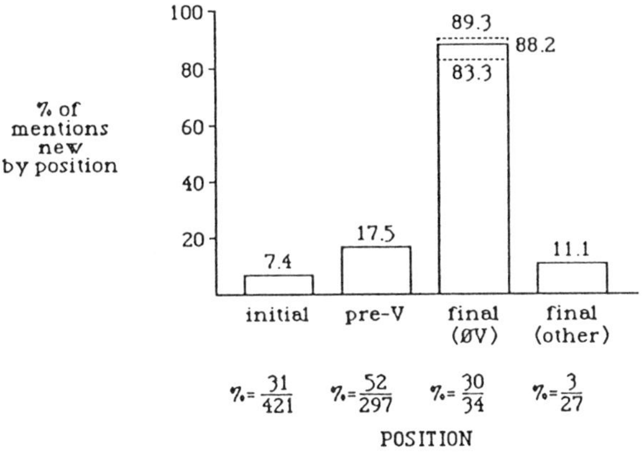

Figure 9. Specialization of positions for new mentions in spoken Tamil

data (87% presentational), reinforcing the view that verbless presentation is predominantly an oral strategy. Figures 8 and 9 represent the relative degree of specialization of each position for new mentions.

At this point, the reader is invited to consult Figure 3 again and to compare it with Figures 8 and 9. Despite differences of degree in written and spoken Tamil involving the verbless construction, the same pattern is evident in both Tamil varieties as is found in Sinhala: Final position is more specialized for new mentions than preverbal position, which in turn is more specialized than initial position. This is so, even though the final presentational strategy in each language is quite different — postposing in Sinhala, and verblessness in Tamil. The common thread appears to be that both provide a means of placing the presentationally focused constituent in sentence-final position, thereby circumventing the verb-final constraint. Thus despite its more rigid degree of verb-finality, Tamil does not support the predictions of the linear order focus hypothesis any better than does Sinhala, at least not for presentational focus.

3.2 *WH-focus in Tamil*

We come at last to the positioning of WH- words in Tamil, the area in which our data stand to confirm or disconfirm the linear order focus hypothesis most directly. From the 7.6% of finite clauses in the Tamil corpus containing WH-words (N=77), we excluded twelve instances appearing in final position in nominal predicate constructions, as was done in the previous analyses. Table 8 shows the distribution of the remaining tokens according to grammatical role and sentential position for the spoken and written data combined.[31]

The strong correlation (90.5%) evident in Table 8 between grammatical objects and preverbal position should by now be a familiar result. More

Table 8. Position of Tamil WH-words by grammatical role

	S	O	Obl	Adv	Interj	Total:
initial	**69.2%**	9.5%	0%	48.0%	75.0%	N=26
preverbal	30.8%	**90.5%**	100%	44.0%	0%	N=35
final	0%	0%	0%	8.0%	25.0%	N= 3
Total:	100% (N=13)	100% (N=21)	100% (N=1)	100% (N=25)	100% (N=4)	N=64

surprising is the correlation (69.2%) between subject WH- words and initial position, a pattern which, taken together with preverbal object WH- words, once again suggests grammatical conditioning, rather than a pragmatically motivated distribution. The distribution of WH- adverbs is also compatible with this view: adverbs are not assigned a fixed position in Tamil grammar, nor do the WH- adverbs in our data favor a single location, but rather are roughly evenly split between initial and preverbal positions. This is clearly not the distribution we would expect if WH- words, as inherently focused elements, were pragmatically conditioned to appear preverbally.

Although the above results were obtained in a manner consistent with Kim's methodological approach — i.e. by treating all WH- words as equally 'focused', in isolation from their contexts of use — in carrying out our analysis, we observed that the position of WH- words in the Tamil data was influenced by discourse functions. More than one-half of the WH- questions in the Tamil narratives are rhetorical; these include CRQs, TRQs, and WH-interjections (whereby the speaker expresses incredulity and/or disapproval without the expectation of a literal 'answer'). The three rhetorical question types are illustrated in (19) - (21).

(19) Tamil (written children's story) [CRQ]
Ēṉ *ippaṭi naṭuṉku-kiṟ-āy? Nay-kuṭṭi-kaḷ-ai nān*
why like:this tremble-PRES-2SG dog-child-PL-ACC I
cāppiṭu-vat-illai eṉṟu cirittu-koṇṭ-ē coll-iṟṟ-u.
eat-FUT:NZR-NEG QUOT laugh-CONT-EMPH say-PAST-3SG:N
'"**Why** are you trembling so? I don't eat puppies," [the bear] said laughingly.' (i.e. "There's no reason for you to tremble so...")

(20) Tamil (oral folk tale) [TRQ]
Uṭaṉē teṉālirāmaṉ ***eṉṉa*** *paṇṇ-iṉ-āṉ;*
immediately Tenaliraman **what** do-PAST-3SG:MASC
mīti pāl elām nallā āṟa va-ccu, avaṉ-um avaṉ
remainder milk all well boil put-PPLE he-and his
kuṭumpam-um uṭkār-ntu, ellātt-aiy-um kuṭi-cciru-cc-u.
family-and sit-PPLE all-ACC-and drink-PERF-PAST-3SG:N
'And then **what** did Tenaliraman do? Having boiled all the milk, he and his family sat down and drank it all up.'

(21) Tamil (oral folk tale) [WH- interjection]
"Tay-ē.. nāṉ uṉṉ-uṭaiya paktaṉ-āka iru-kkiṉṟavaṉ.
mother-VOC I you-GEN devotee-ADV be-one:who:is
Ippaṭi nāḷ kaṇakk-āka, māta kaṇakk-āka, āṇṭu
like:this day measure-ADV month measure-ADV year
kaṇakk-āka vantu-koṇṭiru-kkiṟ-ēṉ-ē; eṉ-akku ***eṉṉa***
measure-ADV come-CONT-PRES-1SG-TAG I-DAT **what**
nī aruḷ paṇṇa-maṭṭ-ēṉ ñ-kiṟ-ēy.
you grace do-FUT:NEG-1SG say-PRES-2SG
'O goddess! I am your devotee. Day after day, month after month, year after year I come to you like this, right? And **what**, you refuse to grant me your grace?!'

The location of WH- words in Tamil according to rhetorical function is summarized in Table 9.[32] Unlike Sinhala WH- words, these data display a noticeable tendency towards preverbal focus, especially in TRQs and information questions. This would seem to suggest that Tamil WH- words can indeed be analyzed as favoring preverbal focus, but only when their rhetorical functions are taken into account.

Upon closer examination, however, even this claim is problematic. Many of the question words in preverbal position are grammatical objects, creating an overall bias in favor of preverbal position — particularly in the case of TRQs — which does not accurately reflect the pragmatic word order preferences of the language. That is, while it is a potentially interesting fact of usage that the vast majority of thematicizing rhetorical questions in Tamil involve an object WH- word (see e.g. example (20)), this distribution cannot be used to

Table 9. Position of Tamil WH-words by rhetorical type (all grammatical roles)

	info Q	**CRQ**	**TRQ**	**Interj**	Total:
initial	3.3%	58.3%	20.0%	60.0%	N=21
preverbal	**62.5%**	41.7%	**80.0%**	0%	N=32
final	4.2%	0%	0%	40.0%	N= 3
Total:	100% (N=24)	100% (N=12)	100% (N=15)	100% (N=5)	N=56

Table 10. Position of Tamil WH-adverbs by rhetorical type

	info Q	CRQ	TRQ	Total:
initial	33.3%	**71.4%**	50.0%	N=11
preverbal	**58.3%**	28.6%	25.0%	N=10
final	8.3%	0%	25.0%	N= 2
Total:	100% (N=12)	100% (N=7)	100% (N=4)	N=23

argue for preverbal WH- focus in Tamil, since the occurrence of objects in preverbal position could equally well be explained by grammatical conditioning. The occurrence of initial subjects in these data is similarly suspect; only adverbs are neutral in their distribution, as indicated in Table 8. What, then, of the distribution of WH- adverbs alone? This is shown in Table 10.[33]

These data show that WH- adverbs in information questions display a preference (58.3%) for preverbal position. In contrast, CRQs (and TRQs as well, although the number of tokens involved is not significant) prefer to situate the WH- adverb in initial position. When the WH- questions in the data are analyzed separately according to rhetorical function, therefore, it becomes possible to perceive a pattern which supports, at least in part, the claims of the linear order focus hypothesis — that is, WH- adverbs in information questions appear to prefer preverbal position. However the claim that preverbal position is favored for WH- words *independent* of their grammatical role or rhetorical function is not supported by the Tamil data, nor is Kim's larger claim extending his predictions to pragmatic 'focus' more generally.

4. Implications and conclusions

In our discussion thus far, we have been primarily concerned to draw attention to the ways in which the placement of focused elements in Sinhala and Tamil provide counter-evidence to the claim that focus position in SOV languages is immediately preverbal. Our findings also enable us to venture several positive observations regarding the expression of focus in Sinhala and Tamil, and to hypothesize about the typological correlates of focus positions in SOV languages more generally.

In the course of our analysis, we discovered intriguing evidence in both languages of sentence-final presentational focus, true to the spirit of Hetzron's (1975) claim. Sinhala focuses presented referents by moving them to the right of the finite verb, in violation of the 'verb-final constraint' characteristic of head-final SOV languages. Tamil circumvents the verb-final constraint by omitting the finite verb, leaving the focused nominal in sentence-final position. However, the Tamil findings suggest that Hetzron's claim, inasmuch as it is formulated in terms of presentative *movement*, needs to be modified to accomodate cases where no movement is involved.[34] Future discourse-based studies of other SOV languages may well turn up evidence of as yet unidentified and potentially even more inventive sentence-final presentational strategies, especially if colloquial spoken usage is considered.[35]

The fact that such differences exist may well reflect a typological dimension. A possible explanation for the differences between Sinhala and Tamil presentational focus is that Tamil is more rigid in its word order, and in particular, in its degree of verb-finality. By allowing greater word order freedom, Sinhala makes it possible to employ different word orders for discourse-pragmatic ends, as is manifested both in its predilection for postverbal presentation, and rhetorically-controlled WH- word placement. Tamil, on the other hand, displays an overall preference for placing subjects initially and objects preverbally, although the position of adverbs is more free. (Note that in omitting the finite verb, Tamil is not violating any word *order* constraint: the resultant structure typically has the form *(Adv) S*).[36] Rigidness of verb-finality, then, may be related to the degree to which a language exercises pragmatic as opposed to grammatical control of word order, which in turn determines the placement of focused elements.

At the same time that we have identified a tendency toward final focus, our findings also provide limited support for the notion of preverbal focus. Both languages 'present' new referents preverbally more often than in any other position, and preverbal position is relatively more specialized for the presentational function than is initial position. In addition, there is some statistical evidence that Tamil favors preverbal position for WH- adverbs in information questions. The problem, however, lies in interpreting these patterns. A precise statistical criterion for preferred focus position has never been proposed — is something a 'preference' if it holds in 60% of the cases? 40%? 20%? Clearly the relative frequencies of other positions must be factored into the analysis as well, along with their degree of functional specialization. Yet what of cases where these differing measures produce conflicting results? Preverbal focus position in our data is preferred for presentation in terms of sheer numbers, but final position is more specialized in the presentational function; which is more basic?

We suggest that these two focus positions are employed in different functions and for different effect, at least in the languages analyzed here. Final position, as a less frequent and hence more marked strategy, is favored for the presentation of central, salient participants. Preverbal position, on the other hand, is used for secondary participants, as well as for a variety of other elements, only some of which are accorded a focus interpretation. This pattern is found in the oral narratives in Tamil, and in both the oral and written Sinhala data. As for WH- focus, Sinhala regularly employs postverbal position for thematicizing rhetorical questions (TRQs), a strategy which is iconic with their function of introducing narrative events in the clauses which immediately follow. Conversely, both languages prefer early sentence positions for WH-words in classical rhetorical questions (CRQs), a reflection perhaps of the non-literal (and hence less focused?) nature of questions of this type.

One obvious conclusion to be drawn from these observations is that 'focus' cannot be treated as a homogeneous category in studies of word order variation. Although our findings do not support the hypothesis that presentational focus is final, and WH- focus preverbal, we have nevertheless discovered systematic differences in the preferred placement of the two focus types in each language. Moreover, WH- words pattern differently according to their rhetorical function, suggesting that it is not enough to distinguish WH- focus from other focus types — one must identify rhetorical WH- subtypes as well. Any typological study of focus phenomena which fails to take these distinctions into account is destined to generate oversimplistic generalizations which make inappropriate predictions for some focus types. The claim that immediately preverbal position is *the* focus position in SOV languages is one such generalization.

Notes

* The authors wish to thank Jim Gair and Tom Givón for reading and commenting helpfully on an earlier draft of this paper, and Rev. Tapowanaya Sutadhara and Rev. Kadurugamuwe Nagita for providing the oral Sinhala data.

1. The actual term used by Hetzron is 'presentative'; we employ the more widely-used term 'presentational' here.

2. Although genetically unrelated, Sinhala and Tamil are spoken in close proximity to one another, and have a long history of contact. A number of grammatical borrowings have made their way into Sinhala from Tamil, including, most notably for the purposes of the present paper, an emphatic or 'contrastive' focus construction (Gair 1986; see also fn.30).

3. The second-language texts are *Advanced Spoken Sinhala Reader*, by W.S. Karunatillake (Kelaniya University, Sri Lanka), and *Tamil Madhu: Sangam Mudal Bharati Varai*, by Kausalya Hart (University of California, Berkeley).

4. Less than 10% of all referents which appear as the focus of a presentational construction were previously introduced.

5. In order to simplify our exposition, which primarily evaluates preverbal as opposed to postverbal focus, we conflate first and second positions into a single 'initial' position. Filled second position slots are infrequent in these data; the majority of 'initial' mentions (85% in Sinhala; 81% in Tamil) appear in (absolute) first position. Moreover, the density of new mentions in first and second positions is similarly low for the corpus overall — 7% of mentions in first position in Sinhala are new, as compared with 4% of those in second position, and the Tamil figures are 9% and 10% respectively.

6. This figure combines the two 'final mention' categories. The first contains postposed mentions which appear after a finite verb. The 'other' category is reserved for sentences in which no finite verb appears, and includes instances of ellipsis as well as nominal predication.

7. The category labelled S includes subjects of both intransitive and transitive predicates. The vast majority of new Ss in the languages considered here are intransitive subjects, however, in keeping with the tendency noted by Du Bois (1987) for speakers to avoid introducing new mentions as transitive subjects. (For an analysis of new mentions by transitivity for Tamil, see Herring (1989).)

8. Excluded from the total are final mentions in the verbless 'other' category, as such instances cannot be used to argue for a particular position vis-à-vis the finite verb.

9. Abbreviations in glosses follow standard practice (see list on p. ix). In addition, the following abbreviations are used: PPLE 'past participle', NZR 'nominalizer', and 3SG:N 'third person singular neuter'.

10. There are two forests in the story, one on either bank of the river.

11. Unlike in English, the postposed nominal in constructions of this sort need not be the subject of an intransitive predicate, but rather may occur in any thematic or case role. Postposed Os and obliques are relatively less frequent than postposed Ss overall, however, a skewing which we attribute to pragmatic principles governing the preferred argument roles for the introduction of new information, rather than to any constraint on the syntax of presentational focus constructions per se.

12. Although the Sinhala examples cited in this discussion are drawn from colloquial written narratives, the tendency toward postverbal focus is equally strong — indeed, somewhat stronger — in the oral narratives.

13. We use the term 'accessible information' to refer to information which the speaker assumes the hearer can infer or otherwise access (Du Bois (1987); cf. Chafe's (1987) 'semi-active' category, and Prince's (1981) 'inferrables'). In our data, accessible mentions are those conventionally associated with a previously mentioned referent, as in e.g. the mention of a body part ('his hand') after the individual as a whole ('a man') has been introduced, mention of 'the villagers' after we have already learned of the existence of 'a village', and '(his/her/its) mother', *except* in cases where the hand, villagers, or mother are themselves thematic narrative participants.

14. By 'functionally complete', we intend 'sufficiently specified to make sense in the discourse context in which it occurs'. Sinhala and Tamil are both zero anaphora languages, and thus completeness cannot be determined by the presence or absence of syntactic arguments alone.

15. In keeping with this last observation, it follows that distinguishing between instances of presentational and afterthought postposing requires taking the discourse context into account.

16. This is the case for true information-seeking questions. In rhetorical WH- questions, a non-emphatic form of the verb is sometimes used.

17. These figures take into account only adverbs and non-WH- lexical NPs — that is, only those elements that could conceivably qualify as new mentions. If we include WH- words and clausal constituents in the count, the distribution shifts: 56.1% preverbal, and 43.9% postverbal.

18. An avenue for further research would be to analyze the functions of the postposed emphatics in the subsequent discourse. If Hetzron's claims are correct, we would predict that postposed mentions would be carried over as thematic material in the immediately following clauses, while preverbal emphatic mentions would not.

19. The occurrence of two subject WH- words in initial position, as compared with one in each of the other positions, cannot be construed as sufficient evidence of a preference for placing subject WH- words in initial position.

20. See Herring (1990) for discussion. An exception is Givón (1990), who argues that initial position is universally preferred for contrastive focus.

21. These terms are from Herring (1991).

22. Of the three instances in the preverbal category, however, two are repetitions of a formulaic expression, *(Api) monawa karanna da* 'Whatever shall we do?' (lit. 'we what to do?'), in which the order of elements is fixed.

23. The verbless category in Sinhala includes nominal/adjectival predication and ellipsis.

24. In addition to postposed new referents, afterthoughts, and emphatics, clausal constituents and quotes may also appear postverbally in Sinhala. This accounts for the higher percentage of postposings than is indicated by the number of postposed elements in Figure 3.

25. This exceptionless adherence to verb-finality reflects the normative, pedagogical orientation of the written texts in our corpus. Word order in modern Tamil short stories and novels is somewhat less strict (Herring, To appear).

26. An analogous distinction exists between Colloquial and Literary Sinhala. Presentational postposing appears in the colloquial language, but is lacking in more literary varieties (Paolillo 1992). Since the present corpus contains only colloquial written and spoken texts, however, this distinction does not surface in our analysis.

27. Excluded from the total in Table 6 are the four instances of final mentions in the 'other' category, along with two adverbial constituents which, for grammatical reasons, could not have appeared in any but preverbal position. Excluded from Table 7 are three instances of final mentions in the 'other' category, and two adverbial constituents.

28. Where a single NP appears preverbally, its position was coded as 'initial' if it was the grammatical subject, and 'preverbal' if it was the object or an oblique argument of the verb. Thus all instances of 'preverbal subjects' involve cases where an S appears immediately before the verb, and is preceded by some other element.

29. In this respect, Tamil is consistent with the claims of Kim for rigid verb-final languages. An example of a postposed given referent is the following:

    (i) Tamil (oral real-life account)
    Appuṟam vantu, oru leṭar pōṭ-ṭ-ā.
    afterwards TOP one letter put-PAST-3SG:FEM
    Añke yār-ukkum paṭi-kka teriy-ātu, ***anta leṭar-ai.***
    there no:one-DAT read-INF be:known-NEG **that letter-ACC**
    'Afterwards, she sent a letter. No one there could read it, *the letter.*'

    Such postposings can be afterthoughts (i.e. repairs or clarifications) or conventionalized 'antitopics' with specific discourse-level functions (see Herring (to appear) for a detailed treatment of this phenomenon).

30. Tamil also has a cleft construction (on which the Sinhala emphatic construction was calqued (Gair 1986)) which allows movement of nominals to the right of the (nominalized) verb. However, there are no instances of this construction in our data.

31. Because of the smaller numbers of tokens in this analysis, we did not separate the spoken and written data. However, no obvious patterned differences between the two varieties emerged on the basis of the examples available.

32. For the purposes of this analysis, eight WH- elements expressing indefinite quantification (*eṉṉa* NP-*um* 'whatever NP'; *eppaṭiyō* 'somehow or the other', etc.) were excluded from the data.

33. The difference between the total number of WH- adverbs here and in Table 8 is a consequence of excluding indefinite quantifiers (see fn.32), two of which are adverbial.

34. It is also possible that Hetzron's claim should be modified to include only SVO and SOV languages, since it is for languages of these types that the most convincing evidence has been adduced. Hetzron's claim that sentence-final presentational focus is 'universal' must be considered suspect, since his data contain no examples from verb-initial languages (save for one Arabic example in which the verb — an optional copula — is deleted). In fact, the available evidence suggests that focus position in verb-initial languages is immediately before or after the finite verb, rather than sentence final (see sources in Herring (1990)).

35. Verbless presentation is never mentioned in grammatical descriptions of Tamil, nor is it accepted as fully grammatical by native speaker informants when examples are presented as isolated sentences.

36. See examples (16)-(18).

References

Chafe, Wallace L. 1987. "Cognitive constraints on information flow." *Cohesion and Grounding in Discourse* ed. by R. Tomlin, 21-51. Amsterdam/Philadelphia: John Benjamins.

Du Bois, John W. 1987. "The discourse basis of ergativity." *Language* 63.805-55.

Erguvanı, Eser E. 1984. *The Function of Word Order in Turkish Grammar*. Berkeley: University of California Press.

Gair, James W. 1970. *Colloquial Sinhalese Clause Structures*. The Hague: Mouton.

Gair, James W. 1986. "Sinhala focussed sentences: naturalization of a calque." *Structure, Convergence and Diglossia* ed. by Bh. Krishnamirti, C.P. Masica and A.K. Sinha, 147-67. New Delhi: Motilal Banarsidass.

Ganesan, S.N. 1975. *A Contrastive Grammar of Hindi and Tamil*. Madras: University of Madras.

Givón, T. 1990. *Syntax: A Functional-Typological Introduction*, Vol. 2. Amsterdam/ Philadelphia: John Benjamins.

Greenberg, Joseph H. 1966. "Some universals of grammar with particular attention to the order of meaningful elements." *Universals of Language* ed. by J.H. Greenberg, 73-113. Cambridge. Mass.: MIT Press.

Halliday, M.A.K. 1967. "Notes on transitivity and theme in English: Part 2." *Journal of Linguistics* 3.199-244

Harris, Alice. 1981. *Georgian Syntax*. London: Cambridge University Press.

Herring, Susan C. 1989. "Verbless presentation and the discourse basis of ergativity." *Proceedings of the Twenty-fifth Annual Chicago Linguistics Society, Parasession on Language in Context*, 123-35.

Herring, Susan C. 1990. "Information structure as a consequence of word order type." *Proceedings of the Sixteenth Annual Berkeley Linguistics Society*, 163-74.

Herring, Susan C. 1991. "The grammaticalization of rhetorical questions in Tamil." In *Approaches to Grammaticalization* Vol. 1 ed. by E.C. Traugott and B. Heine, 253-284. Amsterdam: John Benjamins.

Herring, Susan C. To appear. "Afterthoughts, antitopics and emphasis in Tamil." In *Theoretical Approaches to Word Order in South Asian Languages* ed. by M. Butt, T. King, and G. Ramchand. Stanford: Center for the Study of Language and Information.

Hetzron, Robert. 1975. "The presentative movement, or why the ideal word order is V.S.O.P." *Word Order and Word Order Change* ed. by C.N. Li, 347-388.

Kim, Alan H. 1985. "The functions of linear order in Korean syntax." *Harvard Studies in Korean Linguistics*, 154-167. Cambridge: Harvard University.

Kim, Alan H. 1988. "Preverbal focusing and type XXIII languages." *Studies in Syntactic Typology* ed. by M. Hammond, E. Moravcsik and J.R. Wirth, 147-169. Amsterdam/ Philadelphia: John Benjamins.

Kuno, Susumo. 1978. *Danwa no Bunpo* (The Grammar of Discourse). Tokyo: Taishukan.

Leech, Geoffrey N. and Michael H. Short. 1981. *Style in Fiction: A linguistic approach to English fictional prose*. London: Longman.

Paolillo, John C. 1992. *Functional Articulation in Diglossia: A case study of grammatical and social correspondences in Sinhala*. Ph.D dissertation, Stanford University.

Prince, Ellen F. 1981. "Toward a taxonomy of given – new information." *Radical Pragmatics* ed. by P. Cole. New York: Academic Press.

Word order at the noun phrase level in Japanese

Quantifier constructions and discourse functions*

Alan Hyun-Oak Kim
Southern Illinois University at Carbondale

1. Introduction

In Japanese sentences, arguments have considerable freedom in taking positions without changing their grammatical relations (GFs), a phenomenon which is known as scrambling. The reordering of arguments from one syntactic position to another in a clause or sentence is not, however, completely free. In actuality it is subject to a number of restrictions. First, no elements occur after the predicating verb, so as to keep the verb stationary at the clause-final position (as per the verb-final constraint).[1] Second, when arguments are presented without explicit case-marking, as in the case of casual conversations, such arguments appear in the unmarked basic S-IO-DO-V order. Third, as studies indicate (e.g., Kuno 1973b; Desző 1982; Kim 1988), syntactic positions, particularly the sentence-initial position and the immediately preverbal position, are generally reserved for two distinct discourse functions — Topic and Focus, respectively. Lastly, scrambling is predominantly a main clause phenomenon. It takes place typically at the level of matrix clauses. This may be because the main clause is the domain which is most susceptible to pragmatic influences from discourse contexts.

An NP is another syntactic level which is regarded as highly susceptible to reordering because it very often contains argument-like constituents and a rich array of adjectival modifiers within the structure. However, one may expect that the constituents within an NP (particularly derived nominals) may be reordered with less freedom (particularly when the NP is not derived from a clause by nominalization) for the following reasons: the relatively restricted syntactic domain in comparison with the clause; the lack of syntactic cues for GFs such as case-marking and a predicate (i.e. a verb); and the relatively lower susceptibility to pragmatic influences from the discourse context as a consequence of its being in a syntactically lower locus.[2]

A quantified NP displays rich word order variations, as a result of the interaction of its various structural components. In addition, the presence or absence of a set of particles such as the attributive marker and case markers multiplies the complexity of the word order of quantified NPs in Japanese.[3]

1.1 *The purpose of the study and organization*

The main concern of this paper is to examine the word order effects within quantified NPs. It will show that there are eight distinct word order patterns in Japanese discourse, and that each of these word order patterns is assigned to specific discourse and semantic functions which are involved with semantic features such as Definiteness and Specificity, on the one hand, and discourse features such as Emphasis, New/Given and Anaphoricity, on the other.

This paper is organized in three parts. In the first part some preliminary information regarding the nature of the data and terminologies applied in this study is provided. In the second section the earlier classifications of Q-constructions by Martin and Downing are reviewed, and then contrasted with the typology proposed in this study. The third section, which is the main body of the paper, is devoted entirely to the distribution and functional profile of each of the Q-constructions. I also discuss some issues that fall out as byproducts from the present study, such as relativized Q-Float constructions, the extended notion of specificity, particularly when it is combined with the indefinite feature, a specific role of the quantifier constructions (Q-Shift and Q-Float) in categorical negation, and some diachronic implications of the development of Q-Float in Japanese.

1.2 *Previous studies*

The quantifier constructions, particularly Quantifier Float in Japanese, have drawn considerable attention, mainly from the syntactic point of view. For instance, Shibatani (1977) shows that Quantifier Float co-occurs only with NPs with surface cases of Nominative and Accusative, but not with other oblique cases. Kamio (1977), Inoue (1978), Kuno (1978a), and Haig (1980), and more recently Miyagawa (1989) have made significant contributions to our understanding of the syntactic nature of Quantifier Floating in Japanese.[4] However, the semantics and pragmatics of Quantifier Float (or for that matter, numeral quantifier constructions in general) have largely been left untouched, except for Downing's (1984, 1985, 1986, 1993) systematic studies, which substantiate Martin's (1975) earlier work, and some fragmentary analyses by Kim (1982, 1990).

1.3 *Preliminaries*

This section provides preliminary background information on terminologies and other particulars in data collection.

1.3.1 *Definition of quantifier constructions*

A quantifier construction consists of two parts: a structure containing a quantifier and a noun which it quantifies. A quantifier (Q) refers in this paper to a phrase consisting of two basic elements, namely a numeral and a classifier, as shown schematically in (1).

(1) $[\text{Numeral + Classifier}]_Q$[5]

Numerals in this paper subsume cardinal numbers and two classes of special quantifiers known as universal quantifiers (e.g. *subete*, *zenbu* and *minna* 'all'), and existential quantifiers (e.g. *sukosi*, *zyakkan*, and *ikuraka* 'some'). Ordinal numbers, frequency quantifiers (e.g. *iti do* and *hito tabi* 'once') and adverb-ialized, non-numeral quantifiers like *tyotto* 'a little' and *hotondo* 'almost' are excluded from the present data. A classifier (or 'counter' as they are referred to by some authors) is a marker of genus in counting, as *hai* 'cup,' in *go hai no tya* 'five cups of tea,' *satu* 'volume' in *san satu no hon* 'three books' and *too* 'head' in *ni too no usi* 'two cows.' Classifiers do not appear in non-numerical expressions such as *sukosi/ikuraka* 'some,' *takusan* 'many' and *minna* 'all.'

A quantifier combines with an NP to form a quantifier construction (Q-construction). The schema (2a) or its simplified version (2b) below represents one of the typical quantifier constructions.

(2) a. [[Numeral + Classifier $]_Q$-*no* N $]_{NP}$-κ
b. [Q-*no* N $]_{NP}$-κ
where κ is a case-marker which may be optionally deleted.[6]

A quantifier, Q in the representation of (2a), quantifies NP (hereafter simply N), which refers to the referent (or the base) of Q. The quantifier Q together with the attributive marker *no* forms a modifier phrase for the referent N.[7]

The position of Q varies — Q may appear before or after its referent N inside the NP boundary, but it may also occur outside the NP boundary. A quantifier sometimes appears, not in a sentence where its referent (antecedent) NP resides, but in a separate sentence.

1.3.2 *The data*

In this study, a total of 1,066 examples of the Q-construction were collected from twelve texts of different genres. Efforts were made in selecting the texts to cover a wide range of samples — contemporary novels and texts of Old Japanese.

Besides ordinal numbers, frequency quantifiers (*iti do* 'once'), and numeral quantifiers used for anaphoric pro-forms, such as *hutari* 'the two persons,' 'both,' or *hitotu-wa...moo hitotu-wa* 'one... the other' are also excluded.[8]

2. Previous classifications

In this section I review earlier classifications in Martin (1975) and Downing (1984).

2.1 *Martin's classification*

Martin (1975:777) groups Japanese quantifier constructions under six categories: Basic, Inverted Apposition, Adverbialization, Preposed Adverbialization, Appositional Ellipsis, and Reduced Appositional Ellipsis. As is apparent from the way in which these classes are named, Martin's classification is based on the consideration of syntactic factors (e.g. word order) on the one hand, and semantic factors on the other. These six categories are summarized below. For ease of identification, I have changed Martin's original numbering.

(3) **Martin's Basic Types**

a. ***Basic*** (Number predicated and adnominalized to Noun)
*[**Ni-mai** no irogami] o totta*
two-CLASS-ATT colored paper-ACC took[9]
'I took (the) two pieces of colored paper.'

a'. **Inverted Apposition** (Number [*no*] | N → N || Number)
*[Irogami **ni-mai**] o totta*
colored paper two-CLASS-ACC took
'I took (the) two pieces of colored paper'

b. **Adverbialization** (N-*ga/o* | Number)
*[Irogami] o [**ni-mai**] totta*
colored paper-ACC two-CLASS took
'I took (the) two pieces of colored paper.'

b'. **Preposed Adverbialization** (N-*ga/o* | Number → Number || N *ga/o*)
*[**Ni-mai**] [irogami] o totta*
two-CLASS colored paper-ACC took
'I took (the) two pieces of colored paper.'

c. **Appositional Ellipsis** (N-*no* Number)
*[Irogami no **ni-mai**] o totta*
colored paper-ATT two-CLASS-ACC took
'I took two of the pieces of colored paper.'

c'. **Reduced Appositional Ellipsis** (N-*no* Number → N | Number
*Irogami **ni-mai** o totta*
colored paper two-CLASS-ACC took
'I took two of the pieces of colored paper.'

Martin suggests that (3a'), (3b') and (3c') above are derived from (3a), (3b), and (3c), respectively. In his analysis the derivation of Inverted apposition from the basic type involves two processes: swapping the positions of Q with N, and dropping the Attributive *no* from the Q. Shibatani (1977:798) takes a similar position and calls this transformation Quantifier Shifting. Q-Shifting was generally believed to cause no significant meaning changes. Thus, (4a) and (4b) below are transformationally related by Q-Shifting.

(4) a. **Basic Pattern**

*Kurokawa tantei wa genba de [**san-tyoo-no***
K. detective-TOP site-at three-CLASS-ATT
suiminzai-o] hakkensita.
sleeping pills-ACC discovered
'Detective Kurokawa discovered three sleeping pills at the site'

b. **Inverted apposition pattern (or Quantifier-Shifting)**

Kurokawa tantei wa genba de [suiminzai
K. detective-TOP site-at sleeping pills
***san-tyoo**]-o hakkensita.*
three-CLASS-ACC discovered
'Detective Kurokawa discovered three sleeping pills at the site'

Native speakers of Japanese may find no significant meaning differences between the two sentences above. Even if some semantic differences are perceived, generally such differences would be too subtle to notice. However, in certain situations, semantic differences do emerge. Consider the following:

(5) a. **The basic pattern**

*Sono ziko de [**go-nin-no** keganin ga]*
that accident-by five-CLASS-ACC injured person-NOM
deta
emerged
'There were five injuries in the accident'

b. **The inverted pattern**

*%Sono ziko de [keganin **go-nin**-ga] deta*[10]
that accident-by injured person five-CLASS-NOM emerged
'There were five injuries in the accident'

c. **The adverbialization**

Sono ziko-de [*keganin-ga*] ***go-nin*** deta
that accident-by injured person-NOM five-CLASS emerged
'There were five injuries in the accident'

Many native speakers would take (5a) to be equivalent to (5c) but not to (5b). Unlike the other two, (5b) may be seen as strange because it sounds as if the speaker somehow knew that there would be a specific group of people who would get involved in an accident ahead of time. In other words, the 'inverted' quantifier construction *keganin go-nin* ('five injured persons') in (5b) has a reading of <specificity> in addition to the <indefinite> feature. In general, an NP is interpreted as having the features of <indefinite> and <specific> when the speaker has some specific information about the NP, but the speaker does not share it with the hearer at the time of utterance.[11] In other words, the NP is indefinite to the hearer, but specific to the speaker. Thus, the hearer of (5b) would assume that the speaker possesses a certain "predetermined" or "preemptive" knowledge even before the accident. Hence, the anomaly of (5b). In short, because of such apparent semantic differences between (5a) and (5b), the transformational analysis is difficult to maintain even in traditional terms. We will therefore simply assume that they are two distinct types of the Q-construction.

Martin argues that Appositional Ellipsis (3c) may have an underlying source like (6), from which the square-bracketed part is subsequently deleted. This analysis, however, is untenable because it is apparently based on semantically ill-formed underlying structures. Let us look at sentence (6) more carefully.

(6) *Irogami no* **ni-mai** *[no [irogami]] o* *totta*
colored paper-ATT two-CLASS ATT colored paper-ACC took
'I took two sheets [of paper] of the paper.'

Martin justifies a sentence like (6) by showing the existence of a sentence pattern (7) which is parallel to the pattern of (6).

(7) *Hyaku-mai no* *irogami-no* ***ni-mai**-o* *totta.*
hundred-CLASS-ATT colored paper-ATT two-CLASS-ACC took
I took two of the hundred pieces of colored paper.'

However, such parallelism is ungrounded. Sentence (6) is extremely strange and difficult to process, if not totally unacceptable to many native speakers, including myself. Furthermore, the parallelism between (6) and (7) is simply superficial. That is to say, the first word of (6), *irogami* , and the first word of (7), *hyaku-mai*, are not at all semantically compatible. Sentence (7) is a typical partitive sentence, and perfectly grammatical, while sentence (6) does not allow such a partitive reading. Thus, we will establish a quantifier type equivalent to Martin's Appositional Ellipsis as a separate entity.

Martin suggests that Reduced Appositional Ellipsis is a short version of Appositional Ellipsis via the deletion of Attributive *no*. Thus, *irogami no ni-*

mai in (3c) and *irogami ni-mai* in (3c') are considered to be identical, except for the absence of the Attributive *no* in the latter. However, this deletion analysis seems lack empirical support. Consider the following conversational fragments:

(8) a. *Watasi-wa* ***ni-mai*** *dake torimasita.*
I-TOP two-CLASS only took
'I took only two cards (sheets) of them.'

b. *Ni-mai tte nan-no* ***ni-mai*** *desitaka?*
two-CLASS mentioned what-ATT two-sheets was-Q
'Two cards of what?'

A proper and felicitous response to question (8b) can be (9a), but not (9b).

(9) a. *Sono ni-mai-wa [eisu-no* ***ni-mai*** *] desita*
that two-CLASS-TOP ace-ATT two-CLASS were
'The two cards (that I took) were aces.'

b. *?Sono ni-mai-wa [eisu* ***ni-mai*** *] desita*
that two-CLASS-TOP ace two-CLASS were
'The two cards (that I took) were aces.'

The inverted (or 'shifted') form in (9b) above may become appropriate in the following context:

(10) a. *Nani-o tottan desuka?*
what-ACC took
'What did you take?'

b. *[Eisu* ***ni-mai*** *]-o torimasita.*
ace two-CLASS-ACC took
'I took two aces.'

As I will show in greater detail in the subsequent discussion (Section 3.1.3. and 3.1.4), despite their surface similarities, the Q-constructions [N Q] and [N-***no*** Q] are semantically of different sorts, and there is no reason to regard them as being syntactically related.

Other than the inadequacy of his transformational accounts of some of the Japanese Q-constructions, I find Martin's taxonomy to be basically consistent with mine, which includes two additional categories of clause-external Q-constructions.

2.2 *Downing's classification*

Downing (1984) basically follows Martin's classification, but she reclassifies his categories under four major categories, as we see in (11) below. Downing correctly eliminates the inadequate transformational account from her classification, as is apparent in her analyzing Martin's Inverted Apposition and Appositional Ellipsis as two separate Appositive types with no reference to the syntactic relations between them. The two classifications are contrasted below.

(11)	*Martin (1975)*	*Downing (1984)*	*Patterns*
	Basic	Individualizing	[Q-*no* N]-κ
	Inverted Apposition	Apposition B	[NQ]-κ
	Appositional Ellipsis	Apposition A	[N-*no* Q]-κ
	Adverbialization	Adverbial	[N]-κ X [Q]-κ

Downing maintains a rigorous control of the quality of the data from a large body of discourse material by restricting her data to those Q-constructions which are clearly case-marked. Martin's two other classes, Reduced Appositional Ellipsis and Preposed Adverbializiaton are reduced to the classes of Apposition B and Adverbial.

2.3 *Eight-way syntactic distinction*

Unlike the preceding studies, the classification in this study is exclusively based on the overall syntactic environments in which Q-constructions occur, independent from semantic considerations. In this way, two super-categories are identified according to the relative position of Q with respect to the quantified N. These are NP-internal Q-constructions and NP-external Q-constructions.

The NP-internal type of the Q-construction is further classified into the prenominal Q group and the postnominal Q group. Each has two subordinate members: types Q-*no* N and QN of the prenominal group, and types N-*no* Q and NQ of the postnominal Q group.

The NP-external type has two categories: the locally NP-External Q-construction and S-External Q-construction.[12] The locally NP-External Q-construction also has the prenominal Q type and the postnominal Q type (mnemonically NXQ and QXN, respectively), where an arbitrary element X intervenes between N and Q.[13] Because of the syntactic separation by the intervening X, the Q in the locally NP-external type is often referred to as "floating away" from the "basic" structure of the NP-internal type. Similarly, in the QXN construction, Q also "floats away" from its base NP-internal construction to a position to the left of the NP.[14] In the second super-category, i.e. the NP-external Q-construction, we find two situations. In the one situation, Q and N are separated in such a way that Q is confined within a relative clause, while the referent N is found in the main clause as the Head of that relative clause. Here, Q is external to the main clause, but endogenously, so that it is found in an embedded relative clause. In the other situation, we find a Q and its referent NP in two separate sentences. Hence, we refer to the first class of the NP-external Q-construction as the endogenous type and the second class as the S-external Q construction.

The typology of the Q-constructions in Japanese is summarized in Table 1. The classifications of the Q-construction we discussed in this section are summarized in Table 2.

To recapitulate, the typology of the Japanese quantifier construction established in this study is different from those in the other two studies in two respects. First, the present classification is focused more on the syntactic environments than on the semantic properties of the categories. (The semantic features of each type are introduced separately as the profile.) Second, I include in the present classification two additional quantifier constructions which involve more than two clausal (or sentential) boundaries.

Table 1. Eight-way syntactic classification of Japanese quantifier construction

Type		*Position of Q*	*Pattern*
NP-Internal Q		Prenominal Q	Q-*no* N QN
		Postnominal Q	N-*no* Q NQ
NP-External	Locally NP-External	Postnominal Q Prenominal Q	NXQ QXN
	S-External Q	Q endogenously external to a main clause	$[...Q..]_{RC}N$
		Q external to a main clause	$[...N...]_s$, $[...Q...]_s$

Q = Numeral quantifier; ; N' = Head noun of a relative clause; *no* = Attributive marker; X = Any arbitrary intervening constituents; RC = Relative clause; S = Sentential boundary.

Table 2. Comparison of the three classifications.

Types	*Martin (1975)*	*Downing (1984)*	*The Present Study*
Q-*no* N	Basic	Individualizing	NP-internal, Prenom, attributive-marking
QN	—	—	NP-internal, Prenom, no attributive-marking
N-*no* Q	Apposition. Ellipsis	Appositive B	NP-internal, Postnom, attributive marking
NQ	Inverted Apposition	Apposition A	NP-internal, Postnom, no attributive marking
	Reduced N-*no* Q	—	—
NXQ	Adverbialization	Adverbial	Locally NP-external, Postnom
QXN	Preposed adverbial.	—	Locally NP-external , Prenom
$[..Q..]_{RC}$ N	—	—	Endogenously NP-external, (relative clause) Q
$[..N..]_S$ $[..Q..]_S$	—	—	S-external, Post-sentential

3. Distributions and functional profiles

To see the types of Q-constructions and their distribution patterns in Japanese, a little over one thousand samples of Q-constructions were collected from written texts of various genres, such as fiction, professional essays, and folk tales. From the data, some quantifier expressions — quantifier expressions used as pronouns (e.g. *hutari* 'two persons' or 'both'), adverbials of time, frequency, and manner (e.g. *is-syun* 'momentarily,' *ikkyo-ni* 'all at once,' and *ik-ken* 'at a glance.') — were also excluded. The Modern Japanese samples and the Old Japanese samples were tabulated separately, which led me to appreciate some differences in the distribution patterns between the two groups. As seen in Table 3, the general pattern of the distribution in Modern Japanese corresponds fairly well with the Old Japanese counterpart. Both show three concentrations in the areas of Q-*no* N, QN, and NXQ. One noticeable difference between the two groups is that the relative size of Type Q-*no* N and Type QN is reversed, so that Type Q-*no* N is predominant (45.8%) in the Modern Japanese group, while the predominant type in Old Japanese is shown to be Type QN (42.8%). The second most frequent type is shown to be Type NXQ both in Modern Japanese and Old Japanese, by 21.4% and 27%, respectively. The distribution patterns in the two groups will be discussed in more detail in the later sections.

Table 3. Types of Q-constructions and distribution patterns in Modern Japanese and Old Japanese.

	Modern Japanese		Old Japanese	
Type	Frequency	%	Frequency	%
Q-*no* N	393	45.8	46	22.0
QN	116	13.5	89	42.8
N-*no* Q	67	7.8	0	0.0
NQ	55	6.4	14	6.7
NXQ	183	21.4	56	27.0
QXN	13	1.5	1	0.5
$[..Q..]_{RC}N$	13	1.5	0	0.0
$[..N..]_{S,}Q$	18	2.1	2	1.0
TOTAL	858	100.0	208	100.0
Grand Total: 1,066				

In the rest of the section, I will present the Q-construction types given in Table 1 by sketching their characteristics in syntax and semantics. I will first discuss the NP-internal Q-construction in Section 3.1, then the locally NP-external Q-construction in Section 3.2, and lastly the clause-external Q-construction in Section 3.3.

3.1 *NP-internal quantifiers*

A quantifier (Q) and its referent noun (N) both appear within an NP boundary. Depending on the relative position of Q with respect to N, the NP-internal Q-construction may be further subclassified into Q-*no* N and QN, on the one hand, and N-*no* Q and NQ, on the other. Let us look at each of these subtypes in the rest of the section.

3.1.1 *Type Q-no N*

The numeral quantifier is accompanied by the Attributive *no* marker and it precedes the referent noun. Numerals often appear with no classifiers, particularly in Old Japanese. This pattern, which corresponds to Martin's Basic Type, is the most common form of all in Modern Japanese Q-constructions — 393 cases (45.8%) or nearly half of the total samples, which is close to Downing's figure (45%). In the Old Japanese data, on the other hand, the frequency of Type Q-*no* N (22%, 46 out of a total of 208 samples) is second to the predominant Type QN (42.8%, 89 samples).

Functionally speaking, the prenominal phrase Q-*no* serves as a modifier for the referent N in Q-*no* N construction.

(12) *Kare-wa* ***ik-ken****-no* *aramonoya-o* *mitukeru-to....*
he-TOP one-CLASS-ATT hardware store-ACC found-as
'As he found a hardware store,....' (Shiina:146)

In the above example the phrase *ik-ken no* is a quantifier which is a complex phrase consisting of the numeral *iti* 'one,' *ken* (a classifier for buildings) and the attributive marker *no*. The quantifier phrase modifies the referent noun *aramonoya* 'hardware store.'

(13) *[****Ik-ki****-no* *enban]-ga* *naname ni* *kakatte ita.*
one-CLASS-ATT saucer-NOM diagonally hang-was
'A flying saucer was hung diagonally over the .....' (Mishima:19)

The quantified NP in (13) as a whole carries the nominative marker *ga*, and serves as the subject of sentence (13), while the two quantified NPs in (14) below serve as the object and the indirect object with reference to the verb *wakeru* 'divide.'

(14) *[[****Zyuuni-ko-no*** *] mikan]-o* *[[****yottu-no*** *]* *sara]- ni*
twelve-CLASS-ATT tangerines-ACC four-CLASS-ATT saucer-to
onazi ni *waketara...*
equally divide-if
'If you divide twelve tangerines equally into four saucers, then....'
(Toyama:88)

Table 4. The ratio of definite NPs and indefinite NPs in type Q-no N in Modern Japanese

	Definite NP	Indefinite NP	Total
Subject	53	104	157
Direct object	22	70	92
Others	36	108	144
TOTAL	111 (28.2%)	230 (71.8%)	393 (100%)

As shown in the gloss, the numeral expression *yottu* in *yottu no sara* of (14) is interpreted as being a combination of a numeral *yo* 'four' and *tu*, a sort of generic classifier. Hence numeral quantifiers combined with the morpheme *tu* do not co-occur with other classifiers.[15,16]

The quantified nouns in the above examples happen to be semantically indefinite, and they are all first-mentions in the contexts. However, quantified referents in Type Q-*no* N can also be definite nouns, as shown in (15) and (16) below.

(15) *Sore wa [[tugi no [**hutatu no** gensoku]]-ni] yorimasu*
it-TOP next two-ATT principles-on depend
'It depends on the following two principles.' (Toyama:77)

(16) *[[Kono [**hutatu-no** ryoo]]-wa]....*
these two-att volumes-TOP
'These two volumes are...' (Toyama:17)

Though the NP can either be definite or indefinite in the Q-*no* N construction, statistics indicate that indefinite NPs outnumber their definite counterparts by more than two and a half times in the present Modern Japanese data. See Table 4 above.

3.1.2 *Type QN*

N immediately follows Q to form a unitary NP. Two subtypes are identified — the native QN and the Chinese QN. In the former, Q is a native numeral, e.g. *hito* 'one,' *huta* 'two,' *mi* 'three,' and *yo* 'four.' The latter type takes Chinese numerals, e.g. *iti* 'one,' *ni* 'two,' *san* 'three,' etc. Examples for these two subtypes are shown in (17a) and (17b), respectively.

(17) a. (i) *hito-me* 'a glance' (ii) *huta-go* 'two babies,' i.e. 'twins'
(iii) *mi-ko-ito*[17] 'three-ply-thread'

b. (i) *iti-sakka* 'a writer' (ii) *ni-bun* 'two sentences' (iii) *san-zyuusi* 'three-Musketeers'

The native QN appears in idiomatic expressions, while the Chinese type is preferred in technical and formal writings.

As Martin correctly shows, the QN construction is semantically similar to the Q-*no* N. Even if there appear to be some semantic differences between them, such differences are so subtle that they are hard to pinpoint, except differences in rhetorical style. The QN type sounds more archaic and semantically more restricted than the Q-*no* N type, as we note in examples (18) and (19).

		Type QN	Type Q-*no* N
(18)	a.	*iti-sakka* one writer	*hitori-no sakka* one-ATT writer
	b.	*ni-bun* two sentences	*hutatu-no bun* two-ATT sentences

		(i)	(ii)
(19)	a.	*san-nin-no zyuusi* three-CLASS musketeer 'three musketeers'	*san-zyuusi* three-ATT musketeer 'Three Musketeers'
	b.	*ip-pon-no kasa* one-CLASS-ATT umbrella 'an umbrella'	*ip-pon-gasa* one-CLASS-umbrella 'an umbrella shared by two'
	c.	*san-syoku-no hata* three-CL-ATT flag 'a flag in three colors'	*san-syoku-ki* three-CLASS-flag 'a trois couleur'

The noun phrase *san-nin no zyuusi* 'three musketeers (of any set') in (19ai) may denote any set consisting of three individuals whose social status is 'musketeer,' whereas *san-zyuusi* ('The Three Musketeers') (18aii) denotes a specific set of musketeers, for instance, the flamboyant swordsmen in Dumas' novel. Similarly, *ip-pon gasa* in (19bii) does denote not an umbrella of just any kind but rather one used in a specific context in which a couple in love cuddle each other on the street on a rainy day. This sort of idiomatic or relatively restricted meaning is common in the native QN type as well, as we noticed above. Take, for example, *mi-ko-ito* in (17aiii), which means 'thread of special construction,' that is, 'three-ply thread.' The idiomaticity in examples (20) below is self-explanatory.

(20)	a.	*hito-kuti* one-mouth 'a bite of food'	b.	*huta-gokoro* two-heart 'treachery'	c.	*mitu-dama* three-balls 'three-ball game'

d. *yottu-kado*	e. *hitori-musuko*	f. *san-nin-musume*
four-corner	one-son	three-CL daughters
'a street-crossing'	'an only son'	'three daughters (and no sons)'

Note also that the semantic fusion (idiomaticity) is well represented in the phonological assimilation in the native QN type. For instance, dentals and velars following a Q are voiced as in *huta-go* (not *huta-ko*), *mitu-dama* (not *mittu-tama*), etc.

The specificity reading of this sort is well exemplified in (21) below, where QN *nihon-sugi* 'Twin Cedars' contrasts with *sugi-ga nihon*, 'two cedars' in the NXQ construction.

(21) ***Ni-hon sugi*** *tyuu* <u>*sugi-ga*</u> ***ni-hon*** *arimasu.*
two-CLASS cedar called cedar-NOM two-CLASS exists
'There are two cedar trees called 'Twin Cedars.' (Seki:178)

Some distributional differences between Modern Japanese and Old Japanese are noted. As we see in Table 3, Type QN is predominant (42.8 %, i.e. 89 out of the total 208 samples) in Old Japanese, while we find a less impressive 13.5 % (116 out of 858 cases) in Modern Japanese. The QN type in Modern Japanese is heavily concentrated (roughly 89%) in academic writings (e.g. those by Oe, Doi, Mikami, Toyama) as well as in the novel by Mishima, whose writing style is full of rich metaphors and fabulous allegories. This suggests that the QN type may be regarded as an older form of the Q-construction which survives merely in formal rhetorics and fossilized idioms. In this conjunction, the Q-construction known as Q-Float is particularly interesting. While Type QN has a noticeable archaic flavor, Q-Float is very colloquial and is almost always found in conversations or informal writings. Based on this observation, I devised a statistical index by which one can measure a writer's degree of formality, as shown in Section 3.2.1.

3.1.3 *Type N-no Q*

In the present data, we find a relatively small number (7.8% in our data and 6% in Downing's data) of a Q-construction in which Q follows an attributive *no*-marked N. Type N-*no* Q is not found in the present corpus of the Old Japanese data. Semantically, Q and N in this type are in an appositive relation.

(22) [[*Dokusya, hihyooka, sakka]*$_{NP}$*-no* ***san sya*** *]*$_{NP}$*-ni yotte,*
reader critique author-ATT three-CLASS by
'By the three parties, namely—readers, critics and authors— '
(Oe:29)

In (22) the Quantifier, *san-sya* ('three-CL'), and the three referent nouns (readers, critics, and authors) are in apposition. Since the particle *no* is considered to be the attributive form of the copula *de aru* or *da*, [A-*no* B] may be rephrased as [A-*de aru* B], equivalent to [B who/which is A] in English.[18] So, the underscored part of (22) may be paraphrased as 'the three parties, who are readers, critics, and authors.'

In addition to the appositive reading, the N-*no* Q type frequently appears in partitive readings as well, particularly when the referent N is definite and referential, as shown in (23) below.

(23) *[[Sono sankasya]*$_{NP}$*- no* ***hitori*** *]*$_{NP}$*-to site*
its participant-ATT one- as
'As one of the participants (of the meeting)—.' (Doi:14)

In many cases, however, the distinction between the two readings is not always sharp enough to discern, as shown in (24).

(24) *[[Nakama]*$_{NP}$*-no]* ***hitori*** *]*$_{NP}$*-ga sono Inoue-ni koe o kakeru.*
colleague-ATT a guy-NOM that Inoue-to talk
'A guy who is a colleague (or one of the fellows) talked to Inoue.'
(Shiina:116)

The above sentence exemplifies the typical ambivalence of this sort between the appositive reading and the partitive reading.

3.1.4 *Type NQ*

The constituents N and Q appear immediately next to each other to form an NP unit. The distribution of the NQ type is low to the point of insignificance both in Modern Japanese (6.4 %) and Old Japanese (6.7 %), and it is even lower (5.0 %) in Downing's data.

(25) *[Kanozyo-tati* ***san-nin*** *]-mo hataraita*
they three-CLASS also worked
'The three girls — they worked,too.'

It can easily be shown that the two words *kanozyo-tati* and *san-nin* 'they, three of them' in (25) make up a constituent, by means of suffixing a case-marker to the referent noun or inserting the modal morpheme *mo* 'also' between the two, which yields ungrammatical consequences, as seen in (26a) and (26b). In other words, these two words are inseparable constituents making up a constituent.

(26) a. **Kanozyotati-ga* **san-nin** *-mo* *hataraita*
they-NOM three-CLASS-also worked

b. **Kanozyotati-mo* **san-nin** *hataraita*
they-also three-CLASS worked

There is a strong indication in the present data that the NQ construction seems to serve as a marking device for the semantic feature of <specificity>, regardless of whether a given base NP (i.e. the antecedent of a quantifier) is <definite> or <indefinite>. In this section, I will show two major situations — the 'anaphoric' situation and the other with the combination of the <indefinite> and <specific> features.

3.1.4.1 *Anaphoric NQs* The antecedent NP *kanozyo-tati* 'they' in (25) is anaphorically definite. In (25), the referent noun 'they' is, needless to say, anaphoric, and the information represented by *kanozyot-tati* 'she-PL' or 'they' is necessarily given and old, to the effect that the hearer may already have a good deal of information about who these people are and how many of them there are. Therefore, strictly speaking, the quantifier Q in (25) is simply redundant. However, there must be some reasons for the frequent occurrences of such excessive quantification in well-formed discourse. One possible answer is that such excessive quantification may be a device that draws the hearer's attention to each and every member of the set in an exhaustive manner.[19] I will refer to this discourse function as <emphasis through individuation>, following Downing.

Sentence (27) is another instance of the anaphoric NQ construction. Each of the two NPs in the NQ construction of sentence (27) has an anaphoric reading. The only difference between (26) and (27) is that in (27) <definite> is not explicitly presented. In (27), the farmer's daughter and the peddlers in the story made a deal by which the former will get the peddlers' belongings (a horse and three pieces of cotton cloth baggage), if she indeed could show them her unusual talent. The pair of noun phrases *uma ip-piki* 'horse' and *nimotu san-da* 'three pieces of baggage' are thus actually second mentions and anaphoric in (27), as shown in the translation.

(27) *uma* ***ip-piki*** *to* *nimotu* ***san-da*** *totta*
horse one-CLASS and baggage three-CLASS took
'The girl took away *the* (their) horse and *those* three pieces of baggage from the cotton cloth peddlers' (Seki:202).

In fact, as shown in (28) below, the insertion of demonstrative markers into these NPs does not cause any significant changes in the meaning of sentence (27), which indicates that these NPs indeed represent old information and are semantically definite-referential.

(28) *[[sono[uma* ***ip-piki****]]* *to* *[sono[nimotu* ***san-da****]]* *totta*
that horse one-CLASS and that baggage three-CLASS took
'The girl took away (their belongings, i.e.) *the* horse and *those* three pieces of baggage from the cotton cloth peddlers' (Seki:202).

3.1.4.2 *Indefinite-Specific NQs* The antecedent N of the NQ configuration can also be indefinite. The most typical NQs occurring with indefinite-specific nouns are observed in situations like the following:

(29) a. *Hanako-wa sono siken-de [[mondai* ***ik-ko****]-ga]*
Hanako-TOP the test-in question one-CLASS-NOM
tokenakatta.
solve-unable
'Hanako could not solve *one problem* in the test.'

b. *Hanako-wa sono siken-de [[mondai]-ga]* ***[ik-ko]***
Hanako-TOP the test-in question-NOM one-CLASS
tokenakatta.
solve-unable
'Hanako could not solve *one of the problems* in the test.'

By (29a), the speaker is making a remark that there was *one particular problem* Hanako could not manage to solve, although the speaker did not specify which. The referent noun *mondai* 'question' mentioned in (29a) is not just any question, but a question very special to Hanako (the one which tortured Hanako for two hours!). Thus, the noun *mondai* in (29a) is indefinite-specific — specific to the speaker or the subject (Hanako in this particular case.) In contrast, the speaker introduces by (29b) the existence of one problem, simply as a piece of new information with no specific reference, which Hanako could not handle. In (29b), the antecedent N *mondai* and the quantifier *ik-ko* are found in the NXQ construction of NXQ (i.e. Q-Float), where the N is interpreted as being <indefinite-nonspecific>.

Let us take an example frequently quoted in the literature, "Mary wants to marry a Norwegian doctor." The doctor in the sentence may be interpreted in two ways. In one interpretation, the referent referred to as 'doctor' can be indefinite-nonspecific in the sense that Mary would not be able to tell who such a person will be, except that he would be a professional of a particular type and of a particular origin specified in the sentence. In the other interpretation, the doctor is indefinite-specific just in case Mary has already had an acquaintance with the particular individual whom she wants to marry, but the hearer has no idea who this lucky fellow is. This is a typical kind of indefinite-specificity, and I refer to it as Type A of the feature <indefinite-specific>. In Japanese, such an N with the feature of <indefinite-specific> will typically be presented in the NQ construction, as in *(aru) o-isya-san hitori* ' (a certain) doctor.'

In Japanese, the construction NQ is also frequently used in a physician's prescription or in a cooking class instructor's recipes. A warehouse manager would also read out aloud items on inventory sheets by the NQ format, e.g. *asupirin ni-tyoo* ' two tablets of aspirin,' *o-satoo hito-sazi* ' a spoon of sugar,' and *kompyuutaa san-dai* 'three computers.' In general, items in a program or in an inventory list are considered to be 'prescribed' or 'scheduled' so that such items are regarded in a sense as members of the 'prescribed set' on the part of the person in charge of the program, even though they are referred to for the first time in discourse. What is involved in this kind of situation may also be considered as Type B <indefinite-specific>.

(30) *Ip-poo no hukuro-ni [[Tyawan* ***ik-ko*** *]* *to [koppu*
one-side's bag-into bowl one-CLASS and glass
ik-ko *]]-o ire.....*
one-CLASS-ACC put-in
'In one bag, we put one bowl and a glass, and in the other bag...'
(Toyama:182)

The two instances of the Q-construction (Type NQ) in sentence (30) above may be analyzed as being another instances of the B-type indefinite-specificity. Here, in his explaining a mathematical phenomenon, the author introduces a hypothetical situation in which he divides four objects into two different containers. Although these objects are entirely new information to the hearer, the speaker introduces them as if they are taken granted for as being "objects prepared beforehand for the purpose of illustrating the phenomenon in discussion." Sentence (31) is another example of the Type-B indefinite-specific.

(31) *Minna-ga* *koban* ***iti-mai*** *kuwaite kitewa...*
everyone-NOM gold coin one-CLASS hold-came-then
'Everyone (of the foxes) brought one gold coin, by holding it in his mouth, and......' (Seki:133).

In the context given prior to the utterance of (31), every fox was ordered to bring *a gold coin* to the tyrant. The noun phrase *koban iti-mai* 'gold coin one-CLASS' appearing in (31) is in fact a second mention. In (31), the NP is interpreted as indefinite-specific, because the coins are randomly chosen but specified already in the previous context. However, one must recognize some degree of givenness or specification in *koban iti-mai* because it is mentioned a second time in the discourse. Japanese seems to mark this sort of givenness or specification in discourse by means of the NQ construction.

One other remarkable usage of the NQ construction is found in what I call 'categorical negation,' which is pervasive in Japanese. Consider the following:

(32) *Sora-ni-wa* *kumo* ***hitotu*** *arimasen desita.*
sky-in-TOP cloud one-CLASS exist-not-PAST
'There was not a single cloud in the sky' (Arishima:19).

The speaker of (32) is emphatically expressing the absolute clarity of the sky by mentioning that there is not even a tiny trace of cloud, and the presence of such a trace may otherwise jeopardize the emptiness of the sky. That is, the NP *kumo hitotu* 'a cloud' represents *the minimal condition which may guarantee* the perfect clarity of the sky, and the negation of this condition will annihilate such a state of affairs.

Logically speaking, in order to achieve a negative operation characterized as <categorical negation>, that is, for one to negate an entire set in an exhaustive manner, all that one has to do is choose *one single member in the set* as a "straw man," and "knock" it out, provided that all the rest of the members are conceptually cancelled out. Such an element which has survived the mental operation of negation can be any arbitrary member of the set. Therefore, it is necessarily <indefinite>. And, at the same time it needs to be <specific>, because it is the last member of the given set, and the proof of the existence of that set is at stake, depending entirely upon the proof of the existence of that 'last' member. In reality, such a crucial member is a hypothetical entity — a semantic straw man, so to speak — assumed in the speaker's mind only to facilitate the operation of categorical negation. The numeral *hitotu* 'one (thing)' for an inanimate noun or *hitori* 'one (person)' for a human noun is effectively exploited in Japanese categorical negation. More than 80% of the total number of the NQ constructions (47 cases) in the present Modern Japanese data are used for this purpose.

Incidentally, Japanese speakers' dependence on the straw man 'one' in the NQ-construction for categorical negation seems to be due to a peculiar language-internal restriction of Japanese. That is to say, for some mysterious reason, Japanese has an accidental gap of the negative modifier equivalent to the English negative adjectival morpheme 'no' as in '*No* one showed up.' In general, negative polarity items such as 'none,' 'nothing,' and 'never,' are totally lacking in the lexicon of Japanese, which seems to leave the Japanese speakers little choice for measures but the straw man type of categorical negation. The indefinite-specific NQ serves very effectively to compensate for this peculiar situation.[20]

3.2 *Locally NP-external Q-constructions*

We have examined four types of the NP-internal Q-construction, in which a quantifier and its referent are confined to the same NP domain. In casual conversations, a quantifier often appears apart from its own referent noun, which I refer to as a 'base NP.'

In this section, we will examine two such situations — Q appears after the base NP (Type NXQ), and Q precedes the base NP (Type QXN). Note that although Q is found outside the base NP apart from its referent N, Q is still within the same sentence or clause. For this reason, I prefer to call this type of Q-construction a 'locally NP-external Q-construction.' In other situations, Q presents itself not just outside the base NP, but it appears even beyond the sentence which contains the base NP. We will refer to this situation as the clause-external (or S-external) Q-construction, which we will discuss in Section 3.3.

3.2.1 *Type [NXQ]*

The NXQ type, which is generally referred to as Quantifier Floating, displays several intriguing features.

First, the referent N and its quantifier Q make up one single, semantically cohesive, unit, and yet each of them belongs to a different syntactic domain. That is, the quantifier Q is found outside the base NP, while its referent N is confined in that base NP.

(33) $[...[...[...N...]_{N'}(-\kappa)]_{NP}...Q...]_S$

As (33) shows, N and Q are separated by the NP boundary, which is generally marked by case-markers. Besides the NP boundary, various constituents can separate the two. In (34), for instance, the quantifier *hitotu* 'one' is isolated from the referent noun *eigakan* 'theater' by two intervening elements — the nominative case marker *ga* and the adverb *yatto* 'at last.'

(34) *[Eigakan]$_{NP}$-**ga*** ***yatto*** *hitotu* *atta n desu.*
Movie house-NOM finally one there-was
'Finally, (after all this effort) we found a movie house.' (Shiina: 30)

Likewise, in examples (35) and (36) below, the syntactic demarcation of the two constituents, N and Q, is easily recognizable by virtue of the presence of case markers. Thus, in (35), the accusative *o* marker attached to the referent noun *kippu* 'ticket' syntactically separates the noun *kippu* from the quantifier *ni-mai* 'TWO-CLASS.'

(35) *Anda-wa Shinjuku made [kippu]$_{NP}$- o* ***ni-mai*** *katta*
Anda-TOP Shinjuku-to ticket-ACC TWO-CLASS bought
'Anda bought two tickets for a Shinjuku-bound train.' (Shiina:35)

In the following example, the particle-*n* (a Yamanashi equivalent of the standard Nominative *ga*) intervenes between the referent noun *kodomo* 'children' and *san-nin* 'three-CLASS.'[21]

(36) *Hooka? [kodomo]$_{NP}$-n* ***san-nin*** *to kiitya kotairaren*
is that so kids-NOM three-CLASS heard cannot resist
'Oh yeah? Three kids? I can't wait.' (Seki:83)

Second, Q-Float appears predominantly in informal speech. As we see in Table 6 below, while almost no occurrences of Q-Float appear in the two critical essays by Oe and Doi, we see a large concentration of Q-Float in Seki's folk tales. Another heavy concentration is seen in Toyama's *Invitation to Mathematics* (or more literally *Mathematics —How to Teach and How to Learn),* which is tailored for general readers despite its relatively technical contents of mathematical phenomena.[22]

Table 5. The distribution of Q-construction as per texts (Modern Japanese).

	Arishi	Doi	Fukada	Mikami	Mishima	Oe	Ogawa	Seki	Shiina	Toyama	Total
Q-noN	13	25	8	25	68	7	24	67	29	127	393
QN	1	8	3	20	57	2	7	1	1	16	116
N-noQ		13	4	2	18		4	2	3	21	67
NQ	4	1	2	1	16		3	14	5	9	55
NXQ	7	2	9	12	13		7	65	17	51	183
QXN	4			2	1		4		1	1	13
[Q] N		1	1		2		4	2		3	13
N, Q	1			6	3		3	3		2	18
Total	30	50	27	68	178	9	56	154	56	230	858

Incidentally, in Downing's (1986) study, the frequency of Type NXQ is 54% of the total observations, while Type NXQ in the present research shows 21.4% (183 cases) of the total 858 instances of the Modern Japanese samples. This disparity between the two studies may be in part ascribed to the inclusion of adverbialized quantifiers as well as anaphoric quantifier pro-forms (e.g. *hutari* 'the two persons') in Downing's data. But more crucially, it comes from the difference in the nature of the data used. Namely, half of Downing's data come from oral sources, while our study depends entirely on written texts.

Unfortunately, there are no particular statistics available in the literature that show the distributional differences of Q-Float between written sources and oral material. However, a clear indication of the prevalent occurrence of Q-Float in informal and colloquial discourse can be found in our data. For instance, Tables 5 and 6 clearly show a high correlation between NXQ and colloquialism.

Excluding the category Q-*no* N, which is the most unmarked form appearing both in formal and informal environments, let us take the two most prominent Q-constructions from the table above: QN and NXQ. Type QN is heavily concentrated particularly in three texts (by Doi, Mikami, and Mishima), while Type NXQ (Q-Float) is more frequently distributed in the texts by Arishima, Fukada, Seki, Shiina, and Toyama. What is apparent from this observation is that the first group consists of characteristically technical writings while the latter group's texts are all in the form of narration, folk tale, or casual writing styles. In other words, Type NQ is more frequent in formal writings, while Type NXQ is more casual and discourse-oriented. This contrast can be seen more readily in the Table 6. I will tentatively refer to the ratio of the percentage of QN to that of NXQ as the F(ormality)-index.

The F-index is highest in Oe's literary essay, which is articulate in expression and the least colloquial of all. Mishima comes second after Oe. As critics agree, Mishima has a highly articulate, even poetic style, which is evident in his frequent use of slightly archaic expressions such as *subeki, siranu, naru, ari,* as well as the frequent appearance of connective *V-si,* instead of V-*site*, etc. Doi's academic writing is also very high on the F-index. The text by Mikami is a professional writing in linguistics. Ogawa is just in the middle of the table, as in his writing the classical QN and the colloquial NXQ are equally distributed, and his style is somewhat modest. Fukada is an interesting renegade who left a trading firm to become a fiction writer. One of the works of his that I used in this study is a humorous collection of semi-documentary episodes accumulated during his sojourn abroad as a company

Table 6. Formality index. The ratio of QN and NXQ usage in the Modern Japanese data

Author		% of QN	% of NXQ	QN/(NXQ+1) (F-Index)
1	Oe	22.2	0.0	22.20
2	Mishima	32.0	7.3	3.86
3	Doi	16.0	4.0	3.20
4	Mikami	29.4	17.6	1.58
5	Ogawa	12.5	12.5	0.93
6	Fukada	11.1	33.3	0.32
7	Toyama	7.0	22.2	0.30
8	Arishima	3.3	23.3	0.14
9	Shiina	2.2	30.4	0.07
10	Seki	0.6	42.2	0.01

The calculation of F-index is based on the formula QN%/(NXQ%+1)

representative. His writing style is very casual but his semi-documentary descriptions contribute to the relatively high F-index. Arishima's anthology of nostalgic short stories is based on his childhood experiences, and the style adopted in this recollection is tailored particularly for adolescent readers. Although Shiina is considered a serious story writer, his ideological stance gives a naive and earthy flavor to his writings, which makes his F-index low. The book edited by Seki is a valuable collection of oral history and folk tales in which the storytellers' vivid folksy dialects are kept intact in their storytelling. Since it is expected that the F-index would be lowest in casual conversation or free narration, the frequency of Q-float would be highest. Indeed this is the case, as we can see in Seki's work, where only one instance of the classical QN occurs, while NXQ accounts for 65 out of the total 154 occurrences of Q-constructions.[23] In short, the present study clearly shows that NXQ is used most heavily in conversational or informal discourse in Modern Japanese.

Third, the surface cases that a referent N in Q-Float can take are severely restricted to Subjects and Objects. As we see in Table 6, nearly all of the NXQ constructions in the sample are concentrated in Subjects (60.7%) and Objects (38.3 %) with an insignificant 1% of Oblique cases including Dative. Because of this preponderance of Subjects and Objects, Downing (1993) adequately characterizes Q-Float as "an Absolutive Construction".

Table 7. The distribution of Q-Float with reference to the grammatical relations (subject, direct object, etc.) and (in)definiteness features in Modern Japanese texts

Text	Subject			Direct Object			Other			
	+Def	-Def	SubT	+Def	-Def	SubT	+Def	-Def	SubT	TOTAL
Oe		2	2		1	1				3
Doi	5	5	10	2		2				12
Mikami	1	12	13							13
Mishima		13	13		4	4				17
Shiina	2	4	6		1	1				7
Ogawa		3	3	1	3	4				7
Arishima	1	5	6		3	3				9
Fukada	10	15	25	10	15	25	1		1	51
Toyama	9	24	33	7	23	30	1		1	64
Seki	28	83	111	20	50	70	2		2	183
TOTAL	15.3%	45.4%	60.7%	11.0%	27.3%	38.3%	1.0%	0%	1.0%	100 %

+Def = definite, -Def = Indefinite

Fourth, Q-Float has a remarkable set of semantic and discourse functions. They are: (a) a rhematic reading, (b) a partitive reading, (c) an exhaustive emphasis reading, (d) a categorical negation reading. I will discuss them in detail in the rest of the section.

3.2.1.1 *Rhematic reading* Type NXQ is a unique device specializing in introducing new information into discourse, somewhat comparable to the *there*-insertion construction in English.[24] The Q-Float's rhematic role is evident in the fact that the quantified nouns in the data are invariably presented as being semantically indefinite.[25] As Table 6 shows, of the total 183 occurrences of the NXQ construction in the Modern Japanese data, 133 cases (that is, 71%) are interpreted as indefinite and first-mentions, and only 29% are found to be definite. The rhematic use of Q-Float is exemplified in (34)-(36) above.

3.2.1.2 *Partitive Reading* Q-Float is also interpreted as having a partitive reading. In this situation, the referent N is frequently either a mass noun or a collective noun, and semantically it is most likely to be indefinite. Consider sentence (37) below.

(37) *[Sono kome]$_{NP}$-wa* ***hito-tubu*** *kuu to senninriki-ga*
the rice-TOP one-CLASS eat-if thousand-man-power-NOM
deru mono de atta
come-out things was
'(The rice was so mysterious that) if one eats one grain then he will acquire the power of one thousand men' (Seki:60).

Kome ('rice') in (37) is a mass noun and it carries the demonstrative *sono* 'that' or 'those.' Similarly, the statement 'the portable table' is quadrupedal" in (38) is understood as a piece of presuppositional information. The topic marker *wa* suffixed to the referent N reflects such presupposed information.

(38) *[Tyabudai-no asi]$_{NP}$-wa* ***ip-pon*** *torete ita*
table-GEN leg-TOP one-CLASS missing
'One of the portable table's legs was missing' (Shiina:7).

In (39) below, the referent of the quantifier *mittu* is given in the form of a pronoun, *sore*, which is an anaphoric expression for 'six tiles,' supposedly given in earlier contexts. Like (34), it is not necessary for the referent NP to be a mass noun, for this reading. The demonstrative in (39) represents the referent in a pile or in a mound.

(39) *[Sore]$_{NP}$-o yoko ni* ***mittu*** *atumeru*
those-ACC horizontally three collect
'Then, we put together three of them (six tiles) horizontally' (Toyama:84).

In this regard, the rhematicity is associated only with quantifier *mittu* 'three,' while the given and presupposed information is conveyed by the referent noun, as Downing (1984) correctly observes.

3.1.2.3 *Exhaustive emphasis reading* In this reading, Q emphasizes the references presented by referent nouns in an exhaustive manner by using universal quantifiers and other similar quantifiers (e.g. *hutatu (-tomo)* 'both,' *minna* 'all,' *hitori-hitori*, or *hitori-zutu* 'each/every').

(40) *— [seiziteki ziyuu to kirisutokyoo]$_{NP}$-o* ***hutatu***
political freedom and Christianity-ACC two
nagara appakusita to...
at the same time oppressed-COMP
'—that they oppressed both the political freedom and Christianity' (Doi:106).

In (40) above, Q is used emphatically to refer to each and every one of the members of the referent set in an exhaustive manner. In this type of individuation reading, the referent noun can be given information. The degree of rhematicity in this reading is therefore relatively limited, as in (40).

In the exhaustive emphasis reading, Q can, however, be critically rhematic in certain situations. Consider the following:

(41) *[Ano warumono domo]$_{NP}$-ga kondo wa* ***minna*** *yatte kiyoru zo.*
those gangs-PLNOM this time all are-coming
'Here come all the gangs altogether this time.'

Here, the universal quantifier *minna* 'all' is not just semantically redundant but can be a critical piece of information to the hearer (in this case, the villagers who were harassed by the gang's repeated assaults.) Then, this discourse function of Q-Float — exhaustive individuation — can also be said to be capable of carrying rhematic information, though the degree of such rhematicity may vary depending on contexts.

Besides the universal quantifiers mentioned above, a regular numeral can also serve as a sort of a universal quantifier when it is supported by the morpheme *tomo* 'altogether,' as in (42).

(42) *['watasi-ga,' 'watasi-o,' watasi-ni']$_{NP}$-wa* ***mittu tomo*** —
I-NOM I-ACC I-DAT-TOP three together...
'I-nominative, I-accusative, and I-dative — all three of them are....
(Mikami:138)

3.2.1.4 *"Straw man" reading* Like Type NQ, NXQ is also often used for categorical negation, as shown in (43) and (44).

(43) *Keredomo [gaikotu]-wa* ***hitotu*** *-mo odoranai*
but skeleton-TOP one-even dance-not
'But, there was no skeletons that danced.' (Seki:99)

(44) *Hooroku-ga* ***iti-mai*** *mo ure nai node...*
parching pan-NOM one-CLASS-even sold-not because
'...because he could not sell even one parching pan that day,...'
(Seki:169)

As we noted in Section 3.1.4.1. the numeral 'one' accompanying the modal particle *mo* in categorical negation represents a semantic 'straw man,' which is interpreted as being a member crucial for categorical negation.

Thus, in this regard, NXQ, like NQ, serves for categorical negation in Japanese. However, it is noteworthy that there is a significant difference between the NQ negation and NXQ negation. Compare the following:

(45) a. *Hanako-wa Taroo-kara hagaki-o* ***ip-pon-mo***
Hanako-TOP Taroo-from post-card-ACC one-CLASS-even
morawa nakatta.
received-not
'Hanako has never received post-cards from Taroo.'

b. *Hanako-wa Taroo-kara hagaki* ***ip-pon-mo***
Hanako-TOP Taroo-from post-card one-CLASS-even
morawa nakatta.
received-not
'Hanako has received not even one post-card from Taroo.'

Sentence (45a) is interpreted as a straightforward report of a simple fact that there was no writing from Taroo to Hanako, whereas sentence (45b) carries not just the message in (45a) but also an additional implication that Taroo has never written to Hanako even a post-card (not to mention a ten-page single-spaced letter), despite the fact that Taroo is obliged to write to Hanako for some good reasons. Thus, the NQ negation appears semantically more restricted in comparison with the NXQ negation to the effect that the former has an implicature of some dissatisfaction on the part of the speaker or Hanako with Taroo's behavior.

3.2.2 *Distinguishing NQ and NØQ*

Finally, before I leave this section, I would like to briefly discuss the way in which I distinguish Type NQ and Type NXQ when the latter appears in the form of NØQ, where the intervening X is presented as phonetically null. As we will see, this issue will cast some light on the phenomenon of Q-Float, particularly the diachronic aspect of the construction.

In principle, the distinction between Type NQ and Type NXQ is straightforward. Case-marking indicates the existence of the NP boundary of NQ, so that the case-marker will appear after the NQ phrase as a whole. For NXQ, X is usually preceded by a case-marker, which in turn separates Q from the N. However, problems arise when the case-marking is not explicitly present. This is particularly frequent in casual conversations or informal narration.
I found 28 cases out of the total sample of the NQ type (55 cases) in our Modern Japanese data which occur with no case markers.

In speech, NØQ is easily recognizable, because a prosodic pause always follows the N, which signals that the following Q is syntactically in isolation. This pause is properly expressed conventionally by a comma in written texts. When there are no such syntactic or phonological cues available, the data are analyzed by recourse to contexts in the discourse. I will illustrate this strategy with example (46) below.

(46) a. *[Ko-usagi]$_{NP}$-o* ***san-biki*** *kenzyoosire* [26]
baby rabbit-ACC three-CLASS present IMP
'Present three baby rabbit (to Lord Wolf).'

b. *Kondo* ***Ko-usagi*** ***san-biki*** *kenzyoo seyo*
recently baby rabbit-ACC three-CLASS present IMP
to no koto desuga....
that thing is-but
'I was ordered to present three new-born rabbits to you, my lord, but....'

c. ***[Ko-usagi*** ***san-biki*** *]$_{NP}$-wa moo kenzyoo sen*
baby rabbit-ACC three-CLASS -TOP no longer present
demo yoi
although good
'You no longer need to present three baby rabbits to the Wolf' (Seki:159).

We have three instances of Quantifier constructions in (46) above: the first one is clearly a Q-Float (NXQ) construction where X is the case-marker which clearly signals the NP boundary, and separates Q from it; the second instance is not clear as to whether it is NQ or NØQ because no syntactic or phonological cues are present; but the last occurrence in the same form is clearly understood as NQ because the Topic marker defines the entire NP [*ko-usagi san-biki*] 'three new born rabbits' as an NP.[27]

What is, then, the exact status of the Q-construction of (46b)? I interpret it as an instance of the NQ construction with the Type B indefinite-specific reading discussed in Section 3.1.4.2. The reason for this analysis is as follows:

The NP *ko-usagi san-biki* 'three baby rabbits' in (46b) appears in exactly the same form as in (46a), which is considered to be indefinite. The only difference between the two is that the NP *ko-usagi san-biki* in (46b) is a second mention. (This indefinite feature is retained invariably by the third occurrence of the NP *ko-usagi san-biki* in (46c).) Note that the set of rabbits which is mentioned repeatedly in the discourse does not designate any one particular set of rabbits, rather it remains undetermined until three rabbits are brought to the wolf as gifts. The interlocutors are all well aware of what kind of gifts (i.e. rabbits) and how many of them (three) are to be presented, but what they do not know yet is just *which rabbits* these three rabbits will be. In fact, any arbitrary three baby rabbits will do for fulfilling the wolf's demand. In other words, the set of objects in question is prescriptively specified, and anaphorically repeated in the course of conversation, but the content (i.e. the actual members) of that set is left undefined. Recall that the indefinite-specific reading of this type is referred to in Section 3.1.4.2. as particular to the NQ construction. The Q-construction in (46b) is interpreted, therefore, as an instance of the NQ construction.

3.2.3 *Diachronic implications*

When we turn to the Old Japanese material, we find that most of the NXQ constructions are presented in the form of NØQ without case-making. Of 56 cases of NXQ, only 9 cases are clearly marked by intervening elements such as case-markers and modal particles like *mo* 'too.' Likewise, almost all occurrences of Type NQ are presented with no case-marking. For these cases, too, semantic features as well as discourse contexts are used as determining factors.

From this, I have come to the conclusion that the NØQ construction (i.e. case-less NXQ) is best regarded as a proto-form of the Q-Float construction. In other words, Q-Float is not a recent innovation but is found already operative in Old Japanese. I conjecture that the explicit case-marking convention has become increasingly more prevalent in the course of the subsequent development of vernacular Japanese, and this tendency has led to the emergence of the more explicitly case-marked NXQ from the less clearly marked NØQ. In my opinion, the diachronic change of NØQ→NXQ was completed in Modern Japanese. Incidently, one encounters frequent occurrences of the form NØQ in present-day conversations, as in *Tokyo-yuki kippu iti-mai kudasai* 'Give me a ticket for a Tokyo-bound train,' where the case marker *o* is considered to be deleted from the DO, *Tokyo-yuki kippu* 'Tokyo-bound (train) ticket.' In fact, the majority of NØQ occurring in Modern Japanese need to be analyzed as resulting from the contemporary case-dropping convention in discourse, as in the above example. Therefore, we need to distinguish two kinds of case-less NØQs in Modern Japanese. One kind is found in archaic expressions containing fossilized NØQ from earlier periods. The other is due to the omnipresence of discourse deletion of case-markers in Modern Japanese conversation.

To summarize, in this subsection we discussed the idea that Q-Float is predominantly used for introducing new information into discourse, particularly conversations and informal narration. From this, it follows that the referent in Q-Float tends to be indefinite, and it almost always quantifies either the Nominative argument or the Accusative argument by avoiding non-terms which are prone to serve for background information. We also found that Q-Float may have two other kinds of reading — a partitive reading and an exhaustive individuation reading for emphasis. The present study also supports Downing's observation that it is Q that carries the new information, while the referent N serves as a definite, referential base assumed in previous contexts, when Q-Float has these two readings. Also, I suggested that the contemporary prevalence of NXQ may have derived from NØQ by virtue of case-marking, which has become more normative through the history of Japanese.

3.2.4 *Type [QXN]*

Type QXN is essentially a variation of Q-Float. Martin also characterizes it as "inverted adverbialization." Similar analyses are found in Kamio (1977) and Miyagawa (1989). The only difference between the two forms is the position of Q with reference to the base NP — Q follows in Type NXQ and Q precedes in Type QXN, as shown in schemata (47) below.

(47) a. $[..[N]_{NP}...Q.....\ ]_S$ (Type NXQ)
b. $[...Q, . ..[N]_{NP}..]_S$ (Type QXN)

The prenominal Q in Type QXN is always accompanied by a pause immediately after it, which is expressed by the comma convention in written texts, as shown in (48) below.

(48) *Byoo'in no mae ni-wa,* ***go/rok-ken,***
hospital-in-front-of-TOP five or SIX-CLAS'

[tiisana kasiya ya hanaya o mazieta
tiny cake-shop and flower shop-ACC mixed
[yanami]]$_{NP}$-ga aru ga.....
row of houses-NOM are but
'There are a row of several houses including a cake shop and flower shop, and..' (Ogawa:62).

In (48) the head noun, *yanami* 'a row of houses,' is preceded by the relative clause *tiisana kasiya ya hanaya o mazieta* 'which includes a tiny cake shop and a flower shop' and its quantifier as well. Without the pause marked by the comma after the quantifier, the quantifier may wrongly be taken as modifying the noun immediately following, *tiisana kasiya* '(a) small cake shop.' In this sentence, the quantifier appears before its referent noun, but it is separated by an intervening relative clause, and they form a QXN construction. Below are two more examples from Arishima.

(49) *Tada obaasan-ga boku-ni* ***hito-koto -mo*** *[mono]$_{NP}$-o*
only grandma-NOM me-to one-thing-even word-ACC
iwa-nai-no-ga hen datta
saying-not-NOM strange-was
'Strangely, Grandma didn't say a word to me' (Arishima: 74).

(50) *Hattyan,* ***too-dake*** *[siroi isi]$_{NP}$ kurenai?*
ten-only white marbles give-me-not
'Hattyan, won't you give me white marbles — ten of 'em?' (Arishima:37)[28]

The distribution of Type QXN in the present data is very low (a negligible 1.5%.) I found only 13 such instances in the Modern Japanese texts, and one in the entire body of Old Japanese data, which is given below.

(51) *Kono koromo kituru hito-wa kuruma-ni norite,*
this dress wore person-TOP chariot-on on board
hyaku-nin *bakari [amabito]$_{NP}$ gusite noborinu*
hundred-CLASS around angels accompanied ascended
'(Kaguyahime), i.e. the person who wore the (heavenly) dress, got on the chariot, and ascended (to heaven) accompanied by some hundred angels' (Taketori Monogatari: 55).

In (51), the referent noun *amabito* 'heavenly person' is preceded by the quantifier *hyaku-nin bakari* 'one hundred people or so.'

As we noticed above, the construction in these examples comes with rhematic readings. This discourse function strongly supports our analysis of QXN as a variant of NXQ.

Just as Type NXQ does, Type QXN also presents problems in distinguishing Type QØN from Type QN proper. I have again applied semantic-discourse analysis in discerning these two types. The following exemplifies the application of such a strategy:

(52) a. *Keisatu-wa iede sita Mary to Susan no*
police-TOP ran-away Mary and Susan ATT
*[**hutari-musume**]-o sagasite iru. (QN)*
two daughters-ACC looking-for
'The police are searching for the two girls, Mary and Susan, who ran away from home. (Incidentally, Mary and Susan are the only children to the parents.)'

b. *Reiko-wa riensuru mae-ni* ***hutari**, [musume]- o unde*
Reiko-TOP divorce-before two daughter-ACC gave
iru. (QØN)
birth
'It is learned that Reiko gave birth to daughters (two of them) before she divorced her husband.'

The native quantifier *hutari* (with no accompaniment of classifier) and the head noun *musume* in (52a) are constituents of a single noun phrase which form a semantically tighter unit, as the translation in the parentheses suggests. In (52b), on the other hand, the quantifier, *hutari* 'two' and *musume* 'daughters' are separated prosodically by a distinct pause, which is indicated with a comma after the floated Q, as in (48) above. The preposing of Q in sentences like (48) and (52b) seems to have some emphatic effects. In (48), the preposed quantifier *go rok-ken* 'five or six-CLASS' or 'several houses,' (which is a combination of a Chinese-style numeral and a classifier but with no attributive marker) seems to have an effect of drawing the readers' special attention. Likewise, in (52b), by preposing the floated Q, the speaker seems to put emphasis on Reiko's burden of raising children, not just one but three of them, despite her being single.

(53) *Meziro-wa agari kamati no ue e* ***ni-hon**, [<u>sune</u>]-o*
-TOP framework on-top-of two-CLASS leg-ACC

narabete — nirande ita
line-up was-staring at
'Mejiro was staring at (his mother's tiny shoulder), putting his two legs together on the threshold leading up to the living room' (Ogawa: 149).

If the numeral in (53) above were in the pattern [QN], then the referent noun would be affected phonologically by voicing to result in '*ni-hon zune*' instead of '*ni-hon sune no hiza*,' which a native speaker would be most unlikely to utter. As I have discussed earlier (Section 3.1.2.), the voicing of consonants of this kind is normally restricted to items which form tighter semantic units, as in the examples of (17aii), (20b) and (20c). By preposing the quantifier *ni-hon* in (53), the writer seems to try to create a special effect, by which readers would be made to imagine a scene in which the boy is sitting on the threshold and holding his two shanks between his arms as if they were two unfamiliar objects.

In short, the preposed Q will not be interpreted as a prenominal modifier if the Q is followed by a pause. If Q is a native 'bare' numeral (with no accompanying classifier), and if no phonological voicing ('rendaku') takes place with the initial segment of N, the Q is most likely to be a 'floated' Q instead of a prenominal modifier.

3.3 *Clause-external Q-constructions*

In this section I will discuss quantifiers which appear not only outside the base NP, but even beyond the clause boundary. Two possibilities will be considered: (i) N presents itself as the head of a relative, and Q occurs endogenously within that relative clause; and (ii) Q is located exogenously outside the main clause, that is, in a subsequent sentence. I will discuss situation (i) in Section 3.3.1, and situation (ii) in Section 3.3.2.

3.3.1 *Type [..Q..]$_S$N (the endogenous Q type)*

In some cases the quantifier Q and its referent N are separated, but in an intriguing way. Q is in a relative clause, and N is the head of that relative clause, so that N and Q belong to two different syntactic domains. With reference to the N in the base NP, the position of Q is external, but "inwardly external" or "endogenously"— that is, Q is separated from the N in the relative clause. For this reason, I refer to this type of Q-construction as the endogenous Q type, for convenience. I found altogether 13 examples of the endogenous Q type in the entire body of data.

(54) a. *Keizoo-wa [[**hutatu** naranda]$_{RC}$ [hai]$_{NP}$-ni sasita.*
Keizo-TOP two lined-up cup-to poured
'Keizo poured (sake) into the two cups set side by side' (Ogawa:139).

b. *[hai]$_{NP}$-ga* ***hutatu*** *naranda (or narandeiru)*
cup-NOM two lined-up
'Two cups are set side by side.'

c. [[e_i hutatu]$_S$ [hai_i]$_{NP}$]$_{NP}$

The head noun of the relative clause in (54a), *hai* 'cup,' is construed as the referent of Q (*hutatu*) inside the relative clause. In order to get a correct interpretation of the relation between the referent N and the Q in (54a), we need to assume something like (54b) as a source sentence for the relative clause in (54a). In (54c), as an output of relativization, the referent N of Q is presented as an empty category, and coreferential with the head noun of the relative clause.[29]

(55) a. *[[e* ***hutatu*** *aru]$_s$ [x to y]$_{NP}$]$_{NP}$ no uti,* ***hitotu-o*** *oidasu to,*
two exist and among one-ACC chase-out-when
'If we get rid of one out of the two...' (Toyama:1'30').

b. *[x to y]$_{NP}$-ga* ***hutatu*** *aru*
and-NOM two exist
'There are two (elements), x and y.'

The above example, (55a), is particularly interesting because two kinds of quantifiers, namely, the endogenous Q construction and the S-external Q, are present in the same sentence.

(56) a. *[Butudan-ni kore-made* ***hitotu*** *suwatte gozatta]$_{RC}$*
altar-in now-until one sitting exist-HON
Kannonsan-ga ***hutatu*** *suwatte gozatta. Korya*
Avalokitesvara-NOM two sitting-HON this
okasina kotoda.
strange thing-is
'There was one Kannon goddess (The Goddess of Mercy) sitting in the (family Buddhist) altar a moment ago, and now there are two of them. That's strange.' (Seki:122)

b. *Butudan-ni kore-made Kannonsan-ga* ***hitotu*** *suwatte*
alter-in now-until goddess-NOM one siting
gozatta
exist-HON
'There has been a Kannon Goddess sitting in the altar until now.'

c. *Butudan-ni kore-made e* ***hitotu*** *suwatte gozatta*
altar-in now-until one siting exist-HON
'There has been one Kannon Goddess sitting in the altar until now.'

In the main clause of (56a), the subject *kannonsan* and the "floated" Q *hutatu* 'two' form a Q-Float construction. On the other hand, the same *kannonsan* is regarded as the head of the relative clause, and the head noun has another quantifier, *hitotu* 'one,' in its own relative clause. Relating the head noun *kannonsan* to the Q inside the relative clause would make sense if we assume a source sentence (for the relative clause) like (56b), in which the noun *kannonsan* and the quantifier *hitotu* form a Q-Float construction. Relativization of the noun *kannonsan* would create an empty category *e* or the case-marked *e-ga* to yield a structure like (56c) as a prototype of the relative clause in (56a). Then, we can say that the quantifier *hitotu* relates itself as a "floated quantifier" to the relative clause head noun *kannonsan* by virtue of the intermittent empty category which is assumed to be coreferential with *kannonsan*.

The present analysis of NXQ inside relative clauses explains why the head noun in this type of the Q-construction is interpreted as carrying 'new' information. The function of the relative clause containing an endogenous Q resembles some aspects of the presentational *avoir*-cleft construction in French discussed by Lambrecht (1988:149-150).

I would like to add one minor remark here before moving to the next topic. Consider a sentence like (57) below. In (57), a relative clause contains Q-Float within it. Although the Q-Float involves a relative clause, it must be distinguished from the type of the Q-construction we have been discussing in this section.

(57) a. *[[siki]$_{NP}$ -ga* ***[hutatu]***$_{Q}$ *aru]$_{RC}$ hooteisiki*
formula-NOM two have equation
'an equation in which there are two formulae' (Toyama 1'30')

b. *Sono hooteisiki-ni-wa [siki]$_{NP}$ -ga* ***[hutatu]***$_{Q}$ *aru*
that equation-in-TOP formula-NOM two exist
'There are two formulae in the equation.'

The reason for this distinction is rather straightforward. Namely, what is relativized in (57) is not the referent of the quantifier ([*siki*]$_{NP}$ -*ga*), but the locative NP, *hooteisiki* 'equation.' In other words, the relativization leaves the Q-Float construction untouched, and the former has nothing to do with the latter.

3.3.2 *Type [..N..]$_S$[..Q..]$_S$ (sentence-external Q)*

In the sentence-external Q-construction, a referent noun and its numeral quantifier relate to each other across sentential boundaries, as illustrated below. I found 18 such cases in my data.

(58) *[Himo]$_{NP}$-ga arimasenka? Kono ie-niwa* ***ip-pon-mo***
string-NOM exist-not this house-in-TOP one-CLASS-too
naindesune.
exist-not-TAG.
'Don't you have a ball of string? —Not even a piece!' (Ogawa:69)

In (58), the first sentence contains the referent noun *himo* 'string,' and the following sentence shows its quantifier *ip-pon-mo* 'even a piece of string.'

The question to be asked is how the referent N in the first sentence and its quantifier Q in the second sentence relate to each other. One suggestion I would like to make is that the isolated Q in the second sentence may be generated in a Q-Float construction for achieving categorical negation, as in (59) below.

(59) *Kono ie niwa ([Himo]$_{NP}$-ga])* ***ip-pon-mo*** *naindesu-ne*
this house-in string-NOM one-CLASS-even exist-not-TAG
'There is no string in this house, huh.'

The referent N, *himo-ga* 'string-NOM,' which is coreferential with the identical NP in the preceding sentence, will subsequently be deleted (as shown by parentheses) to leave the "floated" quantifier Q behind. The deleted referent will always be recoverable by virtue of the presence of the identical referent which is available in the first sentence. In this interpretation the referent N of the Q-construction in the second sentence is always anaphorically definite, and coreferential to the noun in the preceding sentence.

Our analysis, which posits Q-Float as the basis for the sentence-external Q, is supported by its special functions, namely, emphasis by individuation, a partitive reading, and categorical negation. Recall that these three functions are particular to Q-Float, which we discussed in 3.2.1. In other words, the S-external Q construction fills all the major functions of Q-Float except the rhematic function, as shown in examples (60) through (62).

(60) a. *Zyotyuu-wa, { [moti]$_{NP}$-mo* ***takusan*** *nokotte ita node, }*
maid-TOP rice cake too many left-over-because

nanatu bakari *kami-ni tutunde yatte.*
seven or so paper-in wrapped gave
'Since there were quite a few rice cake left over, the maid wrapped *seven or so of them* in paper and gave them to (the monk)' (Seki:44).

b. *[sono moti]$_{NP}$ -o* ***nanatu*** *bakari (Q-Float)*
those cake-ACC seven about
'those rice cakes ... sevenof them'

In (60), the second sentence may have a gap created by the deletion of the Object NP *sono moti* 'the rice cake,' which is coreferential to the referent *moti* in (60a). The quantifier *nanatu-bakari* 'about seven' can relate itself indirectly to the referent *moti* in (60a) thanks to the coreferential gap in (60b). It has a partitive reading, as apparent in the translation 'seven or so of them.'

In (61), the quantifier in the phrase *hito-tubu hito-tubu* , (a reduplication form of 'one grain', or 'one (bead) after another (bead)') in (61a) may be interpreted as having an individuation reading in which each and every member of the set *zyuzudama* 'beads' is brought to the hearer's attention.

(61) a. *Nakade [zyuzudama]$_{NP}$-ga kisimi atta.* ***Hito-tubu hito-tubu***
inside beads-NOM squeak one-CLASS
ito-ni toosite-ikeba ...
thread-on pierce-if
'The beads clinks inside my pockets. If we string them one after another, (how long would it be ...)' (Ogawa:177).

b. *[Sono zyuzudama]$_{NP}$ -o* ***hito-tubu hito-tubu***
those beads-ACC one-CLASS one-CLASS
'those beads ... each of them'

In (62b) below, *hito hira* 'one-CLASS' is assumed to have its deleted local referent NP *sono hanabira no yoona tabemono* as in (62c), and it is associated with a partitive reading 'one piece of the petal-like food.' [30]

(62) a. *Are-wa— [hanabira-no yoona tabemono]$_{NP}$*
that-TOP petal-ATT appearance-ATT food
datta—
was
'It was food — something like flower petals—.'

b. ***hito-hira*** *taberu dake de mune-ga sawayaka ni nari—*
one-CLASS eat only by breast -NOM fresh-become
'As you eat them, just one, then your breast becomes fresh and...'(Mishima:209).

c. *[[sono hanabira no yoona] tabemono]$_{NP}$-o* ***[hito-hira]$_{Q}$***
those petals -like food -ACC one-CLASS
'the food like flower petals ... one of those petals'

One last remark to be added to this section is about the distinction between a S-external quantifier and a pronominalized quantifier. Consider the following discourse with multiple utterances.

(63) a. *[Kyoodai]$_{NP}$ -ga* ***hutari*** *ita.*
brothers-NOM two existed
'There lived two brothers (at the beach).'

b. ***Hutari-wa*** *itumo turi ni itta.*
two-TOP always fishing went
'The two went to fishing every day.'

c. *Aru hi* ***hutari-wa—***
one day two-TOP
'one day they (found)—.'

The quantifier *hutari* ('two persons') in (63a) is clearly an example of Q-Float with the referent noun *kyoodai* ('brothers'). However, the two occurrences of *hutari* in the subsequent two sentences, (63b) and (63c), are the pronominal form of the Q, which represents piece of information shared by the interlocutors.

4. Concluding remarks

In this study, I examined some semantic and discourse-functional effects of word order within NPs involving quantifier constructions in Japanese. I identified eight possible types of quantifier constructions on the basis of data collected from both Old Japanese and Modern Japanese written texts. These eight types were classified under three major categories: the NP-internal Q-construction; the locally NP-external Q-construction, and the Clause- (or Sentence)-external Q-construction. In Japanese, the functional roles of Q-constructions in discourse are largely determined by the relative position of Q with respect to its referent N. The locally NP-external type, typically Q-Float, which is characterized as an absolutive construction (à la Downing (1993)), serves as an important discourse device in introducing new information. One of the NP-internal Q-constructions known as Quantifier-Shift was found to be in use for two discourse phenomena — categorical negation and "itemization" as a special form of presentation, as seen in inventory-taking and various types of prescriptions — both of which are characteristically interpreted as being involved with the <indefinite-specific> feature. The study also suggests that there are no essential structural or functional differences between the present-day Japanese Q-Float and the Old Japanese counterpart, except that the latter is typically lacking the explicit case-marking.

Notes

* I thank Pamela Downing and Mathew S. Dryer for their valuable comments. Particularly, Downing's criticism and her recent research on the same subject led me to make extensive revisions of the original version I presented at the symposium. I am also grateful to Janet Fair-Christianson and David Kvernes for their stylistic advice. Needless to say, any errors and shortcomings are mine.

1. In casual conversations, one witnesses the occasional appearance of sentence constituents to the right of the predicating verb. A number of analyses are offered in the literature including Kuno's (1978) afterthought analysis. An excellent quantitative analysis of postposing phenomena in Japanese is found in Fujii (1991). Kim and Shin (1992) is a discourse analysis of Korean postposing on the basis of Fujii's analytical framework.

2. The NP referred to in this paragraph is in particular the kind of NP known as a lexical nominal ("derived nominal") rather than an NP derived via Nominalization.

3. Givón (1984:202) observes that various NP types conform differently to Cross-Category Harmony (à la Hawkins 1983), and suggests the following gradation:

   Most likely to conform to CCH
   - nominal (compounding) modifiers
   - genitive/possessive modifiers
   - noun-complements
   - adjectives
   - relative clauses
   - numerals/quantifiers
   - determiners

   Least likely to conform to CCH

   As seen in the above hierarchy, the quantifier category is found low in the CCH, and the Japanese Q-construction is indeed consistent with the CCH to a significant degree in comparison with other NP types, as Givón predicts.

4. In Kim (1982), I contrasted Rhematic Q-Float in Korean with the English *there*-construction. A study of the rhematic characteristics of Q-Float is found in H.S. Lee (1983), and Downing (1986). The following are some of the syntactic analyses on the Korean Q-Float phenomena in the recent literature: O'Grady (1986), M.-J. Jo (1985), C. Lee (1989), and K.-S. Hong (1990), but none of them is concerned with the discourse-functional effects of Q-Float, except C. Lee's discussion of some semantic implications of Korean Q-Float.

5. As Givón (1984: 223-4) suggests, the quantifier phrase [Numeral + Classifier]$_Q$ itself may be analyzed as an NP.

6. The use of hyphenation between a noun and a case marker is applied throughout this paper whenever the structural makeup is emphatically highlighted.

7. In Japanese the particle *no* plays a variety of functions in sentences. It is used in expressions for possession and association, and used even for the subject marker. Examples of these functions are as follows: Possessive as in *san nin no hon* ('the book owned by the three people'); Attributive as in *sizin* <u>*no*</u> *Frost* ('Mr. Frost, the poet' or 'Mr. Frost, who is a poet'); Partitive as in *zyogakusei* <u>*no*</u> *zen'in* ('all of the female students'), and the grammatical function of Subject as in *Harumi no kikoku sita koto* ('the fact that Harumi returned to her home country'). Linguists like Martin and Kuno recognize Attributive *no* as an adnominal form of the copula *de aru* or *da* . I will use Attributive in a slightly broader sense to include the particle *no* in a phrase like *suna no siro* (a castle of sand), which may be paraphrased as 'a castle which is made out of sand.' The adjectival phrase involved in the combination of a noun and the particle *no* is very much like *N's* in the [*N's N*] construction in English. This sort of particle *no* may be regarded as one of the morphological markers for prenominal modifiers in Japanese.

8. Downing (1986) is entirely devoted to the study of the anaphoric use of the classifiers in Japanese.

9. In (3a), the particle *no* is interpreted as the Attributive form of the copula *da*, as in *syatyoo no Yamadasan* ('Mr. Yamada, (who is) the company president'), following Martin (1975: 777) and Kuno (1973a:25). See footnotes 7 and 18 for more about Attributive *no*.

10. The symbol % refers to the relatively low acceptability of a sentence, notwithstanding the grammatical well-formedness of such a sentence.

11. As for the notion of specificity, I follow basically Enç's (1991) definition.

12. In the locally NP-external type, Q occurs syntactically apart from the NP which contains the Q's referent noun, but remains in the same sentence or clause, whereas Q of the S-external construction is found in a separate sentence.

13. The arbitrary intervening constituents X can be null, which makes the construction indistinguishable from a true NQ construction on the surface. The distinction between NQ and NØQ is elaborated in Sections 3.2.2. and 3.2.3.

14. Following Miyagawa (1989), I do not take the position here that Q is syntactically 'floated' away from its referent NP, which was suggested in Shibatani's (1977) earlier analysis. Instead, I use the word 'floated' as a figurative expression.

15. The Japanese classifier *tu* may be contrasted with the Korean classifier *nas* or its reduced form *-s* for small objects like grain. The Korean *hana* 'one' can be combined to yield /hana-s/ (which is phonetically realized as [hanat] with the arrested dental). Likewise, /twuls/ 'two+CLASS' is analyzed underlyingly as /tul+s/, /sey-s/ 'three+CLASS' for sey+s, /ney-s/ 'four+CLASS' for /ney+s/, and so on. I assume without argument that *hana-s* may

have the derivational source of /han+ nas/, which is semantically equivalent to 'one+unit.' These N+CL phrases in Korean do not appear in the prenominal position, as we see in the ungrammatical string **hana-s chayk* 'a book,' similar to the ungrammatical Japanese equivalent *hitotu hon*. The phonological correspondence between the Japanese /-tu/ and the Korean /-s/ is straightforward. The Japanese anterior dental /t/ and the Korean non-anterior dental /-s/ share the [+coronal] feature. The Japanese dental /t/ is supported by epenthetical /u/ to conform with the Japanese open syllable structure.

If the morpheme *-tu* is analyzed as a classifier (or a form reduced from another form), as we assume in this paper, a numeral/classifier compound like *hitotu* should be transcribed as *hito-tu*. However, I did not make such a specification in this paper.

16. Native numerals (*hito* 'one'; *huta* 'two'; *mi* 'three'; *yo*, 'four', etc.) contrast with Chinese numerals (*iti,ni, san, si,* etc.) For an elaborate description of the usages of the two systems, see Martin (1975: Section 13.6.) Native numerals co-occur with classifiers as well, as in *huta syurui no ringo* ('two kinds of apples).

17. I tentatively interpret the lexical item *ko* in (17aiii) as having a meaning of 'ply,' although ordinary Japanese dictionaries do not list this item as an independent lexical item. The above interpretation is indirectly inferred from the morpheme *ko* in the lexical item *koyori*, 'a *twisted* string, or a *twisted* piece of paper' (Kenkyusha's New Japanese-English Dictionary (1974: 960)). Incidentally, a verb *kko-* in Modern Korean has a meaning of 'to twist.' E.g. '*Sekki-lul kko-n-ta* '(Someone) makes a straw rope.'

18. A remark on the attributive *no* is in order. The structure $[A\text{-}no\ B]_{NP}$ in Japanese is interpreted as a combination of two head-final constructions. First, *A-no* may be analyzed as a postpositional phrase which obeys the head-final constraint. The phrase *A-no* is a modifier in the structure $[\ [A\text{-}no\ ]\ B]_{NP}$, where the head is B, which is placed at the phrase-final position. So, its English equivalent will be [B of A] rather than [A of B]. Or alternatively, the phrase *A-no* may be regarded as an adjectival form of A. In either analysis, the structure $[A\text{-}no\ B]_{NP}$ is to be analyzed as a complex structure like $[\ [A\text{-}no\ ]\ B]_{NP}$.

19. We may find a similar phenomenon in other languages. For instance, Hopper (1986:314) notes that in Malay the parameter specific/nonsecific contrasts only indefinite nouns, and definite nouns. And they are virtually never classified unless there is a strong focus on enumeration.

20. The modal morpheme *mo* 'even,' may often be added to the strawman 'one' in the categorical negation, as in '*Hitori-mo konakatta*,' which may be translated literally '*Even one* person did *not* show up.' (equivalent to 'No one showed up.')

21. The particle *no* serves in Modern Japanese as the attributive marker, but it also serves as the nominative marker in relative clauses. Historically, *no* was used as Nominative, as we see in the remnant usage in the Kyushu region. (Cf. Shibatani 1990:347f.)

22. The high concentration of Q-Float in Toyama's book may also be attributed in part to the specific nature of the book, which deals with numbers.

23. Narration or conversation itself does not seem to ensure the more frequent occurrence of Q-Float in certain situations. In my unprocessed taped data I frequently find that the speaker tends to drop the quantifier expression altogether in many situations (for instance, the number of *Momotaro*'s *kibidango* 'dumplings'). Discourse deletion of quantifier expressions in Japanese deserves further scrutiny in conjunction with pro-dropping or other general ellipsis strategies in the language.

24. In Kim (1982), I contrasted Korean Q-Float and the English *there*-insertion construction to show their functional similarities.

25. In determining the definiteness feature, I relied on the presence of morphological cues such as *wa* or demonstratives. In case neither of them was available, I then relied on the textual contexts where a NØQ candidate appears.

26. The sentence-ending *re* in (43a) is the imperative form of the Niigata dialect.

27. The Q *san-biki* cannot be case-marked by itself apart from the referent N *kousagi*, because this will force the referent N to have no thematic role, or to have a subject role in addition to the alleged subject Q, which will constitute a violation of the theta-criterion. In the Korean Q-Float, the case marker k for an antecedent noun is redundantly added (or copied on) to its corresponding quantifier, without affecting the grammaticality of the sentence, unlike Japanese. Such case-reduplication in Korean Q-Float needs future scrutiny.

28. One may suggest that the constructions in (48) - (50) are of the type of either QN or Q-*no* N. I reserve my discussion of this possibility for other occasions.

39. Various analyses of relative clause formation in Japanese are found in Kuno (1973a), McCawley (1976), and Hasegawa (1981), among others. One may apply Hasegawa's analysis to the present hypothesis of relativization from the Q-Float source for the endogenous Q-construction.

30. One might suggest a structure like Ex. below for the isolated quantifier *hito hira* in (59b).

Ex.	*[[sono*	*hanabira no*	*yoona]$_{AP}$*	*tabemono]$_{NP}$-no*	***[hito hira]**$_Q$-o*
	those	petals	-like	food	-ATT	one-CLASS-ACC

If one takes Ex. for the structure of the isolated quantifier in (59b), the quantifier is expected to take the Accusative case, and, furthermore, deletion is to be applied to the modifier of the referent NP. I will leave open this alternative for future scrutiny.

Appendix

I. *Texts used in this study*

Arishima, Takeo. 1940/1979. *Hito husa no budoo* (A bunch of grapes).Tokyo: Iwanami.
Fukada, Yusuke. 1977. *Shin seiyojijo* (A New version of "Europe today"). Tokyo: Shinchosha.
Doi, Takeo. 1971/1987. *Amae no kenkyu* (A Study of Dependency). Tokyo: Koobunsha
Mikami, Akira. 1963/1988. *Nihongo no ronri: wa and ga* (The Logic of Japanese: wa and ga). Tokyo: Kuroshio.
Mishima, Yukio. 1967. *Utukusii hosi* (Fabulous Stars). Tokyo: Shinchosha.
Oe, Kenzaburo. 1977. "Gendai bungaku kenkyuusha ni nani o nozomuka" (What can one expect from contemporary literary critics?). In: *Nihonbungakukenkyu no hoohoo (ed. by Nihonbungaku kenkyushiryo-kankookai.* Tokyo: Yuseido
Ogawa, Kunio. 1978 *Ryuiki* (A flood plain). Tokyo: Shueisha.
Seki, Keigo. 1969. *Nihon no mukasibanasi (III)* (The folk tales of Japan). Tokyo: Iwanami.

Shiina, Rinzo. 1967. *Eien naru zyosyoo* (An Eternal prelude). Tokyo: Shinchosha.
Takakura, Atsuhiro. 1970. *Taketori Monogatari* (The story of Prince Kaguya. circa 900). Tokyo: Iwanami.
Takeda, Yusuke (annotated) 1974. *Kojiki* (The Record of Ancient Matters of 712AD). Tokyo: Kadokawa.
Toyama, Hiraku. 1972. *Suugaku no manabikata.Osiekata.* (How to learn and how to teach mathematics). Tokyo: Iwanami.

II. *Additional examples of Type [..Q..]N)*

Ex.1 *iti mai sika nai sita o tyongirarete simatta,*
one-CLASS only exist-non tongue-ACC cut-be
'(The monkey) got his only tongue cut (by the earwig)' (Seki:151).

Ex.2 *Mittu yottu matataite iru hi*
three four glittering lamps
'three or four glittering lamps...' (Ogawa:135).

Ex.3 *[musume ni go roku tubu yatta] chocolate no hako ga .....*
girl -DAT five or six-CLASS gave-REL -ATT box-NOM
'the box (was found empty), a few pieces of chocolate from which I gave to the girl' (Fukada:184).

Ex.4 *[hutatu aru] X to Y no uti,.....*
two exist and of
Literally, "among X and Y that exist two in number"
'of the 2 X's ...' (Toyama 1973: 182).

Ex.5 *Kokutetu no eki de hitori zyookyakutati kara hanarete ressya o*
Japan Rail-ATT station-at one passengers-from apart-and train-ACC
matte ita, akanuketa otoko datta no kamo sirenai.
waiting refined man was it-may-be
'That elegant looking person might be the man who was waiting the train apart from other passengers at the JR train station' (Ogawa: 79).

References

Bolinger, D. 1977. *Meaning and Form*. London and New York: Longman
Choi, Y. S. 1988. "A reanalysis of Quantifier Floating in Korean". *Linguistic Journal of Korea* 13. 109-147.
Comrie, B. 1981. *Language Universals and Linguistic Typology*. Chicago: University of Chicago Press.
Desző, L. 1982. *Studies in Syntactic Typology and Contrastive Grammar*. The Hague: Mouton.
Downing, P. 1984. Japanese numeral classifiers: a syntactic, semantic, and functional profile. Unpublished Ph.D. dissertation, University California at Berkeley.

Downing, P. 1985. "Classifier constructions and referentiality-marking in Japanese." Paper presented at Conference on Japanese Language and Linguistics, UCLA.
Downing, P. 1986. The anaphoric use of classifiers in Japanese. *Noun Classes and Categorization* ed. by C. Craig, 345-375. Amsterdam/Philadelphia: John Benjamins Publishing Company.
Downing, P. 1993. "Pragmatic and semantic constraints on numeral quantifier position in Japanese." *Journal of Linguistics* 29.65-93.
Enç, M. 1991. "The semantics of specificity." *Linguistic Inquiry* 22.1-25.
Fujii, Y. 1991. "Nihongo ni okeru gojun no gyakuten." (Reversed word order in Japanese: a discourse-pragmatic analysis). *Gengo Kenkyu.* 99. 58-81.
Givón, T. 1984. *Syntax: a Functional Typological Introduction,* Vol. 1, Amsterdam/ Philadelphia: John Benjamins Publishing Company.
Givón, T. 1979. *On Understanding Grammar.* New York: Academic Press.
Givón, T. 1988. "The pragmatics of word order: predictability, importance and attention." *Studies in Syntactic Typology* ed. by M.E. Hammond, E. Moravcsik and J. Wirth, 243-284. Amsterdam/Philadelphia: John Benjamins.
Haig, J. 1980. "Some observations on quantifier floating in Japanese." *Linguistics* 18. 1068-1069
Hasegawa, N. 1981. A lexical interpretive theory with emphasis on the role of subject. Doctoral dissertation, University of Washington.
Hawkins, J. A. 1983. *Word Order Universals.* New York: Academic Press.
Hong, K.-S. 1990. "Quantifier-Float in Korean." *BLS* 16. 175-186.
Hopper, P. J. 1986. "Some discourse functions of classifiers in Malay." *Noun Classes and Categorization* ed. by C. Craig, 309-325. Amsterdam/Philadelphia: John Benjamins.
Inoue, K. 1978. *Nihongo no Bunpo Kisoku.* Tokyo: Taishuukan.
Jo, Mi-Jeung. 1985. "Constituents in fixed word order and a 'governed' non-Theta position in Korean." *Harvard Studies in Korean Linguistics.* Dept. of Linguistics. Harvard University. 79-87.
Kamio, A. 1977. "Suuryoosi no sintakusu" ('Syntax of quantifiers'). *Gengo* 6(9). 83-93.
Kim, A. H. 1982. "Why quantifiers float?" Paper presented at the Winter Meeting of the Linguistic Society of America. San Diego, CA.
Kim, A. H. 1988. "Preverbal focusing and type XXIII languages." *Studies in Syntactic Typology* ed. by M. Hammond, E. Moravcsik, and J. Wirth, 147-169. Amsterdam/ Philadelphia: John Benjamins.
Kim, A. H. 1990. "Numeral quantifier construction and definiteness restriction in Korean." *Papers from the Seventh International Conference on Korean Linguistics* ed. by E.J. Baek, 121-131.
Kim, A. H. and Shin, H. S. 1992. "Postposing in Korean." Paper presented at the XVth International congress of Linguists, at Université Laval, Quebec, Canada.
Kuno, S. 1973a. *The Structure of the Japanese Language.* Cambridge, Mass: MIT Press.
Kuno, S. 1973b. *Nihon Bunpoo Kenkyuu.* 'The Study of Japanese Grammar.' Tokyo: Taishukan.
Kuno, S. 1978a. "Theoretical perspectives on Japanese linguistics." *Problems in Japanese Syntax and Semantics* ed. by J. Hinds and I. Howard, 213-285. Tokyo: Kaitakusha.

Kuno, S. 1978b. "Japanese: A characteristic SOV language." *Syntactic typology* ed. by W.P. Lehmann, 57-138. Austin/London: University of Texas Press.

Lambrecht, K. 1988. "Presentational cleft constructions in spoken French." *Clause Combining in Grammar and Discourse* ed. by J. Haiman and S.A. Thompson, 135-79. Amsterdam/Philadelphia: John Benjamins.

Lee, C. 1989."(In)definite, case markers, classifiers and quantifiers in Korean." *Harvard Studies in Korean Linguistics 3*. 469-487.

Lee, H .S. 1983. "Word Order and Quantifier Floating in Papago and Pima." UCLA ms.

Martin, S. E. 1975. *A Reference Grammar of Japanese*. New Haven: Yale University Press..

McCawley, J. 1976. "Relativization." *Syntax and Semantics Vol. 5: Japanese Generative Grammar* ed. by M. Shibatani, 295-306. New York: Academic Press.

Miyagawa, S. 1989. *Structure and Case Marking in Japanese.* New York: Academic Press.

O'Grady, W. 1986. "Floated quantifiers and binding in Korean." *Linguistic Journal of Korea* 11.1: 17-23.

O'Grady, W. 1987. *Principles of Grammar and Learning*. Chicago: University of Chicago Press.

O'Grady, W. 1988. "Grammatical relation and Korean syntax." *Linguistics in the Morning Calm*. Vol. 2, 1068-1069. Seoul: Hanshin Publishing Co.

Shibatani, M. 1977. "Grammatical relations and surface cases." *Language* 53. 789-809.

Shibatani, M. 1990. *The Languages of Japan.* Cambridge: Cambridge University Press.

WH-clefts and left-dislocation in English conversation

Cases of topicalization

Kyu-hyun Kim
University of California, Irvine

1. Introduction

In this paper, I examine two different constructions in English, WH-clefts and left-dislocation, and discuss how the particular word orders and syntactic structures displayed by these constructions are put to the service of various interactional enterprises in spontaneous conversation.[1] These two constructions are treated together here because they share the functional characteristic of topic-comment structure (Gundel 1985; Keenan-Ochs and Schieffelin 1976; Geluykens 1986, 1988, 1989). Examples (1) and (2) are instances of WH-clefts and left-dislocation which are excerpted from authentic conversational data:

(1) What that amounts to is that they don't keep comparable books. (WH-cleft)
(2) My father, he is not a heavy drinker. (Left-dislocation)

As example (1) illustrates, what is peculiar about WH-clefts is that, as the name suggests, the proposition is 'cleft' into two parts (cf. Jespersen 1968). Traditionally the initial WH-clause is viewed as containing 'presupposed' or 'given' information, while the utterance following the BE copula carries 'focus', (cf. Akmajian 1970; Gundel 1977; Hankamer 1974; Quirk and Greenbaum 1973). In this respect, the markedness of this construction can be observed in the sense that WH-clefts explicitly delineate the presupposition from the focus (cf. Givón 1982). As for left dislocation, the markedness lies in the word order, which deviates from the canonical SVO word order of English (Ross 1967).

Given the non-canonical structure of these constructions, the present paper aims to explicate how these 'marked' word order constructions are used in the service of the speaker's attempt to achieve some interactional goals which would not be accomplished by using the 'unmarked' counterparts. To this end, I draw upon the functional linguistic perspective and conversation analytic perspective[2] (Sacks, Schegloff, and Jefferson 1974), and attempt to show that the use of these constructions has particular sequential implications to which interactants orient themselves.

The major assumption of this study is that conversation is the primordial mode of language use which constitutes the basis of human social interaction and social organization (cf. Sacks, Schegloff, and Jefferson 1974; Levinson 1983). While conversation has not been given much attention in the field of linguistics, some recent studies analyzing linguistic forms in conversational contexts (e.g., Ford 1993; Fox 1987a) show that conversational data provide contexts which are saliently distinguishable from monologic data, with the factor of interaction shaping functions of linguistic forms in a way that is not found in other genres lacking natural interaction. In this respect, this paper builds on the insights of previous functionally- and interactionally-oriented studies that look at functions of WH-clefts or left-dislocation in authentic discourse (cf. Prince 1978; Keenan-Ochs and Schieffelin 1976; Duranti and Ochs 1979; Geluykens 1986, 1988, 1989), and further explicates the interactional import of these constructions with reference to the sequential contexts where they are situated in spontaneous conversation.

2. WH-clefts in conversation

2.1 *Context of the problem*

While the presupposition/focus distinction has been posited for WH-clefts in the field of generative linguistics in terms of relating the construction to a more basic construction or to other cleft constructions through derivation (Akmajian 1970; Higgins 1973), the examination of WH-clefts in naturally occurring conversation generally shows that such a view is not tenable, even though there are a few cases where the genuine presupposition/focus distinction holds; only three out of 76 instances of WH-clefts examined in this paper are cases where the initial WH-clause of the WH-cleft directly refers to some information retrievable from the preceding context. Example (3) is one such instance where the initial WH-clause contains information that is explicitly picked up from the preceding context; the initial WH-clause of the WH-cleft at line 6 directly refers to A's utterance at line 1:

(3) (SBL, 7-10)
1 A: Uh what he calls it is suggesting to your subconscious,
2 B: Mm hm,
3 A: And it's one and the same thing, exactly.
4 B: Mm hm,
5 (1.0)
→ 6 B: You know what I think I suggests- uh subjects- uh suggest to
7 my subconscious is that I don't feel well, so that I won't haftuh work,
8 (1.0)
9 A: A(hh) // hehh
10 B: Heh hah ha heh!
11 B: That's a terrible thought.

In the majority of cases, it is observed that the initial WH-clause of WH-clefts contains non-anaphoric, non-presuppositional information, as example (4) illustrates:

(4) (GTS 3,11)
1 Louise: Inventory taking of the whole stock every day, ( ),
2 to-(I mean) every other day, an' they hafta- there's
3 this place called Atlas Supply Company which supplies
4 (/ /) drugstores an' beauty shops for most of Los Angeles.
5 And -- got this job there. Where for the rest of this
6 year y'know uh the summer rather, the rest of the term an'
7 the summer, they'll be training me, to do this. // An' I'll
8 be-
9 Dan: Oh sounds good.
→ 10 Louise: The pay goes up- what I'm surprised of is the pay goes up to
11 sump'n like two fifty an hour. At the end. An' that's
12 gonna be nice. hehh

We can readily note in line 10 that the information contained in the initial WH-clause is not presupposed, because the information in the WH-clause can in no way be related to some preceding context, nor is it 'given' in Chafe's (1976) sense, because there is no basis on which the speaker can assume that her internal state of 'being surprised' is in the consciousness of the hearer at the moment of utterance.

In fact, the logico-deductive treatment of 'presupposition' was rejected by Givón (1982), who notes that what is called presupposition can be better characterized in pragmatic terms as presuppositionally backgrounded information or unchallengeable material which the speaker presents as something to be treated by the interlocutor as being presupposed. With specific reference to WH-clefts, this communication-oriented view was proposed also by Hetzron (1975), who notes that WH-clefts can serve as the first instance of communication without true presupposition, and by Prince (1978), who suggests that the information contained in the WH-clause of WH-clefts is information that the cooperative speaker may assume is appropriately in the hearer's consciousness. As I will show in the following discussion, these speaker-oriented and communication-oriented views provide a basis for a more detailed explication of the interactional functions of WH-clefts.

2.2 *Data base*

The data examined in this paper include roughly three types of conversational data:[3]

(i) Casual Conversational Data: Ordinary face-to-face and telephone conversations
(ii) Brad Crandall Radio Talk Show Data (hereafter BC)
(iii) Group Therapy Session Data (hereafter GTS).

Casual Conversational Data subsumes ordinary conversations occurring in non-task-oriented contexts, such as face-to-face or telephone conversations where various casual social goals are negotiated. The BC data are radio call-in show conversations where the show host, Mr. Crandall, talks to different callers. These conversations are often characterized by extended arguments between Mr. Crandall and his callers. The GTS data are conversations among teenagers and a therapist in a loosely structured group therapy session, where the participants talk spontaneously about various personal episodes concerning their life, family, and friends.[4]

A total of 76 instances of WH-clefts occurring in various conversational contexts were examined in this study; 19 are from the Casual Conversation data, 40 are from the BC data, and 17 are from the GTS data. In the next section, I briefly examine the frequency distribution of WH-clefts in these three categories of data in terms of type of verb used in the initial WH-clause as well as the predicate type found in the focus slot, both of which suggest some of the functional and interactional characteristics of WH-clefts.

2.3 *Predicate types in WH-clefts*

The types of verb used in the initial WH-clause of WH-clefts can be roughly categorized as follows:

a. Verbs marking a speaker-internal state (29 tokens): *realize, want, feel, think, know, hesitate, enjoy, see, object to, bother,* etc.
b. Verbs marking a metalinguistic dimension (22 tokens): *mean, say,* etc.
c. Verbs marking meta-actions (6 tokens): *do*
d. Verbs marking meta-events (12 tokens): *happen*
e. Others (7 tokens): *amount to, cash in on*, etc.

Table 1 shows the distribution of WH-clefts in each category in terms of verb types used in the initial WH-clause. The percentage shown in the parentheses refers to the rate of occurrence of each verb type in each conversation type.

First of all, we can note in Table 1 that internal state predicates occurred most frequently in the initial WH-clause of WH-clefts (38%). This tendency is particularly salient in Casual Conversation, where more than half of the WH-clefts (53%) have an internal state predicate. In the other two types of conversation, internal state predicates are still used frequently, occurring in about one third of the tokens of WH-clefts (33% for BC and 35% for GTS). It is to be noted that out of the total of 29 internal state predicates, 24 are used with the first person subject (83%).[5]

Table 1. Verb types in the initial WH-clause of WH-clefts

	Internal state	Metalinguistic predicate	DO verb	HAPPEN	Others	Total
Casual Conversation	10 (53%)	6 (32%)	2 (11%)	1 (5%)	0 (0%)	19
BC	13 (33%)	8 (20%)	4 (10%)	8 (20%)	7 (18%)	40
GTS	6 (35%)	8 (47%)	0 (0%)	3 (18%)	0 (0%)	17
Total	29 (38%)	22 (29%)	6 (8%)	12 (16%)	7 (11%)	76

Table 1 also shows that metalinguistic verbs occurred very frequently in WH-clefts, particularly in the GTS data (47%). While this distributional tendency indicates a function of WH-clefts that refers to the metalinguistic dimension, the relatively high number of metalinguistic verbs in the GTS compared with other data seems to be due to the particular nature of therapeutic discourse where a speaker often metalinguistically refers to what others said for the purpose of 'doing therapy', or making an argument in the context of producing a series of thematically related episodes (see Section 2.4.1.2.).

As for the 'focus' slot of WH-clefts, Table 2 shows the distribution of predicate types in the focus slot of WH-clefts.[6] We can first note in Table 2 that WH-clefts were predominantly used to give focus to a full clause; 64 percent of the WH-clefts counted (48 out of 75) contain a full clause in the focus position.[7] On the other hand, only 24% (18 out of 75) are cases where an NP is given focus. It is noteworthy in this regard that WH-clefts with a focused NP are rather frequently found in the BC data (33%) compared to the other two data sets (17% for Casual Conversation and 12% for GTS). Given that the BC data are radio talk show data which in this case are generally characterized by an argumentative style, this frequency distribution makes one suspect that, while NPs are more frequently focused in a specific context of argument, a more canonical function of WH-clefts in ordinary, everyday conversation is to give focus to an utterance in the form of a clause. This point suggests that, from an interactional perspective, various functions of WH-clefts may be better understood in terms of the speaker's adding the initial WH-clause before the presentation of a major point in the focused utterance rather than in terms of a syntactic operation in which an item is picked up and extraposed to be given focus. As I will point out in the following discussion, we indeed find a general sense in which the focused part of WH-clefts is delayed and framed by the initial WH-clause for specific interactional reasons.

Table 2. Predicate types of focused utterance in WH-clefts

	Full clause	Infinitive	Gerund	NP	Total
Casual Conversation	11 (61%)	3 (17%)	1 (5%)	3 (17%)	18*
BC	23 (58%)	4 (10%)	0 (0%)	13 (33%)	40
GTS	14 (82%)	0 (0%)	1 (6%)	2 (12%)	17
Total	48 (64%)	7 (9%)	2 (3%)	18 (24%)	75

*One token of a WH-cleft with no focused part is not included here.

2.4 *Interactional uses of WH-clefts*

The interactional uses of WH-clefts are globally categorized in terms of (i) discourse-organizational uses as in marking a topic shift, or marking the gist of the prior talk, (ii) interactional management uses as in expressing or dealing with disagreement or initiating repair, and (iii) affect display. These three types of functions, however, are not mutually exclusive. The interactional characteristics of each use are explicated in the following sections with reference to various sequential contexts where WH-clefts are situated.

2.4.1 *WH-clefts in discourse organization*

2.4.1.1 *Topic shift: topic resumption* WH-clefts are frequently found in extended talk at a place where the speaker initiates topic shift. What is noteworthy in this context is that WH-clefts mark a topic shift in such a way that the speaker relates back to a certain topical point which has been temporarily relegated to the background in the immediately preceding context. In this sense, WH-clefts often mark a topic resumption. Example (5) below is an instance where a WH-cleft is used in a story-telling context for topic shift after a digression. In this example, D talks about some experiences he had in a foreign country in response to H's question at line 114 as to what made him the sickest. A WH-cleft is found at line 148:

(5) (After the movie)
114 W: Well what made you the si:ckest.
115 (1.0)
116 C: You could never identify it.=
[
117 D: Mm:
118 H: =You don't kno:w, ye:an=
119 D: No I know. I ('d be) pretty sure it was when
120 (0.8)
121 D: I went to this thing
122 (1.0)
123 D: when a pe(r)- when a ol:d man reaches seventy seven they
124 have this big ceremony (i wu)'s like his re:bir:th or
125 something and they do wha' they (.) carry him on 'iz ba:ck
126 'n put 'im in a chariot n' (.) carry him around all the (.)
127 ki:ds drag him around through th' village an' stuff (they
128 do all this) the(n 'ey 'ave a) big fea:s' an' they drink they

129 'ave these bi:g (.) jars full of this (.) mm-
130 (1.0)
131 D: 'ts like fermen:ted wi(n) er- fermented ri:ce. 'ts like (.)
132 they (.) y'know ri-
133 W: Rice wine?
134 (0.3)
135 D: It's not like wi- I mean it's it's not like wi:ne. It doesn't
136 taste like wine but it's
137 W: Fermented.=
138 D: =White and milky but it's fermented
[
139 H: Oh yeah?
140 (0.3)
141 H: In bo:wls?
142 W: O'that sounds disgusting
[
143 D: Y-yeah well it's in these big
144 (1.0)
145 D: va:ses, you know. Huge.
[[[
146 W: Vats
147 H: Yeah. Yeah.
→ 148 D: But what I didn't realize at the time was I had always
149 been thinking well a:ll anything alcoholic has been (.)
150 distilled and is oka:y.
151 (0.2)
152 D: But this isn't.
153 (0.3)
154 D: It's just made from (.) I mean t'ey jus-
[
155 J: Oh yea:h,
156 D: It's just ferme:nted. It's not disti:lled.
157 (0.3)
158 D: So I drank a lo:t that day'n it jus' about
[
159 W: O:h Go::d

In response to H's question at line 114 ('Well what made you the si:ckest'), D starts to tell an episode at line 121 ('I went to this thing') about a ceremony he had attended. D describes what went on in the ceremony and the particular alcoholic beverage the people drank through line 139, and then a digression ensues when D is asked about what kind of vessel that alcoholic beverage comes in. The WH-cleft at line 148 is then produced at the point where D shifts the topic from the talk about the bowls back to the strange alcoholic substance he drank.

We find that the initial WH-clause in line 148, along with the adversative conjunctive marker *but* that precedes it, projects a contrastive context in such a way that it is highly disjunctive from the immediately preceding talk. It is to be noted, however, that given that the foreign alcoholic substance referred to by the WH-cleft turns out to be the thing that made him the sickest, the WH-cleft is used to orient the interlocutor's attention away from the digressive topic, *bowls*, to the main topic of the story, *the alcoholic beverage*, which was prompted by the interlocutor's question at line 114. Therefore, we find that the disjunction from the immediately preceding context is accorded a thematic coherence by virtue of the fact that the speaker resumes the main story line by means of the topic shift. In other words, 'topic-talking' is what the speaker resumes with the WH-cleft.

2.4.1.2 *Gist-marking* By 'marking the gist of the previous talk', I mean 'summarizing' or 'wrapping up' the previous talk in a cogent manner. WH-clefts with this function often have in their WH-clause metalinguistic verbs, even though other verbs are also found. WH-clefts found in this context are either used for marking the gist of the previous talk by the same speaker, or for marking the gist of what the interlocutor said in the preceding context.

As I mentioned in Section 2.3., the gist-marking WH-clefts are frequently found in the GTS data, where participants, particularly the therapist present among them, often produce a WH-cleft to mark the gist of what a participant said. Example (6) is a case in point, where the WH-cleft is used by Dan, a therapist, in a context where two teenage participants, Ken and Louise, are jokingly exchanging assessments after Ken's story about how his grandmother treats his father as if he were still a child:

(6) (GTS 3, 61)
1 Ken: My-waitaminute. My father's-my father's forty five,
2 my father's forty five, or forty-forty three I think
3 ( ). Uh forty three, an' he'll go over to my
4 grandmother's house, and insteada my grandmother
5 offering him a drink, of beer, she'll say // Wouldju-
6 Louise "Wanna glassa milk?" // hehhh
7 Ken: No "Wouldju like a little bitta he'ing?"
8 Louise: heh // ha ha!

9 Ken: "Wouldja like some crekles?"
10 Louise: ehh ha ha ha ha
11 Ken: "Wouldja like a peanut butter an' jelly samwich?"
→ 12 Dan: So in a way, what you're saying is- is, "you'll never
13 get through that."
14 Ken: heh
15 Louise: ehhehh
16 Ken: You know?
17 Dan: N(hh)o ma(hh)tt(hh)er what! // hhh hehh

In this example, Dan rephrases what Ken said in the WH-cleft format, and invites his confirmation or rejection regarding the correctness of the rephrasing. What is noteworthy in this context is that the speaker uses a WH-cleft to mark the gist of the preceding story as a whole and attempts to direct the talk in a certain direction relevant to the action that he purports to initiate, i.e., for the purpose of 'doing therapy'. That is, Dan produces a WH-cleft in a sequential position where an assessment is due, but by doing so attempts to change the quality of interaction from the story-telling to therapeutic talk. Therefore, what the WH-cleft does is to mark a disjunction in such a way that it evokes the relevance of the current utterance in terms of the current speech event, i.e., a therapy session.

WH-clefts are also frequently used to mark the gist of the previous talk by the same speaker in the context of an argument. Example (7) is a case in point, where A, a radio talk show host, produces extended talk in response to a question from a caller:

(7) (BC, Green, 35)
1 A: When a man commits a murder,
2 A: Uh:
3 A: It would only cost eight cents for a policem'n to put a bullet
4 through 'im. But we don't approve a' that. We'd rather bring 'im
5 into a courtroom, and we — set 'im in a courtroom thet cost a
6 thousan' dollars a day to run, an' we give 'im a trial thet last'
7 three weeks, hh and then we allow an appeal system which runs up
8 another twunty tuh thirdy thousan' dollars before we finally
9 incarcerate 'im fer thirty tuh ninedy da:ys, hh and execute 'im
10 or keep 'im in prison fer life, an' it cost' ten thousan'dollars
11 per year per prisoner tuh do that. hhhh All of thi:s, — to, tuh
12 'spose of a problem thet a man could of done for on an eight cent
→ 13 basis. What that amounts is : thet they don't keep comparable
14 books. When they're talking about the protection of lives an'

property.
(pause)
B: We:ll,

In this example, the gist of the preceding talk is marked by the WH-cleft in lines 13 and 14, and through this, the speaker marks a consequence following from his prior talk. This type of context is frequently found in the BC data, particularly where the radio call-in show host makes an argument in an extended turn in the course of responding to the caller's questions.[8] We can note here that the gist is marked in such a way that the speaker proceeds from the specifics presented for exemplary purposes to the major point of his argument. In this sense, we can say that the speaker marks the gist for the purpose of engaging in an argument in an extended turn.

Therefore, what we find in examples (6) and (7) is that the gist is offered to indicate a particular way of understanding the preceding talk with a view to carrying out a certain action which is contextually licensed, such as 'doing therapy', or engaging in an argument; in both cases, the use of WH-clefts evokes the relevance of the current utterance by way of formulating the sense of the current talk in terms of 'doing therapy' after the interlocutor's 'story-telling', or 'doing an argument' after 'exemplification'. In this respect, while it is 'topic-talking' that the WH-cleft marks in example (5), examples (6) and (7) are cases where a contextually relevant action is being evoked by WH-clefts. Such characteristics of WH-clefts that relate to a broad 'topic' that is the current concern under consideration, or to a 'goal-driven action' that defines the current talk, seem to make the local disjunction with the immediately preceding talk a coherent transition that is relevant to the current interactional context.

What is noteworthy in relation to these observations is that WH-clefts are frequently used by a consultant or specialist in a procedural, direction-giving discourse. For instance, one is likely to hear a number of WH-clefts when he/she consults a specialist in a specialist-novice interaction. This point is illustrated in the examples (8) and (9) below. These examples are from the Garden Lady data in the UCLA Oral Corpus, where a gardening expert on a radio talk show provides advice to people regarding plants:

(8) What you might do is when you go to raise it up check out the root system.

(9) What I would do I would I would keep them evenly moist, not wet.

The frequent use of WH-clefts by the specialist in such a specialist-novice interaction would be explained by the observation that WH-clefts in these cases serve as a device by which the speaker highlights the nature of the current speech situation, while minimizing the role of the speaker as an individual responsible for the action being initiated.

2.4.2 *WH-clefts in interactional management: dealing with a problem*

2.4.2.1 *Disagreement: proposing an alternative* WH-clefts are used in contexts where the speaker disagrees with the interlocutor and asserts his/her point in the course of presenting his/her argument in response to the interlocutor's point. This would be a context in which the contrast-marking function of WH-clefts is used in the service of doing dispreferred interactional work (cf. Pomerantz 1984; Sacks 1987). What is interesting about these contexts is that the speaker often uses WH-clefts for expressing disagreement in the course of reacting to a dispreferred response from the interlocutor, e.g., when the speaker reasserts his/her point after the interlocutor did not quite agree with the speaker's previous point. Example (10) below is a case in point, which is from the BC data. In this example, Speaker A is Brad Crandall, the radio show host, and speaker B is a caller:

(10) (BC, Green, 117)
1 B: And, we j'st can't get it.
2 B: I tried, hh
3 B: Ahm on Medicade no:w but if they take me off- hh what um I
4 going to do:: there's no/-
5 A: Well now waidaminnit dear.
: :
27 A: They won't be taking you off Medicade.
28 B: They will!
29 B: They sayd if you // make-
30 A: No::.
31 B: -over a // certain amount of money.
32 A: Wait a sec,
: :
114 A: The papers, I read.
115 B: Ye:s/
116 A: -have stateduh thet the::, current feelings would apply to those
117 people in that special group we were talking about. Bli:nd, etcetra.
118 B: Ye:s/

119 A: Thet it-
120 A: Those would not change.
121 A: So you would still, be eligible.
122 A: It w-wouldn't cha:nge, you:r eligibility.
123 B: Well
→ 124 B: What I know is that they gave me a ledder an' they never
125 sent me my ca:rd, hh -my:: Medicare ca:rd,

Throughout this segment of talk, A has repeatedly rejected B's point that B would not be eligible for Medicare any more. From line 114 to line 120, A provides a piece of evidence supporting his position, and makes a conclusive remark in lines 121 and 122 that she would still be eligible. In response to A's point, B produces *well* in line 123, a signal that projects a dispreferred response or something less than an agreement (Sacks 1987; Pomerantz 1984), and then uses a WH-cleft at line 124 to reject A's point and reassert her own point.

One of the senses that we make in this example is that speaker B shows disagreement by presenting her point as an alternative to the interlocutor's point, with the presentation of the alternative being initiated by the expression of the speaker's stance, i.e., 'What I know' in example (10). The presentation of the first-handedness of the speaker's experience situated in this type of contrastive context constitutes a basis on which the speaker can implicitly reject the interlocutor's point without directly countering it. We find, in this respect, that there is a sense in which speaker B deals with the interlocutor's disagreement in a highly oblique manner by re-asserting her point on the basis of an independent empirical ground.

While the speaker's expression of his/her stance in the initial WH-clause can be one way of 'doing disagreement', we also found cases where the verb *happen* is used in the initial WH-clause in the context of an argument. This occurs frequently in the BC data; five out of seven WH-clefts whose WH-clause contains the verb *happen* are found in disagreement contexts (cf. Table 1). In such cases, the use of a WH-cleft often proposes an alternative after the interlocutor's point is explicitly rejected. Example (11) below is a case in point:

(11) (BC, Green, 45)
1 A: Now lemme tell yuh dear, It ain't.
2 (pause)
3 A: Yuh see,
→ 4 A: What does happen i:s.
5 A: An' I think you uh- there's a tendency t' forget this,

6 A: The number of Negroes, in Vietnam, or anywhere else, is
7 about- one an' a half out of ten. Fifteen out of a hundred.
8 B: Mmhm,

In the context that precedes this segment of talk, the caller, B, asked Mr. Crandall, A, why there are so many black American soldiers in Vietnam, and in this segment of talk, A rejects the assumption underlying the caller's question. A's use of a WH-cleft in line 4, then, projects an extended turn where the speaker is supposed to provide an account of the basis for his having rejected the caller's point. We can still see that the speaker uses the WH-cleft for providing an alternative, which is obliquely asserted as the right one, as opposed to the caller's idea about what happens. The message of contrastiveness is further strengthened by the emphatic use of the DO verb in the initial WH-clause of the WH-cleft.[9]

With reference to the oblique manner in which the speaker uses WH-clefts to assert his/her first-hand experience as an empirical ground independent of the current point of dispute, the use of a meta-event verb in the initial WH-clause seems to further distance the speaker's self away from the point being rejected. That is, there seems to be a basis on which the speaker can explicitly reject the interlocutor's point by virtue of the fact that the ground for the rejection is furnished by the general external event denoted by verbs like *happen*. Given the function of WH-clefts that evoke an event frame or a prior text through the initial WH-clause, we can say that the use of such a general verb further facilitates the speaker's disengagement from the interactional work of conveying disagreement, thus allowing more leeway for explicit signaling of his/her disagreeing position.

2.4.2.2 *Repair* While WH-clefts are frequently found in the context of disagreement, they are sometimes also used in repair contexts. Even though there are only four such instances in my database, they point to a very interesting way in which a WH-cleft is used in the service of the speaker's attempt to address the interlocutor's misunderstanding of talk. The kind of repair initiated by the use of WH-clefts fits into what Schegloff (1990) calls 'third position repair', which is defined as a type of repair where the speaker notices the interlocutor's displayed misunderstanding of his/her previous turn, and initiates repair. Given that in the majority of cases of third position repair WH-clefts are not used, third position repair contexts provide a well-defined interactional ground for specifically explicating interactional motivations for using a WH-cleft rather than a non-cleft utterance. First, I introduce a typical case of third position repair where a non-cleft utterance is used in the form of 'Well, I mean':

(12) (C/H)
1 H: Let me tell ya, Everybody really had an evening last night. ← *Trouble*
2 C: Oh really. Where'd everybody go. *Source*
3 H: Well I mean everybody that went anywhere. ↞ *Repair*
4 C: Oh.
5 H: Like... ((list))

In this example, H initiates repair at line 3 in response to C's turn at line 2 which displays misunderstanding of the word *everybody*; at line 2, C displays that he understood *everybody* as a referential term referring to a specific group of people whom both H and C know, while the intended meaning of the word is a general and non-referential one. After noticing C's displayed misunderstanding, H specifically goes back to his own trouble source turn, and initiates repair by specifying what he meant by *everybody*.

Third position repair contexts involving WH-clefts display characteristics different from such a typical case in terms of the kind of trouble being addressed as well as the manner of repair. Example (13) illustrates a context where a WH-cleft is used in third position repair. The WH-cleft is found at line 23 in the repair turn:

(13) (BC, Gray, 74-75)
1 B: This is in reference to a call, that was made about a month
2 ago.
3 A: Yessir?
4 B: A woman called, uh saying she uh signed a contract for huh
5 son who is- who was minuh.
6 A: Mm hm,
7 B: And she claims inna contract, there were things given, and
8 then taken away, in small writing.
9 ((pause))
10 A: Mm hm
11 B: Uh, now meanwhile, about a month ehh no about two weeks
12 before she made the call I read in, I read or either heard-
13 uh I either read or heard onna television, where the judge,
14 hadda case like this.
15 A: Mhhm,
16 B: And he got disgusted an' he says "I"- he's sick of these

	17		cases where they give things in big writing, an' take 'em,	
	18		an' take 'em away in	
	19		small writing.	
	20	A:	Mhhnm,	
	21	B:	An' 'e claimed the contract void.	← *Trouble source*
	22	A:	Mhhm?	
→	23	B:	Uh what I mean is it c'd help this woman that called. You	↞ *Repair*
	24		know uh, that's the reason I called.	

In this example, B has been telling a story, which, as he says at lines 1 and 2, he wants to relate to a previous call. Throughout the story, A, the radio host, has been producing the continuer *Mmhm* (Schegloff 1982) in lines 6, 10, 15, 20, and 22. By doing so, A marks the receipt of each previous utterance and signals that he will not take up the turn, thus allowing the interlocutor to go on talking. The trouble arises, however, when A produces a continuer at line 22, even though B's story is over at line 21. After noting that A did not understand that B's story is over, B initiates a repair by using a WH-cleft at line 23.

This instance is different from the typical instance of third position repair in example (12) in that what the speaker deals with in the repair turn is the interlocutor's misunderstanding of the sequential status of talk,[10] rather than misunderstanding the meaning of a term. The WH-cleft in example (13) is not shown to be designed to repair some specific trouble, but is presented as a metalinguistic elaboration of the import of the whole preceding story. That is, the import of the turn containing the WH-cleft as a repair of the preceding turn is to be inferred by the interlocutor, because the speaker does not initiate repair by saying something equivalent to 'My story is over', but simply by referring to the main point of his story.[11] In this sense, the WH-cleft is used for initiating an oblique repair that deals with the interlocutor's sequential misunderstanding by way of not specifically relating the repair utterance to the trouble source.

Example (14) is another instance where a WH-cleft is used in third position repair. In this case, the WH-cleft format is employed to deal with trouble in referent interpretation, but a particular orientation of the speaker to the sequential development of talk can still be observed. The repair turn containing a WH-cleft is found in line 13:

(14) (BB Gun, 2)

1	B:	An' I was wondering if you'd lend me your gun.
2		(0.8)
3	J:	My gun?

	4	B:	Yeah.	
	5		(1.8)	
	6	J:	What gun.	← *Trouble source*
	7		(0.5)	
	8	B:	Dontchu have a beebee gun?	
	9	J:	Yeah	
	10	B:	Oh it's	
			[	
	11	J:	Oh I have a lot of guns. hehh	
	12	B:	Yuh do:?	
→	13	J:	Yeah. What I meant was "which gun".	↞ *Repair*
	14		(0.5)	
	15	B:	Tch! .hhh Oh (0.4) uh::m (0.4) t! .hhh (0.5) well	
	16		D'j'have a really lo:ng one,	

The source of the trouble that the WH-cleft at line 13 is designed to deal with lies in the interlocutor's misunderstanding of the speaker's trouble source turn at line 6 'what gun', which can be interpreted in two different ways, i.e., in terms of the literal, constructive understanding, or in terms of an idiomatic, composite interpretation (Schegloff 1987). That is, while J intended his turn to be accorded the constructive interpretation, B misunderstands it in terms of the idiomatic composite understanding in the sense of 'What gun are you talking about? I don't have any gun', as is reflected in her subsequent query into the availability of a gun at line 8.

Unlike the preceding examples, repair is not initiated just after the turn displaying the interlocutor's misunderstanding.[12] Rather, B is already oriented to the fact that J actually has lots of guns before the repair is initiated through the WH-cleft. In this respect, we find that the speaker adds the WH-cleft to the on-going sequence to retroactively specify what he meant in the trouble source with a greater degree of explicitness than has been implicated in the intervening talk. The repair initiated by the WH-cleft deals with the source of trouble which is thus retrospectively treated as a problem which has caused different sequential understandings on the part of the interlocutors. The use of the WH-cleft, then, joins the interlocutors in intersubjectivity through which the speaker signals that they now clearly share an understanding of the source of the trouble in terms of how they followed different tracks of sequential development. This is a highly oblique repair practice in that the speaker does not relate the repair to the trouble source.

It is interesting to note in passing that in the segment of talk that directly follows example (14), a pseudo-cleft with the initial head noun *all* is produced again to deal with the same kind of trouble in sequential understanding (Schegloff 1990), which suggests a unique interactional function shared by WH-clefts and other pseudo-clefts:

(15) (BB Gun, 2)
((Continued from example (14)))

	14		(0.5)	
	15	B:	Tch! .hhh Oh (0.4) uh::m (0.4) t! .hhh (0.5) well	
	16		D'j'have a really lo:ng one,	
	17		(0.8)	
	18	J:	A really l:ng one.hh [h	
	19	B:	[Yeah.	
	20		(0.2)	
	21	B:	't doesn't matter what ki:nd.	
	22		(1.0)	
	23	J:	Why:: would you like a >really long one.	← *Trouble source*
	24		(0.8)	
	25	B:	Y'don' have a really long one.	
	26		(1.0)	
	27	J:	What?	
	28	B:	Y- Donchuh have a l- really long one?	
→	29	J:	Yea::hhh. A- all I wan' to know why you want a	↞*Repair*
	30		[gun,	
	31	B:	[Oh oh: OH:	

After B's misunderstanding displayed in line 8 in example (14) is resolved, B asks another round of more specific questions inquiring whether J has a long gun. At line 23, then, J asks why she needs a long one. Though this utterance is produced by J as a simple query, B understands it as rejection of her request on the grounds of non-availability of a long gun or J's unwillingness to lend a long gun to her, as her utterance at line 25 shows ('Y'don' have a really long one'). The divergent understandings of the talk in terms of sequence type, i.e., J's understanding of it as a question-answer sequence vs. B's understanding of it as a disagreement sequence, are eventually repaired by the pseudo-cleft at line 29. Therefore, we find a striking structural parallel between example (14) and example (15) (see Schegloff (1990) for a detailed conversation analysis of these examples).

In sum, we find that, unlike the canonical cases of third position repair illustrated by example (12), WH-clefts in third position repair are used in a context where the speaker does not relate repair to the trouble source; they are used not simply for dealing with the misunderstanding of a term occurring in the trouble source turn, but for addressing the interlocutor's misunderstanding of the sequential development of talk by highlighting the contrastive relationship between the speaker's version of sequential understanding as opposed to the interlocutor's alternative understanding. In this sense, a significant interactional motivation for using WH-clefts in repair contexts, as well as in other contexts examined above, can be understood as the speaker's attempt to make a locally disjunctive interactional move meta-discoursally coherent and oblique by exploiting the functional property of WH-clefts that creates discoursal contrastiveness.

2.4.3 *Affect display*

The preceding discussion suggests that WH-clefts have the function of evoking a meta-discoursal, meta-interactional relevance of the current utterance. It is in this sense that the discourse-organizational and interactional work done by WH-clefts bears upon a large discourse domain, often with reference to the preceding sequence of talk and/or a previous point made further back in the prior talk. Important properties of WH-clefts in this regard are those of creating contrastiveness through which the current utterance is posed against the preceding talk, and/or evoking a sense of the current speech event by way of metalinguistically formulating the gist of the preceding talk. What is involved significantly in these discourse operations is the expression of the speaker's internal state, such as his/her epistemic stance, or various kinds of discourse-relevant stances including meta-linguistic reference, or reference to a general state of affairs or action (i.e., *happen*, *do*), which are conveyed in the initial WH-clause of WH-clefts. Therefore, we can say that the initial WH-clause 'foregrounds' speaker stance[13] such as the speaker's epistemological disposition, or meta-linguistic concern of the speaker, thus tuning the interlocutor to some discourse-relevant inferences bearing upon the speaker's communicative goal.

Not surprisingly, in this regard, the initial WH-clause often serves as an affect key (cf. Hymes 1972; Gumperz 1977) whereby the speaker foregrounds his/her affective stance for the purpose of highlighting his/her affective orientation, often in the course of initiating a story, or responding to the interlocutor's prompt. Example (4) introduced above is a case in point, where the speaker initiates a self-repair to add her particular stance towards the current proposition. The example is repeated below:

(4) (GTS 3,11)

Louise: Inventory taking of the whole stock every day, ( ),
to-(I mean) every other day, an' they hafta- there's
this place called Atlas Supply Company which supplies
(/ /) drugstores an' beauty shops for most of Los Angeles.
And — got this job there. Where for the rest of this
year y'know uh the summer rather, the rest of the term an'
the summer, they'll be training me, to do this. // An' I'll
be-
Dan: Oh sounds good.
→ Louise: The pay goes up- what I'm surprised of is the pay goes up to
sump'n like two fifty an hour. At the end. An' that's
gonna be nice. hehh

The speaker abandons the onset of her utterance in line 10 ('The pay goes up-'), and shifts to the WH-cleft in which the WH-clause conveys her affective stance of surprise. Given that her self-interrupted utterance is re-initiated after the affectively loaded WH-clause, we have a sense that the shift to the WH-cleft is motivated by the speaker's wish to add her particular affective stance to the proposition in order to highlight its import.

The affective stance marking function of the initial WH-clause of WH-clefts often initiates a story, which is told in a highly affectively loaded way. For instance, in example (16) below, Louise self-interrupts her utterance at line 1 ('they're talkin-') and shifts to a WH-cleft in line 2 to add her affective stance. As in example (15), the interrupted utterance is re-initiated, this time framed by the initial WH-clause, in the WHEN-clause at line 2 ('what I love is when they're talking about something,...'):

(16) (GTS 3, 69)

Louise: Or like - or you come an' you say- (maybe) they're talkin-
→ what I love is when they're talking about something, (/ /) ohh you
know, "You had radio when you were a little girl?"
(/ /)
Louise: hehh! That doesn't do much for their- for their you
know? Say "Yeah we had-" my mother is w-she was one of
the- they got their radio when it came out, you know,
an' ((story continues))

The affective stance marking function of WH-clefts is sometimes observed in an explicitly contrastive context in which the speaker presents an alternative to what the speaker or the interlocutor said in the prior talk. Example (17) illustrates such a context, where the initial WH-clause is formulated with negative polarity and projects contrastiveness:

(17) (GTS 3, 67)
1 Louise: See, my parents arn't like this at all. Y'know wi'some they are some
→ 2 extent. But what I can't stand is like my father introduces me to this
3 man who has- went some some place an' my two younger sisters an'
4 myself, an' my father.
5 (/)
6 Louise: So "This is uhm Laurie," he goes "Laurie," "This is Judy," "Judy",
7 "This is Loui-", "Loui::se,"
8 (/)
9 Louise: Ya know? "YE::S?" y'kno(hh)w hehhehh
10 Ken: "Ga ga"

While these examples show that the initial WH-clause of WH-clefts functions to assert affect, it also projects an affective domain following the initial WH-clause by virtue of being situated in a story-telling context. For instance, in examples (16) and (17), the expression of affect in the initial WH-clause frames a story which contains some extended background information, and the main point of the story is often presented in a highly vivid, affectively loaded, speaker-involving manner, i.e., in the form of direct quotation.[14]

Such an affect-asserting function of WH-clefts is also observed when the speaker provides an account for his/her answer which was not formulated as a preferred response to the interlocutor's question:

(18) (SBL, 10-10)
1 B: I think I'll call her and ask her if she's
2 interested because she's a good nurse, and I
3 think they would like her don't you?
4 A: Well, I'll tell you, I haven't seen Mary for
5 years. I should- As I remember, yes.
6 B: Well do you think she would fit in?
→ 7 A: Uhm, uh I don't know, what I'm hesitating about is uh- uhm
8 maybe she would, (1.0) uhm but I would hesitate to uhm
9 B: recommend her.
10 A: Yes,

In line 7, A does not give a straightforward answer to B's question ('Uhm, uh I don't know'), and then produces a WH-cleft whose initial WH-clause expresses the speaker's ambivalence. The WH-cleft is not completed, and after the speaker provides a highly modulated preferred response ('maybe she would'), she reformulates the utterance, which is collaboratively completed by the interlocutor. As in the disagreement context where WH-clefts are used in such a way that the initial WH-clause conveys the speaker's epistemic stance, this would be a case in which the initial WH-clause conveys the speaker's affective stance to express disagreement indirectly.[15]

In sum, the initial WH-clause of WH-clefts often serves as as an affect key, while it also expresses the speaker's epistemic stance or other discourse concerns in other contexts. The fundamental interactional meaning of WH-clefts, then, can be generally characterized as foregrounding the speaker's epistemic or affective stance, and/or foregrounding the speaker's meta-discoursal, meta-interactional concerns that are contextually relevant to the current topic or the nature of the current speech event. As I mentioned earlier, these various interactional uses cannot be explained from the informational perspective alone in terms of presupposition/focus or given/new, because what is crucially involved in them is the speaker's interactional exploitation of the grammatical form and functions of WH-clefts as a stance-marker.[16]

2.5 *Foregrounding of the speaker's counteractive stance*

On the basis of the preceding discussion, we can point out that the initial WH-clause is not just a presupposition, as previous studies assumed, but a device whereby the speaker adds a particular stance toward the following focused proposition. What is involved significantly in these discourse operations seems to be a 'relevance-providing' process in which the speaker's counteractive stance towards the preceding discourse is initially 'foregrounded', i.e., brought to the foreground of the listener's mind, and then is accorded discourse/interactional relevance for doing so through the post BE-copula utterance.

What seems to be important to note in relation to this observation is that WH-clefts function to orient the interlocutor to the projected shift of talk by evoking the speaker's first-hand epistemic experience or affect, the speaker's metalinguistic understanding of the prior context of talk, and/or the prior discourse/interactional history, as an 'empirical' ground which, though seemingly independent of the current topic at hand, is presented to be relevant to it. That is, there is a strong sense in which the speaker's generic perception or predisposition, or some prior text, is evoked as a device to facilitate the foregrounding of the speaker's counteractive stance towards the preceding talk.

In this respect, we can note that the oblique interactional works involving the use of WH-clefts are possible because, through the initial WH-clause, the speaker, while foregrounding his/her counteractive stance, concurrently evokes an empirical ground independent of the current interactional business. As a result, the speaker himself/herself is not shown to be personally accountable for the disjunctive and often dispreferred interactional action being initiated. Such a practice distances the speaker from the current interactional move, thus providing a basis on which the speaker can freely and obliquely foreground his/her counteractive stance towards the preceding talk and the interlocutor's point.

2.6 *Contextual features*

The interactional function of WH-clefts that highlights the speaker's stance in various discourse-relevant ways has the interactional import of evoking the relevance of the current utterance to the overall talk and context in which it is situated. Such a stance-foregrounding act predisposes the interlocutors to be oriented to the contrastive relationship of the current utterance to the preceding talk and/or to the kind of action that defines the current speech event. It is on the basis of such a key that the use of WH-clefts triggers the interlocutor's inferential effort and shift of orientation, which interactionally provides coherence to the disjunctive uses associated with WH-clefts. These observations are further supported by the examination of contextual features that often co-occur with WH-clefts. I shall now examine three such contextual features, i.e., self-repair, discourse markers (Schiffrin 1987), and dislocation of the focused utterance.

2.6.1 *Self-repair*

WH-clefts are sometimes preceded by self-repairs in which the speaker shifts to the use of a WH-cleft after abandoning other non-cleft utterance forms.[17] This phenomenon requires our special attention because its explication would show why the speaker bothers to shift specifically to a WH-cleft utterance after abandoning a corresponding non-cleft form. Example (19) illustrates one such case where a WH-cleft follows self-repair in a disagreement context:

(19) (V & B)
52 V: .hhh Oka:y is there any kind of food you want me to g(h)e:t?
53 (0.9)
54 B: Ah-ha well if you do:n't want me to co:me Vaness.

55 V: Wu- of course-I no of course I actually you know
[
56 B: hhhh hhh!huh hhh nuh huh huh hhh
→ 57 V: what I'm doing right now for you tomorrow is I'm vacuuming
[ ] [ ]
58 B: .hhh hhh
59 V: right now.
60 (0.2)
61 B: Oh is it for me:.

This example is from a telephone conversation between a sister and brother, V and B respectively. In the context that precedes this portion of talk, B showed his intention to visit V, but V has implied all along during the talk that she is not very enthusiastic about her brother's prospective visit. At line 54, then, B, who clearly has noticed his sister's implicit dispreferred responses, backs off, and proffers a possible option of not visiting her, thus making explicit the inference he has made in the preceding talk. It is in response to this turn of B that V uses a WH-cleft to counter his point. We can see that the WH-cleft is preceded by disturbances of talk including self-repair whereby V abandons her non-cleft utterance at the onset of its production ('...I no of course...').

What is noteworthy in this segment of talk is that the WH-cleft occurs at a point where the speaker, while responding to the interlocutor's previous turn, makes a rather abrupt topic shift. That is, the speaker suddenly talks about what she is doing, which is highly disjunctive from the interlocutor's query in the preceding turn. In this regard, we find a sense in which the shift to the WH-cleft format is intended to reduce the topical gap by orienting the interlocutor to a non-specific discourse-level contrastive context evoked by the WH-cleft.[18]

The association of self-repair and an abrupt topic shift is also observed in relation to the use of the WH-cleft in a story-telling context. Example (20) is a case in point, where a WH-cleft is found at line 23:

(20) (SBL, 3-1)
1 B: No well this little petty selling stuff isn' fit fer the birds.
2 A: Yeah, becuz I as' the // neighbors, they look at me-
3 B: I'm not a door ringer, and I, I just— can't.
4 B: I don't know.
5 A: Well, I don't like tuh as' the people I know ei//ther.
6 B: No, because you, they sorta feel obligated.
7 A: Yeah,

8 A: I uh as' muh neighbor an' uh, she eh- f-first she said she would
9 c'z we had 'em marked down, so-hh she bought one last year, en'
10 so when I wen' 'n took i' down she didn't wan' it becuz it was
11 sliced. Wul it was sliced last year.
12 B: Mm hm?
13 A: But I mean it's jus' something y- you feel // like they-
14 A: You see, I didn't know it was sliced.
15 B: Huh?
16 A: I didn' even know it was sliced I was so shocked when I put the
17 knife in it 'n it just fell off?
18 B: Yeah.
[[
19 A: Heh heh heh!
20 A: It's- thet's- they're all individually sli:ced.
21 B: Mm hm,
22 A: But uhm, I uhm,
→ 23 A: Anyway I'm ha- ah what I'm having tuh do, to people I know
24 is cut 'em up an' sell 'em, uh a pound an' a half for a dollar
25 sixty five.
26 B: Oh yer doing that?
27 A: Well, I'm doin it t'the few people I know, becuz ever time I say
28 "Three twenty five" they look at me like- hh "You must be nuts
29 woman," you know,

Up to line 7, A and B have been talking about the delicacy required to approach people they know with a sales pitch, with A saying that she does not like selling to people that she knows. At line 14, A begins to tell a story about her experience of selling cakes to her neighbor, who did not want to buy them because they were sliced; the main point of her story is that the customer balked even though she had bought sliced cakes the year before. However, the upshot of the story is not taken by B in spite of A's repeated attempt to mark the main point of her story; B responds only with a continuer ('Mm hm' in line 12), a repair initiator ('huh' in line 15), a receipt marker ('yeah' in line 18), and another continuer at line 21. In response to a non-collaborative attitude of the story recipient, A produces a discourse marker 'anyway' in line 23 to mark the prior talk as tangential to the main point (cf. Schiffrin 1987). Self-repair is then initiated to abandon the onset of the non-cleft utterance ('I'm hav-') in favor of the WH-cleft which is produced at a point where A resumes the main line of talk as she exits from the story. As in the case of example (19), there is a sense in which the self-repair with a WH-cleft is motivated to evoke the discourse and interactional relevance of the abrupt disjunction.[19]

2.6.2 *Discourse markers*

As many of the preceding examples show, WH-clefts often are preceded by various conjunctives like *but*, *so*, *anyway*, *actually*, *and*, or *you know*, which can be collectively subsumed under the heading of 'discourse markers' (Schiffrin 1987); 38 % of the tokens examined (29 out of 76) occurred with some type of discourse marker. If we recall that WH-clefts mark a local disjunction, which is accorded thematic coherence through the evocation of a broader discoursal and interactional relevance of the utterance, the occurrence of these markers just before WH-clefts, often in turn-initial position, can be viewed as participating in this function of WH-clefts. For instance, the preceding examples show that *but* is often used to strengthen the contrastive message of WH-clefts by explicitly marking a local disjunction (e.g., example (5)), and *so* signals that what follows is the gist or consequence of the preceding talk (e.g., example (6)). In some cases, the discoursal and interactional import of a WH-cleft is presented straightforwardly as being disjunctive by way of the preceding discourse marker *oh*, which Heritage (1984) calls a change-of-state marker. Example (21) is a case in point:[20]

(21) (SBL, 12-5)
1 A: Just I had to say "It's rented."
2 B: Mm hm,
3 A: And uh but I was uh I got-
→ 4 A: Oh what I started to say, so I just planned to have this weekend at home,
5 you know,
6 B: Yeah,
[
7 A: All-
8 A: All day Saturday and all day Sunday,

In this example, the discourse marker *oh* projects the following utterance as being triggered by the speaker's sudden recall of some topic which is not necessarily contiguous with the preceding topic. The disjunctive use of *oh* thus provides a ground on which the following utterance can be legitimately disjunctive from the immediately preceding talk by way of alerting the interlocutor to a sudden change of state in the speaker's mind and/or a change in the speaker's interactional stance.

As a whole, the presence of discourse markers provides various clues to the interlocutor regarding the relation of the subsequent talk to the preceding talk, and further specifies the kind of disjunction that is projected by a WH-cleft. What discourse markers do before WH-clefts in this respect is that they more explicitly condition a route through which a contrastive link is supposed to be directed through the use of WH-clefts. That is, the contrastive context set up by a WH-cleft may be conditioned further to relate the current utterance to some prior points in the same speaker's talk, in the interlocutor's utterance in the immediately preceding context, or at some unspecified point in previous interactional history.

2.6.3 *Dislocation of the focused utterance*

The final contextual feature that I will discuss is the dislocation of the focused utterance in WH-clefts, where the focused utterance is preceded by some background information. This feature is found in 20% of the tokens in my database (14 out of 76), and predominantly occurs in an extended turn containing a story or an argument. A relevant portion of example (5) is introduced below for illustration:

```
     (5)   (After the movie)
     143   D:  Y-yeah well it's in these big
     144        (1.0)
     145   D:  va:ses, you know. Huge.
                [      [            [
     146   W:   Vats
     147   H:          Yeah.        Yeah.
→    148   D:  But what I didn't realize at the time was I had always
     149       been thinking well a:ll anything alcoholic has been (.)
     150       distilled and is oka:y.
     151       (0.2)
     152   D:  But this isn't.
     153       (0.3)
     154   D:  It's just made from (.) I mean t'ey jus-
                                          [
     155   J:                             Oh yea:h,
     156   D:  It's just ferme:nted. It's not disti:lled.
```

We can note that the focused utterance of the WH-cleft is dislocated; the focused utterance is found at line 152 ('this isn't'). We can see that the material that is inserted between the initial WH-clause and the dislocated focused utterance ('I had always been.....and is oka:y') provides background information that serves as a preliminary to the main point that is projected to be forthcoming in the subsequent talk.

The sense that we can make out of this feature is that the speaker first presents his/her stance in the initial WH-clause, thus projecting a discourse/interaction-relevant import of the subsequent talk before providing ideational details. That is, there is a sense in which the speaker preempts a step-by-step presentation of an episode for the purpose of marking the import for the story earlier than it is supposed to be marked in the telling. This practice seems to make the disjunction coherent by progressively orienting the interlocutors to what is to come later.[21] The role of the initial WH-clause, in this sense, has a significant interactional value in terms of positioning the interlocutor as a listener for the projected duration of talk. The telling of extended background information following the initial WH-clause, though highly disjunctive from the immediately preceding talk, can thus go on with little possibility of being interrupted or questioned on the basis of the secured attention from the interlocutors, because it is projected to be relevant to the current interaction with reference to an upcoming main point. This observation strongly indicates the discourse framing function of WH-clefts, which projects an extended turn where any relevant background information or the speaker's subjective comment can be provided before or along with the main point.

2.7 *Semantic and functional properties of WH-clefts*

As I have tried to show in the preceding discussion, the various interactional uses of WH-clefts are based on the function of WH-clefts that evokes a meta-discoursal relevance of the disjunctive current utterance towards the current topic or speech event. In this regard, the contrast-marking function of WH-clefts predisposes the interlocutor to make an inferential effort to find such relevance. These discoursal and interactional implications of WH-clefts were treated as deriving mainly from the speaker's use of the initial WH-clause as a counteractive stance-foregrounding device whereby the speaker orients the interlocutor to his/her epistemic or affective stance and/or other discourse-organizational or interactional management concerns. In this light, we find that the initial WH-clause plays a significant interactional role, even though informationally it has been viewed as being very low in 'communicative dynamism (CD)' (cf. Firbas 1964; Huddleston 1984). Therefore, we can roughly characterize the initial WH-clause as a locus of what may be called 'interactional focus', as opposed to the 'ideational focus' given to the utterance following the BE copula.

The interactional use of WH-clefts as a stance-foregrounding device can be traced to the identificational or equative semantic characteristics of WH-clefts, where something to be identified is followed by an identifier (cf. Halliday 1985), particularly in terms of (i) the cataphoric nature of the initial WH-clause, which sets a 'domain' in the context of identification on which some more information is projected (cf. Hetzron 1975; Werth 1984), and (ii) the vague semantic property of WHAT, which is highly unspecific in terms of what it refers to. This second semantic property of WHAT seems to allow it to flexibly refer to some contextually identifiable portion of discourse, rather than some specific entity directly relevant to a real world event. We can posit that this point is responsible for some of the unique tendencies displayed by WH-clefts that Prince (1978) observes. That is, WH-clefts tend to refer to a non-specific entity, or yield a non-agentive reading when the focused element has the nominative case. This contrasts with similar pseudo-cleft constructions with an initial head noun in that they are more likely to refer to a specific referent, and, when the focused element has the nominative case, they yield both agentive and non-agentive readings just as non-cleft utterances do. The following examples, which are excerpted from Prince (1978), illustrate this point:

a. Specific vs. non-specific
 (22) What we need is an inexpensive lawyer. (non-specific)
 (23) The one that we need is an inexpensive lawyer. (specific)
b. Agentive vs. non-agentive
 (24) John made me laugh. (both agentive and non-agentive readings)
 (25) What made me laugh was John. (only non-agentive reading)
 (26) The one that made me laugh was John. (both agentive and non-agentive reading)

Given these observations, we can note that the cataphoric WHAT with an unspecific reference domain interacts with the identificational structure of WH-clefts to serve various meta-discoursal functions. In this light, we can also observe that, unlike pseudo-clefts with a lexical head, the initial WH-clause of WH-clefts, as a free relative, does not anchor any specific referent to the discourse (Fox 1987b). This characteristic of the initial WH-clause seems to further enable it to be specialized for the role of foregrounding speaker stance, which is motivated by some general discourse and/or speaker concerns under consideration.

3. Left-dislocation

3.1 *Background*

Traditionally, left-dislocation (hereafter LD) has been characterized in terms of the fronting of an NP from a proposition into the sentence-initial position external to the proposition, which contains a pronominal copy referring to the left-dislocated NP (cf. Ross 1967). In this respect, the major function of LDs has been noted as that of explicitly foregrounding an informational unit (cf. Duszak 1987), or has been characterized as a process of 'anticipated identification' (Quirk et al. 1985).

Duranti and Ochs (1979), who look at LDs in Italian conversation, observe that they have floor-seeking and competitive turn-taking functions. From a similar perspective, Keenan-Ochs and Schieffelin (1976) provide a cognitive and interactional account of the marked word order of LDs in spontaneous English conversation by treating them as a 'discourse', and not as a sentence-level syntactic operation. According to Keenan-Ochs and Schieffelin, the major discourse function of left-dislocated constructions is that of 'foregrounding a referent'. Treating LDs as a construction that has the format of 'Referent + Proposition', they suggest that the function of this construction is to bring a referent into the foreground of the listener's consciousness, a referent that is usually not currently a 'center of attention'. They argue that such a global function of LD is used by the speaker to introduce discourse-new referents or to reintroduce into the discourse a referent which has temporarily elapsed into the background of the interlocutor's mind (Keenan-Ochs and Schieffelin 1976:243). On the basis of this cognitive explanation of the global function of LD's, they discuss several particular functions of LDs such as (i) suggesting an alternative to something mentioned in a prior utterance or turn,[22] (ii) drawing the listener's attention to a particular case of some general point being discussed, or (iii) giving special emphasis to a particular entity.[23]

Geluykens (1986, 1989) also treats LDs not so much as a syntactic structure, as in terms of a collaborative process through which a new referent is established in discourse. He posits that this process consists of three stages: (i) referent-introduction, (ii) referent-acknowledgment, and (iii) referent-establishment. The utterance of a left-dislocated referent performs (i) with a try-marker, i.e., with an upward intonational contour, which is followed by the interlocutor's acknowledgment in (ii), often in the form of a continuer like *uh huh* (Sacks and Schegloff 1979). The utterance of the proposition, which contains a pronominal gap, constitutes (iii), which predicates upon (ii). Geluykens suggests that LDs are an instantiation of this three-stage process representing a more general interactional pattern of conduct, which points to a characteristic of LDs that potentially engenders a sequence.

A preliminary observation of natural conversation suggests that the phenomenon of LD subsumes a multitude of interactional functions whose domains are extremely diverse. However, in the following sections I focus mainly on one type of sequential context where LDs are frequently found, i.e., story-telling contexts. The major thesis of my argument is that the cognitive account of the function of LDs as foregrounding a referent can be enriched by a more interactional account in which the referent in LDs is considered a vehicle by which the speaker foregrounds his/her stance. While this thesis will be supported by examining several instances of LDs in terms of their role in the sequence organization of storytelling, the findings will suggest a parallel between WH-clefts and LDs in terms of the interactional motivation underlying the use of these constructions, thus shedding light on ways in which linguistic topic-comment structure lends itself to various interactional functions. The data examined are spontaneous conversational data, particularly the GTS data, which are saliently characterized by story-telling activities. Twelve instances of LDs that are found in various story-telling sequences are examined.

3.2 *Interactional functions of LDs in story-telling contexts*

The examination of LDs occurring in story-telling contexts suggests that they have particular sequential import in the story-telling event. In many cases, I found that LDs occur in contexts where the speaker re-initiates a story after some intervening talk, provides a 'second' story following some 'first' story (Jefferson 1978), and/or displays the speaker's affective stance in such a way that a previous story is more vividly formulated or a referent is given a special affective emphasis (cf. Keenan-Ochs and Schieffelin 1976). These functions generally point to a property of LD's that relates the current utterance and the projected talk to the preceding talk by virtue of being situated in the current activity of story-telling.

3.2.1 *Re-initiation of story*

Example (27) shows a case where an LD is used for resuming a story after a turn-by-turn assessment:[24]

(27) (HGII: 12)
1 Hyla: Jewi:sh, 'hh an it's=
2 Hyla: =j's r:rilly s:::a::d,
[ ]
3 Nancy: Guy that sounds so goo::d?
4 Hyla: En ao I mean it jist (.) a f:antastic moo-
→ 5 oh en then the one thet's bigotted,
6 .hhh she's married tih this guy who's, ((Story))

In the context that precedes this segment of talk, Hyla has told a story about a movie she had seen, and at lines 1 and 2 she produces an assessment ('it's j's r:rilly s:::a::d'), which is joined by Nancy's assessment at line 3. At this point, the speaker begins to exit from the story, and at line 4 Hyla produces another piece of assessment. This assessment, however, is not completed as the speaker self-interrupts the utterance, and at line 5, she produces an LD after a change-of-state marker *oh* in the context of resuming the story to tell more about what happened in the movie. We can note that the LD is used at a point where the speaker cuts off the on-going turn-by-turn assessment talk and shifts to re-initiate a story-telling sequence.

LDs are also found in the context where the speaker resumes a story after dealing with the interlocutor's interruption:

(28) (SBL, 12-32, Tape 1)
1 B: Well I, when I was at the Laundromat last Sunday, the most attractive
2 looking girl, in fact she works for doctor uhm-
3 A: No, this one doesn't work, and oon't be working.
4 B: Uh huh,
→ 5 B: Well this gal, she's red headed'n, and freckled, and brown eyes,
6 and uh she had the cutest little boy, and she was telling me he'd be
7 three, in November.

In the preceding context, B attempted to tell a story about a girl she had met, and was interrupted by A, who wonders whether the girl is someone she knows. This digression is followed by the use of an LD at line 5, where B continues her story about the girl.

In these two examples, the speaker explicitly brings up a referent, either in a way that reintroduces it from a set of referents as in example (27), or in a way that refers to a referent in a contrastive context as in example (28). In both cases, we find that the speaker cuts off the on-going turn-by-turn talk in order to resume story-telling. These observations are generally congruent with the findings on LDs in Italian conversation in Duranti and Ochs (1979). They note that LDs "may be used not only to gain access to the speaking floor but also to block or to reduce the access of others participating in the social interaction" (Duranti and Ochs 1979:405). Moreover, they suggest that in story-telling contexts such a competitive turn-taking move operates in the direction of blocking the current turn-by-turn talk in order to re-initiate an extended turn. As I will show in the next section, such a disjunctive move is often realized as a move to produce a story which is thematically related to a previous one in story-telling contexts, i.e., in the fashion of competitive story-proffering.

3.2.2 *Provision of a 'second' story*

One of the most salient discourse characteristics of LDs in story-telling contexts is that they are used to provide a 'second' story which is triggered by some 'first' story that precedes it. The sequential positioning of LDs at a point where the speaker initiates a second or next story which is triggered by a preceding story is predominantly observed in the GTS data where the participants are engaged in providing a series of stories that are thematically linked to some topic at issue. For instance:

(29) (GTS 3, 7)
1 Louise: We didn't go to bed to- t'each other, but- it was so
2 comfortable an' so // nice.
3 Ken: Mh hm, Mh
4 Louise: Y'know? There's everything perfect.
5 (/)
→ 6 Ken: Corliss, the girl that // well I'm not really going with her-
7 Louise: Jo brings her boyfriends back there, too.
→ 8 Ken: mhhhh hhh Corliss the g- this chick that I'm hangin around
9 with now, she's real nice she's gotta real good personality,
10 she's not,- y'know, she's // just real cute little kid. An'
11 last night we went to the Mardi Gras together an' we were
12 both (/) well we were both pooped because I-I ran in the
13 track meet yesterday. And she-she's in the girls'
14 tumbling team. (/) tch I mean she doesn't like it she's
15 just on it because she needs the credits.

16 Louise: Mh hm,
17 (/)
18 Ken: So we took off an' we were havin a good time on the way
19 home, an' ((Story continues))

In the context that precedes this talk, Louise has told a story about when she stayed with her boyfriend in a guest house in the back of her house, which lasts up to line 4. After a pause at line 5, Ken initiates a second story by using an LD format containing background information about the referent ('Corliss, the girl that...'). Ken's LD utterance is then interrupted by Louise's belatedly provided auxiliary comment about her experience, and Ken re-initiates the telling of the second story about one of his dating experiences by repeating the LD format that contains reformulated background information about the referent ('Corliss the g- this chick that I'm hangin around with').[25]

Example (30) is another case in point, which shows a segment of talk that occurs in the context where the interactants talk about adults who exhibit an understanding attitude towards teenagers. We find an LD at line 8, where Ken initiates a story about Mr. Henry following Louise's story about her parents:[26]

(30) (GTS 3, 78)
1 Louise: And they tried to get us in, they got us in, too. Course
2 when the sheriff came they hadda s-shove us in the back
3 room fast, But // uh
4 Dan: hmh hmh hmh hmh
5 Louise: It's then then the uhm manager asked us uh you know, it
6 they'd take us out, because it was too dangerous.
7 (/)
→ 8 Ken: Well, Mister Henry, he came // up.
9 Louise: But these are the kind of people thatchu can have fun with.
10 But there aren't many like that.
11 Ken: He came up to Mammoth this summer. This last summer?
((Story continues))

In sum, the preceding discussion shows that the left-most NP in LDs serves as a pivotal point around which a series of stories is organized. In this regard, the mention of a referent in an LD has discourse organizational implications for relating the current story to the previous story, which points to an essential property of LDs that conveys the speaker's discourse-organizational concerns. It is to be noted that such a function of LDs is contextually situated in, and accorded relevance by, a certain topical point that is currently at issue, as well as by the particular speech event of a therapy session characterized by a continuous story-telling activity. Indeed, as Duranti and Ochs (1979) observe, there is a sense in which the use of LDs is 'warranted' by some dimension of the topical talk at hand (Duranti & Ochs 1979:406), and thus relates the current utterance to some general concern at issue.[27] Why this is the case seems to have much to do with ways in which the initial NP in LDs is interactionally motivated as a device in which the speaker foregrounds his/her discourse-organizational stance. This characteristic of LDs is also observed in contexts where the speaker highlights his/her affective stance, as I will show in the next section.

3.2.3 *Affect display*

One salient interactional feature of LDs can be observed in terms of the role of the left-most NP, which often serves as an affect key (Ochs and Schieffelin 1989) that projects a domain in which the speaker's affective stance is imbued in the following proposition. Such an affect-displaying function of LDs is often observed in contexts where the speaker reformulates a previous point or story in a more vivid, direct speech form. For instance:

(31) (GTS 5, 24-25)
Ken: C'se I- I mean // No-no- all joking aside there's a lotta
kids in my class who c'n be sitting there and saying
absolutely nothing, looking straight // at the teacher,-
Roger: (That was very --),
Roger: An' meaning it, too hehh hehh hh hehh hh
Ken: -looking straight at the teacher, an' acting like they're
paying, complete attention. But yet the teacher could ask
'em what she just said and they'd-they'd sit there and just
be dreaming they-they wouldn't even hear what she said.
Jim: I wouldn't either.
Roger: Wouldju quit talkin about me,
((thud))
Dan: Well isn't that what Jim is talking about when he says that
he's been uh at-at the beach?
Ken: Yeh-well I mean in-in most // of my dreams-
Dan: Mentally he's at the beach.
Ken: In most of my dreams when I'm // sitting in class dreaming,
Roger: An' he's all wet!
(Jim:) hhhh!
Ken: I-

	21	Roger:	hehhehhahahahaha
	22	Jim:	A:ll wet in class,
	23	Ken:	heh
	24	Jim:	Hey gimme a towel.
	25	Ken:	No I-
	26	Roger:	hehhhehh
	27	Ken:	I could be sitting there dreaming but yet I // hear-
	28	Jim:	ha! hhh //hheh
	29	Ken:	when-when my name is // called out I come-
	30	Roger:	Or you pee in your pants in class.
	31	Ken:	I come out of it. Just that fast.
	32	Jim:	((clears throat))
	33	Ken:	But I mean-
	34	Dan:	((clears throat))
→	35	Ken:	Uh:: this guy, you could yell "Hey Jo:hn, hey Jo::hn, hey
	36		Joh-" 'n you c'd go over an' tap him on the shoulder.
	37	Roger:	So he's gotta // good imagination.
	38	Ken:	That's the only way you c'n snap him out of it.

This segment of talk is produced in a context where the participants are telling episodes about daydreaming. In the context that precedes this talk, the participants have talked about a person who tended to daydream while driving at a high speed, which is followed by assessments provided in a joking manner. In lines 1 to 3, Ken talks about his classmates who daydream in class. However, the upshot of Ken's story is not collaboratively taken by the interlocutors, who downgrade the import of Ken's story by saying that they also do the same in class. Ken then goes on to talk about how he daydreams in class in line 17, which is presented as a characterization of 'typical', or 'normal' daydreaming. And in line 35, Ken uses an LD to disjunctively shift the course of talk, and initiates a story about one specific classmate of his ('Uh:: *this* guy, you could...'), and reasserts the tellability of his story by highlighting the extreme depth in which the character daydreams.[28] Here we can also see that the talk about the daydreaming habit of the character is formulated through a direct quotation ('Hey Jo:hn, hey Joh-') in a highly affectively loaded, vivid manner. In this regard, we find that LDs are used where the speaker reasserts the tellability of the story by further upgrading the affective tone of the story in response to the interlocutors' downgrading assessment. This would be a highly effective discourse-strategy in that conveyance of affect would invite the interlocutor's involvement in the story and collaboration with the story-teller (cf. Tannen 1989, Mayes 1990).[29]

In many cases, the reformulated story initiated by an LD is more or less the same as the previous story being targeted. For instance:

(32) (GTS 3, 25-26)
1 Ken: An' I said "Yes I will." An' he started, you know, the
2 normal routine a' "No you won't", you know, "You're-y'
3 just don't have the capability for it"? so after about
4 twenny five minutesa talkin this horse shit I sez "Cram
5 it up your ass" and left.
6 (/)
7 Louise: Good fer you
8 Ken: And uh my father stood there with- you know his jaw
9 dropped down to his knee and my mother- "Hohhhh hohhhh
22 my poor little baby" // An' I got-
:
((Intervening talk))
:
34 Ken: Yeah. He- I think he's an asshole. I really do. That's
35 all I c'n say-
36 Dan: ((coughs, clears throat))
37 Ken: -an' I've just- I was sittin over here, an' I got up an'
→ 38 just walked out an' my father, he w' "Huh? Huh? Huh?"
39 He was (//) He turned green an' I think my father
40 said something before he left, because they were here for
41 another twenny minutes.

In this example, Ken tells the interlocutors about an episode where he got mad at the counselor who discouraged him by saying that he could not be an engineer, and he insulted him in the presence of his parents. The reaction of his father is first described from lines 8 and 9, and is reformulated with an LD at line 38. We can note that, in the reformulated story, the father's reaction is recast in a vivid description where his vocal sound is presented as direct speech ('Huh? Huh? Huh?').

The same pattern is observed in example (33), where two LDs occur at lines 7 and 13 respectively:

(33) (GTS 3, 63-64)
1 Dan: Well then, ok. I-I-I can see what you're // saying,
2 one-one ( )- Huh?
3 Louise: C'n I talk on from here?
4 Louise: C'n I talk on from // there?
5 Dan: Sure, Go ahead.

	6	Louise:	Well my parents are different, I-it isn't my parents
→	7		that do it to me, cause my mother, like my little sister,
	8		she hadda party. So she says to the girls, "Just don't
	9		get pregnant,"
	10		(/)
	11	Dan:	heh heh heh
	12	Louise:	TO TWELVE AND A HALF YEAR OLD GIRLS they-they're
→	13		going out like this y'know? My mother she was making the
	14		food 'n Judy's in there with her- you know, introducing
	15		the girls, Mama sez "Lookit have a nice time, but girls,
	16		remember, just one thing. Just don't get pregnant."
	17		(/)
	18	Louise:	Cause they turned out the lights an' da- That's what my
	19		mother's <u>like</u>. .....

The first LD at line 7 is used where Louise talks about an episode which shows her mother's exceptionally liberal attitude towards her daughter at a party for Louise's sister ('cause my mother, like my little sister, she hadda party. So she says to the girls, "Just don't get pregnant"').[30] We can readily note that the LD frames backgrounded information relevant to the episode and a direct quotation of what the referent said. This story is more or less repeated from line 13, again with the LD format. We find that the reformulated story contains more elaborate background information and more intensified affectively loaded direct speech.[31]

As a whole, we can note that the use of LD initiates a reformulation of a previous story in such a way that the reformulated story carries an upgraded affective stance of the speaker; even when a reformulated story initiated by an LD conveys more or less the same referential meaning as the previous story, we perceive a higher degree of affective strength.

While the examples that I discussed above illustrate the function of LDs that indexes the speaker's affective stance, it is noteworthy that the vivid description in the LDs is often followed by an utterance such as a 'reversed WH-cleft' or a 'reversed pseudo-cleft' (Prince 1978, Geluykens 1988) which explicitly refers to the import of the information in the LDs or the relationship between the referent and the proposition in the LDs. In examples (31) and (33), for instance, such ideational rendering of the import of the affectively presented proposition in LDs can be observed. Relevant portions of the data are marked by an arrow:

(31) (GTS 5, 25)
35 Ken: Uh:: this guy, you could yell "Hey Jo:hn, hey Jo::hn, hey ← LD
36 Joh-" 'n you c'd go over an' tap him on the shoulder.
37 Roger: So he's gotta // good imagination.
→ 38 Ken: That's the only way you c'n snap him out of it.

(33) (GTS 3, 64)
12 Louise: TO TWELVE AND A HALF YEAR OLD GIRLS they-they're
13 going out like this y'know? My mother she was making the ← LD
14 food 'n Judy's in there with her- you know, introducing
15 the girls, Mama sez "Lookit have a nice time, but girls,
16 remember, just one thing. Just don't get pregnant."
17 (/)
→ 18 Louise: Cause they turned out the lights an' da- That's what my
19 mother's like. .....

With reference to the function of LDs that frames an affective domain, these reversed pseudo-clefts can be treated as marking a terminating point of such a frame by way of metalinguistically formulating the sense of the preceding story in a more ideational, less affective style.[32]

3.3 *Summary and additional remarks on LDs*

The preceding discussion shows that in story-telling contexts LDs have the function of disjunctively resuming a story, initiating a second story, or repeating a story in an affectively upgraded manner. The disjunction marked by LDs in relation to the preceding talk is given discoursal/interactional relevance by the the sense of resuming the main story or providing a second story in the context of competitive story-telling, and/or by the projected affective import of the upshot of the story. In this respect, the use of LDs is not only cognitively motivated to foreground a referent it refers to (cf. Keenan-Ochs and Schieffelin 1976), but is also interactionally motivated to foreground the speaker's discourse-organizational and affective stance on the basis of the story-telling context where they are situated. That LDs are often used for initiating a second story disjunctively shows that the speaker invokes the sense of the current activity, i.e., story-telling, in order to furnish a basis on which his/her counteractive stance is displayed. Some additional remarks are in order here, which relate to several characteristics of LDs illustrated by the examples discussed above.

First, many of the examples show that the proposition of LDs contains background information, as was noted by Keenan-Ochs and Schieffelin (1976). Such background information is presented as the initial part of a story being initiated, and leads to the main point in the subsequent context, which points to the discourse-framing function of LDs that is reminiscent of that of WH-clefts.

Second, we can note that, while the referent in LDs is usually identifiable (cf. Duranti and Ochs 1979, Keenan-Ochs and Schieffelin 1976; Du Bois 1980), it usually shares the same membership with a certain referent mentioned in the previous context (cf. Sacks 1972).[33] This point is supported by the examples discussed above where a family member like 'father' or 'grandmother' is often introduced in an LD which is triggered by the use of a reference form in the previous story that refers to the previous speaker's family member. In this respect, the second stage of Geluykens's (1986, 1989) collaborative process represented by LDs, where the interlocutor's assertion of his/her recognition is invited following the try-marked left-most referent, often need not be overtly marked; the referent introduced in an LD can be interactionally established on utterance by way of sharing some membership characteristics in the context of a competitive story-telling sequence.

It is worth noting, in this respect, that even a new referent can be introduced into the current story through an LD as long as it shares membership characteristics with a referent mentioned in the preceding story. For instance, in example (29), the referent ('Corliss') in the LD is new, which refers to the current speaker's (=Ken's) girlfriend. The introduction of the new referent, though informationally disjunctive, is triggered by the previous speaker's mention of her boyfriend, and is accorded referential continuity by virtue of the shared membership and the action context of starting a second story. We can also note in example (29) that each time that Ken attempts to introduce 'Corliss', he provides background information which explicitly identifies her as sharing membership characteristics with a referent mentioned in the preceding story. This observation suggests that preference for 'recipient design' is still operative (Sacks and Schegloff 1979); the existence of shared characteristics alone may not be sufficient grounds to use LDs. Perhaps it must also be the case that the interlocutor be aware of their existence (Downing, personal communication).

As a whole, the discourse-organizational uses of LDs in story-telling contexts display a process in which the initial NP and the following proposition in LDs are respectively brought to bear upon different interactional dimensions. The former brings into relief the speaker's stance relevant to his/her particular communicative goals and has the interlocutor oriented to them, while the latter concerns the speaker's main point, which provides interactional relevance to what the speaker projected by uttering the former. What is crucial in this process is that the interactional relevance of LDs is achieved by the interlocutor's contextually directed inferential effort to relate the current utterance to the broad topic and/or other general contextual concerns at hand.

4. Conclusions: Implications for topicality

The preceding discussion suggests that WH-clefts and LDs share several functional and interactional properties in the area of focus-giving and nominal reference. The common ground that is shared by the two marked constructions is noted in various interactional contexts where the speaker marks a local disjunction and negotiates the relevance of doing so from meta-discoursal contrastiveness and a broader dimension of discourse. These contexts are characterized by the discourse-framing function of the initial element of these constructions, which frames a proposition that is meta-discoursally motivated to be responsive to the prior talk, or frames a proposition in an extended turn where background information and/or affectively-loaded description is often situated. These interactional characteristics are posited as deriving from the interactional function of the initial element of these constructions, which displays the speaker's counteractive stance.

The speaker's display of counteractive stance towards the preceding talk triggers the interlocutor's shifted orientation and inferential effort, and thus negotiates the discoursal and interactional relevance of the current proposition. An important interactional correlate of this function is that it is contextually warranted by some dimension of the topical talk at hand and/or by the invocation of the current action context on the basis of the interactants' co-making of the general sense of the talk (cf. Heritage and Watson 1979). As a result, the foregrounding of the speaker's counteractive stance, though a seemingly subjective countering move that constitutes a serious dispreferred response and/or disjunction in talk, is situated in the concurrently evoked action context with varying degrees of contrastiveness and projection of affect. For WH-clefts, the initial WH-clause provides the speaker-external empirical grounds, or discourse-motivated meta-linguistic grounds, which deal with the prior talk in an oblique fashion, i.e., in a less directly countering manner. For LDs in storytelling contexts, the left-most referent serves as a leverage point by which the current story, which is seemingly disjunctive with the preceding story or assessment, is coherently related to the preceding story as its "second" or as its resumption by virtue of the action context of story-telling that is being invoked, or as an affectively upgraded repetition.

This interaction-oriented characterization of topicality has interesting crosslinguistic implications because interactional contexts where topic constructions in topic-prominent languages like Korean are used (cf. Thompson 1978) are strikingly similar to those where English WH-clefts or LDs are used, even though the linguistic means employed are very different. What is noteworthy in this respect is that most of the cases of WH-clefts and LDs examined in this paper, if translated into Korean, would contain the Korean topic marker *nun*, which is attached to the initial WH-clause or the left-dislocated NP. Indeed, as Kim (1992) shows, the Korean topic constructions that correspond to the English WH-clefts or LDs display interactional characteristics that are observed in these marked English constructions. These observations suggest that, if we define 'topic' in formal terms as referring to a linguistic entity in Korean where the topic marker *nun* is attached, we can cross-linguistically characterize the interactional meaning of 'topic' as counteractive stance-foregrounding (cf. Kim 1991a, 1991b, Lee 1987),[34] which is intertwined with a discourse strategy of situating the meaning in oblique ways by evoking various senses of independent empirical grounds, prior text, and/or action context where the current talk is embedded.

In conclusion, marked word order constructions like WH-clefts and LDs can be viewed as being specially adapted to particular interactional contexts in conversation in such a way that the initial topical element is added to a proposition to refer to some general concern for the current interactional context and/or to convey some non-referential meaning (cf. Besnier 1990; Ochs 1988; Ochs and Schieffelin 1989). The domain for the conversational uses of these marked constructions, then, could be treated as one where the subject-prominent grammar of English is interactionally pressured towards a more topic-prominent side. This point should be further pursued in future research with reference to the different degrees to which interaction shapes the grammar of different languages, or degrees to which grammar indexes particular interactional modes in different languages. An interactional perspective would be essential to such a line of research, because, given the assumption that spontaneous conversation is the basic form of language use, we can say that a grammar of a language is bound to be shaped by or adapted to the primordial interactional context where it is situated and actualized.

Notes

* I would like to thank Prof. Emanuel Schegloff for his insightful comments which helped me formulate the major points of this paper. I am also grateful to Profs. Roger Andersen, Marianne Celce-Murcia, Pamela Downing, Mickey Noonan, Robert Kirsner, and Sandy Thompson for their helpful comments on earlier versions of this paper.

1. Even though the specific terms for these constructions were coined originally in the field of formal linguistics in terms of formal derivations from or to other constructions, I will use the terms 'WH-cleft' and 'left-dislocation' in the following discussion for the sake of convenience. The term 'WH-cleft' is defined as a type of 'pseudo-cleft' (Akmajian 1970), which is treated as a broader notion that subsumes not only WH-clefts but also other similar constructions with a lexical head.

2. The major concerns of the conversation analysis (CA) approach are to provide a systematic account of ordinary conversational interaction in such a way that we can account for the actual course which particular episodes of interaction take, capturing the orientation of participants, and to develop a systematic explication of the recurrent practices of talking in natural interaction (Schegloff 1988).

3. It is to be noted that this categorization of data is not intended to bring into relief differences between them, but is only offered as a rough characterization of the data. While the BC data and the GTS data represent particular types of task-oriented conversation which may be distinct from other more casual conversation, they share common ground with the conversations included in the Casual Conversation data, and this last category of data subsumes a variety of different types of conversation which actually cannot be pigeonholed into a single category. In this respect, it is mainly for the sake of convenience that such a rough categorization is provided, though mention will be made whenever necessary regarding cases where the use of WH-clefts is shown to be influenced by a particular feature of each category.

4. For transcription conventions, see Sacks, Schegloff, and Jefferson (1974) and Atkinson & Heritage (1984).

5. Excluding the categories of "HAPPEN" and "Others", 38 out of 57 instances of WH-clefts (66%) contain a first person subject in the initial WH-clause; 50% of the metalinguistic verbs (11 out of 22) and the DO-verb (3 out of 6) occur with the first person subject .

6. An example of each predicate type is introduced below:

   a. Full clause: What I felt is I pushed Abbey to the wa:ll so that she was always unhappy. (Halloween dinner)

b. Infinitive: What I'm having tuh do, to people I know, is cut 'em up and sell 'em. (SBL)

c. Gerund: What I'm rea:lly enjoy:ing is: uhm:: getting a pa:y check. (Arthur and Rebecca)

d. NP: What he wants is reparations. (BC)

7. Moreover, about 60% of those WH-clefts with a focused sentence (29 out of 48) contained no THAT, sometimes with no BE copula. In such cases, the initial WH-clause is often followed by some background information (see Section 2.6.3.).

8. It is to be noted that the last verb category in Table 1, which was termed 'Others', subsumes cases like example (7); all 7 instances of WH-clefts in this category occurred in the BC data.

9. It is to be noted that the explicit rejection of the interlocutor's point before proposing an alternative to it through a WH-cleft is not characteristic of everyday conversation examined, but is frequently found in the BC data. This seems to be due to the nature of the context, where the interlocutors are frequently engaged in arguments by contradicting the other's point of view. In those disagreements in the BC data where WH-clefts are used, Brad Crandall, the host of the show, often rejects a caller's point and provides an alternative through a WH-cleft as in example (11), whereas callers usually use a WH-cleft turn-initially after some material projecting disagreements as in example (10), or after signaling receipt of Mr. Crandall's point by utterances like 'I see, but...'. This point seems to relate to the power relationship between the caller and the radio show host, with the latter being in control of the talk most of the time.

10. For a more detailed analysis of the way in which repair is done in this example, see Schegloff (1991).

11. We can also note that the sequential/functional status of the WH-cleft in the talk is explicitly formulated in the following utterance in the repair turn ('You know uh, that's the reason I called') (Schegloff 1991).

12. The use of the past tense in the WH-cleft ('What I meant was') seems to be due to this sequential characteristic.

13. According to Biber and Finegan (1989), the notion of speaker stance is defined as referring to the speaker's attitudes, feelings, judgments, or commitment concerning the propositional content of a message. In this sense, foregrounding of speaker stance is defined as an act of bringing such speaker-relevant information to the foreground of the interlocutor's mind for various interactional reasons. This point will be further discussed in Section 2.5.

14. Direct speech has been noted to signal a high degree of speaker involvement and affective meaning (see Halliday 1985; Tannen 1989; Mayes 1990).

15. It is also noteworthy in this example that, in line 4, 'Mary' is referred to by a recognitional, i.e., by name (cf. Sacks and Schegloff 1979), even though the referent was introduced in the preceding context and had since been referred to by pronouns. As Fox (1987a) notes, such an unexpected use of a nominal reference form is often associated with a disagreement context.

16. The presupposition-focus distinction still may be relevant to the consideration of WH-clefts in the sense that it is exploited by the speaker who asserts new information in the initial WH-clause as if it is presupposed, thus creating a collusive bond with the interlocutor (cf. Kim 1992)

17. Such instances of self-repair occurred in 16 percent of the tokens of WH-clefts (12 out of 76). In addition, more general types of self-repair and other forms of disturbance are frequently observed before the use of WH-clefts, which would derive mainly from their frequent occurrences in topic-initial or topic-shifting positions (cf. Schegloff 1979).

18. Given the abrupt shift of talk observed in this example, the need to direct the hearer's attention to the inferential relevance of the current utterance to the preceding talk may be more acute here than in other cases. If non-cleft utterances had been used in this context with no self-repair, the coherence of talk and smoothness of interaction would have been much less apparent because, without the orientation to the contrastive import and meta-discoursal reference achieved through WH-clefts, the listener would have been oriented only to the immediate inter-turn relationship of the current turn and the preceding turn which happens to be highly disjunctive.

19. As Kim (1992) shows, self-repairs towards a WH-cleft are often observed in lectures. In such cases, self-repair often reflects the lecturer's attempt to make his suggestion less personal and more formal by evoking the discoursal/contextual, not personal, basis for the utterance. For instance:

((The instructor talks about the handout being distributed to the students.))
1 Now before I go on. Are there any questions about the syllabus before I
→ 2 go on or the maps and the whatso- whatsoever (.) O.K. Let me- well what
3 I 'd <u>li</u>ke to do today is really cover uh three essential points. ((listing of the three points))
((A student asks a question.))
→ 1 Ah I'd- what I'd suggest to you is to see the TA's as quickly as possible. The
2 TA's uh have office hours now if you (go up) and find them the TA's are <u>he</u>re
3 uh they'll be here after the lecture, I think uh you should try'n find them 'n,
4 and- uh- uh get that (settled) down.

We can see in these examples that the use of the WH-cleft in this context greatly contributes to creating the sense in which the lecturer is not to be personally accountable for the proposition of his utterance. In this respect, WH-clefts in a lecture would be a device which the speaker employs for the purpose of showing that he/she is 'doing lecturing' by way of resuming the proper, formal register of a lecture, after some digressive, informal, casual, colloquial talk (cf. Section 2.4.1.2.).

20. As the WH-cleft in example (21) illustrates, the BE copula is sometimes deleted, which suggests a loose syntactic relation between the initial WH-clause and the focused utterance; there were four such instances of WH-clefts with no BE copula and with no THAT in my database. The loose syntactic relation in WH-clefts is also in line with the fact that the focused utterance of WH-clefts often displays 'main clause phenomena' (cf. Hooper and Thompson 1973). For instance, a question or a request can be placed in the focus slot (cf. 'What I, I s'ppose what I:: would like tuh know is, d'you think that...' (BC, Green, 39)). Moreover, this observation further points to an aspect of the initial WH-clause as a stance-marker which can occur on its own and is somehow added to the following proposition.

21. This strategy can be characterized as a "problem-first-solution-later" practice, by which the speaker initially orients and alerts the interlocutor to a potentially problematic issue at hand, and then provides solutions on the basis of the secured attention of the interlocutor (Du Bois, personal communication).

22. The sense of 'alternative' as intended by Keenan-Ochs and Schieffelin (1976) corresponds to what I mean by 'contrast' in that both notions refer to bringing into the discourse an alternative to some other given item. Keenan-Ochs and Schieffelin seem to avoid the term 'contrast' with the assumption that it refers to a selection of an item from a given set of items, which would be equivalent to what Chafe (1976) calls 'focus of contrast', or what Kuno (1973) calls 'exhaustive listing'.

23. With reference to the interactional functions of WH-clefts examined above, we can see an overall similarity between WH-clefts and LDs in terms of these three particular functions of LDs. The alternative-suggestion function is similar to the contrast-marking function of WH-clefts, and the attention-grabbing function is shared by the property of WH-clefts that causes the interlocutor's shifted orientation. The third emphatic function of LDs reminds us of the fact that the initial WH-clause of WH-clefts conveys the speaker's stance. As a whole, Keenan-Ochs and Schieffelin's characterization of functions of LDs in terms of foregrounding a referent seems to be relevant to the preceding discussion of WH-clefts at the most general level of analysis, even though they pertain to different discourse phenomena that motivate different areas of grammar.

24. Example (27) is from Goodwin and Goodwin (1987), where it is used to illustrate an instance where the speaker exits from a story by providing an assessment.

25. This point will be further elaborated in Section 3.3.

26. As examples (29) and (30) show, LDs are often produced at a turn transition place (cf. Sacks, Schegloff and Jefferson 1974), often after a pause and/or some discourse marker like *well* or *oh*. As in the case of WH-clefts, the presence of a discourse marker seems to anticipate that disjunctive talk is in order.

27. As the preceding discussion of WH-clefts suggests, this point also holds for many contexts where WH-clefts are found.

28. It is noteworthy that the mentions of the two types of daydreaming habits, i.e., the speaker's 'normal' habit (see lines 27, 29, and 31) and his classmate's 'unique' habit, are placed in a contrastive context, which seems to make the transition more coherent.

29. I am not claiming here that direct quotation cannot be used in a non-LD construction. The association of LDs with direct quotation should rather be viewed in the context of the story-telling activity where speakers consecutively attempt to highlight the point of the story in an affectively-loaded manner, i.e., through direct quotation or non-verbal gesture, among other means. While further research should be conducted to see how LDs and non-LDs are used differently to initiate a story, it seems to be the case that LDs constitute one particular way of proposing a story in a seemingly abrupt, though coherent, manner by virtue of the successive story-telling activity where the talk is situated.

30. As Keenan-Ochs and Schieffelin (1976) note, this is a case where an LD is inserted within another LD, with the inserted LD being 'like my little sister, she hadda party'.

31. The reformulated story is also preceded by an affectively loaded utterance produced in a high pitch at line 12.

32. In this respect, what distinguishes reversed WH-clefts most saliently from WH-clefts can be noted in terms of the starting point from which the utterance is initiated; while WH-clefts are often used in initiating a point through the conveyance of the speaker's counter-

active stance with cataphoric orientation, reversed ones are more frequently used for terminating an episode by way of relating the preceding talk to some general point, with the initial demonstrative often referring to the preceding talk as a whole. In this sense, the former highlights the following talk in relation to the preceding talk, while the latter highlights the preceding talk per se by re-asserting the upshot of the preceding talk.

33. In a similar vein, Duranti and Ochs (1979) note that LDs are often used to introduce a topic which is not new, but which is related to the prior discourse by way of being linked to global concerns or themes, e.g., 'frames' (Goffman 1974) or "perspectives that link referents to one another in a semantically coherent way" (Duranti and Ochs 1979:395).

34. Just as interesting is the fact that, in many cases, subject constructions in Korean correspond to reversed pseudo-clefts in English (cf. note 32); if the latter are translated into Korean, the utterance-initial element, which is often a demonstrative, would usually be marked by the subject marker, not by the topic marker. Assuming that different word orders index different speaker stances (cf. Besnier 1990), these observations suggest that different kinds of stance marked by different word orders in English are indexed by different particles in Korean (Kim 1992).

References

Akmajian, A. 1970. "On deriving cleft sentences from pseudo-cleft sentences." *Linguistic Inquiry* 1.149-68.

Atkinson, J. M., and J. Heritage, eds. 1984. *Structures of Social Action: Studies in Conversation Analysis*. Cambridge: Cambridge University Press.

Besnier, N. 1990. "Language and affect." *Annual Review of Anthropology* 19.419-51.

Biber, D., and E. Finegan. 1989. "Styles of stance in English: Lexical and grammatical marking of evidentiality and affect." *Text* 9:1.93-124.

Chafe, W. 1976. "Givenness, contrastiveness, definiteness, subjects, topics, and point of view." *Subject and Topic* ed. by Charles N. Li, 25-55. New York: Academic press.

Du Bois, J. W. 1980. "Beyond definiteness: the trace of identity in discourse." *The Pear Stories: Cognitive, cultural, and linguistic aspects of narrative production* ed. by W. Chafe, 203-74. Norwood, NJ: Ablex.

Duranti A, and E. Ochs. 1979. "Left-dislocation in Italian conversation." T. Givón 1979.377-416.

Duszak, A. 1987. *The Dynamics of Topics in English and Polish*. Wydawnictwa Uniwersytetu Warszawskiego.

Firbas, J. 1964. "On defining the theme in functional sentence analysis." *Travaux Linguistique de Prague* 1.267-80. Academia, Prague.

Ford, C. 1993. *Grammar in Interaction: the pragmatics of adverbial clauses in American English conversation*. Cambridge University Press."

Fox, B. 1987a. *Discourse Structure and Anaphora: Written and Conversational English*. Cambridge: Cambridge University Press.

Fox, B. 1987b. "The noun phrase accessibility hierarchy reinterpreted: Subject primacy or the absolutive hypothesis?" *Language* 63.856-70.

Geluykens, R. 1986. "Left-dislocation as a topic-introducing device in English conversational discourse." *Proceedings of the Second Annual Meeting of the Pacific Linguistics Conference* ed. by S. DeLancy and R. S. Tomlin, 163-71. University of Oregon, Eugene, Oregon.

Geluykens, R. 1988. "Five types of clefting in English discourse." *Linguistics* 26.823-41.

Geluykens, R. 1989. "The syntactization of interactional processes: Some typological evidence." *Universals of Language* 4.91-103.

Givón, T., ed. 1979. *Syntax and Semantics 12, Discourse and Syntax.* New York: Academic Press.

Givón, T. 1982. "Logic vs. pragmatics, with human language as the referee: Toward an empirically viable epistemology." *Journal of Pragmatics* 6.81-133.

Goffman, E. 1974. *Frame Analysis.* New York: Harper and Row.

Goodwin, C., and M. H. Goodwin. 1987. "Concurrent operation on talk: Notes on the interactive organization of assessments." *IPRA Papers in Pragmatics* 1, No. 1.1-54.

Gumperz, J. 1977. "Sociolinguistic knowledge in conversational inference." In *Georgetown University Round Table on Languages and Linguistics* ed. by M. Saville-Troike, 191-212. Washington D.C.: Georgetown University Press.

Gundel, J. K. 1977. "Where do cleft sentences come from?" *Language* 53.543-59.

Gundel, J. K. 1985."'Shared knowledge' and topicality." *Journal of Pragmatics* 9.83-107.

Halliday, M. A. K. 1985. *Introduction to Functional Grammar.* London: Arnold.

Hankamer, J. 1974. "On the non-cyclic nature of WH-clefting." *Papers from the Tenth Regional Meeting of the Chicago Linguistic Society.* 221-33.

Heritage, J. 1984. "A change-of-state token and aspects of its sequential placement." J. M. Atkinson, and J. Heritage 1984.299-345.

Heritage, J. and Watson, D. R. 1979. "Formulations as conversational objects." *Everyday Language: Ethnomethodological Approaches* ed. by G. Psathas, 123-62. New York, London: Irvington Publishers (Wiley/Halstead).

Hetzron, R. 1975. "The presentative movement or why the ideal word order is V.S.O.P." *Word Order and Word Order Change* ed. by Charles. N. Li, 345-88. Austin and London: University of Texas Press.

Higgins, F. R. 1973. "The Pseudo-Cleft Construction in English." Doctoral dissertation, M.I.T., Massachusetts.

Hooper, J., and S. Thompson. 1973. "On the applicability of root transformations." *Linguistic Inquiry* 4.465-97.

Huddleston, R. 1984. *Introduction to the Grammar of English.* New York: Cambridge University Press.

Hymes, D. 1972. "Models of the interaction of language and social life." *Directions in Sociolinguistics: The Ethnography of Communication* ed. by J. Gumperz and D. Hymes, 35-71. New York: Holt Rinehart and Winston.

Jefferson, G. 1978. "Sequential aspects of storytelling in conversation." *Studies in the Organization of Conversational Interaction* ed. by J. N. Schenkein, 219-48. New York: Academic press.

Jespersen, O. 1968. *Analytic Syntax.* New York: Holt, Rinehart, and Winston.

Keenan-Ochs, E., and B. B. Schieffelin. 1976. "Foregrounding referents: A reconsideration of left dislocation in discourse." *Proceedings of the Second Annual Meeting of the Berkeley Linguistics Society*, 240-57.

Kim, K.-H. 1991a. "The role of the Korean topic marker in foregrounding speaker stance." Paper presented at the Seventeenth Annual Meeting of the Berkeley Linguistics Society, Berkeley, California.

Kim, K.-H. 1991b. "Topicality in Korean conversation: Conversation analytic perspective." Paper presented at the Second Southern California Japanese/Korean Linguistics Conference, University of California at Santa Barbara, California.

Kim, K.-H. 1992. "WH-Clefts and Left-Dislocation in English Conversation with Reference to Topicality in Korean". Doctoral dissertation, UCLA.

Kuno, S. 1973. *The Structure of the Japanese Language*. Cambridge, Mass.: M.I.T. Press.

Lee, H.-S. 1987. *Discourse Presupposition and the Discourse Function of the Topic Marker 'nin' in Korean*. Indiana University Linguistics Club Publication.

Levinson, S. C. 1983. *Pragmatics*. Cambridge: Cambridge University Press.

Mayes P. 1990. "Quotation in spoken English." *Studies in Language* 14:2.325-63.

Ochs, E. 1988. *Culture and Language Development.* Cambridge: Cambridge University Press.

Ochs, E., and B. B. Schieffelin. 1989. "Language has a heart." *Text* 9:1.7-25.

Pomerantz, A. 1984. "Agreeing and disagreeing with assessments: Some features of preferred/dispreferred turn shapes." M. Atkinson, and J. Heritage 1984.57-101.

Prince, E. F. 1978. "A comparison of WH-cleft and IT-cleft in discourse." *Language* 54. 883-906.

Quirk, R., and S. Greenbaum. 1973. *A Concise Grammar of Contemporary English.* New York: Harcourt Brace Jovanovich.

Quirk, R., S. Greenbaum, G. Leech, and J. Svartvik. 1985. *A Comprehensive Grammar of the English Language*. London: Longman.

Ross, J. R. 1967. "Constraints on Variables in Syntax." Doctoral dissertation, M.I.T., Cambridge, Massachusetts.

Sacks, H. 1972. "On the analyzability of stories by children." *Directions in Sociolinguistics* ed. by J. J. Gumperz and D. Hymes, 325-45. New York: Holt, Rinehart and Winston.

Sacks H. 1987. "On the preference for agreement and contiguity in sequences in conversation." *Talk and Social Organization* ed. by G. Button and J. R. E. Lee, 54-69. Clevedon: Multilingual Matters.

Sacks, H., and E. A. Schegloff. 1979. "Two preferences in the organization of reference to persons in conversation and their interaction." *Everyday Language: Studies in Ethnomethodology* ed. by G. Psathas, 15-21. New York: Irvington.

Sacks, H., E. A. Schegloff, and G. Jefferson. 1974. "A simplest systematics for the organization of turn-taking for conversation." *Language* 50.696-735.

Schegloff, E. A. 1979. "The relevance of repair to syntax-for-conversation." T. Givón 1979. 261-88.

Schegloff, E. A. 1982. "Discourse as an interactional achievement: some uses of "uh huh" and other things that come between sentences." *Georgetown University Round Table on Languages and Linguistics* ed. by D. Tannen, 71-93. Washington DC: Georgetown University Press.

Schegloff, E. A. 1987. "Some sources of misunderstanding in talk-in-interaction." *Linguistics* 25.201-18.

Schegloff, E. A. 1988. "Other-initiated Repair Sequences in Talk in Interaction". Proposal to the National Science Foundation.

Schegloff, E. A. 1990. "On the organization of sequences as a source of "coherence" in talk-in-interaction." *Conversational Organization and its Development* ed. by B. Dorval, 51-77. Norwood, NJ.: Ablex.

Schegloff, E. A. 1991. "Conversation analysis and socially shared cognition." *Socially Shared Cognition* ed. by L. Resnick, J. Levine and S. Teasly, 150-71. American Psychological Association.

Schiffrin, D. 1987. *Discourse Markers*. New York: Cambridge University Press.

Tannen, D. 1989. *Talking Voices: Repetition, dialogue, and imagery in conversational discourse*. Cambridge: Cambridge University Press.

Thompson, S. A. 1978. "Modern English from a typological point of view: Some implications of the function of word order." *Linguistische Berichte* 54.19-35.

Werth, P. 1984. *Focus, Coherence, and Emphasis*. London: Croom Helm.

Pragmatic relations and word order in Chinese*

Randy J. LaPolla
Institute of History & Philology, Academia Sinica

1. Introduction

In LaPolla 1990, I presented arguments to show that Chinese is a language in which there has been no grammaticalization of the syntactic relations "subject" and "object". This being the case, then syntactic relations cannot be what determines word order in Chinese. In this paper I will argue that, aside from a semantic rule that the actor of a verb, if expressed, must precede that verb, it is pragmatic relations (information structure) that are the main determinants of word order in Chinese.[1] Though writing about a situation that exists for French and Italian, in the following quote Lambrecht could have been talking about Chinese:

> It is interesting to observe that the difference in the pragmatic status of the NP referent as being either already present in the universe of discourse or not is not only expressed by the choice of lexical vs. pronominal encoding but also by the position of the NP in the sentence ... We thus notice a series of correlations between (i) presence of a referent in the universe of discourse, pronominal coding, preverbal position and topic status, and (ii) previous absence of a referent, lexical NP coding, postverbal position and focus status. We may draw from these correlations the preliminary conclusion that certain pragmatic differences having to do with the contrast between the text-external and the text-internal world are formally reflected in the morpho-syntactic structure of the sentence. (Lambrecht 1986:38)

As Li and Thompson (1978:687) argue, "word order in Chinese serves primarily to signal semantic and pragmatic factors rather than grammatical relations such as subject, direct object, indirect object" (see also Li and Thompson 1981:19 for similar arguments). Much has been written about the importance of "topic" in Chinese (e.g. Li and Thompson 1974a, 1976, 1981; Barry 1975; Tsao 1979), but the importance of pragmatic relations ("focus structure" — see definition below) in determining syntactic structure is not that well understood. What I explore then in this paper is focus structure and its grammaticalization in the word order patterns of Chinese.

In discussing information structure, I will generally follow the theory outlined in the work of Knud Lambrecht (1986, 1987, 1988, 1989, to appear). The concept of information structure presented there is an outgrowth of the Prague School notion of Functional Sentence Perspective, though it goes far beyond the simple concepts of "theme" – "rheme". We will discuss two aspects of information structure: focus structure and the cognitive properties of discourse referents.

In the following introduction, it is not my intention to develop a theory of information structure, as this has already been done by Lambrecht. I will here only be presenting a summary of those aspects of information structure (as presented in Lambrecht's work) that are relevant to Chinese. Please see Lambrecht (to appear), for a complete and detailed analysis of information structure.

The concept of focus structure, as defined in Lambrecht (to appear) will be the center of interest in our discussion of information structure:

> *Focus structure*: A grammatical system used to mark the focus of the assertion in a sentence by setting it off against the pragmatic presupposition.

By "grammatical system" is meant a particular use of intonation, morphology, word order, special "constructions", or a combination thereof. We then need to define the terms *pragmatic presupposition, assertion*, and *focus of the assertion*:

> *Pragmatic presupposition*: The set of propositions evoked in an utterance which the speaker assumes the hearer already knows or believes or is ready to take for granted at the time of speech.
>
> *Pragmatic assertion*: The proposition which the hearer is expected to know or believe or take for granted as a result of hearing the utterance.
>
> *Focus* (or *focus of the assertion)*: That portion of a proposition whereby the assertion differs from the presupposition.

The pragmatic presupposition, a propositional notion, must be distinguished from the *topic*, which is the NP (expressed or not) within the pragmatic presupposition that has the function of naming the referent that the assertion is about. As the assertion includes both the presupposition (and the topic) and the focus, it is a pragmatically structured proposition, a proposition *in context*. It is not the case that every utterance has a topic (see below), or that every sentence involves an explicit assertion (as with conventionalized polite greetings, etc.).

Focus structure is not a question of identifiable vs. unidentifiable NPs; it is "an indicator of a semantic *relation* holding on the level of the sentence or proposition as a whole, not ... an expression of information properties of individual sentence constituents" (Lambrecht 1989:3, emphasis in original). For Lambrecht, there is "a threefold distinction ... between *information* as conveyed by propositions, the *pragmatic states* of the referents of individual sentence constituents in the minds of the speech participants, and the *pragmatic relations* established between these referents and propositions" (to appear, p. 42, emphasis in original).[2]

Lambrecht (1986, 1987, 1989, to appear) distinguishes three main types of focus structure: "predicate focus", "narrow focus", and "sentence focus". *Predicate focus* is statistically the most common of the three. It involves an assertion with an unmarked topic-comment structure.[3] There is a topic that is within the presupposition; the domain (scope) of the focus is then the comment (predicate), and within this there is an unmarked focus position, usually the object position (see also Givón 1979b:51-53 on this last point). Lambrecht gives examples (1a-d) (1989:5), to which I have added the Chinese equivalent:

(1)	Q: How's your car?	
A:	a. *My car/it broke **down**.*	English (subject-predicate)
	b. *(La mia macchina) si è **rotta**.*	Italian (subject-predicate)
	c. *(Ma voiture) elle est en **panne**.*	French (topic- subject-predicate)
	d. *(Kuruma wa) **koshoo**-shi-ta.*	Japanese (topic-comment)
	e. *(Wo de che zi) **huai** le.*	Chinese (topic-comment)

In this structure, as the topic is part of the presupposition, it is usually not necessary for it to be explicitly stated for the assertion to be understood, so it is often pronominalized or, in the case of French, Italian, Japanese, and Chinese, completely unexpressed (as shown by the parentheses around the topics).

Lambrecht's second type of focus structure is the *narrow focus* or "contrastive focus" structure. In a narrow focus structure only a single NP is in focus; the rest of the assertion is within the presupposition, as in the examples in (2) ((2a-d) from Lambrecht 1989:8; the focused NP is in bold).

(2) Q: I heard your motorcycle broke down?

A:	a. *My* ***car*** *broke down.*	English (NP focus accent)
	b. *È la mia* ***macchina*** *che si è rotta.*	Italian (*è*-cleft)
	c. *C'est ma* ***voiture*** *qui est en panne.*	French (*c'est* cleft)
	d. ***Kuruma*** *ga koshoo-shita.*	Japanese (*ga*-marking)
	e. *Shi wo* ***chezi*** *huai le.*	Chinese (*shi*-cleft)[4]

Just as it is possible to pronominalize or drop the topic of a predicate focus structure, it is often possible to leave out all but the focused constituent in a narrow focus structure. That is, a single NP could be the whole complete utterance, as in the answer to the question-word question in (3).

(3) a. *Weiyuanhui xuan shei lai dang zhuxi?*
committee choose who come act-as chairman
'Who did the committee choose to be chairman?'

b. ***Zhangsan.***
(personal name)

Again it is important to emphasize that the NP in focus is not necessarily "new information", as "it is not so much the focus noun itself which contributes the new information to the discourse but the relationship between (the referent of) this noun and the entire proposition" (Lambrecht 1989:9). In fact, "information is never conveyed by single words or expressions or even constituents, but by establishing *relations* between words as elements of propositions" (Lambrecht 1986:160, emphasis in original).[5]

In Chinese, intonation can also be used to focus any constituent in the sentence (Teng 1985:166); predicate focus has the intonation on the predicate, and this is the unmarked case; narrow focus can be achieved by using marked intonation on the focused constituent. Therefore, (4), below, could be the answer to *When did Miss Zhao ask for three days' leave of absence?, Who was it that last month asked for three days' leave of absence?*, or *How many days leave did Miss Zhao ask for last month?*, depending on whether the prosodic stress is placed on the temporal phrase, the actor, or the modifier of the final NP respectively (Teng 1985.).

(4)

Zhao	*Xiaojie*	*shang*	*ge*	*yue*	*qing*	*le*	*san*	*tian*
Zhao	Miss	last	CL	month	ask-for	ASP	three	day

jia.
vacation
'Miss Zhao last month asked for three days' leave of absence.'

The third type of focus structure discussed by Lambrecht, *sentence focus*, requires little or no presupposition; the focus of the assertion is the entire sentence. This is the type of sentence referred to by Kuno (1972) as "neutral description" or "themeless". This type is semantically non-binary, as there is no topic-comment or focus-presupposition structure, and so is often referred to as thetic, as opposed to categorical (e.g. Sasse 1987). It is generally presentational, presenting either a state of affairs or a new referent (Sasse's "event-central" or "entity-central"). In languages that have syntactic subjects, the subject is the unmarked topic, so for a subject to be interpreted as not topical it must be "detopicalized", marked in some way, either by intonation, word order, or morphology. As the unmarked focus position is that of the object, most languages detopicalize the subject by giving it markings, intonation, or word order similar to those of an object (Lambrecht 1989:10).

(5) Q: What happened?

A:	a. *My* ***car*** *broke down.*	English (accented subject NP)
	b. *Mi si è rotta la* ***macchina****.*	Italian (inverted subject NP)
	c. *J'ai ma* ***voiture*** *qui est en* ***panne****.*	French (clefted subject NP)
	d. ***Kuruma*** *ga koshoo-shi-ta.*	Japanese (morphol. marking)

Chinese does not have a grammaticalized subject or object, but the relevant NP (what otherwise might be interpreted as a topic) must still be shown to be non-topical in a sentence focus construction. B's answer in (6) is one type of sentence focus structure in Chinese.[6]

(6) A:

Fasheng	*le*	*shenme*	*shi?*
happen	ASP	what	affair

'What happened?'

B:

Gang	*lai*	*le*	*yi*	*da*	*dui*	***liumang****.*
just-now	come	ASP	one	big	group	hoodlum

'A group of hoodlums just arrived.'

In this example the "big group of hoodlums" is marked as non-topical by its postverbal position. It is then not a statement about the hoodlums, but merely asserts that the event of their appearance occured.

One important point we can see from all the examples above is the different ways languages have of marking the different types of focus structure, which gives us a window on the interactions and precedence relations (which type of relation takes precedence over another) between syntactic, semantic and pragmatic relations. We see that in English syntactic relations control the syntactic structure, and are relatively unaffected by pragmatic relations, while in Italian and French pragmatic relations take precedence over syntactic relations in determining syntactic structure. In Chinese pragmatic relations are not subject to syntactic factors, but take a back seat to semantics if the verb has an argument that is an actor (i.e. agent, effector). We will look at the different constructions involved below, but first we will look at the NPs involved in the constructions.

Following I will give a very brief outline of some of the different semantic properties and pragmatic statuses the representation of a referent may have in a discourse. This will be essentially to define the terms to be used in this paper rather than to explicate a theory of pragmatic categories. See Lambrecht, to appear, Chapter 3 for such an explication (cf. also Du Bois 1980).

An NP is *referential* if the speaker intends for it to refer to a particular entity which exists within a particular universe of discourse, with continuous identity over time (cf. Givón 1978:293, Du Bois 1980:208). This referential NP will be either *identifiable* or *unidentifiable* to the addressee. If it is identifiable, it will be in one of three activation states, *active* (currently the focus of consciousness), *accessible* (not the current focus of consciousness, but textually, situationally, or inferentially derivable), or *inactive* (not in the focus or periphery of consciousness, but in long term memory). A referent will often be unidentifiable when first introduced into a discourse, but it can be introduced in two ways, either as a "brand-new" *unanchored* referent, or as an *anchored* referent (these terms from Prince 1981), one where the unidentifiable referent is presented as related in some way to an identifiable referent (as in *a guy I work with*). Further mentions of a referent after its introduction will then treat it as identifiable. A referential NP is *specific* if it is identifiable to the speaker, regardless of whether it is identifiable to the addressee or not. If the individual identity of the referent is not important to the speaker, it is *non-specific* (as in *I'm looking for a mouse* — it could be one I just lost (specific), or any mouse I happen to come across (non-specific)). Generics, predicative NPs, and nouns that occur in compounds (e.g. *bear-hunting*) or are under the scope of negation are all non-referential.[7] This gives us the hierarchy of referential NPs (exclud-

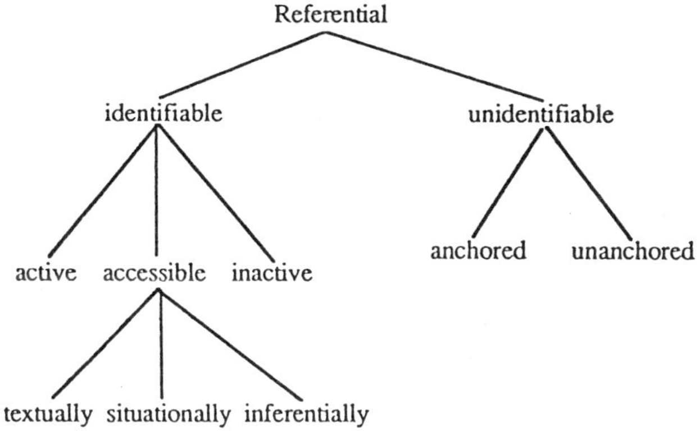

Figure 1. The cognitive states of referential NPs in discourse

ing the specific-non-specific contrast) as presented in Figure 1.

It is important to point out the difference between the (possibly universal) *cognitive* category of identifiability and the (language specific) *grammatical* category of definiteness. *Definiteness* can be said to be the grammatical coding of an NP as to whether or not the speaker assumes the referent of the NP is identifiable to the addressee, though this is a rough definition, as the relationship between definite coding, to the extent that it exists, and the cognitive statuses of referents varies greatly between languages.

It is also important to emphasize the distinction between the activation status of a referent and the information structure categories introduced above. The former involves the cognitive statuses of discourse referents, while the latter involves the relations between discourse referents and propositions.

2. The question of "definiteness"

The first question we will discuss is the types of codings NPs can have in Chinese in relation to their activation states, and whether or not word order is involved in marking "definiteness" or identifiability in Chinese, as is often assumed. Mullie (1932:160-168) outlined a correlation between "definiteness" (what he referred to as "determinateness") and preverbal position, and between "indefiniteness" ("indeterminateness") and post-verbal position, for the single argument of intransitive verbs. Mullie's analysis was quite insightful, as he saw that what determined word order for intransitives was not accurately captured by the use of the terms "determinate" and "indeterminate" ("definite" and "indefinite"); he also understood the use of having the "subject" of intransitives in post-verbal position "when 'a state of affairs' or 'an action', thus the verb rather than the subject, is emphasized" (1932:166) (see below on the event-central thetic sentence); and he understood the possible (though not always necessary) use of the "circumlocution" of the presentative construction for "indeterminate" "subjects" of transitive verbs. (See below for discussion of the presentative constructions.)

Y. R. Chao (1968:76-77) stated that "there is a very strong tendency for the subject to have a definite reference, and the object to have an indefinite reference", but it is "... not so much the subject or object function that goes with definite or indefinite reference as position in an earlier or later part of the sentence that makes the difference". Teng (1975) and Zhu (1982) also give similar analyses. It is significant that each of these scholars stated the tendency with hedges; each recognized the weakness of the generalization. (For examples that violate this tendency (i.e., have "indefinite" sentence initial NPs) see Fan 1985.)

In Li and Thompson 1975, an attempt is made to formalize this relationship between word order and the "definiteness" of the NPs of a sentence in Chinese. They give the following "tendency" (p. 170):

Tendency A: Nouns preceding the verb tend to be definite, while those following the verb tend to be indefinite.

Tendency A is an overgeneralization, so Li and Thompson propose a set of refinements (p. 184):

Refinement 1: The noun in postverbal position will be interpreted as indefinite unless it is morphologically or inherently or non-anaphorically definite.

Refinement 2: A sentence-initial noun must be interpreted as definite, and may not be interpreted as indefinite even if it is preceded by the numeral *yi* 'one'.

Refinement 3: The noun following *bei*, although pre-verbal, is immune to Tendency A.

Refinement 4: Nouns in prepositional phrases are immune to Tendency A.[8]

Tendency A has been supported by data from quantitative discourse analyses of Chinese texts, such as Sun and Givón 1985 and M. Wang 1988.

Sun and Givón (1985) actually claimed to have *disproved* Tendency A with a quantitative discourse analysis of both written and oral texts, but Nichols (1988a) has shown that when run through the relevant statistical tests, Sun and Givón's own data *support* Tendency A. A similar study (M. Wang 1988) done with the same methodology used by Sun and Givón came up with results that also support Li and Thompson's hypothesis.

Though there is this tendency, Li and Thompson point out that

> [t]here is by no means a strict correlation between the definite interpretation of a noun and its position relative to the verb ... [W]ord order plays a significant and systematic role in distinguishing definite from indefinite nouns, although it is not the only means by which definite and indefinite nouns may be distinguished from each other. (1975:184-5)

As Li and Thompson recognize in their discussion of Tendency A, there are two parts to the question of "definiteness" in Chinese: (1) the coding on the NP, and (2) what they consider to be coding by position of that NP in the sentence. We will look at each of these separately to see if they are really two parts of the same thing.

2.1 *Coding on the NP*

Each type of discourse referent in Chinese may be represented in several ways. A referent that is active will often be represented by a zero or overt pronoun, but can also be expressed as a bare lexical NP or one preceded by a genitive phrase or by a deictic pronoun (including a numeral plus classifer phrase if the number of the referents is important).[9]

(7) A: *Zhangsan$_i$ jintian lai guo ma?*
Zhangsan today come ASP Q
'Has Zhangsan come (in) today?'
B: *Ø$_i$ meiyou, keshi (ta$_i$) yi huir hui lai, [ta$_i$ de*
N-A but (3SG) one time will come 3SG GEN
chezi]$_i$ you wenti.
vehicle have problem
'No, but he'll be in in a little while, his car has a problem.'
A: *(([Ta$_i$ de) chezi]$_j$) you you wenti le! Ø$_j$*
((3SG GEN) vehicle) again have problem ASP
zhen shi lan huo.
really COP rotten goods
'His car has problems again! It's really a piece of junk.'

In this example, Zhangsan is inactive (or accessible) in the first utterance, but after being mentioned is then active in the second utterance and so can be represented as a zero or a pronoun. His car is introduced as an inactive (or possibly anchored unidentifiable) referent in the second utterance, and is then active in the last utterance, so can be represented by the bare noun, the noun with the genitive phrase, or a zero.

A referent that is accessible or inactive will generally be encoded as a bare lexical NP or one preceded by a genitive phrase or by a deictic pronoun (see ex. (7)). An unanchored unidentifiable referent which is to become a topic in the discourse will generally be introduced as a lexical noun preceded by a numeral (usually *yi* 'one') plus a classifier:

(8) *Wo$_j$ zuijin mai le yi shuang xiezi$_i$, keshi Ø$_j$ chuan*
1SG recently buy ASP one pair shoes but wear
le Ø$_i$ yi ci Ø$_i$ jiu po le.
ASP one time then break ASP
'I bought a pair of shoes recently, but only wore (them) once and (they) broke.'

Here the shoes are introduced as an unanchored unidentifiable referent in the first clause, and are then active in the following two clauses.

An unanchored referential-unidentifiable referent which is not to become a topic (is incidental to the discourse) will often either not have the numeral plus classifier, or will have the classifer, but not the numeral.[10] An unidentifiable referent can also be introduced as an anchored referent, where it is marked as related, usually by a genitive phrase, to some other element either known to the addressee or within the schema or frame of the discourse, such as is the case with *gongren* 'worker' in the following example:

(9) *Xuexiao de yi ge gongren zuotian chu le*
school GEN one CLASS worker yesterday produce ASP
che-huo.
car-accident
'Yesterday one of the workers in the school got into a car accident.'

Non-referential NPs will be represented as bare lexical nouns or nouns preceded by a numeral plus a classifier or just a classifer:

(10) a. *Ta shi ((yi) ge) gongren.*
3SG COP ((one) CLASS) worker
'He is a worker.'

b. *Bu guan cong nali lai, ren zong shi ren.*
not matter from where come person always COP person
'No matter where (they) are from, people are still people.'

c. *Yi ge ren zai wuliao de shihou hui*
one CLASS person ASP uninteresting GEN time will
xiang he jiu.
think drink liquor
'When a person is bored s/he will think of drinking liquor.'

In (10a), the predicative phrase 'a worker' can be coded in Chinese as a bare noun, a classifer plus noun, or 'one' plus classifier plus noun. In (10b), the generic 'person' is coded as a bare NP, while in (10c) it takes a numeral and classifer.

Following is a summary of the types of representations each type of referent may have:

Type of referent	**Possible codings**
Active	zero, pronoun, bare NP, with deictic pronoun
Accessible	pronoun, bare NP, with deictic pronoun
Inactive	bare NP, with deictic pronoun
Unanchored Unidentifiable	bare NP, (numeral +) classifier
Anchored Unidentifiable	genitive phrase, relative clause
Non-referential	bare NP, (numeral +) classifier

From the point of view of the type of NP which represents a particular referent, we can see that Chinese can generallly distinguish between active and non-active identifiable referents by the use of zero anaphora for active referents, and between identifiable and unidentifiable referents by the use of a deictic pronoun as a modifier on nouns representing identifiable referents.

Chen (1986:16-17) considers all NPs marked with a genitive phrase or relative clause to be "definite" (so, for example, the topic in (9), which represents an anchored unidentifiable referent, would be considered by Chen to be "definite"), and only unanchored unidentifiable referents with overt marking (numeral plus classifier) as "indefinite". The fact that almost any type of referent can be represented by a bare noun with no overt marking leads Chen to posit a third grammatical category, which he calls "indeterminate". The pragmatic states of the referents of these "indeterminate" NPs, according to Chen, are interpreted by the addressee as "definite" or "indefinite" on the basis of "syntactic or discourse contexts" (1986:19). Given these facts, and the fact pointed out by Chafe (1976:39) and Givón (1978:319) that since the deictic (demonstrative) pronouns do not lose their deictic force when used for "definitization" they cannot be seen as simply marking "definitization", I would argue that Chinese does not have a grammatical category of definiteness, but simply several means for expressing the pragmatic category of identifiability.

In terms of position of an NP in a sentence, there are few restrictions based on the semantic or pragmatic status of the referent of that NP.[11] Generic (10b-c), uniquely identifiable (11a-b), and any overtly marked NPs (either definite or indefinite — (12a-d)) can appear before or after the verb, without a change in pragmatic status (Chen 1986:37; see also the refinements to Li and Thompson's Tendency A given above) (The relevant items are in bold type; (12a) is from Fan 1985:322, originally from a New China News Agency bulletin.)

(11) a. ***Taiyang*** *chu lai le.*
sun out come ASP
'**The sun** has come out.'

b. *Wo yi zheng tian dou mei kan dao* ***taiyang***
1SG one whole day all N-A look arrive sun
'I haven't seen **the sun** all day.'

(12) a. ***Liang ge Shaoxianduiyuan*** *xiang Xu Haifeng he*
two CLASS Young-Pioneer(s) towards Xu Haifeng and
Wang Yifu xian le xian hua he hong lingjin.
Wang Yifu give ASP fresh flowers and red scarf.
'**Two Young Pioneers** gave fresh flowers and red scarfs to Xu Haifeng and Wang Yifu.'

b. *Laoshi jintian song wo* ***yi fu huar***.
teacher today give 1SG **one CLASS painting**
'Today the teacher gave me **a painting**.'

c. ***Nei ge ren*** *jintian mei lai.*
that CLASS person today N-A come
'**That person** didn't come today.'

d. A: *Che shang chule nei ge ren yiwai,*
vehicle on aside-from that CLASS person aside-from
hai you shenme ren?
still have what person
'Who else is on the train aside from that person?'

B: *Jiu zuo* ***nei ge ren.***
only sit **that CLASS person**
Only **that person** is sitting there.

It is only the indeterminate category that, according to Chen, is affected by position in a sentence (cf. Chao 1968:76):

(13) a. *Lai le* ***keren.***
come ASP **guest**
'There came **a guest**.'

b. ***Keren*** *lai le.*
Guest(s) come ASP
'**The guest**(s) have come.'

Chen essentially follows the scholars mentioned above in assuming that word order determines "definiteness". Only Givón questions whether the preverbal word order patterns are

> indeed 'mere definitization' or topic-shifting devices. The nouns occurring in them could be definite or generic, which is a general restriction holding to definite NPs as well as topic-shifting. The distributional restrictions in these word order devices in Mandarin, including the *ba* construction, strongly hint that they are topic-shifting rather than definitization devices. (1978:319)

I propose that it is not identifiability that is coded by word order, but focus structure. If we look beyond the identifiability of the referents of noun phrases, we can see that Tendency A is actually only one part of a more general tendency to have the focus at the end of the sentence (cf. note by Dragunov in Wang 1982:106; Huang and Davis 1988:9), or at least postverbal (in the case of cleft constructions). The confusion of focus structure with the representation of referents came about because referents newly introduced into the discourse will almost always occur in the sentence final (post-verbal) focus position (99% of referential-"indefinite" NPs in Sun and Givón's study (1985) were post-verbal), so post-verbal position became associated with "indefiniteness". As a topic is most often identifiable, and as topic position is preverbal, preverbal position became associated with "definite" NPs. Yet an NP of any type of referentiality or identifiability can occur in postverbal position, *if it is focal*, and the same NP can occur in preverbal position, *if it is topical*. We can then make a much stronger generalization than Tendency A, with all its refinements, or the much-hedged statements by other scholars, if we say that *topical or non-focal NPs occur preverbally and focal or non-topical NPs occur post-verbally*.[12] In this generalization I include non-focal NPs with topical NPs because aside from topical NPs, which will generally be sentence initial, non-focal NPs (secondary topics, non-referential NPs used adverbially, etc.) can also appear preverbally, albeit in non-initial position. I also include non-topical (including non-referential) NPs with focal NPs because in a predicate focus structure a focal NP will appear postverbally to mark it as focal, while in an event-central thetic phrase a non-topical NP will appear post-verbally to mark it as non-topical (see below for examples). Focal and non-topical NPs can both appear postverbally because they share the characteristic of NOT being an entity that an assertion is predicated of.

3. Marked focus constructions[13]

Word order in Mandarin is "consistently" verb medial (Li and Thompson 1978) due to the statistical predominance of predicate focus sentences, but there are a number of constructions that deviate from this form because of the influence of marked focus structure. By "marked" I simply mean statistically less common. There is no such thing as a pragmatically "neutral" sentence; all sentences have focus structure, but one type, predicate focus, is more common, and so less "marked". In a language such as English, a sentence focus sentence can have the same syntactic structure as a predicate focus sentence, but the subject NP will not be topical and there will be no prosodic stress on the verb. In Chinese, a sentence focus sentence cannot have the same structure as a predicate focus sentence. A presentative structure must be used to prevent a potentially topical NP from being interpreted as a topic. Following we will examine both entity-central or event-central sentence focus structures, and discuss the focus structure of incorporation constructions.

3.1 *Entity-central presentative sentences*

Entity-central presentative sentences introduce a new referent into a discourse. They do this by placing the new referent in the postverbal focus position.[14] Li and Thompson (1981:509-519) classify these into two types, those which simply state the referent's existence or location (the "existential presentative sentence"), and those which introduce the referent with a verb of motion. This difference is exemplified in (14) (Li and Thompson's (2) and (3), p. 509-10):

(14) a. *(zai) yuanzi-li you yi zhi* ***gou.***
(LOC) yard-inside exist one CLASS dog
'In the yard there is a **dog**.'

b. *Lai le yi ge* ***keren.***
come ASP one CLASS guest
'There came a **guest**.'

Sentences with the existential verb *you*, as in (14a) have two possible structures, the one given in (14a) and that in (15) (Li and Thompson's (7), p. 511):

(15) *You yi zhi* ***gou*** *zai* ***yuanzi****-li.*
exist one CLASS dog LOC yard-inside
'There is a **dog** in the **yard**.'

Li and Thompson point out that there is a pragmatic difference between these two structures, but they see the difference in terms of the "definiteness" of the locus (*yuanzi*). That is, they state that for (14a) to be used properly, the locus must have already been established in the discourse context, as it functions as the topic of the sentence. Yet if we look at the identifiability of *yuanzi,* we see that in both (14a) and (15) the yard is in the same state of identifiability — it is identifiable (this is the unmarked state for locatives — Van Valin 1975); the "definiteness" of the yard then cannot be important here. What is different between the two is the focus structure. In (15) the yard is identifiable, so it is not being introduced as a new referent, as the dog is, yet it is focal (both clauses in (15) contain focal NPs). In (14a) *yuanzi-li* 'in the yard' is not focal, but it is also not a topic about which an assertion is being made. It merely acts as a locative reference point (it is situationally accessible); the locative serves simply to anchor the new referent in the discourse (Lambrecht 1988:15-16). It is generally not the topic of a topic chain, for example, or even simple cross-clause coreference:

(16) a. *Yuanzi li you* ***junren***$_i$*, danshi* Ø$_i$ *bu duo.*
yard inside have soldier(s) but not many
'There are **soldiers** in the yard, but not many.'

b. **Yuanzi li*$_i$ *you* ***junren****, danshi* Ø$_i$ *you kuan,* Ø$_i$
yard inside have **soldier**(s) but also wide
you da.
also big

Li Naicong (p.c.) points out that the following sentence, in which the locative seems to be the topic of a topic chain, is grammatical:

(17) *Yuanzi li you* ***junren****, hai you ji liang*
yard inside have soldier(s) also have several CLASS
tankeche*, suoyi* Ø *xiande hen yongji.*
tanks so appears very crowded
'In the yard there are **soldiers** and some **tanks**, so it looks quite crowded.'

In this case, though, the topic of *xiande hen yongji* 'appears very crowded' cannot be *yuanzi-li* 'in the yard' with a locative sense, but must be *yuanzi* 'the yard' (or possibly *yuanzi-li*, with a nominal meaning, 'the inside of the yard'), as *yuanzi-li* with a locative sense is an abbreviation of *zai yuanzi-li* 'in the yard', with the locative verb *zai*. This difference is significant. In the sentence initial position of (17), *yuanzi-li* and *zai yuanzi-li* are both permissible, but replacing the zero anaphor before *xiande hen yongji* with *zai yuanzi-li* would be ungrammatical. (See also the discussion of (19) below.)

The second type (i.e. (15)), with the locus and presentative phrases reversed is not an existential presentative sentence like (14a), as assumed by Li and Thompson, but is actually an example of what Li and Thomson (1981:611-618) call the "realis descriptive clause sentence", a two-clause structure[15] where a referent is introduced in the first clause, and then an assertion is made about it in the following clause (both of which are part of the same sentence; see below).[16]

A second point about Li and Thompson's analysis of existential presentative sentences is that Li and Thompson equate them with possessives (p. 513). In their analysis, the only difference between a sentence such as (14a) and (18) (Li and Thompson 1981:513, ex. (14)) is that (18) has an animate locus.

(18) *Ta you* ***san ge haizi.***
3SG exist three CLASS child(ren)
'He has **three children**.'

Yet there is an important difference in focus structure between (18) and (14a). In (14a) the locus can take the locative verb *zai;* that is, it is a separate clause (of the type in a serial verb construction), and it can occur either before or after the *you* clause with no change in the truth value of the utterance. The sentence is a sentence focus sentence, i.e., there is no topic. In (18), *ta* is not a separate clause, it is the topic about which the assertion is being made. It cannot occur after the *you* clause. This is a predicate focus sentence, therefore not of the same class of sentences as (14a). Guo (1990:24-25) distinguishes between existential structures and what he refers to as "possessive subject" sentences on the basis of whether there is a "positional" particle (in example (19b), *li* 'inside') in the sentence initial NP. Without the positional particle, the initial NP is a topic in a sentence that says something about what happened to that topic; with the positional particle, the sentence-initial NP is not a topic, it is simply the location of the event or entity. Guo gives the following examples:

(19) a. *Ta si le yi ge erzi.*
3SG die ASP one CLASS son
'One of his sons died (on him).'

b. *Tou li si le yi ge ren.*
head inside die ASP one CLASS person
'Someone among the leaders died.'

This distinction is clearest when the sentence initial NP is a location, as in (20). Without a positional particle, the sentence initial NP is not a locative, as in the existential sentences, but is a topic in a possessor relation to the post-verbal NP:

(20) *Dongwuyuan pao le yi zhi xiongmao.*
zoo run ASP one CLASS panda
'The zoo lost a panda (by its running away).'

A difference similar to that between (14a) and (18) obtains between sentences such as (14a) and those such as (21), which Li & Thompson (1981:514, ex. (17)) also discuss as a type of presentative sentence in that it identifies or characterizes the pre-copula NP, which they also consider a locus.

(21) *Waimian shi yi zhi* ***gou****.*
outside COP one CLASS dog
'What's outside is a **dog**.'

For this sentence to be used properly, "the speaker must believe not only that the listener already knows about the locus but that s/he has some reason to be interested in it and in what it is or what it has or what it looks like" (p. 515). The type exemplified by (14a), on the other hand, simply predicates "the existence of the presented noun phrase at some locus in which the listener need not have had any interest" (p. 515).

Again we can see that these two types are very different in terms of focus structure, and that this is what determines the difference in meaning and usage. In (21), the fact that the pre-copula NP is under discussion is clearly part of the presupposition (cf. the quote in the preceding paragraph), and there is an assertion made about it. It also cannot occur at the end of the sentence. This latter type of sentence and the possessive structure (as in (18)) then are different from the first type of existential presentative sentence (as in (14a), (15)): the first type, similar to *there* sentences in English, is comprised of either a simple thetic statement asserting the existence of an entity in a particular location (15), or a biclausal sentence focus statement involving a statement about the existence of some entity and its location (14a); the other two sentence types are both single-clause sentences with clear topic-comment structures.

The second type of "existential presentative sentence" discussed by Li and Thompson (1981:611-618) (and mentioned just above), they call the "realis descriptive clause sentence". This type is a serial verb construction in which a referent is introduced in the postverbal position of the first clause, then an assertion about the referent is made by the second clause (Li and Thompson say that an "incidental description" is made of the NP by the second clause). The two clauses together are one intonation unit/sentence. (Ex. (22b) is their (75), p. 611):

(22) a. *(Waimian) you yi ge* ***ren*** *xiang jian ni.*
(outside) have one CLASS person think see 2SG
'There's a **person** (outside) who wants to see you.'

b. *Ta you yi ge* ***meimei*** *hen xihuan kan*
3SG have one CLASS **younger-sister** very like look
dianying.
movie
'S/He has a **younger sister** (who) likes to watch movies.'

c. *Wo mai le yi jian* ***yifu*** *hen hao kan.*
1SG buy ASP one CLASS clothes very good look
'I bought a piece of **clothing** (that is) very good looking.'

In all of these examples the structure is a juncture of two clauses, but (22a) does not have exactly the same focus structure as (22b) or (22c): (22a) has a simple presentational clause, which asserts the existence of an entity, as discussed above, followed by a predication. The first clause simply allows the referent to become active in the discourse; the second clause makes an assertion about it.[17] In (22b), on the other hand, there are two topic-comment type assertions, one about the topic *ta,* the other about the sister that is introduced in the unmarked focus position of the first clause and becomes the topic of the second clause. The same structure can be assigned to (22c). It might be argued that in all three of these examples the first clause functions only to introduce a referent, yet the first clause IS making an assertion about a topic (e.g., in (22c) that the topic 'I' bought an item of clothing), even if the proposition expressed is a rather uninteresting or uninformative one. The variety of verbs that can occur in the first clause of this type of construction would also argue against seeing that clause as propositionally empty.

The nature of this type of structure in English is discussed at length in Lambrecht 1988. Lambrecht (1988:15) calls this structure a "presentational amalgam construction". An example of this in English is *I have a friend of mine in the history department teaches two courses per semester* (Lambrecht 1988:1), a construction usually considered ungrammatical in English, but nonetheless used very often. It is a structure where the speaker wishes to express a proposition about a referent being introduced, but is forced by the constraints on information structure (cf. Chafe's (1985:18; 1987:32) "One New Concept at a Time Constraint") to code the proposition in two clauses. The most efficient way to do this with a minimum of syntactic paraphrasing is to code the new referent simultaneously as the focus of the first clause and the topic of the following clause. Sasse (1987:541 ff.) also discusses similar structures in Arabic, Boni and other languages.

This is a type of core-coordination where the two cores share an argument.[18] The structure created, then, is tighter than simple juxtaposition. Though I talk about the referent being introduced in the first clause of a realis descriptive clause sentence and *then* having an assertion made about it, this is not a two-step process; it is not a case of equi-NP deletion in the second clause. The single argument is actually shared by both cores, and so is both new and a topic.

Li and Thompson point out the semantic similarity between these structures and relative clauses,[19] and explain the difference in the following quote:

> [T]he message conveyed by the realis descriptive clause is that the property it names is entirely incidental, while the message conveyed by the relative clause is that there is a preestablished class of such items. By *preestablished* we mean that the item with the property in question is assumed or has already come up at some point in discussions between speaker and hearer; they can be said to have tacitly agreed on the existence of a class of items with this property. (1981:614)

It would seem from this quote that they are talking about identifiability. They give the examples in (23) (their (84), p. 614) as evidence of the semantic difference between realis descriptive sentences and sentences with relative clauses:

(23) a. *Wo mai le yi jian* ***yifu*** *tai da.*
1SG buy ASP one CLASS clothes too big
'I bought an outfit that turned out to be too big.'

b. *Wo mai le yi jian tai da de* ***yifu****.*
1SG buy ASP one CLASS too big REL clothes
'I bought an outfit that was too big.'

They discuss the difference between these two sentences as one of whether or not there is a preestablished class of clothes that are too big. Yet the discourse status of the class of the referent is not what is important here. New information may be presented in the presupposed format of a restrictive relative clause as long as it is relatively unremarkable information, i.e. not the focus of the assertion (Du Bois 1980:223; see also Cumming 1984:369). What is important is that in (23a) an assertion is being made about the clothing, that it is too big. No such assertion is being made in (23b). That is, in (23a) there are two assertions, that I bought a piece of clothing, and that it is too big; in (23b) there is only one assertion, that I bought a piece of (a particular type of) clothing. If anything is incidental, it is the information in the relative clause, not the information which is being asserted. Though it is not clear from the main body of their discussion, Li and Thompson clearly understand this point, as in the last few lines of the section they state that "semantically, a descriptive clause simply adds another assertion to the first one. A relative clause, on the other hand, is a part of the noun phrase naming the item in question, so it is natural that it allows the expression of a preestablished class of items with the property it names" (p. 618).

We now turn to presentative sentences which involve a verb of motion. In this construction, the new referent occurs immediately after the verb of motion (Li and Thompson 1981:517-19), such as we saw in (14b), repeated here:

(14) b. *Lai* *le* *yi* *ge* ***keren***.
come ASP one CLASS guest
'A **guest** came.'

This type of structure cannot be used with all intransitive verbs of motion, though; verbs such as *gun* 'roll', and *pa* 'climb' used alone cannot introduce a referent. They must be in a construction with another clause, as in exx. (14a) and (15), or appear in construction with presentative verbs that act as complements of result, as in (24):

(24) *pa* *chu* *lai* *le* *yi* *zhi* ***laohu***.
climb exit come ASP one CLASS tiger
'A **tiger** climbed out.'

Li and Thompson do not give a reason for this difference, but what seems to be going on involves two different semantic factors. One is the aspect of the verbs involved: only a verb that is temporally bounded can be presentative (cf. Kuno 1972:300). The other factor is the meaning of the verbs involved: verbs such as *pa* 'climb' cannot introduce a referent because they are making a predication about the referent, whereas the general movement verbs, such as *lai* 'come', *qu* 'go', *chu* 'exit', etc. are semantically weak enough (they do not say anything about HOW the movement is done) that they can be used for presentational purposes. The latter, but not the former, also involve a directional component which naturally lends itself to the introduction of new referents. Lambrecht (1989:29) suggests that verbs such as 'arrive' are presentational due to their "inherent lexical content", and verbs such as 'call' may be construed as presentational because of the context. Du Bois (1987:836) also argues that intransitive verbs have two functions: introducing referents and adding semantic material, the difference depending on the discourse.[20]

3.2 *Event-central thetic sentences*

In "event-central" presentative sentences, what is being asserted is the existence (happening) of an event, not the existence of an entity, so this type of structure will often not include referentially specific NPs. It is possible to have a referential NP in this type of structure, but it will be "pragmatically non-referential" (Givón 1981), that is, a referential NP can be treated as non-referential when it is not salient in the discourse (see ex. (26a)). The prototypical examples of the "event-central" sentence are statements about the weather, such as *It's raining*. In Chinese the verbs for *rain* and *snow* do not incorporate the object as in English, though the NPs 'rain' and 'snow' in the sentences in (25), below, are not referentially specific (do not refer to some specific rain or snow — are "non-manipulable" in the framework of Hopper and Thompson 1984, 1985), and not topical, and so are placed in postverbal position:

(25) a. *Xia yu le.*
fall rain ASP
'It's raining.'

b. *Xia xue le.*
fall snow ASP
'It's snowing.'

This type of sentence is sometimes referred to as a type of existential sentence (e.g. Huang 1987), but the pragmatic function of these constructions is not to introduce a new referent; the NP which follows the verb is treated as non-topical, regardless of its identifiability.

An event-central expression can also appear as the comment in a topic-comment structure. In these cases, generally the topic is the possessor of, or is in some way related to, the NP in the event-central expression. We can see the difference between event-central comments about a topic and an unmarked predicate focus structure from the examples in (26):

(26) a. *Ta si le fuqi*n.
3SG die ASP father
'His **father** died.'

b. *Ta de fuqin si le.*
3SG GEN father die ASP
'His father **died**.'

(26a) involves "possessor ascension", and is an example of what is often referred to as an "adversative" construction. The topic has no active control over the action represented by the verb (Guo 1990:27). A better translation for this sentence would be *He was affected by the death of (his) father.* What gives the sentence this adversative reading is the fact that 'father' is made non-topical, by being placed in postverbal position, so that the dying of the father can be expressed as an event-central statement, which is then the assertion about the topic (cf. Kuno's (1987:206) concept of "empathy", the speaker's identification with the person or thing affected by the event being articulated). On the other hand, (26b) is a predicate focus statement about the topic 'his father', who died.

This structure is also possible with proper names appearing in postverbal position, as in the following example, which could be the brigade-leader's response to his superior's request for information about how the battle went, and could not be interpreted as a statement about Zhangsan and Lisi:

(27) *Dui li si le Zhangsan, Lisi.*
Brigade inside die ASP Zhangsan Lisi
'In (our) brigade Zhangsan and Lisi died.'

The unitary nature of the event-central phrase is evident in one type of aspectual marking that can appear with these structures. In general, non-iterative achievement verbs such as *si* 'die' *lan* 'rot', and *chen* 'sink' cannot appear with the "experiential" aspect marker *guo*, yet when these verbs appear in event-central utterances, they CAN take *guo* (Guo 1990). This is because of the verb + post-verbal non-specific NP together being seen as one repeatable event, as in the following example, from Guo (1990:26) (see also the discussion of the use of the adverb *you* 'again' in this type of structure in Teng 1974):

(28) a. *Ta si guo yi pi ma.*
3SG die ASP one CLASS horse
'One of his horses died (on him).'

b. *Ta lan guo wushi jin xiangjiao.*
3SG rot ASP fifty catty banana
'Fifty catties of his bananas rotted (on him).'

Contrast these with the following unacceptable examples, in which the preverbal NP must be interpreted as the topic of the verb and therefore can only experience the action of the verb once:

(29) a. *Ta you yi pi ma si guo.*
3SG have one CLASS horse die ASP
'(He has a horse that died (lit.: has experienced dying).)'

b. **Ta you wushi jin xiangjiao lan guo.*
3SG have fifty catty banana rot ASP
'(He has fifty catties of bananas that rotted (lit.: have experienced rotting).)'

Because of this unity of the verb + post-verbal NP, this structure is the pragmatic equivalent of noun incorporation. In languages with grammatically marked incorporation, incorporation of a subject noun into an intransitive verb converts a simple categorical (topic-comment) judgement into a thetic statement, and incorporation of a subject or object noun into a transitive verb can convert a double categorical (topic-comment within topic-comment) judgement into a simple categorical statement (Sasse 1984:260). In Chinese there is no marking of incorporation other than word order and possibly intonation, but the pragmatic effect is the same (see below for more on pragmatic incorporation).

There are examples of postverbal NPs that are identifiable in structures that look like presentational structures, but these are actually event-central constructions, as in (30) (Li and Thompson's (30), p. 517), where the postverbal NPs are proper names:

(30) *Women de wanhui zhi lai le Zhangsan gen Lisi.*
1PL GEN party only come ASP Zhangsan and Lisi
'Only Zhangsan and Lisi came to our party.'

McCawley (1988:7) considers the postverbal NP in this example as "indefinite" because he feels that the NP is the "focus" of the adverb *zhi* 'only', so "the meaning of such a combination is that of an 'indefinite' NP: *zhi* ... *Zhangsan* means 'no one but Zhangsan'". L. Li (1986:350) also claims that the NP following *zhi* 'only' must be "indefinite" (*wu ding*). The problem here is distinguishing between a referent's discourse status (identifiability) and information structure: it is true that the NP is being treated as non-topical, but being non-topical does not mean it is necessarily "indefinite".

This event-central construction also appears in background or scene-setting clauses (examples from Huang 1987:242):

(31) a. *Suiran lai le Lisi/nei ge ren, keshi ...*
although come ASP Lisi/that CLASS person but
'Although Lisi/that person has come, ...'

b. *Ruguo fasheng zhe jian shiqing, jiu ...*
if happen this CLASS affair then
'If that happens, then ...'

c. *Zicong zou le Zhangsan yihou, jiu ...*
from go ASP Zhangsan after then
'Ever since Zhangsan left, ...'

In these examples the post-verbal referent is identifiable, but it is not focal in the way that *Zhangsan* is in (30) (it is not contrastive). It is also not a topic. In adverbial clauses such as these, the proposition is pragmatically presupposed; there is no predication in the information-conveying sense of this word. The predicate then is not to be construed as being about the postverbal NP; the postverbal NP is presented as part of an event, and the event is simply background information for the assertion to come, as shown by the subordinating (relational) conjunctions.

3.3 *Pragmatic incorporation*

NPs that are not crucially involved in the assertion, that is, that are not topical or focal, can also appear in constructions where they act as modifiers of the verb (and so are within the comment), as is the case with the instruments incorporated into the verbs in (32):

(32)	*qiang-bi*	*huo-shao*	*kou-shi*
	gun-kill	fire-burn	mouth-test
	'kill with a gun'	'burn with fire'	'take an oral exam'

The type of NP in this construction is preverbal but non-topical. We can see from this that simply being in preverbal position does not make an NP "definite", nor does it make it a topic. The fact that it is non-referential may preclude it from being "definite", but it does not preclude it from being a topic, nor does not being in sentence initial position preclude it from being at least a secondary topic (see the discussion of (33) below). It is simply the semantics of the combination, and the lack of any possible relevant topic-comment association that leads the hearer to infer an instrumental meaning for the preverbal NP.

A different type of pragmatic incorporation is the double nominative (Teng 1974) (or possessor ascension — Fox 1981) structure. This structure incorporates a comment about a body part and the body part itself into a comment about the possessor of the body part. As body parts are "universally not conceived of as discourse characters or as independent entities about which information is given during a conversation" (Sasse 1987:571),[21] the body part is pragmatically incorporated into the comment, and the possessor of the body part becomes the topic about which the comment is made.[22]

(33) a. *Wo duzi e le.*
1SG belly hungry ASP
'I'm hungry.'

b. *Wo tou teng le.*
1SG head hurt ASP
'I have a headache.'

In this type of double-topic construction, the main topic ('1sg' in both examples) is semantically the possessor of the secondary topic ('belly'/'head'), but it is not grammatically marked as such, as the secondary topic has been incorporated into the comment about the main topic. There is also a comment about the secondary topic.[23] There are structures where a topic-comment structure is itself an assertion about a more salient topic; that is, constructions exist that function to delineate primary from secondary topics, where the secondary topic is part of the assertion about the primary topic (cf. Tsao's (1987) treatment of the *ba* construction).

Lambrecht (1989) argues that a sentence such as *My stomach hurts* is a sentence focus structure because the subject noun is marked as a non-topic by its prosodic stress, which is usually associated with objects. In Chinese, though, this proposition is not expressed in a sentence focus structure, but in the type of predicate focus structure involving pragmatic incorporation of the body part. In the English form of this proposition, the first person referent is not set off as a separate topic (it simply modifies the subject), but semantically it could also be said to be a statement about the first person referent. In Chinese this is simply made explicit.

4. Conclusions

What I have tried to show in this discussion of word order in Chinese is that

(a) verb medial word order has the function of distinguishing topical or non-focal NPs from focal or non-topical NPs, not "definite" and "indefinite" NPs, and (b) constructions have developed in Chinese which allow the topical (non-focal) and focal (non-topical) elements in marked focus structures to be clearly distinguished. In short, I would argue that in order to understand syntactic structures in Chinese, we need to make clear the role of pragmatic and semantic relations, and the interactions between them, in determining those structures.

Abbreviations used in glosses

LOC= locative verb; N-A= negative aspect marker; NOMLZR= nominalizer; for further abbreviations, see list on pp. ix.

Notes

* I owe a great debt of gratitude to Ivy Cheng, Derek Herforth, Knud Lambrecht, Mark V. LaPolla, Naicong Li, Tsong-hung Lin, Ching-Ching Lü, James D. McCawley, James A. Matisoff, Johanna Nichols, Tian-shin Jackson Sun, Sandra A. Thompson, Robert D. Van Valin, Jr., and the editors of this volume for their very helpful comments on earlier drafts of this paper. The examples, unless otherwise marked, are from asking native speakers, given a particular context, what would be a natural utterance in that context.

1. Cf. Comrie's (1981:72) analysis of Russian word order, which he says is pragmatically determined (with the focus at the end), and unrelated to syntactic functions, and Sasse's (1981) analysis of Boni, a language of the Eastern Cushitic group, which also has pragmatically determined word order.

2. Cf. Kuno's division of information into two different concepts: "the concept applied to lexical items, on the one hand, and the concept applied to the particular semantic relations which lexical items enter into in the given sentence" (Kuno 1972:272).

3. By 'unmarked' here I mean the statistically most common type of sentence, where the comment follows the topic without involving a cleft or other type of 'marked' construction.

4. (2e) would be the equivalent of a "stressed focus *it*-cleft". An example of what would be an example of the equivalent of a *wh*-cleft (contra Teng 1979), as defined in Prince 1978 is (i):

   (i) *Wo mei mai de shi cai.*
   1SG N-A buy NOMLZR COP vegetables.
   'What I didn't buy was *vegetables.*'

   As Prince points out, "though the *it*-cleft presents information (old vs. new) in an aberrant order, it clearly marks which is which" (1978:897).

5. This clearly goes beyond the definition of "new" information in Chafe 1974:112 as that which is "assumed not to be in the addressee's consciousness". It is closer to the concept of "added information" in Chafe 1987, but it seems for Chafe (and also Comrie 1981:56) that "new information" is often simply a "new" constituent.

6. I did not use an example exactly parallel to the ones in (5) because the presence of the first person pronoun and the semantics of the argument in the example complicate the point I am trying to make. These complications are discussed in Section 3.

7. It is possible to consider that with generics the questions of referentiality and identifiability are neutralized, due to the fact that they are unindividuated, as are non-referential NPs, but at the same time can be topical, as if they were referential (Givón 1984:413). For the purposes of this paper I will treat them as non-referential NPs.

8. The need for at least two of these refinements was due to Li and Thompson's earlier analysis (cf. Li and Thompson 1974b) of *bei, zai*, and other phrase-forming morphemes as prepositions. If instead we recognize (as Li and Thompson themselves do in later papers) that these morphemes, which in Old Chinese, and in some cases also in Modern Chinese, are verbs, are still not completely grammaticalized, we can do away with Refinements 3 and 4.

9. For examples other than those given here, see Givón 1978, Xu 1987, and Chen 1986. See Xu 1987 also for discussion of the correspondence of zero form in Chinese with forms marked by the definite article or definite pronoun in English.

10. See C. Sun 1988 for a discourse based study showing that there is a tendency for the representation of a referent which is "thematically important" to have the numeral plus classifier phrase when that referent is first introduced into the discourse, and for the representation of a referent which is not "thematically important" to not include the numeral plus classifier phrase; see also Lambrecht, to appear, p. 67, for cross-linguistic evidence of the numeral plus classifier vs. plain classifer strategy.

11. As mentioned in the Introduction, it is necessary to separate the pragmatic status of the referent of the NP in the mind of the speaker/hearer from the pragmatic relations that the NP is involved in.

12. See Lambrecht, to appear, p. 69, for a similar analysis of Czech. Lambrecht also cites Arabic, Russian, Amharic, Turkish, Japanese, Finnish, and Hungarian as languages where a claim (by Hetzron 1975) of correlation between preverbal definite marking and post-verbal indefinite marking in locative sentences is "unwarranted".

13. Due to space limitations, only sentence focus structures will be discussed here. A number of other word order patterns are dealt with in LaPolla, in preparation.

14. It is not necessarily the case that all new referents are introduced with one of the following presentative constructions. Herring (1989) argues that (at least in the languages she looked at) new referents are often introduced in verbless presentational utterances. Naicong Li (p.c.) has suggested that there may be a difference between those referents introduced in presentative constructions and those not introduced in presentative constructions in terms of their viability as topics in the following discourse. Both of these questions can only be solved by reference to a sizable discourse database, which at the present time is unavailable to me.

15. The juncture here is actually on a level lower than the clause, and a type of nexus different from both coordination and subordination, giving us what has often been called a serial verb construction. See the discussion below of example (22), and particularly note 18.

16. With prosodic stress on *yuanzi*, this could also be a contrastive narrow focus construction, but then the 'one dog' would mean one dog out of a number of dogs introduced in the preceding discourse.

17. This is where we can see the interaction of semantic and pragmatic factors. It is necessary to use this construction in this case, rather than the "inversion" type as seen in (14b), because the argument in focus is the actor of the verb *xiang* 'think' as opposed to the undergoer of the predicate 'arrived'. Since an actor must always precede the verb, the biclausal construction allows the focal actor to both appear in the focal position of the *you* clause and still be in its proper preverbal position vis-à-vis *xiang*.

18. See Van Valin 1984, 1993 for discussion of juncture and nexus types, and Hansell 1993 for a discussion of some juncture-nexus types in Chinese. Essentially, a CORE is the verb and its direct arguments, and does not include the entire clause; *coordination* is a juncture type where the two elements are non-embedded and non-dependent, as opposed to *cosubordination* (non-embedded but dependent) and *subordination* (embedded).

19. Tai 1973:661-663 in fact posits this form as the "underlying" form for all relative clauses. Lambrecht (1988) treats the second clause in this type of construction as a type of relative clause which is a sister to the first clause, whereas Sasse (1987:541) considers all relatives to be non-finite, so believes the second clause is not a relative or some other non-finite clause, but is a finite clause "in a looser appositional connection with the first clause". There are cases where the line is not so clear, as in the following attested example (from H. Sun 1982:297):

(i) *Zang-Mian* *yuzu* *zhong* *hai* *you* *xuduo* *zhongyao* *yuyin*
Tibeto-Burman family middle still have many important phonetic
xianxiang *qi* *genyuan* *zhide* *tantao* . . .
phenomenon GEN origin deserve investigation
'In the Tibeto-Burman languages there are many phenomena whose origins are worthy of investigation.'

This example differs from the earlier examples in the inclusion of the phrase *qi genyuan* 'GEN origin', which makes this look very much like a post-head relative, something that Chinese supposedly does not have!

20. Expressed in the form of a decompositional semantic representation, *lai-le* 'come, arrive' would be [BECOME **be-at**´(x)], where x is a theme (the predicate being a stative verb), whereas *pa* 'climb' would be [**pa**´(x)], where x is an effector/agent (the predicate being an activity verb). As effector/agents cannot appear postverbally, we can see why only in the structure in (24) can the argument appear postverbally with *pa* 'climb': it is a combination of the two predicates, the state predicate providing the theme status, which then allows the argument to appear postverbally: [**pa**´(x) BECOME **be-at**´(x)] (see Van Valin 1993 for discussion of this type of semantic decomposition).

21. See also Hopper and Thompson (1984, 1985) on the "low categoriality" (as nouns) of body parts. Though they are as referential as the person to whom they belong, "*in the discourse* body parts are not in general autonomous, discourse-salient entities" and so "are treated in grammar and discourse as dependent, non-individuated entities" (1984:726, 1985:167, emphasis in original).

22. Nichols (1988b:22) sees possessor ascension as the promotion of the possessor to argumenthood in the clause (the ascended possessor no longer forms an NP with the possessed noun), which makes it a dependent on the verb rather than on the possessed noun. It then becomes a clausal, rather than phrasal, possessive pattern. Givón (1979b:91) sees it simply as topicalization of the possessor because it is a more topical NP. The only difference between these analyses and my analysis is whether we look at possessor ascension from the point of view of the ascended possessor or the incorporated possessed noun.

23. See Teng 1974 for arguments why the sentence initial NP is a distinct topic not in the same NP as the affected body part and why the secondary topic should be seen as incorporated into the predication about the primary topic.

References

Barry, Roberta. 1975. "Topic in Chinese: An overlap of meaning, grammar, and discourse function." *Papers from the Parasession on Functionalism*, 1-9. Chicago Linguistic Society.

Chafe, Wallace L. 1974. "Language and consciousness." *Language* 50.111-33.

Chafe, Wallace L. 1976. "Givenness, contrastiveness, definiteness, subjects, topics, and point of view." C. N. Li, ed. 1976.27-55.

Chafe, Wallace L. 1979. "The flow of thought and the flow of language." Givón, ed. 1979.159-82.

Chafe, Wallace L. 1985. "Information flow in Seneca and English." *Proceedings of the 11th Annual Meeting of the Berkeley Linguistics Society*, 14-24.

Chafe, Wallace L. 1987. "Cognitive constraints on information flow." *Coherence and Grounding in Discourse* ed. by Russell S. Tomlin, 21-52. Amsterdam/Philadelphia: John Benjamins.

Chao, Yuen Ren. 1968. *A Grammar of Spoken Chinese*. Berkeley: University of California Press.

Chen, Ping. 1986. "Referent Introducing and Referent Tracking in Chinese Narratives." PhD dissertation, UCLA.

Comrie, Bernard. 1981. *Language Universals and Linguistic Typology*. Oxford: Blackwell, and Chicago: University of Chicago Press.

Cumming, Susanna. 1984. "The sentence in Chinese." *Studies in Language* 8.365-395.

Du Bois, John W. 1980. "Beyond definiteness: The trace of identity in discourse." *The Pear Stories* ed. by Wallace Chafe, 203-74. Norwood, NJ: Ablex.

Du Bois, John W. 1987. "The discourse basis of ergativity." *Language* 63.805-55.

Fan, Jiyan. 1985. "Wuding NP Zhuyu Ju (Sentences with indefinite NP subjects)." *Zhongguo Yuwen* 1985.321-328.

Fox, Barbara. A. 1981. "Body part syntax: Towards a universal characterization." *Studies in Language* 5.323-342.

Givón, T. 1978. "Definiteness and referentiality." *Universals of Human Language*, Vol. 4: *Syntax* ed. by Joseph H. Greenberg, 291-330. Stanford: Stanford University Press.

Givón, T., ed. 1979a. *Discourse and Syntax*. New York: Academic Press. [*Syntax and Semantics*, 12]

Givón, T. 1979b. "From discourse to syntax: Grammar as a processing strategy." In Givón, ed. 1979a.81-112.

Givón, T. 1981. "Logic vs. Pragmatics, with natural language as the referee." *Journal of Pragmatics* 6.81-133.

Givón, T. 1984. *Syntax: A Functional-Typological Introduction*, Vol I. Amsterdam/Philadelphia: John Benjamins.

Guo, Jimao. 1990. "Ling Zhu Shu Bing Ju (Sentences where the subject possesses the object)." *Zhongguo Yuwen* 1990.24-29.

Hansell, Mark. 1987. "Serial verbs and complement constructions in Mandarin: A clause linkage analysis." *Davis Working Papers in Linguistics* 2.38-54. Reprinted in *Advances in Role and Reference Grammar* ed. by Robert D. Van Valin, Jr. Amsterdam and Philadelphia: John Benjamins.

Hansell, Mark. 1993. "Serial verbs and complement constructions in Mandarin: a clause linkage analysis." *Advances in Role and Reference Grammar* ed. by Robert D. Valin, Jr, 197-234. Amsterdam/Philadelphia: John Benjamins.

Herring, Susan C. 1989. "Verbless Presentation and the Discourse Basis of Ergativity." *Papers from the 25th Regional Meeting of the Chicago Linguistic Society, Part II: Parasession on Language in Context*, 123-37. Chicago: Chicago Linguistic Society.

Hetzron, Robert. 1975. "The presentative movement, or why the ideal word order is V.S.O.P." *Word Order and Word Order Change* ed. by C. N. Li, 345-88. Austin: University of Texas Press.

Hopper, Paul J. and Sandra A. Thompson. 1984. "The discourse basis for lexical categories in Universal Grammar." *Language* 60.4:703-52.

Hopper, Paul J. and Sandra A. Thompson. 1985. "The iconicity of Noun and Verb". *Iconicity in Syntax* ed. by John Haiman, 151-83. Amsterdam/Philadelphia: John Benjamins.

Huang, C.-T. James. 1987. "Existential Sentences in Chinese and (in)definiteness." *The Representation of (In)definiteness* ed. by Eric. J. Reuland and Alice G. B. ter Meulen, 226-53. Cambridge, Mass.: MIT Press.

Huang, Lillian Meei-jin and Philip W. Davis. 1988. "Remarks on the semantics of word order in Mandarin Chinese." Paper presented to the 21st International Conference on Sino-Tibetan Languages and Linguistics, Oct. 6-9, 1988, Lund, Sweden.

Kuno, Susumu. 1972. "Functional sentence perspective." *Linguistic Inquiry* 3.269-320.

Kuno, Susumu. 1987. *Functional Syntax: Anaphora, Discourse, and Empathy*. Chicago: University of Chicago Press.

Lambrecht, Knud. 1986. *Topic, Focus, and the Grammar of Spoken French*. PhD. dissertation, UC Berkeley.

Lambrecht, Knud. 1987. "Sentence focus, information structure, and the thetic-categorial distinction." *Proceedings of the 13th Annual Meeting of the Berkeley Linguistics Society*, 366-82. Berkeley: Berkeley Linguistics Society.

Lambrecht, Knud. 1988. "There was a farmer had a dog: Syntactic amalgams revisited." *Proceedings of the 14th Annual Meeting of the Berkeley Linguistics Society*. Berkeley: Berkeley Linguistics Society.

Lambrecht, Knud. 1989. "When subjects behave like objects: A markedness analysis of sentence focus constructions across languages." (Revised and expanded version of 1987 LSA paper). ms. University of Texas at Austin.

Lambrecht, Knud. To appear. *Information Structure and Sentence Form.* Cambridge: Cambridge University Press.

LaPolla, Randy J. 1990. "Grammatical Relations in Chinese: Synchronic and Diachronic Considerations." UC Berkeley Ph.D. dissertation.

LaPolla, Randy J. In preparation. "Semantic and Pragmatic Principles in the Organization of Chinese Discourse." ms. Institute of History and Philology, Academia Sinica, Taipei.

Li, Charles N., ed. 1976. *Subject and Topic.* New York: Academic Press.

Li, Charles N. and Sandra A. Thompson. 1974a. "Chinese as a topic-prominent language." Paper presented to the 7th International Conference on Sino-Tibetan Languages and Linguistics, Atlanta, Georgia, Oct. 18-19, 1974.

Li, Charles N. and Sandra A. Thompson. 1974b. "Coverbs in Mandarin Chinese: Verbs or prepositions?" *Journal of Chinese Linguistics* 2.257-278.

Li, Charles N. and Sandra A. Thompson. 1975. "The semantic function of word order: A case study in Mandarin." *Word Order and Word Order Change* ed. by Charles N. Li, 163-96. Austin: University of Texas Press.

Li, Charles N. and Sandra A. Thompson. 1976. "Subject and topic: A new typology of language." C. N. Li, ed. 1976.459-89.

Li, Charles N. and Sandra A. Thompson. 1978. "Grammatical relations in languages without grammatical signals." *Proceedings of the 12th International Congress of Linguists* ed. by Wolfgang Dressler, 687-91. Innsbruck: Innsbrucher Beiträger zur Sprachwissenschaft, Universität Innsbruck.

Li, Charles N. and Sandra A. Thompson. 1981. *Mandarin Chinese: A functional reference grammar.* Berkeley: University of California Press.

Li, Linding. 1986. "Shoushi Chengfen Ju Leixing Bijiao (A comparison of sentence types with affected (patient) elements)." *Zhongguo Yuwen* 1986.341-52.

McCawley, James D. 1988. "Notes on Li and Thompson 1981." *Journal of the Chinese Language Teachers Association.* 24.19-42.

Mullie, Joseph. 1932. *The Structural Principles of the Chinese Language.* English translation by A. C. Versichel, 2 vols. Peking.

Nichols, Johanna. 1988a. "On SOV word order in Mandarin." ms. U. C. Berkeley.

Nichols, Johanna. 1988b. "On alienable and inalienable possession." *In Honor of Mary Haas: From the Haas Festival Conference on Native American Linguistics* ed. by William Shipley, 557-609. Berlin: Mouton de Gruyter.

Prince, Ellen F. 1978. "A comparison of *Wh*-clefts and *It*-clefts in discourse." *Language* 54.883-906.

Prince, Ellen F. 1981. "Toward a taxonomy of given-new information." *Radical Pragmatics* ed. by Peter Cole, 223-55. New York and London: Academic Press.

Sasse, Hans-Jürgen. 1981. "'Basic word order' and functional sentence perspective in Boni." *Folia Linguistica* 15.253-90.

Sasse, Hans-Jürgen. 1984. "The pragmatics of noun incorporation in Eastern Cushitic Languages." *Objects: Towards a theory of grammatical relations* ed. by Frans Plank, 243-68. London: Academic Press.

Sasse, Hans-Jürgen. 1987. "The thetic/categorical distinction revisited." *Linguistics* 25.511-80.

Sun, Chao-fen. 1988. "The discourse function of numeral classifiers in Mandarin Chinese." *Journal of Chinese Linguistics* 16.298-321.

Sun, Chao-fen and T. Givón. 1985. "On the so-called SOV word order in Mandarin Chinese: A quantified text study and its implications." *Language* 61.329-51.

Sun, Hongkai. 1982. "Zang-Mianyu Ruogan Yinbian Tanyuan (On the origin of several sound changes in Tibeto-Burman)." *Zhongguo Yuyanxuebao* 1.269-98.

Tai, James H-Y. 1973. "Chinese as an SOV Language." *Papers from the Ninth Regional Meeting of the Chicago Linguistics Society*, 659-671. Chicago: Chicago Linguistics Society.

Teng, Shou-hsin. 1973. "Scope of negation." *Journal of Chinese Linguistics* 1.475-78.

Teng, Shou-hsin. 1974. "Double nominatives in Chinese." *Language* 50.455-73.

Teng, Shou-hsin. 1975. *A Semantic Study of Transitivity Relations in Chinese*. Berkeley and Los Angeles: University of California Press.

Teng, Shou-hsin. 1979. "Remarks on cleft sentences in Chinese." *Journal of Chinese Linguistics* 7.101-14.

Teng, Shou-hsin. 1985. "Gongneng Yufa yu Hanyu Xinxi Jiegou (Functional grammar and information structure in Chinese)." *Proceedings of the First International Conference on the Teaching of Chinese as a Second Language*, 164-68. Taipei: World Chinese Language Association.

Tsao, Feng-fu. 1979. *A Functional Study of Topic in Chinese: The first step towards discourse analysis*. Taibei: Student Book Co.

Tsao, Feng-fu. 1987. "A Topic-Comment Approach to the *ba* Construction." *Journal of Chinese Linguistics* 15.1-54.

Van Valin, Robert D., Jr. 1975. "Existential locatives in Mandarin." Paper presented to the 8th International Conference on Sino-Tibetan Languages and Linguistics, October 24-26, 1975, U. C. Berkeley.

Van Valin, Robert D., Jr. 1984. "A typology of syntactic relations in clause linkage." *Proceedings of the 10th Annual Meeting of the Berkeley Linguistics Society*, 542-58. Berkeley: Berkeley Linguistics Society..

Van Valin, Robert D., Jr. 1993. "A synopsis of Role and Reference Grammar." *Advances in Role and Reference Grammar*. ed. by Robert D. Van Valin, Jr, 1-166. Amsterdam/ Philadelphia: John Benjamins.

Wang, Liaoyi. 1982. *Hanyu yufa gangyao* (Outline of Chinese grammar). (With notes by A.A. Dragunov). Shanghai: Shanghai Jiaoyu Chubanshe.

Wang, Mingquan. 1988. "Comments on Sun and Givón's study of the OV constructions in Mandarin." *Journal of the Chinese Language Teacher's Association* 23.33-53.

Xu, Yulong. 1987. "A study of referential functions of demonstratives in Chinese discourse." *Journal of Chinese Linguistics* 15.132-151.

Zhu, Dexi. 1982. *Yufa Jiangyi (Lecture notes on grammar)*. Beijing: Shangwu Yinshuguan.

Left shifts in strongly VSO languages

Robert E. Longacre
University of Texas at Arlington

0. Introduction

In this paper I consider three VSO languages widely separated in time and space: Chicahuaxtla Trique (Otomanguean) in Mexico[1], Luwo or Jür-Luwo (Nilotic) in south Sudan, and Biblical Hebrew. The special problem studied in this paper is the relationship of left shift to discourse structures in these three languages — and, by implication, in languages of this type.

In classifying languages according to the ordering of clause-level constituents, we need to distinguish a line running from exclusively VSO languages to strongly VSO languages to weakly VSO. The latter includes languages in which the claim is made that they are basically VSO but that statistically some other order, e.g. SVO is much more common. In the case of weakly VSO languages it customarily is necessary to write an article or a monograph to demonstrate the claim that the language is VSO!

At the other extreme of our line is Teposa, another Nilotic language of Sudan. For this language I have two field write-ups (from Martin and Helga Shroeder) involving narrative and hortatory discourse — and in no text cited in either write-up does a subject or object noun ever occur in front of the verb. When first encountering these Teposa data my reaction was almost one of unbelief. I had written somewhat dogmatically several years before:

> Expository discourse is of topic-comment rather than subject-predicate structure. For this reason it is to be expected that VSO languages will necessarily vary to something on the order of S(VO) in expository discourse. In brief, consideration of topic-to-the-left in expository discourse (which is presumably a linguistic and cultural universal) works against a VSO normative order which is applicable to all discourse even in a so-called VSO language (Longacre 1982:484).

Trique, Luwo, and Biblical Hebrew are neither weakly or exclusively VSO; they are in the range which I characterize as strongly VSO. All three conform to Greenberg's generalizations for VSO languages, i.e., they are VSO/Pr/NG/NA, i.e., not only are they verb first languages but they are (1) prepositional rather than postpositional; (2) item possessor ('noun genitive') rather than possessor-item; and (3) head-attribute ('noun adjective') rather than attribute-noun. In all this the generalization is that the head of a construction precedes what is peripheral to it. I illustrate this for Trique below:

(1) (V is central, subject and object are peripheral to the verb.)

da^{3}g^{3}awi^{35}ʔ	*gwi^{35}*	*ža^{5}na^{5}*	*dą^{3}h*	*ngo^{4}*	*de^{2}ʔloho^{54}*
killed	woman		that	a	rooster

'That woman killed a rooster.'

(2) (head of noun phrase is central; adjectives and possessors are peripheral)

a.

č̣ų^{3}	*zaʔa^{54}*
wood	good

'good wood'

b.

ži^{3}č̣ų^{21}	*gwi^{35}*	*ža^{5}na^{5}*	*dą^{3}h*
wood-of	woman		that

'that woman's wood'

Trique distinguishes possessed from unpossessed stems as seen in *č̣ų^{3}* 'wood' and *ži^{3}č̣ų^{21}* 'wood-of' above.

(3) (prepositions act like former head nouns now reduced to prepositional function)

a. *ri^{3}ki^{3}* 'stomach-of', 'underneath'
as in *r. yə^{3}h dą^{3}h* 'underneath that stone'

b. *ži^{3}ʔi^{2}* 'foot-of', 'at the foot of'
as in *ž. č̣ų^{3} dą^{3}h* 'at the foot of that tree'

c. *ru^{3}wa^{23}* 'insides', 'on the inside'
as in *r. we^{3}ʔe* 'inside the house'

Luwo similarly has preposition preceding noun, item preceding possessor and the noun head preceding its attribute. Possessed nouns and unpossessed can differ in form.

(4) (Luwo)[2]

a. *wihy yaadh*
'head-of tree'
'in tree'

b. *yi kood*
'stomach-of basket'
'in basket'

(5) (Luwo)

a. *tuhw* versus *tuhn paa kwaa*
'palmtree' 'palm-of house-of ancestors'
'palmtree' versus 'the palm of our ancestors' house'

b. *luuhd mE cOl* versus *luuhn liEj*
'dust' 'that black' 'dust-of elephant'
'black dust' versus 'the elephant's dust'

The situation in Biblical Hebrew is similar to that illustrated for the other two languages, i.e. in addition to the VSO order within the clause itself, the noun phrase has preposition preceding noun, item preceding possessor, and noun preceding its attribute. Hebrew has the prepositions *bĕ*, 'with', 'by', *lĕ*- 'towards, to' and *kĕ* 'according to', which are not reducible to old head nouns, but has other prepositions which may have once been head nouns. Hebrew also has a special form for the possessed noun ('the construct state') as in

(6) *bayit* 'house' versus *bet Yosep* 'the house of Joseph'

Nevertheless, while we can show that the structure of the noun phrase in Trique, Luwo, and Biblical Hebrew is in accordance with what we might expect in a VSO language, we come up against the fact that the same noun phrase structures are also found in some SVO languages. Furthermore, both orders, VSO and SVO, are found in all three languages here considered. On what, then, do we base the claim that VSO is the norm in these languages? The answer is quite straightforward: *If storyline clauses in narrative discourse in a given language are VSO, then that language should be classified as a VSO language.*

This claim is based on several assumptions:

1. Monologue discourse is a better guide to language typology than dialogue (or conversational discourse) in that the exigencies of repartee presumably make for departures from standard word order at many places.

2. Of all monologue discourse types, narrative discourse has a certain

preeminence in that it is the most universal and most highly structured type of monologue discourse. Narratives emerge in the course of even informal conversation. People recount experiences to each other and often answer inquiries by volunteering accounts of experiences. Such narratives are iconic of reality in that they recount events in sequence. Since most recounted experiences have to do with event sequences which have some unusual or routine-breaking quality, the standard narrative characteristics *inciting incident, mounting tension, climax, and denouement* (Longacre 1983) typically develop even in the telling of informal anecdotes.

3. Within narrative discourse itself the storyline is the most characteristic and indispensable part of the whole. It is the central thread or backbone of the discourse.

Turning the above thesis around somewhat and extrapolating from it, we obtain another thesis: *Strongly VSO languages have a peculiar narrative competence*. In all languages, therefore in languages of all typologies, stories are told, so what can be meant by such a claim?

To support this claim, consider in more detail the fundamental characteristics of narrative. One basic characteristic is that a narrative reports *sequential, punctiliar happenings* which are, at least partially causally connected. Another characteristic of narrative is that it must have a *slate of participants*, one or more of which run through the entire story. Finally, it must weave happenings and participants together into that pattern of rising and falling tension which we call *plot*.

The first concern is of peculiar diagnostic importance in defining narrative. We can discuss the doings of one or more people in an essay without ordering and dramatizing the happenings into a story. On the other hand, we can discuss a problem and its possible resolution(s) and the people involved in those problems without ordering the happenings in sequential fashion. *But we cannot have a story* without sequential, punctiliar, and causally connected happenings (i.e. without a storyline). Let me illustrate this in Diagram 1.

In this diagram I liken the storyline to the keystone of an arch whose two sides are the roster of participants, and problem resolution. When the latter two are joined by virtue of the former we have a narrative; otherwise we have an essay, i.e. some sort of expository discourse.

The "peculiar narrative competence of VSO languages" is seen in their putting the verb first. In going down the storyline from sentence to sentence,

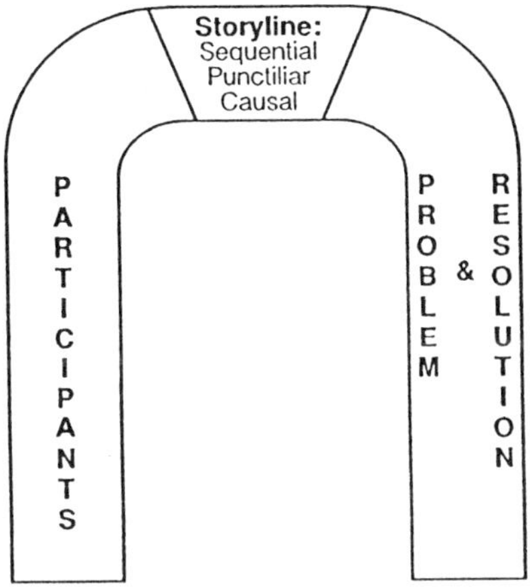

Diagram 1. The crucial nature of the storyline to narrative

the successive initial verbs introduce one by one new happenings into the story, i.e. actions, motions, cognitive events, speech acts, and contingencies (things which happen to people).[3] This natural foregrounding of the happenings leads to a somewhat opposite structure from the theme–rheme distribution which we have learned to expect in Prague School 'functional sentence perspective', because in VSO structures the *most rhematic elements regularly precede the themes*. New participants or props (also rhematic) can presumably be introduced either without departure from the verb-first ordering or with a left shift. The latter is one of the main concerns of this paper and is discussed below. Here, however, I am simply pointing out that the verb-first structure of VSO languages foregrounds the most diagnostic feature of narrative structure.

Granted this peculiar tie-in of narrative structuring to VSO ordering in a language strongly of this type, we must discuss left shifts in such languages in connection with this fact. In the balance of the paper I examine left shifts in narrative in the three strongly VSO languages considered in this study.

1. Trique

1.1 A story in Trique frequently begins with an NV clause which is title-like in function and introduces the main participant. Thus one of the numerous stories regarding 'Peter the Evil One' begins as follows:

(7) *ngo*^{4} *zi*^{21} *dą*^{3}*h* *u*^{3}*ta*^{4} *a*^{3}*če*^{21} *di*^{3}*ga*^{3}*ʔ* *yų*^{4}*ʔų*^{34}*h* *zi*^{3} *gwi*^{354}
a man certain much went-about deceived he people...
'A certain man went about deceiving people'

This sentence continues:

(8) *gu*^{4}*ʔna*^{4}*h* *zi*^{3} *Pedro de Mala.*
called he 'Peter the Evil One'.
he was called 'Peter the Evil One'.

This two-clause sentence has a first clause which displays left dislocation; it shifts the noun phrase 'a certain man' to pre-verb position and refers to him again as *zi*^{3} 'he' in the regular post-verb position after the compound verb 'deceive'. The second clause has a verb which belongs to a class of copulative verbs ('to be' and 'to be named') which take SVO order and characterize expository discourse. These two verbs, however, obligatorily go to VSO when the subject is expressed by an enclitic (here *zi*^{3}). The two clauses of these opening sentences do not display narrative movement; they constitute what I will call the initial *stasis* of the story in which the main participant is introduced, his habitual activity reported, and his name given.

1.2 This same story illustrates a text of the sort where, aside from an initial stasis (descriptive/expository) there are no left shifts (whether left dislocation or topicalization) in the rest of the story. In the first part of this story Peter interacts with a muledriver in whose camp he spends the night. In this stretch of five sentences Peter is the subject in VSO clauses. In the next two sentences there is a subject switch to the mule-driver. This is accomplished in VSO clauses by use of the Spanish loan *arieru* 'muledriver' and subsequent use of the fourth person pronoun *zo*^{2}*ʔ* 'he'. Here a new participant is introduced and becomes thematic without a shift from the VSO ordering. In the next seven clauses Peter replaces the muledriver as subject. Again, this thematic replacement is accomplished without left shift; rather the fourth person pronoun *zo*^{2}*ʔ* gives way again to the third person pronoun *zi*^{3}. In the next sentence the muledriver again replaces Peter as subject and theme. This is accomplished as in the above passage by the reintroduction of *arieru* 'muledriver' and subsequent resort to *zo*^{2}*ʔ*, the fourth person pronoun. The text then enters a final stasis where in three clauses the resultant situation — the upshot of the story — is sketched with the muledriver thematic again; he is referred to as *zi*^{21} *ną*^{3}*ʔą*^{4}*hą* 'mestizo' followed by reference by means of *zo*^{2}*ʔ*. All these subject switches and thematic replacements are accomplished without departure from the basic VSO order. Peter, the central participant or protagonist, is referred to by name in the initial stasis, with subsequent reference as *zi*^{3} 'he' (except in a quoted clause where the mule-drivers call him Peter); the antagonist is referred to as 'muledriver' or 'mestizo' and the fourth person pronoun *zo*^{2}*ʔ*. It is evident that thematic replacement of one participant by another does not require left shift in Trique. It is also of possible interest that the one instance of left dislocation occurs in the initial stasis of the story.

1.3 A much more complicated Trique text with several, instead of just two, participants recounts the death of a young woman who fell (or jumped?) down a vertical pit (the Trique region displays Karst topography[4]). This story has an initial stasis, has five medial stases, but has no final stasis. The story proceeds jerkily with stretches of action clauses interspersed with stases, i.e. expository/ descriptive sections.

The text begins, as do many texts, not with a left shifted clause but with a noun phrase as title:

(9) *zi*^{3}*-gwe*^{5}*ndu*^{5} *ngo*^{4} *gwi*^{35} *za*^{5}*na*^{5} *yą*^{53}
story-of a woman single
'the story of a single woman'

The next few clauses, similarly part of the initial stasis, assert that the young woman was drunk. The time is established in two subordinate clauses: 'where slept-she in the house...when it had been dark for some time and was close to midnight...'
The next three clauses are story-line:[5]

(10) *we*^{3} *dą*^{3} *ni*^{4} *na*^{3}*či*^{3}
lo thus and got-up-she
ni^{4} *gą*^{3}*ʔą*^{3}
and went-she
ga^{3}*wi*^{3} *že*^{5}*ʔe*
exited-she outside
'and then she got up and went outside.'

The last two verbs constitute a Trique sequence sentence which expresses a series of actions without medial conjunction; third person singular is marked by tone 3 on the end of each verb.

The first medial stasis begins with the next clause

(11)

nga^{43}	*ni*^{4}	*nni*^{3}	*ta*^{34}*h*
and-then	mother-her	was-saying	

'And then her mother thought...'

The left shift marks a transition to the world of the mother's inner speech (thoughts). She thought that she (the young woman) had gone outside to urinate. Then she was waiting for a long time for her to reenter the house, but she didn't reenter. This stasis is marked by continuative verbs, by a modal ('that she would reenter') and by a negative (`but she didn't reenter').

Following this passage there is a spate of action verbs (return to the storyline); the action verbs on the storyline are in italics:

(12)
a. And then *went* outside the mother and *looked*.
b. Then *saw* she her (daughter)
c. And was running rapidly she (daughter) up the road
d. Then *said* she (mother) to her other daughters
e. "Let's go follow your sister because she's running rapidly away".'

Here, the story-line references to the mother are by the term 'mother' and *yų*^{2}*ʔ* 'she' (fourth person, older) while references to the young woman, her daughter are by virtue of the tone 3 'third person'. Subject switches are accomplished without left shift. The third clause represents what the mother saw and could be called a field-of-perception clause. Clause (e) represents what the mother said, i.e. a quotation, while the formula of quotation is in the fourth clause. The verbs of perception and speech are considered to be storyline while the field-of-perception clause and the quotation clause are only indirectly connected to the storyline by the verbs of perception and speech.

Two one-clause sentences follow (with a continuative verb and a negative modal) which I am inclined to consider to constitute another stasis, since neither clause reports a punctiliar happening.

(13)

we^{2}	*dą*^{3}	*ni*^{4}	*ni*^{3}*ko*^{35}*ʔ*	*ne*^{3}*h*	*yų*^{2}*ʔ*
lo	thus	and	followed	the	she

'Then she and the others followed'

za^{3}*ni*^{4}	*nų*^{3}	*na*^{5}*r*^{5}*iʔ*	*ni*^{3}
But	not	(could)find	they

'But they couldn't find her'

Again the storyline resumes (storyline verbs in italics):

(14) 'And *fell*-she(or had-fallen-she?) into the pit
'And then *turned about* her mother and sisters, *Returned* they home their
'And-then *told* they this to the town hall the next day
'Then *rose-up* the (they-of) town hall *went gathered-up* the police the ropes of all the people who had cattle.
'Then much rope *gathered*-they, *tied together* they.
'Then *talked* they with two men (to the effect that) would enter the two of them into the pit.
'Then *tied* they rope around the waists of the two men.'

The passage starts off with 'she fell into the hole' — with a tone three indicating third person singular. In the next three clauses ni^3 'they' refers to the mother and her other two daughters. Once the town hall is mentioned, referred to by name, and replaced by 'police' (officers of the town authorities), the third person plural ni^3 is then applied to the latter without a shift to a fourth person form, but the two men mentioned at the end of one clause and made subject of the purpose clause require such a fourth person reference: $ngwe^5he^2?$ 'the-two-those'. But when mention is made of tying the rope around their waists, the whole phrase 'those two men' is reintroduced.

Again, subject and thematic participants are replaced in VSO structures without left shift but with care as to participant identification and tracking. One left shift does occur, however, in the clause:

(15)	u^3ta^4	ni^4ko^3	re^2ta^3	$gi^3ri^{34}?$	ni^3
	great	many	ropes	found	they

Here the left shift is on the storyline and refers to a prop instead of a participant. The left shifted noun phrase u^3ta^4 ni^4ko^3 re^2ta^3 is a superlative transformation of re^3ta^{23} ni^4ko^3 'much rope'. To modify ni^4ko^3 'much' with u^3ta^4 'very' it is necessary that any such superlative adjective phrase be shifted to the left of the governing noun. It is not infrequent in such cases for the whole noun phrase to then be shifted into pre-verb as well. I have several clear examples in my data of superlatives determining left shift both in storyline clauses and in stasis clauses. (See below.)

Again, the storyline is interrupted by another stasis; this time an explanatory bit: 'and then another rope had they (continuative) that would tie (modal) the two around that woman'. There is depiction and mild contrast here: 'another rope' in addition to the rope tied around the waists of the two men.

The storyline resumes again but in specialized fashion. The event of arriving within the pit is described with a subordinated temporal clause: 'And then, when arrived the two inside the hole...' After this demoted event we would expect a storyline verb of perception such as 'and then they saw x'. Instead, as is frequently true of 'moments of truth' at peaks of stories (cf. Longacre 1990:44) the thing perceived is given directly: 'Was on the dead body a maguey-tree down in the hole', i.e. 'the dead body was caught on a maguey tree down in the hole'. Here I consider that such field of perception clauses are implicitly connected to the storyline by virtue of an unexpressed verb of perception (cf. Ex. 12 where such a verb of perception is expressed).

But this clause is followed immediately by another stasis which explains the important role of the maguey-tree:

(16) 'If not-been the maguey-tree
'then they wouldn't have found the woman.
'Because she would have fallen into the lake
(body of water down in the hole).
'And they wouldn't have known how to find her.
'But the maguey-tree did a favor.
'Then found-they'.

This explanatory aside contains contrafactuals and modals. The opening clause is *ni*^{3}*ta*^{4}*h čụ*^{3} *wwe*^{343} with conditional particle *zi*^{3}*zi*^{4} 'if', an emphatic negative verb *ni*^{3}*ta*^{4}*h* and the thematic phrase *čụ*^{3} *wwe*^{343} 'maguey-tree'. In the next to last clause the noun phrase (maguey-tree) is left shifted. Notice that this left shift does not *make* the phrase thematic; it has been thematic since the first sentence of the stasis. Rather it throws the all-important prop into summary relief. The sentence with the left shifted phrase begins with *za*^{3}*ni*^{4} which marks either contrast or expectancy reversal.

After this stasis the storyline briefly resumes — but with one of the events again in a subordinated clause:

(17) 'When *came* the dead outside
And-then *grabbed* her-mother her and much *cried*.'
'when the corpse was finally brought up her mother grabbed her and wept greatly'.

Promptly, however, the text goes into still another stasis in which the scene at the mouth of the hole is described:

(18) 'And then *that young woman herself* much had
come out sweat/moisture on her face.
'And then *all-the-people* much looked.
'Many were the people from all over the village.'

This stasis gives a glimpse of the appearance of the corpse (with left dislocation of the phrase 'the young woman' — perhaps with a topicalization shift here from the mother (who was thematic in the two preceding clauses) back to the corpse of the young woman — only in turn to have the spot-light shifted to the crowd of onlookers in the next clause. It is interesting, however, that both the clauses with left shift contain u^3ta^4 'very', 'much', and are thus similar to superlatives. The left shift may be occasioned by this quasi-superlative structure rather than by topicalization per se.

The storyline then resumes and continues unbroken to the end of the narrative, as it recounts bringing the dead woman in to one of the buildings connected with the priest's residence, laying her out, putting funeral candles to burn in front of her, sending word to Putla (district center) that they had gotten the corpse out of the pit, the sending of a medical examiner, the autopsy, and the burial. The text has no final stasis such as is present in the 'Peter the Evil One' text.

What then? Left shift in this story is associated with stasis, not with the action blocks — except in one case of what we have termed 'superlative fronting'. Two of the items which are left shifted in the stases refer to props ('another rope' and 'maguey tree'); these are somewhat reminiscent of the fronting of nouns which refer to props in some Trique procedural discourses. The fronting of the young woman herself (now a corpse) in the last stasis also refers to a prop of sorts. The fronting of 'all the people' in the same stasis again probably exemplifies 'superlative' fronting. What then of the fronting of nni^3 'her mother' in the first stasis? As we observed above, the fronting of this noun marks the transition to the inner world of the mother's thoughts: 'the mother, for her part, thought that....' The clause in which the fronting occurs is part of that stasis and the mother remains thematic for a few sentences, even on return to the storyline.

While some of the examples cited could be considered topicalization, one thing is certain: *Left shift is not a device of routine participant replace-*

ment in Trique. Frequently there is something implicitly contrastive or surprising about the referent of the noun fronted; and there is a 'world-shift' in each case: to the interior world of the mother's thoughts and anxious waiting; to the world of the preparations for the descent as signaled by 'the other rope'; to the world inside the pit as conjured up by the corpse caught down in the pit on a maguey-tree but poised above the water at the bottom; and to the world at the mouth of the hole: the cold sweat on the corpse's brow and the onlooking crowd. One stasis, the early reference to the mother and daughter following in the road behind the daughter has no fronting. I consider this to be a stasis because the verb is continuative. If it is rightfully considered such, then a stasis may be associated with left shift, but only if something on the order of contrastive pointing is involved; otherwise not.

In contrast with this text the Pedro de Mala text has no left shift. It is a traditional tale with a well-developed protagonist-antagonist structure which replaces participants regularly in VSO storyline clauses and contains no explanatory asides short of a final stasis, but even here there is no left shift. The 'woman who fell down the pit' story is not a traditional tale but recounts a contemporary tragedy. It has neither protagonist nor antagonist — although to be sure it has a victim, sufferers, and two heroes of sorts. The bulk of the participant replacements are performed on the storyline in VSO clauses, but it has numerous asides each with its own thematic structure and fronting as in Trique procedural and expository discourse. The first story has regular storyline movement; the second has broken movement interspersed with stases and accompanying nouns in left shift.

2. Luwo/Jür-Luwo

Luwo, a Nilotic language of southern Sudan, differs from Trique in having a morphologically marked secondary storyline. Not only do many Nilotic languages have a secondary storyline, but a number of other eastern Sudanic languages do as well. In such languages the secondary storyline is perfective but is outranked by the primary storyline, which is typically a special narrative tense (which, of course, is also completive or perfective in meaning) (Longacre 1990).

Luwo has such a primary and secondary storyline division and uses the secondary storyline with considerable frequency. Both the primary and sec-

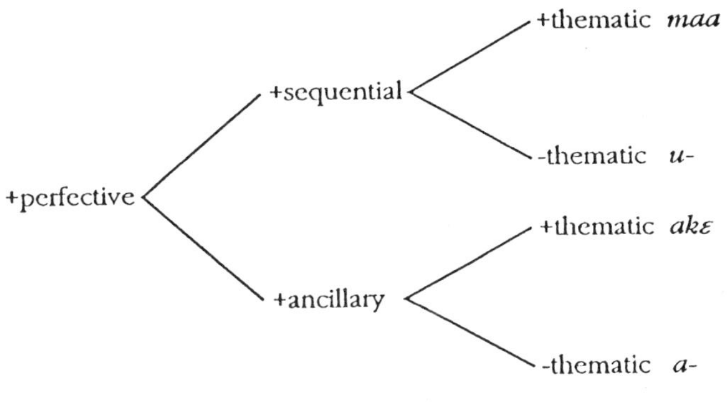

Diagram 2.

ondary storylines have internal split, so that a fourfold distinction has developed. Randall Buth conceptualizes the situation as represented in Diagram 2.

To complete Buth's storyline scheme, we would need to add the imperfective (= the imperfect) as opposed to dependent forms in clauses which are subordinated with *naa* 'when' (+*a-* verb) and *gE* 'whenever' (+imperfective). At the bottom of his scheme (which does not go into matters of irrealis or author intrusion) are clauses with 'be' verbs.

Verbs marked with *maa* or *u-* work together on the primary storyline. Verbs so marked are in VSO clauses, i.e., no noun may occur in front of them. The prefix *u-* marks a consecutive verb, i.e., a form which may continue any tense/mood in the language, so that a *u-* verb following an imperative is semantically imperative, while one following a future is semantically future, etc. Nevertheless, when a *u-* verb occurs without any non-storyline form preceding it, it is in and of itself storyline. *Maa* verbs, in clauses which frequently but not necessarily begin a sentence (or chain), mark the whole sentence as especially significant to the moving of the story. The *u-* forms do not occur discourse initially, but they may occur paragraph initial in subsequent portions of the narrative — or a whole paragraph may consist only of them. While *maa* verbs occur with some frequency in sentence initially clauses, they may, however, occur in sentence-final clauses. At any rate, storyline *u-* verbs are not dependent on the occurrence of a preceding *maa* verb. In the following example, clause 50 has a *maa* verb and the ensuing clauses have *u-*.

(19) (the lines are numbered according to occurrence in Buth's text 'Uriid and the Lions'.)

50. *Maa bEEhn ŋuuh*
Then came lion
51. *u-gOOhdE kii kood*
ran-3SG to-in basket,
52. *u-kahlE nyin kE OOgO*
carried-3SG the-boy to outside,
53. *u-toorE ŋuhd nO toorO*
broke-3SG neck-of him breaking
54. *u-pihyE kE nE nyaam.*
sat-3SG for to eat.
'Then the lion came, ran to the basket, carried the boy outside, broke his neck, and sat down to eat him.'

Notice the strict verb initial order here in all the clauses, but note especially the clauses (52) and (53). Luwo, like many Nilotic languages, has a distinction between definite and indefinite verb stems, with only the former taking direct (that is non-oblique) objects. Both clauses (52) and (53) take direct objects and are easily seen to be the highest grade of transitivity. The whole sentence, marked as it is with *maa* on its first verb, is signalled as encoding pivotal events of the story. Hence, Buth marks *maa* verbs as plus thematic in his scheme, while *u-* verbs are more routine, although still storyline, and thus are marked as minus thematic.

Another basic opposition in Buth's analysis is between *u-* verbs and *a-* verbs. For example, the following sentences occur in the same folktale, 'Uriid and the Lions' which Buth has analyzed:

(20) 55. *RuOhw E ŋuuh adOOa dOm kar dahd*
morrow and lion returned forest place-of hunt
56. *E nyin MOOgO acahg bEEhn kEEhd*
and boy another repeated come again.
57. *u-yEdhE wihy yaadh*
and-climbed-3SG on tree
58. u-cahgE bOOgE kE thOOhr yi pany
repeated-3SG leaves to throw in mortar
'The next day the lion went off again to hunt in the forest and again, another boy came (to the house). He climbed up on a tree and again threw leaves into the mortar.'

Several things are evident in the above example: (1) the past perfective prefix *a-* occurs on the verbs *ad00a* 'returned' and *acahg* 'repeated'; without any other marker such verbs are third person singular; (2) noun subjects occur preceding the *a-* verbs in Clauses 55 and 56; (3) it can be argued that the SVO clauses with *a-* verbs in 55 and 56 report actions that are preliminary in respect to those that are reported with *u-* verbs in clauses 57 and 58 — and this is what Buth argues. Not only are the actions preliminary, but they are identical with those performed by the boy in the preceding episode. These clauses leave the reader with a déjà vu feeling, and at all events, this participant is not a major participant of the story. Such a- verbs fit well, Buth argues, with the notion of a secondary storyline.[6]

But what of verbs marked with *akE*? Buth observed that such clauses with *akE* verbs "can be used to prepare, or set the stage for sequential clauses (either *maa* or *u-*) but not usually the other way around." He also observes that *akE* clauses have SV word order, and may not take transitive verbs with direct (i.e. non-oblique) objects. Broadly speaking, then, akE clauses are similar to a- verbs. The difference is that *akE* clauses "mark very important, crucial backgrounded events in the story." Speaking of an event at the same time as *important* and *crucial*, but *backgrounded* is not contradictory (cf. Jones and Jones 1979:21-3). The *akE* clauses indicate a "change of fortune," a crucial turning point in reference to what is to follow. Thus, to refer again to (19), lines 48 and 49 precede and are marked with *akE*:

(21) 48. *E uthuOnjiEn akE kOOhg kijee*
and rooster crowed that
49. *"CuOr Aywaa nii koodO."*
'man-of Aywaa is-in basket.'
'Then the rooster crowed, saying 'Aywaa's man is in the basket.'

Here the rooster tattled on the boy whom Aywaa had hidden in a basket. The rooster's action is marked as crucial — but not as important as the chain of events that it triggers (22). The story contains several such triggering clauses marked with *akE*.

Thus, to refer again to Diagram 2, *maa* verbs and *u-* verbs are both primary storyline, but *maa* serves to mark the more outstanding events on that line, while *akE* verbs and *a-* verbs are on the secondary storyline with the former especially marking events of special importance although still preparatory to and ancillary to the primary storyline.

The use of *a-* clauses is so frequent, both in staging a story and in laying the groundwork for primary storylines in paragraphs, that there is a striking scarcity of subordinated adverbial clauses (only three such clauses in the whole text from which these examples are taken). English has a choice between independent verbs and subordinated verbs. Luwo has a three-way choice between independent main verbs (*maa* or *u-* marked), independent but ancillary verbs (*akE* or *a-* marked), and subordinated verbs. As a result many *a-* verb clauses come over into English as 'when' clauses in translating a Luwo text.

As for 'left shift' in Luwo, it occurs only with the secondary storyline. We might argue that 'left shift' is somewhat of a fiction in such circumstances. We might rather say that VSO characterizes the primary storyline and NV characterizes the secondary storyline.

3. Biblical Hebrew

Biblical Hebrew, like Luwo, has a split into primary and secondary storylines:

a. Primary storyline is encoded in VSO clauses with the V in a special narrative tense (the *waw*-consecutive + imperfect or better: the *preterite*)[7]. Such VSO clauses do not permit the shifting of S or O into preverbal position. If such a shift is attempted the preterite tense gives way to the perfect, i.e. the primary storyline gives way to the secondary. Similarly, the attempted negation of a preterite clause cannot occur; it provokes a similar shift to the perfect (as does the preposing of *any* particle, e.g. *kî* 'because' or *'ăšer*, 'relative marker').

b. The secondary storyline consists (rarely) of VSO clauses with a verb in the perfect or (much more frequently) of SVO clauses (or of OVS clauses) with a verb in the perfect (Longacre 1989a).

The preterite as the primary storyline form is used generously in Hebrew narrative. Consider the following example (Gen. 37:5):

(22) a. *wayyaḥălom* *yôsēp* *ḥălôm*
and-3SG:MASC-dreamed Joseph dream

b. *wayyaggēd* *lĕ* *'eḥāyw*
and-3SG:MASC-declared to his-brothers

c. *wayyôsipû* *'ōd śĕnō'* *'ōtô*
and-3PL:MASC-added yet to-hate ACC-3SG:MASC.
'And Joseph dreamed a dream. And he told it to his brothers. And they hated him all the more.'

Here the initial verbs 'and-he-dreamed', 'and-he-declared', and 'they-added/ to hate him' are storyline forms. They report sequentially and punctiliously developments in the story. The story proceeds, however, with Joseph recounting his dream [(d) *wayyō'mer 'ălêhem...* 'and-he-said to-them'...], after which we find again in 37:8:

e. *wayyôsipû* *'ōd śĕnō'* *'otô*
and-3PL:MASC-added yet to-hate ACC-3SG:MASC
'al *ḥălōmōtāyw* *wĕ 'al*
on-account-of dreams-3SG:MASC and-on-account-of
dĕbārāyw
words-3SG:MASC
'They hated him all the more on account of his dreams and his words.'

Here it becomes evident that the storyline has got a bit ahead of itself in (c) above — or that the storyline backtracks in (e). Probably the former is indicated. The more normal and expected sense would have been for (d) *wayyo'mer 'ălêhem* 'and-he-said to-them' to have directly followed (b) *wayyaggēd lĕ 'ehayw* 'and-he-declared to-his-brothers' — since speech act clauses ('and-he-reported', 'and-he-answered', 'and-he-commanded', etc.) are typically followed by *wayyō'mer*, 'and-he-said' (plus or minus other elements) and the quotation. Here clause (c) intervenes as a preview of what we can expect. But all these clauses are accorded storyline status by the use of the preterite.[8] We need simply to understand that Biblical Hebrew construes the storyline a bit less rigorously than do some languages. Other cases of such *preview* uses of storyline verbs easily can be found.

Contrast this with a more straightforward sequence (Gen. 39:12):

(23) a. *wattitpĕsē-hû* *bĕbigdô....*
and-3SG:FEM-seized 3SG:MASC by-clothing-3SG:MASC....
b. *wayya'ăzab* *bigdô* *bĕyādāh*
and-3SG:MASC-abandoned clothing-3SG:MASC in-hand-3SF:FEM
c. *wayyānos*
and-3SG:MASC-ran

d. *wayyēsē'* *hahûsâ*
and-3SG:MASC-exited outside-to.
'And she seized him by his clothing. And he left his clothing in her hand. And he ran away. And he went outside.'

So much for the primary storyline. The perfect, which constitutes a secondary storyline, is less sequential in thrust and has a variety of specialized uses. It may occur with or without a preceding noun — although the latter is much more common. It necessary appears after the negative particle lo' and any subordinating particles. Sometimes the perfect (especially in clause-initial uses) marks a preparatory or a resultant action. This can be seen in the following example (Gen. 40:1) — where an adverbial time phrase precedes the verb and its subject:

(24) *wayhî* *'aḥar* *haddĕbārîm* *hā'ēlleh* *ḥāṭē'û*
and-3SG:MASC after matters these sinned-3PL:MASC
mašqēh *melek-misrayîm* *wĕhā'ōpeh....*
the cupbearer of-the-king-of-Egypt and-the-baker....
'And it happened somewhat later that the cupbearer of the king of Egypt and the baker sinned....'

This clause with its perfect verb *ḥāṭē'û* 'sinned-they' is followed by a clause that immediately resumes the storyline: *wayyiqṣōp par'ōh...* 'and-he-got-angry Pharoah....' Here the clause with the perfect verb gives an action which is presented as secondary (as a cause) in regard to the King's anger. Esther 2:21 has an example that is essentially similar but somewhat more complicated.

There are many cases where a perfect verb with a preposed noun (typically subject) seems to relate an action more to a participant than recounting it in its own right. The participant may be (re)introduced or contrasted with some other participant or put to the fore by reasons of etiquette and protocol. Thus in Gen. 39:l, the narrative returns to Joseph as main participant after intervening material (Chap. 38) which deals with Judah and Tamar.

(25) a. *wĕyôsēp* *hûrad* *miṣrāyĕmâ*
and-Joseph was-brought-down-3SG:MASC Egypt-to
(The 3SG:MASC in the Hebrew perfect has nul marking, i.e. is a "zero" category.) 'Now, as for Joseph, he was brought down to Egypt.'

This is a paraphrase of a similar clause at the end of Chapter 38. The storyline resumes with the next clause whose verb is a preterite:

b. *wayyiqnē-hû* *pôṭîpar*
and-3SG:MASC-purchased-3SG:MASC Potiphar
'And Potiphar bought him'

The first clause reports an action but its real function is apparently to refocus on Joseph as central.

In Gen. 40:22 there are two occurrences of the perfect:

(26) *wē'et-śar* *hā'ōpîm* *tālâ* *ka'ašer*
and-the-ACC-prince-of the-bakers hanged-3SG:MASC just as
pātar *lāhem* *yôsēp*
interpreted-3SG.:MASC to-3PL:MASC Joseph.
'But the chief baker he hanged, just as Joseph had interpreted for them.'

The first occurrence of the perfect is in an OV clause, where the preposed object throws the baker and his fate into contrast with that of the cupbearer and his fate as recorded in the previous clauses with verbs in the preterite ('And he restored the chief cupbearer to his position and he again gave the cup into the hand of Pharaoh.') The second perfect pa¢tar is semantically a flashback. The next example is a piece of reported speech (Gen.41:10):

(27) *par'ōh* *qāṣap* *'al* *'ăbādāyw*
Pharoah angry-3SG:MASC at servant-of-3SG:MASC
wayyittēn *'ōtî* *bĕmišmar...*
and-3SG:MASC-put ACC-1SG in-custody...
'Pharaoh got angry at his servant and put him (=me) in jail.'

Here a preliminary event — Pharaoh got angry — is reported via a perfect. Possibly, however, reasons of court etiquette (mentioning the monarch's name first *honoris causa*) are at work here. At any rate, we find not simply a VSO here with its verb in the perfect, but rather an SVO with perfect verb and preposed subject.

Aside from these uses of the perfect to mark preparatory actions and to report on actions with simultaneous focus on a participant — all of which seem to fit well the idea of a secondary storyline (Longacre 1990) — there is also use of a perfect as a pluperfect in clauses introduced by *kî* 'like, as', *'ăšer* (relative particle), and *ka'ăšer* 'just as'. An example of this usage of a perfect was given in (26). Here, again, as a secondary storyline with sequentiality not so basic as in the preterite, the perfect finds use in marking an action/event which is cited out of sequence.

The perfect is also regularly used in negative clauses which report actions/events that 'don't get off the ground.' In Gen. 40:23 the perfect occurs with a negated verb:

(28) wĕlō' zākar śar-hammašqîm
and-not remembered-3SG:MASC the-prince-of-the-cupbearers
'et-yôsēp wayyiskāhē-hû
ACC-Joseph and-3SG:MASC-forgot-3SG:MASC.
'But the chief cupbearer did not remember Joseph; rather he forgot him.'

It happens that in this example the negated clause is in paraphrase relationship with the following storyline clause. Not all negative clauses of course are so used. Again, however, the irrealis (negative) uses of the perfect contrast with uses of the preterite.

Finally, a perfect may be a paraphrase of a preterite in a construction V (Pret) S O V (Perf). The 0 may be here expanded to a string of NP's in which it is difficult to assign with certainty which NP goes with the preceding and which with the following verb. The following example, Gen. 41:48, is comparatively straightforward:

(29) *wayyitten* *'ōkel bĕ'ārîm*
and-3SG:MASC-stored food in-the-cities
'ōkel śedeh hā'îr...
food-of the-field-of the-city...
nātan bĕtôkāh.
stored-3SG:MASC in-midst-of-3SG:FEM.
'He stored food in the cities; the food of the fields of a city he stored inside it.'

Here in sentence initial position occurs the storyline preterite *wayyitten* 'and he stored', while close to the end of the sentence occurs the corresponding perfect form of the same verb, *nātan* 'stored (he)'. In between occurs a pair of NP's as objects; each has *'ōkel* 'food' as its head. Locative phrases with *bĕ-* occur at the end of Clause (1) and in sentence final position. A similar construction inserts a *wĕ-* 'and' before the onset of Clause (2) — thus yielding a paragraph instead of a complex sentence. (Longacre, 1989a) Here in all these uses the perfect does not mark a new action/event but functions in a chiastic paraphrase of the action/event.

What of left shift, then, in Hebrew? We may say that when it occurs it characterizes the secondary storyline. As in the case of Luwo, whole constructions are in contrast: VSO with the preterite, the primary storyline, and NV with the perfect on the secondary storyline.[9]

4. Conclusion

The three languages cited in this paper form an insightful comparison in regard to left shift in strongly VSO languages. Trique, to be true, has no special surface form for a secondary storyline. Nevertheless, the Trique stases within a story — marked by continuatives, modals, and contrafactuals — form a nice comparison with blocks of *a-* verbs and *akE* verbs in Luwo and with passages which feature the perfect tense in Hebrew. While in Luwo SVO is routine on the secondary story line, in Trique NV, i.e. OV or SV structures are found subject to another constraint — that of contrastive pointing (or at least world shift). Nevertheless, aside from superlative fronting, left shift characterizes the stases in Trique, not the storyline.

Jür-Luwo and Biblical Hebrew are alike in having: (a) special narrative tense, (b) a secondary tense. The special narrative tense need not be consecutive on any special initial form when it represents the mainline of a narrative but may function as a consecutive form after some other tense forms and continue their meaning (more markedly in Luwo than in Biblical Hebrew).

The Luwo *a-* verbs (and the *akE* verbs) and the Hebrew perfect function as secondary tenses. The functions of a secondary tense have a certain resemblance across the two languages — and are not unlike the verbs found in stases in Trique stories. A clause with a secondary verb may present a happening that is preparatory, resultant, or in some other way *ancillary* to clauses which have storyline verbs. The clause with the secondary tense may be in paraphrase with a clause whose main verb is storyline. A clause with a secondary verb may picture an action relative to a participant who is often a secondary participant or whose action is contrasted with that of another participant. But again similar functions are found in Trique verbs within stases.

In all three languages NV structures occur off the primary storyline, whether with a secondary tense or in the Trique stasis. The function of such NV clauses is never routine replacement of participants. This is done quite comfortably in VSO narrative clauses without left shift.

So much is this so that we may well question the usefulness of calling such left shifts *topicalizations*.[9] Nor is such topicalization rigidly distinguished from left-dislocation in these languages. The purpose of the left shift is not to regularly replace one participant with another or to topicalize one participant in storyline clauses. Rather, the left shift signals in most cases a departure from the primary storyline into setting, background, or explanation (or even backgrounded events). Within such passages (called stases in Trique) the left shifted item is thematic, but even then the left shift does not per se signal thematic status. The left shift in Trique, e.g. can occur toward the end of a stasis (as a summary) instead of at its beginning; i.e. it may be anaphoric rather than cataphoric. Very probably a kind of identifying contrastive function on the one hand or a déjà vu attitude on the other is involved in these frontings — with functions which are specialized according to each language.

The term *topicalization* within the context of sentence grammar probably signifies something on the order of topic-comment structure ((25): 'And Joseph — he was brought down to Egypt.'). But such 'topicalization' is not necessarily topic-establishing in a discourse. Givón has shown results to sustain his present view that a noun in SV has no more topic persistence than a noun in VS in Biblical Hebrew. It is possible, therefore, that establishing a topic for a stretch of following discourse is not the major function of a noun in a NV clause with a verb in the perfect in Biblical Hebrew.

To go back to the beginning of this paper, I emphasize again the peculiar narrative competence of strongly VSO languages which introduce happening after happening down a string of VSO clauses with participants often introduced, traced, and replaced without departing from the canonical order. Left shift in such languages is a departure not just from the canonical form but into passages which are off the main storyline as background, setting, or explanation, or even backgrounded events. They may treat of participants of secondary importance to the story or restage a major participant.

Notes

1. For ease of reference, in the balance of this paper I will refer to this language simply as Trique. Bruce and Barbara Hallenbach are investigators of Copala Trique and have published variously on that language. The two languages are possibly as distinct as low and high German.

2. M. Noonan suggest to me that in these examples, judging from his knowledge of other Nilotic languages, *wihy* means 'head-of' and *yi* means 'stomach-of'. If so, these Luwo examples would probably be parallel to the Trique forms in (3) above, where body parts come to have a prepositional function.

3. It is plausible to insist that in most narratives action is primary and participants secondary — except in novels where the development of character is portrayed. But even in the latter sort of story, character develops through a series of actions and contingencies. For an early insistence on the primacy of action in narrative see Aristotle's Poetics. For the development-of-character novel, as an expansion of Aristotle's original insistence on the primacy of actions, see Ricoeur (1985. v2. 8-14).

4. This is a geological term named from the Kras region of Yugoslavia. Karst topography is characterized by limestone strata, underground bodies of water, and caverns which in some places collapse leaving sinkholes.

5. I regard punctiliar Trique verbs as storyline, and continuatives as off the line in the type of narrative here illustrated. A type of narrative with continuatives as the storyline throughout would be the Trique equivalent of an English story in the historical present.

   Most Trique verbs have three forms: a contuative stem form, e.g. *a*^{3}*če*^{21} 'walk', a punctilious form with *g-* or *gV-* prefix, e.g. *ga*^{3}*če*^{21}, and a modal form marked with lowering of one or more of the stem tones, e.g. ga^{4}če^{4}. The latter can be regarded as having the functions of a future, subjunctive, and imperative combined. The notional affinity of the future and the subjunctive is wellknown (in that the future is essentially uncertain).

6. For a secondary storyline referring to secondary participants perhaps the classic case is Halbi — as described by Frances Woods (1980:123). But this is possibly true for Biblical Hebrew as well, Consider Gen. 14:18-20, where a minor participant, Melquisedec, bursts suddenly on the scene (in a SV perfect clause)and holds the stage for three verses — and is never mentioned before or after in all the patriarchal narratives. A similar case in Trique is found in a text, 'The Plumed Serpent Rescues a Man' (Longacre 1966), where in a solitary SVO clause 'crows' (providers of food) are mentioned as part of a stasis but never referred to before or afterwards in the same text. The Melquisedec passage in Gen. 14 occurs as part of a contextually backgrounded (and brief) storyline, while 'crows' are in a stasis. In both cases the nouns 'Melquisedec' and 'crows' could be considered to be left shifted as rhematic and non-persisting topics.

7. Thus, Gesenius (1910) insightfully refers to the *waw*-consecutive with the imperfect as "a narrative tense" (p. 326). One would have to plow through the preceding German editions to discover just how early this insight emerged in the history of Hebrew grammatical studies. To me as a theological student in 1945 this remark of GKC sounded somewhat bizarre; now, many years later, I have encountered special narrative tenses in many languages in Africa and elsewhere.

8. I assume that 'storyline' in a given language matches in a high percentage of occurrences with universal semantic judgments as to 'events which carry the story forward', but in the last analysis it is an emic reality within a given language. The storyline forms can sometimes be used somewhat more expansively or more narrowly than our own a prior semantic judgment would suggest. The prior semantic judgments are simply initial heuristic devices which prove to apply in say 90% to 95% of the instances which we encounter.

9. For a lively debate on the analysis of pre-verbal elements in Biblical narrative cf. N. Bailey and S. Levinsohn 1992 with R. Longacre 1992.

References

Bailey, Nicholas A. and Stephen H. Levinsohn. 1992. "The function of pre-verbal elements in independent clauses in the Hebrew narrative of Genesis." *Journal of Translation and Textlinguistics* 5.179-207. Dallas: Summer Institute of Linguistics.

Gesenius, Wilhelm. 1910. *Gesenius' Hebrew Grammar*. Oxford: The Clarendon Press.

Jones, Larry and Linda Jones. 1979. "Multiple levels of information in discourse." *Discourse Studies in Mesoamerican Languages*, Vol 1 ed. by Linda Jones, 3-27. Dallas: Summer Institute of Linguistics and the University of Texas at Arlington. [*Summer Institute of Linguistics Publications* 58.]

Longacre, Robert E. 1966. "The Plumed Serpent Rescues a Man". *Tlalocan* 5(2).114-118. (Mexico City).

Longacre, Robert E. 1982. "Discourse typology in relation to language typology". *Text Processing* ed. by Sture Allén, 476-86. Stockholm: Almquist and Wyksell. [*Nobel Symposium* 52.]

Longacre, Robert E. 1983. *The Grammar of Discourse*. New York: Plenum Press.

Longacre, Robert E. 1989a. *Joseph: a Story of Divine Providence: A textlinguistic and text theoretical analysis of the Hebrew text of Gen. 37 and 39- 48*. Winona Lake, IN: Eisenbrauns.

Longacre, Robert E. 1989b. "Two hypotheses regarding text generation and analysis." *Discourse Processes* 12.413-460.

Longacre, Robert E. 1990. *Storyline Concerns and Word-order Typology in East and West Africa*. Los Angeles: UCLA. [*Studies in African Linguistics*, Supplement 10.]

Longacre, Robert E. 1992. "The analysis of pre-verbal nouns in Biblical Hebrew narrative: Some overriding concerns." *Journal of Translation and Textlinguistics* 5.208-224. Dallas: Summer Institute of Linguistics.

Ricoeur, Paul. 1984, 1985, 1988. *Time and Narrative*. 3 vols. Chicago: University of Chicago Press [translated from the French *Temps et Récit* by Kathleen McLaughlin and David Pellauer].

Woods, Frances. 1980. "The Interrelationship of Cultural Information, Linguistic Structure and Symbolic Representations in a Halbi Myth." Doctoral Dissertations, University of Texas at Arlington.

The pragmatics of verb initial sentences in some ancient Indo-European languages

Silvia Luraghi
Terza Università degli Studi di Roma

0. Introduction

Initial verbs are a rather popular topic in word order studies, as shown by the titles of the papers in this volume. My paper, while approaching the same topic as others, does not fit in the main stream of studies on inital verbs, in that it is not devoted to any verb-initial language. The languages that I will discuss all have a possible verb-initial word order pattern, which, however, does not represent either the basic or the most frequent word order.

Proto-Indo-European is traditionally reconstructed as SOV; however, it certainly did not belong to a rigid sub-type,[1] but was to a large extent a language with pragmatic word order (cf. Thompson 1978). In particular, it certainly had an alternative VSO order. This variant must not have been infrequent, since it has become the basic word order in at least one branch of the Indo-European family, the Celtic group[2].

It is not surprising to find a VSO variant in a SOV language. Virtually all languages posses a verb-initial variant, of which they make use to different extents (cf. Hopper 1987:458). Sometimes, VSO sentences are grammaticalized and have the function of indicating a certain sentence type: in Modern English, for example, initial verbs appear in (direct) questions. Besides, numerous languages have a tendency for imperative verb forms to be placed in initial position: this latter pattern can safely be reconstructed for Proto-Indo-European, as is shown by the daughter languages.[3] I am not going to discuss any constructions of this type in the present paper, since changes in modality, beside sentence type, are involved. I will rather focus on verb-initial declarative sentences.

Among declarative sentences I will not take into account those in which the verb is moved to sentence-initial position because it bears contrastive focus. In fact, in such cases many languages have a rule that the contrasted constituents are moved to the left margin of the sentence, regardless of their grammatical categories. The difference in discourse function between this and other types of initial verbs has been observed in Kroll for Latin:

> Often the verb stands in a more or less explicit contast with some other constituent (most often, obviously, another verb), and it is consequently placed in initial position ... Such occurrences do not, strictly speaking, belong here, since alterations of the habitual word order are also found with constituent belonging to different categories, ... (Kroll 1918:113).[4]

Kroll then goes further to explain that he will include contrasted verbs in his study for the sake of completeness. While not treating them extensively, I will come back to the difference between verbs that carry contrastive focus and other initial verbs in Section 1.2.

Note that the verb initial order in declarative sentences, in all these languges, is a free, pragmatically determined variant, and it is *not* grammaticalized for any specific function. Therefore, while each of the examples quoted for initial verbs is representative of a number of other similar occurrences, it never represents an obligatory pattern. In other words, the conditions under which initial verbs may be used do not trigger their use in the totality of cases. What is noteworthy, however, is that in such conditions there is a possible choice between the basic word order (verb-final, or at least not verb-initial), and its verb-initial variant, a choice that does not exist if the same conditions do not hold.

My article is organized as follows. In Section 1 I will discuss some basic concepts that I will be using in the rest of the paper; I will also summarize the evidence on the function of verb initial sentences in Hittite, which I have already discussed at length in Luraghi (1990a), and discuss Hopper's findings on initial verbs in the Germanic languages (Hopper 1975, 1987). Section 2 contains an analysis of sentences with initial verbs in Classical Latin and Classical Greek. In Section 3 I will discuss the bearing of the data in the first two sections on the reconstruction of Proto-Indo-European word order. Section 4 contains the general conclusions.

I will show that sentences with initial verbs are typically found in connection with some kind of discontinuity or unexpectedness, either in the structure of the discourse, or in the course of the events. As we will see, this connection can explain, among other things, the reason why verb-initial sentences have been taken as either foregrounding (Hopper 1975 1987), or backgrounding devices (Luraghi 1990a).

1. Initial verbs and communicative function

1.1 *Initial position*

Some remarks should be added on what I understand as verb-initial sentences in the present paper. Let us observe the following two sentences from Classical Greek:[5]

(1) *kaì* ***ê:n*** *kaì parà póton he:dù mén,*
and they-were-IMPERF also by drinks sweet PART
kephalalgès dé.
causing-headache PART
'and these made a pleasant morsel also at a symposium, but were apt to cause headache' [Xen., An. 2.3, 15]

(2) ***ê:n*** *dè sphódra kaì toûto kephalalgés.*
they-were PART exceedingly also this causing-headache
'This, too, however, was exceedingly apt to cause headache' [Xen., An. 2.3,16.]

I give here the English translation of the stretch of discourse from which the two sentences are taken:

> As for the dates themselves of the palm, the sort that one can see in Greece were set apart for the servants, while those laid away for the masters were selected ones, remarkable for the beauty and size and with a color altogether resembling that of amber; others, again, they would dry and store away for sweetmeats: *and these made a pleasant morsel also at a symposium, but were apt to cause headache.* Here also the soldiers ate for the first time the crown of the palm, and most of them were surprised not alone at its appearance, but at the peculiar nature of its flavor. *This, too, however, was exceedingly apt to cause headache.* [Xen., An. 2.3, 15-6].

In the remainder of this paper, the position of the verb in (2) will be called initial position, whereas the position of the verb in (1) will be called first position. First position is defined as the position of the first accented constituent in a sentence which is preceded only by an accented connective. Initial position is defined as the position of the first accented word[6] in a sentence which is not preceded by a connective. In this paper, I will be concerned only with verbs in initial position, and will not survey sentences in which the verb stands in first position.

The distinction between first and initial position as defined above has always been recognized as relevant for the discourse function of specific sentences in the Ancient Indo-European languages. The same terminology is used in Justus (1976) and Boley (1985); the Neogrammarians usually referred to first position as 'modified' initial position.[7]

1.2 *Initial verbs in Hittite*

My own interest in the pragmatics of verb initial sentences in non-VSO languages first arose when I was writing my dissertation on the syntax of the simple sentence in Old Hittite (Luraghi 1987). I deepened my study of this subject in Luraghi (1990a, 1990b), and found that verb-initial sentences occur in contexts in which some kind of discontinuity needs to be indicated, and are often used for the purpose of marking some pieces of information as additional, or less important.

Here are some of the relevant Hittite examples:[8]

(3) #[a] apus hantezumni tehhi #[b] wes= a namma anda paiwani
these porch-LOC I-put we PART again insidewe-go

#[c] 2 [D]Hantasepus harwani GIŠ-as #[d] **harkanzi**= ma=
two H-divinities-ACC we-have of-wood they-have PART

an [D]Hantasepes anduhsas harsarr= a [GIŠ]ŠUKUR[HI.A]= ya
PART H.-divinities men-GEN heads and lances and

#[e] sakuwa= smet ishaskanta #[f] **wesanda**= ma isharwantus
eyes their bloodstained they-wear PART purple-ACC

TÚG[HI.A]-us #[g] putaliyantess= a #[h] anda=kan halinas
clothes-ACC bound-NOM and inside PART of-clay

tessummius tarlipit suwamus 2-ki petumini #[i] **tarueni**=
vessels-ACC t.-INSTR full-ACC twice we-carry we-call

ma= at eshar #[j] DUMU.É.GAL-i [D]Hantasepan LUGAL-i
PART it blood page-NOM H-divinity-ACC king-DAT

kissari dai #[k] tessumminn= a pai #[l] SALLUGAL=
hand-LOC he-puts vessel-ACC and he-gives queen

ya *QATAMMA* pai #[m] [NINDA]sarrui= ma= ssan ERÍN[MEŠ]-az
and the same he-gives s.-bread-LOC PART PART troop-NOM

eszi #[n] ser= semet= a GÍR ZABAR kitta
it-sits over them PART dagger bronze it-lies

'#[a] I put those in the front-porch. #[b] We go inside again, #[c] holding two H. divinities, made of wood. #[d] (The H. divinities **hold** human heads as well as spears ; #[e] their eyes are bloodstained. #[f] They **are wearing** purple clothes #[g] and have high belts). #[h] Twice we bring inside the clay vessels full of t. #[i] (we **call** it blood); #[j] the palace servant puts a H. divinity in the hand of the king #[k] and gives him a vessel; #[l] the same he gives to the queen #[m] (a troop-statuette is sitting over the s.-bread, #[n] over it lies a bronze dagger).' *[StBoT* 8 i 21-31'.]

Note that in this example the descriptive passage contains three initial predicates out of four (the two verbs in (3d, f) and the nominal predicate *putaliyantes* (a participle) in (3g)). As we will see below, initial verbs tend to some extent to occur in clusters, in cases where a number of subsequent sentences can be singled out as constituting a textual sub-unit. Uniformity in word order highlights the coherence of the sub-unit.

(4) #[a] KUR Arzawiya [I]Nunnu LÚ [URU] Hurma esta
country A. N. man H. he-was

#[b] KÙ.BABBAR= ya GUŠKIN natta udai #[d] kuit wemizzi
silver and gold not he-carries which he-finds

#[c] apass= a parna= ssa pittaizzi #[e] s= an LÚ [URU]
he= and home= his he-brings PART him man

Huntara isihhis #[f] *ABI* LUGAL *IŠPUR* #[g] s= an
H. he-traced out father king he-sent PART him

sara water #[h] pidi= ssi= ma [I]Sarmassun hatrait
back they-took in-place in-his PART S-ACC he-ordered

#[i] **paizzi**= ma= as nawi
he-goes PTC he not yet

'#[a] In the country of Arzawiya was Nunnu, the man from Hurma, #[b] and he does not turn in the silver and the gold #[c] which he found, #[d] and he takes it to his home. #[e] The man from Huntara traced him out. #[f] The king' father sent (for him); #[g] he was taken back; #[h] (the king's father) ordered Sarmassu to take his place, #[i] but he **has** not **gone** yet.' [KUB 36.104 obv. 9'-13'.]

The initial verbs in the above passages are accompanied by the enclitic particle =*ma*, which has an adversative force, functioning on either the event level, or on the communication level, as suggested in the definition of 'adversativity' given by Halliday and Hasan: "The basic meaning of the ADVERSATIVE relation is 'contrary to expectations'. The expectation may derive from the content of what is being said, or from the communication process ..." (1976:250). In Hittite, =*ma* is often used in order to signal something unexpected in the organization of the discourse. This typically happens when a description is inserted in a text of another type, as in example (3), from a procedural text (description of actions performed in a ritual). Descriptions of this type clearly convey backgrounded information.The connection between =*ma*, or V-initial order, and background is less clear in (4i). The stress here is rather on adversativity in the course of the events, since the event which is referred to is viewed as unexpected and unwanted. The coding is such that it brings about discontinuity in the narrative. Elsewhere, a connection between backgrounding and either the particle =*ma* , or initial verbs is suggested by their relatively frequent use in subordinate clauses, as in (5) and (6) below:

(5) sallanun= war= an kuit ammuk
I-made great PART him because I
'Since I made him great, ...' [*StBoT* 24 iv 11]

(6) man= as lazziyatta= ma
when he he-recovers PART
'When he recovers, ...' [*Laws* § 10 = A i 18.]

However, =*ma* is found with clearly foregrounded information, too, as in (7e) below. The difference in discourse function between verbs in initial position and verbs in first position is also borne out by example (7):

(7) #[a] nu Aparrun *QADU* 3 *LIM* [ ] hulliyat
PART A-ACC with three thousand [...] he-besieged
#[b] n= at= kan kuenta #[c] nu **eppirr**= a mekki
PART them PART he-killed PART they-captured and many
#[d] **kuennirr**= a mekki #[e] Aparrus= ma= kan isparzasta
they-killed and many A-NOM PART PART he-escaped

'#[a] He besieged Aparru with three thousands [troops?]; #[b] he slaughtered them. #[c] Many **were captured** #[d] and many **were killed**, #[e] but Aparru was able to escape.' [KBo 2.5 iii 35-36.]

In this passage, the two verbs *eppir*, 'they captured', in (7c), and *kuennir*, 'they killed', in (7d), are focus of contrast. The verb *eppir* is in first position, i.e. it precedes its subject NP, and is preceded only by the sentence particle *nu*, an additive conjunction ('and then').[9] Besides, sentence (7d) is coordinated to (7c) in a way by which it is clear that the verb *kuennir* is in initial position only because an additive particle would make no sense, since the two events are reported as having occurred at the same time.[10] Here the position of the verb is not connected with any form of discontinuity, either in the organization of the text, or in the course of the events. The events referred to are reported as part of the gist of the narration, as is the event in (7e), in which the particle *=ma* does not have any backgrounding function. The event coded in (7e) is chronologically on a line with those reported before; *=ma* rather marks it as unwanted.

1.3 *Initial verbs in the Germanic languages*

In Hopper (1987) it is argued that the alternation between initial and non-initial verbs has a function in indicating the communicative status of single sentences in the discourse. Hopper took examples from Malay and from the early Germanic languages; he concluded that initial verbs occur in sentences that convey foregrounded information. The Germanic languages, with which we will be concerned here, since they belong to the Indo-European family, have rather free word order, with a tendency for the verb to occur in second position, as in e.g. modern High German; more examples and further discussion are to be found in Hopper (1975). Apparently, Hopper's findings on the Germanic languages are opposite to my own on Hittite. However, this is sometimes due to the fact that many verbs that Hopper considers initial would not be initial in my own terminology, as shown by the following passage in Old Norse:

(8) #[a] ***koma*** *þeir at kveldi til eins bónda* #[b] *ok*
came they at evening to a farmer's [house] and
fá *þar náttstaþ* #[c] *En um kveldit* ***tók*** *þórr*
made there nightplace and on that-evening took Thor
hafra sína #[d] *ok* ***skar*** *băþa* #[e] *Eptir þat* ***váru*** *þeir*
goats his and slew both after that were they
flegnir ok bornir til ketis ... #[f] *þor bauþ til*
skinned and put in pot Thor invited to

matar	*meþ*	*sér*	*bóndanum*	*ok*	*konu*	*hans*	*ok*
meal	with	him	farmer	and	wife	his	and

bornum	*þeira;*	#[g] *sónr*	*bónda*	*het*	*þjalfi*	*en*
children	their	son	of-farmer	was-named	Thjalfi	and

Roskva dóttir
Roskva daughter

'#[a] Toward evening they **came** to a farmer's house, #[b] and **made** their camp there. #[c] And that evening Thor **took** his goats #[d] and **slaughtered** them. #[e] After that, they **were** skinned and put in the pot. ... #[f] Thor had invited the farmer and his wife and their children to eat with him. #[g] The farmer's child was called Thjalfi and his daughter Roskva', [from Hopper 1987: 473].

In this example, only sentence (8a) is truly verb initial, whereas in sentences (8b, c, d, e) the verb is preceded by other accented material. Note especially the occurrence of conjunctions in (8b, d) (*ok*), and in (8c) (*en*); such chaining of narrative clauses is typical of the ancient Germanic narratives, and it indicates chronological ordering and discourse continuity; it is often found in verb final sentences.[11]

As for sentence (8a), which is verb initial and conveys foregrounded information, note that it stands at the beginning of a narrative paragraph. At such junctures in the discourse there is a need to indicate the transition between two units and the resumption of the narrative after an interruption. The occurrence of a word order pattern that indicates discontinuity matches the discontinuity in the communication process.[12] Note also the pattern VS-OV-OV-OV; VS-OV-OV-OV; ... found in Old English (Hopper 1979:221), where the initial verbs in the first sentences function as the marker of each textual sub-unit, and the consistent OV order of the following sentences indicates that they all belong together in the same coherent sub-unit. As Hopper writes

> It is common for a lengthy narrative to be broken up into a series of internal episodes, each of which is initiated by a VS clause. ... Sometimes there is a clear motivation for the break, that is, a distinct thematic shift of some kind. Just as often, however, the break seems to come as a sort of breathpause or, perhaps, an aesthetic effect... (1979:221).[13]

Initial verbs in the Germanic languages are also found in conditional clauses, as shown in Hopper (1975:50-51); the following example is from Old Swedish:

(9) ***Farr*** *annar þroper köpfertþum ok annar hema i asku*
goes one brother to-purchase and other home in hearth

sitær, baþir eighu þer iammykit af arvi
sits both shall-have the half of inheritance

'If one brother **goes** to a commercial venture and the other sits at home by the hearth, both shall have an equal share of the inheritance', [from Hopper 1975:51].

To sum up, initial verbs in declarative sentences are mostly found at text junctures (at the beginning of different paragraphs in the course of a narrative). In the course of a narrative discourse, verbs are often final; otherwise, they can follow a sentence initial connective, or another constituent. In the latter case, we find the typical Germanic verb second order, with the subject following the verb, as in (8c).

1.4 *Grounding of information in the text*

1.4.1 *What is 'non-foregrounded' information?*

The two terms 'foreground' and 'background' are to be found in Hopper (1979) and have been extensively used in the later literature, without being defined clearly enough. Thus, scholars have come to refer to quite different things under the same couple of labels. In origin, the two terms had been created not only in order to refer to the distinction between 'narrative', i.e. chronologically ordered, sentences, and non-narrative, i.e. non-chronologically ordered, sentences (Labov 1972), but mainly in order to distinguish between the most salient information in a discourse, referring to the events that constitute the 'gist' of what the discourse is about, and the 'accessory' information, which has as its main function that of providing a frame for these events. The concept of most salient, i.e. foregrounded, information has later come to be considered equivalent of new information; consequently, backgrounded information has come to be considered old information; see e.g. Givón (1987).

It is easy to see that the two ways of understanding foreground and background present major differences in a number of points. Information contained in sentences which are not chronologically ordered is not necessarily old. In a narrative text, for example, descriptions of places or participants do not convey old information at all; rather, they often introduce new information in the discourse. However, they do not refer to the main course of the events; therefore they cannot be said to be foregrounded.

In fact, there are numerous instances in which the information contained in sentences that are not chronologically ordered is not only new, but also important, as in e.g. presentative sentences. Since it can be deceiving to use the term 'background' in such cases, from here onward I will rather distinguish between foregrounded and non-foregrounded information; I will keep the term 'background' only for truly accessory pieces of information.[14]

To sum up, I will make use of the following definitions:

a. Foregrounded information: the information referring to chronologically ordered events that represent the gist of a narrative.[15]
b. Non-foregrounded information: the information which is not chronologically ordered. Non-foregrounded information includes
   1. information about accessory events, or descriptions of places or participants (normally called backgrounded information);
   2. new information conveyed in sentences that introduce new material (e.g. new participants) into the discourse. This is not foregrounded information, because it breaks the chronological order and does not refer to events; it cannot even be considered accessory, because it concerns referents that are going to play an important role in the subsequent stretch of text/discourse.

1.4.2 *Grounding and subordinate clauses*

It is generally thought that most salient information is coded in main clauses, whereas accessory information is coded in subordinate clauses. Subordinate clauses possess an explicit semantic marker that also indicates their temporal relation to the main clause; therefore they can easily violate the chronological order, which is impossible for (coordinated) main clauses. Beside, subordinate clauses normally do convey backgrounded pieces of information, since they refer to causes, purposes, or conditions for the events referred to in their main clauses, or they provide the temporal setting for them.

However, the connection between main clauses and foreground on the one hand, and subordinate clauses and background on the other is not always straightforward. One must keep in mind at least two important facts:

a. Verbal aspect plays a crucial role in the grounding of information (cf. Hopper 1979). Many languages have a morphological distinction between a perfective and an imperfective aspect, which is especially clear in the past. Languages which have the imperfect as a past tense, as the

Romance languages do, use this tense to code backgrounded information, both in subordinate and in main clauses (see below on the backgrounding function of the imperfect in Latin and Greek).

b. In some special cases, foregrounded information can be coded in subordinate clauses. This is typical of sentences such as

(10) John was skiing, when he fell and broke his leg.

Since point (a) has been widely discussed in the literature, in the next section I will rather elaborate on point (b).

1.4.3 *Cum inversum in Latin*

The construction in (10) is found in numerous European languages (e.g. French, German, Italian) and it was rather frequent in Classical Latin. Very soon, Latinists noted that it was abnormal, in that it is the subordinate clause that conveys the most salient piece of information, and the main clause which encodes backgrounded information, rather than the other way around: "here the *cum* -clause contains the most important idea and indicates most often the start of a sudden or unexpected action ... The tense [in the *cum*-clause] is normally the preterite or the historical present ... A durative tense (imperfect or pluperfect) usually occurs in the main clause" (Leumann, Hoffmann and Szantyr 1965:623).[16]

This construction is commonly called '*cum inversum*'; an example is

(11)

#[a] *iamque*	*ab*	*eo*	*non*	*longius*	*biduo*
yet	from	him	not	longer	than-two-days

aberant	#[b]	*cum*	*duas*	*venisse*	*legiones*
they-were-far-IMPERF		when	two	to-come-PRET	legions

cognoscunt
they-learn-PRES

'#[a] They were not farther away from him yet than two days of march, #[b] when they learnt that two legions had arrived' [Sall., *Jug.* 101.8].

Nehring (1930) contains a study of the theory of subordinate clauses, a part of which is devoted to *cum inversum*. Nehring explains under which conditions the reversal in the communicative function of the main and the subordinate clause is made possible:

> It is obviously by no accident, that in this type of sentence in the majority of cases it is the first clause, syntactically the main clause, which definitely describes a state. ... The structure of the sentences with *cum inversum* is the same in all cases: a state, in which an event takes place. Now, since the event is always more salient than the state which it interrupts, the attention is always moved away from the state, toward the action. (Nehring 1930:149).[17]

Note that in Latin, as well as in the Romance languages, the inversion in communicative function between main and subordinate clause is made possible through an aspectual opposition: a backgrounding tense (usually the imperfect) is used in the main clause, whereas in the subordinate clause we find a foregrounding tense (the preterite or the historical present).

Constructions of this type seem to belong to languages with a rather elaborate literary tradition. In archaic Latin the *cum inversum* construction is in its early development, and it occurs regularly only from Cicero onwards. Nehring (1930:142) notes that the same is also true for German.

1.5 *Text types*

Up to this point, I have been speaking of the discourse function of specific sentences or word order patterns, as if the strategies for indicating discourse functions were the same for all text types. However, this is not true, especially with regard to chronological ordering. In order for the events referred to to be chronologically ordered, sentences obviously need to occur in a text which has a temporal structure: in other words, chronological ordering is typically found in narrative texts.

Beside narratives, procedural texts, too, have a similar strucure, in that they refer to actions that usually need to be performed in a certain order. Therefore narratives and procedures are the text types that can most safely be treated together under the rubric of the grounding of information in a (stretch of) discourse (cf. Grimes 1975:33).

In Section 2 on initial verbs in Latin and Greek, I have worked on two historical texts, Caesar's *de Bello Gallico* and Xenophon's *Anabasis*, both of which contain long and complex narratives. For the sake of homogeneity, I have omitted from my study all instances of indirect and direct speech (frequently found in Caesar and Xenophon respectively).

2. Initial verbs in Latin and in Classical Greek

2.1 *Initial verbs in Caesar*

In his 1918 study of initial verbs in Latin, Kroll found five types of sentences in which initial verbs occur with different discourse functions. About his type (1), Kroll writes: "Initial position of the verb is ... frequent ... where the verb which refers to a progression in the action is placed at the beginning of the main clause" (Kroll 1918:114).[18] The other types are (2) descriptions, (3) occurrences where the verb is preceded by a negation or a conjunction, (4) sentences in which the verb bears contrastive focus, and (5) main clauses whose initial verb is preceded by a temporal subordinate clause.

Only the first two of the above types are relevant for my study.[19] Kroll's type (1) includes sentences which convey foregrounded information. I will further split up Kroll's type (2) into three different groups of occurrences, all of which convey non-foregrounded information: (a) geographic descriptions, (b) sentences in the imperfect which refer to a state or situation holding at the time of a certain event, and (c) presentative sentences.

Latin is a free word order language, with a tendency toward SOV (see Linde 1923; Marouzeau 1938; Panhuis 1982). A rather consistent verb-final word order established itself as a stylistic convention in literary Latin of the Classical period; both archaic and late Latin seem closer to the colloquial language and are less strictly verb final (Panhuis 1982).

For the purpose of this paper, I have looked up all initial verbs in three books of Caesar's *de Bello Gallico* (Books 1, 4, and 6). I have chosen Caesar because of his consistent use of the verb final order,[20] which, as we will see below, renders more fruitful the comparison with the other languages examined in this paper.

2.1.1 *Descriptions*

Descriptions of places usually begin with a sentence which contains the topic in initial position and is typically followed by a series of other sentences, all with an initial verb; the topic is referred to by zero anaphora:

(14) #[a] *Eorum*	*una*	*pars,*	*quam*	*Gallos*	*obtinere*	
of-them	one	part-NOM	which-ACC	Gauls-ACC	to-hold	
dictum	*est,*	*nitium*	*capit*	*a*	*flumine*	*Rhodano;*
said	it-is	beginning-ACC	it-takes	from	river	Rhone

#[b] ***continetur*** *Garumna* *flumine,* *Oceano,* *finibus*
it-is-limited Garonne by-river by-Ocean by-territory

Belgarum; #[c] ***attingit*** *etiam* *ab* *Sequanis* *et*
of-Belgae it-touches also from Sequani and

Helvetiis *flumen* *Rhenum;* #[d] ***vergit*** *ad* *septentriones*
Helvetii river-NOM Rhine-NOM it-bends toward north

'#[a] The separate part of the country which, as has been said, is occupied by the Gauls starts from the river Rhone; #[b] it **is bounded** by the river Garonne, the Ocean, and by the territory of the Belgae; #[c] the river Rhine **touches** it, on the side of the Sequani and the Helvetii; #[d] it **expands** towards the north' [Caes. *G.* 1.1].

It is worth stressing that the topic, rather than the grammatical subject, is omitted. While *eorum una pars, ...* is the subject in (14a, b, d), it functions as the direct object (in 14c). Also in (14c), however, the verb is initial, and the direct object can be omitted just as easily as the subject, in cases of high topic continuity. Therefore the verbs in (14b, c, d) cannot be thought of as standing in initial position for some grammatical reason brought about by the omission of the subject.

Note that here, as in the Hittite example (3), initial verbs occur in a cluster, so as to define the description as a coherent unit.

2.1.2 *Accompanying circumstances*

Sometimes sentences with initial verbs in the imperfect (or pluperfect) convey backgrounded information about certain circumstances which hold at the time when an event takes place, as in (15d) and (16):

(15) #[a] ***Erat*** *inter* *Labienum* *atque* *hostis* *difficili*
there-was between L.-ACC and enemy-ACC hard-ABL

transitu *flumen* *ripis=* *que* *praeruptis* #[b] *Hoc*
to-cross river-NOM banks-ABL and steep-ABL this-ACC

neque *ipse* *transire* *habebat* *in* *animo* #[c] *neque*
neither himself to-cross he-had-IMPERF in mind neither

hostis *transituros* *existimabat* #[d] ***Augebatur***
enemies about-to-cros she-deemed-IMPERF it-increased-IMPERF

auxiliorum *cotidie* *spes* #[e] ***Loquitur*** *in concilio* *palam: ...*
of-auxiliaries daily hope-NOM he-says in council openly ...

'Having learnt the design of the enemy, and in the hope that their recklessness would afford some chance of engaging them, Labienus, leaving a guard of five cohorts for the baggage, ***sets*** off against the enemy with twenty-five cohorts and a large detachment of cavalry. He ***entrenches*** a camp at an interval of one mile.]
#[a] Between Labienus and the enemy **was** a steep-banked river, difficult to cross. #[b] He had no intention of crossing this himself, #[c] nor did he suppose that the enemy would cross it. #[d] Their hope for auxiliaries **was increasing** daily. #[e] Labienus **declares** openly in a council of war, that ...' [Caes. *Gal.* 6.7.]

Sentences (15 a-d) all introduce non-foregrounded information in the discourse. (15a) is a presentative sentence, which comes at a juncture in the narrative: the preceding paragraph reported a series of events (I have highlighted the foregrounded verbs using bold italics), and pictures the physical scene for the events to come. (15b, c) provide some clues to Labienus' thoughts, by which the reader/hearer will be able to understand why the following events took place. Sentence (15d) conveys information which is still additional with respect to what is said in (15b, c); the subject has changed, it is no longer Labienus, with whom the whole passage is concerned; rather, (15d) describes a general feeling of both Labienus and the troops. In (15e) the next chronologically ordered event is referred to in a foregrounding tense (the historical present), the same used to refer to the previously narrated events.

(16) ***Relinquebatur*** *una per Sequanos via,*
it-remained-IMPERF one through S. route-NOM

qua Sequanis invitis propter angustias
by-which S.-ABL unwilling-ABL because-of narrowness

ire non poterant
to-go not they could-IMPERF

'There remained only one other line of route, through the borders of the Sequani, by which they could not march, on account of the narrow ways, without the consent of the Sequani' [Caes. *Gal.* 1.9.]

This sentence is paragraph initial; it is preceded by two narrative paragraphs (§ 7-8); § 6 begins with a presentative sentence:

(17) ***Erant*** *omnino itinera duo, quibus*
there-were-IMPERF altogether routes two by-which

itineribus domo exire possent: unum
by-routes homeland -ABL to-leave they-could-IMPERF one-NOM

per Sequanos, ...: alterum per provinciam nostram
through S. other-NOM through province our

'**There were** two routes, and no more, by which they could leave their homeland, one through the territory of the Sequani, ... the other route, through the Roman Province', [Caes. *Gal.* 1.6.]

2.1.3 *Presentative sentences*

Presentative sentences most often have the verb *esse,* 'be', in initial position. This word order pattern achieves a double result: in the first place, the newly introduced material is placed in a position which is typical of focus constituents; beside, the initial verb brings about discontinuity in the discourse, and marks the sentence as non-narrative, thus calling more attention from the part of the reader/hearer.[21]

(18) *#[a] Provinciae toti quam maximum potest militum*
province-DAT all-DAT as much it-can of-soldiers

*numerum imperat #[b] (**erat** omnino in*
number-ACC he-orders there-was-IMPERF altogether in

Gallia ulteriore legio una) #[c] pontem
Gaul further legion-NOM one-NOM bridge-ACC

qui erat ad Genavam iubet rescindi
which-NOM it-was-IMPERF near Geneva he-orders to-be-cut off

'#[a] From the whole Province he [sc. Caesar] requisitions the largest possible number of troops #[b] (**there was** in Further Gaul no more than a single legion), #[c] and orders the bridge at Geneva to be broken down.' [Caes. *Gal.* 1.7.]

(19) *#[a] **Est** enim hoc Gallicae consuetudinis uti et*
is also this of-Gallic of-habit that both

viatores etiam invitos consistere cogant et ...
travellers-ACC also unwilling-ACC to-stay they-force and ...

['Caesar was informed of these events; and fearing the fickleness of the Gauls, because they are capricious in forming designs and intent for the most part on change, he considered that no trust should be reposed in them.] #[a] It **is** indeed a regular habit of the Gauls to compel travellers to halt, even against their will, and ...' [Caes. *Gal.* 4.5;]

Cf. also sentences (15a) and (17) in Section 2.1.2, and (20a), which I will discuss in Section 2.1.4.

2.1.4 *Foregrounded information*

Initial verbs in the preterite or in the historical present are found in sentences which convey foregrounded information; they often occur in clusters (as in 20d, e, g, i), and refer to rapidly developing events, strictly connected to each other in a single sequence. Typically, such sequences begin with an initial verb just after some non-foregrounded information has been introduced:

(20) #[a] ***Erat*** *aeger cum praesidio* ***relictus*** *P. Sextius*
had-been ill with garrison left P. S.-NOM

Baculus, qui primum pilum ad Caesarem duxerat,
B.-NOM who first javelin by Caesar he-had-driven

cuius mentionem superioribus proeliis fecimus,
whose mention-ACC former-ABL battles-ACC we-have-made

#[b] *ac diem iam quintum cibo caruerat.*
and day already fifth-ACC food he-had-missed

#[c] *Hic diffisus suae atque omnium saluti inermis*
he worrying his and of-all safety unarmed

ex tabernaculo prodit; #[d] ***videt*** *imminere hostis*
from tent he-comes-forth he-sees to-impend enemies

atque in summmo esse rem discrimine: #[e] ***capit***
and in high to-be situation danger he-seizes

arma a proximis #[f] *atque in porta consistit.*
weapons from closest-ones and in gate he-stands

#[g] ***Consequuntur*** *hunc centuriones eius cohortis*
they-follow-PRES this-ACC centurions of-that of-cohort

quae in statione erat: #[h] *paulisper una*
which on guard it-was-IMPERF shortly together

proelium sustinent. #[i] ***Relinquit*** *animus Sextium*
fight they-bear it-leaves consiousness-NOM S.-ACC

gravibus acceptis vulneribus: #[j] *aegre per manus*
severe-ABL received-ABL wounds-ABL hardly through hands

tractus servatur. #[k] *Hoc spatio interposito reliqui*
pulled-NOM he-is-saved this times elapsed others-NOM

sese	*confirmant*	*tantum*	*ut ...*
themselves	they-take-courage	so-much	as-to

'#[a] With the garrison **there had been left** behind, sick, Publius Sextus Baculus, who had been a soldier first under the command of Caesar and has been mentioned by us in previous battles. #[b] He had now been five days without food. #[c] Doubtful of his own and the general safety, he comes forth from his tent unarmed. #[d] He **sees** that the enemies are threatingly close and that the issue is in the greatest danger; #[e] he **takes** arms from the nearest men #[f] and stations himself in the gate. #[g] All the centurions of the cohort on guard **follow** him, #[h] and together for a short time they bear the brunt of the battle. #[i] Sextius **faints** after receiving severe wounds; #[j] with difficulty he is dragged from hand to hand into safety. #[k] In the respite thus given the others take courage so far as to ...' [Caes. *Gal.* 6.38.]

Sentences (20g, h) and (20i, j) refer to foregrounded events and follow the pattern VN-NV; VN-NV. This is a relatively frequent order for couplets of sentences, of which the second is viewed as the logical complement of the first (cf. Marouzeau 1938:71-72).

Sentence (20a) conveys backgrounded information about the circumstances in which the events take place; the predicate, *erat relictus*, 'he had been left behind', is in the pluperfect; note also the occurrence of the verb *relinquere*, 'to leave', as in (16). The separation of the two members of the compound predicate makes this sentence similar to a presentative construction, given the relief that the copula acquires by being placed in initial position. Elsewhere, compound verbs fronted for foregrounding follow a different pattern, as in

(21)	***Pugnatum est***	*ab*	*utrisque*	*acriter.*
	it-was-fought-PRET	by	both-sides	fiercely

'Both sides **fought** fiercely' [Caes. *Gal.* 4.26.]

Sentence (21) stands at the beginning of a paragraph. The action itself is given special relief also through the use of the impersonal passive, which is often the case with the verb *pugnare,* 'to fight'. The form *pugnatum est* is found elsewhere, too, in initial position, in sentences which begin the narration of a battle and follow a description of the conditions under which the battle was going to be fought (cf. Marouzeau 1938:78).

2.1.5 *Summary*

Initial verbs in Latin are found in the following cases:

a. in descriptions of places, examples (14b, c, d);
b. in descriptions of conditions holding at the time of a certain event, referred to later on in the discourse (i.e. accompanying circumstances). In this case, the initial verb is in the imperfect, examples (15d), (16);
c. in presentative sentences, examples (15a), (17), (18b), (19);
d. in sentences that refer to foregrounded events which are presented as taking place suddenly or unexpectedly. In this case, the initial verb is either in the perfect, or in the historical present, examples (20d, e, g, i).

In cases (a), (b), and (c), initial verbs are connected with non-foregrounded information; furthermore, (a) and (b) are similar, because both types of description provide the setting for the subsequent discourse.

2.2 *Initial verbs in Xenophon*

Greek is a free word order language. It is very hard to detect a basic, or more frequent, word order, although clearly a number of rules can be traced out, especially concerning enclitics and other types of particles, pronouns, and conjunctions. The relative order of nominal constituents and the position of the verb are pragmatically determined; the verb can be final, internal, or initial (Dover 1960). The data in the next sections are taken from Books 1 and 2 of Xenophon's *Anabasis.*

2.2.1 *Descriptions*

Topographic descriptions often contain several sentences with initial verbs, similar to Latin in example (14):

(22)

#[a]	*dià*	*mésou*	*dè*	*toû*	*paradeísou*	*rheî*	*ho*
	through	middle	PART	of-the	of-garden	it-flows	the

Maíandros; ...;	#[b]	***rheî***	*dè*	*kaì*	*dià*	*tê:s*	*Kelainô:n*
Maeander		it-flows	PART	also	through	the	of-Celaenians

póleo:s.	#[c]	***ésti***	*dè*	*kaì*	*megálou*	*basiléo:s*	*basíleia*
city		there-is	PART	also	of-great	of-king	palace

en	*Kelainaîs*	*erumnà*	*epì*	*taîs*	*pe:gaîs*	*toû*	*Marsoúou*
in	Celeanea	fortified	on	the	springs	of-the	of-Marsyas

potamoû hupò tê:i akropólei: #[d] ***rheî*** *dè kaì*
of-river under the acropolis it-flows PART also

hoûtos dià tê:s póleo:s
this through the city

'#[a] Through the middle of this park flows the Meander river; ...; #[b] it also **flows** through the city of Celaenae. #[c] **There is** likewise a palace of the Great king in Celaene, strongly fortified and situated at the foot of the Acropolis over the sources of the Marsyas river; #[d] the Marsyas, too, **flows** through the city' [X. *An.* 1.2.7-8.]

Frequently in descriptions of persons or places the copula is placed in initial position. This mostly happens in the imperfect, where the copula is accented (see also 26c):

(23) ***ê:n*** *dè hóte eteleúta amphì tà*
he-was-IMPERF PART when he-died-PRET around the

penté:konta éte:
fifty years

'he was about fifty years old at the time of his death' [X. *An.* 2.6.15].

2.2.2 *Imperfect and background*

The imperfect is the backgrounding tense *par excellence* in Classical Greek, among the finite forms of the verb (cf. Rijksbaron 1988):

(24) #[a] ***etheó:rei*** *oûn ho Kûros prô:ton mèn toùs*
he-inpected-IMPERF PART the Cyrus first PART the

barbárous #[b] *... eîta dè toùs Hélle:nas ...* #[c] ***eîkhon***
barbarians then PART the Greeks they-had

dè pántes kráne: khalkâ kaì khitô:nas phoinikoûs
PART all helmets bronze and tunics red

kaì kne:mîdas kaì tàs aspídas ekkekalumménas. #[d] *epeidè:*
and greaves and the shields uncovered when

dè pántas paré:lase, ... #[e] ***ekéleuse*** *probalésthai*
PART all-ACC he-drove-past-PRET he-ordered-PRET to-throw

tà hópla ...
the weapons

'#[a] Cyrus **inspected** the barbarians first, [and they marched past with their cavalry formed in troops, and their infantry in companies;] #[b] then [he inspected] the Greeks, [driving past them in a chariot, the Cilician queen in a carriage.] #[c] They (=the Greeks) all **had** helmets of bronze, crimson tunics, and greaves, and carried their shields uncovered. #[d] When he had driven past them all, [he halted his charriot in front of the center of the phalanx, and sending his interpreter Pigres to the generals of the Greeks,] #[e] **gave orders** that the troops should advance arms, [and the phalanx moved foreward in a body. The generals transmitted these orders to the soldiers, and when the trumpet sounded, they advanced arms and charged. And then, as they went on faster and faster, at length with a shout the troops broke into a run of their own accord, in the direction of the camp. As for the barbarians, they were terribly frightened; ...]' [X. *An.* 1.2.16-18.]

Here sentence (24a) describes a durative action; it gives information as to what Cyrus was doing when he gave orders to the Greeks (sentence (24e)) to start the unexpected action that frightened the Persian soldiers (referred to as 'the barbarians'). The whole action that starts with *ekéleuse* in (24e) is foregrounded; the verbs in the passage that follows are all in the preterite. So (24a) gives backgrounded information, along with (24c) that provides details about the outfit of the Greek soldiers.

2.2.2.1 *Background sentences with gár* Frequently, a sentence which constitutes a kind of parenthesis in the discourse contains the particle *gár*, a causal conjunction, which can occur in sentences that provide simple explanations, or detailed descriptions of a referent already mentioned, or examples; in such cases, *gár* has the function of confirming or strenghtening something which has just been said. It is usually translated as 'since', 'as', 'for'; note, however, that in Greek it never has the function of a subordinator (cf. Liddell and Scott, 1940:338).[22]

(25)

#[a] hoi	*dè*	*he:déo:s*	*epeíthonto:*	*#[b]* ***epísteuon***	
they	PART	gladly	they-obeyed-IMPERF	they-trusted-IMPERF	
gàr	*autô:i,*	*#[c] kaì*	*labóntes*	*tà*	*hópla*
PART	him	and	having-taken	the	weapons
parê:san		*eis*	*Sárdeis*		
they-set-off-IMPERF		to	Sardis		

[‘he urged the Milesian exiles to take the field with him, promising them that, if he should succesfully accomplish the object for which he was taking the field, he would not stop until he had restored them to their homes.] #[a] And they gladly obeyed #[b] — for they **trusted** him - #[c] and presented themselves, under arms, at Sardis’ [X. *An.* 1.2.2].

(26) #[a] *hápan dè tò méson tô:n teikhô:n*
all-ACC PART the middle-ACC of-the of-walls
ê:san stádioi treîs: #[b] *kaì pareltheîn ouk*
there-were-IMPERF stadia-NOM three and to-cross not
ê:n bía:i: #[c] ***ê:n*** *gàr he: párodos*
was-possible by-force it-was-IMPERF PART the pass
stenè: #[d] *kaì tà teíkhe: eis tè:n thálattan*
narrow and the walls-NOM to the sea
kathe:konta
they-reached-down-IMPERF

‘#[a] The entire distance between one wall and the other was three stadia; #[b] and it was not possible to effect a passage by force, #[c] for the pass **was** narrow #[d] and the walls reached down to the sea’ [X. *An.* 1.4.4].

(27) #[a] *kaì tô:n te Hellé:no:n hoì mè: étukhon*
and of-the and of-Greeks who-NOM not happened-PRET
en taîs táksesin óntes eis tàs tákseis étheon,
in the lines being to the lines they-ran-IMPERF
#[b] *kaì Ariaî:os* #[c] ***etúnkhane*** *gàr eph’*
and A.-NOM he-happened-IMPERF PART on
hamáxe:s poreuómenos dióti etétro:to
chariot travelling because he-had-been-wounded
#[d] *katabàs etho:rakízeto kaì hoi*
having-got-off he-armed-himself-IMPERF *and* those-NOM
sùn autô:i
with him

‘#[a] and such of the Greeks who chanced not to be in the lines proceeded to start to the lines, #[b] and Arieus #[c] (he happened to be making the journey on a wagon because he had been wounded) #[d] got down and put on his breastplate, and his attendants followed his example' [X. *An.* 2.2.14].

2.2.3 *Presentative sentences*

In presentative sentences the verb *eînai,* 'to be', elsewhere enclitic in the present tense, receives an accent and is shifted to initial position, as in (22b). Often, instead of *eînai,* presentative constructions contain the verb *éneinai,* 'to be there':

(28) #[a] *poreuómenoi dè aphíkonto eis kó:mas*
travelling PART they-reached-IMPERF to villages
hóthen apédeiksan hoi hegemónes lambánein tà
whence they-indicated-PRET the guides-NOM to-take the
epité:deia. #[b] ***enê:n*** *dè sîtos polùs kaì*
provisions-ACC there-was-IMPERF PART bread much and
oînos phoiníko:n
wine of-palms
'#[a] The march eventually was leading them to villages, where the guides directed them to get provisions. #[b] **There was** grain in abundance and palm wine' [X. *An.* 2.3.14].

2.2.4 *Foregrounded information*

Sentences which convey foregrounded information can have an initial verb in the aorist (= preterite):

(29) #[a] *boulómenos oûn epideîksai eksétasin* #[b] ***poieîtai*** *en*
willing PART to-show review-ACC he-makes in
tô:i pedío:i tô:n Hellé:no:n kaì tôn barbáro:n.
the plain of-the of-Greeks and of-the of-barbarians
#[c] ***ekéleuse*** *dè toùs Hélle:nas ho:s nómos*
he-ordered-PRET PART the-ACC Greeks-ACC as habit-NOM
autoîs eis mákhe:n hoúto: takhthê:nai... #[d] ***etákhthe:san***
to-them for battle so to-array they-arraid-PRET
oûn epì tettáro:n: #[e] ***eîkhe*** *dè tò mèn*
thus by four he-had-IMPERF PART the PART
deksiòn Méno:n kaì hoi sùn autô:i
right-ACC M.-NOM and those-NOM with him

'#[a] Such an exhibition was what he desired to make, #[b] and accordingly he **held** a review of the Greeks and the barbarians in the plain. #[c] He **ordered** the Greeks to form their lines just as they were accustomed to do for battle, ... #[d] So they **formed** their line four deep: #[e] Menon and his troops **occupied** the right wing, ...' [X. *An.* 1.2.14-15].

Sentences (29b, c) are foregrounded. Whereas (29b) begins the next sequence of events, in (29c) the initial verb resumes the content of the order referred to in (29b). This is a typical function of initial verbs in Classical Greek; see also sentences (30b) and (31). Initial verbs connect an event to the preceding one: this is precisely what Schwyzer (1940: 694) calls the 'connecting' (*anknüpfende*) function of initial verbs. (29d) is a descriptive sentence conveying backgrounded information with an initial imperfect.

(30) *#[a] kaì autoì ebouleúonto ei autoû meínantes tà*
and they decided-IMPERF if there remaining the

skeuophóra entaûtha ágointo è: apíoien
baggage there they-should-bring or they-should-go

epì tò stratópedon. #[b] ***édoksev*** *auto:îs*
to the camp it-seemed-good-PRET to-them

apiénai: #[c] kaì aphiknoûntai amphì dorpe:stòn epì
to-go and they-arrived-IMPERF around supper-time to

tàs skenàs #[d] taúte:s mèn tê:s he:méras toûto tò télos
the tents of-this PART of-the of-day this the end

egéneto. #[e] ***katalambánousi*** *dè tô:n te állo:n*
it-was-IMPERF they-find-on-arrival PART of-the and of-other

khre:máto:n tà pleîsta die:rpasména
of-properties the most plundered

'#[a] So they took counsel for themselves as to whether they should remain where they were and bring the bagagge train thither, or return to their camp. #[b] It **seemed best** to them to leave, #[c] and they reached their tents about supper time: #[d] such was the conclusion of this day. #[e] They **found** most of their property pillaged, ...' [X. *An.* 1.10.17-18].

(31) ***anabaínei*** *oûn* *ho* *Kûros* *labò:n* *Tissaphérne:n*
he-goes-up PART the Cyrus having-taken T.-ACC

ho:s *phílon* *kaì* *tô:n* *Hellé:no:n* *ékho:n* *hoplítas [anébe:]*
as friend-ACC and of-the of-Greek having hoplites-ACC

triakosíous
three-hundred

['Darius and Parysatis had two sons born to them, of whom the elder was Artaxerses and the younger Cyrus. Now when Darius lay sick and suspected that the end of his life was near, he wished to have both his sons with him. The elder, as it chanced, was with him already; but Cyrus he summoned from the province over which he had made him satrap, and he had also appointed him commander of all the forces that muster in the plain of Castolus.] So Cyrus **goes up**, taking with him Tissafernes as a friend and accompanied by three hundred Greek hoplites' [X. *An.* 1.1.1-2].

2.2.5 *Summary*

The occurences of initial verbs in Greek are found in the following contexts:

a. descriptions of places, examples (22b, c, d);
b. descriptions of accompanying circumstances. The tense used in such cases is the imperfect, examples (24a, c);
c. sentences that provide confirmatory information as to the validity of a statement, examples (25a), (26c), (27c);
d. presentative sentences, example (28a);
e. sentences which convey foregrounded information, in connection with the aorist or the historical present, examples (29b, d, i), (30b, e), (31).

The use of initial verbs in Greek matches the use of initial verbs in Latin in the case of sentences that contain descriptions of plces or accompanying circumstances and in presentative sentences; sentences under (c) appear to exploit initial verbs only in Greek, as far as one can judge from the corpus used here. As for sentences with initial verbs that convey foregrounded information, in Greek they seem to fulfill a textual function, rather than being used for encoding unexpected events, as they are in Latin.

3. Discussion

The languages examined in Sections 1 and 2 are very different from each other from the point of view of word order, especially with regard to the degree of freedom in the position of the verb. Moreover, the data that I have provided are from different periods. Hittite is attested exclusively in the second millennium B.C. (about 1750-1250); Greek is documented from the end of the second millennium onwards (Xenophon wrote in the fourth century B.C.), and Latin only from the fifth century B.C. (Caesar's works date to the first century B.C.). The first documents in a Germanic languages date back to the second century B.C., but the literary texts quoted here are all of a much later age. Among the other Indo-European languages, only Old Indic provides us with data that can reach out to the second millennium B.C.; Celtic is known from glosses of the Roman age, but again, literary compositions are more recent. Finally, the Slavonic languages are not documented before A.D. 600.

Delbrück (1900:38-40, 80-83) speaks of a habitual and an occasional word order for Proto-Indo-European, i.e. verb final and verb initial respectively. This reconstruction, which does not allow for a verb internal order, is supported in the first place by Hittite and Old Indic. In these two languages post-verbal constituents in SOVN sentences can only be appostional, so-called afterthought constituents (cf. Luraghi 1990a:106-107; Gonda 1959). The 'occasional' (verb initial) word order was used mainly for imperatives and verbs which bear contrastive focus (Luraghi 1990a:94-95, 102; Delbrück 1900:58-61). Although less frequent than the SOV pattern, the VSO pattern was widely used. In Celtic it became the basic word order; therefore it could not have been confined to imperatives and contrastive verbs in Proto-Indo-European.[23]

On account of its lower frequency, the verb initial order was in a certain sense 'abnormal'. By an iconic principle, it came to be used in cases where something abnormal was going on, either in the arrangement of the discourse, or in the course of the events reported.

A typical condition that triggers the use of an initial verb is a change in discourse type: initial verbs often occur where descriptions interrupt narratives. This is especially clear in Hittite, e.g. in (3). On the other hand, initial verbs are also found in cases where a sudden and important event needs to be referred to, thus being connected with foreground, especially after some additional information has been introduced in the discourse (cf. (15)). Beside marking sub-paragraphs of different text types, initial verbs also occur at the beginning of a new narrative paragraph, which refers to a new episode, regardless of what precedes them. In such a way, initial verbs indicate resumption of the narration after a strong break, thus reestablishing the communication process (cf. (8) and (21)).

In most Indo-European languages presentative and existential sentences with the verb 'to be' are verb initial. Besides Latin and Greek, massive evidence comes from Old Indic (Delbrück 1900:59), and we have numerous examples from the Germanic and the Slavonic (Berneker 1900) languages as well. Athough Hittite does not follow this pattern (cf. Luraghi 1990a:105-106), verb initial presentative sentences can safely be reconstructed for Proto-Indo-European as well. Presentative sentences provide new and focal material, and break the chronological order of narrative discourse by introducing new participants.[24]

Similar to presentative sentences are background sentences that convey information as to the accompanying circumstances of the events in the narrative (15d).

Background and initial verbs are also connected in sentences where the verbal aspect indicates a break in the chronological order: a certain action is presented as contemporary to another one which is given more attention and is consequently foregrounded (24a).

The latter two usages are more characteristic of Latin and Greek than of Hittite. It must be kept in mind that Latin and Greek have much more of a pragmatic word order than Hittite, Old Indic, and, presumably, Proto-Indo-European. In particular they also have a verb internal order, especially frequent in Greek. Initial verbs tend to be used for a greater variety of purposes, not only because of their higher frequency, but rather because of the greater freedom in positioning of the verb. The latter feature renders the opposition between initial and final verbs not so neat as in languages with a more rigid word order.

However, initial verbs still function as discourse organizers. A sequence of initial verbs defines a coherent text sub-unit: this is why initial verbs often cluster together. We have seen this pattern, or some similar ones with systematic VN-NV alternations, in several examples, e.g. (20g-l) and cf. the quotation from Hopper (1979) in Section 1.3; Berneker (1900) also reports it from the Ancient Slavonic languages. Already in Hittite clusters of initial verbs occur in descriptions; this is also true of occurrences such as Latin (14). Note however that initial verbs in this passage do not fulfill the function of interrupting the narrative, which is interrupted by sentence (14a), where the verb is not initial. Rather, the cluster of initial verbs provides unity to the passage in which it appears.

In the course of time many of the Indo-European languages shifted away, to different extents, from the original SOV word order. As they developed an elaborate literary style, the alternation between initial and non-initial verbs acquired wider possibilities of usage for stylistic purposes; also then, the way in which initial verbs are used directly derives from their initial function of marking some sort of discontinuity in discourse.

4. Conclusions

In my paper I have discussed the discourse function of sentences with initial verbs in some of the ancient Indo-European languages. I have argued that sentences with initial verbs constituted a regular variant of the SOV word order, and that, on account of their lower frequency, they acquired an adversative force, thus indicating unexpectedness. Since initial verbs called for closer attention, they were used as discourse organizers in places where some degree of discontinuity in discourse needed to be emphasized. Initial verbs typically occurred at junctures in the discourse, and indicated a shift in style (e.g. descriptive vs. narrative). For this reason initial verbs could be associated with either background or foreground. Such use of verb initial sentences is found in the oldest attested Indo-European language, Hittite, and other languages as well, though having modified some rules or tendencies of word order, provide massive evidence that it existed in Proto-Indo-European already. A more varied use of initial verbs, including different types of stylistic effects, developed later on, along with the development of elaborate literary traditions, and the appearance of possible verb internal variants of word order.

Notes

1. Cf. Greenberg (1963: 110) on the rigid SOV sub-type. Some ancient Indo-European languages, such as Old Indic (Gonda 1959) and Hittite (Luraghi 1990a: 73-75), do in fact meet the requirement set by Greenberg for rigid SOV languages that no nominal constituents can ever follow the verb (in sentences in which the verb is not initial); however, they still have VSO as a possible alternative.

2. On the existence of a VSO variant in Indo-European, see Delbrück (1900:), who calls it the 'occasional' word order, as opposed to the SOV variant, the 'habitual' word order. On the Indo-European origin of VSO as the basic order in Insular Celtic, see Watkins (1963.).

3. This is not only true in languages such as English, where the subject, omitted with the imperative, is normally the only preverbal NP, but also in languages which allow the object NP to be preverbal, cf. the following Latin examples: *da mi basia mille*, 'give (*da* , imperative) me a thousand kisses' [Catul. 5.7], and *tibi in cunis oscula prima dedi*, 'I gave (*dedi*, preterit) you the first kisses in your cradle' [Ov. *Pont.* 2.3.72].

4. "Oft nämlich steht das Verbum in offenem oder latentem Gegensatz zu einem anderen Begriff (meist natürlich einem Verbum) und tritt deshalb in A(nfang) St(ellung) ... Diese Fälle scheiden für unsere Betrachtung aus, da sie eine auch bei andere Wortarten übliche Durchbrechung der habituellen Stellung enthalten, ...".

5. All citations of Greek and Latin authors are taken from the Oxford edition; the English translations are usually taken from the Loeb edition, with minor changes that I have made in order to make the literal meaning more clear. I have not always given a complete morphemic analysis of each form in the glosses; rather, I limited myself to what I found strictly necessary for the understanding of the examples. In particular, verb forms are consistently translated with the corresponding English tense, so the present with the present, the perfect with the present perfect, the pluperfect with the past perfect; only for the imperfect and the preterite, both translated with the simple past, I have added a grammatical gloss.

6. I refer to the initial word rather than to the initial constituent, because initial position in the Ancient Indo-European languages is defined, among other things, by Wackernagel's Law, according to which all enclitics in a sentence are attached to its first accented word; see below.

7. Comparative reconstruction has proved that connectives were important elements for the structure of the simple sentence in Proto-Indo-European; see Watkins (1964). Connectives could be accented of enclitic; they fulfilled the function of marking the left boundary of a sentence. Initial words occurred either in sentences without connectives, or in sentences with an enclitic connective. In the former case, the sentence started without an overt marker of its left boundary, and the initial word was given special emphasis. In the latter case, the initial word was *followed* by the sentence boundary (marked by the enclitic connective); one can regard initial words in such sentences as being left-dislocated. In Luraghi (1990a) I have shown that, in Old Hittite, sentences with initial words (i.e., sentences that did not contain an accented connective in initial position) were not only used in order to indicate a special pragmatic status of the word in initial position. Rather, the whole sentence type could fulfill a number of specific discourse functions. This was especially true of sentences with initial verbs, which were rather infrequent, on account of the strict SOV order of Old Hittite. Since there is evidence that the Old Hittite data partly reflect the syntax of Proto-Indo-European, at least as long as the existence of a VSO sentence type is concerned, in this paper I am going to survey the occurences of initial verbs in a number of Ancient Indo-European sentences, in which the position of the verb was less constrained than in Hittite.

8. I have left out all philological considerations from the Hittite examples, which implies that I have not quoted restorations from different duplicates of the same text, for which the interested reader is referred to the editions.

9. On *nu* see Luraghi (1990a: 49-50).

10. They are viewed as a forked action in the sense of Grimes (1975:42).

11. Cf. Hopper (1975: 27-30) and Enkvist and Warvik (1987). In Hopper (1979), Hopper has shown that foregrounding and discourse continuity are most often found in SOV sentences with sentence connectives in Old English.

12. Hopper (1975, 1987) has more examples of this type.

13. Cf. above, Section 1.2, on Hittite.

14. Grimes (1975:51-70) contains an extensive discussion of what type of sentences encode non-events, and therefore cannot convey foregrounded information.

15. See below, Section 1.5 on the text types from which the examples are taken.

16. "hier enthält die *cum*-Satz den Haupgedanken und bezeichnet meist den Eintritt einer plötzlichen oder unerwarteten Handlung ... Das Tempus ist in der Regel das hist. Perf. oder Praes., ... Im Hauptsatz steht meist ein duratives Tempus (Impf. oder Plqpf.)".

17. "Es ist doch natürlich kein Zufall, dass bei diesem Satztyp in den meisten Fällen gerade der erste Satz, der formale Hauptsatz, einen ausgesprochenen Zustand schildert. ... Die Struktur der Perioden mit *cum* inversumist immer die gleiche: Ein Zustand, in den ein Ereignis hineinplatzt. Da aber das Ereignis immer interessanter ist als der Zustand, den es unterbricht, so lenkt es immer die Aufmerksamkeit auf sich und von dem Zustand ... Hendlung ab".

18. "Anfangsstellung des Verbums findet sich ... häufig ... indem das den Fortschritt der Handlung anzeigende Verbum an den Anfang des Hauptsatzes tritt".

19. I have not taken into account any cases of a main clause preceded by a preposed subordinate clause, since I have considered subordinate clauses in the same way as other types of sentence constituents.

20. Verb final sentences in Caesar's works are 84% of total in main clauses and 93% in subordinate clauses (Linde 1923:154). On pragmatic word order in Caesar, see Panhuis (1982:117-149).

21. It can be claimed that VS word order in presentative constructions is chosen because the subject is focus. However, I would rather say that in SOV languages the VS pattern is used in order to bring about discontinuity, since there is evidence that the contrary happens in VSO languages. Givón (1984: 209) points out that Biblical Hebrew (VSO) has SV in existential sentences with 'to be', which he calls "the discontinuous order".

22. Other factors can intervene and trigger the choice of perfective aspect (e.g. the aspectual context) in sentences similar to the ones quoted below, although less frequently; an example is to be found in X. *An.* 2.1.10, *étukhe gàr thuómenos* , 'for he was performing (pret.) a sacrifice'.

23. See Watkins (1963) on the Indo-European origin of the Old Irish basic word order.

24. In presentative sentences the verb initial order can also be conceived as due to the tendency of indefinite subjects to come toward the end of the sentence; see however note 20.

References

Berneker, Erich K. 1900. *Die Wortfolge in den slavischen Sprachen*. Berlin: Behr.

Boley, Jacqueline. 1985. "Notes on Hittite place word syntax." *Hethitica* 6. 5-43.

Delbrück, Berthold. 1900. *Vergleichende Syntax der indogermanischen Sprache*, vol. 3. Strassburg: Trübner.

Dover, Kenneth J. 1960. *Greek Word Order*. Cambridge: Cambridge University Press.

Enkvist, Nils and Brita Warvik. 1987. "Old English *pa*, temporal chains, and narrative structure." *Papers from the 7th International Conference on Historical Linguistics* ed by G. Ramat, et al., 221-237. Amsterdam/Piladelphia: John Benjamins.

Givón, T. 1984. *Syntax. A Functional Typological Approach*, vol. 1. Amsterdam/Philadelphia: John Benjamins.

Givón, T. 1987. "Beyond foreground and background." *Coherence and Grounding in Discourse* ed. by Russell S. Tomlin, 175-188. Amsterdam/Piladelphia: John Benjamins.

Gonda, Jan. 1959. *Four Studies in the Language of the Veda*. The Hague: Mouton.

Greenberg, Joseph. 1963. "Some universals of grammar with particular reference to the order of meaningful elements." *Universals of Language* ed. by J. Greenberg, 58-90. Cambridge, Mass.: MIT Press.

Grimes, John E. 1975. *The Thread of Discourse*. The Hague: Mouton.

Halliday, M. A. K. and Ruqaiya Hasan. 1976. *Cohesion in English*. London: Longman.

Hopper, Paul J. 1975. *The Syntax of the Simple Sentence in Proto-Germanic*. The Hague: Mouton.

Hopper, Paul J. 1979. "Aspect and foregrounding in discourse." *Discourse and Syntax* ed. by T. Givón, 213-42 New York: Academic Press. [*Syntax and Semantics* 12]

Hopper, Paul J. 1987. "Stability and change in VN/NV alternating languages. A study in pragmatics and linguistic typology." *The Pragmatic Perspective* ed. by J. Verschueren and M. Bertuccelli-Papi, 455-76. Amsterdam/Philadelphia: John Benjamins.

Justus, Carol. 1976. "Relativization and topicalization in Hittite." *Subject and Topic* ed. by Charles N. Li, 213-460. New York: Academic Press.

Kroll, Wilhelm. 1918. "Anfangsstellung des Verbums im Lateinischen." *Glotta* 9. 112-122.

Labov, William. 1972. "The transformation of experience in narrative syntax." *Language in the Inner City: Studies in the Black English Vernacular* ed. by W. Labov, 354-96. Philadelphia: University of Pennsylvania Press.

Leumann, Manu, Johannes Hoffmann, and Anton Szantyr. 1965. *Lateinische Grammatik*, vol. 2, *Lateinische Syntax und Stylistik*. München: Beck.

Liddel, H. G. and R. Scott. 1940. *A Greek-English Lexicon,* 9th ed. Oxford: Claredon Press.

Linde, Paul. 1923. "Die Stellung des Verbums in der lateinischen Prosa." *Glotta* 12. 153-178.

Luraghi, Silvia. 1987. "Studi di sintassi ittita." Pavia, Ph.D. Diss.

Luraghi, Silvia. 1990a. *Old Hittite Sentence Structure*. London-New York: Routledge.

Luraghi, Silvia. 1990b. "Note sulla Legge di Wackernagel e la posizione del verbo in alcune lingue indoeuropee." *Dimensioni della linguistica* ed. by P. Ramat, A. Giacalone Ramat e M. E. Conte, 31-60. Milano: Franco Angeli.

Marouzeau, Jules. 1938. *L'ordre des mots dans la phrase latine,* vol. 2, *Le verbe.* Paris: Les Belles Lettres.

Nehring, O. 1930. "Studien zur Theorie des Nebensatzes." *Zeitung für vergleichende Sprachforschung* 57. 118-58.

Panhuis, Dirk. G.J. 1982. *The Communicative Perspective in the Sentence: A study of Latin word order.* Amsterdam: John Benjamins.

Rijksbaron, Albert. 1988. "The discourse function of the imperfect." *In the Footsteps of Raphael Kühner* ed. by A. Rijksbaron, H. Mulder, and G. Wakker, 237-54. Amsterdam: Gieben.

Schwyzer, Eduard. 1940. *Griechische Grammatik,* vol. 2, *Syntax und syntaktische Stilistik.* München: Beck.

Thompson, Sandra. 1978. "Modern English from a typological point of view. Some implications of the function of word order." *Linguistische Berichte* 54. 19-35.

Watkins, Calvert. 1963. "Preliminaries to a historical and comparative analysis of the syntax of the Old Irish verb." *Celtica* 6. 1-49.

Watkins, Calvert. 1964. "Preliminaries to the reconstruction of the Indo-European sentence structure." *Proceedings of the 11th International Congress of Linguists,* 1035-1045. The Hague: Mouton.

Morphological and prosodic forces shaping word order

Marianne Mithun
University of California, Santa Barbara

0. Introduction

We know that languages differ in their word order. They vary both in their basic orders and in the relative importance of syntactic and pragmatic factors underlying their occurring patterns. Yet we still know relatively little about why different orders occur.

One obvious motivation behind the development of certain orders is a cognitive tendency to proceed from the known to the unknown. As formulated by members of the Prague School, the normal order of elements in the sentence is theme–rheme.

> The theme is that part of the utterance which refers to a fact or facts already known from the preceding context, or to facts that may be taken for granted, and thus does not, or does only minimally, contribute to the information provided by the given sentence-utterance. The other part, now usually called the rheme, contains the actual new information to be conveyed by the sentence-utterance and thus substantially enriches the knowledge of the listener or reader . . . The theme invariably precedes the rheme. This, of course, is in full agreement with the general laws of the psychology of learning: new elements of information can be successfully acquired only if they are organically incorporated into the network of elements known from before. (Vachek 1966: 89-90).

The grammatical category most closely corresponding to the theme or mental starting point of a sentence is the subject. As would be predicted, subjects precede objects in the majority of the world's languages: SOV, SVO, and VSO orders are much more common than OVS, OSV, and VOS.

Yet theme–rheme order is by no means universal. A number of languages show exactly the opposite pattern: constituents appear in decreasing order of newsworthiness. Clearly other factors must shape word order as well. One way to identify these factors is to examine the circumstances surrounding shifts in word order patterns over time.

A good opportunity for such investigation is provided by the Siouan, Caddoan, and Iroquoian languages of North America. These three groups are remotely related genetically (Allen 1931; Chafe 1964, 1976a), so their word order patterns have all developed from the same ancestral system. The modern languages still share a number of structural features that might be expected to affect word ordering strategies: all of them contain pronominal prefixes within their verbs; the pronominal prefixes show agent/patient case organization; all lack equivalents of the independent unstressed pronouns of English; all exhibit noun incorporation. Yet they differ substantially in their word orders. In what follows, it will be shown how patterns already present in their common ancestor evolved into the divergent systems of the modern languages, stimulated by individual morphological innovations and shaped by natural prosodic tendencies.

1. The Siouan languages

The Siouan languages share a number of typological characteristics that might be expected to affect constituent order. Among these are pronominal prefixes based on an agent/patient case distinction, the lack of unstressed independent pronouns, noun incorporation, and constructions involving left- and right-detached nominals.

1.1 *Basic typological features*

In the modern Siouan languages, first person, second person, and inclusive core arguments are expressed by pronominal prefixes on verbs. The pronouns show an agent/ patient case distinction. In the Lakhota paradigm in (1), the pronouns in the verbs on the left represent grammatical agents, participants who actively instigate events. Those on the right represent grammatical patients.

(1) Pronominal prefixes: Lakhota (Stanley Redbird p.c.)

wa-*lówą*	'**I** sang'	***ma***-*hį́xpaye*	'**I** fell'
ya-*lówą*	'**you** sang'	***ni***-*hį́xpaye*	'**you** fell'
u-*lówą*	'**you and I** sang'	***u***-*hį́xpaye*	'**you and I** fell'
lową́	'(he/she/it) sang'	*hixpye*	'(he/she/it) fell'
wa-*ktékte*	'**I**'ll kill (him/her/it)'	***ma***-*ktékte*	'(he/she/it)will kill **me**'

ma-***yá***-*ktekte* '**you**'ll kill **me**'

Number is marked elsewhere in the verbal morphology. There are essentially no third person prefixes; third persons are represented by full noun phrases, separate demonstratives, or by nothing at all. Third persons tend to be identified overtly only when there is change in point of view or possible confusion. There are no third person markers in (2), for example, because the identity of each participant is clear from context. A man had abducted a young woman, then ordered her to delouse him.

(2) Zero anaphora in Lakhota (Deloria 1932:47.14)

č^{h}*ąké*	*wastélašni į́*	*alóslos*	*hįglé*	*č'éyas*	*k*^{h}*ąyé*
so	despise with	repulsed	sudden	but	in.front

'[She] hated [him] so much that [her] whole body cringed but [he] lay down before [her]

hi-yų́ka	*č*^{h}*a*
come-lie	so

wanná	*heyókiẋile*	*ną*	*yuíštįma*	*ke'*^{e}.
now	louse.for.hunt	and	make.eye.close	HEARSAY

so [she] began to hunt lice for [him] and induced [him] to sleep.'

The Siouan languages also contain a kind of noun incorporation, whereby noun roots are compounded with verb roots to yield verb stems, usually with more specific meanings. Examples of such compounds can be seen in (3).

(3) Noun incorporation: Lakhota compounds (Stanley Redbird p.c.)

wa-*ká-žipa*	'**arrow**-by.striking-smooth' =	'(he) whittles arrowshafts'
č^{h}***al***-*wą́ka*	'**heart**-be.brittle' =	'(he) is a coward'

Basic word order is clearly SOV.

(4) Basic SOV word order: Lakhota (Deloria 1932:65.10)

		S	**O**	**V**
yųká	*hehál*	*wį́yą k'ų*	*wógnaka wą*	*gluškį́.*
and.then	next	woman the.PAST	sack a	own.untied

'And then the woman untied her bag.'

As would be expected of an SOV language, complements systematically precede main predicates.

(5) Complement-V Lakhota (Deloria 1932:77.2)

	COMPLEMENT		**V**	
yųkʰą́	*óp*	*yį́kta*	*kéyá*	*ke'ᵉ.*
and.then	with.them	go.will	say	HEARSAY

'He decided to join them.'

On occasion, different word orders occur. Nominals sometimes appear to the left of the nuclear clause. They are typically spoken in a louder, often higher tone of voice, sometimes slightly detached intonationally from the nuclear clause. Additional material may intervene between the nominal and the nuclear clause. A coreferent element, such as a demonstrative, may appear within the nuclear clause. These left-detached nominals usually highlight a focus of contrast or shift from one topic to another. The sentence in (6) comes from a tale in which Iktomi had pretended to sicken and die. When his family looked into the tent where he had been lying, they found only bones, which they took to be his. In fact the bones were not his at all, and this contrast with expectation is highlighted by the left-detachment of the object nominal.

(6) Lakhota left-detachment for focus of contrast (Deloria 1932: 14.20)

	O			S	V	
Leya	**hená**	**sųxpála-huhù**	*čʰa*	*Iktómi*	*tąyéla*	*yasmí.*
actually	**those**	**puppy-bone**	*such*		*well*	*meat.ate.off*

'Actually ***it was the puppy bones*** that Iktomi had eaten all the meat off of.'

Nominals can also appear to the right of the nuclear clause. Right-detached nominals, termed 'antitopics' by Chafe (1976b), typically confirm expected or accessible information, as in the epithet in (7). The separation of the detached nominal 'the idiot' from the nuclear clause can be seen in the confirmatory enclitic =*lo*, added by male speakers to the end of statements.

(7) Lakhota right-detachment to reidentify accessible referents (Deloria 1932:22.19)

V S
Wičákʰe séce=**lo**, **witkó kį.**
be.right perhaps=**m** **fool the**
'The idiot might just happen to be talking sense.'

Right-detached nominals sometimes occur as well when action shifts rapidly back and forth between participants, as in dialogue. Both participants remain active discourse topics throughout the interchange, so they do not need to be reintroduced or recalled to consciousness with each new action or utterance. The right-detached nominals simply confirm matches between the participants and their actions. Although both subjects and objects may appear to the right of the verb, subjects tend to appear more frequently than objects in this position because highly topical arguments are more often cast as subjects than objects.

In Lakhota, as in most spontaneous spoken language, the incidence of full sentences containing both a subject nominal and an object nominal is actually relatively low. A sample count of 500 clauses of Lakhota spoken narrative showed only 21 clauses (4.2%) containing both subject and object constituents. This low proportion is the result of several factors. The two features described above, the absence of independent pronouns and noun incorporation, have some effect. Various strategies for controlling the flow of information are even more important. Usually only one significant new idea is introduced at a time, as in most spoken language (Givón 1975; Du Bois 1985; Chafe 1987; Lambrecht 1987; and others). If a speaker wishes to discuss both a new entity and a newsworthy action, these two pieces of information are usually introduced in separate prosodic phrases or intonation units, that is, phrases uttered under a single intonational and contour, sometimes bounded by pauses. The passage in (8) below, for example, could have been rendered by a single sentence grammatically: 'We Lakhotas held a powwow in memory of Martha St. John's late husband'. The Lakhota speaker, however, presented each major new piece of information in a separate intonation unit, shown here by separate lines of transcription.

(8) Information flow in Lakhota: one new idea at a time (Stanley Redbird p.c.)

O V
a. *wačʰí-piwą ų-káɣa-pi.*
dance-NOM a 1-make-PL
'We had a powwow.

S O V
b. *lakʰóta ikčéya=ča hé wačʰí-piwą ų-káɣa-pi.*
Indian common=REL that dance-NOM a 1-make-PL
We were just ordinary Indians that made the powwow.

c. *Martha St. John ečíya-pi wą*
say.to-PL a
A woman they call Martha St. John

S V
d. *hignį́-ku kį t'a=čʰá,*
husband-her the die=so
her husband died so

e. *hé yuʔónihą kel,*
that to.honor in.a.way
in honor of that

O V
f. *wačʰí-pi he ų-káɣa-pi.*
dance-NOM that 1-make-PL
we held that powwow.'

'We Lakhotas held a powwow in memory of Martha St. John's late husband.'

Several kinds of strategies are used systematically to regulate the flow of information, many of which can be seen here. When an important new entity is introduced, it is presented with a verb of low semantic content, such as 'appear', 'be', 'take', or the 'do' in (8)a. Often complexity is built up piece by piece: a simple statement, like that in (8)a here, is followed by successive elaborations, each introducing additional information, as in line (8)b here. Often demonstratives stand in as place holders in one intonation unit, like *hé* in (8)e here, for referents more fully described in preceding or following intonation units, as in (8)c and d here.

Table 1. Lakhota word order

		Clauses	% of clauses with S/O/C	% of all clauses
Subjects	SV	128	98.5%	25.6%
	VS	*2*	*1.5%*	*0.4%*
	TOTAL	130	100.0%	26.0%
Objects	OV	105	100.0%	21.0%
	VO	*0*	*0.0%*	*0.0%*
	TOTAL	105	100.0%	21.0%
Comps	CV	53	100.0%	17.7%
	VC	*0*	*0.0%*	*0.0%*
	TOTAL	53	100.0%	17.7%
Non-SOV		2	**0.9%**	0.4%

Because of the low proportion of full S-O-V clauses, an examination of word order should not be restricted to clauses with both subject and object nominals. More typical clauses, those that contain only a subject nominal or only an object, should be considered as well. In Lakhota, word order deviates surprising little in either type of clause from a basic SOV, as can be seen in Table 1. In the Lakhota sample, only 0.9% of those clauses with overt arguments (subject, object, or complement) deviated from SOV order.

Strikingly similar patterns appear in comparable material from other branches of the Siouan family. Text counts show a departure from SOV order in only 1.8% of clauses with arguments in a Crow narrative sample from Lowie 1960, and 0.8% in a Mandan sample from Kennard 1936. Narrative material available from Winnebago shows no deviation from SOV order, but Lipkind notes in his grammatical sketch: 'The normal order of words in the sentence is subject, indirect object, object, verb. The verb is generally the final element in the sentence. Occasionally the subject is put last for emphasis but the object almost invariably precedes the verb.' (1945: 56) The similarity of these patterns in most branches of the family indicates that basic word order in Proto-Siouan was SOV.

1.2 *Increased flexibility: Omaha*

Yet not all modern Siouan languages exhibit the same rigidity in word order. Languages of the Dhegiha branch of the family, Omaha, Ponca, Kansa Osage, and Quapaw, show a somewhat different pattern. The Dhegiha languages do share the typological features of Siouan that might be expected to affect word order. There are pronominal prefixes for first, second, and inclusive persons, with an agent/patient case distinction. Third persons need not be overtly specified. There is noun incorporation. Similar strategies are used for controlling the flow of information in these languages as in the other Siouan languages, so that significant new pieces of information are typically introduced in separate intonation units. As in Lakhota, basic constituent order is SOV.

(9) Omaha (Dorsey 1890:154.16-17)

S **O** **V**
Nú amá hi^{n}qpé g¢íza-bi.
man the (MV.SUB.) fine feather took his-they say
'The man took his fine feather.'

Nominals may appear outside of the nuclear clause with the same functions as in Lakhota. Those highlighting a shift in topic or focus of contrast may appear to the left of the nuclear clause, like 'the strong cord' in (10) below. Those reiterating known or accessible information may appear to the right, as in (10) and (11).

(10) Omaha left detached object, right-detached subject (Dorsey 1890:155.8)

O V
Ga^{n}´ hájiñga áwanji ke é ¢izá-biamá
And cord strong the (OBJ) that took-they say
S
nú aká.
man the (SUBJ)
'And **the man** took that strong cord, they say.'

(11) Omaha right-detached object (Dorsey 1890:155.10-11)

S V **O**
itan´ de bisá-biamá ***hájiñga***.
her daughter's husband broke-they say **cord**
'Her daughter's husband broke **the cord**, they say.'

There is morphological evidence here, as in the Lakhota examples, that the detached nominals are outside of the nuclear clause. The clause-final hearsay evidential enclitic *biamá* closes off the nuclear clauses.

Although the Omaha structures that deviate from basic SOV order are similar in function to those in Lakhota and other Siouan languages, they are more frequent. Of the 10 clauses in the sample with both subject and object nominals, 6 (60%) show SOV order, but 4 (40%) show OVS. As in Lakhota, the proportion of full S-O-V clauses is low: in a 300 clause sample of Omaha narrative, 10 clauses (3.3%) contain both subject and object nominals, so any examination of word order should include clauses with only one nominal. Relative ordering within all subject-verb, object-verb, and complement-verb constituent pairs can be seen in Table 2.

In the Omaha sample, order departs from basic SOV in 20.4% of those clauses containing a verb plus at least one other major constituent (subject, object, or complement), considerably more often than the 0.9% of Lakhota.

The greater exploitation of word order for pragmatic purposes can be seen in the Omaha passage in (12). The nominal introducing the Omahas at the beginning of the account appears clause-initially, but each time the Omahas are subsequently mentioned, it is postverbally, since they are accessible information (lines b, f). After we are told about the Omaha preparations for war, our attention is shifted to the Pawnees, who are first introduced with a left-detached nominal (line c). Once introduced, they are subsequently reidentified postverbally (h, i). (Spaced periods . . . indicate ellipsis of material.)

Table 2. Omaha word order

		Clauses	% of clauses with S/O/C	% of all clauses
Subjects	SV	62	71.3%	20.7%
	VS	*25*	*28.7%*	*8.3%*
	TOTAL	87	100.0%	29.0%
Objects	OV	52	85.2%	17.3%
	VO	*9*	*14.8%*	*3.0%*
	TOTAL	61	100.0%	20.3%
Comps	CV	29	100.0%	9.7%
	VC	*0*	*0.0%*	*0.0%*
	TOTAL	29	100.0%	9.7%
Non-SOV		34	**20.4%**	11.3%

(12) Omaha (Dorsey 1890:402-3)

	S	V		
a.	*Uma^n'ha^n amá*	*nuda^n'*	*a¢á-biamá*	*wañ'gi¢e.*
	Omahas the (SUBJ)	to war	went, they say	all

'All of the Omahas went on the warpath . . .

	V	S	S
b.	*Atí-biamá*	*áhigi amá*	*(Uma^n'ha^n amá).*
	Came, they say	many the (SUBJ)	Omahas the

The main body (of Omahas) came . . .

			O
c.	*wapé*	*g¢íze-ma*	*Pá¢i^n-má*
	weapon	those who took theirs	the Pawnee
	ja^n't'e-má	*cti,*	
	those sound asleep	too,	

'They killed some of the Pawnees as they were seizing their

		V
d.	*ca^n'ca^n*	*wáq¢i-biamá.*
	without stopping	they killed them they say

weapons, and the others who were still sound asleep . . .

			O	V	S
e.	*Edíhi*	*ki,*	*wapé*	*g¢ízai te*	*Pá¢i^n amá.*
	they arrived there	when	weapon	took their	Pawnees the (SUBJ)

At that time, the Pawnees seized their weapons;

			V
f.	*Edíhi*	*ki,*	*t'éwac/e-hna^n'i*
	At that time	when,	they killed them regularly
	O		
	Uma^n'ha^n-ma.		
	the Omahas (OBJ).		

and then they killed the Omahas.

g.	*Djúba*	*umúcte*	*ahíi*	*te,*
	A few	remained from shooting	they arrived	when,

When a few of the Pawnees who remained after the shooting arrived,

	V	S
h.	*waji^n´-píbaji*	*Pá¢i^n-ma.*
	in a bad humor	the Pawnees

they were in a desperate mood. [Those on each side killed many.]

	O		V	S
i.	*Cá¢ewá¢e*	*égi¢e*	*t'é¢a-biamá,*	*Pá¢i^{n}amá.*
	Ca¢ewa¢e	at length	killed (him) they say,	Pawnees the(SUBJ)

At length the Pawnees killed Caewae.'

Why does Omaha differ from Lakhota, Crow, Mandan, and Winnebago in this way? An innovation elsewhere in the grammar accompanied the increased use of word order for pragmatic purposes. Languages of the Dhegiha branch have developed a set of definite articles, many from demonstratives that originated as positional verbs. The articles distinguish arguments according to their animacy, number, shape, and position or movement. Several of the articles that appear with animate arguments distinguish case as well. The articles are optional, but their value in disambiguating reference to animate arguments can be seen in (12). The particle *amá* is used with the animate plural agents, while the suffix *-ma* appears with the animate plural patients.

The independent development of case in another branch of the family has affected word order in a similar way. Biloxi, a now extinct language of the Southeastern branch of Siouan, has also developed articles that serve in some contexts to disambiguate case roles. Basic word order is clearly SOV, the order that appears systematically in sentences elicited by Dorsey (Einaudi 1976: 168). Narrative texts in Dorsey and Swanton (1912), however, show a fluidity in ordering not unlike that in Omaha.

2. Caddoan

The Caddoan languages share a number of typological features with the Siouan languages. First person, second person, and inclusive core arguments are specified by verbal prefixes. Agent and patient case are distinguished. There are no pronominal prefixes for basic third persons. Number is marked elsewhere in the morphology. There is noun incorporation. Significant information is typically introduced one idea at a time.

Such structure can be seen in in the Caddo passage in (13) from a narrative told by Mrs. Sadie Bedoka Weller and recorded by Chafe (1977). Instead of opening a tale with a sentence like 'A woman and her husband took a trip', she introduced each important new idea, the woman, her husband, and the trip, in a separate intonation unit.

(13) Caddo information flow (Chafe 1977:37.1-3)

wísc'i?	*náttih*	*háh?í:?a?.*
one	woman	was there.

'A woman lived there.

háyá:nuh	*háhúnt'a?.*
person	had

She had a husband.

síttutáyyakíhnáh	*bah?nah*	*háhwíswá:yah.*
Sometime later	it is said	two journeyed.

Sometime later, it is said, they two took a trip.'

'A woman and her husband took a trip.'

As in the Siouan languages, basic word order in Caddoan could be described as verb final: the majority of subject and object nominals appear before their predicates, as in the Caddo passage in (14).

(14) Caddo (Chafe 1977:29.11-3)

	S				**V**
bah?nah	*ná*	*sah wadu?,*	*ukkih*	*bah?náh*	*háh?áwsa?.*
It is said	that one	Ms. Wildcat	really	it is said	was sitting.

O	**V**
hacihdi?	*háhna:wida:wí:?íh?isa?.*
baby	(she) is pushing in a cradle-hammock.

This order is not rigid. When a deer was first introduced in one Caddo tale, he was identified by a preverbal subject nominal (SV). Two lines later, the same deer, now an established participant, was reidentified with a postverbal nominal (VS).

(15) Caddo subjects: SV and VS (Chafe 1977:30.20-2)

		S	V
bahnah	*nátti?*	*dâ:titi?*	*hákahyâ:ni?a?.*
'It is said	there	little deer	(he) was lying in the brush

(Mr. Turkey was watching.)

		V	S	
bah?nah	*kúsidí,*	*awasá:k'uhah*	*ná*	*dâ:titi?.*
It is said	after a while	(he) yawned	that	little deer.'

Objects show similar ordering alternations. A wren was taking mud to her grandfather when she met a wolf. As she explains her mission, the object 'pipe', new information, precedes the verb 'make'.

(16) Caddo preverbal object (Chafe 1977:33.11)

ibát	*cičandu?nadihah*
Grandfather	I'm taking mud to him

'I'm taking mud to my grandfather

O	V
t'ánk'uh	nah?a?na?.
pipe	so he can make

so that he can make **a pipe**.'

The wolf asks to see her basket, saying that he likes to make pipes himself. This time the now accessible object 'pipe' follows the verb.

Table 3. Caddo word order

		Clauses	% of clauses with S/O/C	% of all clauses
Subjects	SV	37	60.7%	12.3%
	VS	*24*	*39.3%*	*8.0%*
	TOTAL	61	100.0%	20.3%
Objects	OV	30	75.0%	10.0%
	VO	*10*	*25.0%*	*3.3%*
	TOTAL	40	100.0%	13.3%
Comps	CV	5	38.5%	1.7%
	VC	*8*	*61.5%*	*2.7%*
	TOTAL	13	100.0%	4.3%
Non-SOV		42	**36.8%**	14.0%

(17) Caddo postverbal object (Chafe 1977:33.13)

		V	O
wín?t'á?	*kú:?nutah*	*nast'án¡a?na?*	***t'ánk'uh.***
Also	I like	to make them	**pipe**

'I like to make **pipes** too.'

The function of such ordering is similar to that in Siouan languages. Nominals may appear to the left of the clause for added salience, as to highlight a shift in topic or other contrast. They may appear to the right of the clause for reduced salience, as when reconfirming accessible information. Departure from basic SOV order is more frequent than in Siouan, however. Among the three clauses with both subject and object nominals in a 300-clause narrative sample, none shows SOV order (1 SVO, 2 OVS). Relative orders within subject-predicate, object-predicate, and complement-predicate pairs can be seen in Table 3.

In the Caddo sample, order departs from basic SOV in **36.8%** of the clauses with a nominal subject, object, and/or complement in the sample, considerably more often than the **0.9%** of Lakhota and even the **20.4%** of Omaha.

The difference is associated with several factors. One is the development of a special presentative construction in Caddoan. Five of the VS clauses counted in Table 3 are presentatives. An example is in (18).

(18) Caddo presentative construction (Chafe 1977:34.15-6)

		V
Ku?á:na?	*bah?náh*	*hákakkidáwsa?,*
Over there	it is said	sitting on a branch

'Over there was a crow

S
ká:k'ay?.
crow
sitting on a tree branch.'

This construction is used in Caddo to introduce otherwise completely unknown but important participants, usually stating their existence with a verb like 'live' or 'sit'. (Its use has expanded in other Caddoan languages to introduce generally known characters for the first time as well.) The presentative VS structure is not confused with right-detached nominals like that in

(15), which reiterate accessible information, because of a difference in prosody. The nominals in presentatives are uttered with the same intensity and pitch as the verb, while right-detached nominals are typically uttered in a fainter and sometimes lower tone of voice. The motivation behind the development of the presentative construction may actually be the same as that observed by Mathesius: a cognitive tendency to move from a fact that 'does not, or does only minimally, contribute to the information provided by the given sentence-utterance', to the new information that 'substantially enriches the knowledge of the listener' (Vachek 1966:89-90).

Even when the five presentatives are discounted, Caddo exhibits more frequent departure from basic SOV order than the Siouan languages. Yet neither Caddo nor the other Caddoan languages has developed nominal case. Two other morphological developments have occurred in the family that reduce the necessity of relying on constituent order for signalling grammatical relations.

One is a dramatic rise in the productivity of noun incorporation. As in the Siouan languages, noun roots may be incorporated into verbs to yield new lexical items for nameable concepts. The verb stem 'make a fire', for example, consists of the noun root *-nak-* 'fire' and the verb root *-aʔni-* 'make'.

(19) Caddo noun incorporation (Chafe 1977:36.14)
nasánk'aʔniháh
'when (she) made a fire'

The construction has been extended in the Caddoan languages to discourse functions as well. One of these is a variant of the basic statement plus elaboration strategy for controlling the rate of information flow, described earlier. The first line or intonation unit of (20) below consists of a verb with a general incorporated noun, the whole describing a unitary cultural concept, 'to granular substance make'. The nature of the granular substance is elaborated in the following intonation unit with the noun *kišwah* 'parched corn'. The second is used even more pervasively in the Caddoan languages. Incorporation provides speakers with a way of backgrounding familiar information. After the parched corn has been introduced with the independent noun *kišwah*, it is subsequently referred to by incorporated nouns. Since it is already within the consciousness of the listener, there is no reason to draw special attention to it with an independent noun. (Closely spaced periods indicate pauses: .. a very brief pause, ... a slightly longer pause.)

(20) Caddo incorporation (Chafe 1977:30.16)

a. *kassahkún**dân**na?na?*
'you should (*granular substance*) make

b. ... ***kišwah.***
parched corn.

c. *nassahkún**dân**na?niháh*
when you (**granular substance**) have made for me

d. *sínátti? ci:yáhdi?a?.*
then I will go on.

e. *bah?nahwa?, kúhakáhtí? húc'isah**kišwánt**'a?.*
In fact, quickly she had (***parched corn***).'

The extensive use of incorporation reduces the number of independent nominals per clause to a certain extent, and with that, the potential for ambiguity of reference. The average number of major constituents per clause is even lower than in Siouan. In the 300 clause sample of Caddo narrative, only 3 clauses (1%) contain both subject and object independent nominals. The other Caddoan languages show similar proportions: 1% in a comparable Wichita sample from Rood (1977), 2.2% in a Kitsai sample from Lesser (1977), 0.8% in a Pawnee sample from Parks (1977a), and 1.2% in an Arikara sample from (Parks 1977b).

A second innovation in Caddoan reduces the potential for ambiguity even further. As in Siouan, first person, second person, and inclusive core arguments are expressed by pronominal prefixes on verbs. There are no basic third person pronouns. Another pronominal category has been added, however: an indefinite third person 'someone'. The indefinite, also termed a nonspecific or defocused pronoun, allows speakers to avoid direct, focused reference to a participant that they have no interest in specifying or want to avoid mentioning (Chafe 1992 on Caddo). The participant may be unknown or simply 'outside the present field of interest of the hearer' (Rood 1976:117 on Wichita). It may be used where a passive would be used in English (Parks 1976:165 on Pawnee). An example of this usage in Caddo can be seen in (21). No one would help an old woman. One morning when she got up, she found her housework done. The indefinite agent prefix appears here as *i-*.

(21) Caddo defocused pronouns (Chafe 1977:36.12)

*há**ki**t'abíʔsaʔ* *há**ki**tačáywatáhʔnisaʔ,* *hákinčahiʔsaʔ.*
one swept for her **one** cleaned the place **one** washed her dishes.
'Her place was clean and swept and her dishes were washed.'

The function of this pronominal category has been extended in Caddoan in a way that reduces the potential for ambiguity of reference in discourse. Major third person protagonists are not represented by pronominal prefixes within verbs, as would be expected. When additional human participants are involved, the indefinite or defocused prefixes are used for these secondary characters in contexts where they would be cast as subjects in other languages. This use of the defocused pronouns can be seen in (20), which relates a fight between a monster and an elf. An alternation between the defocused pronouns and their absence here clarifies grammatical relations. Verbs without the pronouns describe actions of the major protagonist, the monster. Verbs with defocusing pronouns, here in boldface, describe actions of the secondary participant, the elf.

(22) Caddo defocused pronoun (Chafe 1977:40.47-50)

a. *bahʔnah kwíhʔáwšáyčahah*
It is said as was about to jump (the monster)
As (he) was about to jump

b. *há**ki**:čahšiyah ná yahyašatciʔ.*
defoc shot there that elf
That elf shot (him) there.

c. *bahʔnah kutí áwwí:šiyah.*
It is said on the other side got down, (the monster)
(He) got down on the other side,

d. *kínnakâ:ča:wáyˀhah.*
started to jump over the fire. (the monster)
(He) started to jump over the fire.

e. *bahʔnah áwšahyáh,*
It is said got down, (the monster)
(He) got down

f. *kúkaʔukî:huhnáh hú**ki**:čahsaʔ*
started back **DEFOC** shot just then (monster) **elf**
(he) started back, and **he** shot (him) just then

g. *bah?nah kutí áwwú:šiyah.*
it is said on the other side fell there. (the monster)
and (he) fell on the other side.

The subject, the argument of an intransitive verb or the agent of a transitive, is assumed to be the central protagonist unless the defocused prefix indicates otherwise.

The increased fluidity of word order in Caddoan is thus associated with two morphological innovations: an increase in the productivity of noun incorporation and the grammaticization of a defocused pronominal category. This freer order is felt even in the ordering of sentential complements. While all complements precede the matrix verb in Lakhota and Omaha, only short ones appear in this position in Caddo, usually single word quotations. Full sentential complements generally appear postverbally.

3. Iroquoian

The modern Iroquoian languages share many features with the Siouan and Caddoan languages. Verbs contain pronominal prefixes referring to their agents and/or patients. There is noun incorporation. Similar strategies are used to regulate the flow of information: new entities are introduced in separate intonation units, often with low content verbs; complexity is often built up from a simple basic clause followed by successive elaborations; demonstratives often stand in in one phrase for entities that are more fully identified in another. The pattern of a simple statement followed by successive elaborations can be seen in the Tuscarora passage in (23).

(23) Tuscarora successive elaboration (Elton Greene p.c.)

ǫ́:tši tyahwáhæ:t,
one so it carries
ǫ́:kwœ kayækwarí:yæ?
person they walk
yahkakawǫhrí:yu:,
they were a large group
kyæní:kǫ: nækahsnǫhwáhrǫw,
this it is along the creek
hæ̂?thu tikayækwarì:yœ? uhskú:tkyæh,
there so they walk south to

tikakuyaerá?nǫh.
so they have done
'One time a large group of people was walking southward along the creek.'

As in the Siouan and Caddoan languages, nominals may be placed to the left of the nuclear clause to identify a focus of contrast or significant shift in topic, as in (24). A fox had told a bear to put his tail through a hole in the ice in order to catch fish. The hole froze closed, leaving the bear stuck when people began to arrive. The left-detached nominals highlight the contrast between the bear and the fox and mark a shift in topic.

(24) Tuscarora left-detached nominals for contrast (Elton Greene p.c.)

Ha? katšítšhuh,
the it is crafty
'As for the fox,

θahra?næ̃?ku?.
back he ran
he ran away.

Uhtšíhrǫ?,
bear
The bear,

kyæní:kǫ: .. wahra?nǫ?tyǫ́:?nǫ?,
this he tried
he tried,

wahra?nuryáhnǫ:?.
he struggled
he struggled.'

Nominals also appear to the right of the nuclear clause to reiterate given or accessible information, as in the last line in (25). Here the noun 'corn' confirms the identity of the material that had been introduced a few lines earlier.

(25) Tuscarora right-detached nominal for reidentification (Elton Greene p.c.)

unǫ́ha? unǫ́heh,
then corn
Then corn,

ha? ə̨kwaehə̨̀:wæ yukwanə̨̀hawə̨h,
the real person we corn have
Indian corn,

yahwa?kkə̨?naé :ti?haé?thuh.
I poured it in there there
I would pour in . . .

U:nə̨ wa?kturá:rae?,
then I washed (it)
Then I would wash it,

haení:kə unə̨̀haeh.
that corn
that corn.'

In addition to these features shared with the Siouan and Caddoan languages, and thus presumably reconstructible for their common parent, the Iroquoian languages also share some of the innovations seen in Caddoan. In particular, the use of noun incorporation has been extended to serve discourse functions. As in Caddo, an incorporated noun in one intonation unit can imply an entity that is more fully described in the next. An example can be seen in the Tuscarora passage in (26). Land-discovering is presented as a single concept in the first line, then this particular land is more fully described in the next.

(26) Tuscarora presentative incorporation (Elton Greene p.c.)

*Waktí**haéhn**akə̨?,*
we two **land** discovered
'We discovered **land**,

ha? thawə̨̀ru tkahaehnanù:rə̨?.
the most so it land precious is
the best land.'

Incorporation is also used pervasively in Tuscarora, as in Caddo, to background accessible information. When a Tuscarora head man first asked his people to gather stones for a sacrifice, an independent noun was used to direct attention to the stones, a new entity. When the people carried out his request, the now familiar stones were represented by an incorporated noun root.

(27) Tuscarora incorporation for backgrounding (Elton Greene p.c.)

θtirúhtšrǫ: ***utštə́hraeh***.
you gather **stone**
'Gather **stones**!'

*Wa?kayae**tštǫhr**arúhtšrǫ:? **haé**snǫ:.*
they **stone** gathered that
'So they gathered **stones**.'

Despite these shared features, word orders in the Iroquoian languages differ strikingly from those in both the Siouan and Caddoan languages. There is little basis for positing a basic SOV order at all. As in the other languages, clauses with both subject and object nominals are rare; in a 300-clause narrative sample, only 3 clauses (1%) contain both. Of these three, one shows SOV order, 1 SVO, and 1 OVS. More importantly, of all clauses containing at least one nominal constituent, over two thirds, 67.7%, departed from SOV order. Relative orders within subject-verb, object-verb, and complement-verb pairs in the sample can be seen in Table 4.

Similar text counts in other Iroquoian languages indicate that SOV is not a basic order in Iroquoian at all. In counts of a comparable Mohawk sample, 50.3% of clauses with nominal constituents deviated from SOV order, in Onondaga 70%, in Cayuga 62.4%, and in Seneca 53.6%.

Word order in Iroquoian languages is in fact not syntactically based at all. Elements are ordered according to their relative importance within the dis-

Table 4. Tuscarora Word Order

		Clauses	% of clauses with S/O/C	% of all clauses
Subjects	SV	24	68.6%	8.0%
	VS	*11*	*31.4%*	*3.7%*
	TOTAL	35	100.0%	11.7%
Objects	OV	21	41.2%	7.0%
	VO	*30*	*58.8%*	*10.0%*
	TOTAL	51	100.0%	17.0%
Comps	CV	1	2.0%	0.3%
	VC	*49*	*98.0%*	*16.3%*
	TOTAL	50	100.0%	16.7%
Non-SOV		90	**67.7%**	30.0%

course, rather than according to grammatical relations like subject and object or lexical categories like noun and verb. Constituents appear in decreasing order of newsworthiness (Mithun 1987).

Various features can render a constituent newsworthy. New participants are typically more newsworthy than old. If not introduced in a separate intonation unit, new entities are usually identified early in the clause, and familiar or accessible ones reidentified late. The difference can be seen in the Tuscarora passage in (28). A group of starving people had been walking for a long time on the ice. When they finally discovered land, the head man told them to prepare a sacrifice. The head man, who had not been mentioned before, is introduced with a nominal at the beginning of the phrase, before the verb.

(28) Tuscarora new subject (Elton Greene p.c.)

S			V
haʔ	*uhǫ́ʔnǫʔ*	*ruʔnǫ́ʔǫh,*	*wahrǫ́hrǫʔ, . . .*
the	head	man	he said

the headman said, " . . . "

Once the sacrifice was made, the speaker asked how the headman had known to do this. Here the headman, now an established participant, is represented by a nominal at the end of the phrase, after the verb.

(29) Tuscarora accessible subject (Elton Greene p.c.)

	V	S		
ǫ̀:wæh	*tihruyǫ́hwʔǫh*	*hæní:kǫ:*	*uhǫ́ʔnǫʔ*	*ruʔnǫ́ʔǫh?*
where	he has learned from	that	head	man

'Where had he learned it, that headman?'

Object nominals show similar patterns. The speaker began his recipe for cornbread with the passage in (30). The noun for ashes, a new object, precedes the verb.

(30) Tuscarora new object (Elton Greene p.c.)

Tyahrætšíhǫ	*kǫ:θ,*
first	customarily

'First, I usually

O V
uhsaéharæh .. wa?kkúhae?.
ash I went after
would go after ashes.'

He would then put the kettle on. When it started to boil, he would add the ashes. This time the noun for ashes, now an established referent, appears late, after the verb.

(31) Tuscarora accessible object (Elton Greene p.c.)

		V		O
U:nę	*kę:θ*	*yahwa?kkę?naé:ti?*	*hä¡thu*	*ha? uhsaéharaeh.*
then	customarily	there I poured	there	the ash

'Then I would pour the ashes in there.'

Newsworthiness is not confined to contrast and newness. A historical account opened with the sentence in (32). Neither the Americans nor the British had been mentioned previously, but the purpose of this introductory sentence was to situate the tale during wartime. The predicate 'they fight' thus precedes the subject although both the predicate and subject represent new information.

(32) Tuscarora newsworthiness: VS (Elton Greene p.c.)

				V
U:nę̂ha?	*kyaení:kę:*	*tikahà:wi?*	*kyaení:kę:*	*kayę?rì:yus*
long ago	this	so it carries	this	they fight

'One time long ago

S
kyaení:kę: wahstę̂há:ka:?,
this Bostonians
the Americans

tisnę? kuráhku:.
and British
and the British were at war.'

Similar patterns can be seen with object nominals. A fish peddler had been driving along when he saw a fox. He stopped his wagon to pick it up. He then hopped back in and drove on. The horse had not been mentioned before, although driving had. Still, the object nominal ‘horse’ follows the verb ‘drive’. What was newsworthy here was not the horse, but the resumption of driving.

(33) Tuscarora newsworthiness: VO (Elton Greene p.c.)

		V	O
U:nə̨	*hǽsnə̨:*	*θahraʔnù:riʔ*	*haʔ á:ha:θ.*
now	then	again he drove	the horse

‘Now then he drove his horse again.’

The pattern of newsworthy-first is not limited to relations between verbs and core arguments, but applies to all constituents. The crucial point of (34) was that the Flying Head was *behind* the woman, so the locative appears early.

(34) Tuscarora LV (Elton Greene p.c.)

LOC	V
æʔtǽhsnakw	*wahraʔnáʔnihr.*
behind her	he stood

‘He stood behind her.’

The main point of (35) was the fire, which was to provide the woman with a weapon against the Flying Head, so the verb appears early, and the locative later.

(35) Tuscarora VL (Elton Greene p.c.)

V	LOC
Yú:ʔnæks	*uhə̨́ʔnə̨ʔ.*
it burns	in front

‘A fire was burning before her.’

The newsworthiness peak is systematically the first major constituent of the clause, whatever its grammatical role, apart from various discourse particles that serve to qualify, link clauses or provide other orienting material.

What could have prompted the shift from the basic SOV order of Proto-Siouan-Caddoan-Iroquoian to the completely pragmatically based ordering of Iroquoian? Two morphological developments are pertinent. One is the high productivity of noun incorporation, shared with Caddoan. (This productivity has since faded somewhat in Cherokee, but ample traces remain in the lexicon of its former presence.) The result is a reduction in the number of separate major constituents per clause. The number of occasions on which word order might be necessary to disambiguate grammatical relations is very low. Only 1% of the clauses in the Caddo and Tuscarora samples contain both subject and object nominals. Ambiguity might occur with only a fraction of the 1%, those transitive clauses in which the animacy of the arguments would not be a clue to their roles.

A second grammatical innovation in Iroquoian, not shared with Caddoan, probably served as a final stimulus to purely pragmatic ordering. Neither Siouan nor Caddoan contains basic third person pronominal prefixes. The Iroquoian languages have developed full sets of third person prefixes. A cognate of the defocused Caddo pronoun **yi-* retains the indefinite meaning 'someone' in Iroquoian, but is now used for women as well. The pronominal paradigm has been fully filled out with the development of additional pronouns for the other third persons. The result is that all Iroquoian verbs contain obligatory pronominal prefixes referring to their agents and/or patients, whatever their person. Some of the Tuscarora prefixes can be seen in (36).

(36) Tuscarora pronominal prefixes: all core arguments specified

***k**-araerúha?*	'**I**'m running'	***wak**-nə̨́hwaks*	'**I**'m sick'
***s**-araerúha?*	'**you**'re running'	***θa**-nə̨́hwaks*	'**you**'re sick'
***ra**-raerúha?*	'**he**'s running'	***ru**-nə̨́hwaks*	'**he**'s sick'
***yə**-raerúha?*	'**she**'s running'	***yaku**-nə̨́hwaks*	'**she**'s sick'
***w**-araerúha?*	'**it**'s running'	***yu**-nə̨́hwaks*	'**it**'s sick'
***khæ**-tkáhnæ?*	'**I**'m chasing **him/her**'	***rakæ**-tkáhnæ?*	'**he**'s chasing **me**'

Singular, dual, and plural number are also distinguished in all persons.

The pronominal prefixes appear in every verb whether additional nominals are present in the clause or not. Grammatical roles are thus always specified within the verbal morphology, as relations between the pronominal prefixes and verb stem, rather than between independent nominals and the verb. In a sense the relative order of predicates and arguments is an even more rigid SOV in Iroquoian than in Siouan, but in Iroquoian the order is among morphemes rather than words.

The foundation of modern Iroquoian word order was already present in the Proto-Siouan-Caddoan-Iroquoian system. In the parent language, nominals could be positioned to the left of the clause for added salience or to the right of the clause for reduced salience, but these structures were highly marked. In Iroquoian, an increase in the productivity of noun incorporation and the completion of the pronominal paradigm freed word order from its role in distinguishing grammatical relations. The pragmatic force of left-detachment for added salience and right-detachment for reduced salience of nominals was generalized to a general ordering principle. Now elements are ordered entirely according to their relative importance to the discourse, regardless of their syntactic roles, in descending order of newsworthiness.

4. The intonation factor

The origin of the pragmatic word orders of the Dhegiha Siouan, Caddoan, and Iroquoian languages can thus be traced to left- and right-detachment constructions in the common parent language that became more frequent, and correspondingly less marked, with various morphological developments in the languages. The newsworthy-first principle is still not entirely explained, however. Why should left-detachment be utilized for focus, highly important information, and right-detachment for reiteration of already known information. If it is cognitively more natural to move from the known to the unknown, then all of this pragmatic ordering, from the left-and right-detachment of Siouan to the purely newsworthy-first ordering of Iroquoian, seems not merely unmotivated, but counterintuitive.

Of course speakers of Iroquoian languages speak as coherently as speakers of other languages. Scenes are typically set before sequences of events are detailed. This order need not be reflected among the core arguments of every clause. Appropriate orientation can be accomplished with the ordering of larger units: adverbial phrases, clauses, and sentences. The relative order of core arguments and verbs within clauses in Iroquoian does differ in an important way from that in many others, including Proto-Siouan-Caddoan-Iroquoian. With the grammaticization of pronominal affixes, predicates and core arguments are processed simultaneously within a single word, not sequentially.

The ordering of constituents from high to low newsworthiness may stem from a quite different kind of motivation, one rooted in prosody. We know that speakers of all languages identify intonation units, the aural counterparts of phrases and sentences set off by commas and periods. In most languages, the unmarked contour of the intonation unit involves descending amplitude and pitch among other things (Pierrehumbert 1980, Cruttenden 1986). Cruttenden notes that this phenomenon is physiologically motivated:

> The explanation for declination has often been related to the decline in transglottal pressure as the speaker uses up the breath in his lungs. A more recent explanation suggests that an upward change of pitch involves a physical adjustment which is more difficult than a downward change of pitch, the evidence being that a rise takes longer to achieve than a fall of a similar interval in fundamental frequency. (1986:168)

Speakers learn to disregard the decrease in pitch when identifying contrastive tones in tone languages, but remain attuned to falling pitch and amplitude contours when delineating aural phrases, sentences, and paragraphs.

In the polysynthetic languages discussed here, particularly those of the Caddoan and Iroquoian families, such intonation contours are particularly easy to identify. Intonation units typically consist of only one or two major words, plus particles. The location of tone and stress is determined for the most part by regular phonological rules whose domain is the word. Individual morphemes within words are rarely if ever given constrastive stress for pragmatic purposes. Prosodic contours of Lakhota, Caddo, and Tuscarora examples discussed here can be seen in Figures 1-12. All were taken from recordings of spontaneous connected speech. The figures were produced with Cecil, a device for the Computerized Extraction of Components of Intonation in Language produced by the Summer Institute of Linguistics. The upper graph indicates amplitude (essentially volume), the lower fundamental frequency (essentially pitch). The most prominent syllables, stressed in the case of Lakhota and Tuscarora, high toned in the case of Caddo, are indicated by numbers above those syllables. Arrows have been inserted to locate these syllables.

Figures 1 and 2 show typical prosodic contours in Lakhota. There is a general fall in both volume and pitch. Within the single intonation unit in Figure 1 'They're staying in a church', the pitch of successive stressed syllables is 127 103 87-84Hz. Successive phrases in a sentence show a general fall both within each phrases and over the series. Each intonation unit begins slightly lower than the beginning of the last, and ends lower than the last, as in Figure 2, 'Her husband died, so in honor of that, we put on a powwow': 135 107, 120 110, 97 87Hz. Similar contours can be seen in the Caddo example in Figure 3, 'He was unable to get over the log' (254 248 243, 238Hz) and the Tuscarora example in Figure 4, 'Now then one time, three of them went out hunting' (127 111 108 93 89, 95 88 86Hz).

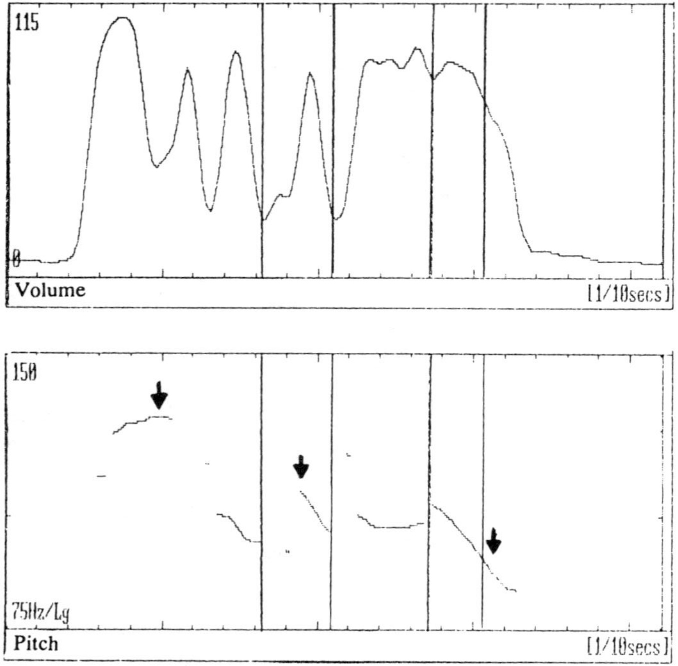

127	103			87-84
Owácʰekiya	*tʰípi*	*wą*	*el*	*ų́pi.*
church	house	a	there	stay-pl

'They're staying in a church.'

Figure 1. Prosodic fall in Lakhota

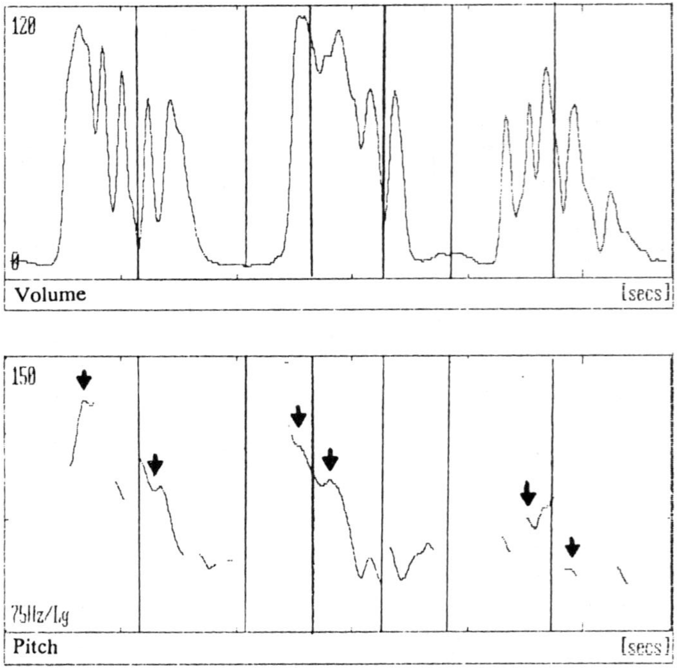

135	107	120	110		97	87
Higənákukį	*t'áčʰa,*	*hé*	*yuʔónihą*	*kel*	*wačʰípi he*	*ųkáɣapi.*
her husband	die so	that	honoring	so	dance that	we made.

'We put on a powwow in honor of her late husband.'

Figure 2. Prosodic fall over multiple intonation units in Lakhota

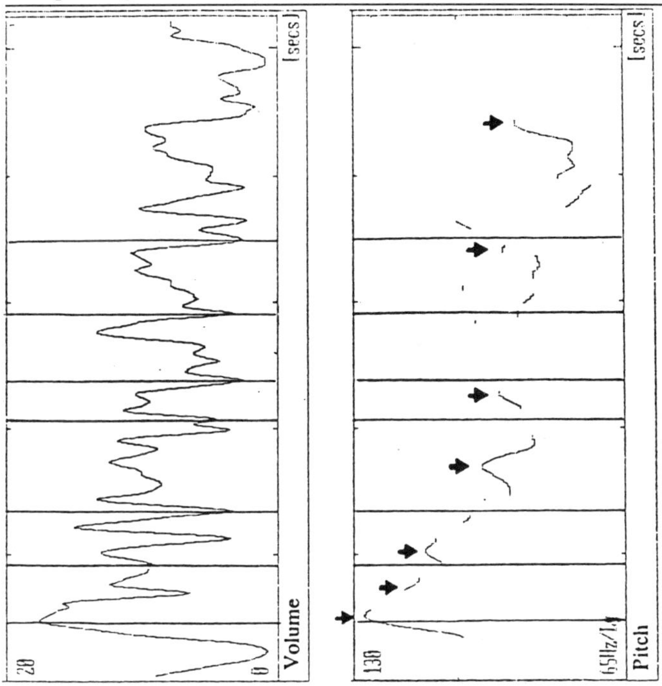

127 111 108 93 89 95 88 86
U:nę hǽ snǽ ę̄:tši tyahwáhæ:t kyæní:kę, áhsę tikayá:kę wa?kayętųrá:tha?
now then one it happend this three of them they went hunting
'Now then one time, three of them went out hunting.'

Figure 4. Prosodic fall in Tuscarora

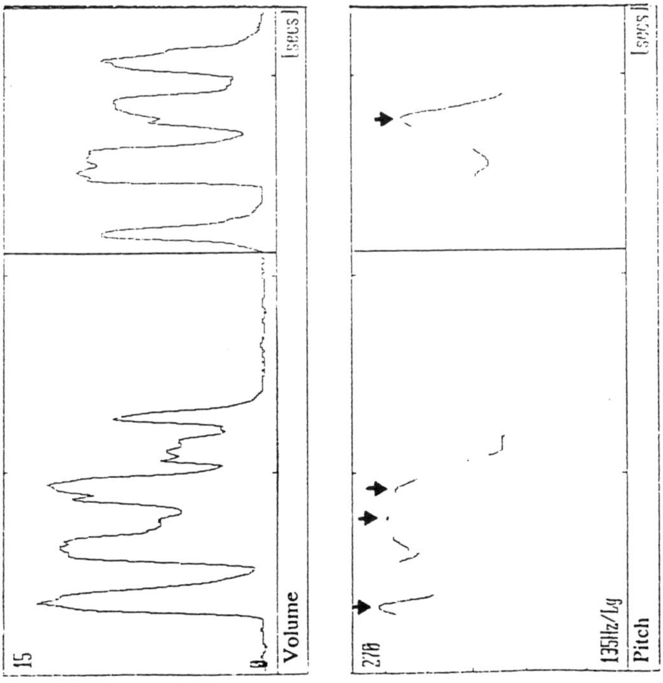

254 248 243 238
kúyatáyánnáhdu? natdah?ni:way
He was unable to get over the log.

Figure 3. Prosodic falll in Caddo

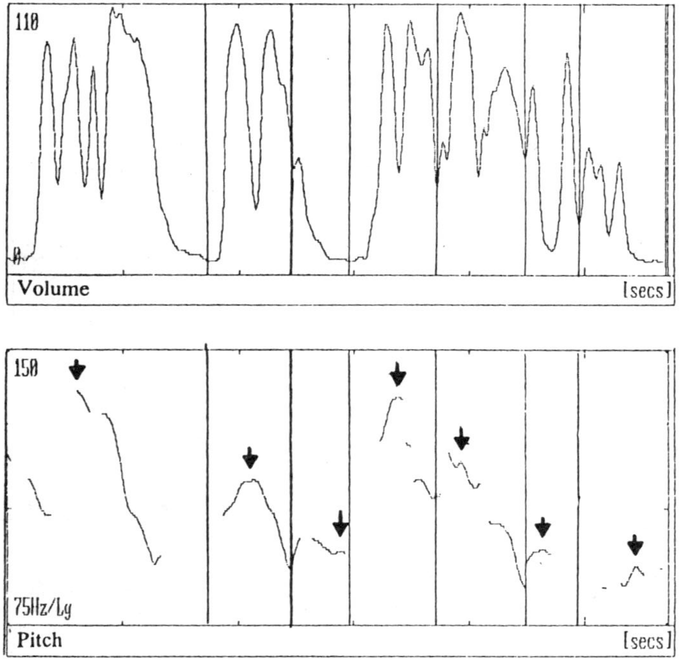

135 107 93 133 111 89 82
Makʰásitomniyą oyáte eya áhi? tʰiyátahą kʰoláwičʰaųyapi eyá hípi nakų́
all over the world people some come from home our friends some come too
'People came from all over. Some friends from home came too.'

Figure 5. Left-detached subject in Lakhota

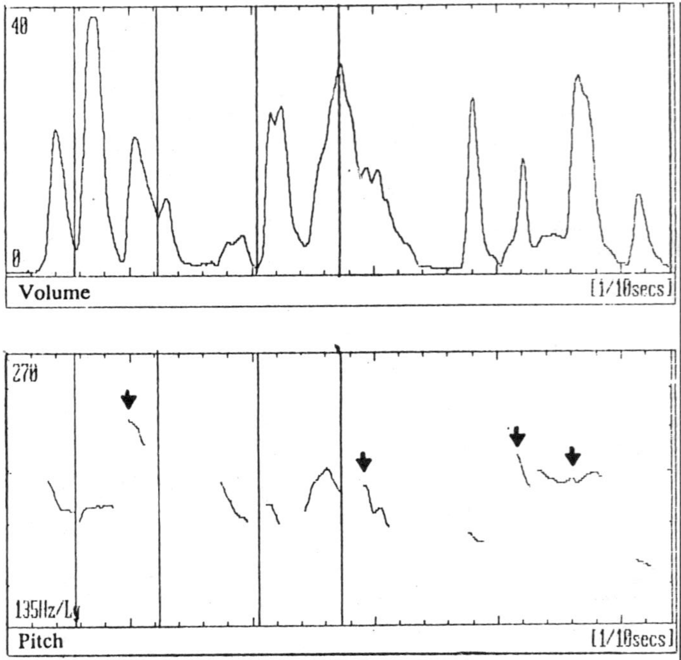

227 192187 205-191198-6
cah wadu? ukkih bah?nah háh?áw?isdakánná:sa?.
Mr. Wildcat really it.is.said is stooping over
'Mr. Wildcat, it said, was stooping over.'

Figure 6. S-V in Caddo

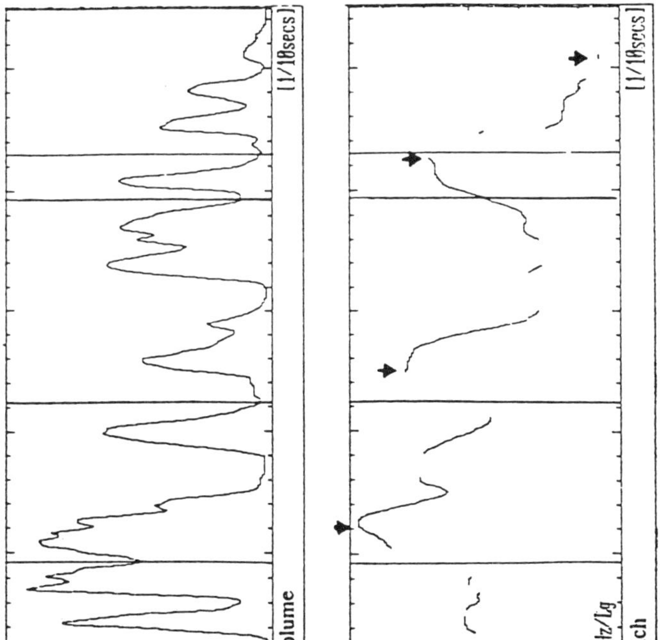

262		236	222	142
Bahʔnah	*áwwissiyah,*	*kúhbisahʔaʔ*	*ná*	*cahwaduʔ.*
it is said	he arrived	where house was	that	Mr. Wildcat

Figure 7. *V-S in Caddo*

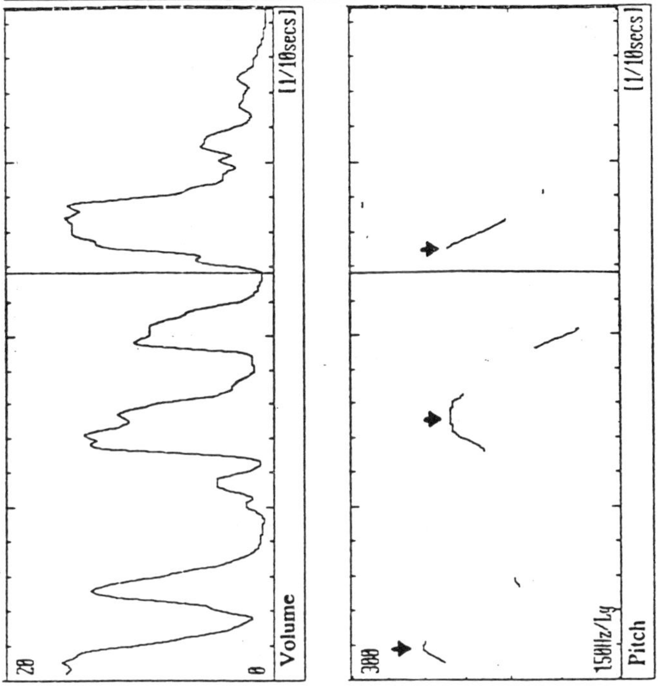

250	232	232
Hákakkidáwsaʔ,		*ká:k'ay*
was sitting		crow

'There was a crow sitting on a branch.'

Figure 8. *Presentative V-S in Caddo*

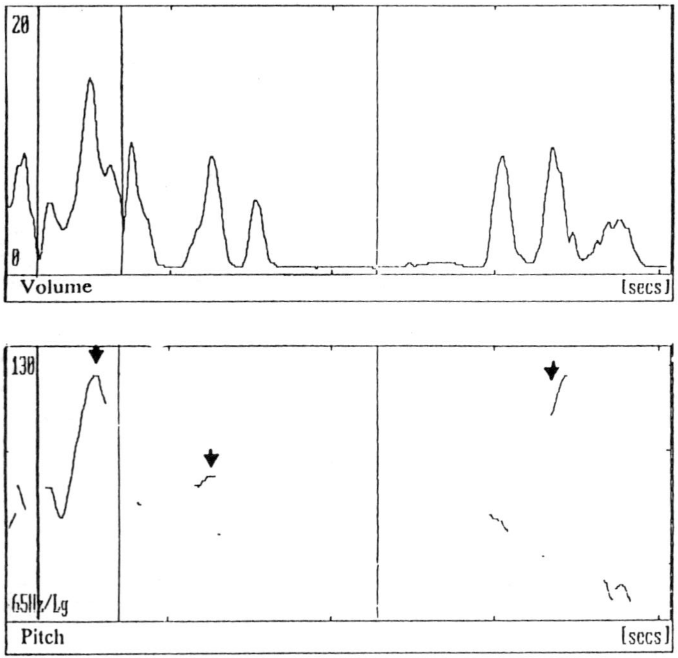

122		93
Haʔ	*uhę́nęʔ*	*ruʔnę́ʔęh,*
the	head	man

'The head man said,...'

Figure 9. S-V in Tuscarora

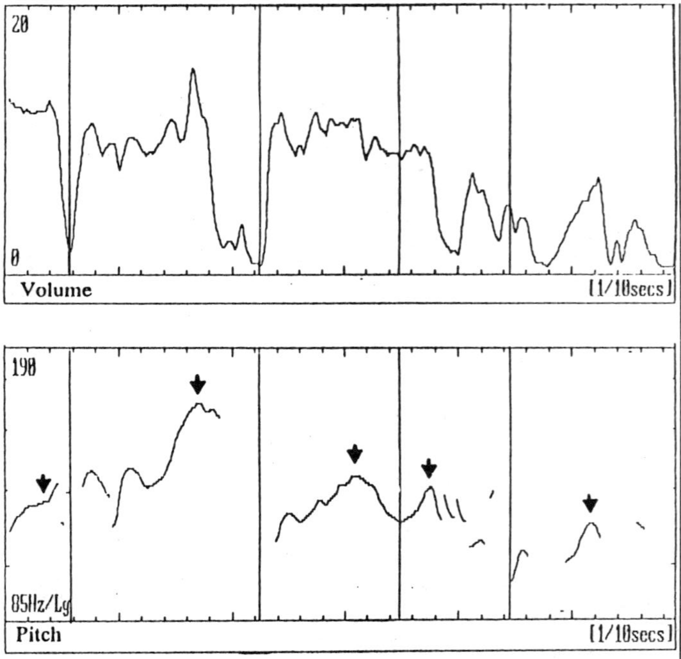

109-120	121	162	128	125	113
wahrę́hręʔ	*ę́:wæh*	*tihruyę́hwʔę,*	*hæní:kę:*	*uhę́:ʔnęʔ*	*ruʔnę́ʔęhʔ*
he said	where he	got it from	that	head	man

'Where did he get it from, that head man?'

Figure 10. V-S in Tuscarora

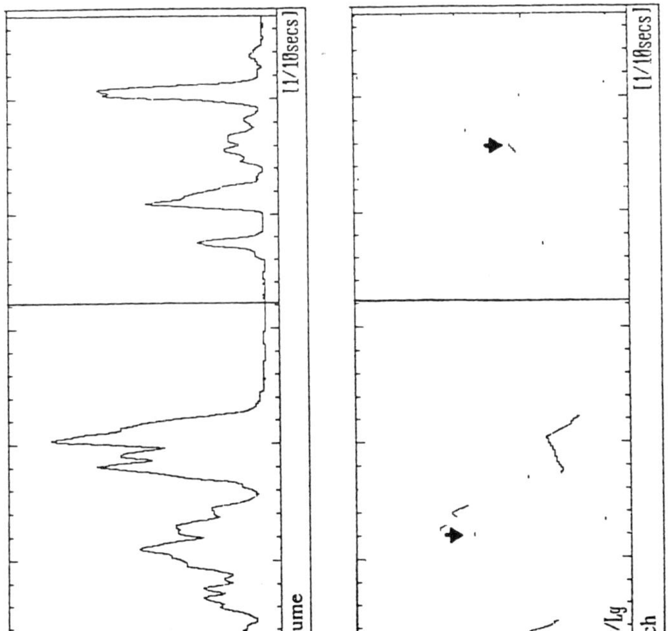

118	101-104
uhsǽharæh	*waʔkkúhæʔ.*
ash	I go after

'I go after ashes.'

Figure 11. O-V in Tuscarora

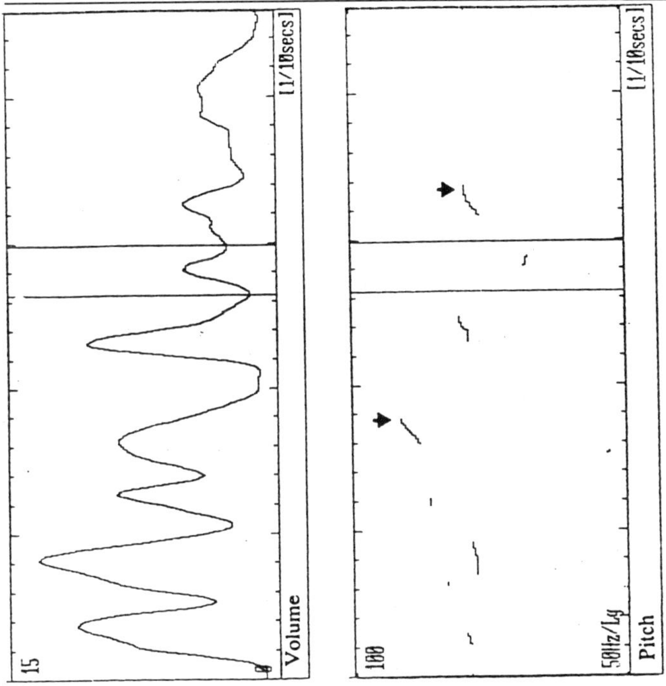

89		75
Nęθkayętkáhnęʔw	*haʔ*	*θútahr.*
they willl wake them	the	soldier

'They will wake up the soldiers.'

Figure 12. V-O in Tuscarora

The widespread development of left-detached and right-detached constructions, with similar functions across a variety of languages may be motivated by such prosodic contours. Left-detached nominals, those conveying important information such as a significant focus of contrast or shift in topic, appear at the most prominent portions of prosodic units, at the points of highest volume and pitch. Right-detached nominals, those reconfirming already familiar information, appear at the least prominent portions of prosodics units. Presumably this pattern characterized the left-detached focus constructions and right-detached antitopic constructions of Proto-Siouan, as it does in the modern languages. (See for example Lambrecht 1987 on French.) The prosodic contour of left-detachment in Lakhota can be seen in Figure 5. This sentence followed a statement that a lot of people had come to the powwow. The new information supplied by the left-detached element 'from all over' is at the prosodic peak.

The increased frequency of left- and right-detached nominal constructions in Caddoan resulted in a more frequent correspondence between pragmatic importance and prosodic salience. A contrast in the prosodic salience of preverbal and postverbal subjects in Caddo can be seen by comparing Figures 6 and 7. The clause in Figure 6, 'Mr. Wildcat was stooping over . . . ', introduced a new protagonist. The stressed syllable of the subject 'Mr. Wildcat' is the most prominent of the clause (**227** 192 187 205-191 198-196Hz). The sentence in Figure 7, 'He arrived at the house, that Mr. Wildcat', appeared later in the same tale, when Mr. Wildcat was a well-established figure. Here the same nominal, now a right-detached subject, simply reconfirms his identity and has the least prosodic prominence in the clause (262 236 222 **142**Hz).

Volume and pitch need not fade at the end of an intonation unit. The special VS presentative construction in Caddo is characterized by a distinctive amplitude contour in which the introduced argument is nearly as loud as the preceding verb. The VS clause in Figure 8, 'There was a crow sitting on a branch' introduced an important new character. Unlike the VS clause in Figure 7, this shows little fall. The noun 'crow' was pronounced in a separate intonation unit, as loudly as the verb 'sit', and its high toned syllable was as high as that of the preceding verb (250 232, **232**Hz).

Figures 9 and 10 contrast similar pairs in Tuscarora. In Figure 9, the initial subject of 'The head man said', introduces a new topic and appears at the prosodic peak (*122 93*, 109-120Hz). In Figure 10, the same subject provides a simple reiteration of a continuing topic and appears finally, with minimal prosodic salience (121 162 **182 125 113**Hz). Figures 11 and 12 show a similar contrast between Tuscarora OV and VO structures. The OV clause in Figure 11, 'I go after ashes', opened the description of how corn soup is made. The noun 'ashes' is the most important element of the clause, so it appears initially, at the prosodic peak (**118** 101-104Hz). In the VO clause in Figure 12, 'They will wake up the soldiers', the most newsworthy element is the verb 'wake up'. The soldiers were already familiar at this point. Accordingly, the verb appears at the prosodic peak, followed by the less prosodically salient, already familiar, object (89 **75**Hz).

The generalization of pragmatic ordering to all constituents in Iroquoian has resulted in the best fit of all between the flow of information over clauses and their prosodic contours. The most newsworthy elements are generally uttered with the highest volume and pitch, followed by successively less important elements uttered with decreasing prosodic salience.

5. Conclusion

A variety of factors can shape word ordering strategies. One is of course a general human cognitive propensity to proceed from the known or given to the unknown or new, which may account for the theme–rheme pragmatic structure observed in so many languages, and ultimately the high frequency of basic subject–object syntactic order.

Yet neither theme–rheme nor basic subject–object order is universal. In a number of languages, constituents systematically appear in decreasing order of newsworthiness. These languages also fail to show basic subject–object order. In fact, they show no basic syntactic word order at all: order is entirely pragmatically based. The existence of these languages indicates that a cognitive preference for given–new order is not the only factor shaping word order. Here, the effects of two other kinds of factors have been illustrated: morphological and prosodic structure.

A number of morphological innovations were described in Siouan, Caddoan, and Iroquoian languages. They are diverse, including the grammaticization of nominal case (Omaha), increased productivity of noun incorporation (Caddo, Tuscarora), the grammaticization of a defocused pronominal category (Caddo), and the grammaticization of complete sets of third person pronominal prefixes (Tuscarora). Yet they have affected word order in similar ways, reducing its syntactic role in distinguishing grammatical relations. Order has become more fluid, exploited more often for pragmatic purposes.

It is possible that the pragmatic ordering patterns themselves were shaped by a second kind of factor: natural prosodic tendencies. In the parent language, nominals could be placed to the left of the nuclear clause for increased salience, or to the right for reduced salience. Such constructions were relatively rare, as they are in many of the daughter languages, but they were iconic. The leftmost position in the sentence is intonationally the most prominent, normally the location of highest volume and pitch. The rightmost position is intonationally the least prominent, the location of lowest volume and pitch. As the morphological innovations in various branches of the family freed word order from its syntactic function, it was these constructions that were increasingly exploited for pragmatic purposes. Ordering strategies in these languages now reflect an ever better fit between form (the intonation contour) and function (pragmatic importance).

References

Allen, Louis. 1931. "Siouan and Iroquoian." *International Journal of American Linguistics* 6.185-93.

Chafe, Wallace. 1964. "Another look at Siouan and Iroquoian." *American Anthropologist* 66.852-62.

Chafe, Wallace. 1976a. *The Caddoan, Iroquoian, and Siouan Languages.* The Hague: Mouton.

Chafe, Wallace. 1976b. "Givenness, contrastiveness, definiteness, subjects, topics, and point of view." *Subject and Topic* ed. by Charles N. Li, 25-55. New York: Academic Press.

Chafe, Wallace. 1977. "Caddo texts." Parks 1977c. 27-43.

Chafe, Wallace. 1987. "Cognitive Constraints on Information Flow." *Coherence and Grounding in Discourse* ed. by Russell S. Tomlin, 21-52. Amsterdam: John Benjamins. [*Typological Studies in Language,* 11.]

Chafe, Wallace. 1992. "Uses of the defocusing pronominal prefixes in Caddo." *Anthropological Linguistics* 32.

Cruttenden, Alan. 1986. *Intonation.* Cambridge: Cambridge University Press.

Deloria, Ella. 1932. *Dakota Texts* New York: G. E. Stechert. [*Publications of the American Ethnological Society,* 14.]

Dorsey, James Owen. 1890. *The C/egiha Language.* Washington: Government Printing Office. [*Department of the Interior U.S. Geographical and Geological Survey of the Rocky Mountain Region,* 6.]

Dorsey, James Owen and John R. Swanton. 1912. *A Dictionary of the Biloxi and Ofo Languages.* BAE Bulletin 47. Washington: Government Printing Office.

Du Bois, John. 1985. "Competing motivations." *Iconicity in Syntax* ed. by John Haiman, 343-65. Amsterdam: John Benjamins. [*Typological Studies in Language*, 6]

Einaudi, Paula Ferris Einaudi. 1976. *A Grammar of Biloxi.* New York: Garland.

Givón, T. 1975. "Focus and the scope of assertion: Some Bantu evidence." *Studies in African Linguistics* 6.185-205.

Kennard, Edward. 1936. Mandan grammar. *International Journal of American Linguistics* 9.1-43.

Lambrecht, Knud. 1987. "On the status of SVO sentences in French discourse." *Coherence and Grounding in Discourse* ed. by Russell S. Tomlin, 217-61. Amsterdam: John Benjamins. [*Typological Studies in Language*, 11.]

Lesser, Alexander. 1977. "Kitsai texts." Parks 1977c. 44-64.

Lipkind, William. 1945. *Winnebago Grammar.* New York: King's Crown Press.

Lowie, Robert H. 1960. *Crow Texts.* Berkeley: University of California Press.

Mithun, Marianne. 1987. "Is basic word order universal?" *Coherence and Grounding in Discourse* ed. by Russell S. Tomlin. Amsterdam: John Benjamins. [*Typological Studies in Language* 11.] Reprinted in *The Pragmatics of Word Order Flexibility* ed. by Doris Payne. Amsterdam/Philadelphia: John Benjamins.

Parks, Douglas R. 1976. *A Grammar of Pawnee.* New York: Garland Press.

Parks, Douglas R. 1977a. "Pawnee texts: Skiri and South Band." Parks 1977c. 65-90.

Parks, Douglas R. 1977b. "Arikara texts." Parks 1977c. 1-19.

Parks, Douglas R. 1977c. *Caddoan Texts.* Chicago: University of Chicago Press. [*International Journal of American Linguistics Native American Texts Series*, 2.1.].

Pierrehumbert, Janet. 1980. *"The Phonology and Phonetics of English Intonation."* Ph.D. Dissertation, MIT.

Rood, David S. 1976. *Wichita Grammar.* New York: Garland Press.

Rood, David S. 1977. "Wichita texts." Parks 1977c. 91-128.

Vachek, Josef. 1966. *The Linguistic School of Prague.* Bloomington: Indiana University Press.

The word order of two-constituent constructions in spoken Spanish*

Francisco Ocampo
University of Minnesota

1. Introduction

Languages can be considered as having a flexible or a rigid word order according to their utilization of word order variation (Givón 1984:188). Spanish belongs to the first type, as seen in the following examples of VS and SV constructions:

(1) *Fueron los chicos* V S
went the kids
'The kids went'

(2) *Los chicos fueron* S V
the kids went
'The kids went'

This paper studies the motivation of word order variation in declarative constructions with a verb and another constituent in spoken Spanish.

Previous studies on spoken Spanish (Silva-Corvalán 1983; Bentivoglio 1985; Bentivoglio and Weber 1986) have pointed out the importance of pragmatic and cognitive factors in the analysis of word order variation. Within the same orientation, I will try to show that there is a correlation between word order, the type of construction, the informational status of the NP referent (in the case of constructions that have a NP), and the pragmatic function conveyed by the proposition.

This work is based on a corpus of nine hours of casual conversations. It includes a total of twenty one middle-class Rioplatense speakers residents of La Plata, Argentina.

The constructions considered in the analysis are: VS, SV, VDO, DOV, VIO, IOV, VPP, PPV, VADV, and ADVV. In the case of NPs, I examine only lexical NPs, i.e. I do not include personal pronouns (*yo* 'I', *tú*, 'you', etc.), because a preliminary analysis of the data shows that there may be additional factors — besides the ones postulated here — that motivate their word order.

As the number of constituents affects word order and as at present it has not been established for Spanish if main and subordinate clauses share the same word order restrictions, I take into consideration only those two-constituent constructions that are independent or main clauses. For example, a VPP construction like the one shown in (3) is excluded because it is not a main clause and because in addition to the V and the PP it has a third constituent: the adverb *siempre* 'always'.[1]

(3) recuerdo que lo lleva siempre en la cartera 1a12
I remember that it carries always in the purse
'I remember that (she) carries it always in the purse.'

In the data, direct objects may or may not co-occur with a clitic, as illustrated in the following examples:[2]

(4) pido el libro 12a5
I ask the book
'I ask the book.'

(5) lo traje el papelito 23b6
CL I brought the piece of paper
'I brought the piece of paper.'

(6) Doce años tenía 14a17
twelve years I had
'I was twelve years old.'

(7) la lección no la daba 14b21
the lesson no CL I gave
'I didn't know the lesson.'

In (5) the direct object, *el papelito* 'the piece of paper', has the coreferential clitic *lo*, and in (7) the direct object, *la lección* 'the lesson', the coreferential clitic *la.* Silva-Corvalán (1984) regards cases like (4) to (7) a variable phenomenon of object-verb agreement, which is in the process of diffusion. Therefore, in my analysis I consider examples like (4) and (5) as constructions with a postverbal direct object, and cases like (6) and (7) as constructions with a preverbal direct object, at different stages of the spread of object-verb agreement.

In the analysis of the data I attempt to find out the following: (i) whether the status new/given of the NP referent has any influence on the order of the constituents, and (ii) whether there is any relationship between primary stress placement, pragmatic function, and word order.

I adopt Prince's typology of new and given referents (Prince 1981). After classifying the data under Prince's six types (brand-new, brand-new anchored, inferrable, unused, textually evoked, situationally evoked) I discovered that these values cluster in two broader categories that correlate with word order variation: new, and given. New referents are those that are introduced into the discourse for the first time. I classify as new Prince's values brand-new, brand-new anchored, inferrable, and unused. Given referents are those that have already been introduced (Prince's textually evoked), or those that are present in an extratextual context (Prince's situationally evoked: any person or object within the speaker's visual field).

The pragmatic functions found to motivate word order variation are: conveying information,[3] contrary to expectation, focal referent, focus of contrast, and topic.

Table1 shows the interaction between syntactic factors (type of construction), pragmatic function, status of the NP referent, and word order.

Presentatives are those one-valency stative verbs that have the possibility of taking NP arguments whose referents are brand-new or brand-new anchored: *haber* 'there is/are', *estar* 'to be (locative)', *existir* 'to exist'.[4] No other verbs in the data (with the exception of *tener* + DO 'to have') show this feature. Presentatives do not take exclusively brand-new and brand-new anchored referents; like other verbs, they can also have NP arguments whose referents are inferrable, unused, and evoked.

NP arguments of presentatives are not prototypical subjects because they lack the feature of agency (Keenan 1976) and — in the case of *haber* in Rioplatense Spanish — also agreement. For these reasons I will refer to them as 'NP arguments' and not as 'subjects.'

Verbs belonging to the *gustar* 'to like' type share the following features: (i) the verb agrees with a NP that lacks agentivity, and (ii) the experiencer is obligatorily expressed by an indirect object clitic,[5] as in (8).

Table 1

type of construction			pragmatic function	cogn. status NP refrnt.	tokens	word order
verb and NP	one valency verbs	intransitives	conveying information	new	33	V S
				given	23	S V
			contrary to expectation	new	2	S V
				given	9	V S
			subject focus of contrast	new	1	S V
				given	1	S V
			unclear cases	new	1	S V
				given	1	V S
		presentatives	conveying information	new	81	V NP
				given	24	V NP
			contrary to expectation	new	0	
				given	3	NP V
			NP focus of contrast	new	3	NP V
				given	5	NP V
			verb focus of contrast	new	1	V NP
				given	0	
			unclear cases	new	1	NP V
				given	0	
	two valency verbs	verb and subject	conveying information	new	6	S V
				given	15	S V
			contrary to expectation	new	0	
				given	2	V S
			subject focus of contrast	new	2	S V
				given	2	S V
			unclear cases	new	1	V S
				given	1	V S
			conveying information	new	273	V DO
				given	185	V DO
			contrary to expectation	new	6	DO V
				given	4	DO V
			topic direct object	new	1	DO V
				given	5	DO V

	two valency verbs	verb and direct object	dir. obj focus	new	7	DO V
			of contrast	given	2	DO V
			verb focus	new	0	
			of contrast	given	1	V DO
			focal direct	new	2	DO V
			object	given	2	DO V
			focal	new	0	
			verb	given	1	V DO
			unclear	new	4	DO V
			cases	given	1	DO V
		verb and indirect object	conveying	new	5	V IO
			informat	given	5	V IO
			indir. obj focus	new	1	IO V
			of contrst	given	1	IO V
		gustar type	conveying	new	3	V NP
			information	given	2	V NP
			topic	new	0	
			NP	given	1	NP V
			NP focus	new	0	
			of contrast	given	2	NP V
verb and prepositional phrase			conveying	new	132	V PP
			information	given	53	V PP
					16	V PP
			contrary to	new	3	PP V
			expectation	given	1	PP V
					3	PP V
			PP focus	new	4	PP V
			of contrast	given	3	PP V
					6	PP V
			focal	new	1	PP V
			PP	given	0	
			verb focus	new	1	V PP
			of contrast	given	4	V PP
			unclear	new	1	V PP
			cases	given	1	V PP
				new	3	PP V
				given	2	PP V
					3	PP V

verb and adverb	class 1 adverbs	conv information	94	V ADV
		contr exp	8	ADV V
		ADV focus of contrast	9	ADV V
		verb focus of contrast	1	V ADV
		focal ADV	1	ADV V
		unclear	5	ADV V
	class 2 adverbs	conv information	69	ADV V
		contr exp	1	V ADV
		verb focus of contrast	1	V ADV
		unclear	1	ADV V

(8) *me* *gusta* *el* *té*
to me (CL) pleases the tea
'I like tea / tea pleases me'

The only verbs behaving like *gustar* present in two-constituent constructions in the data are: *encantar* 'to charm', and *interesar* 'to interest.'

In the following sections I will interpret the results of Table1. My exposition is ordered by pragmatic function. In each case I will define the notion. In the final section I will outline some generalizations.

2. Informational word order

When a construction has only the pragmatic function of conveying information, I call its word order informational word order. Primary stress falls on the focus, as in (9):

(9) *nos metímos en la alcantarílla* 14a19
we entered in the culvert
'We entered the culvert'

The context is (10)[6]

(10) 14a19

T: acá en el ferrocarril, salía un tren de carga,
F: mhm
T: que tenía como ***cinco guardas****, qué sé yo. Entonces,*
[
M: claro
T: arrancaba despaci:to así, no? Y en y los los ***vagones****, llenos de pie:dras, llevaba, j este: - teni - tiene unos fierros cruzados para reforzar el - la=*
F: =aha
T: para reforzar el ***vagón****.*
E: claro, porque es tanto peso el que lleva
[[
T: unos unas vigas. [riéndose] Y con otro: chico fuimos nomás, - <u>nos metimos en la alcantarilla</u> - y si agarramos y - ¿vamos a subir acá? Estaba parado, el tren.
M: o sea que estaban en - de debajo de las ruedas

T: here at the railroad station, there was a freight train
F: mhm
T: that had like ***five brakemen****, I don't know. So, it used to*
[
M: right
T: start very slowly like this, you see. And in and the the ***cars*** *were full of stones, er - it had - it has a - like supports to reinforce the - the=*
F: =I see
T: to reinforce the ***car***
E: yes, because it carries a lot of weight
[[
T: some some supports. [he laughs] And I and another boy we went there - <u>we entered the culvert</u> - what if we - let's climb under the car. The train was stopped.
M: this means that you were un - under the wheels

Here the construction in (9) only conveys information.

Primary stress falls on that constituent which, according to the speaker, asserts the crucial piece of information. I will call this focus. I take the notion of 'crucial information' from Comrie 1981: "The essential piece of new information that is carried by a sentence will be referred to as its focus" (Comrie 1981:57). This definition is somewhat vague, because of the lack of precision about what exactly the term 'essential' means. The focus does not necessarily have to be new information in Prince's sense — i.e., introduced into the discourse for the first time. It is the relation between the focus and the rest of the proposition that is considered by the speaker as new to the hearer. In (9) the focus of the sentence *nos metimos en la alcantarilla* 'we entered the culvert' is *alcantarilla* 'culvert'. It contains 'the essential piece of new information'. The newness attributed to this information resides in the relationship between *alcantarilla* 'culvert' and *nos metimos en* 'we entered'.

Lambrecht (1986, 1987b) utilizes this relationship between the referent and the rest of the proposition to define focus:

(11) focus is to be understood as a formal *scope indicator*, i.e. as a grammatical signal indicating the scope of the assertion expressed by a sentence or proposition. The focus indicates which portion of the sentence are asserted and which portions are pragmatically presupposed. (Lambrecht 1987b:374).

This definition sets clearer boundaries for the members of the set 'focus'. The problem is that if we utilize only this definition, in some cases the focus domain encompasses more than one constituent. Notice that the usefulness of the notion of focus for my analysis is its correlation with primary stress placement, which falls on one syllable of one constituent. If the focus domain can include more than one constituent, then in some cases we cannot explain why primary stress falls on a particular item. For example:

(12) 11b3

S: ¿no se enteraron que hubo una marcha pagana? [...] había: m doscientas personas

A: mhm

S: e:n general chicos jóvenes, de las juventudes políticas, () feministas en especial, ***no****. No había sido organizada por feministas. Este:: m () y:: habían:: creo:: hecho dos muñecos gigantes, desnudos, un hombre, una mujer*

F: mhm

S: *y qué sé yo si les habran hecho hacer* ***movimientos****, no sé, llevaban* ***carte:les***

S: *do you know that there was a pagan demonstration? [...] there were um two hundred persons*
A: *mhm*
S: *mostly young people, from political organizations, () there were no feminists. It hadn't been organized by feminists. U::m () a::nd they ha:d I belie:ve, they had made two giant naked puppets, a man and a woman*
F: *mhm*
S: *and I don't know if they made the puppets make* ***movements*** *I don't know, they carried* ***signs***

The whole sentence *llevaban* ***carteles*** 'they carried signs' is asserted, and therefore within the focus domain, but primary stress falls on the direct object *carteles*, as seen in (13):

(13) *lleva̋ban carté:les* 11b3
(they) carried signs
'they carried signs'

Lambrecht himself also notes that "the focus is often not restricted to a single lexical item — the word receiving prosodic prominence — ...focus prominence on a word can indicate a larger focus *domain*." (Lambrecht 1986:172). He later concludes that "the term 'focus' is thus a shorthand for 'focus of the assertion'" (p.178). To solve the assignment of focus in the case of sentences like (13) he postulates "a rule of *default focus assignment*":

(14) This rule assigns focus prominence to (a syllable in) an NP or PP rather than to a verb in any sentence in which both the verb and its complement are in the scope of the assertion...The existence of this rule is based on the (repeatedly mentioned) fact that the pragmatic status of a verb tends to be more neutral or at least less important than the status of an argument constituent. (Lambrecht 1986:188).

This rule would work for most of the cases in my data. In my view, what is behind this rule is the subjective opinion of the speaker who decides, and indicates — by primary stress placement — what is the most important, crucial, piece of the information asserted. This is why I include in my definition of focus the subjective notion of importance. Example (15) illustrates this notion of crucial constituent within the scope of the assertion:

(15) *invitás a una mujer* 8a3
you invite PREP a woman
'you invite a woman'

Primary stress falls on the verb. The context is (16):

(16) 8a3
[speaker C speaks about the bad financial situation of the Argentine middle class]
C: *Yo lo veo en muchos e de: mis compañeros, y demás que l - les decís, mirá, esta noche: los invito a un cu:rso. (0.4) Vengan a un cu:rso, entrada pa:ga, un lanch, e que viene después del curso. (Me dicen) no, pero no tengo qué ponerme. (0.4) Dice y p - son* ***profesionales***, ***universitarios****, no? No, pero: l inv -*
[
A: *hhh*
C: <u>*invitás a una mujer*</u> *y te dice,* ***no****, pero yo n:o voy a ir con - las pilchas que tengo, no puedo ir.*

C: I see it in most of er of: my colleagues when you - you tell them, look, this night um I invite you to a conference. (0.4) Come to a conference, it's free, there are refreshments after the conference. (They tell me) no, I don't have anything to wear. (0.4) He says and p - they are **professionals**, they are **doctors**. But you
[
A: hhh
C: inv - <u>you invite a woman</u> and she says **no**, but I won't go with - the clothes that I have, I can't go.

Speaker C wants to emphasize the financial hardship of Argentine middle class. In (15) the whole construction is asserted. The crucial constituent is the invitation — refused because of lack of appropriate clothes — and not the woman. This is the reason why primary stress falls on the verb, which constitutes the focus.

In the remainder of the section I will try to find a motivation for each of the informational word orders shown in Table1.

In most of the constructions that involve a verb and a NP (intransitives, presentatives, verb and subject, and verb and direct object) there is a correlation between the new/given status of the NP referent and informational word order.

If we take into consideration the cognitive status new/given of the NP referent for all the constructions present in Table1, we have the following results. In constructions with presentatives most NP referents are new (86/118; 73%), which is also the case of constructions with a verb and a direct object[7] (293/494; 59% of new NP referents). In these constructions there is, then, a correlation between a majority of new NP referents and the rigid postverbal position of the NP in the informational word order.

As Table1 shows, in constructions with a two-valency verb and a subject, most NP referents are given (20/29 69%). In this case we see a correlation between a majority of given NP referents and a rigid SV informational word order.

On the other hand, in constructions with intransitives, approximately half of the NP referents are new (37/71; 52%). The informational word order of these constructions, as Table1 shows, is flexible: NPs whose referent is new appear postverbally, and NPs whose referent is given appear preverbally. There is a correlation here between the balanced frequency of both categories of referents and a flexible informational word order.

For constructions with indirect objects and for verbs like *gustar*, it was not possible to find a clear correlation between the cognitive status of the NP referent and the postverbal position of the NP when the construction only conveys information. Half of the indirect object referents are new (6/12), and in the case of *gustar* type the majority of NP referents are given (5/8; 62.5%). A possible cause for this is the very low rate of occurrence of these two constructions in the data.

The correlations stated above confirm that Spanish informational word order follows the theme–rheme type pattern first defined by Mathesius and later refined by Firbas (Firbas 1964). This is an instance of what Mithun (1987:282) calls a pragmatic ordering and, as she shows in her work, does not constitute an universal.

Behind the theme–rheme ordering is the cognitive motivation of moving from which is known to which is unknown. In this sense it is possible to postulate that a majority of new NP referents motivates the rigid postverbal position of the NP, and a majority of given NP referents motivates its rigid preverbal position. When there is a balance between the occurrence of new and given NP referents, informational word order is flexible and varies in direct response to cognitive factors.

In the case of constructions with a verb and a PP, as shown in Table1, when one of the constituents of the PP is a NP, the majority of the referents are new (142/206 69%).[8] On the basis of this correlation it is possible to hypothesize a cognitive motivation for the postverbal position of the PP in informational word order constructions.

In 12% of the cases (28/234) the constituent after the preposition is an adverb or a non-prototypical noun like *vez* 'time, occasion'. The postverbal position of these PPs in informational word order could also be attributed to the cognitive motivation stated above. This is shown in the following example:

(17) *y* *estâba* *de* *allá* 12b2
and it was of there
'and it was towards that side'

The context is (18):

(18) 12b2
[The previous discourse topic is the car of V's mother, so old and unreliable that thieves can't start it and abandon it in frustration].
F: *¿y cuántas veces se lo robaron?*
V: *cinco* ***veces***. *Cinco veces pero ya te digo,* ***nunca*** *más de tres cuadras. El día que estuvo más lejos estaba - dos cuadras para allá. Otro día acá a la vuelta. Otro día movido, viste? Salió Mamá por acá y no lo vió: ()* ***Nena***, *me robaron el auto () y yo me vi:sto, viste, [riéndose] toda porque est - era a la mañana siempre, no? () me levanto, me visto, salgo a buscarlo y estaba -* ***allá***, *en la otra* ***esquina***, *en la misma es - la misma* ***cuadra***. *Otra vez, también, no sé si par - lo habían - mandado para atrás* <u>*y estaba de* ***allá***</u> *[hace gestos].*

F: and how many times they robbed it?
V: five **times**. Five times but as I have told you, **never** beyond three blocks. The furthest they moved it it was - two blocks in that direction. Another time it was around the corner. Another time they moved it, you see. Mom went out to the street and didn't see it. **Girl**, they stole the car () and I got dressed, you see, [laughing] because it - it always happened in the morning

> () I get up, I get dressed, I go out to look for it and it was - **there**, in the the **corner**, in the same **street**. Another time, also, I don't know if th - they have - they have pushed it backwards <u>and it was towards **that** side</u> [she makes gestures].

Here it is the location of the car that is unknown to the hearer. The verb *estar* 'to be located' could be seen as a link between the previous discourse and the information delivered by the PP. What is new to the hearer is the relationship between the adverb and the verb, expressed by the preposition. Therefore, the flow of information moves forward from what is known to what is unknown. Notice that *allá* 'there' is the focus and receives primary stress.

The remaining construction in Table1 involves a verb and an adverb. In the corpus, the adverbs *ahora* 'now', *casi* 'almost, *después* 'later', *entonces* 'so', *todavía* 'still', *ya* 'yet', *siempre* 'always', *nunca* 'never', and the adverbs that end in *-mente* '-ly': *difícilmente* 'seldom', *directamente* 'simply', *simplemente* 'simply', *lamentablemente* 'unfortunately', *propiamente* 'actually', *realmente* 'really', henceforth 'class 2 adverbs', exhibit an ADVV informational word order. 'Class 1 adverbs' includes all the other adverbs, their informational word order is VADV, as shown in Table1. Interestingly, with the exception of *después* 'later' and *entonces* 'so', all of the adverbs listed above as class 2 have been found to occur preverbally in English (Jacobson 1978).

The motivation for the preverbal position of most class 2 adverbs in Spanish can be attributed to their syntactic function in the sentence. In his study of *-mente* adverbs in Spanish, Egea (1979) distinguishes the class of *adverbios oracionales* 'sentence adverbs.' These adverbs modify the whole sentence. Egea cites all of the aforementioned class 2 *-mente* adverbs as sentence adverbs. He observes that their preferred position is initial. He affirms that "these adverbs are independent, functioning at the periphery of the sentence or clause without integrating with it"[9] (p.253). What these adverbs have in common is that they, in some manner, relate the construction to the previous context. This function may be considered to be comparable to the one that conjunctions have.[10] In Spanish, conjunctions always occupy the first position in the construction. It is possible, then to hypothesize that the preverbal position of most of class 2 adverbs is motivated by this relational function.

The relational function, however, does not account for the preverbal position of the following adverbs: *casi* 'almost', *siempre* 'always', *nunca* 'never', *todavía* 'still', *ya* 'yet'. This group shares a semantic feature: its members modify aspectually the action of the verb.

The postverbal position of class 2 adverbs in informational word order cannot be accounted for clearly. The only correlation is that the majority of them express focus and the constituent with a focus referent most often appears postverbally in informational word order constructions.

3. Contrary to expectation

An utterance expresses the feature of 'contrary to expectation' when it conveys a message not expected, given the previous discourse, knowledge of the world or the culture, knowledge of the other discourse participants, etc. This pragmatic function includes two related notions: (i) unexpected or surprising news, and (ii) denial of a previous assumption. In the first case, what the utterance communicates is not expected, given the previous discourse situation, knowledge of the world, etc. In the second case, something in the previous discourse has led the speaker to believe that the hearer has a false assumption. Therefore, the speaker tries to clarify the situation. For example, (19) is a case of unexpected news:

(19) *no víno Bő́rga* 6b5
not came B.
Borga didn't show up

The context of (19) is (20):

(20) 6b5
C: Borga [...] estaba de profesor en la Alianza de Buenos Aires,
F: sí
C: y:: andaba en el ***teatro*** *allá. (1) Y:: por ahí murió el hermano.*
F: ¿quién? el - el=
C: =el hermano, creo que se - ***Telmo*** *o algo así. Mayor que él, me parece.=*
F: =sí, que era médico.
C: tonces digo bueno, ahora, este: - digo, voy a ir al entierro, voy a ir al entierro y lo voy a ver a ***Borga****, tantos años. <u>No vino Borga</u>.*

C: Borga [...] was instructor at the Alliance Française in Buenos Aires.
F: mhm
C: a::nd he was involved in the **theatre** there. (1) A::nd suddenly his brother died.
F: who? the - the=
C: =his brother, I believe that his - **Telmo** or something like this. He was his elder, I guess=
F: =ah yes, the one who was a doctor
C: so I said, well now, u:m - I said, I will go to the funeral, I will go to the funeral and I will see **Borga**, so many years. <u>Borga didn't show up</u>.

In the context of Rioplatense culture a person is expected to attend his/her brother's funeral. Failure to do so would be socially inappropriate. Therefore, the absence of Borga constitutes a case of unexpected news. Note that primary stress falls on the focus of the deviation from expectation: the verb *vino* '(he) came' in (19).

In two-constituent constructions, deviation from expectation motivates an inversion of the corresponding informational word order, as seen in Table2.

Given an informational word order AB, the feature 'contrary to expectation' is expressed by a BA ordering. For example, the informational word order of constructions with an intransitive verb and a subject whose referent is given is SV, as shown in Table1. In (19) this same type of construction expressing deviation from expectation exhibits an inverted VS word order. It is important to keep in mind that the term 'inversion' is only a useful descriptive metaphor. I do not wish to imply here any ordered process in the mind of the speaker/hearer.

Examples with verbs like *gustar* and cases of verbs with indirect objects are not very common (as seen in Table1), and there are no instances in the data analyzed of these two constructions expressing deviation from expectation.

Table 2

Pragmatic function	Word order	
informational word order	A	B
contrary to expectation	B	A

4. Focus of contrast

The focus of contrast is the constituent that stands in opposition to a closed number of alternatives, members of the same semantic set. What is asserted is which candidate is the correct one (Chafe 1976; and Silva-Corvalán 1983). The other alternatives, members of the set, must be identifiable. For example:

(21) 19b6

V: *El padre, ¿con los hijos? (0.4) no fue para nada afectuoso. Ahora, <u>(a) la perra la adora</u>. A la perra le* ***habla****, a la perra le - ¿te das cuenta lo que es - eso es terrible. A la perra le le le le - le habla como si fuera una persona, e: le le*
[
A: *a:h*
V: ***juega****. Ahora, a los hijos, no. <u>Al canario le habla</u>, al canario lo lo lo* ***besa****, y a los hijos, no.*

V: the father never showed affection to his children. Now, <u>the dog, he loves it</u>. He **speaks** to the dog, he - do you realize this? - this is terrible. He speaks to the dog as if it was a person, u:m he he
[
A: oh
V: **plays** with him. But never with the children. <u>he talks to the canary</u>, he **kisses** the the the canary, not the children.

Speaker V contrasts the direct object referent of *perra* 'dog' and the indirect object referent of *canario* 'canary' with the referent of *hijos* 'children'. The contrast is based on opposite predications *hablar* 'to talk' versus *no hablar* 'not to talk', and *besar* 'to kiss' versus *no besar* 'not to kiss'.

In spoken Spanish the constituent whose referent is focus of contrast appears first and receives primary stress, as in Table 3.

In a two-constituent construction AB, if constituent A is focus of contrast

Table 3. Focus of contrast

Pragmatic function	Word order	
constituent A focus of contrast	ˈA	B
constituent B focus of contrast	ˈB	A

the word order will be AB with primary stress on A; if constituent B is focus of contrast, the word order will be BA, with primary stress falling on B.

Examples (22) and (23) are the constructions presented in context (21):

(22) ahôra (a) la pe̍rra la adő̈ra 19b6
now PREP the dog CL loves
'now the dog he loves it'

(23) al cana̍rio le ha̍bla 19b6
to the canary CL (he) talks
'He talks to the canary'

Primary stress falls on the foci of contrast, *perra* and *canario.*

5. Focal referent

In a question-answer exchange, the referent of the constituent that provides the information requested — the focus of the answer — is the focal referent (Silva-Corvalán 1983:135). The following is a case of a focal PP:

(24) en el oche̍nta nos fu̎imos 15a5
in the eighty (we) left
'We left in 1980'

This construction appears in the data in a question-answer exchange. The initial PP, also the focus of the utterance, provides the information requested:

(25) 15a5
Q: ¿cuándo hace que [...] se fueron?=
M: =pero vos sabés
[
F: <u>*en el ochenta nos fuimos*</u>

Q: when did you [...] leave [the country]?=
M: =but you should know
[
F: <u>we left in 1980.</u>

A focal referent is expressed in the same manner as a focus of contrast: it appears in first position and receives primary stress.

The expression of focal referents is not very common: only VDO, VPP, and VADV constructions have been found in the corpus, as shown in Table1.

6. Topics

According to Lambrecht (1984) "the topic of a sentence is what the sentence is about." In Rioplatense Spanish the constituent whose referent is topic appears in preverbal position. In the data topics occur only with direct objects, and with subjects of verbs like *gustar*, as seen in Table 1. The following is a case of a direct object topic:

(26) 12a11

*V: **Vos**, para presentarte a un concurso tenés, un: código () e formado por una letra y un número. No firmás no figurás, no sos nadie, sos un número. () Es decir que: - tu **prueba**,*

F: m

V: no se puede relacionar con vos, () no es cierto?

[

F: es claro, está bien, así no se sabe nada.

[

*V: entonces ya es **bien** objetiva, se supone, la este:m () e la calificación. () Entonces, <u>a esa prueba la - la leen</u>:, la analizan, la la entre todos, pa:sa por un montón de de - de filtros, primero la lee uno, después la lee otra, ha hacen acotaciones neee () hasta que, resuelven, si la aprobaste o no la aprobaste.*

V: in order to be considered for the job you have a: code () um formed by a letter and a number. You don't sign, your name doesn't show up, you are anonymous, you are a number. () This means that your exam,

F: m

V: cannot be related to you, () see?

[

F: ah, all right, in this way nobody will

know

[

V: so your grade is very objective, we suppose. () So, this exam, they read it, they analyze it, it passes a lot of filters, first one person reads it, then another one reads it, they make comments eee () until they decide if you pass it or not.

Speaker V is talking about an exam. Speaker F's reaction makes her switch to a related topic: grading. Then, she switches back to the previous topic. The referent of *la prueba* 'the exam' is the topic of the sentence. Also, as we can see in (26), the DO referent becomes the topic of the stretch of discourse that follows. In the data, sentence topic DOs are used by the speakers to return to a previous topic (in the majority of the cases), or to introduce a new one. Although this is an open empirical issue — because new data can falsify this statement — it is very likely that the preverbal position of the DO does not correlate with topics in general, but only with new or resumptive topics.

7. Generalizations

Table4 synthesizes the previous discussion. The informational word order of constructions with a verb and a NP, or a verb and a PP, is pragmatically motivated by the new/given status of the NP referent. The preverbal position of most Class2 adverbs seems to be syntactically motivated. Given an informational word order AB, deviation from expectation motivates an inversion, BA. The constituent whose referent is focus of contrast, focal, or topic appears in

Table 4. The word order of two-constituent constructions in spoken Spanish

Pragmatic function	Word order		Tokens	%
Conveying information	A	B	1019	88
Contrary to expectation	B	A	41	3
Constituent A or B focus of contrast or focal	{A	B}	65	6
	B	A		
Constituent B topic	B	A	7	1
unclear cases			26	2
Total			1158	100

first position and — in the case of focus of contrast and focal — it receives primary stress.

It seems that there are two general principles influencing word order in these constructions: cognition, and iconicity. In the case of the pragmatic function that solely conveys information — informational word order — the principle of communicative dynamism (Firbas 1964) plays a role: constituents carrying the highest degree of communicative dynamism are placed at the end. This could be conceived as a cognitive principle, motivated by the manner in which the mind processes information.

When the utterance, in addition to communicating information, conveys another pragmatic function, iconicity plays a role. Deviation from expectation is iconically expressed by an unexpectedly inverted word order. In the case of topic, focus of contrast, and focal referent, the principle at play is the one described by Givón (1988:275): "more important information is fronted"; the referent that occupies the first place in attention comes first.

One question is whether there is any connection between the notions presented in Table4. Focus of contrast, focal constituent, and focus indicate a relationship between the referent of a constituent and the rest of the proposition expressed by the sentence.[11] Deviation from expectation, on the other hand, is a relationship of contrast between a proposition and the previous context.

Almost all two constituent constructions express only one pragmatic function.[12] In the only case found in the data where two pragmatic functions are expressed, both notions are compatible:

(27) *en la Pla̋za Itália está̋ba* 12b4
at the (it) was (located)
'it was at Plaza Italia'

The context is (28):

(28) 12b4
V: el hermano de Beatriz [...] tiene un Citroën [...] un día lo ***deja*** *en la puerta de la casa, sube, al departamento a hacer no sé qué () habrá tardado una hora, cuando bajó el Citroën no estaba. () Le habló por teléfono - a un este amigo y le pidió de ir a buscarlo*
F: mh
V: y empezaron a recorrer La Plata hasta que lo ***encontraron****. [...] lo empezaron a buscar, a buscar, primero empezaron por la periferia, no en la* ***Plaza Italia*** *estaba.*

V: Beatriz's brother [...] has a Citroën [...] one day he parks it in front of the house, he goes upstairs to his appartment to do I don't know what. One hour later, when he came back the Citroën wasn't there. () He asked a friend to drive him to look for his car

F: mh

V: and so they drove all over La Plata until they **found** it. [...] They started the search in the suburbs but no, it was at **Plaza Italia**.

(27) conveys contrary to expectation: the point of the story is the unusual place where they found the car, *Plaza Italia*, located in downtown La Plata, where there are always people around — an unlikely place to abandon a stolen car. (Notice that in Argentina middle-class people live downtown. The poorer neighborhoods are in the suburbs, where stolen cars are more likely to be abandoned). At the same time, there is a contrast between *periferia* 'suburbs' where they expected to find the car, and *Plaza Italia,* where they finally found it, not far from home. Primary stress falls on Plaza Italia whose referent is contrasted and is also the focus of deviation from expectation.

To conclude, as Table 4 shows, the majority of the constructions in the corpus are instances of informational word order (88%), only 10% express a pragmatic function (besides that of conveying information), and the hypothesis is followed by 98% of the data.

Notes

* I would like to express my deep gratitude to Carmen Silva-Corvalán for stimulating my interest in the question of word order in spoken Spanish. Her perceptive criticism, enthusiasm, and encouragement were most inspiring to me. I am particularly indebted to the editors of this volume, Mickey Noonan and Pamela Downing. Their insightful questions and observations made me rethink many portions of my work. Any errors that remain are, of course, my own.

1. The numbers and letters at the right indicate the location of the example in the corpus.

2. The symbol (') indicates primary stress, (") secondary stress, and (^) tertiary stress.

3. This is to be understood in a very broad sense as 'communicating something'. I am not excluding social or interactional factors here. This pragmatic function could alternatively be defined in a negative way: it does not convey any of the other pragmatic functions, such as contrary to expectation, or focus of contrast.

4. For a more detailed report on the introduction of new referents into the discourse cf. Ocampo (1990, 1991).

5. The experiencer can be optionally expressed, in addition, by an indirect object NP, but the clitic is always present.

6. The conventions used in the transcription are as follows. A single bracket '[' between two utterances indicates that they overlap. The sign '=' marks partial overlapping between the end of a turn and the beginning of another. Utterances appear between parentheses when I am not sure of the accuracy of the transcription. Three periods between parentheses '(...)' mean that it was impossible to ascertain what the speaker said. Three periods between square brackets '[...]' indicate that data is omitted. A hiatus of any kind in the speech flow is marked by '-'. A pause is indicated by parentheses: '()'. A number between parentheses '(1.4)' shows the length of the pause (in seconds and tenths of seconds). Words or utterances in bold mark that this portion is perceived as salient (strong primary stress, or high pitch, or uttered with louder voice, etc.). Lengthening is indicated by ':' after a vowel or a consonant. Any additional information appears between square brackets: '[risas]'. The constructions relevant for the analysis are shown underlined.

7. In Spanish, the subject is not obligatory.

8. Although in some instances it was difficult to ascertain if the status of the NP referent in PP constructions was brand-new or inferrable, there was no problem in assigning it to the more general categories new or given.

9. The translation is mine.

10. That adverbs can function as also conjunctions was noticed by Bello (1951) (quoted by Egea 1979:210).The Real Academia Española (1973:501) states that some conjunctions are former adverbs.

11. Notice that Lambrecht (1986) divides focus into broad focus and narrow focus. Under his classification, what I call focus of contrast and focal constituent fall under the category of narrow focus.

12. With the exception of conveying information, which all of them express (in addition to focus of contrast, deviation from expectation, etc.).

References

Bello, Andrés. 1951. *Estudios gramaticales*. Caracas: Ediciones del Ministerio de Educación.

Bentivoglio, Paola. 1985. "Función y significado de la posposición del sujeto nominal en el español hablado". Instituto de Filología 'Andrés Bello', Universidad Central de Venezuela.

Bentivoglio, Paola and Elizabeth Weber. 1986. "A functional approach to subject word order in spoken Spanish". *Studies in Romance Linguistics* ed. by Osvaldo Jaeggli and Carmen Silva-Corvalán, 23-40. Dordrecht: Foris.

Chafe, Wallace. 1976. "Givenness, contrastiveness, definiteness, topics, and point of view." *Subject and Topic* ed. by Charles Li, 27-55. New York: Academic Press.

Comrie, Bernard. 1981. *Language Universals and Linguistic Typology*. Chicago: University of Chicago Press.

Egea, Esteban. 1979. *Los adverbios terminados en mente en el español contemporáneo.* Bogotá: Publicaciones del Instituto Caro y Cuervo.

Firbas, Jan. 1964. "On defining the theme in functional sentence analysis". *Travaux linguistiques de Prague* 1.267-80.

Givón, T. 1984. *Syntax.* Amsterdam/Philadelphia: John Benjamins.

Givón, T. 1988. The pragmatics of word order: predictability, importance and attention. *Studies in Syntactic Typology* ed. by M. Hammond, E. A. Moravcsik, and J. R. Wirth, 243-84. Amsterdam/Philadelphia: John Benjamins.

Jacobson, Sven. 1978. *On the Use, Meaning, and Syntax of English Preverbal Adverbs.* Stockholm: Almqvist & Wiksell.

Keenan, Edward. 1976. "Towards a universal definition of 'subject'". *Subject and Topic* ed. by Charles Li, 303-33. New York: Academic Press.

Lambrecht, Knud. 1984. "A pragmatic constraint on lexical subjects in spoken French". *Chicago Linguistic Society* 20.239-56

Lambrecht, Knud. 1986. "Topic, Focus, and the Grammar of Spoken French". PhD Dissertation. UC Berkeley.

Lambrecht, Knud. 1987a. "On the status of SVO sentences in French discourse". *Coherence and Grounding in Discourse* ed. by R. Tomlin 217-61. Amsterdam/Philadelphia: John Benjamins.

Lambrecht, Knud. 1987b. "Sentence focus, information structure, and the thetic-categorial distinction". *Berkeley Linguistic Society* 13.366-82

Mithun, Marianne. 1987. "Is basic word order universal?" *Coherence and Grounding in Discourse* ed. by R. Tomlin 281-328. Amsterdam/Philadelphia: John Benjamims.

Ocampo, Francisco. 1990. "The pragmatics of word order in constructions with a verb and a subject." *Hispanic Linguistics* 4.1.87-127.

Ocampo, Francisco. 1991. "Word order in constructions with a one-valency verb, a subject NP, and a PP in spoken Rioplatense Spanish." *Hispania* 74.2.

Prince, Ellen. 1981. "Toward a taxonomy of given-new information". *Radical Pragmatics* ed. by Peter Cole, 223-55. New York: Academic Press.

Real Academia Española. 1973. *Esbozo de una nueva gramática de la lengua española.* Madrid: Espasa-Calpe.

Silva-Corvalán, Carmen. 1983. "On the interaction of word order and intonation: some OV constructions in Spanish." *Discourse Perpectives on Syntax* ed. by Flora Klein-Andreu, 117-40. New York: Academic Press.

Silva-Corvalán, Carmen. 1984. "Semantic and pragmatic factors in syntactic change." *Historical Syntax* ed. by J. Fisiak, 555-73. Berlin: Mouton.

Verb initial languages and information order*

Doris L. Payne
University of Oregon & Summer Institute of Linguistics

1. Introduction

The better attempts at determining word order frequencies estimate that roughly 10% of the world's languages are verb initial (VI).[1] Families with such languages principally include Austronesian, Salishan and Wakashan and perhaps other families of the northwestern United States and Canada, Otomanguean, Mayan, southern Arawakan, Celtic, Semitic, Nilo-Saharan, and isolates scattered here and there (e.g. Yagua, Taushiro, both located in the Peruvian lowlands).[2]

In summarizing what either were, or what he thought might prove to be, characteristics of VI languages, Edward Keenan once stated that "topicalization may be done by fronting, though there is a tendency in Nilotic to move old information to the end of the clause."[3] Yagua provided my first in-depth experience with a VI language. Order of postverbal objects and obliques could vary and I eventually concluded that Keenan's statement about Nilotic was not too far off in predicting the Yagua variation. I was happy to think that Yagua was, at least to that extent, a well-behaved VI language. So far, so good (I thought).

Keenan's claim about Nilotic was almost certainly based on Chet Creider's work (1975, 1977, 1979). Creider (1975) hypothesized that "in verb-initial languages the theme is placed in sentence-final position in what speakers feel are unmarked sentences." Creider (1979) stated it in the reverse order, suggesting that languages in which "themes" or "topics" come last and "focused" elements come initially, are VI.[4] In conceptualizing theme, Creider (1975; see also 1979, 1983) appealed to Functional Sentence Perspective works of Firbas (1964) and Trávníček (cf. Trávníček 1939), but further stated that theme must "be defined with reference to the pragmatic notion of discourse topic, i.e. in terms of the textual and extra-linguistic context in which sentences in discourse are found". Evidently, a theme for Creider was a referent around which a section of discourse is oriented, which is not asserted, and about which further talk is possible. He defined rheme as "that part of a sentence which is most closely related to the assertion of the sentence."

This paper discusses VI languages from three genetic groups relative to what comes initially in the clause, what comes right after the verb, and what comes finally. Two languages reported on are fairly rigid VI languages: Yagua (Peba-Yaguan of Peru) and Maasai (Eastern Nilotic of Kenya and Tanzania). Austronesian languages are less rigid, showing more VN/NV alternation (Hopper 1987; Quakenbush 1992).

The present study assumes a cognitive-pragmatic perspective and simultaneously hopes to keep sight of the morphosyntactic properties of individual languages. In adopting this perspective, I presuppose that an understanding of discourse production must consider (a) the speaker's goals *vis-à-vis* the hearer's current knowledge network and subsequent possible behaviors, (b) the speaker's ongoing evaluation of the hearer's mental representation of incoming information and the status of information in the hearer's memory and attention, and (c) the concomitant speech acts that the speaker chooses to perform.

There is an increasing amount of work on the role of cognitive processing in determining choice of one linguistic form over another. Here I note just two ideas in the psycholinguistic literature that seem especially relevant to word order variation. These are the rather severe limitations on how much can be focally attended to at any one time; and the process of building a mental representation, including what it means to "establish a foundation" for a section of a representation. I will consider these in reverse order.

In a series of comprehension-based studies on English, Gernsbacher (1990) and Gernsbacher and Hargreaves (1992) claim that comprehension involves building coherent mental representations or structures. They metaphorically refer to the first part of this building process as "laying a foundation." On the basis of experimental data, they argue that information which occurs first in a phrase, clause, sentence, or passage gains privileged, foundational status in comprehenders' minds. Another cognitive process is "mapping," whereby incoming information that coheres or relates to previous information is integrated into the developing structure. If the incoming information is less coherent or less related, a third process occurs: comprehenders automatically shift and develop a new substructure. Most mental representations of discourse thus consist of branching substructures.

I do not believe it is too far afield to see Gernsbacher's experimentally-validated "foundation" of a mental representation as roughly what the Functional Sentence Perspective school and Creider himself were getting at in talking about the "theme" or "topic" of a discourse section. I suggest that whatever a comprehender takes as the foundation for a mental structure can linguistically be referred to as the **thematic** concept or referent of that structure — this is the concept onto which other information is mapped.

Gernsbacher and Hargreaves' concern is with what comprehenders do with linearly initial material in a sentence or other linguistic unit, particularly with first-mentioned participants. But most certainly the foundation for a mental representation need not correspond to the literally initial element in some clause. If a Maasai audience heard a traditional story with (1) as its first sentence, it is almost certain that *enkítojó* 'the hare' would be established as the foundation of the first (sub)structure, rather than *etíi ɔpá* 'he-be-there formerly'. That is, comprehenders would likely try to relate additional incoming information to the referential concept of 'the hare', and not to the nonreferential, existential '(he) formerly existed'. The very point of referentiality is that a referential concept has continuous identity over time, and as an enduring entity, additional information can be mapped to this concept.[5]

(1)	*e-tíi*	*ɔpa*	*en-kítojó*
	3-be.in.place	formerly	FS-hare

'Long ago there was/lived the hare...' (Hollis, p. 103).

Relative to discourse production, Gernsbacher and Hargreaves cite MacWhinney (1977:152) who claims that in English, speakers use the first element of a "sentence as a starting point for the organization of the sentence as a whole."

A second relevant concept is "focus of attention". In an experimental study of Mandarin, Tomlin and Pu (1991) describe focal attention as follows:

> "From the set of activated elements [in short-term memory], it is possible for a further subset to receive even more specialized and localized processing. Elements which receive this more focused processing fall within **focal**

> **attention**. They represent elements which have been selected to form novel associations against information in long term memory. Focal attention is a particularly limited kind of processing state, requiring sustained expenditure of rather limited attentional resources. Consequently, only one or two elements ordinarily receive focal attention at any given time."

One may infer from Tomlin and Pu that when speakers intend their hearers to establish a concept as the theme (i.e. as the foundation for further information), they do so by directing the hearers' attention to it. While an item has status as theme, it remains in active memory and even in focal attention. Nevertheless, it would appear that the limited attentional resources can **simultaneously** be extended or oriented to additional information which the speaker wishes the hearer to relate to the now-established theme.[6]

One crucial thing to note is that information in the focus of attention and information which constitutes the foundation of a mental representation are potentially distinct cognitive parameters, but that a particular piece of information can realize them both in a given clause.

Finally, although morphosyntax may be sensitive to whether information is in the focus of attention, it is also sensitive to the speaker's goals and speech acts *vis-à-vis* the hearer. That is, knowing whether information is in the focus of attention (whether as the already-established theme, or as information to be related to that theme) may not be enough to predict morphosyntax; one of several constructions might be chosen depending on the more specific job to be achieved. Consider the following Yagua data. Ex. (2) contrasts 'with leaves' and 'with mud.' In the story prior to these two clauses there is a clear presupposition that Mocayu ('he') and two wasp twins ('they.two') have made shelters. The specific building materials are new information and set up Mocayu as an intelligent individual who will ward off the night-time rain, while the witless the wasp twins will get a soaking when their mud shelter disintegrates in the rain:

(2) ***Návɨɨ-ta*** *sa-sų́tąy-day*
leaves-INST 3SG-make.shelter-CONSECUTIVE
'With leaves he made shelter;

múcadíí-ta *naada-sų́tay-day*
mud-INST 3DL-make.shelter-CONSECUTIVE
'with mud they.two made shelter.' (KT027-030)

Ex. (3) introduces an old woman who is one of two main characters in the final section of a discourse. She has not been referred to before, and all subsequent references are by bound clitics only:

(3) *Naada-jųsitya-rįį-maa* *jį́į́*
3DL-follow-enroute-PERF DISCONTINUITY
rimityu-jáda-dee-rųy-níí
old.one-FEM-DIMIN-DL-3SG
'A dear little old woman (had) followed him (= a wounded warrior).'

In (2-3) the focus of attention is most likely newly extended to the information in the boldfaced phrases.[7] But in (2) there is contrast or pragmatic markedness, while (3) simply introduces a new major participant. Thus out of all information that is likely in the focus of attention, only a subset is placed preverbally in Yagua.

In some languages a certain (e.g. clause-initial) position might serve to direct attention to information that is somehow novel — if not in itself, at least in terms of its links to other information.[8] In most VI languages, however, it is likely that only a subset of information to which attentional resources are specifically directed occurs initially. In what follows I suggest this is roughly equivalent to the sum of certain pragmatically marked information, plus the verbal element in temporally-sequenced clauses.

2. The functions of initial position

When an item is initial in a sentence, it may be ambiguous what kind of structure it is initial within. In a Government Binding treatment of Mayan, for instance, Aissen (1992) argues that an initial lexical item may be initial within CP, IP, or XP. Based on Niuean, Chamorro, Breton, and Jacaltec, Woolford (1991) argues that in VI languages, an initial lexical phrase may be initial within IP, VP, or V'.[9] Perhaps to my own detriment, in this study I generally ignore such differences under the hypothesis that when a language does allow order variation for cognitive-pragmatic reasons, some particular job may be achieved by, or a coherent set of conditions may motivate, placing an item in initial position regardless of what structure is used to get the phrase into initial position. That is, there may be a conspiracy among different structures, all serving to achieve a preferred information order for the job in question. This is certainly consonant with the theories expressed by MacWhinney (1977) and Gernsbacher (1990), who are concerned with the memory representation of initial elements. I approach this study inductively, attempting to determine what cognitive-pragmatic functions initial elements appear to serve in VI languages. In the process I will address how these various functions might cohere.

2.1 *Predicates in temporally sequenced clauses*

Most claims about word order have undoubtedly been based on narrative data and, without conscious awareness, the typological cubby-holes to which languages have been assigned are likely biased by formal features correlating with temporal sequentiality. It is most certainly true that in any language which has been labelled "verb initial", the verb (plus or minus auxiliaries, adverbs, modals, negatives, perhaps clitics, etc.) will come initially in temporally-sequenced main event line clauses, before the nominal arguments of the verb.[10] An explicit correlation between temporal sequencing and VI clause choice has been argued for Early Biblical Hebrew (Givón 1977; Longacre, this volume and 1982), Tzotzil, and Chorti (Mayan; Myhill 1992), Agutaynen (Austronesian; Quakenbush 1992), Yagua (D. Payne 1993), and Tashelhit Berber (Bailey 1991).[11]

Temporally sequenced event line clauses narrate events (Hopper 1987). Assuming participants have already been established, attentional resources are most certainly extended to predicate elements in such clauses, which come initially. In terms of event line clauses, then, novel attention redirection is associated with initial position.

If a language tends toward a rigid VI type, predicates also come first in many clauses that are not temporally sequenced but which serve to introduce and describe referents, state background conditions, or describe events which are out of sequence with the main event line.

2.2 *Delimiting phrases*

Edward Keenan observed that no language is rigidly VI in the same sense that some languages are rigidly verb final. Under specifiable conditions some arguments of the verb can always come initially (cf. Greenberg's 1963

Universals 6 & 12). In this and following sections, we consider conditions under which this happens.

Relative to preverbal phrases, I do distinguish left-dislocated phrases which are outside the syntactic clause proper, from phrases which are inside the clause (at some structural level) but before the verb. Formal differences between the two are language-specific, but a rule of thumb is that a left-dislocated phrase occurs under a separate intonation contour and may or may not be related to the verbal case frame. If it is related to the verb's case frame, then a resumptive reference may occur within the clause proper. A non-dislocated preverbal phrase also may or may not be related to the verbal case frame, but if it is, a resumptive reference will likely not occur.

I will not consider in depth differences in what these two preverbal phases cross-linguistically convey, except to note that left-dislocated phrases often delimit a time, location, or some other conceptual frame of reference for what follows. In some languages they may express contrastive topics for an ensuing section of discourse — i.e. they may "lay the foundation" for other incoming information. It should be noted that both delimiting expressions and contrastive topics can be expressed in other ways than just by a left-dislocated phrase; in (14) below, for example, the participial or gerundive clause *Ore apa tenkiterunoto* 'long ago at the beginning of time' sets a delimiting frame of reference.

2.3 *Pragmatically marked phrases*

In all VI languages, non-dislocated preverbal phrases express at least a subset of pragmatically marked (PM) information.[12] I use the term "pragmatically marked" firstly because of the vagueness associated with "focus." One traditional meaning of "focus" is for asserted, nonpresupposed information; under such a definition, preverbal position does not express all "focused" information in VI languages (if it did, the language would likely not be called VI).[13] Nor does it include all the information in the focus of attention (cf. the Yagua example in [3] above). Secondly, by "pragmatically marked" I have something broader in mind than strict "focus of contrast" (cf. Dik *et al.* 1981 for additional discussion), something closer to information which is to some degree counter to what the speaker assumes are the hearer's current expectations or presuppositions. Such PM speech acts include types of single focus contrast, multiple foci of contrast, establishing an entity as the unique item related to some other information, negation, information questions, answers to information questions, some yes-no questions, threats, added detail restatement, semantic augmentation (e.g. superlatives) or diminuation, and other situations. In etic terms, a continuum exists between highly marked speech acts that express information or a relation between pieces of information that speakers assume to be downright contrary to their hearers' assumptions, versus those that express information assumed to be in accord with, or only incrementally different from, the hearers' current expectations. I will only give a brief introduction here, starting with the most highly marked situations, and will then extend the discussion to information questions and answers. For reasons of space, a full treatment of PM speech acts cannot be given here, but the reader is referred to D. Payne (1990) for some discussion.[14]

The most highly PM speech acts include those in which the speaker assumes the hearer holds some proposition to be true, or assumes the hearer has certain established links in his or her information network. But there is a further assumption that (I) the hearer has information incorrectly linked with other information, or that (II) a propositional link is missing between certain pieces of information which really must be established. In (I), the speaker can instruct the hearer to unlink the incorrect information. Morphosyntactically, this is often done by simple negation. In VI languages, negated constituents often occur before the verb; this is, for instance, required in Mam (Mayan; England 1983). Consider also the following complaint from Maasai (Eastern Nilotic), which is likely uttered against the normal assumption that a woman does have children.

(4) *Mmɛ ɛn-kɛ́ráy á-áta*
Neg FS-child 1SG-have
'I have no child.' (Hollis, p. 161)

In (5) several members of a laggardly coward's party fear that the coward has killed some forbidden monkeys. The coward explains why he has not kept up with the others:

(5) a. *Mmɛ nɪncɛ́ á-ar*
NEG they 1SG-kill
'Not them I kill,

b. *en-amʊ́ke na-tu-dúng-e á-ytɔbɪr.*
FS-sandal REL-PFTV-break-MIDDLE 1SG-prepare
'The sandal which has broken I'm fixing.' (Hollis, p. 130)

Beyond unlinking incorrect information, in many contrast situations a limited set of possibilities is assumed to be in the addressee's mind which could rectify the missing or incorrect information (Chafe 1976; Dik *et al.* 1981). In situations of either type (I) or (II), the speaker can instruct the hearer to link up the correct information from the assumed set. In (6b) the speakers assert that there is one item wished for against the not-quite-right backdrop of 'we don't wish for anything'. In (7) the presupposition is that the kick should have landed squarely on the opponent's body; but in actuality it only connected with his shield.

(6) a. *Mi-kí-yó-u* *áytoki*
NEG-1PL-wish-PFTV anything

b. *o-sárgɛ́* *l-inó* *ki-yó-u*
MS-blood M-your 1PL-wish-PFTV
'We won't wish for anything, (only) your blood we will wish.
(Hollis, p. 106)

(7) *n-e-rua* *to-l-kimojino*
C-3-kick OBL-PL-toe
kake *ellongo* *ake* *e-ta-rua*
but shield only 3-PERF-kick
'He kicked (him) with his foot, but only the shield he kicked (i.e. instead of the person).' (Hollis, p. 113)

Answers to information questions share the same pragmatic parts as do most contrast situations: (a) there is a background assumption with some piece of information missing, (b) a set of candidates which could supply the information is normally assumed to exist, and (c) the correct candidate is asserted. Similarly, information questions contain (a) a background presupposition but with certain information missing. If the question is felicitous, the questioner also (b) assumes that a set of possible candidates exists which could supply the missing information, though its contents may be unknown to the questioner. In place of asserting the correct candidate, an information question (c) solicits the missing information (see [9] below). Given their shared pragmatic makeup, it is not surprising that contrast and information questions and answers often share the same morphosyntax. In nearly all VI languages, question phrases come before the verb (Greenberg's Universal 12: 'If a language has dominant order VSO in declarative sentences, it always puts interrogative words or phrases first in interrogative word questions'; p. 111).

In Maasai, clauses with preverbal subjects syntactically resemble predicate nominal or cleft expressions in which the non-initial verb takes on a relative clause form initiated with *na-* (feminine gender) or *o-* (masculine gender). Clefts iconically partition the clause into two portions: the first contains the single constituent to which the limited attentional resources are being directed, while the remainder contains largely presupposed information. This structure is used for subject questions, answers, and in some contrastive contexts (ex. 8); it is not used for fronted objects (ex. 9). In Irish, cleft constructions are used with any kind of fronted material, including information question pronouns (Noonan, 1994).

(8) *ángay ná-to-rik-u-ó ɪntáy*
who FS-PFTV-bring-AL-PFTV you
ol-mʊ́rráni ó-to-rik-ú-o iyyóók
MS-warrior MS-PFTV-bring-AL-PFTV us
'Who brought you here? The warrior brought us here.' (Hollis 134)

(9) *áάynyɔ́ɔ́ í-ncɔ iyyóók*
what 2-give us
'What will you give us?' (Hollis, p. 106)

Tennet (Surmic) can place question phrases initially within clefts, leave them *in situ,* or at the end of the clause, with decreasing degrees of exclusivity of contrast (Scott Randall, p.c.). Creider (1989) asserts that in Nandi (Southern Nilotic), question phrases occur postverbally *in situ*; they can also occur initially in cleft constructions. These are two of the very few exceptions known to the VI portion of Greenberg's universal 12 and are surely also two of the most strongly VI languages. Maasai and Yagua are both strongly VI in that aside from left-dislocation, only PM phrases occur preverbally. But Maasai is more strongly VI than Yagua: in elicitation, even adverbials are said to be "wrong" when placed before the verb in Maasai (Morompi Ole-Ronkei, personal communication). Second, although information question words are always initial for subjects (in the relative-like construction), and preferably initial for objects, answers to information questions can occur after the verb. In this respect Maasai — akin to Nandi — differs from many VI languages. Consider the following (exs. from Ole-Ronkei):

(10) a. *Káynyɔ ɛ́-tɔ́-dúá ɛn-kɛráy*
what 3-PFTV-saw FS-child
'What did the child see?'

b. *ɛ́-tɔ́-dúá* *ɛn-kɛráy* *ɪn-kíshú*
3-PFTV-saw FS-child FP-cattle
'The child saw the cattle.' (possible answer to a.)

c. *ɪn-kíshú* *ɛ́-tɔ́-dúá* *ɛn-kɛráy*
FP-cattle 3-PFTV-saw FS-child
'The child saw the cattle.' (possible answer to a.)

According to Ole-Ronkei, (b) is the most common answer to a question like (a). The (c) form is appropriate for asserting that the child saw cattle rather than donkeys or goats, for example. Thus (c), with the preverbal phrase, more closely approximates a focus of contrast situation in which there is a limited set of possible answers, while in (b) the set of possible answers extends to the whole universe. In numerous VI languages, parallels to (b) are simply not an option for answers to questions.

Why a limited set of items which could rectify the missing or incorrect information produces a particularly contrastive situation likely has to do with short term memory activation. When the set is limited and the contents are assumed to be known to the hearer, all items in the set may receive some degree of excitation or activation and thus to some extent are "expected information." The item finally selected from the set must be signalled out from amongst other somewhat activated items. When the set is unlimited, potentially extending to the universe, it is impossible for all its elements to receive some degree of activation. Since no items are particularly activated, the final selection is less clearly counter to any other expectations.

Although it is the norm, it is not true that questioned phrases must be fronted in all VI languages. This is shown by such Austronesian languages as Toba Batak and Niuean. In Toba Batak, a questioned internal argument (i.e. an argument which forms a constituent with the verb) cannot be fronted at all (Schachter 1984:126; AT = 'actor trigger'; according to Schachter, in the AT form the patient is an internal argument):

(11) *Mangida aha si John?*
AT.see what PN John
'What is John seeing?'
**Aha mangida si John?*

However, a questioned external argument (i.e. an argument which is external to the verb phrase) can optionally be fronted; Schachter does not indicate whether the (a) or (b) form is most common.

(12) a. *Mangida turiturian ise?*
AT-see play who
'Who is seeing a play?'

b. *Ise mangida turiturian?*
'Who is seeing a play?

Niuean interrogative words may occur post-verbally, though as in "good" VI languages it is more common for them to occur initially, introduced by the "predicate marker" *ko* (Seiter 1980:106). Neither Seiter nor Schachter discuss answers to information questions or contrast.

We listed above a number of additional PM situations that involve correcting or filling in specific information and which, in VI languages, commonly correlate with preverbal phrases. For reasons of space we cannot explore these further here. In the next sections we turn to use of preverbal phrases that affect the architecture of a mental representation, regardless of whether the specific information is counter to particular expectations.

2.4 *Foundations and substructures in the mental representation*

Most Austronesian languages are commonly said to be VI. However, many place phrases before the verb under specifiable conditions which are not particularly pragmatically marked. These situations concern the establishment of foundations, the initiation of new subsections in the representation, and descriptive clauses (Section 2.5). Languages of this sort are less rigidly VI than are Maasai and Yagua.

Fronting typically occurs in VI Austronesian languages when foundations are laid.[15] Cooreman (1992) reports a high correlation between the (re)introduction of a subject participant and placing that participant before the verb in Chamorro.[16] Surely the establishment of a foundation must heavily consume the limited attentional resources. A foundation in Gernsbacher and Hargreaves' sense differs from a delimiting phrase in that a foundation is that concept to which subsequent information is specifically mapped. A delimiting phrase is more likely to express orienting circumstances relative to which the foundation and information related to the foundation are to be interpreted. Example (14a-b) below illustrates the difference: *Ore apa tenkiterunoto* 'long ago at the beginning of time' is not the primary concept about which other information is verbalized but instead tells us within which universe of discourse the subsequent participants and events are to be interpreted. *Naiterukop* 'Beginner-of-the-earth' is the primary concept to which the remaining information in (14a-b) is related.

Fronting also correlates with the initiation of a new discourse substructure. This is discussed by Fox (1985) for Tagalog relative to participant, temporal, locational and other types of discontinuities. Pebley (1990) illustrates it for Kagayanen. The following initiates the narrative section of a story. It does not establish new participants as the "three friends" have just been introduced in a short series of existential and descriptive clauses.

(13) *Isya adlaw tallo i na mag-arey gapanaw*
one day three FOC LINK AF-friends AF-walk
munta ta bukid
AF.go NONFOC mountain
'One day the three friends went walking going to the mountain.' (GT 4, from Pebley 1990)

Following this sentence, VI clauses carry on the action.

Unlike the typical Austronesian VI language, only particularly contrastive foundations or themes come before the verb in Maasai. This is likely when the theme is a member of a limited set, some other member of which has previously been theme. Thus, it is very like a focus of contrast situation, only that the background presupposition has to do with the global construction of the mental representation. The default expectation is that an already-established theme will be continued. Establishment of a subsequent theme may be contrastive in that the speaker asserts (just via choice of construction) that "I as speaker am no longer going to talk about X as theme (as you may expect), but Y. I now want you the hearer to establish Y as the foundation and relate incoming information to it, instead of to X." In the following Maasai example, clause (d) has a resumptive pronoun *ninye*; whether or not this is a dislocated structure is somewhat unclear because intonation is not available. Allan (1989) suggests that all Maasai sentences beginning with *ore NP* make theme (or topic) switches, (SwT).

(14) a. *Ore apa t-enk-iteru-noto n-e-atai Na-iteru-kop*
SWT long.ago in-FS-begin-ger C-3-exist REL.FS-begin-earth
'Long ago at the beginning of time, lived a demigod called Naiterukop (Beginner-of-the-earth).'

b. *N-e-yam Naiterukop in-kituaak are*
C-3-marry FP-wives two
'Naiterukop married two wives.'

c. *Ore en-kitok edukuya n-e-isho n-kishu naa-nyokioo.*
SWT FS-woman first C-3-gave FP-cattle REL.FP-be.red
'Now as for the first wife, he gave (her) red cattle.'
(Two more clauses about the first wife follow. Then ...)

d. *Ore en-kitok eare n-e-isho-ri ninye n-kishu*
SWT FS-woman second C-3-give-PASS 3 FP-cattle
naa-rook
REL.FP-be.black
'As for the second wife, she was given black cattle.'
(Text continues on about the second wife.)
(Example from Allan, who cites Kipury 1983)

Except for such contrastive contexts, new foundations in Maasai are simply introduced in postverbal position, as suggested by the following excerpts from two different texts. Boldfaced phrases are the first mentions of major participants who continue throughout a major portion of the discourse.

(15) a. *e-tíi ɔpá* ***ɪláláshara áare****...*
3-be formerly brothers two
'Once upon a time there were two brothers...'

b. *N-é-yshɔ nabó-ɔlɔ́ng mɛnyɛ́ ɔlkítɛ́ng ...*
C-3-give one-day father bull
'One day their father gives them a/the bull...'

c. N-*é-lótú* ***enkúkuu*** *kɛwáríé...*
C-3-come devil night
'The devil comes at night ...' (from Hollis 108-116)

(16) *E-tíi ɔpá* ***ɔl-páyyan***
3-be formerly MS-old.man
'Once upon a time there was an old man'

n-é-yú ***ɪnkɛ́ra uní,*** *intóyye are, o ólayyóni obô ...*
C-3-bear children three girls two boy one
'and he bore three children, two girls together with one boy...'

óre *nabó-ɔlɔ́ng* *n-é-pwɔ́nú* ***ɪl-mángatɪ́*** ...
now one-day C-3-come MP-enemies
'Now one day the/some enemies come...'

N-é-mʊr-ɪta ***síankikín*** ***ɛ́nk-ang*** *ink-ájíjík*
C-3-plaster-PROG young.women FS-homestead FS-huts
'The young women of the homestead are plastering the huts' (from Hollis 117-122)

Conditions on preverbal phrases in Yagua are partially similar to those in Maasai in that PM phrases come before the verb, and new themes for a section of discourse are normally postverbal. Consider the following Yagua story, given in English translation.[17] The only preverbal NPs in the Yagua are indicated by bold. Note particularly that when the protagonists and the antagonists are introduced at the beginning of the text, and later on the "little old woman", they are postverbal (italicized items are ideophones).

(17) Long ago lived the warrior Moquɨɨ, the warrior Cąduring also, and the warrior Jamuchęę also.

The savages arrived around their house during the night. Completely the savages had surrounded their house. *Jiiin*. They[i] now began burning their[j] house with fire. It was engulfed in flames now from the house's peak. He said to Jamuchęę: "You now lead us." I will collect your price [= I will avenge your death]". *jta*. Jamuchęę lost courage. He said to him again: "You now lead us." *jta*. Didn't he lose courage? He says to him again: "The house is now finished burning. You now lead." At last Jamuchęę runs out. *Júúyin*. There (they) spear (him) in his sternum. "*Jee*! I have been killed!" He goes running out. Lost (i.e. killed). Moquɨɨ runs out behind him, from there also Cądu. There they spear at him. *ta*. Going out he has dodged it (the spear). From there again Cądu says... [false start?] Going out he has dodged it (the spear). He just really ran out. There now they fight. Then he spears at him. *jta*. He has grabbẹd it. He spears at him. *jta*. He has grabbed it. He has swept them (away). Then he spears. Then he spears. He really terminates the savages there. The remaining ones fled. Without dying remained Moquɨɨ and Cądu too. *ti*. **Only Jamuchęęy** was wounded/killed.

A dear little old woman had followed him. "**There** (I believe) he went." She saw upon arrival there he was lying down. **Only his heart now** it was (that was speared). She digs out now a worm. Now she rubs the worm in the wound. She squeezes a little cane juice in it too. He then recovers from it.

2.5 *Descriptive clauses*

In many Austronesian languages preverbal phrases further occur when a clause describes or identifies a referent, but not when clauses report temporally sequenced actions of referents (cf. Section 2.1). Quakenbush (1992) discusses this for Agutaynen, Hopper (1987) for early 19th-century Malay, and Pebley (1990) for Kagayanen. Perhaps the best summary comes from Hopper, who states: "Verb-initial clauses narrate, noun-initial clauses describe" (1987:471). Because VI clauses advance the time line, noun-initial clauses often occur not only in introductions of major themes (discussed above), but also in background clauses within narrative genre. Consider (18) from Kagayanen. Although it reports the activity of 'getting food', Pebley describes it as a "verbal clause which tells about the customary action of the younger brother" (AF = 'actor focus,' following certain Philippine terminology):

(18)	*Uyi*	*mangngod*	*i*	*naan*	*nang*	*ga-kamang*
	DET	younger.sibling	FOC	LOC	only	AF-get

'This younger brother only got

ta	*pag-kaan*	*ta*	*iya*	*na*	*magulang,*	*kanen*	*an*
NONFOC	NR-eat	NONFOC	3	LINK	older.brother	3	FOC

his food from his older brother.' (TB7)

In Agutaynen genres not characterized by temporal sequencing, Quakenbush (1992) finds a frequency of about 25% VI clauses to about 75% noun-initial clauses. In narratives and procedures, percentages are reversed, squaring with the traditional designation of Philippine languages as VI. Quakenbush questions whether Agutaynen is, after all, VI and shows up the long-standing habit of basing claims on narrative.

In summary, the facts we have reviewed for Yagua, Maasai, and some Austronesian languages show the clear error of saying that either "rheme" or information in the focus of attention comes initially in all VI languages. What does appear to be true is that a subset of information in focal attention comes initially. This includes PM information and predicates in at least temporally sequenced clauses. In less rigid VI languages, more global considerations having to do with construction of mental representations also correlate with order. These less rigid VI languages still differ from so-called "free" word order languages such as Papago, Warlbiri, and Wayampi. In "free" order languages — but not in VI languages of the Austronesian type — order is far more sensitive everywhere to such things as identifiability, perhaps coupled with discourse "importance" or "newsworthiness" (Mithun 1987).

3. The functions of postverbal positions

We now turn to what happens after the verb in VI languages. Languages of interest are those in which postverbal order is not strictly determined by grammatical or other syntactic relations. To recall some of the initial motivations for this research, Creider (1975) predicted that in VI languages thematic information would come finally. Creider (1977) suggested that the "natural" order in VI languages is new-old, that for Nandi in particular it is asserted-presupposed, and that final position in sentences with more than two constituents is associated with the "topic", i.e. "the element in the sentence which most closely relates to what the sentence is about" (1977:332). Essentially the same claim was maintained for Nandi in Creider (1983).

Creider (1975) presented data substantiating his claim from all major VI families except Arawakan, Otomanguean, and those of the northwest U.S. and Canada. But the data are essentially from sentence-level elicitation, and not insignificant support in all his papers come from question-answer pairs, sometimes involving predicate nominals which have just two constituents. He distinguishes thematic or presupposed from rhematic or asserted information. But he does not distinguish PM from non-PM information.

It is easy to see how such data and framework would support the claim that: "theme comes finally." If part of a sentence is questioned or is the answer to a question — hence, pragmatically marked — it will come first (an almost universal strategy in VI languages). The remaining constituent(s) perforce come at the end. Furthermore, it is most certainly incorrect to equate presupposed with thematic information, even though most discourse sections are made coherent by maintaining a particular referent as thematic, resulting in statistical correlations to the effect that: "If a referent is thematic, then more often than not it will be presupposed."

In what follows I review quantified text studies of Yagua and Cebuano and present an analysis of Maasai. These studies are based on clauses with postverbal references to at least two nominal concepts. References may be by full NPs or by pronouns, but not just by verb agreement. The studies employ quantified methodologies actually presaged in Creider (1975) and inspired by Clancy (1980) and Givón (1983). Since the methodologies are scalar, I sometimes speak in terms of relative topicality, rather than what is or is not the particular theme for a discourse section. Though the studies are not identical, they all point away from final position as characteristic of thematic information. There may be one partial exception in that Yagua tends to place certain presupposed information at the end of the clause (and here I specifically back away from using the term "theme"). But other evidence from Yagua also supports the hypothesis that when there are two or more postverbal referents, the more thematic one occurs closer to the verb.

3.1 *Maasai (Nilotic, Kenya and Tanzania)*

We have already presented Creider's hypothesis on information ordering for the Southern Nilotic language Nandi. Dimmendaal describes Turkana, an Eastern Nilotic language more closely related to Maasai, as VSO. But he notes that "VOS is also a basic word order pattern in [Turkana], not being marked for any specific context" (1983:57). He suggests that if the subject is more salient than the direct or indirect object, the surface order is VSO; if the direct object is more salient, the order is VOS. For Dimmendaal "salience" or "prominence" involves definiteness and animacy. He claims that "definite noun phrases referring to animate entities precede indefinite ones in a sentence" (p. 83) and he proposes the following prominence hierarchy: participants > non-participants / proper names > animate nouns > inanimate nouns. Within any clause, an entity to the left on the hierarchy will precede an entity to the right. These descriptions do not say what happens if both participants are of equal rank (e.g. both definite or both indefinite), or what happens if a clause contains definite inanimate plus indefinite animate referents, etc.

Based on a sheerly statistical evaluation of narrative text, Maasai would be termed a VSO language. In elicitation speakers will generally allow VOS renderings of clauses, though VSO is usually offered first. For most nouns, subject and nonsubject case forms are well differentiated by tone, and order variation does not result in interpretation problems. In the Maasai texts from Hollis (1905) a few clauses have VOS syntax, and in a few the subject follows obliques.[18] Order of postverbal objects and obliques also varies. Native speakers have judged propositions with various orders to be "good Maasai," repeat them without difficulty, and claim that they "mean exactly the same thing." Thus, in terms of grammatical possibilities, Maasai allows more order variation after the verb than does a VSO language like Yagua.

In an analysis of one Maasai text taken from Kipury (1983), Allan (1989) suggests that the normal information order is given–new. In so far as given information is presupposed and new is commonly asserted, Allan's claim for Maasai would appear counter to Creider's hypothesis for Nandi. For the most part, Allan's observation accurately describes Maasai when a clause contains one given and one new postverbal phrase. However, there are many places in the Hollis texts and elsewhere where two postverbal phrases both contain given, or both contain new information. Is there any larger generalization predicting order in such clauses, which will include given-new order as a typical subcase?

In Maasai clauses which are neither information questions nor in some other well-defined way pragmatically marked, I find it inaccurate to say that thematic information comes finally. Instead, I propose the following hypothesis for Maasai:

> Thematic but otherwise unmarked information goes right after the verb.
> Less topical information strongly tends to come at the end of the clause.

There is one sentence type which, on the basis of the methodology employed, cannot be said to fit the generalization; it will be elaborated below. My conclusions are based primarily on a study of 20 traditional narratives from Hollis (1905), comprising some 2,965 clauses. Hollis gives little information about how the texts were collected, but they have a fluent oral feel, including ubiquitous clause chaining and many clauses without full NPs.

Though statistical counts are not the same as cognitive categories or statuses, they can provide an objective heuristic for getting at cognitive statuses. As I am working with oral texts produced under non-experimental conditions, I use a density methodology. "Density" is the number of references to a particular participant in the ten clauses preceding, or in the ten clauses following, a particular clause. References may be as subject, object, dative, oblique, possessor, by a verb agreement form, noun phrase, or zero — all that matters is that the participant is somehow referred to in the clause. If two formal devices refer to a participant in any one clause, I count the clause only once. For example, in *John's mother hit him (=John),* the referent *John* would be counted once for this clause.

Density is clearly not equivalent to thematicity. But I take the former as heuristic of the latter under the supposition that a thematic participant is more likely to persist — and thus be rementioned — throughout a portion of discourse than is a non-thematic one. What makes a referent thematic is not how often it is mentioned in a stretch of text, but whether the speaker **intends** for it to be the cognitive foundation for the section under development.[19]

The density tool yields some apparent exceptions to the hypothesis. These clauses were evaluated in further detail as to whether they are truly exceptional, or whether the density methodology simply provides a rough — but not 100% accurate — reflection of thematicity. I considered further features such as animacy, referentiality in the discourse (cf. D. Payne 1992), and importance in the culture. Other things being equal, I assume that human or anthropomorphized animals are more likely candidates for cognitive foundations than are non-human ones. In Maasai culture cattle are of central significance. Indices of their status include evaluation of one's wealth in terms of cattle, all animals in the herd have individual names, it is impolite to point at cattle when you count them, the vocabulary for cattle is well elaborated, and in greetings not only are family members asked after but also the welfare of one's cattle. I assume that cattle outrank other animals and inanimate entities in terms of inherent likelihood of serving as foundations. I assume that referential concepts are higher than nonreferential ones in inherent likelihood of serving as foundations.

I count as a clause anything which contains one non-nominalized verb, excepting *ajo* 'to say' when it functions as a complementizer or an adverbial conjunction. I considered all NPs in the corpus except those constituted of nominalized verbs which have their own overt NP arguments or adverbial modifiers. Such nominalized clauses were excluded in an attempt to control for possible effects of "heavy NP shift".

Table 1 summarizes average densities and standard deviations for several different clause types. A clause was excluded from the preceding density (PD) measurement if fewer than ten clauses preceded it; a clause was excluded from the following density (FD) measurement if fewer than ten

Table 1. Average densities (standard deviations in parentheses); Maasai

	Preceding densities		Following densities	
	Linearly first argument	Linearly second argument	Linearly first argument	Linearly second argument
VSO (N=83)	4.1 *(2.8)*	1.2 *(2.1)*	4.2 *(2.9)*	1.6 *(2.3)*
VOS (N=9)	3.8 *(2.3)*	1.7 *(1.8)*	5.4 *(2.4)*	1.8 *(1.6)*
V-S-Obl (N=55)	2.5 *(2.4)*	0.3 *(0.6)*	3.3 *(2.7)*	0.4 *(1.0)*
V-O-Obl (N=41)	1.6 *(1.8)*	0.4 *(0.6)*	2.7 *(2.7)*	0.5 *(0.8)*
V-O-O (N=31)	2.1 *(2.3)*	0.3 *(0.8)*	2.4 *(2.6)*	0.3 *(0.6)*
Rare:				
V-Obl-S (N=4)	0.5 *(0.9)*	0.3 *(0.4)*	0.5 *(0.5)*	3.0 *(2.0)*
V-Obl-O (N=2)	not calculated			

clauses followed. For example, there are 93 VSO and 10 VOS clauses in the corpus; but 83 VSO have at least ten clauses preceding them, and 9 VOS clauses have the requisite ten clauses following them.

For both VSO and VOS orders, linearly second arguments cluster in the low range of values (0-2), while linearly first arguments are more evenly distributed across all values. In approximately 90% of the text data higher density referents precede lower density ones. Out of 103 total VSO and VOS clauses, there are only 11 exceptional instances in which PD for the second argument is higher than that of the first argument, and 11 exceptional instances where FD is higher for the second argument (two of the clauses are exceptional for both PD and FD).

However, it is unlikely that the real order explanation has anything to do with density; instead, the crucial factor is likely to be thematicity, where thematicity is based on the speaker's intentions. A closer look at the apparently exceptional clauses supports the hypothesis presented at the beginning of this section. I will discuss representative examples of the "exception" types here, taking up PD cases first.

In 100% of the VSO and VOS clauses where pronouns express an argument, the pronoun immediately follows the verb. In no clauses are both S and O expressed by free pronouns. The O is pronominal in 50% of the VOS clauses; the S is pronominal in 14% of the VSO clauses. In the one "exceptional" VOS clause where PD is higher for the S than for the O, the O is a pronoun. Universally, proforms or zero are the most likely way of expressing already established referents.[20] This universal pattern is consonant with the possibility that if the O participant in this clause was, in terms of the speaker's mental representation, an already-established participant, it was more likely the expected foundation, compared to the participant expressed in the NP.

Most of the apparent exceptions express both arguments by full NPs. Example (19) is illustrative (surrounding context is presented just in English translation):

(19) The old man (had) **left** his wife *skinning* the ox, and while she was *skinning* the ox, just when she had *reached* the dewlap, she *stabbed* herself (in) the eye with the knife, and she *ran* to *go lie down* and the birds came, and they finished the whole ox.

Well, the old man **drove** the cattle to the kraal. Now when the cattle were opposite the gate,

n-é-ning ol-mórúó engóroyyoni,
C-3-hear MS-old.man woman
the old man heard the woman

weeping "Oh, my eye!", and the old man **said**, "My one who has born, who told you [that our child has been burnt]?" (Hollis, p. 158)

The italicized predicates all have the woman as their (understood) subject; those in bold have the man as their subject. There are clearly more references, including those made just by verb agreement, to the woman than there are to the old man in the ten clauses preceding the pertinent clause. However, it is likely that a new section or perspective in the mental representation is initiated with the clause "Well, the old man drove the cattle to the kraal," and that "the old man" is the principle foundation for the new developing section.

In another apparent exception type, both participants have very low PD values; the second argument is inanimate and objectively has the higher density, but the one immediately after the verb is animate:

(20) And he [=the child] does this only when the sun is opposite to him, and he comes (to) the *kraal*. And the woman says to him, "go to the foot of the bed; bring the bag where the razor is." And the child goes where the hole is which the woman dug, and he falls into it, not seeing it. Well, the woman comes and puts a big stone in the hole.

N-é-pwónú in-kíshu áng téypa
c3-come FP-cows kraal evening
And the cows come (to) the kraal in the evening

and the woman goes and does the milking ... (Hollis, p. 192)

I would not argue that either 'cows' or 'kraal' is particularly thematic in this instance, despite the technically higher density of 'kraal' in the preceding context. (The clause in fact probably serves to convey temporal discontinuity.) But do note that cows are inherently more likely to serve as foundations compared to with kraals, and 'cows' takes the syntactic position characteristic of higher thematicity. An alternative hypothesis here is that when neither participant is truly the foundation of the section, a default VSO order occurs. This hypothesis would require further investigation.

The facts are similar for following densities. In all instances where FD is higher for the second-mentioned argument, a new section or perspective in the mental representation appears to be initiated shortly after the clause in question; and the second-mentioned participant may later stand as the foundation of the new section. The following illustrates:

(21) *N-é-dɔl en-kítojó en-túa*
c-3-see FS-hare FS-frog
'And the hare sees the frog

and says to him "come, please, see if you are able to take out the man whom they have been unable [to dislodge] who is in my hut."

And the frog says to him, "Let's go." And they go and arrive there, and the frog says.... (Hollis, p. 182)

Although 'frog' is mentioned second in the clause in question, a new section or perspective in the mental representation is likely opened with 'and the frog says to him...', with the frog as its foundation.

In all, the only instance that may be genuinely exceptional in the Hollis texts is *e-ipir-a enderit il-Lumbwa* (3-face-DIR dust PL-Lumbwa) 'The dust faces (toward) the Lumbwa.' Here the dust ominously portends the hostile Lumbwa's approach. 'Dust' does not appear elsewhere in the story (Hollis, p. 185), though the Lumbwa are mentioned both before and after this clause. In sum, density is simply not a foolproof index of thematicity or order; it is only a helpful heuristic.

What, now, about clauses with two nominal expressions after the verb, but where one or both is neither subject nor object? Whether these clauses also support the "thematic before non-thematic" order hypothesis may depend on whether a dative argument is involved. We first consider clauses without a dative.

In clause types where there are sufficient data to draw firm numerical conclusions, density patterns are compatible with the hypothesis (cf. Table 1). This is true for V-subject-oblique, V-object-oblique, and V-object-object clauses.

By V-object-object, I have in mind clauses like (22-24). The verb *pik* 'put' requires expression of, or understanding of, both a patient that gets 'put', and some location where it gets put (Renoi, p.c.).

(22) *n-é-pɪk ɪl-ashɔ́ ɔl-álɛ́*
c-3-put.in MP-calves MS-shed
'And he puts the calves in the shed/hedge.' (Hollis, p. 124)

In (23) 'eye' and 'devil' are not in a genitive relationship (which would display the opposite order and additional morphology). In (24) an applied dative suffix occurs on the verb.

(23) *N-é-ybʊ́ng en-kʊ́kuu ɛnk-ɔngʊ́*
c-3-seize FS-devil FS-eye
'And he seizes the devil the eye.' (Hollis, p. 113)

(24) *n-é-an-ikí ɔl-áshê ɔl-kɪdɔngɔ̂y*
c-3-fasten-to MS-calf MS-tail
'And he fastens to the calf the tail.' (i.e. he fastens the tail on the calf) (Hollis, p. 126)

I will not explore here whether one "object" is actually oblique-like or fails to hold a grammatical relation to the verb (i.e. a demoted chomeur), though this is certainly a relevant question to pursue: in terms of density the second object does appear oblique-like, having an average PD of 0.3 and an average FD of 0.3. In contrast, the object closest to the verb has an average PD of 2.0, and an average FD of 2.4.

Despite the size of the data base (2965 clauses), there are extremely few instances of some order types (see Table 1). However, even those with very few tokens are telling. The scarcity of V-oblique-subject (N = 4) and V-oblique-object (N = 2) clauses is surely due to the way that thematicity normally maps onto grammatical relations: thematic participants are likely introduced as subjects of intransitive clauses or perhaps as objects of transitive clauses, and then tend to continue on as subjects of either (Du Bois 1987). If the unmarked position for thematic information is immediately after the verb, then we would predict essentially no examples of the low frequency orders. This is because cross-linguistically a participant is unlikely to be expressed as an oblique whenever it holds tenure as the thematic participant of a discourse section. For Maasai this is corroborated by density: regardless of what else occurs in the clause, the average PD for all obliques calculated over all order positions is 0.5 (actual range 0-3); the average FD is 0.4 (actual range 0-4).

Though the low number of V-oblique-subject clauses makes any claims tenuous (N = 4), the values for these final subjects is striking: average PD for the obliques is 0.5, while for the subjects it is a mere 0.3. (The following densities in the V-oblique-subject clauses are characteristic of oblique and subject overall, with oblique showing 0.3 and subject showing 4.0.) In the two V-oblique-object instances, actual preceding densities for the obliques are 3 and 1, and for the objects are Ø and Ø. Again the data are too few to draw density-based conclusions, but the observed zero values for final objects are teasing. (Actual following densities are characteristic of oblique and object overall: obliques have Ø in both cases, and objects have 3 and 1.)

To summarize, given universal mapping tendencies between thematic or topical information and grammatical relations, and if the hypothesis about Maasai order is right, we would be extremely surprised to see a high incidence of V-oblique-subject and V-oblique-object clauses. Clause types where there are enough data to draw density-based conclusions support the hypothesis that for postverbal phrases, thematic information precedes non-thematic information.

We now turn to clauses with semantic datives.[21] In terms of density, clauses with postverbal subject plus dative participants do not support the hypothesis that thematic precedes non-thematic information. However, they also do not support the hypothesis that thematic information comes at the end of the clause. The vast majority of such clauses involve the verb *ajo-ki* 'say/ tell.' Grammatically, arguments of this verb (as of other verbs that take datives) may surface in the order V-subject-dative or V-dative-subject. There are 33 tokens of the first order and only two of the latter (which will not be considered further).

Table 2. Average densities for V-subject-dative clauses (standard deviations in parentheses); Maasai

	Subject	Dative
Preceding density	5.2 *(2.3)*	4.8 *(2.9)*
Following density	4.9 *(2.4)*	5.8 *(2.4)*

Table 2 gives average PD and FD values for V-subject-dative clauses (clauses without the requisite ten preceding or following clauses are excluded).

Table 2 suggests that subject and dative are roughly equal in terms of potential thematicity. Examination of each individual clause also does not lend any particular support to the Maasai information order hypothesis: in 18 out of 33 clauses the second-ordered dative argument is actually higher in FD than is the subject. In 7 out of 33 the dative is higher in PD than is the subject. I do not have any firm explanation for this pattern, but find that what follows a verb of saying is usually a quote. Sometimes the quote content is heavily dative-oriented. Consider (25). The italicized predicates all have the hyena as their subject, which is the dative of the 'say' clause; the subject 'hare' does not even appear in the following ten clauses.

(25) *N-é-jo-kí en-kítojó ɔl-ngɔjínɛ*
C-3-say-DAT FS-hare MS-hyena
'And the hare says to the hyena:

"When you *enter*, *say* 'Stone, open.' Now when you *go* within, *say* 'Stone, close.' Now when you *wish,* and *come out, say* 'Stone, open.'" And the hyena *says... (Hollis 205)*

Another factor potentially accounting for the 18 "exceptional" V-subject-dative clauses is that in conversation, turn taking is frequent. By the very nature of reported conversation, any particular token of 'say' is likely to soon be followed by a clause which does not have as its subject/agent the participant who was the subject/agent of that 'say' verb. Insofar as thematic shifts may occur when there are shifts in reported speaker, the density measurement breaks down as an index of what is likely to be the thematic participant.

3.2 *Cebuano (Austronesian, Philippines)*

Cebuano verbs have two voice options commonly referred to as "Actor Focus" and "Goal Focus." As in Maasai, order of postverbal arguments can vary. In a study of the function of Cebuano Actor Focus (AF) vs. Goal Focus (GF) clauses, T. Payne (1991) presents quantified data bearing on whether Cebuano patterns like Maasai, or whether thematic information comes clause finally as Creider claims for Nandi. The conclusion drawn here is that Cebuano is very like Maasai in that higher density phrases immediately follow the verb.

T. Payne's Cebuano study is based on some 2,670 clauses of written narrative in which there are 114 perfective, independent, declarative, semantically transitive clauses with overt postverbal references to both "A" and "P" arguments (cf. Comrie 1978). In both Actor Focus and Goal Focus voices, the majority of such clauses display VAP order.

Table 3 presents density measurements calculated in the same manner as for the Maasai study. For purposes of exposition let us consider VAP clauses as providing some type of baseline values. In VPA clauses, the P has PD and FD values much higher than the baseline found in VAP clauses. Although A density is not extremely low in VPA clauses, it is still lower than the baseline value.

Table 3 conflates Actor Focus and Goal Focus clauses, which likely perform different discourse-pragmatic functions. Table 4 presents figures just for Goal Focus clauses, which display the same density patterns as do the composite figures in Table 3.

Table 3. Average densities; Cebuano VPA and VAP clauses

	Preceding density		Following density	
	Linearly first argument	Linearly second argument	Linearly first argument	Linearly second argument
VAP (N = 88)	5.0	0.9	4.6	1.1
VPA (N = 26)	3.1	3.3	2.6	3.9
Total N = 114				

Table 4. Average densities; Cebuano Goal Focus clauses only

	Preceding density		Following density	
	Linearly first argument	Linearly second argument	Linearly first argument	Linearly second argument
VAP (N = 58)	5.4	1.2	4.8	1.4
VPA (N = 19)	4.1	3.0	3.4	3.7
Total N = 77				

3.3 *Yagua (Peba-Yaguan, Peru)*

Yagua differs from Maasai and Cebuano in that pragmatically unmarked subject NPs must precede postverbal object NPs. This relative order is strictly determined by grammatical relations. However, relative order of objects and obliques may vary. Indepth discussion of what might motivate the variation is found elsewhere (D. Payne 1990); here I summarize only selected data.

In approximately 1500 clauses from both oral and written narrative, 120 clauses contain postverbal references to both object and oblique participants. The order is object-oblique in 45% of these clauses, and oblique-object in 55%. This shows that grammatical relations hardly predict order. In my first study of Yagua, I concluded that order was predicted by something akin to Creider's "(more) thematic information comes finally in the clause" principle, due to figures such as those found in Table 5. The incidence of new–

Table 5. Relative order of object and oblique when clause contains mixed informational statuses; Yagua

	Object-oblique	Oblique-object	Total	
Given-New	7	2	9	20%
New-Given	16	19	35	80%
Total			44	100%
Definite-Indefinite	9	3	12	27%
Indefinite-Definite	18	14	32	73%
Total			44	100%

Table 6. Morphosyntactic form relative to object-oblique versus oblique-object orders; Yagua

	Object-oblique	Oblique-object	Total
NP = Object & NP = Oblique	30	13	43
NP = Object & Pronoun = Oblique	18	8	26
NP = Oblique & Pronoun = Object	4	34	38
Pronoun = Object & Pronoun = Oblique	2	11	13
Total	54 (45%)	66 (55%)	120 (100%)
	Chi-Square = 41.6 (df = 3), p < .001		

given and indefinite–definite orders are much higher than the alternative orders. Although 'given' and 'definite' are not synonymous with 'thematic', we might expect some correlation between given/definite and theme when there is also a new/indefinite NP in the clause — and certainly this is not out of line with Creider's definitions and methodology.

Reference to object and oblique can be either by NPs or by unstressed pronominal clitics which come toward the end of the clause.[22] NP-NP, NP-pronoun, pronoun-NP, and pronoun-pronoun references all occur, and the initial or the final reference can be to either object or oblique. These data are summarized in Table 6. There is a significant association between morphosyntactic form combination and order.

Calculation of the Lambda-b statistic, successively leaving out various of the encoding choices, shows that the strongest association occurs when a NP codes the oblique and a pronoun codes the object (the NP = oblique & pronoun = object category). The association may be particularly strong for two reasons. NP-pronoun order is particularly likely, regardless of grammatical relation (NP-pronoun = 81%; pronoun-NP = 19%). Second, objects are somewhat more likely than obliques to be expressed by pronouns.[23]

How are we to interpret these data relative to the question of this paper? First, other things being equal, topical participants are more likely to be expressed by pronominal clitics than by NPs. This is substantiated in T. Payne (1992) for Yagua and is consonant with numerous other studies of the relationship between discourse status and morphosyntactic form. Given that NP-pronoun order is particularly likely, it follows that there is an apparent tendency to move more topical information to the end of the clause. Second, cross-linguistically there is a clear difference in discourse status between referents expressed as obliques and those expressed as objects: the former are typically incidental and hardly persist (cf. the overall figures on Maasai obliques), while objects at least stand a chance of playing a major role in the story. Insofar as pronominal objects tend to come finally, it also follows that more topical information tends to come finally (recall that subject is excluded from this generalization). This same pattern of placing direct object pronouns finally in the clause, following even new obliques, is also found in Irish (Noonan 1994); Irish thus constitutes another case of placing at least a restricted set of topical information at the end of the clause.

However, what I have described so far is not the whole story. Calculation of the Lambda-b statistic over the data in Table 6 also shows there is a fairly high probability of the object-oblique order occurring when both object and oblique are expressed by NPs. Here, we see the reverse order of grammatical relations: object precedes oblique in 70% of the instances (30 out of 43).

How are we to interpret this? When speakers choose to express objects via NPs rather than via pronouns, they do so based on the judgment that the informational content is cognitively less-expected or uncertain, and that correct processing will require expenditure of attention. Simple introduction of new information (without additional pragmatic or semantic marking) may be one such situation. There is a clear difference between participants that are introduced as obliques, and those introduced as objects or as subjects of intransitives: the former hardly persist at all, while any major, thematic participant almost certainly comes onto the discourse stage in the absolutive role. Insofar as the object is more likely to be thematic than is the oblique, the order is thematic information precedes nonthematic information, at least when referents are being established.

Crucial in understanding the Yagua data is realizing that presupposed information is not synonymous with the theme or foundation of a mental representation. Although between object and oblique there is a clear tendency in Yagua for presupposed information to come at the end of the clause (Tables 5 and 6), this does not necessarily imply that the theme comes at the end, nor that "theme final" is an accurate generalization for all of Yagua clause structure.

Establishing a particular participant as thematic may require different cognitive processing than does the tracking of an already-established theme. Morphosyntax is likely sensitive to these different processings. Theme establishment may be accomplished in Yagua by expressing a referent via a subject or object NP and placing that NP as close after the verb as possible (cf. example [3] again). Tracking already-introduced non-subjects may be accomplished via pronominal clitic forms which occur toward the end of the clause. Only in this subcase is there a tendency for the object to occur after less presupposed information.

4. Conclusion

In languages commonly identified as VI, predicates occur initially in temporally sequenced clauses. Pragmatically marked information is also initial. In etic terms there are different degrees of pragmatic markedness. In more rigid VI languages only the most marked situations (e.g. focus of contrast) will trigger preverbal position, while information question words, answers to information questions, and other less highly marked information may follow the verb. Third, when new foundations are laid down, these come initially in some languages. Laying down a new foundation may be mildly contrastive in that the speaker is saying "I am no longer going to talk about X as theme (as you might expect), but Y. Now establish Y as the foundation." Fourth, nominal phrases may be initial in descriptive or background clauses, even when there is nothing particularly marked.

I suspect there is a general direction of predictability from the fourth situation to the first two, such that if a VI language places phrases before the verb to accomplish any function to the left on the following hierarchy, all phrases that accomplish functions to the right on the hierarchy will also occur before the verb:

NP in descriptive or background clause	>	NP establishing a foundation	>	Pragmatically marked NPs
				More marked > Less marked

Among PM phrases, if a VI language places a somewhat less-marked phrase type before the verb, then it will also place more marked types before the verb. Languages that fall to the left on this hierarchy are clearly less rigidly VI than are languages to the right.

In terms of postverbal phrases, syntactic constraints must not be ignored. But when languages do allow variation, it is not universally true that thematic information occurs finally. Rather, there is evidence that thematic NPs may come right after the verb.

Even if two languages are roughly equivalent in terms of rigidity, questions may remain in trying to make direct comparisons simply because of different morphosyntactic hardware available in the two languages. In the instances we have seen here, Yagua has object and oblique clitics that operate on a sentence level; Maasai and many Austronesian languages have forms bound to the verb. Given that clitics are phonologically light forms, what influence might this have on their placement that may invalidate trying to make comparisons with languages where the only elements that can vary in order are full NPs?

Finally, I have restricted my attention to languages that would typologically be identified as VI. But it remains an open research question as to what extent the hypotheses advanced here for VI languages are specific to just these languages.

Abbreviations

In examples taken from other linguistic works (see note 5), I have generally retained glosses given by the original authors. Abbreviations used are: AF = actor focus, AL = allative, AT = actor trigger, C = continuing clause chain, DAT = dative, DET = determiner, DIMIN = diminuitive, DL = dual, FEM = feminine, FOC = focus, FS = feminine singular, FP = feminine plural, INST = instrument, M = masculine, MP = masculine plural, MS = masculine singular, NONFOC = nonfocus, NR= nominalizer, PERF = perfect, PFTV = perfective, PL = plural, PN = personal name marker, REL = relative clause form, SG = singular, SwT = switch topic

Notes

* Those who have influenced this study notably include Robert Longacre, Edward Keenan, Desmond Derbyshire, Paul Hopper, T. Givón, Russell Tomlin, Morton Gernsbacher, and David Hargreaves, though they do not always agree with my interpretation and application of their work. I gratefully acknowledge the importance of Paul Powlison's extensive Yagua text collection, Renoi and Morompi Ole-Ronkei's help with Maasai, and helpful commentary from Keith Allan, Chet Creider, Pamela Downing, John Myhill, Mickey Noonan, Tom Payne, Stephen Quakenbush and Scott Randall.

1. See Tomlin (1986) for one study plus review of several others. As far as I am aware, all the large-scale typological studies Tomlin cites assume that subject, object, and verb are the relevant categories for evaluating constituent order. In my view, they may mistakenly include pragmatic order languages in which grammatical relations may have little or nothing to do with order generalizations.

2. Some languages have been called VI which are probably best viewed as pragmatic order languages (cf. Mithun 1987); Scancarelli 1987; and D. Payne 1987 and 1992 (ed.). In such languages order depends not on grammatical relation but on whether the information expressed is nonidentifiable-important vs. its opposite, or "newsworthy" vs. "non-newsworthy," and possibly other cognitive-pragmatic factors. In narrative a majority of sentences may happen to be VI because NPs are frequently omitted and most overt NPs display whatever properties determine postverbal placement. Other than frequency, there may be no particular reason to call them VI. If some speech event contained more situations motivating preverbal placement, the frequencies would automatically change in that particular discourse token, but the rules of the language would in no way change. See Quakenbush (1992) for one enlightening study in this regard.

3. Keenan's observations were presented in UCLA class handouts from the late 1970s, and have been published in Chapter 2 of D. Payne 1990.

4. Though they overlap, note that the 1975 and 1979 hypotheses are not equivalent.

5. Maasai texts used for this study are largely from Hollis (1905). Hollis' orthography is not phonemically adequate; all examples from Hollis have been checked with a native speaker of Maasai (either Renoi or Morompi Ole-Ronkei, Ilwuasinkishu dialect) and are rewritten in a phonemically more precise way. Renoi and Morompi have found the Hollis texts to be natural, well-spoken Maasai. Excerpts from Kipury (1983) are not altered.

6. Tomlin and Pu actually state "...the notion of **theme** or **topic**, quite slippery to define in text analysis, seems reasonably replaced by 'current focus of attention' in terms of the model described [in Tomlin and Pu 1991]. If a speaker wishes or needs the focal attention of the hearer to be on a particular parameter at a given point in time during the discourse production process, the speaker will, via a specific functional interaction, either a structural coding or a pragmatic signaling, direct the focal attention of the hearer to the targeted parameter." Tomlin and Pu thus equate theme with focus of attention. However, it seems too restrictive to equate foundation/theme as used here with focus of attention, as the limited attentional resources can also be directed to information which is to be mapped onto an already-established foundation.

7. The portion in regular type in (2) repeats presupposed information, and in (3) it simply serves as a presentational form.

8. Papago (Uto-Aztecan) is a language where experimental exploration of this hypothesis would seem especially promising.

9. Presumably she would also allow that in information questions, items could also be initial within CP. Haegeman (1991) provides an easily accessible introduction to definitions of CP, IP, V', etc.

10. For now I ignore initial temporal, locative, and adverbial phrases.

11. Also see Hopper (1987) for important discussion, though Hopper is concerned with more than just traditionally VI languages.

12. Dimmendaal (1983:426) and Allan (1989) suggest that in Turkana and Maasai, respectively, immediately post-verbal position may also express a subset of PM elements, though they do not comprehensively discuss the differences between PM elements that occur before the verb, versus those that occur right after the verb. This is also true for Tennet (Surmic). For Turkana, some of the conditions involve phonological size. Placing even a subset of PM information postverbally does not appear to be true for all VI languages.

13. See Givón (1991, Ch. 16) on the implicational relation holding between PM and asserted information.

14. Some may object that I have too narrowly appropriated "pragmatically marked" for degrees of counter-expectation or counter-presupposed knowledge (Dryer 1991). Nevertheless, I hope the way the term is used in this paper is clear, and I have not found anything better in the literature.

15. Existential clauses performing this function may remain VI.

16. Cumming (1984) claims that in Toba Batak fronted NPs present "thematic" information and are a cohesive device since some 80% of fronted NPs express given information. This claim might seem somewhat at odds with the claims of this paper that, typically in Austronesian, themes are preverbal only when they are being established. However, Cumming does not discuss the possibility that any of these fronted NPs might simultaneously be pragmatically marked, or whether they correlate with new discourse sections, even though they may be given.

17. For the Yagua with morpheme analysis, see Payne and Payne (1990). It does not appear that the preverbal locative 'there' which occurs in the last section of the following text is contrastive, but the only other preverbal noun phrases clearly are. For a fuller accounting of pre- vs. post-verbal placement of phrases in Yagua, see D. Payne 1990 and 1993.

18. Hollis' transcription system is linguistically underspecified because he does not indicate tone. However, in these culturally well-known stories, grammatical relations can be confirmed by checking tone patterns with native speakers.

19. Russell Tomlin has pointed out that in at least some instances morphosyntax is sensitive to whether a referent is locally thematic, rather than globally thematic. Density measures within ten contiguous clauses likely reflect local thematicity, whether or not a referent is globally thematic.

20. Mickey Noonan (p.c.) has observed that VI languages do not generally use zero forms for already-established referents, but rather bound clitics or pronominal forms. Why VI languages should avoid true "pro-drop" is surely linked with Nichols (1986) observation that VI languages are dominantly head-marking languages, where verbs are indexed for features of their arguments.

21. One V-object-dative and three V-dative-object clauses occur. These are not considered further here.

22. Reference can also be made by a combination of noun phrase and clitic pronoun (T. Payne, 1992; D. Payne 1990). Here I subsume such references under 'NP'.

23. This distribution barely misses significance (Chi-square with Yates' correction = 3.5, 1 df., $p < .06$).

References

Aissen, Judith. 1992. "Topic and focus in Mayan." *Language* 68.43-80.

Allan, Keith. 1989. "Discourse stratagems in a Maasai story." *Current Approaches to African Linguistics* ed. by J. Hutchison and V. Manfredi, 7:179-91. Dordrecht: Foris.

Bailey, Pamela. 1991. "Word Order Variation and Temporal Sequencing in Tashelhit Berber." University of Oregon ms.

Chafe, Wallace. 1976. "Givenness, contrastiveness, definiteness, subjects, topics, and point of view." *Subject and Topic* ed. by Charles N. Li, 25-55. New York: Academic Press.

Clancy, Patricia. 1980. "Referential choice in English and Japanese narrative." *The Pear Stories* ed. by Wallace L. Chafe, 127-202. New York: Academic Press.

Comrie, Bernard. 1978. "Ergativity." *Syntactic Typology*, ed. by Winfred Lehmann, 329-94. Austin: University of Texas Press.

Cooreman, Ann. 1992. "The pragmatics of word order variation in Chamorro narrative text." D. Payne (ed.) 1992.243-63.

Creider, Chet. 1975. "Thematization and word order." Paper presented at the Annual Meeting of the Linguistic Society of America, San Francisco.

Creider, Chet. 1977. "Functional sentence perspective in a verb-initial language." *Language and Linguistic Problems in Africa (Proceedings of the VII Conference on African Linguistics)*, ed. by Paul Kotey and Haig Der-Houssikian, 330-43. Columbia, S.C.: Hornbeam.

Creider, Chet. 1979. "On the explanation of transformations." *Syntax and Semantics 12: Discourse and Syntax*, ed. by T. Givón, 3-21. New York: Academic Press.

Creider, Chet. 1983. "Topic–Comment relations in a verb-initial language." *Journal of African Languages and Linguistics* 5.1-15.

Creider, Chet. 1989. *The Syntax of the Nilotic Languages*. Berlin: Dietrich Reimer Verlag.

Cumming, Susanna. 1984. "The syntax and semantics of prepredicate word order in Toba Batak." *Studies in the Structure of Toba Batak* ed. by Paul Schachter, 17-36. [=*UCLA Occasional Papers in Linguistics* 5.]

Dik, Simon, Maria Hoffmann, J. R. de Jong, Sie Ing Djiang, Harry Stroomer, and Lourens De Vries. 1981. "On the typology of focus phenomena." *Perspectives on Functional Grammar* ed. by Teun Hoekstra, Harry van der Hulst, and Michael Moortgat, 41-74. Dordrecht: Foris.

Dimmendaal, Gerrit. 1983. *The Turkana Language*. Dordrecht: Foris.

Dryer, Matthew. 1991. "Frequency and unmarked word order." Paper presented at the 1991 Milwaukee Linguistics Symposium. University of Wisconsin-Milwaukee.

Du Bois, John. 1987. "The discourse basis of ergativity." *Language* 63.805-55.

England, Nora. 1983. *A Grammar of Mam, a Mayan Language*. Austin: University of Texas Press.

Firbas, Jan. 1964. "On defining the theme in functional sentence analysis." *Travaux Linguistiques de Prague* 1.267-80.

Fox, Barbara. 1985. "Word order inversion and discourse continuity in Tagalog." *Quantified Studies in Discourse* ed. by T. Givón, 39-54. [=*A special issue of Text* 5.1/2].

Gernsbacher, Morton. 1990. *Language Comprehension as Structure Building*. Hillsdale, NJ: Erlbaum.

Gernsbacher, Morton and David Hargreaves. 1992. "The privilege of primacy: experimental data and cognitive explanations." D. Payne (ed.) 1992.83-116.

Givón, T. 1977. "The drift from VSO to SVO in biblical Hebrew: the pragmatics of tense-aspect." *Mechanisms for Syntactic Change*, ed. by Charles Li, 181-254. Austin: University of Texas Press.

Givón, T. (ed.) 1983. *Topic Continuity in Discourse*. Amsterdam/Philadelphia: John Benjamins.

Givón, T. 1991. *Syntax: A Functional-Typological Introduction* Vol. 2. Amsterdam/ Philadelphia: John Benjamins.

Greenberg, Joseph. 1959. "The origin of the Masai passive." *Africa* 29.171-76.

Greenberg, Joseph. 1963. "Some universals of grammar with particular reference to the order of meaningful elements." *Universals of Language*, ed. by Joseph Greenberg, 58-90. Cambridge, Mass.: MIT Press.

Haegeman, Liliane. 1991. *Introduction to Government & Binding Theory*. Oxford: Blackwell.

Hollis, A. C. 1905. *The Masai, Their Language and Folklore*. Oxford: Clarendon Press.

Hopper, Paul. 1987. "Stability and change in VN/NV alternating languages: a study in pragmatics and linguistic typology." *The Pragmatic Perspective (Selected papers from the 1985 International Pragmatics Conference)*, ed. by Jef Verschueren and Marcella Bertuccelli-Papi, 456-76. Amsterdam/Philadelphia: John Benjamins.

Kipury, Naomi. 1983. *Oral Literature of the Maasai*. Nairobi: Heinemann Educational Books.

Longacre, Robert. 1982. "Discourse typology in relation to language typology." *Text Processing*, ed. by Sture Allen, 457-86. Stockholm: Almquist & Wiksell.

MacWhinney, Brian. 1977. "Starting points." *Language* 53.152-68.

Mithun, Marianne. 1987. "Is basic word order universal?" *Coherence and Grounding in Discourse*, ed. by Russel S. Tomlin, 281-328. Amsterdam/Philadelphia: John Benjamins. [Reprinted in D. Payne (ed.), 1992.]

Myhill, John. 1992. "Word order and temporal sequencing." D. Payne (ed.) 1992.265-78.

Noonan, Michael. 1994. "A tale of two passive in Irish."*Voice: Form and Function* ed. by Barbara Fox and Paul Hopper. Amsterdam/Philadelphia: John Benjamins.

Nichols, Johanna. 1986. "Head-marking and dependent-marking grammar." *Language* 62.56-119.

Noonan, Michael. 1994. "A tale of two passives in Irish." *Voice: Form and Function* ed. by Barbara Fox and Paul Hopper. Amsterdam/Philadelphia: John Benjamins.

Payne, Doris L. 1987. "Information structuring in Papago narrative discourse." *Language* 63.783-804.

Payne, Doris L. 1990. *The Pragmatics of Word Order: Typological dimensions of verb initial languages*. Berlin: Mouton de Gruyter.

Payne, Doris L. 1992. "Nonidentifiable information and pragmatic order rules in 'O'odham." D. Payne (ed.) 1992.137-66.

Payne, Doris L. (ed.) 1992. *The Pragmatics of Word Order Flexibility*. Amsterdam/ Philadelphia: John Benjamins.

Payne, Doris L. 1993. "On the function of word order in Yagua narrative." *International Journal of American Linguistics* 59. 1-15.

Payne, Doris L. and Thomas E. Payne. 1990. "Yagua." *Handbook of Amazonian Languages,* Vol. 2. ed. by Desmond Derbyshire and Geoffrey Pullum, 249-474. Berlin: Mouton de Gruyter.

Payne, Thomas E. 1991. "Goal Focus and Actor Focus in Cebuano narrative." Paper presented at the Sixth International Conference on Austronesian Languages. Honolulu, Hawaii.

Payne, Thomas E. 1992. *The Twins Stories: Participant coding in Yagua narrative.* Berkeley: University of California Press.

Pebley, Carol Jean. 1990. "Participant referencing in Kagayanen." SIL, Philippines. ms.

Quakenbush, Stephen. 1992. "Word order and discourse type: An Austronesian example." D. Payne (ed.) 1992.279-303.

Scancarelli, Janine. 1987. "Grammatical Relations and Verb Agreement in Cherokee." UCLA Ph.D. dissertation.

Schachter, Paul. 1984. "Semantic-role-based syntax in Toba Batak." *Studies in the Structure of Toba Batak* ed. by Paul Schachter, 122-49. [=*UCLA Occasional Papers in Linguistics* 5.]

Seiter, William. 1980. *Studies in Niuean Syntax.* New York: Garland.

Tomlin, Russell. 1986. *Basic Word Order: Functional principles.* London: Croom Helm.

Tomlin, Russell and Ming Ming Pu. 1991. "The management of reference in Mandarin discourse." *Cognitive Linguistics* 2.65-93.

Trávníček, F. 1939. "Slovosled Pri Durazu." *Slovo a Slovesnost* 5.131-144.

Woolford, Ellen. 1991. "VP-internal subjects in VSO and non-configurational languages." *Linguistic Inquiry* 22.503-540.

On the discourse functions of possessor movement in Emai prose narratives*

Ronald P. Schaefer
Southern Illinois University-Edwardsville

Introduction

The complex relationship between the word order of major sentence constituents and the internal structure of narrative storyline in African languages is examined closely in Longacre (1990). He begins with the assumption that a text's storyline is not presented at a single level of tension, i.e. "a story goes somewhere," and that resulting tension peaks are manifested in a variety of linguistic strategies collectively identified as "peak marking." Despite the range of data analyzed by Longacre, there has been little investigation of how word order within sentence level constituents might reflect storyline tension and, perhaps also, other discourse functions. The following paper examines word order variation affecting genitive constructions in Emai, a Benue-Congo language of southern Nigeria, and relates it to the discourse functions of secondary topic and peak marking.[1]

Possessor movement

Emai, a strict SVO verb-serializing language, exhibits word order variation with respect to genitive or, more accurately, associative constructions. Although the entire range of grammatical conditions governing this re-ordering phenomenon await complete description (Schaefer and Egbokhare in preparation), the relative positioning of the genitive's head and modifier constituents is readily describable. In one variant, the associative marker *isi* intervenes between the possessed object and its following possessor. In the other, characterized by obligatory omission of *isi*, the possessor precedes the possessed object.

In some respects the process relating these contrasting genitive constructions is reminiscent of what has been called "possessor ascension" (Aissen 1979; Croft 1991). That is, the possessor element assumes the erstwhile position of the possessed object and thereby the latter's grammatical function. As illustrated below however, the possessor modifier in Emai, when moved, does not consistently assume the position of its head. The genitive phrase, in fact, does not delimit the boundary for movement of the possessor, since in certain grammatical circumstances, the possessor is located outside this phrase. Because the possessor does not consistently usurp the grammatical position of its possessed object, I will simply refer to the possessor as moving and to its repositioning relative to the possessed object as possessor movement.[2]

Possessor ascension aside, constraints on possessor movement in Emai appear, in part, related to the possessor constituent's information status in postverbal position. The Emai process appears to reflect a discourse function of secondary topic marking. Initial support for this interpretation comes from the fact that possessor movement fails to occur in subject position. In (1a) the genitive phrase serving as subject has the order possessed-possessor, whereas in (1b), where the order is reversed, the sentence is ungrammatical.

(1) a. *éli ikposo ísi oje tóó á.*
the women ASS king burn CS
'the women of the king burned up'

*b. *oje éli ikposo tóó á.*
king the women burn CS

Grammatical positions affected by possessor movement are consistently postverbal. Relative to the direct object, the constituents of a genitive phrase can occur in one of two orders. The possessed object precedes the possessor in sentences like (2a) where the associative marker *isi* is present, whereas it follows the possessor in the corresponding paraphrase (2b), where *isi* does not and cannot occur.

(2) a. *élí íkpósó húá ikpun ísi oje.*[3]
the women carry cloth ASS king
'the women carried the cloth of the king'

b. *élí íkpósó húá ójé ikpun.*
the women carry king's cloth
'the women carried the king's cloth'

Similarly, a genitive construction occurring in the subcategorized locative complement of a verb can exhibit possessor movement. In this case the possessed object retains its post-locative position, the associative marker is omitted, and the possessor immediately follows the verb, as in (3a) and (3b). As the ungrammaticality of (3c) attests, the possessor cannot be stranded in post-verbal position by deleting the locative marker and the possessed object.

(3) a. *éráín ó vbí íwé ísi oje.*
fire enter L house ASS king
'fire entered the house of the king'

b. *éráín ó ójé vbí íwe.*
fire enter king's L house
'fire entered the king's house'

*c. *éráín ó ójé.*[4]
fire enter king's

Possessor movement applies as well to stative verbs requiring a locative complement. Relevant examples with the verb *rii* 'to be located' occur in (4a) and (4b). However, when a locative is not in a verb's subcategorization frame, e.g. the outer locatives shown in (5), possessor movement cannot apply.

(4) a. *évbii rii vbí íkpún ísi oje.*
palm oil be L cloth ASS king
'palm oil is on the cloth of the king'

b. *évbii rii ojé vbí úkpun.*
palm oil be king's L cloth
'palm oil is on the king's cloth'

(5) a. *éli ikposo gbé vbí íwé ísi oje.*
the women dance L house ASS king
'the women danced at the house of the king'

*b. *éli ikposo gbé ójé vbí íwe.*
the women dance king's L house

Although realized only in postverbal grammatical positions, possessor movement's occurrence is further constrained by parameters reflecting animacy, its subordinate status relative to grammatical subject and, more generally, its exclusion from preverbal position. Regarding animacy, possessor movement in direct object or locative complements can occur only if the possessor constituent is a human or animate noun, never an inanimate such as *egho* 'money.'

(6) a. *élí ívbekhan dóó úbélé ísi egho nwú.*
the youths steal gourd ASS money carry
'the youths stole a gourd of money'

*b. *élí ívbekhan dóó egho ubele nwú.*
the youths steal money gourd carry

Movement of the possessor is also restricted under conditions of referential identity between possessor and clausal subject, (7a) and (7b).

(7) a. *éli ikposo húá íkpún ísi iyáin.*
the women carry cloth ASS their

*b. *éli ikposo húá iyain íkpun.*
the women carry their cloth (their own cloth)

Transporting direct object or locative complements to preverbal positions likewise limits possessor movement. It cannot apply when the direct object or locative is grammatically topicalized, compare (8a) to (8b), or clefted, compare (8c) to (8d).

(8) a. *ikpun isi oje, élí íkpósó húá iyain.*
cloth ASS king the women carry them
'as for the king's cloth, the women carried them'

*b. *ójé ikpun, élí íkpósó húá iyain.*
king's cloth the women carry them

c. *íkpun ísi oje lí élí íkpósó húái.*[5]
cloth ASS king PF the women carry-F
'it is the king's cloth that the women carried'

*d. *oje íkpun lí élí íkpósó húái.*
king cloth PF the women carry-F

Although the postverbal complements direct object and locative can manifest possessor movement, indirect objects cannot. Indirect object position does not exhibit genitive word order variation, as a comparison of positions marked by *lí* in (9a) and (9b) indicates. Such cases might be ruled out by assuming that secondary topics are limited to the grammatical slot immediately following the verb.

(9) a. *élí ívbekhan nwú úkpún lí íkpósó ísi oje.*
the youths carry cloth APP women ASS king
'the youths carried cloth to the women of the king'

*b. *éli ívbekhan nwú úkpún lí ójé ikposo.*
the youths carry cloth APP king's women

Another factor constrains possessor movement which is not as easily related to the function of enhancing the secondary topic. Cognition or psychological verbs limit movement of the possessor. Genitive word order variation is not found in the complement of verbs like *zawo* in (10b). Why this should be the case remains to be explored.

(10) a. *éli ikposo záwó agháé ísi ojé.*
the women see knife ASS king
'the women saw the knife of the king'

*b. *éli ikposo záwó ójé agháé.*
the women see king's knife

Data base

We turn now to the analysis of possessor movement in Emai oral tradition narratives. Over the past few years Emai-speaking colleagues and I have transcribed and translated prose narratives from tape-recorded sessions of spontaneous oral tradition presentations (Schaefer and Egbokhare in preparation). For this study, I examine twelve narratives from two separate sessions presented by the same storyteller.[6]

Thirty-one genitive constructions exhibit possessor movement in the twelve prose narratives under consideration. In Appendix 1 the possessor forms (underlined in the interlinear translation) are presented along with a minimal amount of surrounding discourse. For instance, in 29.1, the direct object complement of the verb meaning 'climb' consists of a possessor followed by a possessed object, i.e. 'her body'; and in 29.2 the locative complement is comprised of the locative marker *vbi* and the possessed object *ihue* 'nose,' with a possessor meaning 'her' preceding both. Two of the twelve narratives in this set contain no examples of possessor movement.[7]

Grammatical character of possessor movement

Closer scrutiny of the distributional and grammatical properties of possessor movement is revealing. I will initially consider its distribution in the twelve narratives and follow with assessment of its grammatical characteristics vis-à-vis the constituents possessed object and possessor.

As an initial step, consider genitive constructions in the twelve narratives, irrespective of the application of possessor movement. Table 1 provides frequency information regarding the occurrence of genitives in two grammatical positions: preverbal (PREV) encompasses the grammatical position subject as well as topicalized and clefted noun phrases, while postverbal (POSV) covers direct object and locative complements licensed by a verb. Table 1 also distinguishes postverbal genitives showing possessed-possessor order (-PM)

Table 1. Instances of genitive constructions exhibiting possessor movement (+PM) or its absence (-PM) in preverbal (PREV) and postverbal (POSV) positions.

	-PM PREV	-PM POSV	+PM POSV	TOTAL
28	6	10	1	17
29	2	0	5	7
30	5	6	0	11
31	10	3	8	21
45	4	4	3	11
46	7	8	1	16
47	2	4	1	7
48	2	4	2	8
49	6	3	2	11
50	0	6	0	6
51	14	21	6	41
52	13	10	2	25
	71	79	31	181

Table 2. Grammatical characteristics of possessor (first-, second-, third-person pronoun, third-person logophoric pronoun, or full noun) and possessed object (body-part or non-body-part noun) constituents in possessor movement constructions.

	Possessor					Possessed	
	1	2	3	3L	FULL	+body part	-body part
28	0	0	1	0	0	1	0
29	0	0	5	0	0	5	0
30	0	0	0	0	0	0	0
31	0	3	1	3	1	6	2
45	0	0	2	0	1	3	0
46	0	0	0	0	1	1	0
47	0	0	1	0	0	1	0
48	0	0	0	0	2	2	0
49	0	1	0	0	1	2	0
50	0	0	0	0	0	0	0
51	0	0	5	1	0	6	0
52	0	1	1	0	0	2	0
	0	5	16	4	6	31	0

from those showing possessor-possessed (+PM), thereby highlighting instances of possessor movement.

From the figures in Table 1 one significant fact emerges. Possessor-possessed order is considerably less frequent than possessed-possessor, irrespective of the latter's occurrence in either preverbal or postverbal position. Of more immediate interest in Table 1 are the thirty-one instances of possessor movement. Closer scrutiny of these examples reveals two salient grammatical characteristics. First, the possessor constituent tends to be a third-person pronoun rather than a full noun or a pronoun indicating first-, second-person or third-person logophoric.[8] Second, the possessed object tends to be a body part. The dominant nature of these properties is evident in Table 2. Strictly speaking, a body part is not involved in one case, Narrative 31's wound or sore, but its close association with the body argues for its inclusion.

When measured against the characteristics of all genitive constructions in postverbal position, the figures in Table 2, particularly those for the third person possessor, assume a somewhat different cast. Table 3 expresses the characteristics of possessor movement exemplars in terms of the overall

Table 3. Relative to postverbal genitives, percentage of possessor movement exemplars occurring in possessor (first-, second-, third-person pronoun, third-person logophoric pronoun or full noun) and possessed object (body-part or non-body-part) categories.

Possessor					Possessed	
1	2	3	3L	FULL	+body part	-body part
0	56%	34%	15%	21%	63%	0%

properties of genitive constructions in postverbal position. Although third-person pronoun may be the more frequent realization of possessor in Table 2, it is less likely in the overall context of the narratives to express possessor movement than a second person pronoun. Nonetheless, it is still more likely to do so than a full noun or a logophoric pronoun. From Table 3 it is also evident that body-part terms, when occurring as possessed objects in postverbal genitives, exhibit a significant tendency to evince possessor movement.

Additional grammatical characteristics of genitives displaying possessor movement are indicated in Table 4. The left column indicates that possessor movement more often affects locative than direct object complements. The middle and right columns indicate that, overall, possessor movement occurs with nearly equal frequency in main and embedded clauses. There is a slight tendency for narratives which exhibit only a single instance of possessor movement to do so in a main clause. As the middle columns indicate, there is a much stronger tendency for possessor movement to occur in clauses expressing perfective aspect, thus being part of the narrative storyline or the foregrounded portion of the narrative (Hopper and Thompson 1980). Only narratives 28 and 29 exhibit possessor movement in imperfective clauses. Interestingly, narratives 31 and 51, which exhibit the greatest amount of possessor movement in embedded clauses, contain the longest and most complicated plot lines, for each essentially depicts a quest in which a single character undergoes a repeated series of trials with a range of other characters, or two contrasting characters undergo an identical series of trials. The remaining narratives are basically aetiological in nature as well as shorter in length.

Within the context of all genitives in postverbal position, the Table 4 figures stand in relief. As shown in Table 5, possessor movement genitives are much more likely to occur in locative position than direct object position. Genitives displaying possessor movement also exhibit a strong tendency to appear in imperfective clauses and an even greater tendency to occur in complements dominated by non-say verbs.

Table 4. Possessor movement exemplars classified as to complement type (direct object or locative), clause type (main or embedded), aspect type in main clause (perfective or imperfective), and verb type dominating the embedded clause.

	Position		Main		Embedded	
	DO	LOC	PERF	IMPERF	'say'	'non-say'
28	1	0	0	1	0	0
29	1	4	1	3	0	1
30	0	0	0	0	0	0
31	0	8	0	0	6	2
45	0	3	3	0	0	0
46	0	1	1	0	0	0
47	0	1	1	0	0	0
48	1	1	2	0	0	0
49	1	1	1	0	1	0
50	0	0	0	0	0	0
51	2	4	4	0	1	1
52	2	0	1	0	1	0
	8	23	14	4	9	4

Table 5. Relative to postverbal genitives, percentage of possessor movement exemplars classified as to complement type (direct object or locative), clause type (main or embedded), aspect type in main clause (perfective or imperfective), and verb type dominating the embedded clause.

Position		Main		Embedded	
DO	LOC	PERF	IMPERF	'say'	'non-say'
11%	67%	29%	44%	20%	67%

Analysis of possessor movement

The preceding section established that the genitive order possessor-possessed is far less frequent than its thematic paraphrase in the converse order. It also demonstrated that when possessor movement occurs the possessor nominal tends to be a third-person pronoun and the possessed object a body part. Having briefly outlined its grammatical shape, we turn to a closer scrutiny of possessor movement and its discourse conditions.

A fundamental assumption of the following is that the act of reference associated with nominal elements in discourse includes opening a cognitive file (Givón 1984b; Du Bois 1987; Chafe 1987; Croft 1991), a knowledge state recording the degree of participation of a discourse referent. As outlined by Du Bois (1987) and Fox and Thompson (1990), cognitive files may be active, inactive, or accessible. The active/inactive dimension refers to the extent the nominal referent is in the hearer's focal consciousness, while accessible refers to a referent in a hearer's peripheral consciousness which can be activated by the immediate situation, prior discourse, or general knowledge. Relative to this tripartite scheme, the question to ask is "What is the activation status of the cognitive file pertaining to possessor nominals which have undergone possessor movement and to their associated possessed objects?"

Table 6a. Referential distance (in number of clauses) to preceding and following mention of possessed object referent in possessor movement exemplars; grammatical function (GF) of preceding and following referent; their clause type (main or non-main); and clause type encoding possessor movement (PM).

		Preceding mention			Following mention			PM
		GF	#C	CT	GF	#C	CT	CT
28	1.	-	-	-	-	-	-	- M
29	1.	-	-	-	-	-	-	- M
	2.	-	-	-	L	1	- M	- M
	3.	L	1	- M	L	1	- M	- M
	4.	L	1	- M	L	12	- M	- M
	5.	-	-	-	-	-	-	+M
30		0	0	0	0	0	0	0
31	1.	DO	11	+M	-	-	-	- M
	2.	-	-	-	-	-	-	- M
	3.	-	-	-	-	-	-	- M
	4.	-	-	-	-	-	-	- M
	5.	-	-	-	-	-	-	- M
	6.	-	-	-	-	-	-	- M
	7.	-	-	-	L	2	- M	- M
	8.	L	2	- M	-	-	-	- M

Table 6b. Referential distance (in number of clauses) to preceding and following mention of possessed object referent in possessor movement exemplars; grammatical function (GF) of preceding and following referent; their clause type (main or non-main); and clause type encoding possessor movement (PM).

		Preceding mention			Following mention			PM
		GF	#C	+M	GF	#C	+M	+M
45	1.	-	-	-	-	-	-	+M
	2.	-	-	-	-	-	-	+M
	3.	-	-	- M	-	-	-	+M
46	1.	-	-	-	-	-	-	+M
47	1.	-	-	-	-	-	-	+M
48	1.	DO	5	- M	-	-	-	+M
	2.	-	-	-	DO	7	+M	+M
49	1.	-	-	-	-	-	-	+M
	2.	-	-	-	-	-	-	- M
50		0	0	0	0	0	0	0
51	1.	DO	2	- M	-	-	-	+M
	2.	-	-	-	-	-	-	-M
	3.	-	-	-	-	-	-	- M
	4.	-	-	-	-	-	-	-M
	5.	S	1	- M	-	-	-	+M
	6.	-	-	-	-	-	-	+M
52	1.	-	-	-	-	-	-	- M
	2.	-	-	-	-	-	-	+M

Using a technique advanced in Givón (1983), I tracked the referent of each possessor and possessed object nominal in possessor movement constructions. Accordingly, the referential distance, in number of clauses, between relevant possessor or possessed object nouns and their preceding and subsequent mention in the narratives was computed. This led directly to the Preceding Mention and Following Mention categories in Table 6 and Table 7.

Besides clause count to previous and subsequent mention, these tables specify the syntactic function of the referent in its previous and subsequent position as well as its occurrence in a main or non-main clause, i.e. on or off the storyline. Also indicated is possessor-movement's status relative to the primary storyline, again either main or non-main clause.

Turning initially to possessed objects in Table 6, we note evidence of one dominant feature bearing on referential continuity. Across both the preceding and following mention domains, possessed object nominals framed by possessor movement tend to exhibit an extremely inactive cognitive file. A full 94% (29 of 31 instances) of the possessed objects display either no preceding or no subsequent mention within 20 clauses of their occurrence in the narratives. With regard to these domains individually, 78% of possessed objects display no preceding mention while 84% show no following mention. Possessed objects in possessor movement constructions, therefore, tend to manifest a cognitive file which is not active.

Possessor nominals exhibit a contrasting referential character which has two manifestations. With regard to Table 7, one pattern is evident in the Preceding Mention category. The first instance of possessor movement in Narrative 29.1, for example, requires that one look back six clauses to locate

Table 7a. Referential distance (in number of clauses) to preceding and following mention of possessor referent in possessor movement exemplars; grammatical function (GF) of preceding and following referent; their clause type (main or non-main); and clause type encoding possessor movement (PM).

		Preceding mention			Following mention			PM
		GF	#C	CT	GF	#C	CT	CT
28	1.	DO	1	- M	S	1	- M	- M
29	1.	S	6	+M	L	1	- M	- M
	2.	DO	1	- M	L	1	- M	- M
	3.	L	1	- M	L	1	- M	- M
	4.	L	1	- M	DO	3	+M	- M
	5.	DO	5	- M	-	-	-	+M
30		0	0	0	0	0	0	0
31	1.	S	1	- M	S	1	+M	- M
	2.	IO	1	- M	S	1	+M	- M
	3.	DO	1	- M	DO	1	-M	- M
	4.	S	2	+M	-	-	-	- M
	5.	IO	1	- M	DO	1	- M	- M
	6.	S	1	+M	DO	1	- M	- M
	7.	DO	1	- M	DO	1	- M	- M
	8.	DO	1	- M	S	1	+M	- M

Table 7b. Referential distance (in number of clauses) to preceding and following mention of possessor referent in possessor movement exemplars; grammatical function (GF) of preceding and following referent; their clause type (main or non-main); and clause type encoding possessor movement (PM).

		Preceding mention			Following mention			PM
		GF	#C	+M	GF	#C	+M	+M
45	1.	DO	6	+M	DO	1	- M	+M
	2.	L	8	+M	S	3	- M	+M
	3.	S	7	+M	DO	3	+M	+M
46	1.	DO	40	- M	S	1	- M	+M
47	1.	DO	1	+M	DO	2	- M	+M
48	1.	IO	4	- M	IO	1	+M	+M
	2.	S	2	- M	S	1	+M	+M
49	1.	S	1	+M	S	2	+M	+M
	2.	S	3	+M	S	1	+M	- M
50		0	0	0	0	0	0	0
51	1.	DO	2	- M	DO	1	+M	+M
	2.	S	1	+M	L	1	- M	- M
	3.	L	1	- M	DO	1	+M	- M
	4.	S	1	+M	S	4	+M	- M
	5.	S	2	+M	DO	1	- M	+M
	6.	DO	1	- M	DO	1	+M	+M
52	1.	S	1	- M	S	2	- M	- M
	2.	S	1	+M	S	1	+M	+M

mention of the possessor referent. For another example in this same narrative, Narrative 29.5, one must look back five clauses for mention of the possessor referent. Likewise, in Narrative 45, a number of clauses intervene between the possessor nominal and its preceding mention, six in the case of Narrative 45.1 and eight in Narrative 45.2. However, it is only in Narratives 29 and 45 that look-back values of five to eight clauses occur.

The remaining examples in Table 7 do not demand extensive tracking of the possessor referent. In the typical case, Narrative 28.1, for example, mention of the possessor referent occurs in one of two immediately preceding clauses. 74% of possessor movement exemplars, in fact, require a look-back of only one or two clauses, a point further substantiated by an average distance of 1.2 clauses to preceding mention when the exceptional examples in Narratives 29 and 45 are excluded.

Subsequent mention or persistence of the possessor referent follows this latter pattern, too. The first or second clause immediately following possessor movement mentions the possessor referent in over 80% of the cases in Table 7. The average subsequent mention distance using all examples is 1.3 clauses. None of the examples show persistence values higher than four clauses, although there is one instance, Narrative 29.5, where the possessor referent is not mentioned again.[9]

Based on the figures in Table 7, it is evident that cognitive files for possessor nominals undergoing possessor movement reflect contrasting degrees of activation. For most exemplars, the activation level is high, mention of the possessor's referent being in the preceding as well as subsequent clause. The cognitive file in these cases is active. In a few other instances the activation level is lower, but not at a level which one would call inactive (Du Bois 1987). Less involved possessor nominals of the type found in Narratives 29 and 45 are better thought of as exhibiting accessible cognitive files.

Secondary topic

To this point we have established the tendency for possessor movement to consist of a body-part possessed object whose referent is unlikely to be mentioned in preceding or subsequent discourse and a pronominal possessor whose referent typically is mentioned in this same discourse range. Furthermore, preceding mention of the possessor referent most often, 78% in Table 7, occurs in the position of grammatical subject (13/31) or grammatical direct object (11/31), positions accorded nouns of high discourse topicality: respectively, the primary and secondary topic of Givón (1984a). Within this theoretical framework one discourse function of possessor movement begins to emerge. Specifically, possessor movement shuttles a nominal of relatively high discourse salience, as measured by preceding mention in subject or direct object position, into a slot immediately following the verb, the position accorded secondary topics. Had possessor movement not applied, an animate or human participant syntactically registered as topical in the preceding narrative would be signaled as outside the range of discourse salience, a seemingly unsatisfactory state of affairs.

Regarding the secondary topic notion, contrasting hypotheses have attempted to identify its grammatical underpinning. Givón (1984a) proposes that it be specified in terms of a thematic relations hierarchy: DAT/BEN < ACC < LOC < INSTR < OTHERS. The most likely relation to manifest secondary topicality is DAT/BEN, based on the cross-language prevalence of shift sentences like *John built Mary the house.* vs *John built the house for Mary.*, compared to shifts involving the remaining relations. On the other hand, Croft (1991) suggests that secondary topics reflect Silverstein's (1976) and Dixon's (1979) animacy hierarchy: first/second-person pronoun < third-person pronoun < proper name < human common noun < animate common noun < inanimate common noun. Pronouns in first/second-person are then most likely to be secondary topics.

Of these, the animacy hierarchy more adequately characterizes the grammatical properties of possessor-moved nominals in Emai narratives. But to assess the thematic relations hypothesis first, we see that it is not a head noun expressing a thematic role which undergoes possessor movement but a modifier. The possessor nominal, however, does express the ultimate animate recipient of the clausal event or the animate participant affected by the verb's action or state. For instance, in Narrative 28, it is the possessor 'man' whose liver the puff-adder wanted to eat, and in Narrative 29 it is the young child which is affected by the climbing action of the millipede and its entrance into her nose. As a representation of the ultimate recipient of the verb event, possessor nominals are akin to those functioning as thematic datives or benefactives, the highest roles on the hierarchy.

A related line of inquiry may be to recognize that the possessor nominal is the principal affected entity participating in the verb event. This approach would tie possessor movement to a range of studies noting that post-verbal position is reserved for more affected clausal entities (Fillmore 1977; Anderson 1970), e.g. differences in the interpretation of *He loaded the wagon with hay.* vs *He loaded hay onto the wagon.* Dative and benefactive shift sentences might then be subsumed under this approach along with possessor movement exemplars. Although the range of construction types involved, to say nothing of the discourse data needed to assess NP shifts, makes the task of articulating this approach formidable, the convergence on post-verbal position suggests an initial point of entry for further investigation.

As for the animacy hierarchy, it is indeed personal pronouns rather than full nouns which more often undergo possessor movement. Although the data in Table 2 indicated that first/second-person pronouns, contrary to the animacy hierarchy, participate less frequently in possessor movement than third-person pronouns, they are more likely in a narrative to manifest possessor movement than the latter. The percentages in Table 3, that is, are generally consistent with the animacy hierarchy: in the context of all postverbal genitives, the occurrence of a second person pronoun is more likely to signal possessor movement than a third person pronoun, and this, in turn, is more likely to participate in possessor movement than a full noun. Finally, inanimate nouns, positioned lowest on the animacy hierarchy, never undergo possessor movement. More detailed investigations will undoubtedly be required before the relationship between the animacy hierarchy and secondary topic can be adequately captured.

Assuming that secondary topics reflect the relative weighing of clausal participants in terms of animacy and affectedness, one naturally returns to those genitive constructions in the narratives which exhibit the constituent elements characteristic of possessor movement but which nonetheless fail to undergo this process. Distributional information concerning all genitives in postverbal position not reflecting possessor movement is shown in Table 8, where the grammatical character of their constituent elements is recorded.

Table 8. Grammatical characteristics of genitive constructions in postverbal position failing to exhibit possessor movement.

	+animate possessor +body part possessed	+animate possessor -body part possessed	-animate possessor -body part possessed
28	6	3	1
29	0	0	0
30	1	5	0
31	0	1	2
45	1	2	1
46	1	7	0
47	1	3	0
48	0	4	0
49	1	1	0
50	0	5	0
51	2	19	0
52	2	8	1
	15	58	5

An initial aspect to note about Table 8 is that genitives not involving possessor movement generally exhibit an animate possessor but lack a body-part possessed object. Far fewer exemplars exhibit neither an animate possessor nor a body-part possessed. Genitives exhibiting both a body-part possessed and an animate possessor constitute the remaining 19%. Two questions arise at this point: Why do body-part possessed objects lend themselves to possessor movement? and Why does possessor movement not occur when its constituency conditions are met? I will deal with each of these in turn.

Regarding body-part nominals, Hopper and Thompson (1984) note their atypicality as autonomous and salient discourse entities, as discourse participants distinct from their possessors. The relationship between body parts and their animate possessors appears to reflect the undifferentiated state of the former relative to their possessors. It may be this unique dependency which allows, and in some cases requires, the possessor to be dislodged through possessor movement from its position to the right of the possessed object. The Emai possessor, especially given its active cognitive file as judged by preceding and subsequent mention, is likely to perform a substantial grounding or identifying function (Fox and Thompson 1990) for a possessed object referent which, as Table 6 indicated, exhibits an extremely inactive cognitive file. Building on this, I hypothesize that the possessor nominal's inextricable link to its body-part companion allows the possessor to perform a grounding function, even at some remove from the possessed object, by virtue of its discourse salience, while at the same time reinforcing through the change in word order the status of an animate and affected participant as secondary topic.

To deal with our second question, we will examine more closely the grammatical properties of body-part possessed and animate possessor pairs not manifesting possessor movement. Of the exemplars identified in Table 8, a sizeable number do not inhabit a grammatical environment conducive to possessor movement. Constraints on identity between the possessor and the grammatical subject block possessor movement in examples 30, 46, 49, and 51; and a cognition verb blocks movement in example 47. The examples in 52 involve a character who has died and therefore is not an animate, sentient being.

More problematic are the remaining seven examples shown in Appendix 2. The six in Narrative 28, all in close proximity in the narrative, re-tell the main storyline, a condition in which possessor saliency may give way to other discourse priorities and thus may no longer be of immediate value. Finally, 45

Table 9. Referential distance (in number of clauses) to preceding and following mention of possessed object referent in genitive constructions with animate possessor and body-part possessed failing to exhibit possessor movement; grammatical function (GF) of preceding and following referent; their clause type (main or non-main); and that of the possessed object-possessor construction (POP).

		Preceding mention			Following mention			POP
		GF	#C	CT	GF	#C	CT	CT
28	1. -	-	-	-	L	14	- M	- M
	2.	L	4	- M	L	1	- M	- M
	3.	L	1	- M	-	-	-	- M
	4.	-	-	-	-	-	-	+
	5.	-	-	-	DO	1	- M	- M
	6.	DO	1	- M	-	-	-	- M
30.	1.	-	-	-	-	-	-	+M
45.	1.	-	-	-	-	-	-	+M
46.	1.	-	-	-	DO	1	+M	+M
47.	1.	-	-	-	S	1	- M	- M
49.	1.	-	-	-	-	-	-	- M
51.	1.	-	-	-	-	-	-	- M
	2.	-	-	-	-	-	-	- M
52.	1.	S	9	+M	S	2+	M	+M
	2.	-	-	-	DO	1	+M	+M

occurs in an episode bounded by two instances of possessor movement. Why possessor movement does not occur in this case is not clear, although it may be related to the high look-back values of possessor movement exemplars in this narrative and thus the operation of a derivative discourse function for possessor movement, as discussed below.

Analysis of the constructions identified in Table 8 suggests that genitives consisting of an animate possessor and body-part possessed which fail to manifest possessor movement frequently lack the requisite grammatical environment. We might also ask whether these examples otherwise reflect possessor movement's discourse conditions. Partial reply to this question is found in Table 9 and Table 10, where the referential distance of animate possessors and body-part possessed objects is recorded. As with earlier examples, the number of clauses to preceding and subsequent mention of the possessed object and possessor referent was computed.

Referential distance patterns for possessed objects in Table 9 do not differ substantially from those of possessed objects in possessor movement constructions. 87% exhibit no preceding or no following mention, although there is a greater tendency for possessed objects in these constructions to show no preceding mention, 73%, as opposed to no following mention, 53%. Generally, cognitive files for possessed objects differ little across genitive constructions, irrespective of possessor movement.

The same conclusion does not apply to possessors. From Table 10, we can infer that it is not only grammatical conditions which are lacking; general discourse conditions, as measured by referential distance, are at variance with

Table 10. Referential distance (in number of clauses) to preceding and following mention of possessor referent in genitive constructions with animate possessor and body-part possessed failing to exhibit possessor movement; grammatical function (GF) of preceding and following referent; their clause type (main or non-main); and that of the possessed object-possessor construction (POP).

		Preceding mention			Following mention			POP
		GF	#C	CT	GF	#C	CT	CT
28	1.	S	4	+M	DO	2	- M	- M
	2.	S	1	- M	L	1	- M	- M
	3.	L	1	- M	S	4	- M	- M
	4.	S	6	+M	DO	5	- M	+M
	5.	DO	5	+M	DO	1	- M	- M
	6.	DO	1	- M	S	9	- M	- M
30.	1.	S	2	- M	S	13	- M	+M
45.	1.	L	1	+M	L	11	+M	+M
46.	1.	S	2	- M	S	1	+M	+M
47.	1.	DO	1	+M	DO	1	- M	- M
49.	1.	S	1	- M	DO	1	- M	- M
51.	1.	DO	1	- M	S	1	- M	- M
	2.	S	1	- M	S	2	+M	+M
52.	1.	DO	1	+M	DO	1	+M	+M
	2.	DO	1	+M	DO	1	+M	+M

those supporting secondary topics. The average distance to preceding mention of the possessor referent is 2.0 clauses for the non-possessor movement exemplars in Table 10 compared to 1.3 in Table 7. Average distance to subsequent mention is even higher, 3.6 clauses compared to 1.3 in Table 7. Both of these figures suggest that possessors associated with body parts but not exhibiting possessor movement are not as integrated into discourse as possessor nominals in Appendix 1, i.e. especially those with active cognitive files.

It thus seems that one function of possessor movement is to enhance the discourse topicality of the possessor nominal referent, specifically the latter's role as secondary topic. For this function, the cognitive file of the possessor nominal is not only open but active in the immediately preceding discourse, usually the immediately preceding clause.

Peak marking

The topicality enhancing function of possessor movement appears to be exploited for additional discourse purposes. As we saw earlier in Table 7, some possessor nominals exhibited less active cognitive files compared to others. In particular, what were identified as nominal referents with accessible cognitive files had preceding mention values of 6-8 clauses. When examined closely relative to storyline tension, they appear to reflect peak marking, Longacre's (1990) term for linguistic strategies signaling a story's intuitive climax or denouement.

Longacre maintains that a variety of surface level strategies are employed to encode moments of storyline tension. One of these, Maximum Interlacing of Participant Reference, essentially maximizes the presence of participants at moments of storyline tension. My hypothesis is that the instances of accessible cognitive files, such as we saw in 29 and 45, perform this discourse function. Support for this contention exists in the co-occurrence of possessor movement with other peak marking devices discussed by Longacre such as repetition, presence of ideophones, abrupt changes in aspect and sentence length, etc.

Indeed, the examples in 29 and 45 occur in the context of abrupt changes in sentence syntax. In 29 the expression of storyline events switches from perfective to imperfective aspect with the onset of possessor movement. In addition, possessor movement is expressed in a series of repeated clauses.

Peak marking devices are also evident in Narrative 45, where possessor movement co-occurs with verb repetition in the immediately preceding clause and with the appearance of ideophones.

One might assume from this discussion that the functions of peaking marking and secondary topic are consistently reflected in distinct levels of cognitive file activation, accessible for peak marking and active for secondary topic. This does not appear to be the case however. There is some evidence that a short-distance look-back, a very active cognitive file, may also be associated with peak marking. Consider Narrative 48 in Table 7, which has exemplars with preceding mention distances of 4 and 2 clauses. What is interesting about this example is that it represents two of six instances in this entire set of narratives where a full noun rather than a pronoun evinces possessor movement. Relative to pronominal forms, a full noun is more characteristic of an inactive cognitive file. Why then is a full noun used when similar preceding mention conditions relied on a pronoun?

Intuitively, possessor movement in Narrative 48 occurs at the climax of the storyline. It is at this point that the tortoise makes his decisive step to seek revenge on the dog by inserting a smoldering yam-rod into his nose. Support for this intuition resides in the convergence of peak marking devices at this juncture in the narrative. A switch in sentence length is typical of the peak-marking strategy Longacre (1990) calls Augmented Sequence. Immediately following the possessor movement clause in Narrative 48.2, which itself has been preceded by a series of complex sentences, most immediately one involving an adverbial and an embedded clause, a series of brief sentences follows, one using a main verb meaning 'to say' and the other 'to do.' Peak marking is also evident in these following sentences, since an ideophone, or a series of ideophones, occurs as the verb complement. Finally, the full noun *awa* 'dog' occurs as the grammatical subject of these following sentences, as if to emphasize further its significance at this moment in the narrative. Evidence thus exists that the peak marking function of possessor movement does not require the five to eight clause look-back of the examples in Narratives 29 and 45, provided the possessor is realized as a full noun rather than a pronoun.

Are the same characteristics evident in other instances of possessor movement employing a full noun? One's first impression is that peak marking is not evident, for there are no ideophones or dramatic changes in sentence length. Nonetheless, other peak marking strategies discussed by Longacre are present. In Narrative 31.8, for instance, possessor movement occurs in an embedded clause dominated by the cognition verb *gaze* 'to realize.' It thus gives the appearance of being off the main clause story line. Furthermore, repetition is evident, since the possessor movement sentence is identical to the one immediately preceding, which employed a pronoun rather than a full noun for the possessor. Finally, the full noun undergoing possessor movement occurs as subject of two following sentences. Since pronominal forms are frequent in these same circumstances, the use of a full noun is unusual. It is made more unusual by its relative late occurrence in the narrative when identity of the referent is well-known.

Intuitively, this final instance of possessor movement in Narrative 31 does not occur at the story's climax, which occurred earlier when the wife character was taken up into the branches of the tree. Instead, it appears to reflect the denouement, since at this juncture the remaining characters in the story, recognizing the possessor no longer holds his wife, cease pursuing him. It is essentially with this event that the sequence of storyline actions come to a halt. Consistent with this overall analysis, I summarize in Table 11 the functions of possessor movement exhibited in the Emai narratives analyzed.

Table 11. Designation of Emai narratives with respect to possessor movement functions: peak marking and secondary topic marking.

	Peak marking	Secondary topic
28		*
29	*	*
30	-	-
31	*	*
45	*	*
46	-	-
47		*
48	*	*
49		*
50	-	-
51		*
52		*

Conclusion

In this paper I examined the discourse functions of possessor movement in Emai oral tradition narratives. These functions, limited to genitives consisting of an animate possessor and a body-part possessed object, are typically reflected in contrasting activity levels of the possessor's cognitive file. In its basic function as a secondary topic serving to ground a body part, the possessor exhibits an active file relative to immediately preceding discourse. As a device exploited to enhance storyline tension, peak marking, its cognitive file is accessible.

Notes

* An earlier version of this paper entitled "Genitive Word Order and Action Peak in Emai Prose Narratives" was presented at the 20th Annual University of Wisconsin-Milwaukee Linguistics Symposium. I am grateful to conference participants, Russ Tomlin and Matt Dryer, for their comments on that presentation. Analysis of the Emai narratives was supported by Fourth Quarter Research Fellowships from Southern Illinois University-Edwardsville. Data for this paper were analyzed with the support of National Science Foundation Grant BNS - 9011338.

1. Within Benue-Congo Emai is a member of the North-Central branch of the Edoid language family (Bendor-Samuel 1989).

2. Since the construction in which the possessor precedes the possessed object cannot occur in subject position, we can infer that "movement" is specified relative to the construction in which the possessed object precedes the possessor.

3. Emai sentences are presented in the orthographic system developed in Schaefer (1987) where *e* and *o* represent lax front and back mid-vowels, respectively, and vb represents a voiced bilabial fricative.

4. Emai expresses this notion using a phrase in which the possessed object is ellipted from the genitive construction, e.g. *éli ikposo ó vbí ísi óje* 'the woman entered the king's' (e.g. entered the king's house).

5. Cleft constructions in Emai are signaled by the positive focus (PF) marker *li*. In these examples the *-i* morpheme attached to the verb is the Factative marker.

6. The narratives were recorded in the village of Afuze, Bendel State, Nigeria on 27 November 1983 and 12 February 1984.

7. The original numbering scheme for the narratives has been retained primarily for purposes of reference to the larger set of narratives. Abbreviations in the Emai text refer to the following:

RD= Right Dislocation, ANT= Anterior, APP= Applicative, ASS= Associative, C=Continuous Aspect, CL= Change of Location, CMP=Comparison, COMP=Indicative Complement, CS= Change of State, EMR= Emphatic Repetition, G= Goal, HOR= Hortative, HYP= Hypothetical, ID= Ideophone, JUS= Jussive, LOC= Locative, NEG= Negation, PCT= Punctual, PRED= Predictive, R= Relator, REFL= Reflexive.

8. Logophoric pronouns in Emai, confined to third-person singular and plural, indicate that co-reference obtains between a pronoun in an embedded complement clause and the grammatical subject of the matrix clause, or, more generally, between a pronoun and the discourse participant whose speech is reported in indirect disourse or whose knowledge state is being reported. It appears limited to indicatives and, therefore, does not occur in subjunctive or conditional complements.

9. In this case possessor movement occurs only a few sentences from the end of the narrative.

Appendix

1. Instances of Possessor Movement in Prose Narrative Samples from Emai Oral Tradition.

Narrative 28

íyóín	ní	yón	fáán	*é*	lí	*ó*vb*é*	í	i	kónó	w*é*
he	R	he	rescue	you	APP	puff-adder	it	NEG	pick	*your*

iban	é,	iy*o*in	ú	ló	ke	gbé	*ó*	vbí	ufáánmí	ní	yón
liver	eat	it	you	PRED	ANT	kill	CL	L	rescuing	PF	it

fáán	*é*?
rescue	you

Narrative 29

1.

é	gázé	ikpékpéhimi	*o*	héén	*óí*	égbe.
they	discover	millipede		it	climb	*her*	body

2.

o	*ó*	o	*oí*	vbí	íhue.
it	C	enter	*her*	L	nose

3.

ikpékpéhímí	áin	*o*	*ó*	o	*óí*	vbí	íhue.
millipede	that	it	C	enter	*her*	L	nose

4.

o	*ó*	o	*óí*	vbí	íhue.	*ó*	ké	k*oo*	ré	kéré. ...
it	C	enter	*her*	L	nose	it	ANT	remain	G	small-bit

5.

é	sí	*óí*	k*é*k*é*k*é*k*é*.	ikpékpéhímí	fán	á	kpá.	*ó*lí
they	pull	it	continuously	millipede	snap	CS	ID	the one

ó	k*óó*	re,	*ó*	sí*ó*	ó	*ói*	vbí	*é*k*é*ín	úhumi	l*é*.
it	remain	G	it	crawl	enter	*her*	L	inside	head	depart

Narrative 31

1. *ó* r*ó*í kpaa íy*o*in gbé údi ní íy*ó*ín
she say help her fell palm tree APP she

mi*e* eny*ó* vbi *o*. óf*é* r*é* *é* w*é* lí ú
find wine L it. rat SEQ say you R you

ú vbiavbíá na, a gúá erain *ó* w*é* vbí úhumi.
do repulsive this, one heap fire CL *your* L head

2. *é*r*ú*é r*ó*í y*o*n l*ó* ku éhia *ó* w*é* vbí *é*máí enyáa.
deer say it PRED thrust hoof CL *your* L wound now

3. íkoíkó r*ó*í y*o*n kha hían *e*kpa *ó* w*é* vbi efen,
gorilla say he HYP strike punch CL *your* L side

á l*ó* hoo *é* bá kun.
one PRED search-for you grope in-vain

4. *é*kp*é*n r*é* *é* *ó*í ébé ú ké mí*é* égbé ísi *é*
leopard SEQ tell her where you ANT see REFL ASS your

s*é*? ... sh*oo* íy*ó*ín vbí ísao ré.
reach leave *its* L front G

5. íní r*ó*í y*o*n kha gbé úkpak*o*n *o*kpá *ó* w*é* vbi ef*e*n,
elephant say it HYP hit tusk one CL *your* L side

ó ré *é* órán ní y*ó*n l*ó* fi *é* khúán,
it SEQ say tree R it PRED throw you hang

ó i sí k*ee* égbe ena.
it NEG draw near side-of these

6. *ó* r*ó*í, wo *o*í, khi *é*máí lí *ó* ri íy*ó*ín vbí *óé* na,
she say look-at it COMP wound R it be *her* L leg this

lí á *é* íy*ó*ín ya r*é* *ó*i *ó* ... lí *ó* í r*e* fóó.
R one tell her JUS put it CL APP it HOR SEQ heal

7. a kha ké khú isi, a gázé khi isi,
one HYP ANT chase pig one discover COMP pig

*o*kposo í i ké e *ó*í vbí ób*o*.
woman she NEG ANT be *its* L hand

8. a kha ké khú isi, a gázé
one HYP ANT chase pig one discover

khi *o*kposo í i ké e isí vbí ób*o*.
COMP woman she NEG ANT be *pig's* L hand

Narrative 45

1. ó róó úháí áin. ó róó *ó*i ó vbi *e*tekun. ó fí *ó*í
he pick-up arrow that he pick-up it CL L bow he shoot it
iváóó. ó shán *ó*í vbí *égégé*n íhúánb*o* ráá re.
ID it proceed *its* L under tip-of-wings pass G

2. ó róó *ó*i, ó róó *ó*i ó vbí *o*, ó gbó nwú áb*o*
he pick-up it he pick-up it CL L it he EMR put hand
ó *ó*lí áfiámí áín vbí égbé k*éé*, ó ú váo.
CL *the bird that* L body steadily it do ID

3. ó íy*ó* nwú áb*o* ó *ó*í vbí ídáma. ó ú fáa.
he that way put hands CL *its* L chest it do ID

Narrative 46

1. ó déé ákhé únu ré vbí ókhúmí óm*e*h*e*n, ioo.
she turn pot opening G L top sleeper ID
ó éyé ó íny*ó* *ó*d*ó*n *ó*í égbe. óe!
she spill CL *mother husband her* body INT

Narrative 47

1. ó kú éhi*é*n ó *ó*í vbí égbe. ú h*ó*n ighiriri.
it put claws CL *its* L body you hear ID

Narrative 48

1. á ré évbii, á ré *ó*i gb*ó*ó éín *e*hai.
one take palm-oil one use it rub *tortoise's* forehead

2. éín ghé nwú úbósún áín vbi éráín váó. ó ghé fí
tortoise PCT take yam-rod that L fire swiftly he PCT insert
*ó*i ó áwá vbí íhue. áwá ré é fún, fún, fún. áwá ú gbíólo.
it CL *dog's* L nose dog SEQ say ID ID ID dog do ID

Narrative 49

1. éín ghé ré úkpaw*e* vbéé *ó*m*ó* áín úkpaw*e*.
tortoise PCT use leg entangle *child's that* leg

2. éín ré é iy*o*in tá iyó. íny*ó* *ó* lí
tortoise SEQ say he speak that-way mother your PF
ó zé ona ó w*é* vbí égbe, í khi okpokpo.
she cause this CL *your* L body AF COMP agitation

Narrative 51

1. ó zá nwú ikitib*é* sh*óó* íyáín vbí íhue ré.
he RES take pipe exit *their* L nose G

2.

ó	súghú	únu	kú	*ó*	vbí	úkó.	*ó*	gázé	íkpékh*ó*í	ésó	lí
he	rinse	mouth	spit	CL	L	cup	she	discover	worms	some	R

é	ó	*ó*í	vbí	*égégén*	ak*o*n,
they	enter	*his*	L	between	teeth

3.

e	ríi	*o*í	vbí	*é*k*é*ín	am*e*.
they	be-F	*his*	L	inside	water

4.

*ó*n*ó*í	r*ó*í	u	ya	kp*óó*n	íy*ó*ín	ák*ó*n	vbí	únu.
other-one	say	you	almost	collapse	*his*	teeth	L	mouth

5.

ó	fíló	*ó*í	aw*e*	sh*óó*	vbi	erain	ré	píípíí.
he	throw-DS	*her*	legs	exit	L	fire	G	ID

6.

íní	gbó	gbé	ak*o*n	*ó*	*ó*í	vbi	ef*e*n.
elephant	EMR	hit	tusk	CL	*his*	L	side

Narrative 52

1.

úvbíúk*ó*	r*é*	*é*	*e*kp*e*n	*wewe*	m*oe*	ob*ó*	lí	ú	l*ó*	*re*
billy-goat	SEQ	tell	leopard	you	have	hand	R	you	PRED	use

gbé	íy*o*in?	w*é*w*é*	li	*e*kp*e*n,	émé	y*ó*n	l*ó*	*re*	*é*	*eo*
kill	him	you	R	leopard	what	he	PRED	use	*your*	face

mí*é*,	únu	*ó*	l*ó*	ya	tá	*ó*i.
see	mouth	it	PRED	JUS	say	it

2.

o	t*éé*	*e*d*e*d*e*,	*ó*	nwú	úríáí	ísi	*e*kp*e*n.	*ó*	só	*ó*í
it	be-long	earlier	it	take	tail	ASS	leopard	it	touch	*its*

úkpá	vbi	ót*ó*í	g*ó*.
tip	L	ground	stabbingly

2. Genitive Constructions in Postverbal Position Exhibiting an Animate Possessor and a Body-Part Possessed Object but not Possessor Movement.

Narrative 28

1.

*ó*vb*é*	í	i	ké	amá	sh*oo*	vbí	*é*k*é*ín	ísi	*o*m*ó*hé
puff adder	it	NEG	ANT	agree	leave	L	belly	ASS	man

lí	*ó*	fáán	*ó*í	ré	o.
R	he	rescue	him	G	INT

2.

y*o*n	ké	táán	únu	á,	*ó*	zá	ó	vbí	*é*k*é*ín	ísi	iy*ó*ín.
he	ANT	spread	mouth	CS	it	RES	enter	L	belly	ASS	his

3.

ó	*ó*	diá	vbí	*é*k*é*ín	ísi	iy*ó*ín.
he	INC	stay	L	belly	ASS	his

4. *ó* dé égbéegbé óó ísi *oí* ré. *o*
he reach edge opening ASS his G it

ké *é* *óí* khi *o* l*ó* ya gúé
ANT say it COMP it PRED JUS present

ezón, *ó* *ré* *é* "*ó*vb*é*." *ó* r*óí* "heé."
case it SEQ say puff-adder it say yes

ó r*óí* y*ó*n kha h*o*n emé ú a gúé.
it say it-NEG HYP hear what you H present

5. "si k*éé* únú ísi *oí* vbi ean ré,
move near mouth ASS his L here G

6. gbe únu ráá únú ísi *oí* ré dé ean ré."
dip mouth pass mouth ASS his G reach here G

ó r*óí* "he." *ó*vb*é*, *o* ké ghe yí úhumi ré.
it say ok puff-adder it ANT PCT push head G

Narrative 45

1. íkpihai eéá ré... *ó* *ó* shan vbí égbégbé úgúítíhán
arrows three G it INC proceed L beside tail-feather

ísi *oí* ráá re.
ASS its pass G

References

Aissen, J. 1979. "Possessor ascension." *Papers in Mayan Linguistics*. Columbia, MO: Lucas Brothers.

Anderson, S. 1970. "A Little Light on the Role of Deep Semantic Interpretation." NSF Report No. 26. Cambridge, Mass: Harvard University.

Bendor-Samuel, J. ed. 1989. *The Niger-Congo Languages*. New York: University Press of America.

Chafe, W. 1987. "Cognitive constraints on information flow." *Coherence and Grounding in Discourse* ed. by R. Tomlin, 21-52. Amsterdam/Philadelphia: John Benjamins.

Croft, W. 1991. *Syntactic Categories and Grammatical Relations*. Chicago: University of Chicago Press.

Dixon, R.M.W. 1979. "Ergativity." *Language* 55. 59-138.

Du Bois, J. 1987. "The Discourse Basis of Ergativity." *Language* 63. 805-855.

Fillmore, C. 1977. "The case for case re-opened." *Grammatical Relations* ed. by P. Cole and J. Sadock, 59-82. New York: Academic Press. [*Syntax and Semantics* 8.]

Fox, B. and S. Thompson. 1990. "A discourse explanation of the grammar of relative clauses in English conversation." *Language* 66.297-316.

Givón, T. ed. 1983. *Topic Continuity in Discourse: Quantitative Cross-Language Studies*. Amsterdam/Philadelphia: John Benjamins.

Givón, T. 1984a. "Direct object and dative shifting: semantic and pragmatic case." *Objects: Towards a theory of grammatical relations* ed. by F. Plank, 151-182. New York: Academic Press.

Givón, T. 1984b. *Syntax: A Functional-Typological Introduction*, Vol. 1. Amsterdam/ Philadelphia: John Benjamins.

Hopper, P. and S. Thompson. 1980. "Transitivity in grammar and discourse." *Language* 56.251-99.

Hopper, P. and S. Thompson. 1984. "The discourse basis for lexical categories in universal grammar." *Language* 60.703-752.

Longacre, R. 1990. "Storyline concerns and word order typology in East and West Africa." *Studies in African Linguistics* Supplement 10.

Schaefer, R. 1987. *An Initial Orthography and Lexicon for Emai, An Edoid Language of Nigeria*. Bloomington: Indiana University Linguistics Club.

Schaefer, R. and F. Egbokhare. In preparation. *An Emai Reference Grammar.*

Schaefer, R. and F. Egbokhare. In preparation. *Narrative Prose Samples from Emai Oral Tradition.*

Silverstein, M. 1976. "Hierarchy of features and ergativity." *Grammatical Categories in Australian Languages* ed. by R.M.W. Dixon, 112-71. Canberra: Australian Institute of Aboriginal Studies.

Focal attention, voice, and word order

An experimental, cross-linguistic study*

Russell S. Tomlin
University of Oregon

0. Introduction

Historically, functional linguists investigate the factors which determine the selection of alternative word orders or voice constructions in text and discourse. Typically, specific analyses postulate some pragmatic notion, like *theme*, or *topic*, or *focus*, as the functional basis for understanding alternative orders (for example SVO versus OSV in Russian or Czech) or the selection between active and passive voice (for example, English or Indonesian). While such analyses have been appealing for their intuitive grasp of how functional grammars work in managing discourse, they nonetheless suffer from a number of serious problems:

- Theoretical weaknesses in the definitions of the central pragmatic notions like *theme* or *topic*.
- Empirical difficulties identifying instances of *theme*s or *topic*s in actual discourse data.
- Failure to distinguish form-function *correlations* from causal functional interactions.
- Difficulty in cross-linguistic comparisons due to uncertainties regarding comparability of discourse data.

Two central problems, then, in discourse study are how to articulate plainly hypotheses about form–function interactions and how to examine such hypotheses empirically. This paper argues that hypotheses about theme/topic interactions with word order and voice can be recast more clearly in terms of cognitive processes of attention amenable to experimental manipulation. It also shows that it is possible to devise an experimental paradigm that permits an unequivocal test of coding claims regarding the function of alternative main clause word orders and voice constructions.

To this end the paper deals with three concrete issues. One, we will consider a number of fundamental issues and problems we face in developing an adequate theory of functional grammar. We will do this with specific reference to the classical problem of investigating the interaction of so-called clause-level theme or topic[1] with voice and word order. Two, we will present the details of an experimental paradigm in which the classical notion of clause-level *theme* is replaced by the cognitive notion of *focal attention*, a cognitive notion which is well-grounded in the psychological literature and which is amenable to experimental manipulation. This paradigm will be examined for English discourse production data involving the selection of active versus passive voice. Three, we will extend this paradigm cross-linguistically to explore the grammatical means employed by several languages to code focal attention.

The theoretical significance of this kind of work is threefold. First, the theoretically undefinable and empirically vague pragmatic notions of theme or topic can be discarded in favor of well-motivated and independently manipulable cognitive processes like focal attention, giving us a theory of discourse and syntax that links production more directly with cognition. Second, the experimental paradigm, and potential developments within it, better permits cross-linguistic comparison by controlling the conditions under which discourse production is managed. Third, the analytically severe problem of distinguishing correlations from causal interactions is neatly reduced through a genuine experimental paradigm.

1. Functional approaches to linguistics

As a descriptive enterprise, functional approaches to linguistics seek to account for interactions between grammatical form and semantic or pragmatic function. In general, descriptive questions assume one of two basic forms. The first explores the function of some given grammatical alternation, asking the question what are the semantic or pragmatic conditions that lead to the selection of one grammatical form over its alternative(s). The second considers the grammatical means employed to code or signal some semantic or pragmatic function. The selection of nominal versus pronominal NPs to manage reference in discourse production is an example of the first kind of question. The comparison between word order and grammatical morphology to signal "contrastive" information is an example of the second.

This basic, descriptive enterprise is commonly conflated with a second, explanatory one. As an explanatory enterprise, functional approaches to linguistics seek to account for why grammars turn out to be organized as we describe them. For example, it seems unlikely to be an accident that languages seem universally to use phonologically shorter units to refer to arguments which are more easily identified by the hearer (Givón 1983a, 1983b).

Increasingly, functional linguists organize both descriptive and explanatory efforts around cognitive matters, what one might call the Cognitive Rationale. Languages are said to be organized the way they are to make discourse easier to produce or comprehend. But appeals to a cognitive basis for functional explanation do require one to show that concrete cognitive processes are involved in grammatical alternation at the descriptive level; otherwise, one has merely substituted a new set of vague functional categories for the old ones.

1.1 *Problems in functional linguistics*

While there are numerous problems facing the functional paradigm (Tomlin 1990), there are four which are of particular interest here: (1) the definition and identification of central pragmatic notions, (2) the specification of the kinds of functional interaction permitted in a functional grammar, (3) the standard of empirical prediction required for functional claims, and (4) the proper management of cross-linguistic comparison.

1.1.1 *The definition and identification of central pragmatic notions*

No one working with discourse data is unfamiliar with this fundamental problem. While theoretically respectable and empirically sound analysis requires precise stipulation of the central pragmatic notions utilized in a given study, virtually all contemporary and traditional analyses of discourse rely on problematic definitions. We still cannot say clearly what a clause level theme or topic is, despite decades of trying and despite relatively sympathetic tolerance among our colleagues for the definitions ultimately employed. We end up relying on vague definitions whose application in specific data analyses requires too much dependence on introspection or indirectly permits the use of structural information in the identification of instances of the key category.

The two most common solutions really do not address the problem. The first route is to proliferate additional terminology and distinctions. For example, Mithun uses the term *newsworthy* to capture what has traditionally been captured by the categories of *rheme* or *contrastive*. Payne's use of the expression "focal attention" (this volume) aligns well with both Mithun's "newsworthy" and traditional "rheme".[2] The principal advantage of this strategy is that it permits one to avoid the intellectual baggage associated with more extensively used terms, but it still does not address at all the serious problems one faces in using these definitions actually to identify instances of the category in discourse data.

The second route is to develop operationally sound definitions based on the distribution of items in text data. This route, best represented in the work of Givón and his associates[3] (Givón 1983a, 1989), addresses the practical problem of data analysis by providing operational formulas for calculating the distribution of linguistic forms in text data. These methods, the calculation of referential distance and referential persistence, increase the *reliability* of data analysis markedly over their introspective competitors. However, they do not address directly the theoretical question of precisely what it is such measurements are measurements of.

1.1.2 *Kinds of functional interaction*

Functionalists are routinely vague about the theoretical and empirical status of claims made regarding the interaction of form and function (Tomlin 1987, 1990). While there may be all sorts of correlations and pseudo-correlations observable between linguistic form and function, only a small set of these are of significant interest to understanding how functional grammars actually work. These form-function interactions are ones in which either the speaker and hearer share an automated, invariant rule governing the use of some linguistic form (grammatical *coding*) or where the hearer can routinely and conventionally infer some meaning given the occurrence of some linguistic form (pragmatic *signaling*) (Tomlin 1987, Tomlin and Pu, 1991).

It is extremely difficult to determine the nature of a specific functional interaction from the statistical analysis of text data, principally because the analytical tools available do not permit one easily to draw the causal inferences required (Tomlin 1984, 1985; 1987; Tomlin and Pu 1991). Experimental studies, however, can permit more direct testing of hypotheses regarding coding in functional grammars precisely because they reduce the analytical problems associated with text analysis.[4]

Another problem functional approaches should face more explicitly is the theoretical standing of so-called functional correlations or functional rules. It is commonly assumed outside of functional work per se that functional correlations at best represent psycholinguistic statements on language use which fall outside of grammatical knowledge, outside of the grammar as traditionally conceived. Functionalists, on the other hand, tend to behave as though functional interactions represent rules of the grammar, though it is most common simply not to consider such questions. Yet it is ultimately of interest to know where and how so-called functional rules (if there are any) are to stand in a grammar.

1.1.3 *Standards of prediction*

Traditionally, linguists embraced the toughest standard of evidence of any intellectual field I am aware of: no counterexamples permitted, no residue allowed. Argumentation within competing schools of structuralist syntax still adheres to this important standard, despite their methodological dependence on introspection.[5] However, the kinds of linguistic behaviors functional linguists investigate, like most other kinds of cognitive behavior, are not amenable to introspection. This means that introspective judgments of grammaticality[6] are inadequate for exploring conditions of use for linguistic forms. Consequently, other methods of garnering empirical data are required, methods which are certain to generate error of one kind or another.

The combination of weak definition and unclear theoretical or empirical criteria for so-called coding relationships invites functional research to embrace a weak standard of prediction, actuarial prediction.[7] Actuarial prediction specifies the probability that an event will occur given some set of circumstances. To say that there is a tendency (in language or in some particular language) for *old* information to come first in the sentence is to make an actuarial statement. To say that VS order is a marked order in a particular language is to make an actuarial statement. To say that 85% of the time a pronoun is used if its antecedent is only one clause away is to make an actuarial statement. In none of these situations can the researcher indicate on an utterance by utterance basis whether old information will show up in a particular place, whether a VS order will occur, or whether a pronominal or nominal NP will show up. Instead, one substitutes statements of the probability of occurrence for statements of the precise conditions which lead to the actual occurrence of a putative form-function correspondence.

The key question is whether probabilistic distributions in linguistic data reflect indeterminacy in the system or in the analytical rigor of the linguist. Actuarial prediction retreats from the tough-minded standards of evidence previously embraced and substitutes appeals to probability and tendency instead. The alternative to actuarial prediction is individuated prediction. An individuated prediction describes the output of a given system on a trial-by-trial basis. It would predict, if the first putative generalization above were correct, that each instance of old information in fact show up as the initial element in the sentence. The failure to observe this, the residue of exceptions, is not attributed to the system but to limitations either in theory or in methodology.

1.1.4 *Cross-linguistic comparisons*

It has been observed consistently that cross-linguistic comparisons of form–function interactions are difficult. The difficulty arises in no small measure because the discourse data samples used for cross-linguistic comparison may not be sufficiently comparable to permit cross-linguistic comparison. Comparison of informally collected narratives or conversation is extremely problematic, despite their so-called naturalness[8], largely because the conditions which lead to the selection of grammatical alternatives are localistically controlled and fall outside the range of what can reasonably be controlled by general selection or management of discourse topic.

2. Thematic management in discourse production

When reporting a simple event like that represented by the proposition in (1), speakers of English can use either of two grammatical alternatives to relate that event to the hearer, active or passive voice (2a, 2b).

(1) E_1 = EAT (RED FISH, BLUE FISH)

(2) a. The red fish eats the blue fish.
b. The blue fish gets eaten by the red fish.

The ordinary use of these alternatives is well illustrated in the play-by-play descriptions produced by hockey announcers (Tomlin 1983):

(3) *Hockey play-by-play data*
1 Puck knocked away by Dale McCourt,
2 Ø picked up again by Steve Shutt/
3 Now Shutt coming out,
4 into the Detroit zone/
5 He played it out in front/
6 There's Lemaire with a shot,
7 and it was blocked by Reed Larson/

There is a long tradition, both within linguistics and within cognitive psychology, of trying to determine the conditions under which these two alternants are selected. Weil, in his early treatise on word order (Weil, 1877), distinguishes "syntactical order", the order of grammatical relations, from the "march of ideas", the theoretical precursor to Prague school notions of theme. Mathesius (1929) observed that "das Thema der Satzaussage womöglich zum grammatischen Subjekt des Satzes [gemacht wird]". The overall development of Prague school work in functional sentence perspective develops the principal classical notions of *theme~rheme*, *topic~comment*, *given~new*, etc. (Dahl 1974; Daneš 1974, 1987; Firbas 1964a; 1964b, 1966, 1974; Jones, 1977). These efforts share the general observation that the difference in English between the active and the passive resides primarily in whether it is the agent or the patient[9] which is the more central or salient or important referent in the sentence. This centrality or salience is captured theoretically in concepts of *theme* or *topic*, and such a concept is then associated either with subject or initial position. Patient themes become the subjects of passives and agent themes those of actives.

More contemporary work develops these original insights in two principal directions. One, clause-level topic or theme is a function of the overall or global theme of a larger discourse unit. Two, local topic or theme arises out of the saliency of a referent or its realization in discourse.

2.1 *Global control of theme or topic*[10]

In this view the selection of active versus passive derives from the comparative significance of the two referents competing for subject assignment in relation to some higher level theme. So, a story that is globally about, say, the red fish, will tend to encode the red fish as subject, resulting in active or passives when the red fish is, respectively, the agent or the patient of a transitive verb.

Experimental study of the selection of active versus passive clauses has tried to exploit this apparent connection. By manipulating what the subject takes to be the most significant or global character, the researcher tries to stimulate actives when that main character is the agent of some target event the subject describes and passives when it is the patient. Prentice (1967) and Turner and Rommetveit (1968) used pictures to prime a character prior to eliciting sentences about a targeted event. When the primed character was the agent, subjects routinely produced active sentences. When the primed character was the patient, subjects produced some passives, generally doing better than chance ($p<.05$), but certainly not demonstrating individuated prediction.

In a similar vein, some researchers have used verbal cues rather than pictures to prime a particular character. Carroll (1958) used questions to prime a particular character and showed better than chance performance on sentence production tasks. More recently, Bates and Devescovi (1989) have used linguistic cues (e.g. "Tell me about the hippo") to prime one or another character in their film based discourse production task.

Tannenbaum and Williams (1968) read paragraphs to subjects prior to their reading sentences and collecting reaction times on actives versus passives congruent with or not congruent with the overall verbal priming. Flores d'Arcais (1975) provided single word cues for a test of production in Italian. Priming the agent led to actives 77% of the time; priming patients led to passives 67% of the time.

In all of these cases, the researcher tries to stimulate the production of active or passive clauses by using a general, global priming of a given character just prior to a targeted event involving that character. Actives are expected whenever the primed character is the agent of the targeted event, and a passive is expected when the primed character is the patient. All researchers report the experience of generating uniformly active clauses when the agent is primed. All researchers also clearly observe better than chance performance on the production of passives when the patient is primed. But the residue, those cases in which a primed patient results in the unexpected active clause, remains a pesky problem, and most have been content to conclude that the active form is the unmarked or default form chosen, without much regard for specifying the detailed conditions under which the choice actually gets made.[11]

2.2 *The saliency of characters*

In this view the assignment of a referent to subject is a function of the saliency of that referent. The more salient the referent is, the more likely it is that the referent is assigned to subject. Saliency derives from one of two sources: inherent, physical saliency or discourse/grammatical saliency. Physical saliency includes the comparative size, humanness, imageability of objects to be described. Sridhar (1988) conducted a series of cross-linguistic experiments in which the perceptual saliency of objects was manipulated to see whether more salient referents were encoded either earlier in a sentence or as subjects. Flores d'Arcais (1987) also manipulated physical characteristics to show that perceptually more salient objects tended to show up earlier in sentence production. More interesting work in this area is currently being done by Bock. She has argued that referents whose lexical accessibility is higher tend to be encoded first and consequently placed in positions of greater grammatical prominence (Bock 1987; Bock and Warren 1985).

Discourse saliency involves two main dimensions. One, referents which are definite or pronominal or "old" information are argued to occur before indefinites, nominals, or "new" information. Two, it is argued by some that certain semantic roles, notably *agent*, tend to be inherently more topical than other roles (Hawkinson and Hyman 1974). Arguments in either dimension generally are based on a higher text frequency for the more salient entity. For example, agents are inherently more topical than patients because agents show up in more prominent grammatical positions with much greater frequency than do patients. Similarly, definite or "old" information is inherently more topical because these attributes, too, show up more frequently in text counts in grammatically more prominent positions.

2.3 *Local control of theme or topic*

Both prior directions are partially correct in their assessment of the conditions leading to the alternative selection of active and passive in English. Yet neither provides an adequate account of the phenomenon largely because the analytical residues left by each are too large to warrant claims of a general solution. The global topic model leaves too large a residue of cases in which the subject of a sentence, even of a passive clause, turns out *not* to be the global topic. For example, in the crab film protocol fragment (Tomlin 1984, 1985) in (4), the global topic is the little goldfish (*fish* in the example below), yet in numerous clauses, in fact in 67% of those for which there is an alternative possible, the subject of the sentence is *not* the global topic at all.

(4) *Crab film data sample: subject 11*
1 There's a fish
2 swimming in the ocean/
3 It's a cartoon like/
4 A cráb just popped up/
5 Ø chasing him/
6 Ø trying to get him/
7 And the fish is going back and forth real quick/

The global model fails precisely because it cannot account for subject assignment on a clause by clause basis. Thus, one is left with empirically weaker claims about tendencies for global topics to be clause level themes. The saliency model fails for much the same kinds of reasons. While there may be a correlation between perceptual or discourse saliency and subject assignment, neither is adequate to predict speaker behavior on an utterance by utterance basis. Saliency also permits weak generalizations, or tendencies, but it fails to provide a deterministic account of how actives and passives are selected. It is in fact precisely the occurrence of passive clauses and so-called marked word orders which provides the critical evidence that saliency models are in principle inadequate.

Both kinds of model fail for the same fundamental reason: each focuses on aligning general and global characteristics of the discourse setting with clause level theme or topic and the concomitant selection of subject. But such global considerations do not determine directly how voice selection is made. Our model embraces the insight of these earlier efforts but provides a more localistic account of the selection of active and passive. We will claim that there is a rule within the grammar of English which maps the locus of focal attention onto syntactic subject at the moment of utterance formulation. Whatever referent on which focal attention is allocated within the speaker's dynamically unfolding mental representation of events at the moment an utterance is formulated shows up as the subject of the clause, without exception, every time. Matters of global theme or saliency will influence how focal attention is allocated and thus play only an indirect role in the details of this functional alternation.

The hypothesis that we are testing in this paper is that there is a rule within the functional grammar of English which stipulates:

(5) At the time of utterance formulation, the speaker codes the referent currently in FOCAL ATTENTION as the SYNTACTIC SUBJECT of the utterance.

The hypothesis entails the following:

- If a referent falls within focal attention at the moment of utterance formulation, it shows up as syntactic subject. If it does not fall within focal attention, it does not show up as subject.
- Given an event reported by transitive verb, if the agent is in focal attention, one will observe a corresponding active clause. Likewise, if it is the patient that is focally attended, one will observe a corresponding passive clause.
- This mechanism is localistically controlled, which means that neither global theme nor local saliency is adequate to determine the selection of linguistic form, though both may contribute to the assignment of focal attention during the discourse production process.
- This rule is invariant and automatic. It is invariant in that it governs the discourse production behavior of all native speakers in exactly the same way. It is automatic in that it applies to each and every instance of sentence production without easy or noticeable conscious access by the speaker.

3. The experiment

The experiment designed for this study is a simple one in conception, though difficult to implement. If one could independently manipulate the locus of focal attention in speakers about to perform a sentence production task, one should be able to see a dependent assignment of the focally attended referent to syntactic subject in discourse production. And, if the event were described with a transitive verb, one would expect to see active clauses if and only if the focally attended referent were the agent of the action and one would expect to see passive clauses if and only if the focally attended referent were the patient of the action.

We designed a computer animated film[12] to permit a within-subjects test of the interaction between focal attention and syntactic subject in sentence production. The film is composed of a set of thirty-one trials in which one fish eats a second fish. The fish are identical in shape and size, differing only in color[13]. They approach each other from opposite sides of the video display, moving at equal speeds. At the center of screen, at the very last moment, one fish swallows the second, taking about 50 ms. to do so. The colors of each pair of fish and the outcome of each eating event were randomly determined. The direction of the agent, either from the right or from the left, was counterbalanced.

Subjects are instructed to produce on-line descriptions of the events they witness. In the on-line procedure the subject describes events as they unfold, simultaneously with their initial display. Given that in any production protocol, including recall protocols, speakers always formulate utterances with respect to the current state of some mental representation, the on-line procedure offers the advantage that the representations on which the speaker operates in formulating utterances will have had a minimal amount of time for reformulation (the intrusion of additional, and perhaps interpretive, cognitive processing) prior to description. The speaker's mental representation of events in the on-line procedure, then, is the most iconic representation possible of the events as they are witnessed.

In each trial, one of the two fish is visually primed to attract focal attention to it just prior to the subject's formulation of an utterance to describe the eating event. The priming consists of displaying a large arrow which points to the targeted fish.[14] The timing of the priming is crucial. Attention moves about quite fleetingly in such a visual display, and any new transient movement subsequent to the arrow prime, such as the opening of the agent fish's jaws to swallow the patient, can itself attract focal attention away from the primed fish. Ideally, then, one must time the priming action so that the time between successfully attracting attention to the targeted fish and the

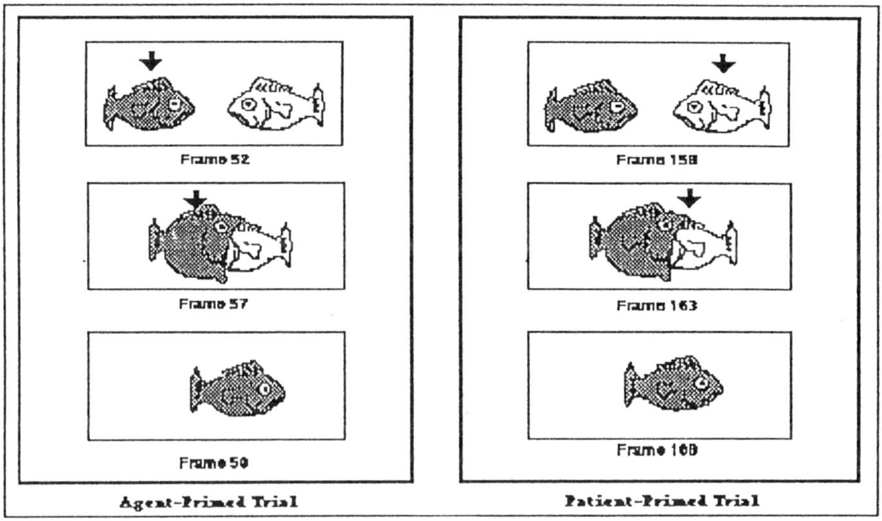

Figure 1.Frames from sample trials

initiation of the utterance describing the eating event does not permit attention to have been attracted elsewhere. The trials were created, then, under the assumption that utterance formulation begins immediately upon closure of the agent's jaws on the patient fish. The time between priming the targeted fish and jaw closing is less than 150 ms., effectively blocking movement of attention anywhere else, if the subject begins utterance formulation at the moment the eating act is completed. It should be noted that if the subject begins utterance formulation much later than the end of the eating act, it may well have been possible for attention to have shifted elsewhere during the intervening period. Figure 1 presents film frames extracted from both agent- and patient-primed trials.

3.1 *Expectations for English data*

The trials, then, fall into two types: agent-primed trials, of which there are 15, and patient-primed trials, of which there are 16. We expect to see that whenever the agent is primed, the subject will encode that argument as subject and an active clause will occur. Further, we expect no actives other than actives produced under agent priming. We expect also that whenever the

	Active	Passive
Agt Primed	15	0
Pat Primed	0	16

Figure 2. Expected outcome for each subject

patient is primed, the subject will encode that argument as subject and a passive clause will occur. We expect no passives produced other than passives produced under patient priming; and we expect no actives to be produced under patient priming. Thus, for each of the 31 total trials we make a specific prediction of the form of sentence production, an individuated prediction we expect to hold for each subject tested. This ideal expected outcome is displayed in Figure 2.

3.2 *Results*

The performance of each subject can be assessed to determine the extent to which his or her individual performance deviates from the ideal represented in Figure 2. The sign test can be performed on the total number of hits and misses to reveal the general congruence of subjects with the expected outcome. The Irwin-Fisher exact test can be used to calculate the precise probability of a chance distribution matching the one observed. So, for example, for subject 8, the observed performance is shown in Figure 3.

Altogether subject 8 produced 28 hits, the items in the upper left and lower right cells, and 3 misses, the items in the upper right and lower left cells. The sign test shows that there is no more than one chance in 100 that the observed pattern of hits could occur by chance. The Irwin-Fisher exact test shows that the probability of the observed table in Figure 4 occurring by chance is exactly .0000027. One can thus conclude that for this subject there is a significant interaction between where the subject's focal attention was

	Active	Passive
Agt Primed	15	0
Pat Primed	3	13

Figure 3. Observed performance of subject 8.

allocated at the moment of utterance formulation and the assignment of an argument to syntactic subject.

Overall, for 10 of 12 subjects tested this same pattern holds true. The exact probability of this occurring by chance alone is only 2%.[15]

There is a systematic pattern of error in two of the subjects. These deviated from the observed pattern in a consistent fashion. Both of these subjects produced only active clauses for all 31 trials. But a closer look at their data reveals that these subjects appear to have significantly longer delays in the initiation of their utterances than do the other subjects. It thus appears that these subjects may well have been performing a different task, something like an immediate recall task, rather than the on-line production task performed by the other subjects. One subject who produced no passives indicated in the debriefing session that she was a journalism major and that, having been taught to avoid the use of passive, she actively suppressed its use during the protocol.

3.3 *Summary findings for English*

In this experiment the independent manipulation of the locus of focal attention within a dynamic visual stimulus led to the dependent assignment of a primed referent to syntactic subject. Since the depicted events were all of the same type, eating events, and all were reported by semantically transitive verbs (*eat, swallow, devour*, etc.), we see a direct and routinized alternation in voice corresponding exactly to the manipulation of priming. Simply put, we are able to determine the selection of voice on a trial by trial basis by directing focal attention to particular referent, causing this referent to be coded as syntactic subject according to the rule stated in (5). There is virtually no substantive individual variation.

This experimental paradigm offers advantages over traditional methods of discourse analysis. First, it avoids the definitional problems associated with classical notions of theme or topic. Theoretically speaking, there seems to be no compelling reason to sustain either notion as critical to a theory of discourse. In fact, it seems likely that these notions represent the logical consequences of theory building dependent upon the relatively weak methods of introspective analysis and text counting. That is, the notions of theme and topic may well represent the reified outcome of the post hoc analysis of textual artifacts rather than a cognitively motivated linguistic category.

Irrespective of whether focal attention should be taken to replace notions of theme and topic, this experimental paradigm permits a highly systematic investigation of cross-linguistic differences in the coding of focal attention. One can investigate whether some languages employ voice to manage this phenomenon, whether others use word order, and whether yet others may have no rule which manages focal attention in discourse production.

4. Cross-linguistic comparisons: some pilot data

The tight interaction between focal attention and syntactic subject in English, reflected in the selection of voice during on-line discourse production, invites systematic comparison cross-linguistically. This section considers for a handful of languages the second kind of fundamental functional question posed above: what grammatical means, if any, are employed in a language to code a focally attended referent?

4.1 *Burmese data*[16]

Little is known about how Burmese manages so-called clause level theme or topic, or, as we have recast it, a focally attended referent. One reasonable hypothesis is that Burmese, an SOV language, manages focal attention through word order, putting focally attended referents in initial position.

	Active	Passive
Agt Primed	11	4
Pat Primed	1	15

Figure 4. Burmese: observed outcome for single subject

Under this hypothesis one should see SOV orders for agent-primed cases and OSV orders for patient-primed cases.

A second, low probability hypothesis is that Burmese codes focal attention with its syntactic subject, just as English does, with the same kind of voice alternation displayed as a result. This hypothesis is a low probability one because the Burmese passive shows up with such low frequency in text counts.

A single Burmese subject performed the experimental fish film task. The results are displayed in Figure 4. Examples of the Burmese data are presented in (6) and (7).

(6) Trial 9 — AgtPrimed

nga‘ kha’ram‘ rawng ka’ nga‘ ?anak ko ngu~ lok tay /
fish purple color SUBJ fish black OBJ swallow AUX TAM
‘The purple fish eats the black fish.’

(7) Trial 14 — PatPrimed

nga‘ mi‘kho‘ rawng ka nga‘ ?ani ?a-ngu~ kha~
fish grey color SUBJ fish red NOM-swallow suffer
lok ra’ tay /
AUX AUX TAM
‘The grey fish is eaten by the red fish.’

The syntax of the Burmese passive is different from that of its English analogue. Like English, Burmese assigns the focally attended patient to subject, indicated with the *ka* postposition. The agent and the semantic predicate form a nominalized clause which is a complement to the passive auxiliary *ra*. The alternation in this case is not a simple variation in order, no more than such is the case in English.

The Burmese results show no significant deviation from that expected for the analogous English case. The probability is less than .01 that a pattern of 26 hits and 5 misses would be observed (sign test). In fact, by the Irwin-Fisher exact test, the probability of observing precisely this outcome as a matter of chance is exactly .00015.

4.2 *Indonesian data*

Among linguists who study the functional syntax of Indonesian there has been a longstanding debate about the functional similarity of the Indonesian *oleh* passive to English passive. Data collected from a single Indonesian speaker shows that there is a striking parallelism between Indonesian and English passives, both in their syntax and in the conditions which call for their use. Like English, Indonesian appears to code the focally attended referent as its syntactic subject, with a resulting selection of voice when the depicted events are described by transitive verbs.

The basic results are displayed in Figure 5. Examples follow in (8) and (9).

	Active	Passive
Agt Primed	15	0
Pat Primed	0	16

Figure 5. Indonesian: observed outcome for single subject

(8) Trial 5 — AgtPrimed

Ikan merah muda ber-temu dengan ikan putih / Dan
fish red light INT-meet with fish white And
me-makan ikan putih
ACT-eat fish white
'The pink fish meets the white fish. And Ø eats the white fish.'

(9) Trial 14 — PatPrimed

Ikan merah muda ber-temu dengan ikan putih / Dan
fish red light INT-meet with fish white And
di-makan oleh ikan putih
PASS-eat by fish white
'The pink fish meets the white fish. And Ø is eaten by the white fish.'

The Indonesian results show no significant deviation from that expected for the analogous English case. The probability is less than .01 that a pattern of 31 hits and 0 misses would be observed (sign test). In fact, by the Irwin-Fisher exact test the probability of observing precisely this outcome as a matter of chance is exactly .0000000033.

4.3 *Mandarin data*

In Mandarin there is an alternation between two voice-like constructions: the *bei* construction and the *ba* construction. It is not clear the extent to which this alternation represents a Mandarin analogue to English passive or to which it represents merely word order variation with concomitant differences in prepositions. It is possible to examine this alternation with the fish film experiment.

Unlike prior cases in which single subjects were available, there were six Mandarin speakers, three from Taiwan and three from the PRC. The expected outcome for each of these subjects, displayed in Figure 6, is for agent-primed trials to display the agent argument in initial position and the patient marked with *ba*, while patient-primed trials should display the patient as the initial argument and the agent marked by *bei*. Subject performances which are congruent with expectations are shown in (10) and (11).

	ba	bei
Agt Primed	15	0
Pat Primed	0	16

Figure 6. Mandarin: expected outcome for six subjects

(10) Trial 9 — AgtPrimed

hóng sè de yú ba hui sè de yú chi d iao le
red color DE fish BA grey color DE fish eat fall ASP
'The red fish ba the grey fish ate.'

(11) Trial 16 — PatPrimed

qihong sè de yú bèi hóng sè de yú chi diao le
purple color DE fish BEI red color DE fish eat fall asp
'The purple fish bei the red fish ate.'

The results obtained with this small group turn out to be intriguing results. First, three of the subjects performed exactly as expected, with virtually no deviation from the expected results. Again, the probability of such congruence is less than .01 for the sign test on hits versus misses and less than .01 for each individual contingency table. Whenever the agent was primed, one observed the *ba*-construction; whenever the patient was primed, one observed the *bei*-construction.

Whether the two constructions are merely order variants or represent a true voice alternation cannot be decided with this experimental paradigm. That problem is strictly a syntactic one, one which cannot be legally resolved by an appeal to the facts of use revealed here. One suspects that some of the impetus to call the *bei*-construction a passive may stem from its analogous function to the English passive, rather than from the syntactic facts alone.

In the other three subjects, a quite different pattern was observed than that just described. These three speakers all used only *ba*-constructions. Their performances deviated from the expected performance, but they did so in a consistent manner. There are several possible explanations, though none can be argued for with the existing data. First, it may just turn out that these three speakers, like the two odd English speakers, did not perform the task as requested, but instead performed immediate recall production rather than on-line production. Second, it may turn out that Mandarin does not have a functional rule like the one we see in English, so that more variability is revealed in subject performance.

Third, it may turn out to be dialectal. Of the six subjects, the three who performed as expected were all from Taiwan, while the three who departed from the expected pattern were all from the mainland. While the data here are not adequate to examine this possibility, the experimental paradigm developed here does permit the more systematic examination of just such questions.

4.4 *Polish, Russian, and Bulgarian data*

Small groups of Polish and Russian speakers and a single Bulgarian speaker were able to participate in the experiment. For each of these languages one could again consider the grammatical means employed to code a focally attended referent. For Polish and Russian one might consider either hypoth-

	Active SVO	Passive V-obj S
Agt Primed	15	0
Pat Primed	0	16

Figure 7. Expected outcomes for Polish and Russian speakers

eses involving initial position, leading to word order variation, or hypotheses involving subject, with an expectation of a voice alternation. Bulgarian, on the other hand, is typologically a quite rigid SVO language, so that no order variation was expected, though a voice alternation remained logically possible.

The expectations for the Polish and Russian speakers are displayed in Figure 7.

Some examples of Polish production are found in (12) - (14). Russian examples reveal much the same kind of linguistic form.

(12) Trial 5 — AgtPrimed (Active)

szara *spotyaka* *sie* *z* *fioletow-a /* *ø*
grey-FEM:NOM meet REFL with violet-FEM:ACC/ (She)
poz'era *ja...*
devours her
'The grey fish meets the violet and ø eats her.'

(13) Trial 4 — PatPrimed (Passive)

zielon-a
green-FEM:NOM
zo-sta-l-a *po-z'ar-t-a*
PFTV-become-PFTV:Act-FEM:NOM:PFTV-devour-PFTV:PASS-FEM:NOM
przez *róz'ow-à*
by pink-FEM:ACC
'The green is eaten by the pink.'

(14) Trial 12 — PatPrimed (V-obj S)

zielon-a *wychodzi* *z* *lev-ej* / *polyka-jà*
green-FEM:NOM comes out from left-Genfem / swallow-her
liliov-a /
lilac-FEM:NOM
'Green comes out from the left. Swallows her the lilac.'

The general pattern of results for both Polish and Russian does not permit one to conclude that either subject assignment or initial position is systematically employed to code a focally attended referent. Most of the time these speakers produced simple, active SVO sentences. While this was expected for agent-primed trials, it most certainly was not for patient-primed trials.

Nonetheless, the productions of subjects are intriguing. For example, on some patient-primed trials, one observes a voice alternation, while on other patient-primed trails one observes the subject postposed after the verb with an object enclitic. Both structures represent reasonable ones for these languages, but neither is used in a systematic fashion across the full set trials.

It is not clear what this much variability is due to. One strong possibility is that subjects, very much unexpectedly, found the task unclear to them. For example, despite instructions, both in English and in the native language, to produce simple descriptions, several of the subjects spent overt time and energy trying to determine what the experiment was *really* about. One subject tried to predict which fish would be the agent on each trial, a daunting task since that was randomly determined. Another subject insisted on a metaphorical interpretation of each event seen. It may well be that a different set of general instructions may be required to solicit the kind of participation the experiment requires.

In Bulgarian, where there is no systematic word order variation, it is not surprising none was found. Nor is there employment of a voice alternation either.

4.5 *Akan (Fante) data*

There is no classical passive in Akan, nor does it appear that word order alternations between SVO and OSV or VOS are particularly productive. These observations led an associate, Emmanuel Osam, to hypothesize that

	Active	Anything Else
Agt Primed	15	0
Pat Primed	16	0

Figure 8. Akan: expected outcomes for three subjects

Akan will reveal no alternation sensitive to this manipulation of focal attention. Thus, as displayed in Figure 8, one expects Akan speakers to uniformly produce active, SVO ordered clauses only.

Three speakers of Akan (Fante) participated in the experiment. As anticipated, no one produced anything other than active, SVO clauses, exemplified in (15) and (16):

(15) Trial 5 — AgtPrimed

nam	*blue*	*n'*	*amen*	*nam*	*red*	*n'*
fish	blue	the	PFTV-swallowed	fish	red	the

'The blue fish swallowed the red fish.'

(16) Trial 4 — PatPrimed

purple	*n'*	*amen*	*green*	*n'*
purple	the	PFTV-swallowed	green	the

'The purple swallowed the green.'

Given the expectations in Figure 8, the Akan speakers performed exactly as expected. The probability of chance outcomes for the observed performances matching the expected performances is less than .01 (sign test) and for each individual table is exactly .0000000033 (exact test).

The Akan data seem radically different from all of the other cases examined. There clearly seems to be no grammatical alternation employed to code the focally attended referent[17] While there are only three subjects, their full congruence across all individual trials makes it unlikely that increasing the sample size will reveal dramatically different results.

5. Discussion

5.1 *Summary findings*

The experimental paradigm presented in this paper provides worthwhile comparative information on the grammatical means employed by diverse languages to code a focally attended referent.

English. A focally attended referent is coded as the syntactic subject. When the event described requires a semantically transitive verb, one observes an active clause just in case the focally attended referent is the agent, and ones observes a passive just in case the focally attended referent is the patient.

Burmese. A focally attended referent is coded as the syntactic subject, marked as such by the postposition *ka*. Like the English case, Burmese exhibits an alternation between active and passive exactly congruent with the focally attended referent.

Indonesian. A focally attended referent is coded as the syntactic subject. The Indonesian *oleh*-passive is employed, as is its canonical active, exactly as its English analogues.

Mandarin. A focally attended element is coded as the initial argument in the clause. When the event described requires a semantically transitive verb, one observes a *ba*- clause just in case the focally attended referent is the agent, and ones observes a *bei*-clause just in case the focally attended referent is the patient.

Polish. No clear pattern emerges of grammatical use sensitive to focal attention, though instances of both voice and word order alternations do occur.

Russian. No clear pattern emerges of grammatical use sensitive to focal attention, though instances of both voice and word order alternations do occur.

Bulgarian. There appears to be no grammatical coding of a focally attended referent. Bulgarian uses its canonical SVO, active clause structure no matter which referent is focally attended.

Akan (Fante). There appears to be no grammatical coding of a focally attended referent. Akan uses its canonical SVO, active clause structure no matter which referent is focally attended.

5.2 *Some possible objections*

There are a couple of kinds of objections to the claims and proposals offered in this paper which require some comment.[18] First, one might object that the research reported here does not achieve the status of individuated prediction precisely because the experimental results display "correlations" of less than 100%. Such an objection misunderstands both the distinction of actuarial versus individuated prediction and the role of experimental results in argumentation for theoretical issues. The principal difference between an actuarial statement and an individuated one is that the actuarial statement makes its claims about *types* of structures in terms of a general array of conditions whose specific contribution to the state of any single observation is unknown. Thus, statements about the weather are actuarial. For example, "The chance of precipitation today, August 13, 1992 in Eugene is 10%" makes no claim about August 13 per se. Rather , it claims that given a constellation of circumstances, whose contribution to precipitation we do not readily understand, we have seen before that it rains about 1 of each 10 days which display this particular constellation of circumstances. Individuated prediction makes its claims about specific *tokens* of a category in terms of an array of contributing causes whose specific contribution to the state of any single observation is specifically asserted, either as known or as hypothesized.

The experiments reported here do make individuated predictions. They claim that given a set of circumstances which the experimenter controls (the priming of visual attention), we can predict the form of each utterance produced by each subject as a direct function of the control of visual attention. Restated more plainly, our model predicts the form of any given specific utterance by any given subject if the conditions for the selection are well met. So what should one make of the exceptions we do in fact see? There are only a few possibilities. One, the experimenter may have made some error in accounting for the data; some item may be placed in the wrong category. There are no such errors in these data. Two, there may be some other variable, some third intervening variable, which interacts with or interferes with the one the experiment purportedly manipulates. But what might such a variable be? In this case, the burden of proof must lie with those postulating the intervening variable.

Three, the experimental manipulation has failed to maintain full control at all possible moments within the experimental presentation. This seems to me the most likely reason for our exceptional data. In most of the exceptional data — largely unexpected actives —, I suspect that subjects moved their attention back to the agent when the patient was primed before they began to formulate their sentences. Such a movement of attention is certainly possible, but must occur outside the parameters of the manipulation employed. That is, the subject must have also shifted the temporal moment at which utterance formulation begins to permit that re-allocation of attention. In fact, for a large proportion of the exceptional data the onset of the utterance is substantially later than is the case for most of the utterances produced. Such exceptions are not counterevidence to the hypothesis, nor does it make the claims or manipulations merely actuarial. It seems likely, though we cannot know it for sure, that the exceptional utterances still conform to the hypothesis, that the subject put the currently attended referent into syntactic subject; it's just that we cannot see it when we do not manage to sustain control over the subject's attentional states. An occasional failure within an experiment to maintain control over the cognitive states of an experimental subject does not reduce the merits of the experiment and it most certainly does not make the predictions actuarial rather than individuated.

A second objection is that the on-line production task is too narrow a task to permit generalization about the function of syntactic subject in English. This view sees the on-line production task as unnatural, as something one seldom does in ordinary speech settings. There are two points to make here. First, the task is in no way unnatural. It is not unnatural because speakers in fact do produce spontaneous descriptions of witnessed events in many kinds of ordinary settings.[19] More importantly, it is not unnatural in another sense. Our view is that linguistic production requires that the speaker access a concrete mental representation prior to formulating an utterance (Levelt 1989; Tomlin and Pu 1991). For many ordinary narrative or descriptive tasks the mental representation accessed will be a particular memory of a witnessed or created event, and attention is allocated to the component parts of that memory as the speaker accesses it. Recall protocols are problematic for studying production processes because one can never be certain what the details are of the mental representation at the critical moment of utterance production. In the on-line task we try to minimize the opportunity for subjects to modify or reconstrue witnessed events before their report, and we try to control where the speaker's attention is allocated as they witness those events. The experimental subject does not report directly the events in the world, rather the subject reports on his or her mental representation of events very, very recently perceived. In this regard, then, on-line production is in fact *no* different from any other sort of remembered narrative production.

A third objection is that the experimental paradigm employed here, specifically the examination of voice and word order with the films we employed, is too restricted to permit generalization beyond this highly restricted transitive setting. In a limited sense, this objection is correct. No one who does experimental work expects that a single experiment or experimental paradigm is adequate to establish a particular model or hypothesis as certain. External validation is required, either in the form of replication of the study or by devising independent experiments whose results converge with the original study. Both sorts of evidence are available. First, the multiple employment of the fish film with numerous languages, most with results highly congruent with the original English data, represents a kind of replication. It is not an accident that it is virtually always precisely the same subset of trials, agent primed versus patient primed, that receive differential treatment grammatically. Second, there is additional research (Forrest 1992) which generates the same kind of result (focally attended referent into syntactic subject in English) but which employs very different techniques for manipulating attention. Forrest looks at locative sentences like those in (17):

(17) The star is above the heart.
The heart is below the star.

Briefly, Forrest cues the speaker's attention to a given location on the computer monitor. She then presents two objects simultaneously, say a star and a heart in vertical alignment, whose spatial arrangement the speaker must describe immediately. On half the trials it will be the star that is placed at the cued location; on the other half of trials it is the heart that is placed at the cued location. The object which is placed at the cued location — that is brought into the speaker's attention — is generally assigned to syntactic subject with the rest of the sentence dependent on that assignment. This is very much the sort of converging evidence required to increase the external validity and plausibility of the results reported here.

A final objection is that in more ordinary discourse there are a multitude of factors — some linguistic, some cognitive, some social — which conspire to determine the form of an utterance. Thus, the effort reported here is too narrow to predict voice or word order in *real* discourse because it does not take these additional factors into account. For the long term, this objection is quite right. One cannot ignore the interaction of factors or variables in formulating how a functional grammar operates. But it is my belief that the proper research strategy to take is one which sorts out the contribution made by each specific factor contributing to utterance formulation. Observations that multiple factors do contribute to utterance formulation cannot contribute to formulation of a serious functional grammar unless and until the details of how those contributions affect utterance formulation are articulated. The effort reported here tries to contribute to that important functional goal by carefully examining one putative factor. Importantly, it is my suspicion that other factors one might think contribute to subject selection — point of view, empathy, story theme, desire to "suppress" the agent, and so on — will turn out to be factors which guide a speaker's attention to referents in mental representation in a non-linguistic way, but that once an attention assignment is made to a referent (again in real, on-line time), it will be precisely that referent which is assigned to syntactic subject at the moment of utterance formulation.

5.3 *Implications for a theory of functional grammar*

The experimental paradigm presented in this paper provides concrete means to address the four critical problems facing functional linguistics described above.

First, it addresses well the problem of adequate definition. The traditional notions of clause-level *theme* or *topic* remain difficult to pin down, and this difficulty is compounded when trying to identify instances of theme or topic in discourse data. When these traditional notions are examined closely, one sees in them, in their appeal to "starting point" and "importance" and "saliency", very much the kinds of descriptions one also finds in the literature on attention. The notion of "focally attended referent" proposed here is well-grounded in that literature, and the manipulation employed in the experimental film has been carefully established within cognitive psychology. Since the general idea of "theme" and "topic" is intuitively so congruent with general ideas of attention, and since the specific manipulation of attention provided here produces such strong effects in the production of speakers, there seems to be no particularly compelling reason to sustain a pragmatic category called theme or topic unless one is to re-define clause-level theme as "the referent which is focally attended at the moment of utterance formulation".

Second, the experimental paradigm contributes to the problem of understanding what counts as coding in a functional grammar. It does not address the theoretical issue of coding (Tomlin 1987), but it does show one way in which successful argumentation about coding can be conducted. As long as one relies on textual analysis as the principal methodology for investigating functional claims, one will be hindered by the problem of distinguishing correlation from causation in functional mappings, principally because the statistical methods required to reach the kinds of theoretical conclusions functional analysis requires are not yet fully developed.[20]

But the experiments performed for this study do permit reasonable causal inference in the following way. Unlike textual analysis, the experimental paradigm manipulates directly some pertinent attribute of the discourse production setting. In a well-constructed experiment, all other independent influences on the use of alternative orders or voice constructions are controlled for either by their random distribution across all trials or by counterbalancing. Thus, in the logic of well-done experimental work nothing other than the independently manipulated factor can be the cause of the dependent effects one records.[21] The syntactic subject in English grammatically codes the focally attended referent precisely because whatever we direct the speaker's attention to is put by that speaker into syntactic subject, virtually every time by every individual.

Third, the experimental paradigm does not require a retreat to actuarial tendencies from our traditional tough-minded standards of evidence and prediction. The design and outcomes of the experiments conducted here permit individuated prediction rather than actuarial prediction. The predictions of the forms used by speakers under the experimental conditions we control are predictions of the form of each individual utterance made by each individual subject. From what I can see, the assignment of the focally attended referent to subject in English is deterministic, not probabilistic, and thus I see the appeal to probabilistic description and explanation in functional linguistics as reflecting our collective analytical weaknesses rather than probabilistic organization within natural language grammars themselves.

Fourth, this experimental paradigm offers an additional tool for cross-linguistic work. Under the reasonable, though not certain, assumption that the cognitive processes of attention employed during the experiment are universal, then the results so obtained represent the best one can do in assuring cross-linguistic comparability of discourse production data. Still, there are two critical shortcomings here that must be noted. First, it is clear that in at least some cultures the specific sort of task required in this experiment will prove difficult, even in cultures whose Western foundations might suggest there should be no problem. Second, even where cultural expectations might well permit use of the experiment, the practical constraints of transporting technology to the field will preclude such work in most field (applied) settings. Still, the logic supporting the use of Chafe's pear film (1980) or my crab film (Tomlin 1984, 1985) in quasi-experimental discourse elicitation is the same logic supporting this experimental task. The difference is that in the experimental task we more tightly control the organization of the film and thus can know better what it is we are comparing.

Finally, the results produced in this study also offer some insight into the place of functional, discourse-based generalizations within a cognitive grammar. Most non-functional linguists would attribute the kinds of behavior revealed by this experiment as evidence only for rules of language use, knowledge of which falls outside the grammar itself, as do general conversational conventions like Grice's maxims (Grice 1975). Alternatively, the observed behavior may well be explained as the employment of more general cognitive information processing strategies, like "moving attended information first", applied to these language use cases.

The data collected here argue well for these form-function interactions constituting rules within the grammar. First, the interactions, at least for English, where the quantity of data is clearly sufficient, satisfy the same epistemological requirements as do ordinary examples of linguistic rules: (1) their use is automatic and (2) their use is invariant. In this sense the subject assignment rule for English described here is a significantly better candidate for rule status than older proposals which linked subject assignment to semantic role, even as this was restricted to underlying representations.

The Akan data, and apparently similar data for Finnish, add an additional wrinkle. The Akan case represents one in which speakers clearly do nothing linguistic to manage the focally attended referent.[22] If it were general cognitive processes alone that accounted for the kinds of data seen in all of the other cases, then it would seem that Akan should reveal some sensitivity to focally attended elements as well. But it does not, which suggests that Akan lacks a rule for focal attention management, which in turn means that it cannot be general cognitive principles alone that account for the cross-linguistic behavior we see in Akan. The critical point is that if Akan speakers have no rule which codes the focally attended referent, then the difference between a child learning Akan and a child learning English will in part be whether this automatic, invariant rule of adult production is learned.

Overall, it is my hope that the kind of experimental paradigm offered in this paper can prove useful in helping us understand how grammatical alternations of voice and word order are employed in discourse production. While the pilot data presented here are somewhat limited, and while this particular experiment may seem primitive in some ways, this direction may well help us to formulate functional generalizations which are empirically stronger and theoretically more transparent. If we are to make good use of the Cognitive Rationale in developing the functionalist research agenda, then we will surely find it important to cast basic questions in cognitive terms which can be concretely and explicitly managed.

Notes

* The following individuals have all contributed helpful suggestions and criticisms or concrete technical assistance to this project: Linda Forrest, Matthew Dryer, Pamela Downing, Michael Noonan, Ray Vukcevich, Michael Posner, Larry Hayashi, Scott McGinnis, Scott DeLancey, Gloria Olness, Kathie Carpenter, Emmanuel Osam, Lynne Yang, Myint Soe, and Walter Rybarkiewicz.

This research was supported in part by a grant from the Office of Research and Sponsored Programs, University of Oregon.

1. To avoid confusion let me stipulate here that the terms *theme* and *topic* are to be taken in their most classical senses: each refers to information the speaker believes is the more central, salient, or important at the moment of speech. For the Prague School, this has been cast as the starting point of the utterance (Daneš 1974, 1987; Mathesius 1929). For Halliday, this has been cast as "what is being talked about" (Halliday 1967, 1976).

   These notions should not be confused with North American departures from this tradition. Thus, theme is sometimes associated with paragraph or discourse level theme, meaning something like the general matter a paragraph is about. Topic has also been used to refer to the referential status of an argument in discourse (Givón 1983, 1988) or to a quasi-grammatical unit incorporating information importance with initial position (Li and Thompson 1976).

2. This exemplification is not intended to indicate rejection of either researcher's claims; it is meant only to illustrate this common research strategy.

3. There is, of course, an extensive tradition of European text studies in which the function of particular grammatical structures was determined from the statistical distribution of linguistic form.

4. An appropriate analogy here is the comparison of epidemiological studies of tobacco and health and the absence of human experimental studies. If it were possible to conduct medical experimentation on humans, one could examine directly whether or not the active chemicals in tobacco or tobacco smoke actually caused cancer. Since this cannot be done (and ignoring the value of animal research), the medical community relies on epidemiological studies of tobacco use/cause of death/incidence of disease correlations to establish the "causal" link between tobacco use and various kinds of disease. The otherwise self-serving defence of the tobacco industry against the claims that tobacco is unhealthful is that such studies are merely statistical analyses of correlations, any of which might yet be explained away by additional variables not incorporated into the study design. That is, correlational studies logically cannot permit inferences of causal interactions. Properly designed experimental studies can better permit such inferences.

5. It is important to note, as M. Noonan has pointed out to me, that the functionalist research program tends to be more ambitious than the structuralist program (cf. also Tomlin 1990) and that the structuralist research agenda, in its preoccupation with structural syntax, tends to restrict its conception of what constitutes relevant data, making it easier to meet this higher standard of evidence. A wider range of problems and data will certainly make it harder to meet higher standards of evidence, but that can be of little solace to our functional efforts, because failure to meet higher standards of evidence is still failure and the success of our structuralist colleagues in meeting such higher standards remains laudable independent of how restricted the data examined might be.

6. Actually, as Matthew Dryer has pointed out to me, there really is no direct access to *grammaticality*. Judgments of grammaticality are really judgments of acceptability, as occasional debate about grammaticality judgments clearly illustrates.

7. I use this term as it is used in Hildebrand *et al.* (1977).

8. Even this naturalness must to some extent be suspect. The presence of any non-native speaking person in the elicitation setting may well set up conditions for use of "foreigner talk" (Ferguson 1975), that register of discourse in which native speakers systematically alter their production to make it more comprehensible by a non-native speaker. As far as I know, no one has investigated this phenomenon in either the field or laboratory setting.

9. Some recent work by DeLancey (1991) argues convincingly that the semantic category *patient* could well be collapsed into a more general category. This category, following Anderson (1971), is called *theme*. While this usage of the expression 'theme' is a common one, it is not related to the expression as it is used in discourse studies. To avoid confusion, then, I will continue to use the expression *patient* rather than (semantic) *theme*.

10. This summary derives in part from the excellent summary found in Levelt (1989: 260-283).

11. Similar techniques were used in the original films produced for this study. A film segment was produced in which only one character was present, and this segment juxtaposed to target events in which the character was either the agent of the patient. While we could replicate the kinds of results others had achieved, we still could not fully control the details of production on each utterance, the goal of individuated prediction.

12. Copies of this film are available upon request. The film requires a Macintosh computer with a color monitor (such as the Macintosh cx, si, or LC) and at least 4 MB RAM. Those interested should include with their request a double-sided, double-density 3.5" floppy.

13. Color is the essential visual parameter by which the otherwise identical fish are distinguished from one another (red fish, blue fish, etc.) We used eight different colors: red, blue, green, black, white, gray, yellow, and purple. Use of patterns on a monochrome display failed because subjects could not rapidly lexicalize the distinguishing features of different patterns ("the checked fish", or "the cross-hatched fish", etc.). It should be noted that speakers of languages without color terms for some of the colors used may also experience difficulty in formulating referential expressions identifying the various fish.

14. The literature on the orienting of focal attention is an extensive one (Cowan 1988; Kahneman and Treisman 1984; Posner 1982, 1989; Posner and Petersen 1990). In general, visual stimulation which disrupts a previously habituated display will attract

attention to the locus of the disruption. It takes on the order of 150 ms. for attention to be attracted to a given location and for the fovea to re-locate on that new locus of focal attention.

The physical changes to a stimulus which can be used to manipulate focal attention include changes in color, changes in relative speed, changes in relative direction, jiggling an element, introduction of an element. Our manipulation introduces a new element, the arrow, at the location of the targeted fish.

15. The use of only 12 subjects poses no problem as the power of the statistics employed, for this size sample is more than adequate.

16. The Burmese data were produced and transcribed by Myint Soe, Dept. of Linguistics, University of Oregon.

17. Nor does it appear to be that case that intonation cues are used to deal with attentional priming either.

18. My thanks to P. Downing for her clear and helpfully skeptical reactions to an earlier draft of this paper.

19. When a parent calls to a child, "What are you doing in there?" Or, when an anchor says to a reporter, "What's happening there right now?" Or, when someone says to another, "What are you thinking about?"

20. The problem is that the data we collect through textual analysis are complex contingency tables composed of cross-classified nominal data. While log linear analysis and analysis of the proportionate reduction of error are of value in text analysis, they do not provide the means needed to deal with the logical problem of inferring causation from text counts. The casual use of chi square or the simple reporting of proportions (percentages) remains unequivocably inadequate.

21. Obviously, one does not want to oversimplify this too much. Experimentation is always complicated by issues of whether the independently manipulated factor might be derivative from some as yet unidentified, but more general, variable, or whether the details of the manipulation are in fact adequate in themselves.

22. This should not seem much more surprising than the fact that there are languages which do not employ grammatical means such as tense systems to deal with time.

Appendix A

Sample data from one English-speaking subject

Trial	**Primed**	**referent**	**Utterances**
1	RED	AGENT	There's two fish swimming towards each other/
			A red one just ate the gray one/
2	RED	PATIENT	There's now a blue fish with the red fish
			And the red fish was eaten by the blue fish/
3	BLUE	PATIENT	There's a blue fish and a green fish/
			The blue fish - oh- the green fish ate the blue fish/

4	GREEN	PATIENT	There's a green and purple fish/ The green fish was just eaten by the purple fish/
5	PURPLE	AGENT	There's two more fish A purple one and a white one And the purple one ate the white one/
6	PURPLE	PATIENT	There's two fish again swimming towards each other And the purple one was just eaten by the black one/
7	BLACK	AGENT	There's two fish swimming towards each other/ And a black one ate a yellow one/
8	BLACK	PATIENT	There's a black fish and it was just eaten by the red fish/
9	RED	AGENT	The red fish just ate the gray fish/
10	RED	PATIENT	This time the red fish was eaten by the blue fish/
11	BLUE	PATIENT	The blue fish was eaten by the green fish/
12	GREEN	PATIENT	The green fish was eaten by the purple fish/
13	PURPLE	AGENT	The purple fish just ate the white fish/
14	PURPLE	AGENT	The purple fish ate the black fish./
15	PURPLE	AGENT	The purple fish ate the yellow fish/
16	PURPLE	PATIENT	There's two more fish/ And this time, um the purple fish was eaten by the red fish/
17	RED	PATIENT	The red fish is swimming to:wards the gray fish who eats the red fish/
18	GRAY	PATIENT	The gray fish was just swallowed by the blue fish/
19	BLUE	PATIENT	This time the purple fish ate the blue fish/
20	PURPLE	PATIENT	The purple fish was eaten by the white fish/
21	WHITE	PATIENT	The white fish is swimming towards the black fish The white fish was eaten by the black fish/
22	BLACK	AGENT	Black fish is swimming towards the yellow fish/ The black fish ate the yellow fish/
23	BLACK	AGENT	The black fish swallowed by the red fish/
24	BLACK	PATIENT	The black fish is swimming towards the gray The black fish was eaten by the gray fish/
25	GRAY	AGENT	The gray fish ate the blue fish/
26	GRAY	AGENT	The gray fish is swimming towards the green fish It ate the green fish/
27	GRAY	AGENT	The gray fish ate the purple fish/
28	GRAY	PATIENT	There's gray and a white fish/ The white fish ate the gray fish/
29	WHITE	AGENT	The white fish ate the black fish/
30	WHITE	AGENT	The white fish is swimming towards the yellow The white fish ate the yellow fish/
31	WHITE	AGENT	The white fish now ate the red fish/

References

Anderson, John 1971. *The Grammar of Case: Towards a localistic theory*. Cambridge: Cambridge University Press.

Bates, Elizabeth, & Devescovi, Antonella 1989. "Crosslinguistic studies of sentence production." *The Crosslinguistic Study of Sentence Processing* ed. by Brian MacWhinney and Elizabeth Bates, 225-256. Cambridge: Cambridge University Press.

Bock, J.K. 1987. "An effect of accessibility of word forms on sentence structures." *Journal of Memory and Language* 26. 119-137.

Bock, J.K., & Warren, R.K. 1985. "Conceptual accessibility and syntactic structure in sentence formulation." *Cognition* 21. 467-484.

Carroll, J.M. 1958. "Process and content in psycholinguistics." *Current Trends in the Description and Analysis of Behavior* ed. by R. Patton, 175-200. Pittsburgh: University of Pittsburgh Press.

Chafe, Wallace (ed.). 1980. *The Pear Stories: Cognitive, cultural, and linguistic aspects of narrative production*. Norwood, New Jersey: Ablex.

Cowan, Nelson 1988. "Evolving conceptions of memory storage, selective attention, and their mutual constraints within the human information-processing system." *Psychological Bulletin* 104(2). 163-191.

Dahl, Östen 1974. "Topic-comment structure in a generative grammar with a semantic base." *Papers on Functional Sentence Perspective* ed. by F. Daneš, 75-80. The Hague: Mouton.

Daneš, František 1974. "Functional sentence perspective and the organization of the text." *Papers on Functional Sentence Perspective* ed. by F. Danes, 106-128. The Hague: Mouton.

Daneš, F. 1987. "On Prague school functionalism in linguistics." *Functionalism in Linguistics* ed. by R. Dirven and V. Fried, 3-37. Amsterdam: John Benjamins.

DeLancey, Scott 1991. "Theme, Goal, and Patient." Paper presented at the Second International Cognitive Linguistics Association Conference, Santa Cruz, CA, August 1, 1991.

Ferguson, Charles 1975. "Towards a characterization of English foreigner talk." *Anthropological Linguistics* 17. 1-14.

Firbas, Jan 1964a. "From comparative word-order studies (thoughts on L.V. Mathesius' conception of the word-order system in English compared with that in Czech)." *Brno Studies in English* 4. 111-128.

Firbas, Jan 1964b. "On defining the theme in functional sentence perspective." *Travaux linguistiques de Prague* 1. 267-280.

Firbas, Jan 1966. "Non-thematic subjects in English." *Travaux linguistiques de Prague* 2. 239-256.

Firbas, Jan 1974. "Some aspects of the Czechoslovak approach to problems of functional sentence perspective." *Papers on Functional Sentence Perspective* ed. by F. Daneš, 11-37. The Hague: Mouton.

Flores d'Arcais, G.B. 1975. "Some perceptual determinants of sentence construction." *Studies in Perception* ed. by G.B. Flores D'Arcais. Milan: Martello.

Flores d'Arcais, G.B. 1987. "Perceptual factors and word order in event descriptions." *Natural Language Generation: New results in artificial intelligence, psychology, and linguistics* ed. by G. Kempen, 441-451. Dordrecht: Martinus Nijhoff.

Forrest, Linda. 1992. "How grammar codes cognition: syntactic subject and focus of attention." Unpublished MA thesis, University of Oregon.

Givón, T. (ed.). 1983a. *Topic Continuity in Discourse: Quantitative cross-language studies*. Amsterdam: John Benjamins.

Givón, T. 1983b. "Topic continuity in spoken English." *Topic Continuity in Discourse: Quantitative cross-language studies* ed. by T. Givón, 343-363. Amsterdam: John Benjamins.

Givón, T. 1988. "The pragmatics of word order: predictability, importance, and attention." *Studies in Syntactic Typology* ed. by Michael T. Hammond, Edith A. Moravcsik, and Jessica R. Wirth, 243-284. Amsterdam: John Benjamins.

Givón, T. 1989. *Mind, Code and Context: Essays in pragmatics*. Hillsdale, NJ: Lawrence Erlbaum.

Grice, H.P. 1975. "Logic and conversation." *Speech Acts* ed. by Peter Cole and Jerry C. Morgan, 41-58. New York: Academic Press.

Halliday, M.A.K. 1967. "Notes on transitivity and theme in English (part 2)" *Journal of Linguistics*. 3. 199-244.

Halliday, M.A.K. 1976. "Theme and information in the English clause." *Halliday: System and Function in Language* ed. by Gunther Kress, 174-188. London: Oxford University Press.

Hawkinson, A., & Hyman, Larry 1974. "Hierarchies of natural topic in Shona." *Studies in African Linguistics* 5. 147-170.

Hildebrand, David K., Laing, James D., & Rosenthal, Howard 1977. *Prediction Analysis and Cross Classifications*. New York: John Wiley & Sons.

Jones, Linda K. 1977. *Theme in Expository English*. Lake Bluff, Illinois: Jupiter Press.

Kahneman, Daniel, & Treisman, Anne 1984. "Changing views of attention and automaticity." *Varieties of Attention* ed. by Raja Parasuraman and D.R. Davies, 29-61. New York: Academic Press.

Levelt, Willem J.M. 1989. *Speaking*. Cambridge, MA: MIT Press.

Li, Charles N., & Thompson, Sandra A. 1976. "Subject and topic: a new typology of language." *Subject and Topic* ed. by Charles N. Li, 457-489. New York: Academic Press.

Mathesius, Vilém 1929. "Zür Satzsperspektive im modernen Englisch." *Archiv für das Studium der neuren Sprachen und Literaturen* 155. 202-210.

Posner, Michael I. 1982. "Cumulative development of attentional theory." *American Psychologist* 37. 168-179.

Posner, Michael I. 1989. "May I have your attention please?" *Science and Public Policy Seminars*, Federation of Behavioral, Psychological, and Cognitive Sciences.

Posner, Michael I., & Petersen, S.E. 1990. "The attention system of the human brain." *Annual Review of Neuroscience* 13. 25-42.

Prentice, J.L. 1967. "Effects of cuing actor vs. cuing object on word order in sentence production." *Psychonomic Science* 8. 163-164.

Sridhar, S.N. 1988. *Cognition and Sentence Production: A cross-linguistic study*. New York: Springer-Verlag.

Tannenbaum, P.H. & Williams, F. 1968. "Generation of active and passive sentences as a function of subject and object focus." *Journal of Verbal Learning and Verbal Behavior* 7. 246-250.

Tomlin, Russell S. 1983. "On the interaction of syntactic subject, thematic information, and agent in English." *Journal of Pragmatics* 7. 411-432.

Tomlin, Russell S. 1984. "The treatment of foreground-background information in the on-line descriptive discourse of second language learners." *Studies in Second Language Acquisition* 6. 115-142.

Tomlin, Russell S. 1985. "Foreground-background information and the syntax of subordination." *Text* 5. 85-122.

Tomlin, Russell S. 1987. "The Problem of Coding in Functional Grammars." Paper presented at the UC Davis Conference on the Interaction of Form and Function in Language, Davis, California, January, 1987.

Tomlin, Russell S. 1990. "Functionalism in second language acquisition." *Studies in Second Language Acquisition* 12. 155-177.

Tomlin, Russell S., & Pu, Ming Ming 1991. "The management of reference in Mandarin discourse." *Cognitive Linguistics* 2. 65-93.

Turner, E., & Rommetveit, R. 1968. "Focus of attention in recall of active and passive sentences." *Journal of Verbal Learning and Verbal Behavior* 7. 543-548.

Weil, Henri 1877. *The Order of Words in the Ancient Languages Compared with that of the Modern Languages* (C. Super, Trans.). Boston: Ginn & Co.

Noun incorporation and object placement in discourse

The case of Guaraní*

Maura Velázquez-Castillo
University of California, San Diego

0. Introduction

This paper is concerned with the use of noun incorporation (NI) in discourse. The study will be based on data from Guaraní, a South American Indian language spoken in Paraguay, parts of Brazil, and Argentina. The main goal of the paper is to elucidate the type of knowledge the speaker of the language should have in order to properly use and interpret this type of linguistic structure in discourse.

In Guaraní, the subject or the object of the verb can be "incorporated" into (i.e., affixed to) the stem of a predicator to form a compound predicator.[1] Most compounds generally have a corresponding unincorporated structure. Sentences (1)-(3) provide a sample of the different grammatical structures that can result from NI. Examples (1a)-(3a) are the phrasal equivalents of the incorporated structures, which are given in (1b) through (3b).

I. NI of a body-part noun:

(1) a. *A-johei-ta* *che-juru*
1SG-wash-FUT my-mouth
'I'll wash my mouth'

b. *A-je-**juru-hei**-ta*
1SG-REFL-mouth-wash-FUT
'I'll wash my mouth out'
(lit: I'll mouth-wash myself)

(2) a. *Maria resay o-syry*
Maria tear 3SG-flow
'Maria's tears flow'

b. *Maria* ***hesay-syry***
Maria 3SG=tear-flow
'Maria is crying profusely'

II. NI of a non-body part noun:

(3) a. *A-jogua-ta petei mba'e*
1SG-buy-FUT one thing
'I will buy something'

b. *A-**mba'e-jogua**-ta ko ka'aru*
1SG-thing-buy-FUT this afternoon
'I'll go shopping this afternoon'

There are some obvious surface differences between the compounds and their phrasal counterparts. Among them, word order (compare sentences in (1) and (3)) and "possessor ascension" (compare sentences (a) and (b) in (1) and (2)) figure prominently. Recent studies of NI within formal theories try to account for such differences in strictly structural terms (Baker 1988; Rosen 1989). Functional studies of the phenomenon, however, have suggested that the formal differences are symptomatic of underlying semantic and functional differences (Mithun 1984; Hopper and Thompson 1980, 1984; Haiman 1985). Most studies of NI, including the functional ones, have been based on context-free sentences. The present paper will build on the insights of functional studies by analyzing the factors which influence the speaker's choice of linguistic structure in actual speech situations and by showing how different aspects of the formal resources of the language "conspire" to create the same communicative effects.

The paper will analyze the semantic and communicative effects of NI in a number of speech situations excerpted from folk tales. It will be shown that the discourse use of Guaraní NI has a descriptive function with the following possible semantic effects: (i) portraying bodily actions as reflections of emotional states, (ii) construing bodily activities as characteristic behavior, and therefore as a reflection of an attitudinal characteristic, (iii) portraying bodily qualities as manifestations of a permanent personal trait, and (iv) construing an action and its object as a unitary predicate to designate a routinized or institutionalized activity. The study will also show that incorporation serves the communicative function of signaling lack of discourse topicality and/or prominence of the incorporated noun. It will be shown that noun incorporation interacts with other formal devices, such as object preposing and "possessor ascension", to signal lack of discourse prominence or topicality. Finally, it will be argued that the proper characterization of the semantic and communicative function of NI requires that the data source be expanded beyond context-free sentences to include wider linguistic and situational contexts. Only this sort of data makes explicit the speaker's communicative intent and the local conditions which license the use of NI as opposed to its phrasal counterpart.

The discussion will be organized as follows: (i) outline of the general methodological framework; (ii) a discussion of the communicative motivation of NI, and (iii) the role of word-order in facilitating the speaker's communicative purpose.

1. General methodological approach

In the first part of the study, the communicative function of NI in a short story will be analyzed. The discussion will concentrate on the different emergent factors which license the use of an incorporated structure as opposed to its unincorporated counterpart. The analysis will invoke the notion of discourse modes presented in Du Bois (1980). In particular, the notions of descriptive vs. narrative mode will play an important role.

According to Du Bois (1980:227), "a clause is in the narrative mode if it serves to advance the story line to some degree". Mentions which occur in the narrative mode tend to be topical and persistent in subsequent discourse. Noun phrases in this mode are "used to speak about an object as an object, with continuous identity over time .... and can be thought of in cognitive terms as activating a mental "file" for some object or referring back to a previously opened file".[2] The descriptive mode "is a cover term which includes categorizations, descriptions, statements of relations to other discourse participants and so on (p. 227)". Mentions which occur in non-subject positions in the descriptive mode often lack topicality and discourse persistence.

In the second part of the study a text-counting methodology developed by Givón (1983) is used in which the difference between pre- and postverbal objects in terms of topic continuity and discourse prominence is measured. The methodology is fully explained in Section 3.

Before we begin our study, a few words are in order regarding the data source. In a previous study of Guaraní NI (Velázquez 1989b), I used context-free utterances as a data source. My study consisted of discussions of the semantic differences between carefully constructed incorporated and unincorporated structures. During the course of the study, it became evident that a discussion of meaning differences necessitated the mention of some background knowledge and communicative context, but the type of data I used limited my ability to show how this background knowledge or communicative intent would influence the speaker's choice of linguistic structure in a given speech situation. It has been pointed out (Cicourel 1988) that context-free utterances presuppose a considerable amount of implicit background knowledge whose effect in the grammatical structure under study is seldom discussed by the analyst. A similar concern is present in the work of a few linguists, such as Hopper (1988) and Du Bois (1985). Hopper claims that grammar "emerges" from discourse and is not detachable from discourse-building strategies, and therefore that isolated, context-free sentences as a data source have marginal usefulness in the study of language. Similarly, Du Bois argues in favor of an "adaptive" grammar whose patterns are the result of the interplay between language-internal forces and external pressures, among which he includes discourse building strategies. In this paper, I attempt to make explicit the background information and the local conditions in which the utterances of my data occur. In order to illustrate and clarify the aspects of background knowledge that are implicit in my previous analysis of NI, I analyze the use of NI in a folk tale.

In general, I relied on my own native speaker intuition to provide semantic interpretations for the sentences that occur in the texts. Occasionally, when I was in doubt, I consulted other native speakers to corroborate my judgements.[3] The same was true for acceptability judgements when they were needed.

2. The communicative motivation of incorporation

2.1 *Data source*

This section will be based on a single folk tale which happens to have a high number of incorporated structures.[4] The story belongs to a particular type of tale involving animal characters. As it is common in folk tales the world over, human characteristics are attributed to animal characters in these stories. For example, they talk, have cultural values, and participate in the same social activities as humans do. Each animal embodies certain personality traits characteristic of well-known human types. The art of telling this type of story, therefore, lies primarily in the successful portrayal of the different human types through the descriptions and actions of the animal characters.

There is a limited number of animals that can have the status of main characters in this culture. One of the most popular main characters of animal stories is the monkey. Typically, the monkey is a hyperactive, crafty, clever and creative character who is always thinking of new ways to achieve his ends or have fun at the expense of others. In this particular case, the characters are the monkey and the crocodile. I will provide an English translation of the story in order to make explicit the contextual and situational conditions that license the use of incorporation. I will then give the original incorporated structures and discuss their communicative function in the story.

The monkey and the crocodile

It had just stopped raining and the monkey was at the bank of a river looking down at the water which rolled furiously as if it were going to leap out of the river bed. On the other side of the river, he could see lots of ripe yellow pakuris in the pakuri trees. The monkey's mouth watered at the sight of the fruit but he couldn't figure out how to get across the river. He paced back and forth at the river's edge for a while and then, trying to call attention to himself, climbed to the top of the tallest tree and started to howl. He thought perhaps he could find a friend to go "pakuri-eating" with him on the other side. Having no luck, he climbed back down to a branch which bent right to the edge of the river.

At that moment he saw the crocodile swimming down the river. The monkey gave the crocodile a very friendly greeting, and asked him why he no longer came to the places where women talk so fondly about him. The crocodile, clearly flattered, laughed and asked what places he meant, but the monkey answered very vaguely. The crocodile then asked what kinds of things the women say about him, and the monkey replied that all the women think he is incredibly handsome. The crocodile laughed again, and said: "You're not just trying to flatter me, are you?", to which the monkey replied: "Of course not. Why would I lie to you?" The crocodile then asked the monkey why he came to the river bank, and the monkey told him that he was waiting for his friend to go "pakuri-eating".

The crocodile asked the monkey how he was planning to cross the river, but the monkey simply answered that he and his friend would find a way to do it. The crocodile offered to carry the monkey on his back to get him across the river. The monkey pretended to be a little worried about his friend, but soon decided to accept the offer. When they were half-way across the river, the crocodile asked the monkey to please tell him once more what the women say about him, and the monkey repeated what he had said before, embellishing it with details.

When they reached the other side of the river, the monkey jumped off the crocodile's back onto the branch of a tree, and yelled : "Here's where I get off. Don't forget what I told you". Still not satisfied, the crocodile asked once more: "How did it go again?". This time the monkey replied: "I will tell you so you can have it with honey and cheese: They call you a big-mouthed, rough-skinned old crocodile, whose eyes tremble in their sockets, and who is nothing but a laughingstock."

2.2 *Bodily actions as reflection of emotional states*

In this section I will analyze one of the communicative effects of incorporation, namely that of construing bodily activities as a reflection of the emotional or mental state of a given participant. In all the examples of incorporation excerpted from the story, the complex predicates resulting from NI will be highlighted to facilitate their identification. Consider example (4):

(4) *Ka'i* ***o-ne-ndy-moko,*** ***o-ne-mbe-su'u,***
monkey 3SG-REFL-saliva-swallow 3SG-REFL-lip-bite
o-jete-poka,
3SG-body-twist
'The monkey's mouth waters, he bites his lips, twists his body,'

Line (4) contains the first set of incorporated structures in the story. The sentence is used with the purpose of *describing* the emotional effect that the sight of the ripe fruits had on the monkey. The story teller is not interested in *narrating* what happened to the monkey's saliva, lips, or body; the external appearance of the monkey's body is important only insofar as it reflects the feelings and emotions of the monkey at the sight of the fruit. Despite the availability of a referent in the immediate context for the incorporated nouns, the story teller does not direct the attention of the listener to those objects. It is clear from the context and the reflexive marker *je-/ñe-* that the story teller is talking about the monkey's body/body-parts. But the nouns lack "continuity of identity" in the discourse (Du Bois' term), or in Givón's terms, "discourse persistence". That is to say, the referential content of these nouns is not exploited for further references in the discourse. Thus the monkey's saliva, lips or body are not referred to in the rest of the story. In fact, I would like to claim that, by incorporating these nouns, the story teller gives a signal to the listener that the referents of these nouns will not enter the discourse at all, and therefore a "file" should not be opened for them. Incorporation, then, is a device used by the story teller to tell the hearer: "I'm using these nouns to describe the monkey, not to report what happened to his body or his body-parts".

Given that incorporation here has the effect of backgrounding the body part of the monkey so that the monkey himself (and his emotional reaction) can be brought into focus, it would be interesting to see to what extent incorporation is a necessary linguistic structure for the expressive needs of the story teller. Without incorporation, the sentences containing the highlighted verbs in line (4) would have the form given in line (4'):

(4') *Ka'i o-moko h-endy, oi-su'u h-embe,*
monkey 3SG-swallow his-saliva 3SG-bite his-lips
oi-poka h-ete.
3SG-twist his-body

The unincorporated predicates in (4') do not convey the emotional overtones present in the original sentences. The sentence merely reports the actions as objective facts. Thus the action of biting the lips, for example, could as well be referring to an accidental lip-biting on the part of the monkey. The unincorporated predicates of (4') would be awkward in the context in which they appear. In the line immediately following (4), the listener is informed why the monkey was so uneasy. The awkwardness arises from the fact that the unincorporated structures set the expectation that the monkey's saliva, lips and body are going to play a role in the discourse. The context, however, clearly indicates that the story teller is trying to *describe* the emotional state of the monkey.

The linguistic structure reflects the intent of the story teller to focus on the monkey's emotional state as opposed to what happened to his body. This is clearly seen when we compare the structures in (4) and (4'). If we focus our attention on the linguistic coding of the objects in both lines, we can see that in line 4' the body/body-part is coded as the clausal object, and the monkey as the possessor. In line (4), however, the noun *ka'i* 'monkey' has the "privileged" status of clausal object (as evidenced by the reflexive markers). This phenomenon, of course, is what is known in formal linguistics as "possessor ascension"(PA) (Perlmutter 1983). Unlike in other languages, PA in Guaraní does not occur independently from NI. The role of incorporation is to background the noun designating the body/body-part by attaching it to the verbal root, and thus "depriving" it of its independent coding as the clausal object. PA provides an alternative element for focal attention.

Example (5) contains another example of incorporation as a means of *describing* the emotional affectedness of the participant involved:

(5) *O-puka* *Jakare,* ***o-mbo-py'a-kyryi*** *chupe.*
3SG-laugh crocodile 3SG-CAUS-chest-tickle to=him
'The crocodile laughs, (the monkey's words) made him feel good.'

This time, the description applies to the crocodile, who feels extremely flattered by his alleged reputation as a handsome young "man" among women. Here, using an unincorporated structure would be even more awkward than in the preceding case:

(5') *O-puka* *jakare* *o-mo-kyryi* *i-py'a*
3SG-laugh crocodile 3SG-CAUS-tickle his-chest
'The crocodile laughed, because it made his chest tickle.'

The unincorporated structure in (5') suggests that the crocodile was being physically tickled, even though from the context it is clear that what the crocodile is reacting to is the remarks of the monkey about his good looks. While the incorporated structure in this context is unequivocally referring to the emotional reaction of the crocodile, the unincorporated structure would unduly confuse the listener by signaling the *narration* of a tickling event when what is intended is a *description* of the crocodile's emotional reaction. For the story teller, it is important to portray the flattering effect of the monkey's words on the crocodile to the greatest possible degree so s/he can make the point that the monkey fooled him by appealing to his vanity. S/he achieves this via the choice of linguistic structure.

Again, the intention of the story teller is reflected in the linguistic structure used, since body-part incorporation backgrounds the part and allows the main participant to be encoded as the clausal object and thus given its due prominence via PA.

2.2 *Bodily activity as a reflection of attitudinal characteristics*

Another *descriptive* meaning that body-part incorporation can convey is that of an attitudinal characteristic. Although object incorporation can also have this effect, most commonly, this semantic effect is achieved with the incorporation of a body-part noun in the role of subject of an intransitive predicator. Examples of this communicative effect of incorporation occur five times in the story. Consider examples (6) and (7):

(6) *Neipamiro guãrã o-hecha Jakare* ***huguai-vava-vava***
In=no=time 3SG-see crocodile his=tail-move-move
'Hardly any time passes before the monkey sees the crocodile with his tail moving back and forth (as he comes down the river).'

(7) ***o-ne-mbo-huguai-pu'a,*** *ha o-kañy-manera'e*
3SG-REFL-CAUS-tail-raise and 3SG-disappear-right= a=way
pakuri-ty-re.
tree-field-at
'Lifting his tail, the monkey immediately disappeared among the pakuri-trees'

In (6), it is said of the crocodile that he came with his tail moving back and forth when the monkey first saw him swimming down the river, while in (7), it is said of the monkey that he disappeared among the bushes, lifting his tail after fooling the crocodile.

As in the cases discussed in the previous section, the main interest of the story teller is not in narrating the body activities of both participants, but to offer a quick interpretational comment on some aspect of the characters involved. This time, using incorporation and PA, the story teller *describes* an aspect of the character's personality. Thus, rather than *narrating* a bodily activity per se, the story teller portrays the physical activity as a habitual or characteristic action, which in turn signals the character's permanent emotional or attitudinal characteristic. In both (6) and (7), the incorporated structure suggests that it is expected of the participants to move in the way described. It is perceived as natural for the calm and slow crocodile to come moving his tail back and forth in a leisurely manner; and for the irreverent monkey to leave lifting his tail (and showing his rear end) after he accomplished his objective by making fun of the crocodile.

As was the case for the incorporated nouns discussed in the previous section, these incorporated nouns lack continuity of identity in the discourse in the sense that the designated entities are not exploited for subsequent reference in the discourse. In fact, as suggested earlier, it is likely that their incorporation signals that their mention should not be considered an entry into the discourse.

Again, alternative unincorporated structures, such as (6') and (7'), would fail to portray these bodily actions as characteristic of the participants since the predication would apply to the body-parts rather than to the participants:

(6') . . . *o-hecha jakare ruguai o-vava-vava*
3SG-see crocodile tail 3SG-move-move
'. . .he saw the crocodile's tail move back and forth.'

(7') . . . *o-mo-pu'ã huguai*
3SG-CAUS-raise 3SG-tail
'he lifted his tail'

In addition, it would create the expectation that the body parts themselves will become of interest in the development of the story. In order to maximize the effect of the monkey's mockery, the story teller needs to portray the deceived participant as a slow, naive individual, and the deceiver as an energetic and irreverent individual. The incorporation of the noun designating the body-part along with PA helps achieve this portrayal of the two characters since it allows the predication to apply to the participants themselves, rather than to their body parts.

2.4 *Properties of body-parts as a reflection of a permanent physical quality*

A third *descriptive* effect of NI is to construe a property of a given body-part as a permanent physical quality that applies to the participant, not merely to the body-part. Examples of NI involving this effect are provided in (8) and (9). Both examples involve subject incorporation.

(8) *Karia'y pora resa-mburukuja,* ***ape-syi-asy,***
young=man handsome eye-passion=flower surface-soft-nice
rembe-pyta *jakarati'a-aju, he'i nde-rehe.*
lip-red fruit-ripe say=they you-about
'Handsome young man with eyes like passion flowers, with nice soft skin, with red lips like ripe fruit. — that's what they say about you.'

(9) *Jakare tuja* ***ape-korocho, resa-kua-ku'e, juru-guasu.***
crocodile old surface-rough eye-hole-move mouth-big
'That old rough-skinned crocodile, with eyes trembling in their sockets, big mouth'.[5]

Here the monkey talks about the physical appearance of the crocodile, first to flatter him, and then to make the mockery clear to the crocodile. In both cases the story teller has the option of using incorporated or unincorporated structures, and s/he opts for the first. Again, the important semantic difference between the two structures is that in the first case the predication is about the participant, while in the second case the predication would be about the body-part. Since the intent of the monkey here is to flatter the crocodile, he chooses the incorporated structure, which has the effect of downplaying the part and emphasizing the whole. It is important for the story teller to communicate that the monkey attributes the positive qualities to the crocodile, as a "person", rather than to his body-parts only. Specifying the positive qualities of the different parts is important only insofar as it serves to suggest attractiveness of the crocodile. Similarly, when he later decides to tell the truth of what he really thinks about the crocodile (9), he chooses the incorporated structure because his intention is to make fun of the crocodile himself, not merely of how his skin or eyes look.[6]

In summary, we have seen that incorporation of body-part terms serves a descriptive purpose in the discourse. Using both NI and PA the story teller offers an interpretational comment on some aspect of the character's current or permanent emotional state or attitude. The description can be of three types: (i) a portrayal of the emotional or mental state of discourse participants through bodily manifestations of those states, (ii) a construal of bodily activities as characteristic or habitual behavior, and (iii) construal of body-part quality as a permanent physical characteristic of the participant. The phenomenon known as "possessor ascension" plays a crucial role in portraying bodily activities as attributes of the participants themselves, and not of the parts mentioned. Thus, both incorporation and possessor ascension receive here a functional explanation: the incorporated status of these nouns signals lack of discourse prominence, while the body-part possessor is brought into focus by being given the status of clausal objects or subjects. It is worth reiterating that "possessor ascension" in Guaraní is possible only in case a part–whole relation holds between the possessor and the possessed entity. Implications of this fact for the distinction alienable-inalienable were explored in Velázquez (1989a).

In the next section, I will discuss cases of incorporation which do not trigger "possessor ascension" since they don't involve body-part terms. The result is not a comment on the character's emotional state or personality, but a comment on the nature of a given activity.

2.4 *Institutionalized, or routinized activity*

The last communicative function of NI that I will discuss in the present paper is that of naming a routinized, or socially relevant activity. There is one such instance of NI in the story that I am analyzing here, and it is used twice. It first comes up when the story teller describes what the monkey wants to do at the other side of the river, and then, when the monkey himself tells the crocodile what he wants to do:

(10) *A-ha'aro-a-ina* *che-iru-me* *ro-ho-hagua* ***pakuri-'u-vo***.
1SG-wait -1SG-PROG my-friend-to 1PL-go-PURP fruit-eat-DIR
'I'm waiting for my friend so we can go "pakuri-eating" together.'

As in the previous cases, the speaker has the option of using an incorporated or unincorporated structure. The unincorporated structure of (10) would look like (10').

(10') *A-ha'aro- a-ina* *che-iru-me* *ro-ho hagua ro-'u* *pakuri*.
1SG-wait-1SG-PROG my-friend-to 1PL-go PURP 1PL-eat pakuri.
'I'm waiting for my friend to go and eat pakuri.'

In (10'), the only purpose of the monkey is to satisfy his craving for the fruit at the other side of the river. The incorporated structure, however, suggests that the purpose of the monkey is to engage in a social activity besides the mere act of eating pakuri. It is clear from the context that, besides having a physical craving for the fruit, the monkey does want to share the activity with a friend. Even though it is clear that the monkey wants to treat himself to some pakuri, the first thing he tries to do is not to find a way to cross the river, but to find a partner in the "pakuri-eating" activity (that is the reason why he climbs on the tree and makes noise). This type of incorporation conforms to Mithun's Class I NI, in that it designates a unitary, institutionalized activity (Mithun 1984). Also, this type of incorporated structure has a very similar communicative effect to what Du Bois (1980) calls "predicate conflation", in which a noun and an object together are used to express a "unitary predicate concept rather than to refer to an actual object" (p. 214). The concept of 'pakuri-eating' evokes the social activity of eating pakuri with friends. Conversations, jokes, and the pleasure of eating among friends figure more prominently in the concept than the actual fruit. The unincorporated expression, however would evoke no such social situation. It is therefore appropriate for the story teller and the monkey to use the incorporated structure, and not the unincorporated one. The reason why *pakuri* is incorporated here is because the unincorporated structure would not convey the idea that eating *pakuri* is a social thing to do.

In this case, it is more difficult to show that the incorporated noun lacks discourse persistence or prominence, since the referent for *pakuri* appears at least twice in the whole story. The referent is introduced in the discourse when the monkey sees it for the first time. The noun is used with the modifier *aju* 'ripe', which further establishes its discourse referentiality. The referent reappears at the end of the story, when the monkey disappears among the pakuri trees. It is clear that these instances are meant to refer to specific entities in the discourse, and that therefore a "file" must be kept open for them. Even though the '*pakuris*' are part of the story setting and have some, if not much, discourse prominence or persistence, I would still like to claim that the referential link is either nonexistent or irrelevant when the tree/fruit is mentioned in the incorporated structures. When the speaker incorporates "pakuri", the fruit is not important in itself; it is important only insofar as it serves the purpose of characterizing the action as an established type of social activity. Thus, it doesn't matter which particular fruits are eaten; what matters is the type of activities people are engaged in when eating that kind of fruit.

In this section, we have seen that, once more, incorporation serves the purpose of characterizing or *describing* the type of activity rather than *narrating* an actual event that involves a specific object. The difference between this type of incorporation and that of body-part terms is that, while an alternative focus is provided in the latter, in an incorporation of a non-body-part term the effect is only defocusing, without an alternative focus being provided. In Section 3, I will argue that object placement in NI serves the purpose of reinforcing the defocusing effect of incorporation.

3. The discourse function of object placement in Guaraní

As was stated above, another surface manifestation of NI (more specifically, object incorporation) in Guaraní is the discrepancy in object position vis-a-vis the verb between incorporated and unincorporated structures. In the first case, the object is preverbal, while in the second, the object is generally postverbal. In this section I will offer a possible explanation for why this is the case.

According to some linguists, similar discrepancies in other languages are the result of a diachronic shift in basic word order whereby an originally OV language adopts the new order of VO. The position of incorporated objects is then a relic of an older OV order, and the postverbal unincorporated objects are instances of the more innovative VO order (cf. Lehman 1975; Givón 1984: 214). Despite the fact that we do not have conclusive historical evidence that the same thing happened in Guaraní, there are reasons to believe that the language must have undergone a word order change along the lines suggested above.

First, the language presents structural characteristics associated with OV types: postpositions instead of prepositions, prenominal genitives instead of postnominal ones, predominantly suffixal morphology instead of prefixal morphology. At the same time, however, the language also presents characteristics of a VO type: a noun-modifier order instead of a modifier-noun order, and a noun-relative clause order instead of a relative clause-noun order. This typological ambivalence, plus the fact that most independent objects are postverbal, suggests that the language might be undergoing a change from a OV type to a predominantly VO type.

Second, a survey of the first recorded records of this and other related languages (16th-17th centuries) suggests that the OV order was more common then than it is now. For example, in Montoya's Catechism (Montoya 1640), I was able to find 103 independently occurring object NPs. A total of 73 of these were preverbal, while 30 were postverbal. It seems then that there are sufficient reasons to believe that the language has been undergoing a basic word order shift.

This hypothesis provides a possible explanation for the existence of the two object-orders, but it does not provide a possible motivation for why the innovative order affected some objects and not others. In particular, it does not help us answer the question of what the incorporated objects have in common with the other objects which have also kept the old order. According to Givón (personal communication), it is possible that the incorporation was already an established morphological pattern by the time the shift in word order started.[7] But we do not have to necessarily assume a rigid, syntactically motivated word order as a starting point in the historical development. It is also possible that, in Guaraní, the object-verb order was pragmatically governed. In other words, there is the possibility that there had been a stage at which preposing or postposing the object played a functional role which determined the order split, and that the position of incorporated objects has the same functional motivation as that of other preposed objects.

Since we do not have access to historical records to trace the development of the new order and its possible functional motivations, we cannot offer certain proof that object preposing has had a functional motivation. Nevertheless, we can appeal to two data sources to test our hypothesis: (i) present day narrative discourse, and (ii) the first documents written in the language by 17th-century missionaries.

3.1 *A quantitative study of topicality and object placement in present-day discourse*

Since the language still presents the OV order in some contexts, I have decided to conduct a study of the discourse role of both orders in present-day discourse. The structures studied include independent objects only. The study assumes that despite the relatively uncommon occurrence of the unincorporated OV order, some pattern would emerge that would indicate some traces of the communicative motivation behind this split order.

In order to determine the discourse role of object ordering in Guaraní, a study of discourse continuity and thematic importance of pre- and postposed independent objects was conducted following Givón (1983). The data base consists of a collection of 9 folk tales, including the one analyzed in the previous section. All of them belong to the same type of folk tale, namely, they are all based on stories whose main characters are animals representing well-known human archetypes. Givón's text counting methodology of *lookback* or referential distance, and discourse *persistence* or decay was applied to the transcripts of the tales, which were previously divided in clauses.

Lookback measures thematic continuity and is defined as the average distance in number of clauses between the present mention and the first mention preceding the present mention. When there was no previous mention within 20 clauses, a lookback of 20 was assigned; in the case of new mentions, the maximum lookback of 20 was assigned. A highly topical participant will have a very low average of lookback, in other words, a high degree of continuity; while a non-thematic participant will have a high average of lookback.

Persistence measures the degree of thematic importance of a given discourse participant and is defined as the average number of consecutive following clauses in which the referent is mentioned in some way. The counting stops when a clause is found in which the referent in question is not mentioned. An important discourse participant is expected to have a relatively high average of persistence while a non-thematic participant is expected to have a low average of persistence.

Following Givón, all clauses except relative clauses were counted, and no-mentions in directly quoted texts were not counted as gaps. The results are reported in Table 1.

Table 1 shows that the most continuous and important participants are coded by pronouns, as suggested by their low lookback average and their high persistence average. This result is to be expected given previous studies of topic continuity (Givón 1983). What is interesting for our purposes is that these highly continuous and important participants occur post-verbally, never pre-verbally. Despite the fact that animate nouns are never incorporated, this result is significant for the present discussion in that it suggests that pre-verbal position of objects indicates lack of topic continuity and/or importance, while the post-verbal position is available for NPs of varying degrees of topicality.

As for nominal objects, the figures indicate that NP objects in general have very low continuity and persistence when compared to pronouns, again, a result that is to be expected given previous studies. What is significant for our purposes, though, is that when we compare preposed and postposed NP objects, the latter show more continuity and persistence than the preposed ones. Furthermore, preposed objects have consistently the maximum possible numerical value for lookback and the minimum possible value for persistence. In other words, they have no continuity and 0 importance for subsequent discourse. In this sense, they are identical to incorporated objects (which are also preposed), whose average for lookback is also 20 and 0 for persistence.

Despite the fact that the figures for postposed NP objects show a high lookback (indicator of low continuity), this coding device has the potential for

Table 1. Lookback and persistence of post- and preverbal objects

Category	Lookback	Persistence	N° of tokens
VO (pron)	1.18	4.83	12
VO (NP)	13.01	1.16	43
OV (pron)	N/A	N/A	0
OV (NP)	20	0	14

high continuity, as suggested by some low lookback values in the sample under study: of the 43 postverbal NP objects, four have a lookback value of 1, three a value of 2, and five a value of 3. This suggests that postposed NP objects, while not the coding device of choice for highly continuous topics, have the potential to code a continuous topic. Preposed objects, on the other hand, never code a continuous topic. Thus, while thematic participants are only sometimes coded by direct objects, when they *are* coded by a direct object, they must follow the verb.

The figures for persistence given in Table 1 indicate results similar to those for lookback. That is, postposed NP objects have a relatively low persistence when compared to, say, the highly thematic participants coded by pronouns, but higher than their preposed counterparts, whose persistence value is consistently 0. These figures suggest that preposed NP objects have no importance whatsoever for subsequent discourse while postposed NP objects could be slightly more important, but not significantly so.

I believe that the figures for persistence are a bit misleading, however, due to the way persistence was measured. Assigning a value of 0 to a given item when the following clause contains no mention of its referent ignores the possibility of reappearance of the same referent in later clauses. Thus the possibility exists that an item that occurs only once will be assigned the same value (0) as one which re-occurs more than once, even though those occurrences are not in immediately subsequent clauses. This is precisely what happened in many cases of preposed and postposed NP objects in the present study. The referents of preposed NP objects almost always enter the discourse only once, while the referents of postposed NP objects reoccurred more than once in many cases. In both cases, the persistence value was 0 because the re-occurrence of postposed NP referents was not necessarily in immediately subsequent clauses.

A particularly telling example of how this method of measuring persistence can be misleading pertains to a tale whose main characters are the monkey and the armadillo. The former, desperate because he could not round up his scattered horses, goes and asks his friend, the armadillo for help. The word for 'horses' is introduced by a postposed NP object in the first clause, and is also the referent of the postverbal NP object of the last clause. Altogether 'horses' was coded 8 times in the form of a postverbal NP object, these together average a persistence value of only 1.5 according to the method of persistence measurement described above. This is a low figure if we consider that there is a total of 20 mentions of the same referent in a tale of 68 clauses.

The example of 'horses' described above is not as thematic as, say, the main characters of the tale. Nevertheless, it is not insignificant for the development of the main events of the story, as suggested by its repeated reappearance in the discourse. At the very least, it seems clear that the hearer must keep an open "file" for this referent during the length of the whole story. Since the method of measuring persistence in Table 1 is not devised to reflect the type of "intermediate" persistence that postverbal objects seem to have, and given its potential significance for the present study, I decided to expand the notion of persistence in a way that would reflect the difference between intermediate persistence and non-persistence. I decided to measure persistence based on the average number of occurrences of the same referent in a fixed length of discourse. In keeping with the arbitrary maximum number of 20 clauses for lookback set by Givón, I decided to count the number of mentions of the same referent in the subsequent 20 clauses to determine persistence. The results are given in Table 2.

The figures in Table 2 suggest a much more significant difference in persistence between post- and preverbal objects than that originally suggested in Table 1. There was only one item in the category of preverbal objects whose persistence value was more than 0; that value was 2. In the case of postverbal objects, however, values as high as 19, 13 and 12 were found. Of course there was also a significant number of postverbal objects with low persistence value, hence the average value of 3.48.

Overall, the results of the text counts suggest that objects coding relatively thematic and continuous discourse participants do not occur preverbally and that the postverbal position for objects could potentially be filled by nouns with highly continuous and thematic referents. While preposed objects are generally ungrounded in the discourse, there is a potential grounding purpose in object postposing. Thus it seems that if a thematic participant is coded as object, it must follow the verb (but the opposite implication does not hold).

Table 2. Persistence of post- and preverbal objects within 20 clauses.

Category	Average	N° of tokens
VO (NP)	3.48	43
OV (NP)	0.14	14

Since postverbal objects can introduce significant participants in the discourse, postposing an object gives a clue to the hearer that a "file" must be kept open for that participant.

We can speculate that the results of the present text count are traces of an earlier stage in the development of the language in which there was a clearer functional split between pre- and postposed objects. This functional split was such that only topical objects were postverbal, while non-topical ones were preverbal. At this developmental stage, object position could have been used to signal definiteness or discourse continuity/thematicity. The shift in position of non-topical objects followed later, conceivably aided by the introduction of a definite article borrowed from Spanish.

The possible explanation for the consistent preposing of incorporated nouns then would be as follows: NI as a pattern emerged at a stage in which there was a functional split between pre- and postverbal objects. Since incorporated nouns are totally ungrounded in the discourse, it is natural for them to be preverbal rather than postverbal. Their preverbal position could then be the result of a historical discourse-controlled object position whose traces can still be found in the language. Thus, even today, postposing an incorporated object could unduly confuse the hearer, leading him/her to believe that the object has a referent which could become important in the discourse; especially since definite nouns in Guaraní often do not have a specialized definite marker. This is changing, though, with the introduction of the definite article, *la/lo* borrowed from Spanish.

I will now turn to 17th-century texts to look for further support for this hypothesis.

3.2 *Object placement in 17th-century Guaraní*

As stated above, the oldest Guaraní text recorded is a 17th-century Catechism prepared by Antonio Ruiz de Montoya. This data source is probably not the most representative of 17th-century Guaraní for two reasons. First, it was written by a non-native speaker, and the structure of the language was probably influenced to some degree by the author's native language. Additionally, the language of the text had to be adapted to the rigid format of Catholic ritualistic prayers and recitations of doctrine. Therefore, we cannot derive any conclusive evidence of the discourse role of object position from this data source. Nevertheless, in most cases, the grammatical structures used are different enough from the Spanish translation provided along with the Guaraní texts that we can safely assume that they must have some validity. As a starting point, I conducted a lookback and persistence text-count similar to the one conducted for present-day discourse. The results are given in Table 3.

Table 3 shows results similar to the text-count conducted on present-day discourse. The number for lookback of postposed objects indicates slightly more continuity than that found in present-day discourse, while the number for persistence suggests that these objects are slightly less persistent than in present-day discourse. Preposed objects of Montoya's Catechism are slightly more continuous and more persistent than those of present-day discourse. All in all, this text-count indicates that the split of object position with respect to the verb had some sensitivity to functional motivation. But it does not confirm my hypothesis, which would predict a clearer split between preposed and postposed objects than that found in present-day discourse. In other words, the postverbal position would be reserved for continuous and persistent objects only. As it was, there were a good number of non-continuous and non-persistent objects in this position. We also saw that although the overwhelming majority of object NPs in preverbal position were non-thematic, this position was not reserved exclusively for non-thematic object NPs.

While the hypothesis was not definitively proved by the text count, the results cannot be taken as proof that the hypothesis is wrong. First, as was pointed out before, the text was not produced by native speakers. The fact that pre- and postverbal objects do not behave more neatly according to the hypothesis of functionally motivated order split could be due to lack of mastery of discourse building strategies on the part of the author of the text. Second, the nature of the text is such that it can hardly be considered a piece of normally flowing discourse, for which the measures of lookback and persistence are designed. Most of the text consists of units of a maximum of five or six questions and answers on a given command or Catholic teaching, which were meant as a tool for raw memorization and testing of doctrine. The units that come closest to normally flowing discourse are the few prayers included in the document.

Table 3. Lookback and persistence of post- and pre-verbal objects in Montoya's Catechism.

Category	Lookback	Persistence	N° of tokens
VO (NP)	9.63	2.56	73
OV (NP)	17.76	0.24	30

Some of the units in Montoya's "Catecismo" which come relatively closer to qualifying as normal discourse (such as prayers and sustained questions and answers on a given topic) contain a fair number of examples that seem to give more positive support to my hypothesis than the entire text-count. Consider examples (11) and (12), which contain preverbal objects:

(11)	*Ore-rembi'u*	*ara*	*navo-guara*	*eme'e*	*ko-ara*	*pype*	*oreve.* (p. 2)
	our-food	day	every-of	give	this-day		to us

'Give us this day our daily bread'

(12)	*Mbaerehepe*	*cruz*	*i-poravogi*	*o-mano-haguama*	*ra'e.* (p. 58)	
	why	cross	3SG-choose	3SG-die-in=order-to	PAST	

'Why did he choose the cross (as a way) to die?'

In both "The Lord's Prayer", from which (11) was excerpted, and the series of questions about Christ's humanity from which (12) was excerpted, the referents of the preposed objects do not play an important role in subsequent discourse. Thus, the word for 'bread' is mentioned only once in "The Lord's Prayer", and the cross is the topic of one single question among many others, each dealing with one aspect of the humanity of Christ. In (13), however, the object refers to the topic of the "Apostles' Creed", and is therefore postposed:

(13)	*A-rovia*	*Tupa*	*Tuva*	*opakatumba'e apo* . . . (p. 5)
	1SG-believe	God	Father	all-mighty

'I believe in God the Father almighty'

The prayer goes on to say 'the creator of heaven and earth, ... who gave his only son', and so on. In other words, 'God' is *the* topic of the prayer, and is therefore postposed when coded as a clausal object.

In a different passage, which is titled "Charitable Works" and which contains a list of actions one must do as a good Christian, the objects appear before the verb. Sentences (14) and (15) are some examples of this:

(14)	*Ijypi-vae,*	*hasy-vae*	*pohu.* (p. 21)
	weak-which	sick-which	visit

'To visit the sick'

(15)	*Ñembyavo*	*mo-ngaru.*
	hungry	CAUS-eat

'Feed the hungry'

The "discourse" from which these examples were excerpted is a mere list of actions which are not viewed as closely connected with each other. In all of the infinitival sentences which contain an object, the objects are preposed. I would like to suggest that this is the case because the referents for the object nouns do not play any role in the rest of the discourse, and therefore a 'file' need not be kept open for them. All these examples from 17th-century Guaraní seem to indicate a tendency which suggests a functional split in object placement in the language along the following lines: highly topical objects, for which a 'file' must be kept open, tend to be post-posed, while objects with non-topical, non-persistent referents are preposed.

While these examples do not constitute conclusive evidence for the soundness of my hypothesis, they are suggestive that the split in object position was sensitive to functional motivations along the lines suggested by the hypothesis. Be that as it may, one conclusive remark one can make about pre-posed objects both in present-day and 17th-century Guaraní is that the overwhelming majority have low discourse continuity and persistence, and that in this sense, they are functionally very similar to incorporated nouns.

4. Concluding remarks

NI was found to be a device of the expressive needs of the discourse builder. Thus NI is a quick and effective way of providing additional (interpretational) information without blocking the flow of the narration. In this sense, NI is primarily a descriptive rather than a narrative device. Four types of semantic effects were found in the descriptive capabilities of incorporation: (i) portraying bodily actions as reflections of emotional states; (ii) construing bodily activities as characteristic or habitual behavior, (iii) construing a body-part quality as a permanent physical characteristic of the participant, and (iv) portraying an action as an institutionalized social activity.

The study shows that the incorporation of nouns in Guaraní serves the function of defocusing attention on a given entity, sometimes to create a unitary new concept, and in the majority of cases, to promote an alternative discourse entity to the level of focal attention. We have seen that despite the availability of referents in the immediate situation described by the story teller, this potential referential link of incorporated nouns is not exploited in the discourse. They are not integrated into the structure of the discourse since their referents lack discourse continuity/and or prominence. Thus NI is, among other things, a formal clue to the listener that s/he will not need to keep track of a given referent.

It was suggested that incorporation interacts with other formal resources of the language to create the same communicative effect. Thus we have suggested that the preverbal position of incorporated objects might reinforce the formal signal that the incorporated noun lacks discourse persistence and/or prominence. Support for the hypothesis that object preposing in NI serves this discourse function was found in a study that compares the discourse prominence/topicality of the referents of independent pre- and postposed objects in present-day Guaraní. It was found that, while postposed objects have the potential to code prominent/topical participants, preposed objects consistently code participants that have a very insignificant, or no role at all, in subsequent discourse. Additional support for this hypothesis was found in 17th-century texts. Much like in present-day discourse, preposed objects were found to be of low discourse thematicity.

It was also pointed out that "Possessor Ascension" is another formal device that interacts with NI to achieve the expressive effects described above. This formal device has the effect of creating an alternative focal participant in the case of part-whole relations.

Finally, the paper also makes a statement regarding the data source for incorporation studies. The data for previous analyses of Guaraní NI consisted mainly of context-free utterances, which were carefully constructed in such a way that they would be self-contained (i.e., they could be understood without reference to a specific situation or previous elements in the discourse). Extra-linguistic factors such as communicative intent and cultural knowledge of the speaker have to be invoked for the characterization of the semantic differences between incorporated and unincorporated structures. But in order to make a valid claim that these extra-linguistic factors play an important role in the use of NI, it is necessary to use a different sort of data. Specifically, we need a body of data that includes a wider linguistic and situational context, and an explicit indication of the background knowledge on which the speakers in the speech situation need to rely for the proper use of NI.

Notes

* I am thankful to Aaron Cicourel for discussing with me the ideas that originated this paper and for his valuable suggestions and ecouragement. I am also grateful to Suzanne Kemmer, Kathy Carey, and the editors of this volume, Pamela Downing and Mickey Noonan, for providing comments on earlier versions of this paper.

1. NI is usually defined as a compounding process involving a *verb* and a noun. In this paper, I am expanding the use of the term to include a compounding process that involves any *predicator* since, in Guaraní, forms designating qualities and states can be directly used as main predicators, just as canonical verbs can. As we will see later, these predicators can incorporate their subjects, in the same way as more canonical verbs can.

2. Du Bois refers to this property as "discourse referentiality", but I will continue using the terms "discourse persistence" and "discourse topicality" to avoid confusion given the already numerous and confusing senses of the term "referentiality" in the literature.

3. Consultation was not done on a systematic basis, as it always involved long distance calls due to the scarcity of other native speakers in the area where the study took place.

4. The story was taken from the magazine *Ñemity* (1981, No. 7), which, besides publishing studies on the grammar of Guaraní, encourages the submission of poems and popular stories such as this, written in the native language.

5. Examples (8) and (9) are considered instances of NI here because predicatives such as 'soft', 'red', 'rough', and 'big' are capable of functioning as main predicators, as evidenced by their ability to take morphological markings characteristic of verbs, such as the discontinuous negative morpheme *nda- ... -i*, the desiderative *-se*, and the future marker *-ta*. Furthermore, once they incorporate their subjects, as in (8) and (9), they retain these morphological capabilities: *nda-ij-ape-korocho-i*, *ij-ape-korocho-se*, *ij-ape-korocho-ta*. In addition, the semantic effect of these compounds is exactly parallel to those originating from more canonical verbs, such as *ku'e* 'move' in (9). That is to say, a quality or action that technically applies to a body-part is construed as descriptive of the body-part possessor as a whole.

6. Of course, in order to interpret the story in the intended way, the listener needs to know not only the different effects in prominence of the two linguistic structures, but also what counts as "handsome" or physically unattractive in their particular culture. Thus having very red lips, or big eyes and long eye-lashes are not necessarily universal attributes of masculine beauty, but in Guaraní culture they are. Similarly, having a rough appearance is not necessarily a universal indication of unattractiveness. It might even be considered attractive in a man in many cultures.

7. It is important to point out that this hypothesis would hold despite the fact that relatively new compounds still maintain the old OV order, as can be attested by examples such as: *vaka-ami* (cow-milk) 'to milk a cow', where the incorporated object is a borrowed word from Spanish.

References

Baker, Mark. 1988. *Incorporation: A theory of grammatical relation changing.* Chicago: University of Chicago Press.

Cicourel, Aaron. 1988. "Semantics, pragmatics, and situated meaning". Paper presented at the 1987 International Pragmatics Conference. Antwerp, Belgium.

Du Bois, John W. 1980. "Beyond definiteness: the trace of identity in discourse". *The Pear Stories: Cognitive cultural, and linguistic aspects of narrative production* ed. by Wallace Chafe, 203-274, Norwood, N.J.: Ablex.

Du Bois, John W. 1985. "Competing motivations". *Iconicity in Syntax* ed. by John Haiman, 343-66. Amsterdam/Philadelphia: John Benjamins.

Givón, T. 1984. *Syntax: A Functional-Typological Introduction*, Vol. 1. Amsterdam/ Philadelphia: John Benjamins.

Givón, T., ed. 1983. *Topic Continuity in Discourse: A quantitative cross-language study.* Amsterdam/Philadelphia: John Benjamins.

Haiman, John. 1985. *Natural Syntax.* Cambridge: Cambridge University Press.

Hopper, Paul. 1988. "Emergent grammar and the a priori grammar postulate". *Linguistics in Context: Connecting observation and understanding* ed. by Deborah Tannen. Norwood, N. J.: Ablex.

Hopper, Paul and Sandra Thompson. 1980. "Transitivity in grammar and discourse". *Language* 56.251-99.

Hopper, Paul and Sandra Thompson. 1984. "The discourse basis for lexical categories in universal grammar". *Language* 60.703-52.

Lehmann, Winfred. 1975. "A discussion of compound and word order". *Word Order and Word Order Change* ed. by Charles N. Li, 149-62. Austin: University of Texas Press.

Mithun, Marianne. 1984. "The evolution of noun incorporation". *Language* 60.847-94.

Perlmutter, David, ed. 1983. *Studies in relational grammar,* Vol. 1. Chicago: The University of Chicago Press.

Rosen, Sara T. 1989. "Two types of noun incorporation". *Language* 65.294-317.

Ruiz de Montoya, Antonio. 1640. *Catecismo de la Lengua Guaraní.* Reprinted in 1870. Leipzig: Oficina y Funderia de W. Drugulin.

Velázquez, Maura. 1989a. "Guaraní possessive constructions". *The Fifth Annual Meeting of the Pacific Linguistic Conference*, 489-506. University of Oregon.

Velázquez, Maura. 1989b. "Noun incorporation in Guaraní". Unpublished paper. University of California, San Diego.

SUBJECT INDEX

D

E

R

S

AUTHOR INDEX